D1738087

Friar, Reformer, and Renaissance Scholar

Life and Work of Giles of Viterbo
1469-1532

THE AUGUSTINIAN SERIES
VOLUME 18

Friar, Reformer, and Renaissance Scholar

Life and Work of Giles of Viterbo
1469 -1532

by
Francis X. Martin, O.S.A.

with a Foreword by
John W. O'Malley, S.J.

edited by
John E. Rotelle, O.S.A.

Augustinian Press
1992

Cover: *School of Athens* by Raphael
Cover design: Jaroslaw Dziewicki

Library of Congress Cataloging–in–Publication Data
Martin, F. X. (Francis X.)
Friar, reformer, and Renaissance scholar: life and work of
Giles of Viterbo, 1469-1532 / by Francis X. Martin;
with a foreword by John W. O'Malley; edited by John E. Rotelle.
p.   cm. — (The Augustinian series; v. 18)
Originally presented as the author's thesis (Ph. D. —Cambridge University)
under title: Egidio da Viterbo, 1469-1518.
Includes bibliographical references and index.
ISBN 0-941491-51-X. —ISBN 0-941491-50-1 (pbk.)
1. Egidio, da Viterbo, Cardinal, 1469?-1532.
2. Augustinians-—Italy—Rome—Biography.
3. Cardinals—Italy—Rome—Biography.
4. Rome (Italy) —Biography. I. Rotelle, John E. II. Title.
III. Series.
BX4705.E32M37   1992
282'.092—dc20   92-2863
[B]   CIP

Augustinian Press
P.O. Box 476
Villanova, PA 19085
Printed in R.O.C.

Contents

Foreword

In the past thirty years Giles of Viterbo has become a familiar name to scholars from a variety of disciplines researching the culture of Rome and the Church during the High Renaissance. I have been told that when a seminar on "Rome Under Popes Julius II and Leo X" was held a while ago at a large American university a student complained at the end that under the rubric of Renaissance Rome they had in fact studied nothing but Giles of Viterbo! The student's complaint may have been unfair or the teacher's emphasis exaggerated, but the anecdote graphically suggests the attention Giles has received from art historians, scripture scholars, students of the classical heritage and Jewish literature, scholars interested in the Reformation, the Catholic Reform, the history of religious order, the history of the papacy, and the history of Rome during the Renaissance. The list is not exhaustive.

Partly because of this attention directed to Giles, we are now much better informed about Renaissance Rome during the early years of the Cinquecento than we have ever been. This means that our understanding of the role Giles played has been redimensioned, and scholars see more clearly that he and the rich cultural diversity he embodied represent in fact only a small portion of the forces at work in Rome during that crucial period of western history. Some years ago a distinguished art historian commented to me on my own book on Giles that it was "a good book that had done a great deal of harm." By that he meant that it had given Giles an undue importance in the eyes of some scholars, as if Giles were almost the unique key to understanding the high culture of Renaissance Rome — a misconception, I assure you, that I had no intention of engendering or propagating.

Scholarship is now well beyond that misconception. Nonetheless, we must admit that Giles remains a special source for understanding certain aspects of the Renaissance. The reasons are several. He played many roles — orator at the papal court, reforming prior general of the Augustinians, synthesizer — almost syncretizer — of certain strains of Renaissance culture. He was in significant ways a child of the Renaissance, but medieval influences on him sometimes seem stronger. He knew the mainstream of Ficinian Neoplatonism and Paduan Aristotelianism, but also ardently pursued *esoterica*. A reformer, he was worlds apart from his most famous subject in the Augustinian Order, Martin Luther. Perhaps most important of all, he left behind a large *corpus*, in which we find a curious mix ranging from practical directives as superior general of an important religious order to the most abstruse speculation on theological, historical, and other subjects. Almost every literary genre is represented — correspondence, orations and sermons, translations, poetry, official registers, commentaries and treatises.

Whence did current interest in him arise? As the following pages indicate, Giles was not unnoticed before the middle of the twentieth century. Local historians like Giuseppe Signorelli and especially historians of the Augustinian order called attention to him. He was mentioned and given a certain due in larger works of synthesis. But his writings, the vast majority of which lay unpublished in manuscript, were forbiddingly extensive, complex, and uncharted. They had never been studied in any systematic way. Giles' profile remained blurred and almost unrecognizable. Only in the 1950s did scholars like Eugenio Massa and François Secret begin to suggest that there was more to Giles than we had heretofore imagined.

At about the same time Francis X. Martin was independently preparing at Cambridge University his doctoral dissertation entitled "Egidio da Viterbo, 1469-1518: A Study in Renaissance and Reform History." Shortly thereafter he began to share some of the results of his research in several articles, including the influential "The Problem of Giles of Viterbo: A Historiographical Survey," published in two parts in *Augustiniana* in 1959 and 1960. A turning-point had been reached.

From that time forward it was to Father Martin, by now Professor of Medieval History at University College, Dublin, that scholars from around the world first turned for guidance on the until then elusive Giles. Father Martin continued to publish on the subject. Principally through those publications the contours of Giles' career and the location and richness of the sources pertaining to him began to emerge.

Just as important, however, was the unfailing encouragement Frank Martin offered to others whose curiosity about Giles his writings had provoked. His generosity in this regard was sometimes reckless, as no one knows better than I. His articles had helped me determine to do my own dissertation on Giles. When as a self-invited guest I stopped to meet him in Ireland in 1963 on my way to Rome to begin my research, he took me in as if I were a long-lost member of the family. A friendship began that is among my most cherished.

More pertinent to the subject at hand, however, is a request I made of him at the time. With the bold naïveté of which only a young doctoral candidate is capable, I asked him if I might have a copy of his recent dissertation. Although he had known me for only a few days and had no idea how devious I might be, he provided me with one (which I have in front of me at this moment). Now that I am so much better informed about the ways of the academic world and the apprehensive concern with which scholars guard their unpublished lucubrations, I am all the more amazed at his decision. It spared me many months (or more) of work, saved me from countless errors, and provided me with a reliable *vade mecum* as I plowed through the confusing maze of Giles' manuscripts.

Frank Martin's decision, as I soon learned, was characteristic of the helping hand he extended to other scholars. Part of the result was the burgeoning of what he and I have come to refer to jokingly as "the international Giles industries." One of the most palpable results of this phenomenon was the international congress on Giles held in Rome and Viterbo in 1982, largely inspired by Frank and at which he was the pivotal figure.

The results were published in Rome the next year in a volume entitled *Egidio da Viterbo, O.S.A., e il suo tempo*. Although the volume gives a fair indication of the directions research had taken, it still does not touch many aspects of Giles' career that scholars have been exploring — his possible relationship to Renaissance painting, his cultivation of the "Christian Cabala," to name only two. Since the congress, publications concerning him have continued to appear. Among the most important are the edition of Giles's registers by Alberic de Meijer and two editions of his letters — one of his official correspondence as prior general by Clare O'Reilly and the other of his *familiares* by Anna Maria Voci Roth.

What we have been missing up to this point, however, has been Frank Martin's Cambridge dissertation, a fundamental instrument for putting the pieces together. The present volume fills that lacuna. It contains supporting materials in the appendices prepared by other scholars, but the body of the text is a revised form of the dissertation. Frank's concern for exactitude, his many writings on other subjects, his academic and administrative duties at University College, his editorship of the *Oxford History of Ireland*, his civic engagements, especially his courageous efforts in the Wood Quay controversy — these are some of the factors that have occasioned postponement of publication until now.

The book is simply all the more welcome. Moreover, it brings us full circle in accounting for most of the scholarship on Giles of Viterbo during these some thirty years.

John W. O'Malley, S.J.

Weston School of Theology
Cambridge, Massachusetts

Editor's Note

The material in chapters 1 to 8 of this book has been culled from various sources. The primary source is the unpublished thesis of F. X. Martin, O.S.A., *Egidio da Viterbo, A Study in Renaissance and Reform History*, Cambridge University, England, 1959.

For chapter 1 see F. X. Martin, O.S.A., "Giles of Viterbo and the Monastery of Lecceto: the Making of a Reformer," *Analecta Augustiniana* 25 (1962) 225-263; also F. X. Martin's thesis, chapter I, pages 1-6;

For chapter 2 see F. X. Martin's thesis, chapter IV, pages 99-150.

For chapter 3 see *ibid.*, chapter V, pages 151-173.

For chapter 4 see F. X. Martin, O.S.A., "The Augustinian Observant Movement," *Reformbemühungen und Observanzbestrebungen im spätmittelalterlichen Ordenswesen*, ed. Kasper Elm, Berlin 1989, 325-345; see also F. X. Martin, O.S.A., "The Registers of Giles of Viterbo. A Source on the Reform before the Reformation, 1506-1508," *Augustiniana* XII (1962) 142-160.

For chapter 5 see F. X. Martin, O.S.A., "The Augustinian Order on the Eve of the Reformation," *Miscellanea Historicae Ecclesiasticae* 2 (1967) 71-104; also F. X. Martin's thesis, chapters VI and VII, pages 174-212.

For chapter 6 see F. X. Martin, O.S.A., "The Problem of Giles of Viterbo. A Historiographical Survey," *Augustiniana* IX (1959) 357-379; X (1960) 43-60; see also F. X. Martin, O.S.A., "The Writings of Giles of Viterbo," *Augustiniana* XXIX (1979) 141-193.

For chapter 7 see F. X. Martin's contribution to *Egidio da Viterbo, O.S.A., e il suo tempo*, Atti del V Convegno dell'Istituto Storico Agostiniano, Roma-Viterbo, 20-23 ottobre 1982, Roma: Studia Augustiniana Historica 9, 1983, 191-222.

For chapter 8 see F. X. Martin's thesis, epilogue, pages 389-400.

For over forty years Father Martin has been publishing various articles on Giles of Viterbo and at the same time updating his masterful work on Giles written at Cambridge University, England.

Chapter 1

Friar and Scholar

Early Influences

Giles was born in Viterbo in 1469 of Lorenzo Antonini and Maria del Testa and entered the Augustinian monastery there in June 1488.[1] In those days youths usually joined religious orders about the age of fifteen. Giles however was aged eighteen and had completed his studies of humanities and a course in philosophy.

Little is known of Giles' early years. He went to school in Viterbo[2] and it is likely, but not as certain as Signorelli would wish, that the Augustinian friars were among Giles' teachers.[3] He shared the devotion of the people of Viterbo to the "Madonna della Liberatrice," a shrine of the Blessed Virgin in the Augustinian church.[4]

It has been suggested that his decision to join the Augustinians was influenced by Mariano da Genazzano, a renowned preacher, who came to deliver a course of sermons at Viterbo in 1485, when Giles was at the impressionable age of sixteen.[5] Whatever the accuracy of that suggestion it is undoubted that Mariano was a decisive influence in Giles' life twelve years later. Giles had the good fortune to pass his novitiate years in a house where a satisfactory standard of discipline and a respect for studies had been maintained throughout the fifteenth century. The prior of the monastery was a Viterbese, Giovanni Parentezza.[6] In later years Giles paid tribute to his learning and exemplary life when he made the following entry in his register under 20 August 1514: "We raise Friar John of Viterbo from bachelor to master because of his learning, good example, and age and because he was our mentor."[7]

Giles was sent after his profession in 1489 to teach philosophy for a year at Amelia in Umbria.[8] In the autumn of 1490 he resumed his studies, this time at Padua in the college of Saints Philip and James, a studium generale of the Order.[9] Presumably he was then studying theology, but it is curious that there is no record of the date or place of his ordination to the priesthood. In the autumn of 1493 he published an edition of three works of Giles of Rome (*Questiones de materia coeli* and *De intellectu possibili* were printed together and finished on 25 September 1493; *Egidii Romani, com-*

mentaria in VIII libros Physicorum Aristotelis was taken off the printing presses on 15 October 1493).[10] His achievement will be appreciated when it is realized that he was only twenty-four years of age and that this was the first printed edition of the three works.

Giles' years at Padua brought him something more than the zest of intense intellectual application. Living as he was in the college of Saints Philip and James with friars from different countries in Europe he had his first opportunity to learn of the grave problems facing the Augustinians in common with the Church in general. The major issue was reform. Throughout the fifteenth century the priors general were sympathetic to reform and often active on its behalf. Theirs was the right to nominate students and professors to the *studia generalia*; in consequence the spirit of reform was cultivated at the study centers. The little we know of Giles' student years indicates that at Padua he first made the acquaintance of those bent on a spiritual revival. In the dedication of his edition of Giles of Rome's commentary on the *Physica* of Aristotle he stated that he undertook the work due to the encouragement of one of his professors, Gabriele Della Volta. This Venetian friar was in later years a constant support for Giles' reforming efforts and succeeded him as general of the Order in 1518.[11] Giles dedicated the edition of the commentary to Graziano Ventura, the procurator general of the Order, who left a reputation for piety and learning.[12] The prior general at the time, Anselmo da Montefalco, knew Giles sufficiently well to refer to him as "familiaris noster."[13] Anselmo was noted for his exemplary life and his support of the reform movement; he had a particular affection for the Congregation of Lecceto, of which he was a member.[14] These three friars unquestionably turned Giles' mind toward their own ideals of a spiritual revival.

From Padua Giles went to study Plato under Marsilio Ficino at Florence; thence after some months he was appointed to lecture on theology at Capo d'Istria.[15] The effect of his visit to Florence remained, and whenever he had a free moment at Capo d'Istria he gave himself to a study of Plato. There was a natural affinity of soul between Marsilio and Giles; their common interest was Plato. Marsilio was not merely an intellectual fashion in the Europe of his day but was the leader of a group at Florence who were formulating a new exposition of Christianity, the *theologia platonica*, to counteract what they condemned as the insidious errors of Averroistic Aristotelianism.[16] Giles' concept of reform, infused with the spirit of Marsilio and the Platonic Academy, embraced a whole outlook on life and not merely a disciplinary rejuvenation of the

Augustinian Order. Special care was given by Ficino, and in turn by Giles, to the program of studies.

Florence

Giles remained at Capo d'Istria for two years. He was called to Rome in the winter of 1496 or spring of 1497 by Mariano da Genazzano, now vicar general, to undergo an examination for the magisterium in theology. He had to withstand a fierce assault by the examiners on his Platonic exposition of Christian doctrine, but he emerged successfully from the test.[17] He was sent to Florence to teach theology, happy beyond measure at the prospect of being near Ficino whom he so much admired. However, he found Florence a changed city, with the scene dominated by the apocalyptic Savonarola and its perfervid reformers. Political events now began to cast shadows across Giles' path. Mariano da Genazzano, vicar general of the Augustinian Order, was both a rival of the Dominican as preacher and a trusted agent of the Medici.[18] It was to favor Mariano that Lorenzo the Magnificent built the splendid monastery of San Gallo for the Augustinians.[19] Savonarola, in a sermon preached during Lent 1497, denounced Mariano for intriguing against him at Rome and "crawling after great lords and potentates."[20] Mariano's authority and prestige at Rome were greatly increased when he was elected prior general at the Augustinian general chapter of May 1497. He returned for a visit to Florence, carefully watched by Savonarola and his adherents. In August 1497 an informer, Lamberto dell'Antella, alleged that a plot was afoot to restore Piero de' Medici, and that Mariano and a group of citizens were implicated. Mariano was warned that countermeasures were being taken and fled to Rome.

The Council of Eight acted decisively. Five of the ringleaders in the supposed plot were condemned to death by a special tribunal on 21 August and beheaded that same evening.[21] This was the political Florence in which Giles was living, and he could not escape the fact that the head of his Order was reckoned to be a leading critic of Savonarola. Though it is likely that the Augustinians at Florence were as a body opposed to the Dominican friar,[22] the suggestion has been made that Giles sympathized at least in retrospect with Savonarola.[23] This theory is based on a patent misunderstanding of one phrase in a letter of Giles.[24] There is no proof that Savonarola with his harsh methods and uncompromising denunciation of the "pagan" vanities touched any chord in

Giles' heart. The Dominican and Augustinian were poles apart in personality and outlook.

Rome

Giles escaped the storm which was about to burst on Florence and engulf Savonarola. He was called to Rome to preach before Alexander VI.[25] The Augustinian general stood in favor with Alexander and probably aroused his interest by telling him of Giles' oratorical ability. Yet, curiosity alone on the part of Mariano and the pope to hear a promising preacher does not explain why when Giles wished to leave Rome the permission was refused.[26] It was perhaps fear on the part of the Roman authorities of what might befall him if he returned to Savonarola's Florence. In a letter written to Della Volta about December 1497 he stated that he left Florence with the intention of returning there shortly afterward, but that he was balked of his wish.[27] We remain in the dark about the causes and motives for his detention in Rome.

Rome of the fifteenth century fitted ill with Giles' ideals. Twenty years later when surveying the reign of Alexander VI he castigated the Borgia pope for his baneful influence on spiritual affairs.[28] He dismissed Alexander's reign in one lapidary thought — "There was then no regard for justice, human or divine. All was ruled by gold, violence, and lust."[29] In 1508, when writing to a friend, Giles broke out into a lament which applied with even greater force to the Rome in which he found himself in 1498. If, he cried, Rome is to deserve its claim to be the leader of the Christian world "why does it not lead in sanctity, probity, virtue, religion? Why are these not the principal concern?"[30] Throughout the winter of 1497 and the Lent of 1498 these same barbed questions were being thundered by Savonarola from the pulpit in San Marco and Santa Maria del Fiore. Both Giles and "the new Ezekiel" ardently desired reform but their methods were different. Savonarola would force reform on what he described as "the prostitute Church." Giles, for all his impatience with the corruption at Rome, believed that a lasting reform must come from inside the Church. His view was expressed in that famous phrase which he coined at the Lateran Council in 1512: "Men must be changed by religion, not religion by men."[31] There is no reason to believe that his attitude was any different in 1498.

Giles was called upon to preach before Alexander VI, probably on 18 March 1498.[32] Shortly afterward Mariano set out for a visitation of the Augustinian houses in the province of Naples and took Giles with him as companion. Mariano was a zealot for reform and a member of the Congregation of Lecceto. It is significant that he selected Giles as his companion, and Mariano's example undoubtedly helped to confirm Giles' interest in Lecceto. Mariano's health was already in precarious condition before they left Rome. The strain of the journey, and the shock of a storm which all but wrecked the ship in which they were traveling, accelerated his end. The ship put in at Gaeta, and Mariano made his way to Suessa where he died on 14 December 1498.[33] Giles was stricken with illness, perhaps with one of those tertian fevers which were a feature of Neapolitan medical history. He despaired of life, and in his hours of depression and weakness resolved that the values of the world were transient and that henceforth he would cast all his care upon God.[34] Glad to escape with his life, he returned to Viterbo where he arrived on 18 December.[35]

Naples

The attraction of the *Mezzogiorno* was strong, and he traveled to Naples in the spring of 1499. Here he remained until June 1501. Giles stated that he withdrew for two years to Mount Posilipo close by Naples in order to meditate in solitude.[36] This is true up to a point. The lack of letters to and from Giles during the year 1499 is a convincing indication that he turned his back on normal social intercourse for the sake of the gifts of self-knowledge and contemplation of the divine. It is corroborated by the fact that he did not stay with the Augustinian Conventuals at Sant'Agostino alla Zecca, but with the Augustinian Observants at San Giovanni in Carbonara on Posilipo.[37] A stricter standard of religious life was expected of the Observants. But Giles' self-imposed isolation was not to last long. His was a warm though delicate nature instinctively drawn to friendship. All his protestations during the next twenty years about withdrawing from the world must be taken with a grain of salt. He himself may not have realized it, but what he really sought was not so much an eremitical existence as a sheltered life in which to study and to hold converse with a select number of friends. He believed, or affected to believe, that his happiness lay in the *vita solitaria* as expounded by Petrarch, and as expressed religiously in the hermitages of the Observant friars. In reality his natural element was in a Platonic Academy such as flourished under Ficino at Florence.[38]

The high literary life of Naples found its social crown in the Pontanian Academy, presided over by the founder, Giovanni Pontano. Giles was readily accepted by these humanists and won the hearts even of Pontano and Sannazzaro who were not accustomed in their writings to spare the clergy.[39] In order to wean several members of the Pontanian Academy from a materialistic concept of life Giles presented Christian doctrine in Platonic form and terms. His success in these private discussions led to his being called upon to preach in similar fashion to the public. This was to be the undoing of his retired life on Posilipo.

Lecceto

The popularity of his sermons attracted the attention of King Frederick of Naples, who sent him to preach in Puglia in the late spring of 1501. Giles was not long there before he was summoned to Rome, probably in June 1501. It is likely that Pope Alexander VI, then secretly negotiating with Spain and France for an unwarranted attack on Naples, suspected that Giles was on a political mission in Puglia.[40] Giles did not return, or perhaps was not allowed to return, to Naples until September 1501. By that time Frederick was a prisoner in exile in France, while the kingdom of Naples had been overrun by French, Spanish, and papal troops. Giles spent some weeks at Naples and was back in Rome by the end of November.[41] What he witnessed of political chicanery at Naples, with pope and kings involved, only served to confirm his desire to escape from all entanglements with politicians and the practical men of affairs. This was the immediate background to his decision to join the Observant Congregation of Lecceto. He became a member of the congregation sometime during 1502 or 1503, most probably in April 1503. It is opportune at this point to explain the significance of Lecceto, its place in Augustinian history, and the attraction it held for Giles.

The Augustinians formed one of the four "great" mendicant orders who were synonymous with the "preaching friars." Since the thirteenth century it was the friars rather than any group in the Church who preached the gospel to the masses of the people.[42] It was they almost exclusively, Augustinians, Carmelites, Dominicans, and Franciscans, who led local and national revivals of religion up to the time of the Reformation. The Augustinians were not as noted as the Franciscans for popular preaching, but their contribution to popular piety by means of the sermon was considerable.[43]

The Dominicans owed one of their most renowned preachers to the Augustinians; Savonarola was converted to the religious life by the sermon of an Augustinian friar.[44] Until Savonarola rose to notoriety the Augustinian Mariano da Genazzano was the leading Italian pulpit orator of the day.[45] Contemporary with Mariano was the Florentine Augustinian, Aurelio Lippi Brandolini (d. 1497), a virtuoso both as preacher and as poet.[46] Giles' fame overshadowed the merits of two other outstanding Augustinian preachers, Mariano da Cave and Ambrogio Flandini, whose sermons drew large crowds during the first decade of the sixteenth century.[47] Giles could not disregard such a persistent tradition of his Order.

There was a contrary Augustinian tradition to which Giles could and did appeal. The Augustinian Order came into existence in the thirteenth century when various congregations of Italian hermits, following the *Rule* of Saint Augustine, were united by a papal bull, *Licet Ecclesiae* (9 April 1256).[48] This union is known as the "Great Union" since it had been preceded by at least three smaller aggregations of the Augustinian hermits in Tuscany.[49] The official title adopted by the new Order in 1256 was "Hermits of Saint Augustine."[50] The name was in fact somewhat of a misnomer, and of value as an historical signpost to the origins of the Augustinians rather than as an indication of the spirit and work of the new Order. The purpose for which the Augustinians were welded together in 1256 was to add a new order of preaching friars to the Church. Pope Alexander IV (1254-1261) had found that not even the rapidly expanding orders of Franciscans and Dominicans were sufficient to cope with the religious problems of a Europe which was passing through an economic and intellectual revolution. It was for this reason that the pope summoned the hermits from their seclusion.[51] The Augustinians amply justified Alexander's hopes, as their history showed during the hundred years following the Great Union.[52] Within that span of years the Order gave at least eighty-two bishops to the Church, joined wholeheartedly in the intellectual life of the university cities, founded a distinctive school of scholasticism which included figures such as Giles of Rome and James of Viterbo, devoted itself with signal success to preaching and pastoral work in the towns, and produced friars of notable sanctity as exemplified by Saint Nicholas of Tolentino (d. 1305) and Blessed Angelo of Foligno (d. 1312).[53]

Thus the Augustinian hermits were officially committed to the active apostolate and were juridically recognized as mendicant friars on an equal footing with Franciscans and Dominicans.[54]

Nevertheless, the eremitical spirit remained as a living force among the Italian Augustinians. Its influence may be seen in a friar such as Blessed Simon of Cascia (d. 1348), who sighed for a solitary life in which he could devote all his powers to prayer and penance.[55] This mentality was strengthened by the example of the Franciscan "spirituals," whose rigid asceticism and denunciation of worldly values were potent factors in late medieval Italy.[56] The pseudo-Augustine *Sermones ad Fratres in Eremo* gave a justification and a spiritual basis to those Augustinians who were of an eremitical frame of mind. This work was supposedly by Saint Augustine of Hippo, the father of Augustinian monasticism, and became the inspired word for those who believed that a revival of true religion would come with a return to the monastic life as practiced by Augustine and his companions at Thagaste.[57] Just as the Franciscan "spirituals" were firmly rooted in Umbria and the Marche because of the association of Francis of Assisi with these regions, so the Augustinian eremitical tradition was strongest in Tuscany. The Tuscan hermits were the dominant group among the five congregations who were brought together by the papal bull of 9 April 1256.[58] They believed that after Saint Augustine had been baptized in Milan in 387 he lived for some time in retirement in Tuscany and there instituted the first monastery of Augustinian hermits.[59] This apocryphal story gave to Centumcello the honor of being the first Augustinian foundation. It was also believed that Augustine visited the hermitage of Lecceto, a few miles west of Siena.[60] The brethren of this house looked upon themselves as the heirs of the monastic ideal as set forth by Augustine. The hermitage, and the tradition that it formed a direct link with Augustine, exercised a fascination over Augustinians in the fourteenth and fifteenth centuries.

Giles of Viterbo was one of the strongest exponents of the ill-founded theory about Lecceto. His belief was set forth in a lyrical work, *Panegyricus pro coenobio Ilicetano*.[61] The tradition that the history of Lecceto could be traced back to the time of Augustine was an expression of the reform movement among the Augustinian friars. They dreamed of a golden age in the past when religious life was perfectly observed by the hermits. This they fondly assumed was in the lifetime of Augustine. They believed that Lecceto, by reason of its supposed association with Augustine, had retained something of his soaring spirit and ardent zeal. A parallel is to be seen in the Franciscan "spiritual" movement with its insistence on a return to the austere life followed by Saint Francis and the observance of his rule to the letter, "without gloss or marginalia."[62] It was a mentality common among Renaissance scholars, men devoted to a cult of the past, hypnotized by the thought that "they were giants in those days."[63]

Lecceto became the inspiration of the reform movement among the Augustinians. The Avignon Captivity (1309-1378) and the Black Death (1348-1352/1361) had brought about a sharp decline in religious observance among all branches of the clergy, including the friars.[64] There was hardly time for a breathing space before the Schism of the West (1378-1417) disrupted the unity of western Christendom. The centralized religious orders, because of their tightly-knit organization, were first to recover from the general confusion.[65] A chapter of the Augustinians was held at Gran, Hungary, in May 1385, and Bartholomew of Venice was unanimously elected prior general. He was bent on reform but realized that the wind must be tempered to the shorn lamb. He did not attempt the virtually impossible task of enforcing a universal stringent reform on the Order. He set about raising the religious tone of his friars in general. At the same time he selected Lecceto as the light which was to shine before the Augustinians, the house where strict religious observance was to be practiced. His hopes were happily fulfilled. Already by the middle of the fourteenth century the hermitage had been famed as a center of mystical piety.[66] Saint Catherine of Siena (c.1347-1380) found there some of her most resolute supporters. Its reputation drew one noted English mystic, William Flete, across the seas in 1359; he remained at Lecceto for the remainder of his life.[67]

A description of Lecceto by E. G. Gardner recaptures something of its medieval charm:

> It lies beyond Belcaro, a few miles westward of Siena, in what still remains of a once glorious forest of ilex trees. The place was originally known as the Convento di Selva (Convent of the Forest), and it was also called the Selva di Lago because of the lake or swamp (afterward drained) that lay at the foot of the hill upon which, solitary and austere, the convent still rises. From remote middle ages, wonderful legends had lingered round the convent and forest. Miraculous waters had gushed out of the arid soil; the stones had taken mystical colors in commemoration of him who was crucified; the flowers of the forest had wonderful healing properties, all evident signs that here flourished a continual spring of Paradise. Angels had descended in human form to eat with the hermits in their refectory, or to succor them in their need; Christ himself had appeared in the wood to confirm the young friar,

Giovanni di Guccio, in his vocation; but fiends lurked in it, ready to ensnare the souls of the unwary, even as the young Sienese knight, Ambrogio Sansedoni, walking heedlessly under the ilexes, had been confronted with what seemed a beautiful girl bound by two ruffians, who was only revealed in her true nature at the sign of the Cross.[68]

Bartholomew's decision to set Lecceto apart for model religious observance was taken at Gran on 19 May 1385.[69] He appointed two exemplary friars, Cerretani and Bandinello, to lead the reform.[70] So that Lecceto might have a unique position and would not feel the envy of lukewarm brethren at nearby Siena, he took the house from the jurisdiction of the Sienese provincial and by a decree of 3 March 1387 put it directly under the rule of the prior general.[71] Though Lecceto suffered from growing pains during the subsequent two decades it fulfilled all the hopes placed in it by Bartholomew.[72] The seal of the monastery conveyed its own message. It showed three mountains, symbols of the mystical ascent of the soul; a cluster of ilex trees, the peculiarity of Lecceto; overshadowing all was the figure of Christ. Underneath ran the motto "Who by his cross and blood redeemed us."[73] The reputation of Lecceto brought Count Carolo Sforza of the Milanese ruling family to join the Observants as a simple friar in 1442. He became novice master in 1454 and was nominated archbishop of Milan in the same year.[74] Alessandro Oliva, perhaps the most admirable Italian Augustinian of the fifteenth century, considered it an honor to be affiliated to the congregation. Oliva was elected prior general of the Order in May 1459 and was created a cardinal by Pius II in 1460.[75] He had sent a young man, Anselmo da Montefalco, to be trained as a novice at Lecceto in 1447.[76] This pious friar became prior general of the Order in 1486. Mariano da Genazzano joined the Congregation of Lecceto in 1482 and succeeded Anselmo in 1497 as prior general.[77] It can be seen how important a position Lecceto had assumed in the Augustinian Order.

The reform or "observant" movement spread with a firm vigor throughout the Italian provinces. Naples was first to follow the example of Lecceto. The reform was introduced there in the early fifteenth century and was formally established as a separate congregation, styled "San Giovanni in Carbonara," by a decree of the prior general, Agostino Favaroni, on 7 February 1421.[78] We have seen Giles as a guest of the congregation during his stay at Naples in 1499-1501.

Giles at Lecceto

When Giles went, however reluctantly, to preach the Lenten sermons at Siena in 1502, he was not without personal motives for the visit. Lecceto lay a few miles west of Siena, and after he concluded the Lenten sermons he was sent by the prior general, Graziano Ventura, to spend the summer months amid the cool woods of Lecceto.[79] His letters show that he was there from May until at least the second half of August.[80] Giles, who had more in mind than a holiday in the hermitage, was preparing the way for his affiliation to the congregation of Lecceto. Giles became a member of Lecceto probably on 30 April 1503.

Giles' enthusiasm for Lecceto was unbounded. During these years when he was not yet burdened with high administrative offices he saw it as the means by which he could attain that peace of soul and opportunity for study which would lead to close union with God.[81] He assured the Leccetan friars that when he first walked under the shade of the ilex trees he cried out with Jacob of the Old Testament: "Truly this place is holy and is none other than the house of God and the gate of heaven."[82]

Spiritual Itinerary

Giles' spiritual ideals explain his decision to become an observant at Lecceto. According to him, it was the example of Christ Crucified which spurred him on to seek a life of prayer and self-immolation.[83] The friar's sermon recorded in *Aegidius* may well be dressed up in Pontano's words, but it is dominated by a vision of Christ Crucified which almost certainly came from Giles.[84] When he wrote to the friars of Lecceto in July 1506 he described how he sought union with God by taking his model from the Crucified Savior.[85] To do so, he declared, he decided to make of himself a perfect holocaust by means of a triple sacrifice. Three things, he stated, were pleasing to him: ease of the body, personal possessions, intellectual satisfaction.[86] By fasts, vigils, and hardships he tried to bring his body into subjection, though he ruefully admitted that his delicate health did not allow him to practice the austerities which he believed would be of benefit to his soul.[87] The desire for personal possessions he sacrificed by sharing all in a common use with his fellow friars. This he did to such an extent that, according to him, visitors to the hermitage on the Cimino shook their heads at what they considered to be his extreme interpretation of poverty. Far from being ashamed of his lot Giles affirmed that the better part was to endure miseries, to beg for maintenance, to feel the pangs of hunger.[88] But for him the real holocaust lay in the things of the mind. This, he admitted, was a personal matter. He explained his attitude from the words of Christ, *He who wishes to come after me must take up his cross and follow me* (Mt 16:24). The Lord, Giles pointed out, did not counsel that one should carry a cross with others or bear somebody else's cross, but one's own.[89] Giles therefore devoted himself "with incredible purpose" to meditation, to communion with God, to a secluded life of prayer. This he believed was his particular road to heaven.

Giles' interpretation of Christ's words while undoubtedly sincere was nevertheless tendentious. He selected a hard road to heaven but it was the way of his own choosing. Therein lay the fallacy of his reasoning. His knowledge of ascetical theology should have made him aware that the very nature of a cross is that it is imposed not selected. He admitted that the way he chose, a life of seclusion and study, was most pleasant despite its rigors.[90] To his distaste he found that he was not to be allowed this life.

The five years, 1501-1506, saw an increasing tension between two aspects of his life. Giles the scholar grew plaintive in his appeals that he be allowed to follow a life of solitude, of prayer, of study. Giles the preacher was in constant demand, and popular taste would not be denied opportunities of hearing "the Christian Cicero."[91] He had gone to Posilipo in 1499 for a quiet life, but his own gifts of self-expression and friendship, as much as the admiration of the humanists at Naples, made him a popular figure. In 1503 he joined the Congregation of Lecceto in order to regain the peace which he had found then lost at Naples, but the proximity of Lecceto to Siena meant that he was not immune from urgent requests for preaching. He withdrew in 1503 to an island in Lake Bolsena only to be summoned back to the pulpit by popular acclamation and a papal command. After an exhausting round of sermons in central and northern Italy he sought refuge in July 1504 in a hermitage on Mount Cimino near Viterbo. The peace he desired was forever shattered when messengers arrived on 27 June 1506 from Julius II, with a brief appointing Giles vicar general of the Augustinian Order.

Vicar General

It was not blind instinct which dictated the pope's decision, nor was the choice made because Giles was then acclaimed as a preacher in Italy. His success in the pulpit had undoubtedly made him the most talked of Augustinian in those years, but a preacher, particularly in Italy, might well be a voice and nothing more. The della Rovere pope, hardened by years of sharp feud and bitter exile, was too realistic to be gulled by a torrent of words. He selected Giles to rule the Augustinian Order because he knew him to represent a program of reform. Though it seemed a gamble to appoint as general a friar who had no practical experience of administration, there had been one affair in 1502 which demonstrated Giles' ability in negotiation.

Until the year 1502 Giles had been concerned mainly with his own spiritual and intellectual development. It was this which caused him to study in isolation at Capo d'Istria; it led him to the stimulating atmosphere of the Platonic Academy in Florence; it drew him to what he believed would be the peace of Posilipo at Naples. Though it was uppermost in his mind when he sought to live at Lecceto he also showed an active interest in the spiritual welfare of the Augustinian community at Viterbo. Writing to an intimate Augustinian friend, Serafino Ferri, in December 1503, Giles told almost in passionate terms how Viterbo and its Augustinian monastery were always before his eyes.[92] Like a true Italian of the Renaissance he looked upon his native city as the *dolce patria*. In addition, he knew that it was because of the Augustinian friary that his entire life had been changed and that his feet had been set on a road which he believed led securely to heaven. His delight with the religious life as he found it practiced at Lecceto urged him to introduce the same spirit and observance to the friary at Viterbo. He had an added stimulus because of his belief that the Augustinians at Viterbo were falling short of the ideals of the Order.

To Giovanni Botonti

In a way typical of your conscientious piety you made out your case with great labor and zeal when you urged us not to disdain our monastery at Viterbo, but rather to seek out holy men from every quarter and bring them there like a new swarm to colonize the house, so that they may restore and care for it, and build up the community. You declared that love for our own native province and kindred ought to move us, and that we owe this service to the age-old kindness of Our Lady, who has defended the city against demons, darkness, and long-lasting night. You further asserted that the desires and feelings of nearly all the citizens demand this, and that they will soon begin to threaten those men who falsely claim the name of religious, for they long to see the place occupied by men worthy of it. Moreover, you stressed that you personally attach the utmost importance to your request, and that if we are in any way indebted to your faithfulness, your goodwill, and your service, we ought to grant it out of love for you.

Well then, I have yielded to your persuasion, I have turned my eyes toward the tutelary gods of my homeland, and the whole matter has been arranged without delay; but there is one condition. The man who blew the trumpet to signal the advance must himself lead with spear and sword in the battle. Yes, you have played a major role in the consultations and decisions, and you must be in charge of implementing them and making a success of the enterprise. If you agree, then listen to what I have settled, relying on you.

With Serafino beside me I discussed the matter with the Leccetans; they put pressure on the senate, and eventually all the senators came to promulgate their decrees with great joy, declaring that they would take no action unless I myself were present when the work of building begins.

They also entrusted the province to Serafino as consul-designate; the general consensus among both elders and young men was that the consul's very name was a pledge of victory.

It now remains to prepare for you whatever you will need for your campaign. Concerning the Holy Father's orders, I will enquire of Antonio Zoccoli. We are writing to the city fathers, gently encouraging them to make progress, and attempting to arouse in the citizens a willingness to help with resources. We are awaiting a papal brief as a matter of urgency, however, lest any enemy sow tares among the wheat and the emerging crop be ruined.

Farewell to you in the Lord. Be sure to let us know what you decide and what you achieve in all these matters.[93]

However, local patriotism was so strongly ingrained in Renaissance Italy that considerable tact was needed if the Viterbesi, citizens and friars, were to allow the monastery to be incorporated with a congregation centered in Sienese territory. Giles, for all his eremitical leanings and literary preoccupations, now showed some of that subtlety in negotiation which was to stand him in such good stead when he became prior general of the Order. It is this which gives the event a special significance.

Giles stood high in the esteem of the Leccetan friars and shared his project with one of them, Serafino Ferri, a close friend who had lived with him in San Giovanni in Carbonara at Naples.[94] Serafino's words carried weight with his own community.[95] He acted as intermediary when Giles visited Lecceto to discuss the scheme: "With Serafino beside me I discussed the matter with the Leccetans."[96] Before Giles left Siena in May 1502 the agreement of the Leccetan congregation had been secured.[97] It was equally important to have the consent of the interested parties at Viterbo. Giles prepared the ground by writing to some friends in the monastery and among the townsfolk.[98] As Viterbo lay in the patrimony of Peter the sanction of the papacy had also to be obtained. Giles wisely decided that the crucial stage of the proceedings would be best undertaken by an influential third party, outside the Augustinian Order. For this purpose he had the cooperation of Antonio Zoccoli and of two Viterbesi clerics, Giovanni Botonti and Giovanni Battista Almadiani. Zoccoli was a Roman aristocrat, a layman who attained high office in the administration of the city under Julius II.[99] Botonti and Almadiani were important officials in the Roman curia. Botonti was president of the papal camera, and on 30 June 1502 was appointed governor and commissary of Benevento.[100] Almadiani began his curial career as secretary to Cardinal Giovanni Colonna, became a protonotary apostolic, and at the time of the negotiations concerning Lecceto was in the service of Cardinal Carafa.[101] It is uncertain how Giles first became acquainted with Zoccoli, Botonti, and Almadiani, but it is likely that they met when he was called to Rome in the autumn of 1497 to preach before Alexander VI. Almadiani was a humanist and, like Giles, belonged to the literary group who were accustomed to meet at the house of the German prelate, Johann Goritz.[102] Despite the malodorous reputation of the papal curia in these years both Botonti and Almadiani were known as men of virtue.[103]

In mid-June 1502 Botonti went for a health cure to the baths near Viterbo. He used the occasion to obtain from the city council letters asking the Leccetan friars to accept the Viterbese monastery for their congregation.[104] He then wrote to the Augustinians at Viterbo exhorting them to cooperate with the city council in the good work. There was a large amount of make-believe in Botonti's appeal. He knew that a month previously Giles had so advanced the enterprise that the consent of the Leccetan friars had been secured, and that the papal brief confirming the jurisdiction of the Leccetan congregation over the monastery at Viterbo was being prepared.[105] Had the Viterbesi friars but known it, they were being asked to agree to a *fait accompli*. Botonti's appeal was made about 20 June.[106] The papal brief had been granted four days earlier.[107] Giles showed more than the simplicity of the dove in his manipulation of the negotiations. Nevertheless there was a real danger that opposition from certain citizens at Viterbo would upset the scheme. Botonti dwelt on this disturbing possibility in a letter of 24 June to Giles, but added that he was confident of the support of the majority of the city council, and that he relied in particular on his cousin, Domenico Cordelli, the most influential voice in Viterbo.[108]

All went as Giles wished. Lorenzo Scarmiglioni, a man of authority among the Viterbesi friars, approved of the proposed affiliation with Lecceto, and acted as superior until the arrangements had been completed. Serafino Ferri was appointed prior and arrived to take possession of the monastery on 1 September 1502.[109] Giles remained at Viterbo until November,[110] probably to safeguard that Serafino's first months as prior would proceed smoothly, without offense either to the Augustinians or to the citizens of Viterbo. Subsequent events justified the introduction of the Leccetan reform to Viterbo. Giles wrote to Serafino on 15 July 1505 congratulating him on having achieved a thorough success within less than three years. It was not so much the material renovation of the monastery church which pleased Giles. In his eyes the real success was the reform which had taken place among the friars, the increased discipline and sanctity of life which was evident in the monastery. The success was all the greater, he assured Serafino, because the Viterbesi far from being opposed to the new regime were loud in their praise of the change which had taken place.[111]

It is unlikely that at this stage Giles had the intention of attempting to introduce the reform to any other Augustinian friary. Even had he wished to do so his continuous activity as a preacher between December 1502 and June 1506 made it impossible in practice. Yet there was an intimate connection between his success in the pulpit and his appointment as vicar general and reformer of the Augustinians by Julius II in June 1506. His eloquence made him a power to be sought after by cardinals, princes, city states, and even by the imperious Julius II. The fact that he had the entrée to the highest civil and ecclesiastical circles in Italy meant that he would be treated with respect by the various powers in whose territories there were Augustinian houses. This was important if the reform was to be advanced with any reasonable measure of hope. The attitude of the Augustinians was equally important. They, with a sense of corporate pride, welcomed as vicar general the man acclaimed as the greatest orator in Italy. It is important, therefore, for an understanding of Giles' life to observe him as a preacher during the years 1502-1506.

Notes

1. Giuseppe Signorelli, *Il Cardinale Egidio da Viterbo, Agostiniano, umanista e riformatore, 1469-1532*, Florence, 1929, pages 1-2: hereinafter *Egidio*. These and other basic facts about Giles' early life have been established beyond reasonable doubt by G. Signorelli, the most competent authority on Viterbese history.

2. See funeral oration given by Giles' contemporary, Bishop Lorenzo Grana of Segni, Appendix 1.

3. Signorelli, *Egidio*, page 1.

4. Letter to Giovanni Botonti, Siena, 7 May 1502, see Signorelli, *Egidio*, page 218, and Anna Maria Voci Roth, *Egidio da Viterbo, O.S.A., Lettere Familiari*, I (1494-1506), Institutum Historicum Augustinianum, 1990, pages 155-156: hereinafter *Lettere Familiari*.

5. *Egidio*, page 121, note 15.

6. For Parentezza see Signorelli, *Egidio*, page 121, note 17.

7. Alberico de Meijer, *Aegidii Viterbiensis, O.S.A. Registrum Generalatus 1514-1518*, vol. 18, Rome, 1984, page 63, number 130.

8. Giles wrote to a friend, Niccolò Mannio, in the summer of 1504, "When I was eighteen I entered the Augustinian Order and was ordained to the priesthood. I then read for a year at Ameria," in Martène and Durand III, 1249, and *Lettere Familiari*, I, pages 234-236 (see Appendix 3). In those days ordination to the priesthood at times took place before theological studies.

9. Padua was one of the four studia generalia established by the Augustinian general chapter at Florence in 1287.

10. G. Bruni, *Catalogo critico delle opere di Egidio Romano*, Florence, 1936, pages 60-62(9); 73 (22).

11. For della Volta (1468-1537) the best notices, though woefully incomplete, are D. Perini, *Bibliographia Augustiniana*, II, Florence, 1931, pages 22-23.

12. For Ventura see Perini, *op. cit.*, IV, Florence, 1938, page 48.

13. See entry from Anselmo's register in Signorelli, *Egidio*, pages 125-126 note 33.

14. For Anselmo (1422-1495) see Herrera, *Alphabetum Augustinianum*, I, 18. At his own request Anselmo was buried at Lecceto, see Signorelli, *Egidio*, page 126, note 34.

15. See letter to Niccolò Mannio, written in 1504 (note 8 above). Giles there omits to mention his stay in Florence, but we know of it from a letter which he wrote to Ficino about the summer of 1499, in *Supplementum Ficinianum*, ed. P. O. Kristeller, II, Florence, 1937, pages 315-316; the version of this letter in Martène and Durand, III, 1250-1252, is somewhat inaccurate. See also *Lettere Familiari*, I, pages 101-104.

16. See P. O. Kristeller, "Florentine Platonism and its relations with humanism and scholasticism," in *Church History* VIII (1939), pages 201-211; *idem*, "Lay religious traditions and Florentine Platonism," in *Studies in Renaissance Thought and Letters*, Rome, 1956, pages 99-122.

17. Giles in his letter to Ficino describes his experience in graphic terms (see notes 15 above).

18. For Mariano, see D. Perini, *Uno emulo di Fr. Girolamo Savonarola: Fr. Mariano da Genazzano*, Rome, 1917. Perini attempts on pages 62-86 to clear Mariano of the charges made against him by admirers of Savonarola, particularly by P. Villari, *Life and times of Girolamo Savonarola*, London, 1897. Despite Perini's able defense of Mariano the charges made by Villari still stick, and are repeated for example by R. Ridolfi, *Vita di Girolamo Savonarola*, Rome, 1952, pages 62-65, 285, 339. See David Gutiérrez, "Testi e note su Mariano da Genazzano (d. 1498)," *Analecta Augustiniana* 32 (1969) 117-204.

19. Perini, *op. cit.*, page 21.

20. *Ibid.*, pages 68-72; Villari, *op. cit.*, page 157. One of the most frequently quoted charges against Mariano is his supposed anti-Savonarola sermon, "Abrucia! Abrucia! Santo Padre, lo strumento del diavolo!" (Burn, burn, Holy Father, the instrument of the devil) before Alexander at Rome, mentioned in the Pseudo-Burlamacchi, *Vita del beato Jeronimo Savonarola*, ed. R. Ridolfi, Florence, 1937, page 29. The authenticity of the sermon has been inpugned by Perini.

21. Villari, *op. cit.*, pages 557-575.

22. Signorelli, *Egidio*, page 5, states that the Augustinians were in the anti-Savonarola camp. This is likely because of professional rivalry between the Augustinians and Dominicans, and because of Augustinian loyalty to Mariano. Nevertheless, no evidence has been produced to resolve the question.

23. U. Mariani, "Egidio da Viterbo," in *Enciclopedia Cattolica*, 5 (1950) page 142, states "Egidio partecipò, ma con moderazione, alla campagna contro il Savonarola, verso il quale, in seguito, cambiò alquanto opinione e contegno, sino a manifestare una certa stima per lui." Mariani misinterprets the facts. There is no evidence that Giles joined in the attack on Savonarola; the phrase in Giles' letter of June 1516 criticizes rather than approves of Savonarola. Mariani was probably depending on Signorelli, *Egidio*, page 6.

24. "Memor tamen esse debes quod nec Praedicatorum Fr Hieronymum Ferrariensem nec ordo Minorum Fr Bonaventuram et alios deceptores potuit coercere, adeo potest est aura favorque populorum," Giles to della Volta, Rome, 14 June 1516, in Angelica, MS 688, fol. 59r and *Lettere Familiari*, II, pages 202-204. Signorelli, *Egidio*, page 6, assumes that the Bonaventure in question was Saint Bonaventure (1221-1274), and that Giles was equating the work of Savonarola with that of Saint Bonaventure. Giles was obviously referring to Fra Bonaventura, a fanatical preacher who appeared at Rome in May 1516 and ended as a prisoner in the Castle Sant'Angelo. For this Fra Bonaventura, the self-styled "Angelic Pope," see L. Pastor, *History of the Popes*, V, London, 1950, pages 224-225. Giles explicitly ranked Fra Bonaventura among the "deceptores" of the people, a stricture which could not have had any relevance to Saint Bonaventure.

25. "Revocor mox Romam facturus ad Alexandrum pontificem verba, quae, cum non obscure habuissem abire prohibeor," Giles to Mannio (see note 8 above).

26. *Ibid.*

27. "Recessi isthinc post paulum rediturus, sed ita, Deo O. M. disponente, restitimus. Quidquid erit, in bonum Deus ferat," in Angelica, MS 688, fol. 10v.

28. This section of Giles' *Historia XX Saeculorum* has been edited by K. Höfler in *Archiv für Kunde oesterreichischer Geschichts-Quellen*, XII (1854), 379-382.

29. "Nihil ius, nihil fas. Aurum, vis et Venus imperabant," *ibid.*, page 381.

30. Giles to Antonio Puccio, Cimino, 5 July 1508, in Siena, MS G.X. 26, page 191 (Signorelli, *Egidio*, pages 234-235).

31. "Homines per sacra immutari fas est, non sacra per homines." Giles' oration is printed in P. Labbé and G. Cossart, *Acta Conciliorum*, ed. J. Harduin, IX, Paris 1714, cols. 1576-1581; critical edition, C. O'Reilly, "'Without Councils we cannot be saved.' Giles of Viterbo addresses the Fifth Lateran Council" in *Augustiniana* XXVII (1977), 166-204, at 182-204; see Appendix 2.

32. Giles to Mannio (see note 8 above). Signorelli, *Egidio*, page 130, note 20, concludes that Giles' sermon was delivered on the Third Sunday of Lent (that is, 18 March) because the Augustinians had the right to preach *coram pontifice* on that day.

33. D. Gutiérrez, "Testi e note su Mariano da Genazzano (d. 1498)," *Analecta Augustiniana* 32 (1969) 119. The precise date of the death is known from a note by Giles in Augustinian General Archives, MS Cc 37, fol. 116r.

34. Giles to Mannio (see note 8 above).

35. Signorelli, *Egidio*, page 131, note 28.

36. Giles to Mannio (see note 8 above).

37. For San Giovanni in Carbonara see Herrera, *Alphabetum Augustinianum*, II, pages 205-207, and the documents edited in *Analecta Augustiniana* 14 (1932), 353-358; 382-398.

38. For the clash among Renaissance thinkers about the "vita solitaria" as against the "vita activa-socialis," see H. Baron, *The Crisis of the Italian Renaissance*, Princeton, 1955, pages 4-8; 88-93.

39. There is a wealth of background material on the Pontanian Academy in E. Pèrcopo, "La vita di Giovanni Pontano," in *Archivio Storico per le Province Napoletane* LXI (1936) 116-250; *idem*, "Gli scritti di Giovanni Pontano," *ibid.* LXII (1937) 57-228. For Giles in this setting see F. Fiorentino, "Egidio da Viterbo ed i Pontaniani di Napoli," *ibid.* IX (1884), 430-452; E. Gothein, *Die Kulturentwicklung Süd-Italiens in Einzel-Darstellung*, Breslau, 1886, pages 449-459; G. Toffanin, *Giovanni Pontano: fra l'uomo e la natura*, Bologna, 1938, pages 15-35 and *passim*.

40. In his letter to Mannio, Giles protested that Frederick had none other than a religious purpose in sending him to Puglia, "You yourself can testify with what good reason and with what holy and loyal intention I was sent to Apulia by King Frederick, by whom I have always been more highly esteemed than one mortal man should be by another. I was recalled to Rome" (see note 8 above). For the political background see Pastor, *op. cit.*, pages 83-84; Signorelli, *Egidio*, pages 9; 132, note 37.

41. Giles to Fra Deodato, Rome, 16 November 1501, in Angelica, MS 1001, 194v-195r; see *Lettere Familiari*, I, pages 129-130.

42. See J. Burkhardt, *Civilization of the Renaissance in Italy*, London, 1951, pages 286-296; P. Hughes, *History of the Church*, III, London, 1942, page 212; P. Monnier, *Le Quattrocento*, Paris, 1901, II, pages 189-203; Pastor, *History of the Popes*, I, pages 31, 34; V, 97-108, 175-181.

43. A. De Romanis, *L'Ordine Agostiniano*, Florence 1936, pages 44-45; 83; 88-90; 113-115. See Gutiérrez, *The Augustinians in the Middle Ages 1256-1356*, History of the Order of St. Augustine, volume I, part I, pages 23-54; *The Augustinians in the*

Middle Ages 1357-1517, History of the Order of St. Augustine, volume I, part II, pages 121-138; 175-190.

44. R. Ridolfi, *Vita di Girolamo Savonarola*, I, Rome 1952, page 11.

45. G. Tiraboschi, *Storia della letteratura italiana*, 2nd ed., VI, part 3, Modena, 1791, pages 1149-1152.

46. *Ibid.*, pages 968-973; 1149.

47. Pastor, *History of the Popes*, V, page 180. Perini, *Bibliographia Augustiniana*, I, pages 218-219; II, 72-73.

48. The only satisfactory study of this question is by F. Roth, "Cardinal Richard Annibaldi, first protector of the Augustinian Order, 1243-1276: a study of the Order before and after the Great Union in 1256," in *Augustiniana* II (1952) 26-60, 108-149, 230-247; III (1953) 21-34, 283-313; IV (1954) 5-24.

49. For a union before 1223 see *ibid.*, III, 292 (34); for the union of 1228 see *ibid.*, II, 112-114; for the union of 1244 see *ibid.*, II, 114-121.

50. R. Kuiters, "*Licet Ecclesiae Catholicae*: Commentary," *ibid.*, VI (1956) 19-23. The title of the Order explains why Giles is often described in contemporary Latin books and documents as "Eremita."

51. The bull, "Licet Ecclesiae," stated "et ex pluribus cuneis acies una con- surgeret fortior ad hostiles spiritualia nequitie impetus conterendos." See critical edition of the bull by A. de Meijer, *ibid.*, VI, 9-13.

52. E. van Moé, "Recherches sur les ermites de Saint-Augustin entre 1250 et 1350," in *Revue des questions historiques* LX (1932) 275-316.

53. See Gutiérrez, *The Augustinians in the Middle Ages 1256-1356*, History of the Order of St. Augustine, volume I, part I. *The Augustinians in the Middle Ages 1357-1517*, History of the Order of St. Augustine, volume I, part II.

54. It is not clear at what precise date the Augustinians were recognized as mendicant friars, but they were accepted as such by Boniface VIII in a declaration of 3 March 1290, see Kuiters, *op. cit.*, in *Augustiniana* VI, 28-29, note 33.

55. See P. Bellini, *Blessed Simon Fidati of Cascia*, Villanova, 1988, pages 11-27; 30-31; 68-72; M. G. McNeil, *Simone Fidati and his "De Gestis Domini Salvatoris,"* Washington, 1950, pages 32-34; 129-130.

56. There were close relations between the famous Franciscan Spiritual Angelo da Clareno and Blessed Simon of Cascia, see Bellini, *op. cit.*, pages 14-18.

57. For the *Sermones ad Fratres in Eremo* see R. Arbesmann and W. Hümpfner, *Jordani de Saxonia: Liber Vitasfratrum*, New York-Würzburg, 1943, XXIV-XXIX. For the authentic teaching of Augustine on monasticism see A. Zumkeller, *Augustine's Ideal of the Religious Life*, New York, 1986; A. Manrique, *La vida monástica en San Augustín*, El Escorial-Salamanca, 1959.

58. Roth, *op. cit.*, pages 108-121.

59. R. Arbesmann, "Henry of Freimar's 'Treatise on the origin and development of the Order of the Hermit Friars, and its true and real title,'" *Augustiniana* VI (1956) 53-55.

60. A. Landucci, *Sacra Ilicetana Sylva, sive origo et chronicon breve coenobii et congregationis de Iliceto, Ord. Erem. S. P. Augustini in Tuscia*, Siena, 1653, pages 14; 77-78 (hereinafter *Sacra Ilicetana Sylva*).

61. The work was used by Landucci, who quoted extracts in *Sacra Ilicetana Sylva*, pages 43; 44; 78, and referred, on pages 14 and 49, to other extracts. This work by Giles is not to be confused with his *De laudibus Congregationis Ilicetanae*, now Angelica, MS 1156. See Appendix 4.

62. R. M. Huber, *History of the Franciscan Order, 1182-1517*, Milwaukee-Washington 1944, pages 181-232, 255-360.

63. F. Chabod, "The concept of the Renaissance," in *Machiavelli and the Renaissance*, London, 1958, 149-200; W. K. Ferguson, *The Renaissance in Historical Thought*, Cambridge (MA) 1948, pages 8-28.

64. It has been estimated that during the years 1348-1352 some 5,084 Augustinian friars succumbed to the Black Death; see J. Pamphilius, *Chronicon Ordinis Fratrum Eremitarum Sancti Augustini*, Rome, 1581, page 56r. It would be difficult to appreciate the harm done to discipline and the moral fiber of the Order by the ravages of the pestilence; see also Gutiérrez, *The Augustinians in the Middle Ages 1357-1517*, History of the Order of St. Augustine, volume I, part II, Villanova, 1983, pages 97-98.

65. For the damage done to the Augustinians by the Great Schism see F. Roth, "The Great Schism and the Augustinian Order," in *Augustiniana* VIII (1958) 281-298; Gutiérrez, *op. cit.*

66. *Gli assempri di Fra Filippo da Siena*, ed. F. C. Carpellini, Siena, 1864. Fra Filippo came as a novice to Lecceto in 1353, and wrote his *Assempri* between 1397-1416.

67. A. Gwynn, *The English Austin Friars in the Time of Wycliff*, London, 1940, pages 139-140; M. B. Hackett, "The Spiritual Life of the English Austin Friars of the Fourteenth Century," in *Sanctus Augustinus Vitae Spiritualis Magister*, Rome, 1959, II, 471-492. Flete died in 1395 or thereabouts.

68. E. G. Gardner, *Saint Catherine of Siena*, London 1907, pages 94-95. Apropos of Gardner's description it may be added that the ilex forest has once more grown to its former luxuriance. A surviving extract from Giles' lost work, *Panegyricus pro coenobio Ilicetano*, expresses the spirit of which Gardner wrote. "Nemus, in quo sancta et regularis vita semper floruit, mira et mirabili innumerabilium Patrum luce ac sanctitate clarum, cuius habitatores non modo Deo chari ob sanctissimum vitae institutum, verum etiam ob multa magnaque prodigia, quae diversis apud eos apparuerunt stupori hominibus et miracula fuere," cited in Landucci, *Sacra Ilicetana Sylva*, page 43.

69. This is the date given by Landucci, though there does not appear to be a contemporary document to prove it. The prior general, Agostino Favaroni, in a declaration of 18 April 1420, attributed the foundation of the observant movement at Lecceto to Bartholomew, but without giving a precise date. See *Analecta Augustiniana* 6 (1915-1916), 258.

70. Landucci, *op. cit.*, pages 22, 40, 46. For Nicola di Cerretani, who was considered to have set the high standard for the observations at Lecceto, see Herrera, *Alphabetum Augustinianum*, II, page 173.

71. This was confirmed by decrees of the general chapter of Rimini in June 1394, of Munich in June 1397, and of Aquila in June 1400; see Landucci, *op. cit.*, pages 40, 47.

72. An upheaval in the community caused the friars to change their allegiance to the Canons Regular of Saint Augustine in 1408. However, most of the commu-

nity returned to their former mode of life during that same year, see Landucci, page 23.

73. This was the seal of Lecceto as early as 1422, see Landucci, page 24; when Giles became a cardinal in 1518 he adopted the Lecceto crest for his coat-of-arms.

74. Landucci, page 25; Perini, *Bibliographia Augustiniana*, III, pages 201-202.

75. For Oliva (1407-1463), *Bibliographia Augustiniana*, III, pages 31-35. See the warm compliments paid to Oliva by Pius II in his *Commentarii rerum memorabilium*, ed. Frankfurt 1614, pages 179, 329-605.

76. Landucci, page 26. For Anselmo, see above, note 14.

77. Landucci, page 26.

78. *Ibid.,* page 41.

79. Giles to Zoccoli, Lecceto, 1 May 1502, in Angelica, MS 1001, fol. 221v-222r; *Lettere Familiari*, I, pages 149-150.

80. Signorelli, *Egidio*, page 134, note 49, who however overlooked Giles' letter to Serafino, Lecceto, 3 August 1502, in Angelica, MS 1001, fol. 3r; see *Lettere Familiari*, I, pages 169-170.

81. "Congregatio vestra et aetate antiquissima et institutis commendatissima adeo nobis semper cordi fuit, ut illam (ut scitis) universae religionis preposuerimus et habitandam, quasi certiorem coeli viam, elegerimus," Giles to the friars of Lecceto, Rome, 13 September 1509, in Siena, MS G.X. 26 page 167.

82. *Ibid.* He expressed the same thought in his *De Ilicetana Familia*. "Reliquum est ut experrecti dicamus cum Jacob: Vere locus iste sanctus est; et non est aliud nisi Bethel et porta coeli; vos illius claves habetis," in Angelica, MS 1156, fol. 10r; see Appendix 4.

83. Giles to the friars of Lecceto, Cimino, July 1506, in Martène and Durand, III, cols. 1235-1238; see *Lettere Familiari*, I, pages 337-342.

84. No other christological passage is to be found in Pontano's works. Even in *Aegidius* the sermon stands out in contrast with the rest of the work.

85. Giles to the friars of Lecceto, Cimino, July 1506 (see note 83 above).

86. *Ibid.,* col. 1235.

87. *Ibid.*

88. *Ibid.* His spartan hermitage on the Cimino, though in ruins, still bears witness to his words.

89. *Ibid.,* col. 1236.

90. *Ibid.*

91. "Eloquentia tua, qua, christiane mi Cicero, animis hominum dominaris . . . Nam cum eloquentium longe sis religiosissimus, id etiam felicitate ingenii consecutus es, ut et religiosorum omnium, quoscumque haec tulit aetas, idem facile sis eloquentissimus," Summonte in the preface of *Aegidius* in *Opera Omnia Johannis Joviani Pontani*, II, Venice 1518, fol. 154v.

92. Giles to Serafino, 15 December 1503, in Angelica, MS 1001, fol. 70v; *Lettere Familiari*, I, page 207.

93. Giles to Giovanni Botonti, Siena, 7 May 1502, in Angelica, MS 1001, fol. 112v; Signorelli, *Egidio*, page 218; *Lettere Familiari*, I, pages 155-156.

94. Giles to Serafino, Rome, 28 July 1517, in Angelica, MS 1001, fol. 32v; *Lettere Familiari*, II, page 229.

95. He was appointed procurator general of the congregation in Rome in 1508, was elected prior of Lecceto in 1512, again in 1514 and 1515, and vicar general of the congregation in 1516. See Landucci, *Sacra Ilicetana Sylva*, pages 30, 31, 59, 61, 147.

96. Giles to Botonti, Siena, May 1502, *Lettere Familiari*, I, page 156.

97. *Ibid.*

98. *Ibid.*

99. Signorelli, *Egidio*, page 134, note 51, found himself almost baffled for biographical facts about Zoccoli. He overlooked the useful note by L.-G. Pélissier, "Pour la biographie du Cardinal Gilles de Viterbe," in *Miscellanea di studi critici edita in onore de Arturo Graf*, Bergamo 1903, page 805, note 1, which serves to correct Signorelli. There are letters between Giles and Zoccoli in Angelica, MS 1001.

100. For Botonti see Signorelli, *Egidio*, pages 262-263.

101. The facts of Almadiani's life are threaded together in an admirable fashion by Signorelli, *Egidio*, pages 259-262.

102. For Almadiani in the Goritz circle, see Signorelli, *Egidio*, page 260; for Giles' attendance at Goritz's house, see Tiraboschi, *Storia della letteratura italiana*, VII, part 4, 1596.

103. Signorelli, *Egidio*, pages 260-262.

104. Botonti to Giles, Rome 24 June 1502, in Angelica, MS 1001, fol. 59r-v (printed in Signorelli, *Egidio*, pages 250-251, but with wrong foliation mentioned); see also *Lettere Familiari*, I, pages 162-163.

105. Giles to Botonti, Siena, 7 May 1502. This letter and that of Botonti to Giles, Rome, 24 June 1502, show how the negotiations were guided. Signorelli did not explain the inner working of events.

106. Botonti to Giles, Rome, 24 June 1502, states that he had asked for and received the letters from the Viterbo city council a few days previously.

107. Landucci, *Sacra Ilicetana Sylva*, page 59.

108. Signorelli, *Egidio*, page 251.

109. *Ibid.*, pages 134-135, note 53, from MS 31, *Archivio della Cattedrale di Viterbo*, fol. 372.

110. Signorelli, *Egidio*, page 135, note 58.

111. Giles to Serafino, Cimino, 15 July 1505, in Angelica, MS 1001, fol. 77v, Signorelli, *Egidio*, page 222; *Lettere Familiari*, I, pages 270-271.

Chapter 2

Preacher

It can be deduced that Giles began preaching in the year 1493 when he was studying at Padua. In his oration at the opening of the Fifth Lateran Council in April 1512 he stated that his career as a preacher went back for about twenty years.[1] A more precise date is given in a letter of July 1507 to the prince of Macedonia, where Giles mentioned that for fourteen years he had been accustomed to preaching.[2] However, his success in the pulpit was not meteoric. His first notable appearance as a preacher was in 1497 when he was summoned to be heard by Alexander VI in Rome. His effort was sufficiently successful to warrant another sermon *coram pontifice* before he and Mariano left for Naples in the late spring or early summer of 1498. It was due to Mariano that Giles gained these opportunities to preach before the pope, and it was likewise because of the patronage of such a recognized master of eloquence that the humanists at Naples were predisposed in favor of Giles. Ultimately it was on his own merits that he gained their approval. Eloquence for them, and for the critical audiences in any city of Renaissance Italy, was not a matter of words and gesture. It was the art of presenting doctrine in the cultured language of the humanists. Part of the success achieved by Savonarola and other revivalist preachers of the time such as Girolamo da Siena, Fra Bonaventura, and Girolamo da Bergamo was due to the very novelty of their harsh words in contrast with those of typical preachers like Mariano da Genazzano.

Giles' friends, the humanists, were to be his undoing in life as they were also after his death. The price which Giles paid for his success with the Pontanian Academy was the loss of the seclusion dear to his heart. Though Renaissance scholars were sometimes ruthless toward one another they as often displayed the qualities of a mutual admiration society. This was noticeably true of Italy where each academy formed a group of elite. A member of an academy was addressed in superlative terms by his colleagues in their letters and writings. The constant correspondence and visits between members of different academies kept these scholars well-informed about the studies and personalities of the various Italian cities. The Pontanian was one of the foremost academies and acted as host to the *literati* of other academies such as that of Pomponius Laetus at Rome and the Platonic Academy at Florence. Though Giles' permanent connection with Naples was severed by his departure from the city in autumn 1501 his fame went before him by means of the humanists. While at Naples in October 1501 he was already committed against his will to preach at Siena before Christmas. An illness laid him low at Viterbo in December, but he was at Siena by the third week of January 1502, and was fully occupied with the course of Lenten sermons there during February and the first half of March. An Augustinian, Raffaele Brandolini, wrote from Rome to Giles on 30 April mentioning the praise which the sermons had drawn from many sources. Such direct compliments to a preacher generally need to be reduced considerably in order to arrive at the strict truth. In this case there is a reassurance that Brandolini was not exaggerating unduly. Five months later, in September 1503, when Siena was ablaze with joy at the news of the election of Francesco Piccolomini as Pius III, the Signoria summoned Giles from the isle of Martana so that justice might be done to the occasion by his eloquence.

Mariano da Genazzano

There is further testimony from Brandolini's own native city, Florence, where Giles preached in April 1502. Among his listeners was a layman, Piero Parenti. As Parenti had also heard Mariano da Genazzano and Savonarola his remarks are worth noting:

> I shall deal with the Augustinian friar, Giles of Viterbo, who is so like Fra Mariano da Genazzano that you would not believe it possible. Their resemblances are as follows: the same stature, the same pronunciation, the same method when introducing the sermon, the same vehemence in developing the theme, the same eloquence and erudition. Indeed, in learning Giles surpasses Mariano. He is skilled in Greek, Hebrew, and Latin. He is a philosopher and a profound theologian, a Platonist and an Aristotelian, and is versed in profane and sacred history. All this is accompanied by a perfect knowledge of, and dexterity with, the scriptures.[3]

The resemblance to Mariano also struck Paolo da Genazzano, a nephew of Mariano. When dedicating a theological work to Giles in the year 1502 he remarked: "All who have been present at your sermons declare that you are a double person, not Mariano da Genazzano, not Giles of Viterbo, but a fusion of both, and yet better than either."

What impression did Mariano make on his contemporaries? If Parenti and Paolo were accurate in their observations we can glimpse Giles and catch his accents as we watch and listen to Mariano in the pulpit. Poliziano, who embodied the poetry and classical learning of the Medici circle, wrote in April 1489 to Tristano Calchi at Milan on hearing that Mariano was to preach in that city. He urged Calchi not to miss the opportunity of hearing the friar. He recalled that when Mariano came to preach for the first time in Florence he himself went to listen to the sermon, not for any worthy motive, but to sneer at this much-vaunted preacher. From the moment Mariano appeared in the pulpit Poliziano found himself spellbound. The preacher's stance and expression held his gaze. Poliziano continued:

> he began to speak and I pricked up my ears. I heard a harmonious voice, apt words, elevating and pious sentiments. He divided his subject and I found nothing incongruous, nothing superfluous, nothing bombastic. His proofs convinced me, his illustrations delighted me, and I was enraptured by the music of his pronunciation. When he chose to joke I laughed, when he pressed home a point I was left no option, I surrendered; I was overcome. When he treated of delicate emotions I wept, when he was aroused and threatened I grew terrified and wished I had not come. In short, he varied his illustrations and voice according to his thoughts, and by his gestures supported and heightened the effect of his words.[4]

Poliziano went on to state that it was hard to credit such a slight frame with this fire and spirit. Yet one did not tire of Mariano as of a novelty; the more often one heard him the greater seemed his variety and his power to stimulate. In private life he did not bore his friends with the preacher's itch to moralize. Poliziano found that when Mariano mixed in the company of Lorenzo the Magnificent, Pico della Mirandola, and the Florentine humanists, his moderate opinions and grace of manner made him welcome to all.

The Accepted Preacher

With such a memory still bright in Florence Giles found a ready welcome. Lorenzo de' Medici, because of his esteem for Mariano, had caused the magnificent monastery and church of San Gallo to be built for the Augustinians. The friars there insisted that Giles would give two series of sermons during Christmas 1502 and the new year 1503. Giles wrote to Serafino from Florence on 6 January 1503 commenting that the walls of the church were almost in danger, so tightly packed were the crowds who came to hear him at San Gallo. He was not drawing the long bow in describing his popularity at Florence. Parenti wrote in December 1502 that Giles held the Florentines under his sway, and had produced a reform of morals by his denunciation of blasphemy and gambling. Four months later Parenti reported that the city flocked to hear Giles, men and women, nobility and common people. Giles, in a letter of 6 January 1503, told Serafino with evident delight of the many people at Florence whom he had led back to God. He then mused from experience on how the different cities in Italy reacted to a preacher:

> At Naples any speaker is welcome as long as he is not foreign to the muses and literary grace. Genoa gives ear to the unusual. At Milan the crowds press upon the preacher. Once the Venetians approve of an orator they treat him with the greatest veneration and liberality. Rome, if you except a sprinkling of people and pious women, does not readily listen, nor does it pay much attention unless he is a most learned man. At Florence not alone do they attend and listen, and pay attention and relish, but they venerate and even idolize. I doubt if the apostles preached to any people more dedicated to religion and piety.[5]

Peacemaker

Giles passed from Florence into Emilia, going by way of Bologna and Ferrara to Viterbo.[6] When he preached at Bologna and Ferrara he found audiences who were still terrified by the earthquakes which had recently shaken the countryside.[7] He could not resist the popular preacher's device of warning the people that such upheavals were manifestations of God's wrath.[8] At Ferrara he paid a visit to the notorious Lucrezia Borgia, wife of Alfonso d'Este, son and heir of the prince of Ferrara.[9] Whatever the alleged excesses of her previous years it is generally agreed that after her marriage with Alfonso in December 1501 her conduct was above reproach.[10] Some of the credit for her decorous behavior is given to Giles.[11]

Whatever pleasure he may have experienced in meeting Lucrezia was spoiled by another member of the Borgia family when he reached Viterbo late in February. For a long time Viterbo had been torn by disputes between two factions, the Maganzesi and the Gatteschi.[12] After the fall of the house of Naples in 1501 Caesar Borgia set about establishing a kingdom in central Italy. With this end in view Alexander VI dispossessed or heavily mulcted the Roman barons, the Colonna, Orsini, Savelli, and Gaetani. Not all of them submitted meekly. Some of the Colonna united with the

Gatteschi of Viterbo, while the Maganzesi automatically joined forces with the Orsini, the traditional foes of the Colonna. Confusion, bloodshed, and uncertainty reigned at Viterbo and in its neighborhood.[13] Giles vividly described the state of affairs:

> Never before were there such savage dissensions in the cities of the patrimony of Peter, never such frequent pillaging, never such bloody slaughter, never had bandits such a free hand on the roads, never was the lot of travelers more endangered.[14]

To add to all these miseries Caesar Borgia, then grimly set on reducing the Orsini citadels at Cere and Bracciano, arrived at Viterbo on 5 February 1503 with an army of six thousand foot soldiers and one thousand horsemen.[15] These he quartered in the unfortunate city. The citizens were despoiled of their valuables and according to Giustiniani, the Venetian ambassador at Rome, some of the poorer inhabitants died of sheer starvation.[16] Giles' estimation of Caesar Borgia was summed up in one phrase, "a master of deceit and treachery."[17] Caesar's army did not leave until 25 February. When Giles returned to the city, he found that the Viterbesi had reached the limit of their endurance. According to a reliable local historian it was Giles who organized the religious procession which brought an end to turmoil in the city.[18] All reports agree that his sermon was the climax of the occasion.[19]

A procession of women and children, dressed in white and carrying olive branches, left the Augustinian church bearing with them a picture of the Blessed Virgin. As they wound their way around the city, they chanted, "Peace! Peace! God and the Virgin Mary want peace!" More and more people were drawn to join the procession as it moved through the streets and back toward the slope on which stood the Augustinian church. The tumult brought the magistrates and the governor of the city, Bishop Niccolò d'Este, hurrying to the scene, alarmed that another bloody riot or an attack on the city was afoot. Relieved beyond words to find a religious demonstration they too joined in the procession. It was met by Giles and the friars who led it into the church. In such an electric atmosphere and to such a highly emotional audience Giles delivered a resounding sermon on peace. As he concluded the people burst out into cries of "Peace! Peace!" It was thus that tranquility returned to Viterbo. The citizens signed a public instrument, binding themselves to peace and to a fine of one thousand gold ducats on anyone who would disrupt law and order in the city.[20]

Viterbesi historians have exaggerated Giles' role in the advent of peace to their native city. Before he had returned to the city, all were heartily sick of the factional fighting, and had already manifested their desire to make peace with one another and with Alexander VI.[21] Nevertheless, it required something such as a religious demonstration to soothe the hatreds and lull the passion in the city. Giles' intervention supplied the occasion which was commonly desired. To that extent the outcome of events at Viterbo was bound to enhance his reputation. Niccolò d'Este, governor of Viterbo, was a brother-in-law of Lucrezia Borgia. According to Lingeri he was profuse in his thanks to Giles.[22] Viterbo straddled the Via Cassia, the main road leading north to Florence, and it was of utmost concern for Alexander VI that the city be internally united and loyal to its papal allegiance.

Giles went from Viterbo to preach in the Augustinian church of Saint Stephen at Venice, probably for the Holy Week sermons in mid-April.[23] His reception there confirmed the comment which he had made to his friend, Serafino Ferri, that "once the Venetians approve of a preacher they treat him with the greatest veneration and liberality."[24] After this visit to Venice he wrote to Serafino that he feared for his own humility, so many were the gifts and marks of honor conferred upon him.[25] The Venetians were not satisfied until he agreed to return for a course of sermons the following year.[26] His popularity as a preacher made evident that the solitude he desired would not be found at Lecceto. The friars there were animated by a religious spirit and sustained by a strict discipline which satisfied Giles' ideals, but the hermitage was too readily accessible from Siena. He foresaw that he would be in frequent demand as a preacher. In order to put a physical barrier between himself and importunate visitors he went to live in a hermitage on the isle of Martana in Lake Bolsena.

Martana

Martana seemed to fulfill Giles' hopes. He was living near his native city, yet in circumstances which made him difficult of access. Lake Bolsena lies about ten miles northwest of Viterbo, on the way to Orvieto. A circle of the Cimino hills, wooded with chestnut and beech, surrounds the lake and gives it an air of retirement. This is the country of the Tuscan tombs, where since pre-Roman times the *mystique* has been a tranquil consciousness of death and of the life hereafter. Enshrined in the lake are two small islands, Martana and

Bisentina, their air of mystery deepened by clusters of plane trees and evergreen bushes. Martana, the larger of the two islands, rises high out of the water sloping gently upward to a hillock from which one can survey lake and hillside. It is an ideal retreat for contemplation, and at least since the eleventh century harbored a church dedicated to Saint Stephen.[27] At a later stage Benedictine nuns founded a convent there, and a chapel dedicated to Saint Mary Magdalene was built upon the hillock.[28] In the year 1459 the bishop of Montefiascone entrusted the buildings to the care of the Augustinians.[29] A friary and a new chapel dedicated to the Magdalene were erected at the expense of Cardinal Domenico della Rovere and completed by the year 1500.[30] It was probably about the same time that the friary became a hermitage of the Congregation of Lecceto. Certainly at the time Giles went to live there during the summer of 1503 it was part of the Leccetan reform.[31]

He was living on Martana by 21 July 1503,[32] in an atmosphere which he described as "so suitable for the religious life and contemplation."[33] His peace was short-lived. Alexander VI died of fever at Rome on 18 August 1503; Caesar Borgia was then prostrate with illness, and with his menacing figure removed from the scene the cardinals hurried to a papal election. A deadlock ensued between the Spanish, French, and Italian parties among the cardinals. Finally, as a compromise the aged Francesco Piccolomini, cardinal of Siena, was elected on 22 September, taking the name of Pius III in honor of his uncle, Pius II. Siena was thrilled with jubilation on hearing the news. Elaborate preparations were made for a public celebration to take place in the piazza on 8 October, the date of the pope's coronation in Rome. The city council of Siena would be satisfied with nothing but the best for the occasion. A letter was dispatched to Giles on 27 September, telling him of Piccolomini's election, of the forthcoming celebration, and urgently requesting that he preach in the piazza. The council explained that Giles alone would do justice to so great an event in the history of the city. They asked with an exaggerated anxiety that as soon as he received the letter he would ride with all speed by horse so that he might be in Siena by the eighth of October.

There was a special satisfaction in acceding to the request. Giles regarded Pius III as a shining light in the college of cardinals, a welcome contrast to Alexander VI.[34] The new pope might be able to effect the reform so necessary for the well-being of the Church. Indeed, Giles overreached himself in his effort to do justice to the Piccolomini pope. Sigismondo Tizio who was among the exultant crowd in the piazza has left on record that though the Augustinian friar delivered a brilliant oration he tired his audience by the length of the discourse and by frequent repetition of the verse from Psalm 103: *He made the moon for seasons; the sun knows its going down.* The verse was chosen to point out the significance of the sun and moon on the Piccolomini coat of arms. Giles, in a letter written from Lecceto six days later, revealed the central idea of the discourse and the principal authorities from whose writings he wove the text of his oration.[35] His theme was the divine harmony in events. To this purpose he quoted liberally from Saint Augustine, Boethius, Ptolemy, and the *Timaeus* of Plato. Giles here showed himself the humanist and neoplatonist, harmonizing the writings of the Grecian and Christian worlds.

Rome and Julius II

Giles went from Siena to Lecceto,[36] then to Florence,[37] and was in Rome by 25 November.[38] The hopes which he had built on Pius III had vanished with the death of the pope on 18 October. Giuliano della Rovere, a man cast in a different mold from Piccolomini, was elected pope on 31 October after the shortest conclave known up to that time in papal history. His past life could hardly have inspired Giles with the hope that the urgently needed reform of the Church would be set afoot. However, as we shall see later Giles was to trust that the martial ardor of Julius would be turned to a crusade against the Turks. The pope for his part looked with friendly interest on the friar. It was an initial advantage for Giles that he was an Augustinian. The della Rovere family treated the Augustinian church of Santa Maria del Popolo as their favorite.[39] Julius commissioned Raffaele, Bramante, and Sansovino, among other artists, to embellish the church.[40] The favor which the pope was to show for Giles was due to more than the connection of Santa Maria del Popolo. Julius valued the friar as a reformer and preacher. He also regarded him as a useful diplomatic agent. The Augustinian historian, Torelli, states that Giles was summoned to Rome by a papal brief of 14 December,[41] and though this appears curious in view of the fact that Giles wrote a letter from the city on 15 December,[42] the fact of the summons, whatever its date, is corroborated by another letter in which he stated that he was recalled to Rome when he had returned to the isle of Martana and was preparing for a visit to Venice.[43] The Venetians resented the interference by authorities in Rome. The diarist, Sanudo, mentions a letter written on 6 February 1504 by the Venetian ambassador at Rome affirming that Giles was prevented from going to Venice by the opposition of certain cardinals.[44] Giles himself in a letter of 31 January 1504 informed his friend Serafino that the college of cardinals had made plain to the pope that it would be a shame if in this matter Venice were to receive preference over Rome.[45] In the same letter Giles commented that it was practically impossible to disentangle himself from commitments at Rome. It was not merely that the cardinals, the Augustinians, and his friends urged him to stay in the city. The Roman populace were truculent in their desire to hear him preach, though Giles was dubious of any good which might be effected among them. He had previously expressed his skepticism about the religious interest of a Roman audience.[46] To add to his dissatisfaction he was not allowed to preach in an Augustinian church but had to deliver his sermons in the basilica of San Damaso, the titular church of Cardinal Riario.[47] It would not have been wise to gainsay the wishes of Riario, protector of the Augustinian Order and nephew of Julius II. Early in February the Venetian ambassador was advised by the college of cardinals that he should desist from his attempts to have the friar for Venice. Why this effort to obtain a particular preacher for San Marco, and the resolute refusal of the Roman authorities to allow him leave the city? It should not be imagined that Giles in himself had any political significance, but it is probably true that the affair was part of Julius' insistence that the Venetians should return the papal possessions seized in the Romagna. Refusing a preacher for Venice was only part of the diplomatic game. Though Giles announced on 31 January 1504 that he had received permission from Riario to go where he wished,[48] five weeks later he was willy-nilly preaching at San Lorenzo. In the same letter of 31 January he commented that he was free to go where God would lead him, and when he did leave Rome he turned his footsteps to Viterbo and Lake Bolsena.[49] He seems to have assumed that his own personal preferences coincided with God's will.

Literary Interests

Once back in his hermitage on the isle of Martana he was able to give free rein to his literary tastes. The evidence which remains indicates that at this time his interest in the learning of the ancient classical world remained unabated. His copy of Valla's published translation of Homer's *Iliad* has survived.[50] The book is heavily annotated by Giles, and the last folio bears the date June 1504.[51] Bound in with this volume, and probably in use at the same time, is a copy of Bessarion's *In Calumniatorem platonis,* published by Manuzio at Venice in July 1503 and copiously annotated in Giles' handwriting.[52] In a letter of July 1504 Giles mentioned that during his time on Martana he wrote "the eclogues."[53] Fortunately these three compositions have survived, and show Giles' modeling his poetry on the pastoral hexameters of Vergil. Homer and Vergil, Plato and Aristotle, along with the Bible were to be the authorities most frequently quoted by Giles in his letters and literary works. In the year 1504 he was aged thirty-five, coming toward the prime of life. The literary interests which he had formed by that year remained for the rest of his life, though in his later years there was to be added a marked enthusiasm for the cabala and rabbinical studies. The catalogue of the manuscripts which he possessed as a cardinal (1517-1532) reveals that though his main concentration was then on scriptural and rabbinical works he had maintained his interest in Homer, Plato, Aristotle, and Vergil. In a letter of 2 July 1504 he disclosed the interesting fact that four years previously he had written a novel in Italian, entitled *Cyminia.*[54] Though this work has not survived there is an obvious suggestion about the background to its composition. In the year 1500 he was living at Naples, a member of the Pontanian Academy. Masuccio Salernitano's *Novellino,* published in 1476, had set the fashion at Naples for prose works in the vernacular, but it may be safely assumed that Giles' novel had none of the moral traits which Masuccio showed in his.

The eclogues give a valuable insight into Giles' mentality. They show that he was attempting to Christianize the pagan world of the classics rather than allowing the spirit of the classical authors to permeate his religious thought. It is often supposed that the Renaissance use of classical terms and figures of speech meant submission to a pagan ethos. At least with Giles it was an expression of his belief that what was good in the classical world could be made to serve the Christian message. Two of his eclogues have the birth and resurrection of Christ as their main theme. Giles described in graceful terms how the angels who appeared to inform the shepherds of the birth of Christ were spirits more beautiful than Phyllis and Chloe. Giles believed that such presentation was a fruitful method of conveying the story of Christ to Renaissance readers. It has yet to be proved that given the circumstances of his Italy the method was unsound or unsuccessful.

Though Giles found peace on Martana, separated as he was by a barrier of water from the complications of normal social life, the island was not suitable for his health. There was inadequate cover during winter and spring when the searing *tramontana* swept over the Cimino hills and across the lake. It will be remembered that his stay at Capo d'Istria ended in 1497 because of the harsh winter and spring weather which he experienced on the Dalmatian coast. He suffered likewise during the summer months on Martana, when the mirrored surface of Lake Bolsena sent waves of heat across the isles of Martana and Bisentina. His friends, Almadiani, Botonti, Serafino, Zoccoli, and others, feared for his health and pressed the cardinal protector, Riario, to allow Giles to settle in a healthier refuge. Yet Giles had practically to be forced by friendly threats and exhortations to leave Lake Bolsena in July 1504.[55] Though he quit Martana sadly, even, according to his words, with tears, he was never to regret the change. Up on Cimino he found himself in circumstances which corresponded with the *vita solitaria* as idealized by men of the Renaissance like Petrarch.

Cimino

Cimino is the highest hill in the region of Viterbo, rising at its summit to over a thousand and fifty meters. Clinging to one of its ridges is the town of Soriano, "the jewel of the Cimino," with its sloping streets dominated by the formidable thirteenth century Orsini citadel. The hermitage lies far above the town, nestling among the beech trees in a place which even today is difficult of access. The Augustinians founded a small friary and church there in the thirteenth century, but by the year 1504 it had been abandoned and was in a ruined condition.[56] Giles stated in 1506 that if it had not been rebuilt, the mountain streams would have washed him and the hermitage away.[57] For its reconstruction he received liberal support from the governor of Soriano, Bertrando Alidosi, and from his brother, Francesco, the unsavory cardinal bishop of Pavia.[58] Before Giles left Martana he was guaranteed an annual income for the hermitage by Giulia Farnese, Giulia La Bella, then living at Castel Bassanello near Soriano.[59] Francesco Alidosi became a confidant of Julius II during these years, and in 1505 Giulia's only daughter, Laura, married Niccolò della Rovere, a nephew of the pope. In the light of these facts it is easier to understand how Giles was a persona grata with Julius II.

It was one of the apparent paradoxes of Giles' career that though of unblemished life as far as is known, and not a place-hunter, he was regarded with favor by the members of the hard sensual world of the Borgia, the Alidosi, the della Rovere, and the Farnese. It was part of this paradox that the more he sought to live apart in solitude the louder became the demands for him to appear in the pulpit. He wrote to a friend, Mannio, during the summer of 1504 lamenting that when he had withdrawn to Cimino he found that even in this area there was no village or hamlet which did not insist on claiming him for a sermon.[60] His mother and a sister of his were living nearby at Canino,[61] and it would have been difficult for him to refuse to preach in the church there. Soriano now had a special claim upon him, as had his native city, Viterbo. However, he had no distant excursions to make until the following winter.[62]

More Preaching

He delivered a course of sermons at Ferrara in December 1504. In a letter to Serafino he related that he used the occasion to inveigh against the evil morals of the time.[63] Members of the ruling d'Este family were present, and doubtlessly included Lucrezia Borgia, wife of the heir apparent, Alfonso, who was then hurrying back from England where his visit to the court of Henry VII had been cut short by the news that his father, Duke Ercole I, was seriously ill. Alfonso's depraved brothers, Giulio and Cardinal Ippolito, can hardly have taken Giles' severe admonitions to heart if one may judge from the sordid affair of Angela Borgia which took place during 1505. The cardinal had Giulio seized and succeeded in having one of his eyes torn out. It was an event which had the direst consequences for several members of the d'Este family. Whatever was true of Giulio and Ippolito, other members of the family were so swept away with enthusiasm by Giles' preaching that they refused to allow him continue on to Venice.[64] His protestations were of no avail until he promised that he would return sometime during 1505.[65] He fell seriously ill at Ferrara, and the rumor reached Rome that he was dead. The story assumed a sinister color in Venice, where it was reported that the friar had been poisoned at the behest of Cardinal Riario and of his follower, Bishop Giacomo de Ruelis.[66] A natural death or illness was often attributed to poisoning by the men of the Renaissance, and Venetian suspicion of the della Rovere family showed itself in what in this case was an unfounded rumor.

Giles reached Venice in January 1505 and remained there for more than three months. Sanudo, the Venetian diarist, mentioned that Giles delivered a course of sermons to packed congregations in the church of Saint Stephen, and recorded the fact that Giles baptized a Jew on Palm Sunday, 23 March.[67] It is tempting to believe that the Jew was the Hebrew scholar, Felice da Prato, who was converted to Christianity sometime before 1506, became an Augustinian, was in correspondence with Giles, and edited the first rabbinical Bible in 1518.[68]

Pastoral Sensitivity

During April Giles preached in the basilica of San Marco, the architectural glory of Venice. He denounced the then prevalent vice of blasphemy and invoked the aid of the senate to enforce civil penalties against the offenders.[69] Such intervention by the state was not an unusual procedure at this time, but the information is illuminating as evidence that Giles dealt with practical issues in at least some of his sermons. Böhmer believed that Giles as a preacher was a voice and nothing more, eloquent in discussing the abstract vices and virtues in the manner of Cicero and Seneca, but without any lasting effect on the crowds which flocked to hear him in so many Italian cities.[70] Böhmer refers by contrast to Savonarola's startling success as a preacher at Florence. The comparison is unfortunate. Savonarola's triumph was dazzling but short-lived. It is very difficult, almost impossible, to decide how enduring is the impact of any popular preacher on his contemporaries.

Böhmer would have it that Giles' ultimate failure in the pulpit emerges from the fact that, as far as the evidence goes, his sermons were not copied down by any of his listeners. This is an arbitrary measure of success. Giles' fame as a preacher coincided with the diffusion of printing and the abandonment of the custom of copying by hand. He himself is primarily to blame for the absence of his sermons in printed form. However, this was a feature common to all his literary work and was partly explained by the demands made upon his time by administration, diplomatic missions, and preaching tours. He was conscious of the criticism that he was not committing himself to print and commented sarcastically in July 1505 that in view of all his engagements the wonder was not that he was writing so little but that he was alive.[71]

One obvious reason why he has left no copies of his "normal" sermons is that these in all likelihood were delivered extempore or at best from skeleton notes such as are found in his *Themata sermonum de tempore*, now in the Bibliothèque Nationale, Paris.[72] He possessed the gift of ready eloquence, choice words, and a mind adapted to the people and movements of his Italy. It is unlikely that, except for special occasions, he prepared his sermons in detail beforehand. Two of his more famous orations were printed during his lifetime but they can hardly be described as examples of his typical sermons; they were composed for special occasions. One was the discourse delivered at the opening session of the Fifth Lateran Council in May 1512;[73] the other was the official oration on the occasion of the treaty between the Emperor Maximilian and Pope Julius II in November 1512.[74] We also have the text of a discourse delivered on 21 December 1507 in St. Peter's at Rome, at thanksgiving celebrations for the Portuguese successes in the Far East, and three other compositions have survived which, although they may be classed as sermons, are of a special type — two directed to the friars of Lecceto and the third addressed to Antonio Zoccoli and the Romans.[75]

His sermon notes in the Bibliothèque Nationale, Paris, are the basis for a series of his workaday sermons but unfortunately they represent no more than the bare outline of what he intended to preach. In this sketchy form they convey no sense of that extraordinary power which electrified his Italian listeners during the first two decades of the century. We are thus left without the text of what may be termed his normal sermon, one of those delivered as part of the series he preached during Advent or Lent at Rome, Siena, Ferrara, Venice, and the other cities of Italy. Nevertheless, there is evidence to contradict Böhmer's belief that Giles was little more than a word spinner, or at best a mere rhetorician and theorizing professor in the pulpit.

The most convincing proof of Giles' practical bent of mind are his registers and letters as general of the Augustinian Order, 1506-1518.[76] In these he often legislated for details in the daily lives of his friars. His comments on the clergy are biting. There is also evidence that in his sermons to lay people he could come down to earth.

It has been already noted that when Giles preached at San Marco in April 1505 he dealt with the abuse of blasphemy and sought the help of the city council to have it curbed. The friar undertook a much more delicate topic and faced a cynically interested audience on one occasion in Rome during Lent 1508, when he preached to the prostitutes of the city. The traffic in vice was perhaps greatest in Venice where the number of such unfortunate women was estimated at the beginning of the sixteenth century to be 11,000 out of a population of 300,000,[77] but at Rome also the numbers assumed alarming proportions. Infessura, a writer admittedly given to exaggeration, states that in the year 1490 there were 6,800 women plying this trade in Rome.[78] An observer from Mantua who was present in Rome during Giles' sermon reported that the Augustinian won the enthusiastic attention of his listeners and worked such a change in some that they left Rome to return to their homes, while others entered the religious houses of San Giorgio and San Sisto as penitents.[79] Though in fact the friar's appeal made no substantial difference to such a deeply rooted practice at Rome the immediate results of his sermon were a tribute to his common sense and virtuosity.

At first sight it would seem that Giles could have no comprehension of, or sympathy with, these women of easy virtue. He aspired to a life of study and prayer and was reputed to be of blameless morals. However, he had the artist's sensitivity to an audience. Besides, in Rome of the Renaissance, Vice treated Virtue as an equal and sometimes as an inferior. Giles in his public life had to meet and pay honor to men and women of evil repute. Vanozza di Cattanei, mistress of Alexander VI, was a devotee of the Augustinian church of Santa Maria del Popolo. Imperia, a famous Roman courtesan, was mistress of Agostino Chigi, who was a liberal benefactor of Santa Maria del Popolo. Association with such people was part of Giles' education as a reformer. An appreciation of the weakness of human nature was to be a very necessary quality in his role as prior general of the Augustinian Order.

Criticism

There is evidence which seems to support Böhmer's contention about Giles' preaching. We have seen that when Giles delivered a discourse at Siena on 8 October 1503 he dwelt on the divine harmony in events and drew largely from the thought of Augustine, Boethius, Ptolemy, and Plato. There we gain no sense of an application of the theme to the daily humdrum lives of the people. It was thus that Giles intended it. He was delivering not a sermon but a panegyric, a song of praise for Siena and the Piccolomini family.

There is other evidence, criticism of Giles, which cannot be so easily dismissed. Pietro Pomponazzi, the Aristotelian professor, published his *Apologia* in 1518. This was a defense of his teaching on the immortality of the soul, which he believed could not be proved by reason alone. In his final paragraphs he launched out into a searing denunciation of preachers who used the pulpit to demonstrate their own learning. What use is it, he heatedly demanded, for a preacher to quote Latin, Greek, Hebrew, and Chaldaic in his sermons, puffing up his own vanity with a display of erudition, while he neglects to speak in the vernacular and in the manner which would be understood by the simple, the unlettered, and the ignorant?[80] Is this the gospel? Where is the message of Christ? So Pomponazzi swept on to end his *Apologia* with this glorious philippic which might well have been a denunciation by one of the early Protestant Reformers.

Pomponazzi did not blame any particular preacher, but the unexpected introduction of this trenchant condemnation leaves more than a suspicion that he had a particular person in mind. A year later his views on the soul were answered by the Augustinian bishop, Ambrogio Flandini, in *De animarum immortalitate.* In his preface Flandini referred to Giles' virtues and to his firm conviction of the demonstrability of the immortality of the soul by reason alone.[81] Still, he gave no indication that it was Giles who had been under fire in the conclusion of Pomponazzi's work. Four years later Flandini published a book of sermons which is generally overlooked because of its rarity. He availed himself of a sermon for the feast of Saint Augustine of Hippo, and having as its topic the active and contemplative life, he praised Giles' spiritual and intellectual gifts.[82] He then revealed that Pomponazzi's criticism had been directed against Giles.

It is not too difficult to conclude why Pomponazzi should have had a grudge against Giles. Ever since his student days at Padua in the early 1490s Giles had been set in his opposition to the Averroists, and manifested his opinion by editing the *De intellectu possibili: contra Averoym* of Giles of Rome. During the first two decades of the sixteenth century, when writing his two major works, one historical, the other philosophical and theological, he denounced what he termed the incredulity and the pagan philosophers of Padua. Pomponazzi was an obvious target for the friar's remarks. Although the above-mentioned works were never printed, Giles had so many opportunities to express himself publicly that Pomponazzi was bound to know of his criticisms. Professor Kristeller states that Giles endorsed and perhaps inspired the dogmatic definition of the Fifth Lateran Council, 19 December

1513, condemning what in fact was Pomponazzi's teaching on the philosophical demonstrability of the immortality of the human soul.[83] Here was cause for deep resentment. It is in the light of Giles' stand against rationalism that we should view Pomponazzi's harangue against "learned preachers."

Preaching Method

It is true that Giles studded his sermons, and his letters also, with references to and quotations from Plato, Aristotle, Homer, Vergil, and other masters of Greek and Roman thought. But almost always these references were ancillary to a scriptural quotation. The same method was used by the Franciscan, Roberto da Lecce (1425-1495), whose preaching helped to produce a religious revival in many parts of Italy.

Giles and the neoplatonists of his time looked on the history of human thought as having a pattern in which all the great figures of classical thought were witnesses to the one truth. For the neoplatonists therefore it was not incongruous but a corroboration of their belief when an authority such as Plato or Homer could be summoned to testify in its favor. Nor did it appear a desecration of the Christian revelation to use classical mythology when illustrating God's dealings with humankind. So Giles saw the love affairs of Jupiter as a representation of divine affection for the human race; the transport of the beautiful infant, Ganymede, to Olympus was an image of man deified by the Holy Spirit; Saturn devouring his children was the divine nature absorbing in itself all things which it had created; Acolus, the god of winds, was inferior reason, inconstant and fickle. Giles was not conscious of any need to defend his use of such symbols for sacred purposes, but he implicitly justified his practice by referring to the *Song of Songs* where the Hebrew author utilized the sensuous expression of human love to represent the relationship between the chosen soul and its creator.

In Giles' *Sententiae ad mentem Platonis* there is a striking example of the fusion of Greek, Latin, and Hebrew imagery to demonstrate the Christian message. He pictured the soul as Juno, sister and wife of Jupiter, and quoted Vergil's "Jovis soror et coniux." He capped the reference by adding the "soror mea, sponsa mea" from the Song of Songs. These classical quotations, far from grating on the feelings of Renaissance readers and listeners, served to enhance the message. There is a parallel with the modern preacher who uses

illustrations from contemporary events in order to capture the
imagination and goodwill of his audience. Now, as in the time of
the Renaissance, a preacher first strives to arouse the interest of his
listeners before moving them to good resolutions.

Certain characteristics can be observed in Giles' extant sermons.
He used the repetition of one scriptural text to keep the central
point prominent.[84] He had the art of so building up the argument
that one is kept in a state of increasing anticipation for the climax.
He spiced his sermons with illustrations from the ancient classics,
the Old and New Testaments, but did not allow mere erudition,
whether sacred or profane, to obscure the devotion to Christ Crucified which was at the center of his thought. Even the sermon in
Aegidius, which Pontano probably touched up in the style of the
humanists, is clearly christological in character. The sermon is built
around the saying of Christ: *I am the way, the truth, and the life* (John
14:6). Giles' attraction to the Congregation of Lecceto was partly
because its members nurtured the thirteenth century devotion to
the passion of Christ.[85] When Giles was created a cardinal in 1517
he made a profession of faith by selecting the crest of Lecceto —
three crosses on three hills — as his coat of arms. It was the
combination of piety, eloquence, and learning which assured his
success as a preacher. His method was designed for the cities of
Renaissance Italy. It was not until the time of the Reformation that
preachers such as the Capuchins, who paid as much attention to
the countryside as to the cities, revived the direct simple style
which was in the medieval Franciscan tradition.

Notes

1. P. Labbé and G. Cossart, *Acta Conciliorum,* ed. J. Harduin, IX, Paris 1714,
col. 1576; see Appendix 2.

2. Writing of his efforts on behalf of a crusade, Giles stated "Ego incredibili
animi dolore stimulatus quatuordecim iam per annos saepe universam Italiam
peragravi, principes adivi, populos congregavi," Giles to the prince of Macedonia,
Cimino, July-August 1507, in Martène and Durand, III, 1245-1248; Signorelli,
Egidio, page 146, note 11.

3. P. Parenti, "Istorio Fiorentino," Florence, Biblioteca Nazionale MS II.LL.133.

4. Poliziano to Calchi, 22 April 1489, *Opera Omnia Angeli Politiani,* Basle 1553,
pages 52-53.

5. Signorelli, *Egidio,* pages 219-220.

6. Giles to Serafino, 6 January 1503, *Lettere Familiari,* I, pages 180-181; Giles to
Serafino, 19 January 1503, *Lettere Familiari,* I, pages 182-183; Signorelli, *Egidio,* page

140, notes 88-89. Signorelli here misdates the letter of 19 January 1503; there is a copy in Angelica, MS 1001, fol. 62r-v.

7. Giles to Serafino, 27 January 1503, *Lettere Familiari*, I, pages 183-184; see also Signorelli, *Egidio*, page 140, note 89, for a note on the earthquake of this year.

8. *Lettere Familiari*, I, page 184.

9. *Ibid.*

10. See F. Gregorovius, *Lucrezia Borgia*, London 1948, page 211; Pastor, *History of the Popes*, VI, pages 111-113.

11. "Egidio of Viterbo . . . maintained his connection with Lucrezia Borgia while she was Duchess of Ferrara. He exercised a deep influence upon the religious turn which her nature took during the second period of her life," Gregorovius, *Lucrezia Borgia*, page 83. See Signorelli, *Egidio*, page 140, note 93.

12. See Signorelli, *Viterbo*, II, pages 204-216, 305-320.

13. See Signorelli, *Viterbo*, II, pages 306-307, quoting contemporary sources.

14. *Historia XX Saeculorum*, ed. K. Höfler in *Archiv für Kunde oesterreischischer Geschichts-Quellen*, XII (1854), page 381 (hereinafter *Höfler*).

15. Signorelli, *Viterbo*, 5 II, page 314, note 38; *idem*, *Egidio*, page 136, note 64 bis, carefully works out the time when Caesar and his army were at Viterbo.

16. "Il Valentino [that is, Caesar Borgia] trovasi ancora a Viterbo, et ha redutto quella terra in tanta penuria che si morono di fame, con gran querimonie de tutti quelli meschini," *Dispacci di Antonio Giustiniani, 1502-1505*, ed. P. Villari, Florence, 1876, I, page 402.

17. *Höfler*, page 380.

18. V. Lingeri, *Breve et historico racconto*, Viterbo, 1681, pages 49-50 (hereinafter Lingeri).

19. "Cronico della Chiesa e convento della santissima Madonna della Trinità di Viterbo dell'ordine di Sant'Agostino," Archivio Cattedrale di Viterbo, MS 28, fol. 504-507; Bussi, *Istoria della città di Viterbo*, Rome, 1742, page 291; Signorelli, *Egidio*, pages 11-12.

20. Signorelli, *Egidio*, page 136, note 65, stated that this document was not to be found in the communal archives. But the fact was vouched for two centuries earlier by Bussi, *Istoria della città di Viterbo*, page 291, who examined the archives.

21. The municipal records show that delegates were sent to the pope on 7 March to thank him for a brief of 23 January granting pardon to those outlawed, mulcted, and guilty of sedition, see Signorelli, *Egidio*, pages 12, 135, notes 63 and 65. The papal brief is printed on page 251.

There are contradictory dates given for the procession and Giles' sermon. Bussi, page 291, decides on 16 January, as does MS 28, Archivio Cattolico, Viterbo, fol. 504; Lingeri, page 50, gives 6 January; A. Bonnanni, *Il Santuario della Madonna Liberatrice in Viterbo* (Viterbo, 1901), opts for 15 January. Signorelli, *Egidio*, page 136, note 65, points out that the usual date accepted, 15 January, cannot be true, as Giles had not then returned to the city. If we accept the detailed history as given by Lingeri, but assume that his date, 6 January, is a mistake for 6 March, we are probably as near to the truth as the evidence allows.

22. Lingeri, page 54.

23. This was an engagement which he had accepted a year previously. See Giles to Serafino, 13 August 1502, where he mentions that since he was already committed to preach at San Stefano, he could not accept the offer to preach in the Cruciferi church in Venice, in Angelica, MS 1001, fol. 3r-v; *Lettere Familiari*, I, pages 169-170.

24. Giles to Serafino, Florence, 6 January 1503, in Signorelli, *Egidio*, page 219; *Lettere Familiari*, I, pages 180-181. For Serafino, a member of the congregation of Lecceto, see Landucci, *Sacra Ilicetana*, page 147; Perini, II, page 58; Signorelli, *Egidio*, page 135, note 54.

25. Giles to Serafino, Martana, 21 July 1503, in Angelica, MS 1001, fol. 64r; *Lettere Familiari*, I, pages 196-197.

26. Giles to Mannio, Summer 1504, in *Martène and Durand*, III, col. 1250; *Lettere Familiari*, I, pages 234-235.

27. See Signorelli, *Egidio*, pages 268-269, for a documented brief account of Martana.

28. The chapel possessed some supposed relics of Saint Mary Magdalene. Giles valued these highly, and during his stay on the island caused greater care to be taken of them, Giles to Zoccoli, 1504(?), in Angelica, MS 1001, fol. 223v.

29. Herrera, *Alphabetum Augustinianum*, II, page 127, gives a precise account of the transfer to the friars, drawing his facts from records in the Augustinian general archives, Rome. The transfer was completed by a bull of Pius II, dated from Rome, 20 February 1461.

30. *Ibid.*

31. After July 1504, when Egidio left the island for good, the Congregation of Lecceto relinquished the hermitage. See Landucci, *Sacra Ilicetana Sylva*, page 59.

32. Giles to Serafino, "Ex Insula, In vigilia Mariae Magdalenae 1503," in Angelica, MS 1001, fol. 64r; *Lettere Familiari*, I, pages 196-197.

33. Giles to Zoccoli, 2 July 1504, *ibid.*, fol. 9r, published in part by Signorelli, *Egidio*, pages 220-221; *Lettere Familiari*, I, pages 231-232.

34. See the comparison which Giles makes between Alexander VI and Pius III in his *Historia XX Saeculorum*, ed. Höfler, page 383.

35. Giles to Serafino, Lecceto, 14 October 1503, in Angelica, MS 1001, fol. 65r-v; *Lettere Familiari*, I, pages 203-206.

36. *Ibid.*

37. Giles to Serafino, Florence, 15 November 1503, concludes with the comment, "cras abeo Florentia." *Ibid.*, fol. 8v; *Lettere Familiari*, I, page 206.

38. Giles to Serafino, Rome, 25 November 1503: *ibid.*, pages 69v-70v; *Lettere Familiari*, I, pages 206-207.

39. Sixtus IV, uncle of Julius and founder of the della Rovere and Riario fortunes, was so attached to this church that he visited it almost every week. Many of the chief events of his reign were celebrated there. See Pastor, *History of the Popes*, IV, page 456.

40. Pastor, *ibid.*, IV, pages 492, 495, 591. It was probably Julius' partiality for Santa Maria del Popolo which caused Agostino Chigi to pay for the well-known Chigi chapel in the church, see Pastor, page 497.

41. Torelli, *Secoli Agostiniani*, VII, Bologna 1682, page 539.

42. Giles to Serafino, Rome, 15 December 1503, in Angelica, MS 1001, fol. 70v-71v; *Lettere Familiari*, I, pages 207-209. He went to Viterbo later in December, see Giles to D. Florentis, Viterbo, 2 January 1504; *ibid.*, fol. 247v-248r. Signorelli's belief in *Egidio*, page 141, note 100, that Giles preached before the pope on 1 January 1504 is no more than conjecture.

43. Giles to Mannio, Summer 1504, in Martène and Durand, III, col. 1250; *Lettere Familiari*, I, pages 234-235. The comments of Sanudo, *Diarii*, V, cols. 796, 839, 845, show that Giles was due at Venice in the spring of 1504.

44. Sanudo, *Diarii*, V, col. 796.

45. Giles to Serafino, Rome, 31 January 1504, in Angelica, MS 1001, fol. 75r-v; *Lettere Familiari*, I, pages 214-215.

46. Giles to Serafino, Florence, 6 January 1503, in Signorelli, *Egidio*, page 219 (V); *Lettere Familiari*, I, pages 180-181.

47. Giles to Serafino, Rome, 5 March 1504, in Angelica, MS 1001, fol. 69r-v; *Lettere Familiari*, I, pages 219-221.

48. Sanudo, *Diarii*, V, col. 845.

49. There is a letter of Giles to Antonio Zoccoli, Viterbo, 21 May 1504, Angelica, MS 1001, fol. 225v-226r (see *Lettere Familiari*, I, pages 223-224); and a number of letters from Giles to Serafino, covering the period from 10 June to 17 July 1504, all addressed from the isle of Martana; *ibid.*, fol. 71v-73v; *Lettere Familiari*, I, pages 229-231; 233-234.

50. "Homeri poetarum supremi Iliae per Laurentium Vallen.," in *Latinum sermonem traducta*, Brescia, 1497. Now Incunabulum 1261a in the Casanatense Library, Rome.

51. The folios of this edition are unnumbered; the last folio (recto) of the text bears an inscription in Giles' hand, "In insula pharrnesia, 1504 Junio." This apparently refers to a visit to Isola Farnesina, a few miles from home, before he returned to Martana.

52. Giles' copy is now Incunabulum 1261 of the Casanatense Library, Rome. The marginalia and notes by Egidio on this work and on Valla's translation of Homer's *Iliad* deserve a special study.

53. Giles to Zoccoli, 2 July 1504, in Angelica, MS 1001, fol. 8v-9r; part of the letter is printed in Signorelli, *Egidio*, pages 220-221; *Lettere Familiari*, I, pages 231-232. See Appendix 3.

54. *Ibid.*

55. Giles to Mannio, Summer 1504, in Martène and Durand, III, col. 1250 (see note 43 above). See also Giles to Serafino, Martana, 27 June 1504, in Signorelli, *Egidio*, page 220, where the letter is mistakenly dated 10 June; see *Lettere Familiari*, I, pages 230-231 and the copy of the letter in Angelica, MS 1001, fol. 243r-v.

56. For the hermitage on the Cimino, see F. Roth, "Cardinal Richard Annibaldi," in *Augustiniana* III (1953) 293; Signorelli, *Egidio*, pages 269-270; E. Peretti, *Frammenti di Storia di Soriano nel Cimino*, Vatican, 1945.

57. Giles to Serafino, 26 January 1506, in Angelica, MS 1001, fol. 82r; see Signorelli, *Egidio*, page 269 (II); *Lettere Familiari*, I, pages 304-305.

58. Giles to Zoccoli, Cimino, 1 July 1507, *Lettere Familiari,* II, pages 19-20. See Signorelli, *Egidio,* page 162, note 3; Pastor, *History of the Popes,* VI, pages 335-336, 348-351.

59. Signorelli, *Egidio,* page 137, note 77.

60. Giles to Mannio, Summer 1504, in Martène and Durand, III, col. 1250 (see note 43 above).

61. See Signorelli, *Egidio,* page 137, note 71.

62. Giles' letters between 26 July and 15 November 1504 are addressed from Cimino, see Angelica, MS 1001, fol. 71v-74v, 117v-135v; *Lettere Familiari,* I, pages 234-252.

63. Giles to Serafino, Venice, 15 January 1505, in Angelica, MS 1001, fol. 9v; *Lettere Familiari,* I, pages 256-257.

64. Giles to Serafino, Cimino, 8 November 1505, in Angelica, MS 1001, fol. 86r; *Lettere Familiari,* I, pages 290-291.

65. Giles to Cardinal Riario, Cimino, May 1505; *ibid.,* fol. 203r; *Lettere Familiari,* I, pages 262-263.

66. Giles to Serafino, Venice, 15 January 1505, in Signorelli, *Egidio,* page 221; *Lettere Familiari,* I, pages 256-257.

67. Sanudo, *Diarii,* VI, col. 141.

68. Perini, III, pages 100-102.

69. Sanudo, *Diarii,* VI, cols. 145-146.

70. Böhmer, *Luthers Romfahrt,* Leipzig, 1914, pages 40-41.

71. Giles to Serafino, Cimino, 2 July 1505, in Martène and Durand, III, col. 1233; *Lettere Familiari,* I, pages. 266-267.

72. *Themata sermonum de tempore,* MS Latin, 3461, fol. 57. These are sermon notes, based on the Old and New Testament, and arranged for Advent, Lent, and Easter. This manuscript has been overlooked by Giles' biographers.

73. *Oratio prima synodi Lateranensis habita per Aegidium Viterbiensem,* Rome, 1512, reprinted in P. Labbé and G. Cossart, *Acta Conciliorum,* ed. J. Harduin IX, Paris, 1714, cols. 1576-1581 (see Appendix 2 and Chapter 1, note 31).

74. *Oratio habita post Tertiam Sacri Lateranensis Concilii sessionem . . . per Fratrem Egidium Viterbiensem,* Rome, 1512(?). There is also from Giles' library the *Oratio ad Carolum Caesarem,* Bibl. Nat., Paris, MS Latin 7863, fol. 15. Hitherto this manuscript has escaped the notice of Giles' biographers; it is not certain that Giles was author of this oration.

75. Text of discourse at Rome, ed. John W. O'Malley, "Fulfillment of the Christian Golden Age under Pope Julius II: text of a discourse of Giles of Viterbo, 1507," in *Traditio* XXV (1969) 265-338, at 280-338. *De Ilicetana Familia,* Angelica, MS 1156, which Pélissier classes as a sermon. Of the same character is the letter from Giles to the Leccetan friars, July 1506, in Martène and Durand, III, col. 1235-1238, and *Lettere Familiari,* I, pages 337-342. See Appendix 2 below. John W. O'Malley, "Man's Dignity, God's Love and the Destiny of Rome. A text of Giles of Viterbo," in *Viator* 3 (1972) 389-416, at 398-416.

76. Böhmer made only a cursory examination of Giles' first register, Dd 11, and did not know of his letters in Siena Bibl. Comm., MS G.X. 26.

77. Sanudo, *Diarii,* VIII, col. 414.

78. "Talis effecta est vita sacerdotum et curialium, quod vix reperitur qui concubinam non retineat, vel saltem meretricem, ad laudem Dei et fidei christianae. Et ea forte de causa numeratae sunt meretrices, quae tunc publice Romae sunt, ut ex vero testimonio habetur, ad numerum sex millium et octingentarum meretricum; exceptis illis quae in concubinatu sunt et illis quae non publice sed secreto cum quinque vel sex earum exercent artificium, ut unaquaeque earum vel unum vel plures habent lenones. Consideretur modo qualiter vivitur Romae, ubi caput fidei est, et vocatur civitas sancta," S. Infessura, *Diario della città di Roma*, ed. O. Tommasini, Rome, 1890, pages 259-260.

79. Pastor, *History of the Popes*, V, page 131.

80. P. Pomponatius, *Apologia*, Bologna, 1518, car. xxxiiii.

81. *De animarum immortalitate contra assertorem mortalitatis, nempe Petrum Pomponatium*, Mantua 1519. See "Ad lectorem." For Flandini (1462-1531) see Perini, II, pages 72-73; IV, pages 75-76.

82. Ambrosius [Flandinus], *Quadragesimalium concionum liber*, Venice, 1523, fol. 481v-482r. There are copies of this work in the Angelica Library, Rome, and the Bibliothèque Nationale, Paris.

83. P. O. Kristeller, *The Classics and Renaissance Thought*, Cambridge, (MA), 1955, page 63; *idem*, *The Philosophy of Marsilio Ficino*, New York, 1943, page 347. Pomponazzi maintained that he was merely recording Aristotle's theory, and not necessarily agreeing with it. Nevertheless, he was called upon by Leo X to make a formal recantation of the theory. See Pastor, *History of the Popes*, V, pages 156-157.

84. This was a method which he overdid in his oration at Siena in October 1503. It is to be seen to full advantage in his address to the Leccetan friars in July 1506, by use of *Ecce in pace amaritudo mea amarissima* (Isaiah 38:17), in Martène and Durand, III, col. 1235-1238; *Lettere Familiari*, I, pages 337-342.

85. For this characteristic of the Leccetan friars, see *Gli Assempri di Fra Filippo da Siena*, ed. D. F. C. Carpellini, Siena, 1804; the same spirit runs through Giles' *De Ilicetana Familia*, Angelica, MS 1156, see Appendix 4.

Chapter 3

Unwilling Protégé of Julius II

Giles set out from Venice about the beginning of May 1505 riding a mule which he had been loaned during his visit to Ferrara in December 1504. Writing to Serafino he commented with a flash of humor that his further plans for travel were upset because on reaching Ferrara the mule died, thus showing that it knew it had returned to its owner's house.[1] Giles went from Ferrara down along the Adriatic coast on a preaching tour which took in the cities of Ravenna, Rimini, Pesaro, Fano, and Ancona.[2] Ten years later a citizen of Fano, Francesco Poliardo, recalled the friar's visit and commented that the Fanesi were unanimous in acclaiming him as a prince of preachers.[3] Giles was by now established in the front rank of Italian preachers, but was not without his peers. The city council of Pavia wrote to the Augustinian general, Agostino Faccioni, on 14 April 1505 asking that he send either Giles or his fellow friar Giovanni Benedetto Moncetto to preach the Lenten sermons at Pavia in 1506. Equal tribute was paid to the piety and learning of Giles and Moncetto.[4]

When writing to Serafino about his journey back from Venice Giles included a vivid passage in which we glimpse his personal piety. Having passed through Ancona he made a pilgrimage to the holy house of Loreto where he shed tears of emotion on beholding what he believed was the dwelling in which Jesus had dwelt at Nazareth. From Loreto he passed to Tolentino, and there at the shrine of the Augustinian thaumaturge, Saint Nicholas, religious emotion again drew tears from his eyes. The climax was a visit to honor the relics of the Augustinian nun, Saint Clare of Montefalco. The sensible evidence which purported to show how one holy soul could so unite herself to Christ Crucified that an image of the Savior was reproduced in the tissues of her heart made him all but swoon. There, he informed Serafino, was a unique and startling argument for Christianity.[5] Giles for all his Renaissance culture had none of Erasmus' disdain for relics.

Return to Cimino

He was back in his hermitage on Cimino by the second week of May, exhausted from preaching and traveling but filled with a sense of peace now that he had returned to "the holy mountain with its pleasant arbors and sacred recesses."[6] In a letter of 2 July to Serafino he was still complaining of the after-effects of his preaching tour of the previous winter and spring.[7] He remained on Cimino for a further two months, and then went to Perugia as one of the eighty delegates at a general chapter of the Augustinian Order.[8] Agostino Faccioni, who had been ruling the Order as vicar general since the death of Graziano Ventura in July 1504, was unanimously elected prior general.[9] Giles who consistently fought shy of ecclesiastical office could hardly have guessed that within less than nine months he would be appointed to succeed Faccioni. With the election completed Giles returned to his hermitage.[10]

Signorelli states that he went to Viterbo during the last week of September to be present for a visit which Julius II was then making to the city.[11] Though it is very likely that Giles did so, there is no solid proof to warrant the statement.[12] Whether or not Julius met the friar at Viterbo he was determined to have him at his disposal. Giles was safe in his hermitage during the month of October, but a papal brief of 4 November commanded him to come to Rome, "so great is the desire you have left among all who seek their eternal salvation in the law of God."[13] The summons held no attraction for him, and he risked the pope's wrath by staying on Cimino while he sought the intercession of Cardinal Riario to free him from the obligation of going to Rome.[14] Even before Giles' appeal had been answered he received a further papal brief instructing him to preach at Siena.[15] Julius' interest in Siena should be seen in the context of his political program. At this stage the pope had three immediate political objectives.[16] The first was to restore order in the Patrimony of Peter, principally by bringing the Roman barons to heel, either by naked force or through marriage alliances. The second was to check the power of Venice and to recover, if necessary to wrest back, the territories in the Romagna which the republic had gradually been occupying on various pretexts since the death of Alexander VI. The third was to reestablish papal authority in the states of the Church; this meant driving the Baglioni from Perugia and the Bentivogli from Bologna. By summer 1505 the pope and Venice had come to an agreement, which though replete with mutual distrust allowed Julius a free hand to pursue his other aims. During the winter of 1505 and the first half of 1506 a series of marriage alliances between members of the Della Rovere family and those of the Farnese, Orsini, and Colonna families gave the pope a greater measure of security in the neighborhood of Rome.

Meantime he was preoccupied with plans for the recovery of Perugia and Bologna. In order to prevent any last minute interference from states bordering on the Romagna he negotiated for alliances with Florence, Siena, Mantua, Ferrara, and Urbino. There is no evidence that Giles was used as a political agent in Siena, but it was undoubtedly pleasing to the Sienesi when the friar received a papal instruction to preach in their city. Though Giles complained privately of their possessiveness[17] he bowed to Julius' inflexible will and went to Siena in January.[18] Agreement between the pope and Siena was reached in April 1506.[19]

Toward Rome

Giles' efforts to remain away from Rome were of no avail. The cardinal protector insisted that he comply with the pope's wishes, and he was in Rome by 6 February 1506.[20] Here, according to his own words, he was kept much against his will.[21] He does not disclose whether Julius' purpose was other than to have him as a preacher in the city. Giles was impatient to leave and made arrangements for a visit to Naples which he had not seen since the winter of 1501. He was on the point of entering a ship which was to carry him to Naples when he received word from Cardinal Alidosi that he was to betake himself to Viterbo and there await the pope's arrival.[22] It is uncertain whether Julius really intended to visit Viterbo at this time or by recalling Giles wished to show his displeasure with Ferdinand of Aragon who was refusing to pay the feudal dues which the pope claimed from Naples. In fact Julius did not visit Viterbo for a further four months. Giles returned to Cimino, and though he had intended to preach at Viterbo in May the Leccetan friars decided that he should go instead to Siena.[23] He accepted this assignment wearily, as something unavoidable from the hand of God. He fulfilled his mission, and was back in the hermitage by mid-June.[24]

What took place on 27 June 1506 was described in a letter, a little masterpiece of dramatic narrative, which Giles wrote to the community at Lecceto announcing his appointment as vicar general of the Augustinian Order.[25] He described how he and a few fellow friars were sitting in their small garden beside the hermitage, chanting divine office in the cool shade of a great overhanging crag while the evening sun sank down toward the distant horizon. Unexpectedly they saw a lay brother, who had been dispatched to Soriano a short time beforehand to buy provisions, come running up the hillside track, perspiring in his haste and anxiety to reach the hermitage. On reaching the garden he gasped out that Antonio Zoccoli was nearby on his way up to the hermitage. Zoccoli, it will be recalled, was an influential nobleman, holding office in the civil administration of Rome, and a friend of Giles. The friars, who seem to have made a quick end to their divine office, moved rapidly down the hillside. They met Zoccoli and two companions, Fra Girolamo, an Augustinian,[26] and Niccolò Mannio, another friend of Giles.[27] When the visitors had been greeted and embraced, Zoccoli was asked why he was paying this surprise call to Cimino. Giles' presentiment that something serious was afoot was banished by Zoccoli's ready reply that the visit was nothing other than a friendly occasion to see with his own eyes the haven of peace which Giles had so often described in lyrical terms.[28] Animated conversation went on for the rest of that evening and late into the night. A solid meal was laid before the guests before they retired to bed, though Giles and his fellow friars observed the customary fasts for the vigil of the feast of Saints Peter and Paul. It seemed but natural that Zoccoli followed Giles to his cell for a private discussion.

Having closed the door Zoccoli broke the news, "Giles, your friends can keep up this pretense no longer," and he thereupon produced the letter in which Julius II informed the friar that he was appointed vicar general of the Augustinians. What followed is so abnormal by present day standards of behavior that we are made sharply aware that here we are seeing not merely an incident from the Italian Renaissance but are witnessing the reactions of a highly emotional character in stress. Giles was thunderstruck by the news and fell to the floor with a cry of pain. The other guests and friars heard the commotion and came hurriedly to his cell, where they found him on the floor weeping and lamenting. They heard the news and overcome with emotion also began to cry. At this point in the letter Giles realized that the histrionic scene he was describing might seem to be the creation of literary imagination. He assured the Leccetan friars that if they wished to check his story they might consult those who had been present in the hermitage on 27 June.

During the scene enacted in his cell Giles poured forth a spate of reasons why he should not undertake the government of the Order, his weak health, his total inexperience of administration, his lack of years and of the qualities necessary to rule a religious order, the hostility of many and powerful critics. Yet he did not conceal from the Leccetan friars that his overriding concern was the knowledge that once he assumed the office of vicar general his life of study and seclusion was at an end.[29] We have already noted that this was a motivating factor in his life ever since his student days at Capo d'Istria. His listeners in the hermitage were sympathetic but firm. When Giles tried to delay his consent by asking for time to consult with the Leccetan friars he was told that the papal summons was imperative and would allow of no delay. The next day he sent an urgent message to Fra Basilio de' Mendaldi, prior of the Augustinians at Viterbo.[30] De' Mendaldi came promptly but gave unqualified advice that duty beckoned from Rome. Giles' friends gave him a sop of consolation, saying that the authorities in Rome might reverse the decision on hearing his statement of the case. According to his own words he found the visit to Rome so bitter, as he went around the city in the company of his friend, Fra Ambrogio Flandini, that "I wished I were dead."[31] Cardinal Riario was obdurate despite Giles' tears and explanations. When the friar persisted in his position the cardinal protector remarked with some heat that Giles' preaching would seem as so much hypocrisy when it was seen that he himself had not learned to obey and apparently was not satisfied to be placed in charge of the Augustinian Order but desired some greater office. Reduced to silence by these comments Giles went for an audience with the pope who stood by his decision but promised that he would give the friar as much assistance as possible to bear the burden. Giles had no option but to accept his responsibility.

Vicar General

His appointment as vicar general was a stopgap, to tide over the period until a general chapter would meet and elect a prior general. Though in fact his efforts as a reformer of the Order date from July 1506[32] he could do little more than exhort as long as he and the Augustinians knew that his position was merely temporary.[33] Before considering his program and activity as a reformer it is well to glance briefly at the salient events which lay between his appointment as vicar general in June 1506 and his election as prior general in May 1507. They indicate the esteem in which he was held by Julius II.

The pope startled political observers in August 1506 by setting out in person with his troops against Perugia and Bologna.[34] Perugia fell without a struggle, and Giles was called there to preach twice before Julius as part of the victory celebrations. His sermon during the solemn high Mass in the church of Saint Francis on 16 September may have been an implied reproof of Julius. It was mainly an exhortation for a crusade against the Turks.[35] This was to become a favorite theme of Giles' preaching during the next ten years. While the papal army was advancing by difficult mountain roads toward Bologna, Giles was on his way to Naples. Since he would have done so only with Julius' consent the permission may be seen as an expression of the pope's policy to conciliate Ferdinand of Aragon who was then on a visit to his Neapolitan kingdom. Early in November Giles preached before the king, again appealing for a united effort against the infidel. The Venetian ambassador reported that the king was so moved by the friar's eloquence that he inquired what assistance might be expected from Venice for a crusade.[36] The Aragonese historian, Zurita, states that Ferdinand commissioned Giles to assure Julius of his support for the undertaking and even for the recovery of the States of the Church in Italy.[37] The king's message expressed exactly what Julius had announced as his policy — a crusade against the Turks, but first the recovery of the lawful possessions of the Church in Italy. Whether the pope and Ferdinand seriously considered a crusade may be questioned, but it served as a diplomatic feeler for Julius. Giles was recalled to Bologna where on 28 December 1506 he preached in the presence of the pope, once again dwelling on the need and the opportunity for an expedition against the power of the Emperor Bayezid II.[38]

Foremost in Julius' mind was the recovery from Venice of the papal possessions in the Romagna. He was aware that Giles was a persona grata with the Venetians, and that he had shown independence of spirit by speaking in favor of Venice during his sermon before King Ferdinand, though all knew that Julius and the republic were then at daggers drawn. In January 1507 the pope sent Giles to discuss with the doge and his council the launching of a crusade, but as a preliminary — and this was the rub — the restitution of the Romagna or at least of Faenza to the papacy.[39] The Venetians did not allow sentiment for Giles to cloud their political judgment. The shrewd old doge, Leonardo Loredano, blandly refused to yield an inch and raked up Julius' political past with the barbed comment that Venice would hardly give way to one who by word and deed had been the first to offend against papal sovereignty. The Venetian determination was expressed in the pithy phrase recorded by Giles that Faenza would be handed over as readily as the Tower of San Marco.[40] He arrived in Rome at the end of March, and when he reported the result of his mission the pope's indignation was aroused. "If," he snapped, "they refuse to return the little I have asked for, they will be obliged to return all. They who would not heed you will have to submit to force." It was the Venetian refusal to deal with Julius that caused him to join the League of Cambrai with all the grave consequences which this was to have both for the pope and the Republic.

Toward Prior General

The approaching general chapter of the Augustinians was of more personal interest for Giles. His original intention was that it should be held in Siena, and for this he had the approval of Julius and the cardinal protector.[41] While at Venice in January 1507 he sent a circular letter to members of the Order informing them that the pope had granted special indulgences to be preached in favor of the general chapter.[42] In view of the later Luther-Tetzel controversy it is piquant to find that Giles took special care to have the indulgence preached in Germany, writing on their behalf to the Emperor Maximilian and to the Venetian ambassador in Germany.[43] The rendezvous of the chapter was decided by the generosity of *El Gran Capitan*, Gonzalo de Cordoba, then viceroy of Naples. He offered to pay all expenses of the chapter on condition that it be held in Naples.[44] The pope, anxious to conciliate King Ferdinand and to draw Naples into a coalition against Venice, gave his blessing to Gonzalo's offer in a brief of 7 April 1506.[45] Julius indicated his mind on the choice of a prior general by appointing Giles president of the chapter, with the right to nominate delegates in place of those who would be absent.[46]

As if the pope's intentions were not sufficiently plain for the electors, Giles' friends, Augustinians and lay people, made the general chapter an occasion to demonstrate their support.[47] Giles' obvious reluctance to accept office does not alter the fact that the election seems to have been an example of "guided democracy." The chapter opened on 21 May, with the secular power present in the persons of the viceroy, Gonzalo de Cordoba, Fabrizio Colonna, duke of Amalfi, and Prospero Colonna, duke of Salerno. Cardinal Ludovico Borgia attended on behalf of the pope. Agostino Nifo, Giles' former professor at Padua, and Jacopo Sannazzaro represented the philosophy and humanism of the Renaissance. Eight hundred friars assembled for the chapter, and the Neapolitan chronicler, Giacomo, tells with gusto of the liberal hand with which

Gonzalo fed them, with meat, fowl, sugared dainties, and wine.[48] Eighty-four delegates came on behalf of the provinces of the Order in the Iberian penisula, France, England, the Low Countries, the Germanic lands, Hungary, Italy, and the Grecian Islands.[49] Also present were about seventy outstanding Augustinian theologians who were to take part in the traditional disputations.

The chapter opened on Pentecost Sunday, 23 May, and the preliminary oration by the procurator general, Giovanni Antonio Aprutino, made plain to the electors on whom their choice should fall. The speech was an undisguised eulogy of Giles and culminated in the exclamation, "What happy times we live in! O fortunate, O thrice and four times blessed are those Augustinians to whom it is granted to behold a leader in whom experience and wisdom are so providentially united."[50] The conclusion to be drawn from Giovanni Antonio's oration was so obvious that Giles made one final effort to prevent his own election. It was normal procedure for the outgoing general to hand over the seals of office in a public formal ceremony. Giles laid aside his cloak, knelt in front of the capitulars and asked forgiveness for any mistakes he had made during his year as vicar general. So far he was merely following the prevailing custom. Without further ado he went on to explain why he should not be chosen as prior general. He described himself as a man from the woods, addicted to solitude. In what amounted to a direct contradiction of Giovanni Antonio's final statement he pointed out that he had no experience of administration and practical affairs, and sagely commented that it was unreasonable to expect that a man would suddenly find himself invested with these qualities. He concluded his appeal with the statement that he was not shirking responsibility but was refusing to be presumptuous.[51] He handed over the seals of office, overcome with tears and emotion. His appeal was to no purpose and he was chosen as prior general by a unanimous vote. The result was hailed with delight by Gonzalo and the other notables who had gathered at Naples to do Giles honor. When the election was confirmed with evident satisfaction by Julius II in a brief of 7 October 1507,[52] Giles' role as reformer had begun in earnest.

Notes

1. Giles to Serafino, Cimino, 2 July 1505, in Martène and Durand, III, col. 1233; *Lettere Familiari*, I, pages 266-267.

2. *Ibid.*

3. Francesco Poliardo to Giles, Fano, 18 November 1515, in Martène and Durand, III, cols. 1256-1257; *Lettere Familiari*, II, pages 197-199.

4. R. Maiocchi and N. Casacca, *Codex diplomaticus Ord. E. S. Augustini Papiae*, III (1907), 25.

5. Giles to Serafino, Cimino, 2 July 1505 (see note 1 above).

6. Giles to Zoccoli, Cimino, 10 May 1505, in Angelica, MS 1001, fol. 86v; *Lettere Familiari*, I, page 261.

7. Giles to Serafino, Cimino, 2 July 1505 (see note 1 above).

8. "Mag. Egidius de Viterbio, Diffinitor," is listed among the delegates as a representative of the Roman province; see *Analecta Augustiniana* IX (1921) 12-15.

9. *Ibid.*, page 11.

10. Giles to Serafino, Cimino, 18 October 1505, in Angelica, MS 1001, fol. 80r-v.

11. Signorelli, *Egidio*, pages 18, 143.

12. The indications in favor of Giles having been in the city at this time are: the gap in his correspondence between 13 September and 18 October, the proximity of the Cimino to Viterbo, the visit which Julius made to the Augustinian friary at Viterbo on 27 September 1505.

Julius had two purposes in visiting Viterbo. He wanted to end the smoldering feud between the Maganzesi and the Gatteschi, see Signorelli, *Viterbo*, II, 324-325. He was to preside at the requiem Mass for Cardinal Peraudi in the Augustinian church, see Signorelli, *Egidio*, pages 18, 143, notes 115-116.

13. Vatican Archives, Brev. Julius II, XXII, page 452; Pastor, *History of the Popes*, VI, page 635.

14. See Signorelli, *Egidio*, page 143, note 122.

15. Giles to Zoccoli, Cimino, 25 October 1505, in Angelica, MS 1001, fol. 87; *Lettere Familiari*, I, pages 286-287. Signorelli, *Egidio*, page 19, mistakes the time of Giles' visit to Siena; the brief, dated Rome, 28 April 1505, is registered in Vatican Archives, Armadio XXXIX, 23, fol. 275r-v.

16. See Pastor, *History of the Popes*, VI, pages 232-289.

17. Giles to della Volta, Rome, 6 February 1506, in Angelica, MS 688, fol. 14r; Signorelli, *Egidio*, page 144, note 124.

18. Giles to Serafino, Siena, 6 January 1506, in Angelica, MS 1001, fol. 81v; *Lettere Familiari*, I, pages 303-304.

19. See Pastor, *History of the Popes*, VI, page 263, note 4, citing a brief of 19 April 1506 in the State Archives, Siena, by which Julius II promised to protect the people of Siena in return for their fidelity to the Holy See.

20. Giles to della Volta, Rome, 6 February 1506 (see note 17 above).

21. Giles to della Volta, Rome, 20 February 1506, Angelica, MS 1001, fol. 279v-280v.

22. Giles to Deodato, Viterbo, 15 April 1506, *ibid.*, fol. 178r; *Lettere Familiari*, I, pages 310-311.

23. Giles to Serafino, Cimino, 6 May 1506, in Angelica, MS 1001, fol. 89r.

24. See letters of Giles from Soriano, 24 May; Lecceto, 28 May; Soriano, 17 June; *ibid.*, pages 93r-94v; *Lettere Familiari*, I, pages 316-320.

25. Giles to the friars at Lecceto, July 1506, in Martène and Durand, III, col. 1235-1238, *Lettere Familiari*, I, pages 337-342; there is also a copy in Angelica, MS 1001, fol. 102r-105v. The letter is undated but from internal evidence it can be inferred that it was written in early July after Giles had returned from his visit to the cardinal protector in Rome.

26. Signorelli, *Egidio*, page 19, mistakenly states that the Augustinian visitor was Niccolò Foresio, papal sacristan and titular archbishop of Durazzo. Fra Girolamo was a chaplain to Foresio.

27. For Mannio, of whom very little is known, see Signorelli, *Egidio*, page 144, note 129. There are several letters between Mannio and Giles in Angelica, MS 1001.

28. Giles to Zoccoli, Cimino, 17 August 1504, in Angelica, MS 1001, fol. 231r. Giles to the cardinal protector, May 1507, cited by Pélissier in *Miscellanea*, page 799. The remainder of the letter deserves to be read for an appreciation of Giles' mentality.

29. Giles to the friars at Lecceto (see note 25 above). The same thought is to be found in a brief of Julius to Giles, 7 October 1507, which refers to his appointment as vicar general, *Analecta Augustiniana* IX (1921) 18.

30. Giles does not supply the prior's name, but it has been established by Signorelli, *Egidio*, page 144, note 131, who adds some biographical facts. See Perini, I, pages 221-222.

31. Giles refers the Leccetan friars to Fra Ambrogio Flandini as a witness of these events in Rome, in Martène and Durand, III, col. 1238.

32. His extant letters to the friars on reform began on 15 July 1506 and continued throughout his eleven months as vicar general; there is a selection of them in Siena MS G.X.26, pages 3-60.

33. The papal brief of appointment, 27 June 1506, in *Analecta Augustiniana* IX (1921) 17, gave him the powers of prior general until the general chapter would take place.

34. Signorelli, *Egidio*, page 23, assumes that Giles joined Julius at Viterbo. This is quite possible, but there is no evidence to prove it.

35. Sanudo, *Diarii*, VI, col. 427; see also Eubel, *Hierarchica Catholica*, III, page 9, note 3; Pastor, *History of the Popes*, VI, pages 271-272. He also preached before Julius in the church of Saint Peter, but according to De Grassis, *Diarium*, page 48, did not please the pope on the occasion. De Grassis shows no friendship toward Giles and his statements must be accepted with caution.

36. Sanudo, *Diarii*, VI, pages 494-495.

37. G. Zurita, *Annales de la Corona de Aragon*, VI, Zaragoza 1610, fol. 120v.

38. Giles to the prince of Macedonia, Cimino, c. July 1507, in Martène and Durand, III, page 1247; De Grassis, *Diarium*, page 181; Signorelli, *Egidio*, page 148, notes 23-24.

39. See Sanudo, *Diarii*, VI, col. 528, 533, who mentions one meeting which Giles had with the Venetian authorities on 16 January.

40. *Historia XX Saeculorum*, page 335.

41. Circular letter from Giles to members of the Order, perhaps August 1506, in Signorelli, *Egidio*, page 224 (XIII) and *Lettere Familiari*, I, pages 354- 355; brief of Julius to Giles, Perugia, 18 September 1506, mentioned in *Analecta Augustiniana* IX, 17, note 3; Serafino to Giles, Lecceto, 10 January 1507, in Angelica, MS 1001, fol. 99v-100r; *Lettere Familiari*, II, page 7.

42. Giles to the Order, Venice, 19 January 1507, in Signorelli, *Egidio*, pages 224-225 (XIV). G.X.26, pages 51-53. The papal grant was dated 18 September 1506, see *Analecta Augustiniana* IX (1921) 17, note 3.

43. The letters, dated 24 January 1507, are published in Signorelli, *Egidio*, pages 225-226 (XV-XVI); see *Lettere Familiari*, II, pages 8-9.

44. A. de Meijer, *Aegidii Viterbiensis O.S.A. Resgestae Generalatus I, 1506-1514*, vol. 17, Rome, 1988, pages 30-34.

45. *Analecta Augustiniana* IX (1921) 17-18.

46. *Ibid.*, 18.

47. See note 44 above.

48. *Cronaca di Napoli di Notar Giacomo*, ed. P. Garzilli, Naples, 1845, page 302.

49. Such was the number of delegates at the chapter of 1497. See *Analecta Augustiniana* VIII (1920), 29. There had been no increase between that time and the year 1507 in the number of delegates entitled to vote.

50. A. de Meijer, *op. cit.*, page 32.

51. *Ibid.*

52. *Analecta Augustiniana* IX (1921) 18-19.

Chapter 4

The Augustinian Observant Movement

The Augustinian observant movement is a subject which is of considerable importance both for late medieval Europe and for the origins of the Reformation. This applies not only to Germany, but to Italy, France, Spain, the Low Countries, and Ireland.

The Followers of Augustine

Saint Augustine of Hippo (354-430) was a monk in North Africa and for his followers wrote a *Rule*, embodying principles and practical directives for a monastic form of life.[1] This *Rule* was also a constant factor in the evolution of monastic life in western Europe.[2] Its considerable influence in his own native North Africa was limited, of course, to his own lifetime.

The Vandals, and later the Muslims, put an end to Augustine's legacy in North Africa. The *Rule* was taken overseas by refugee monks to Spain, France, and Italy. It continued to be followed in variant fruitful forms as a way of religious life by groups of women and men who can loosely be described as Augustinians. However, during the early middle ages the *Rule* of Saint Augustine was largely overshadowed by the *Rule* of Saint Benedict (c.480-c.530), and it was not until the tenth century and the reform movement of Pope Gregory VIII (c.1021-1085) that the *Rule* of Saint Augustine came back into vogue. Its very flexibility meant that it could be rapidly adopted by, and adapted to, communities of men and women who are generally known as Augustinian canons and canonesses. The most notable of these were the Canons Regular of the Lateran, the Victorines, and the Praemonstratensians. All were expressions of religious renewal and more efficient organization. They usually lived in substantial monasteries, with incomes and properties.

While the *Rule* of Saint Augustine was thus being adapted to the needs both of feudalism and of an emerging urbanized Europe it continued to be practiced in simpler form by men and women who lived withdrawn from centers of population. These were generically described as "Augustinians," and more specifically, in the case of men, as "Hermits of Saint Augustine." They were not solitary hermits, but lived in communities, and usually in austere

73

conditions. In due time these hermits were to form one of the bodies from which came the Augustinian observant movement.

Observant Movement and the Reformation

Since the time of the Reformation our view of the observants has been bedeviled by prejudices and preconceptions. The Augustinians themselves have not yet given adequate attention to the observants. One obvious reason for their attitude, at least until recently, was Luther. For 400 years — until Vatican Council II — he was regarded officially by the Order as the black sheep of the flock. Not only was he an observant but many other observants in Germany and elsewhere were involved in the Protestant revolution. The Augustinians therefore shied away from that chapter in their history.

The situation is further complicated by the prejudice with which both Protestant and Catholic historians have considered the observants. For many Protestant historians the observant movement was regarded as a typical exaggerated spiritual development within the late medieval Catholic Church. For them it was another example of Catholic decadence. On the other hand, Catholic historians viewed the observant movement with suspicion. They believed it began in dubious circumstances in the fourteenth century, among the restless Franciscan "spirituals," and spread its fever to other religious orders such as the Augustinians. In due time it produced its controversial results at the time of the Reformation.

The most obvious connection between the observant movement and the Reformation was Luther — a source of pride for Protestants, of bitter sorrow, even anger, for Catholics. In addition he was for Augustinians a cause of shame and chagrin. But he was not a lone bird among his brethren. The prominence of Augustinian friars in the Protestant reform cannot be denied.[3] In Germany there were, to mention but a few, Martin Luther, Wenzeslaus Link, Johann Lang "the Greek," and Gabriel Zwilling; in England, George Browne (first Anglican archbishop of Dublin), Miles Coverdale (the first to translate the whole Bible into English), and Robert Barnes (who was to perish at the stake); in Ireland, Richard Nangle (first Anglican bishop of Clonfert); in the Low Countries, a group of Augustinians at Antwerp with their prior, Jacob Praepositus and the well-known Hendrik van Zutphen whose companions here and at Tournai supplied the first Lutheran martyrs in the Netherlands; in France, the friaries at Paris, Toulouse, Narbonne, and Bourges had even in the 1520s earned the reputation of being heretical centers, and the Augustinian, Jean Chatelain, died at the stake in Metz in 1524, while the Circle of Meaux had its Augustinian members, of whom the best known is Michel d'Arande, adviser to Marguerite de Navarre; in Italy, Agostino Mainardi da Piemonte (who by paradox implicated Ignatius of Loyola with the Roman Inquisition), Giulio della Rovere, Ambrogio da Milano, and Nicolò da Verona were apostles of that "evangelism" which in several cases fringed imperceptibly into defiant heresy.

While an historian such as Pastor judiciously summed up the problem with the statement that "The Order of the Augustinian Hermits, from which Luther emerged, contained many dangerous elements,"[4] another standard work of Catholic scholarship surveyed the number of Augustinian defections to Protestantism under the more outspoken heading, "Déchéance des Augustins."[5] Not all the Augustinians who joined, or sympathized with, the Protestants were observants, but even conventual Augustinians who took the Protestant side were influenced by the observants, as in the cases of Coverdale and Barnes in England, who admitted their debt to Luther's teaching and example.

Augustinians and Reformers

The problem becomes something of a puzzle when it is noted that not a few of the prominent Catholic reformers and anti-Lutherans were also Augustinians.[6] In Germany, one of Luther's former professors, Bartholomew Arnoldi von Usingen, earned Luther's wrathful attention, while the death of the Augustinian Johann Hoffmeister, in August 1547, robbed German Catholics of one of their most doughty defenders; Wolfgang Kappelmaier (d. 1531) of Munich had entered the lists at an early stage against Luther; in Switzerland, Konrad Treger (d. 1542) of Freiburg resolutely opposed the new teaching; for Italy one needs but mention the two reformers, Cardinal Giles of Viterbo and his disciple, Cardinal Jerome Seripando; in England, John Stone was executed and parboiled at Canterbury in 1539 for his defense of papal supremacy; Portugal had its Luis de Montoya (1497-1569), founder of a new reforming movement within the Augustinian Order; in Spain, Saint Thomas of Villanova, "The glory of the Spanish Church," who was received into the Order in 1518, had before his death in 1555 anticipated many of the reforms of the Council of Trent in his archbishopric of Valencia; in the Low Countries and

Rhineland it was Roger de Jonghe (1492-1579), the restorer of the Cologne Province, who exemplified the Catholic reform.

The paradoxical picture emerges of an Order with its members apparently divided between their traditional allegiance to Rome and on the other hand a strong attraction to Luther and to the doctrines of the Protestant reformers. This puzzling impression sets a challenge, obliging us to examine that period of Augustinian history preceding the year 1517 and to inquire into the reasons why this religious Order found itself in the foreground of the convulsive movement which was to rend the politico-religious structure of Europe. What emerges from the inquiry is a paradox, not a contradiction. The Catholic and the Protestant reforms were both products of the same movement. This is well exemplified if we take, not the whole Church picture, but one significant section, the Augustinian Order of the mendicant friars. With the aid of this microcosm, we can evaluate the macrocosm.

The Background

In 1955 I was fortunate enough, while a doctoral student at the University of Cambridge, in England, to live in the same community, Blackfriars, with the internationally famous French Dominican theologian, Yves Congar. He was later, at Vatican Council II (1962-1965), to receive due recognition for his theological, and in particular his ecumenical, ability, but at the time we were colleagues at Cambridge he was in effect in voluntary exile, keeping a low profile away from the sharp scrutiny of zealous heresy-hunters at Rome.

On one occasion, when we were discussing the Reformation, he commented that since the religious divisions of Europe began with Luther, those same divisions will never be healed until we go back to Luther and try to understand the spiritual forces which impelled him to challenge, and then to break with, Rome.[7] I would go one step further than Yves Congar and suggest that unless we go behind Luther, far behind him to at least the early fourteenth century, we shall not properly understand the man and the ideals which inspired and sustained him. It is in that context that we must evaluate the observant movement. It is not the sole or the master key to Luther, but if we do not give it serious attention we shall not understand Luther and many of those who rekindled their religious fervor from the blaze he ignited in 1517. Luther began something momentous but he in his turn was the product, one might say the end product, of a much earlier religious process.

Just as the appearance, the decisive appearance, of Luther on the German stage cannot be understood unless he is seen in his national background, so his Augustinian background cannot be assessed unless it in its turn is fitted into its wider European context. It was not just a combined German and Augustinian problem; it concerned the whole Christian western Church. This was shown by the involvement in the Reformation of other religious orders, secular clergy, princes, merchants, professors, and the common people. Understandably the clergy played a major role in events, and among the clergy the friars were outstanding.

Characteristics

Let me crystallize my point with what I may term a joint, triple example. There was a medieval quotation: *Omne trinum perfectum* (all perfect things come in threes), and my example will seem to prove the quotation. One may legitimately argue that the three most dynamic religious figures in Europe between 1490 and 1520 were Girolamo Savonarola (1452-1498) in Italy, Francisco Ximinez de Cisneros (1436-1517) in Spain, and Martin Luther (1483-1546) in Germany. Historians have hitherto studied what divided these three men, not what they had in common. One significant feature which they had in common, and which is almost universally overlooked, is that they were observant friars. They are usually thought of either in national terms — that they were respectively, Italian, Spanish, and German — or as members of three separate religious orders, Dominican, Franciscan, and Augustinian. It is of considerable relevance, in terms of religious reformation and of the Reformation, to realize that the three were committed to religious renewal antecedent to the Reformation.

The tragedy and paradox is that such men and their followers, dedicated to religious revival within the Catholic Church, should eventually be found in bitter opposition to one another, and in some cases in open and convinced revolt against the central Church authority at Rome. However, my intent is not to deal with that tragic development, but with the earlier and happier phase, when there was still unity and when the vision of a renewed Church was a binding, not a divisive, force.

There were at least seven characteristics of the Augustinian observant movement: 1) it owed a great deal to the example of the

Franciscan observants; 2) it was Italian in origin and in continuing influence; 3) it upheld the eremetical ideal as a main principle, and looked back in particular to the Hermits of Saint Augustine in Tuscany in the early middle ages as the link with Saint Augustine; 4) it was formally initiated in 1385 by the Augustinian prior general, the central authority of the Order in Rome, and was consistently supported by a succession of priors general up to the time of the Reformation and later; 5) the observants remained under the jurisdiction of the priors general, who became their protectors. Several of the priors general were observants; 6) the observant movement was not co-terminous with the Augustinian Order. It was encouraged, but not imposed, by the priors general. It depended on local support for its beginnings in different countries, but inevitably this was a matter of chance and opportunity. For that reason it was not to be found in France and England; 7) the observants encouraged learning. This was a policy of the Augustinian Order since the late thirteenth century, and owed much to the example of the Dominicans.

One of the most powerful spiritual forces in the high middle ages was that released by an Italian genius, Francis of Assisi, and astutely canalized into institutional forms by the Holy See and by the sage legislation of another religious genius, the Spaniard, Dominic Guzman, and his early followers in the Dominican Order. Between them these two holy men, Francis and Dominic, produced, almost unconsciously, a revolutionary change in the character of what had hitherto been the settled, and almost inflexible, appearance of monastic life.

Mendicants

The mendicant friar was a new phenomenon. Many conservatives said it was a dangerous phenomenon. The solidly established, well-financed monasteries of Benedictines had been an integral part of feudal Europe since the Dark Ages, as were the later Benedictine reforms at Cluny (910) and Clairvaux (1115). The spread of the admirable canons regular of Saint Augustine was part of the same process during the eleventh and twelfth centuries. Then the religious scene was changed, utterly changed, by the appearance of the friars on the scene. Here was an adaptation of the monastic life to the new dynamic evolution of an urbanized civilization in which an educated generation of lay people challenged the dominant position of the literate clerics. Rarely was religion so urgently needed by the masses of the population, particularly by the workers in the towns; rarely was a new look for religious life so desired by the body of the faithful. Then came Francis of Assisi with his happy — some would say his hippy — genius for arousing enthusiasm and love. When these were harnessed and disciplined in a generous partnership with Dominic Guzman there emerged the mendicant friars. It was these mendicant friars who played a principal part in the religious transformation of western Europe in the high middle ages. They operated at every level and in every sphere of society. Pastoral life, social services, the universities, foreign missions, all gave scope to the tireless activity of the friars.

Yet even this phenomenal activity was not sufficient to cope with the religious needs of a rapidly expanding, inquisitive, impatient Europe. It was at this point in the mid- thirteenth century that the papacy, mindful primarily of its pastoral obligations, summoned two groups of hermits, the Carmelites and the Augustinians, to join in the care of souls, especially in the towns and cities. It was thus that the Augustinian hermits became Augustinian friars. As a reminder of their origin (real or fictional) not only from the medieval hermits but from Saint Augustine, they took as their official title the name "Friars Hermits of Saint Augustine."

Augustinian Mendicants

In March 1256 representatives of five different groups of hermits assembled in the church of Santa Maria del Popolo in Rome, under the leadership of an influential papal legate, Cardinal Richard Annibaldi. The delegates represented 200 houses throughout Europe, but with the major concentration in Italy. The final act in the legal process of transformation from hermits to friars was the papal bull, *Licet Ecclesiae,* of 9 April 1256.[8] It is the charter of the Augustinian Order, and commemorates a most unusual decision — an Order founded not by negotiation among groups of religious, nor even (as is more normal) by the inspiration of a saint or holy individual, but by the intervention of the papacy. That act of direct foundation by the papacy was to influence profoundly the history of the Order. In consequence the Augustinians felt themselves particularly bound to the papacy and were among the most loyal defenders of the claims of the papacy from this time forward until the Reformation — one need mention only Giles of Rome (d. 1316), James of Viterbo (d. 1308), Augustine of Ancona (d. 1328), Alexander of San Elpidio (d. 1326), and William of Cremona (d. 1356). Paradoxically, it was this same Order of Friars Hermits of Saint Augustine which produced Martin Luther, the man who led the greatest ever assault on the papacy in the medieval period. Between 1256 and 1517 the emergence of the Augustinian observant movement was to take place.

Undoubtedly the Augustinians were influenced by the Franciscan observants, but on one important aspect, on learning, they differed noticeably from them. To appreciate this difference we must look, even if briefly, not just at the Franciscans but at Francis of Assisi. Franciscan history has always had the problem of the "two Saints Francis" — Francis the popular preacher, and Francis the solitary on Mount Alvernia. Francis, unlike Dominic Guzman, was not a man of the Schools, he was not a bookman. He believed in *docta ignorantia* but, even during his own lifetime and at an accelerated rate shortly after his death, his Order attracted some of the most brilliant young minds in the universities. Then, after the death of Francis, there appeared a division, a bitter division, among the Franciscans between those who claimed to follow the lifestyle of *Il Poverello* literally, and those who believed a compromise was necessary on the crucial questions of property and education. The dispute continued throughout the thirteenth century and was brought to a head in the early fourteenth century by the Franciscan zealots — the "spirituals" and the Fraticelli. Pope John XXII thought he had solved the recurrent crisis when he issued his *Cum inter nonnullos* on 12 November 1323. This granted the Franciscans the right to corporate ownership, despite the ideal upheld by Francis of absolute poverty. The Franciscans were thus established with property, with convents, and became "conventuals."

Augustinian Observants

Within little more than a decade of *Cum inter nonnullos*, a Franciscan reform, linked with the preceding "spiritual" party through that controversial individual, Angelo Clareno (d. 1337), began to spread through Italy under the title of "observant." This new reform, unlike that of the "spirituals," did not have the taint or reputation of heresy about it, and it spread widely. The observant influence was not confined to the Franciscans. The same spirit made itself felt among the Augustinians, as among the Dominicans. There were close relations between Angelo Clareno and the Augustinian, Simon of Cascia (d. 1348).[9] Simon was a notable preacher, ascetic, and writer, whose orthodoxy was put beyond question when the Church declared him to be a blessed. Simon was one of those who paved the way for the Augustinian reform, the observant movement, and who set the standards which were to be characteristic of the Augustinian, as distinct from the Franciscan, observants. While Simon believed in the eremitical tradition and that spiritual perfection, at least for Augustinians, would best be achieved by withdrawal from the "world," he was also a learned man, as shown in his monumental *De gestis Domini Salvatoris.*[10] Nobody who claimed to be a spiritual descendant of Augustine of Hippo could turn a disparaging eye on learning, be it sacred or profane. On this issue the Augustinians were a contrast with Francis of Assisi who put little store by books and the world of learning.

The eremitical tradition had a hypnotic effect on those Augustinians who favored and fostered a reform movement in their Order under the title of "observant." They believed it linked them directly to Saint Augustine, and they expounded their argument as follows. The Augustinian Order came into existence in the thirteenth century when various congregations of hermits, mainly Italian, who were already following the *Rule* of Saint Augustine, were united by a papal bull, *Licet Ecclesiae*, on 9 April 1256. It is called the "Great Union," having been preceded by at least three smaller aggregations of Augustinian hermits in Tuscany.[11] The official title "Friars Hermits of Saint Augustine" was in fact something of a misnomer. It was meant as an historical signpost to the origins of the Augustinians rather than as an indication of the spirit and work of the new Order. They were no longer hermits. They were now friars, mendicant friars, called in by the papacy to the streets and marketplaces of towns and cities, to preach and teach by word and example. They well fulfilled the purpose for which they had been summoned, but they continued to cast a backward glance whenever opportunity allowed. It was the widespread observant movement, common to Franciscans, Dominicans, and Augustinians, and in its turn part of a general reform movement within the western Church, which gave Augustinians an historical argument to support a spiritual revival.

They had a basis of some facts, and they imaginatively bridged the yawning gaps between isolated facts with a delicate structure of supposition, suggestion, and intuition. Whether that structure can bear the heavy weight of modern historical criticism is an extremely doubtful matter, but there may be more reality to the suppositions and intuition than has been conceded by the unimaginative historians of the previous generations in this and the previous century.[12]

Lecceto

Just as the Franciscan "spirituals" were firmly rooted in Umbria and the Marche because of the association of Francis of Assisi with these regions, so the Augustinian eremitical tradition was strongest in Tuscany. It was historically true that the Tuscan hermits were the dominant group among the five congregations which were brought together by *Licet Ecclesiae* on 9 April 1256. A tradition, already in existence in the mid-thirteenth century, or newly created by the Augustinian publicists in the mid-fourteenth century, held that Augustine, having been baptized at Milan in 387, lived for some time in retirement in Tuscany and there instituted the first monastery of "Augustinian" hermits. This apocryphal story gave to Centumcello the honor of being the first Augustinian foundation. It was also conveniently believed that Augustine visited the hermitage of Lecceto, a few miles west of Siena. The brethren of this house looked upon themselves as the heirs of the monastic ideal as originally set forth by Augustine. The hermitage, and the tradition that it formed a direct link with Augustine, exercised a fascination over Augustinians in the fourteenth and fifteenth centuries.

Already during the medieval period they were encouraged not merely by oral traditions but by the creation of a sympathetic literature. The pseudo-Augustine *Sermones ad Fratres in Eremo* gave a justification and a spiritual basis to those Augustinian friars who were of an eremitical frame of mind. This work, supposedly by Augustine, became the inspired word for those who believed that a reflowering of the true religion would come with a revival of the monastic life as practiced by Augustine and his companions when they settled at Thagaste on their return to North Africa in 388.[13] The advocates of the Augustinian monastic revival in the middle ages did not realize that there was a genuine work of Augustine, *The Work of Monks*, which proved much of what they were laboring to express. However, the hermitage at Lecceto gave them apparently visible evidence of the direct connection with Augustine. This concentration on Lecceto became an expression of the reform movement among the Augustinian friars. They dreamed of a golden age in the past when religious life was perfectly observed by the hermits there. This, they fondly assumed, was in the lifetime of Augustine. They believed that Lecceto, by reason of its supposed association with Augustine, had retained something of his soaring spirit and ardent zeal. It was a mentality then common among Renaissance scholars, men devoted to a cult of the past, hypnotized by the thought that "they were giants in those days."

Reform Congregations

Lecceto became the inspiration of the reform among the Augustinians. Already by the middle of the fourteenth century the hermitage had been famed as a center of mystical piety. Saint Catherine of Siena (d. 1380) found there some of her most resolute supporters. Its reputation drew one noted English mystic, William Flete, across the seas in 1359, and he remained there for the rest of his life. When the Augustinians decided to promote officially the reform movement within the Order they selected Lecceto as the first designated house of the observance. This took place at a general chapter of the Order at Esztergom (Gran) in Hungary on 18 May 1385, when Bartholomew of Venice was elected prior general. He appointed two exemplary friars, Nicola de Ceretanis and Bandinello, to supervise the reform at Lecceto. It was realized that it would be virtually impossible to impose a universal reform on the Order, but instead Lecceto was selected as the light to shine before Augustinians. So that it might have a unique position, and would not suffer from the possible envy of lukewarm brethren at nearby Siena, Bartholomew took the house from the jurisdiction of the Sienese provincial and, by a decree of 3 March 1387, put it directly under the rule of the prior general. This was confirmed by decrees of the general chapter at Rimini in June 1394, at Munich in June 1397, and at Aquila in June 1400.

The reform or "observant" movement spread with a firm vigor throughout the Italian Augustinian provinces.[14] As would be expected in a country with such strong regional patriotism several regions created their own separate congregations, though each one was subject to the prior general, who was also supreme head of the Augustinian conventuals. Naples was the first to follow the example of Lecceto. The reform was established there in the early fifteenth century, and was formally established as a separate congregation, styled San Giovanni in Carbonara, by a decree of the prior general, Agostino Favaroni, on 7 February 1421. But already the observant movement had made its first steps beyond the Alps into Germany and across the seas into Spain. The strict observance was introduced at Ramsau, Bavaria, in 1419, and spread rapidly to the friaries of Saxony and Bavaria. By 1459 there was a separate German (or Saxon) Congregation, and among its members in the beginning of the sixteenth century was Martin Luther. Parallel with the Congregation of Saxony had grown the already mentioned Congregation of Naples, San Giovanni a Carbonara, which was to have as its most distinguished member a contemporary of Luther, Jerome Seripando (1463-1563), prior general of the Augustinian Order (1538-1551), and cardinal legate at the Council of Trent (1561-1563). In the simultaneous appearance of these two individuals, Luther and Seripando, within the same movement in one religious order is encapsulated the problem of reform within the Catholic Church.

The observance took root in Spain, also in the beginning of the fifteenth century, in Castile, and by 1505 had become the major Augustinian influence in the Iberian peninsula.[15] Before the close of that century all the provinces of Spain and Portugal had transferred their allegiance to the observants. The most memorable of the Spanish observants was Saint Thomas of Villanova (d. 1555), archbishop of Valencia, also a contemporary of Luther.

Almost without exception, the appearance of the Augustinian observance in any region was a local and spontaneous effort. It should also be emphasized that it was equally true that the initial impetus for those regional efforts was often due to some young friar who had studied in Italy and come in contact there with the observants. For example, a leading figure among the early German observants was Heinrich Zolter, who had been a student at Pavia in the 1420s. Later the guiding spirit in Germany was Andreas Proles (1429-1503), who was a lector of theology at Perugia in 1455. The same is true for several of the early Spanish observants: the pioneer of Augustinian observants in Spain was Juan de Alarcón (d. 1453), who had been a lector at Florence in 1420.

It is no great surprise, in view of the political and cultural developments of the fifteenth century, that the Augustinian observants did not establish themselves in either France or England. Yet the observants were introduced to Ireland in 1423 and by 1479 had a separate congregation, politically within the theoretical jurisdiction of England, but religiously responsible directly to the prior general in Rome.[16] The fact remained that no matter what developed in different parts of Europe the most important geographic area for Augustinians was Italy. That is where the action took place, where the papacy and the prior general operated directly.

By the last quarter of the fifteenth century there were eleven observant congregations — seven in Italy (Lecceto in Tuscany, Naples, Perugia, Monte Ortone for Venetian territory, Lombardy, Dulceti in Apulia, and Genoa), two in Spain (Castile and Toledo), one in Germany (that of Saxony), and one in Ireland (centered at Callan, Co. Kilkenny). While the Franciscan observant reform suffered a checkered history, and had to contend with determined opposition even from the central government of the Order, the Augustinian priors general were the protectors of the observants. So successful was their patronage that the observant movement captured the leadership of the Order during the second half of the fifteenth century. The priors general, Giuliano Falciglia (1443-1458), Alessandro Oliva (1458-1460), Anselmo da Montefalco (1485-1495), and Mariano da Genazzano (1495-1498) were observants. Two of the most remarkable priors general during the crises of the sixteenth century were also observants, Giles of Viterbo (1506-1518) and his protégé, Jerome Seripando (1539-1551).

Augustinian Observant Reform

At this point one may well ask, almost impatiently, "What was the Augustinian observant reform? What did it have to attract a Martin Luther in Germany, a Jerome Seripando in Italy, a Thomas of Villanova in Spain?" To be an observant friar meant that one belonged to a reformed house or branch of the Order. In what did the reform consist? The word "observant" is its own answer. The reformers did not expound revolutionary policy. Their purpose was to observe strictly, yet as far as humanly possible, the vows of poverty, chastity, and obedience, the *Rule* of Saint Augustine, and the constitutions of the Order. But there were noticeable differences between the observant branches of different orders. For Franciscans the touchstone was poverty. For Augustinians the ideal was expressed by "devotion to the common good" of the group, as against the personal benefit or ambition of individual friars. In effect, a reformed or observant friar was one who sought neither privileges nor exemptions from the "common life." It was socialism long before that word had come into political and sociological parlance. Inevitably, any renascence of religious life brought an increase of austerities, stricter discipline in the community, fresh interest in prayer and in liturgical services.

The observant reform was somewhat introverted. It did not immediately concern itself with pastoral activity. Yet inevitably, in an active Order such as the Augustinians, renewed zeal for religious life created a keener awareness of the need to attend to the sacramental life of the laity. However much the medieval Augustinians might sigh for the eremitical style of life they could not ignore the fact that they had been called out of their hermitages by the papacy to become friars in urban centers. An obvious consequence was that they appeared there as preaching friars, not as hermits. Nevertheless, it should be noted that preaching was one activity which the Augustinians, even as hermits, had already undertaken before 1256. One of the many merits of Professor Elm's work on the Tuscan hermits is his contention that they were not recluses in the tradition of the "Fathers of the Desert" in Egypt and the middle east.[17] The Tuscan hermits lived in community, not as individuals, and they worked as a group. While it is true that they resided outside the towns and cities, in woods and on the hillsides, they had a positive policy of evangelization of the people, the much-neglected people, of the countryside. The change came in 1256 when they were directed by the Holy See to translate themselves and their activity to centers of population.

Preaching

As spiritual sons of Saint Augustine they could console themselves that the monk-bishop of Hippo had devoted much of his energies to preaching, most of it in urban centers. Nor did they fail to rise to the challenge after the "Great Union" of 1256. The first generation of Augustinian friars produced preachers such as Saint Nicholas of Tolentino (d. 1305) and Blessed Angelo of Foligno (d. 1312). That became a feature of the Augustinians in all of their provinces, but it was particularly strong in Italy. Unexpected but striking evidence of Augustinian preaching activity is that two of the most outstanding preachers of the middle ages, the Franciscan, Saint Bernardine of Siena (1380-1444), and the Dominican, Girolamo Savonarola (1452-1498), were both converted to the religious life by sermons delivered by Augustinians. Savonarola's fame as a preacher was almost equaled by that of his contemporary and opponent, the Augustinian, Mariano da Genazzano (d. 1498). It should not be overlooked that Mariano was both an observant and prior general of his Order.

Preaching was not a feature peculiar to the Augustinian observants. It was equally a characteristic of the Franciscan and Dominican observants, as of the reformed congregations of the Carmelite
and Servite orders. And it would be a manifest injustice to disregard the preaching activity of the conventuals of the mendicant
orders, as of individual secular priests. Furthermore, a detailed and
illuminating study has revealed the outstanding theological quality of the sermons preached at the papal court (of all places!) during
the very height of the Italian Renaissance.[18] Nevertheless, it was in
the very character of the observants of all orders that they should
be the revivalist preachers. It was an external expression of their
raison d'être as observants. The need to preach the word of God did
not begin with the Reformation, however much it may have been
emphasized at that time. A significant example is Giles of Viterbo,
an Augustinian who was an observant and was prior general
during the period of Luther's most important theological forma-
tive years. Giles was by common repute in the very front rank of
preachers in Italy and acclaimed by many as the greatest in his own
day.[19]

Learning

Preaching was one thing, learning was another. No true Christians can question the need to have the word of God preached. Nor
would they query the obligation of studying the Bible in all its
theological implications. That is where much trouble begins. How
far do you go in your queries? Do you confine yourself strictly to
the biblical text, and how far do you branch out into theology,
linguistics, philosophical and sociological presuppositions? And
what of "mere" secular literature, with all the light it throws on the
background to the Bible, and on the Roman empire which received
the good news so unwillingly.

It was here that the Augustinian observants, who owed much to
the inspiration of the Franciscan spirituals and observants, differed
sharply from them. The tradition of the Franciscan spirituals was
to believe in the *docta ignorantia*, which Francis himself had advo-
cated in his single-minded devotion to Christ. Why indulge in
secular learning when Christ was waiting? What profit was there
for the Christian in the pagan literature of Greece and Rome? This
is the language of Christian fundamentalists at all stages in the
history of the Church, it is the mentality of the revivalist for whom
human life is short and eternity is long. But it was not the mentality

of Augustine or of the Augustinian observants. In 1259, within three years of the "Great Union" of 1256, the first Augustinian prior general, Lanfranco of Milan, had established a house for students at Paris at what was then the leading university center of western Europe.[20] Its main purpose was, of course, theological, and that objective might placate even the fundamentalists, but the Augustinians pursued learning on a more liberal basis. From the time of the "Great Union" they adopted the intellectual program of the Dominicans, rather than the fundamentalist attitude of the Franciscans. There were many current influences to explain the Augustinian policy, but these friars could point to the example of Augustine himself, the last great classical stylist of the Roman world.

The Augustinians succeeded during the fourteenth century in establishing a further tradition in their Order — patronage of, and participation in, secular vernacular learning. This tradition they were to communicate to their observants. The tradition was immortalized by the association of the Augustinians with Petrarch and Boccaccio, the two luminaries of the early Italian Renaissance.[21] Petrarch was closely bound by friendship with four Augustinians, Denis of Borgo San Sepolcro (d. 1342), Bartholomew of Urbino (d. 1350), Jean Coci (d. 1364), and Cardinal Bonaventure Baduario da Perago (d. 1389). We know that Petrarch's devotion to Saint Augustine, which was both spiritual and literary, was fostered by the Augustinians. When Petrarch died in 1374 it was Bonaventure Baduario who delivered the funeral oration at the poet's tomb.

Boccaccio had not as many Augustinian friends as Petrarch, but in Friar Martino da Signa he found intelligence and sympathy. In August 1374 Boccaccio bequeathed his library to the Augustinians at Florence and asked that his body be laid with the friars at Florence or Certaldo. These golden years of Augustinian friendship with Petrarch and Boccaccio took place at the time when members of the Order were astir with the notion of formally founding the observant reform. That came in 1385 when the Augustinian house of study at Florence, Santo Spirito, in the description of Gian Francesco Poggio Bracciolini, "was frequented by the best and most outstanding men of the city." The magnet who drew the artists, scholars, and literati was Fra Luigi Marsigli (d. 1394), who though known as "the apostle and soul of the literary renaissance in Florence" was equally intent on Church reform.[22] It was thus by a happy coincidence of circumstances that the scholarship of the Renaissance and the Augustinian observant movement became associated from an early stage. It was to be a characteristic of the Augustinian observants, but was to be less in evidence in the Germanic and Nordic lands than in the Latin countries.

The premature death of Marsigli in 1394 did not interrupt the Augustinian association with humanism. A notable contribution was made by a Milanese friar, Andrea Biglia (d. 1435), who, though only forty years old at the time of his death, has left his mark in Renaissance literature.[23] Nor was the humanism confined to Italian friars. The French Augustinian, Jacques Legrand (d. 1360-1415), was both a preacher of national fame and a humanist of repute.[24] Though neither of these friars was an observant they do illustrate the continuing Augustinian association with learning, including secular learning such as the classics. Two English Augustinians, John Capgrave (1393-1464) and Osbern Bokenham (1393-1467), have their place in middle-English literature as humanists.[25] It is important to bear in mind that, unlike the Franciscans, there was no ideological division between Augustinian conventuals and observants over the issue of scholarship. On the interpretation of the *Rule* of Saint Augustine and the constitutions they did differ, but not on the value of human learning.

The hour of apparent triumph for the Augustinian observant movement came in June 1506 with the nomination of Giles of Viterbo as vicar general of the Order by Pope Julius II. Here in one person had come together, at an eminent level, a superb combination of four elements which had been gathering force among the Augustinians since the mid-fourteenth century: the reform movement, the eremitical ideal, preaching the word of God, and the humanism of the Renaissance.

Notes

1. The modern magisterial work on the *Rule* is the study by L. Verheijen, *La Règle de Saint Augustin*, I: *Tradition manuscrite*, II: *Recherches historiques*, Paris, 1967. For an appreciation of Verheijen's work, see R. Arbesmann, "The Question of the Regula Sancti Augustini," *Augustinian Studies* 1 (1970) 237-259. See also T. van Bavel, *The Rule of St. Augustine: masculine and feminine versions, introduction and commentary*, London, 1984; Sister Agatha Mary, S.P.B. *The Rule of Saint Augustine. An Essay in Understanding*, Villanova, 1992.

2. There are three essential works to consult on Augustine the monk: A. Manrique, "La vida monastica en San Agustin: enchiridion historico-doctrinal y Regla" (*Studia Patristica, Sección de Estudios* 1) El Escorial, Salamanca, 1959; A. Zumkeller, *Augustine's Ideal of the Religious Life*, New York, 1988. J. J. Gavigan, *De*

vita monastica in Africa Septentrionali inde a temporibus S. Augustini usque ad Invasiones Arabum, Turin, 1963. See also L. Verheijen, *Saint Augustine: Monk, Priest, Bishop*, Villanova, 1978.

3. There is no even near-adequate study of the Augustinians at the beginning of the Reformation, but see: D. Gutiérrez, "Al margen de libros y articulos acerca de Lutero," *Ciudad de Dios* 169 (1956) 609-637; A. Zumkeller, "Martin Luther und sein Orden," *Analecta Augustiniana* 25 (1962) 254-290; F. X. Martin, "The Augustinian Order on the Eve of the Reformation," in *Miscellanea Historiae Ecclesiasticae* (1967) 71-104; D. Gutiérrez, "I primi Agostiniani italiani che scrissero contro Lutero," *Analecta Augustiniana* 39 (1976), 5-74.

4. L. Pastor, *History of the Popes*, London, 1912, page 493.

5. C. J. Hefele-J. Hergenroether, *Histoire des Conciles*, ed. J. Leclercq, VIII, 2, Paris, 1921, pages 865-871.

6. There is a treasure trove of pertinent information in H. Jedin, *Girolamo Seripando. Sein Leben und Denken im Geisteskampf des 16. Jahrhunderts* (Cassiciacum 2-3) Würzburg, 1937, especially pages 154-164. See also D. Gutiérrez, *Analecta Augustiniana* 21 (1947-1950), 55-177; *idem, The Augustinians from the Protestant Reformation to the Peace of Westphalia 1518-1548*, History of the Order of St. Augustine (Volume II), Villanova, 1979. For an erudite investigation of the Augustinian background to Luther's theological training: A. Zumkeller, *Erbsünde, Gnade, Rechtfertigung und Verdienst nach der Lehre der Erfurter Augustinertheologen des Spätmittelalters* (Cassiciacum 35), Würzburg, 1984.

7. See Y. Congar, *Martin Luther, sa foi, sa réforme. Etudes de théologie historique* (Cogitatio fidei 119), Paris, 1983.

8. Critical edition by A. de Meijer, *Augustiniana* 6 (1956), 9-13, with commentary by R. Kuiters, *ibid.*, 14-36.

9. P. Bellini, *Blessed Simon Fidati of Cascia*, The Augustinian Series, vol. 13, Villanova 1988.

10. See M. G. McNeill, *Simon Fidati and his "De Gestis Domini Salvatoris"* (Studies in Medieval and Renaissance Latin Language and Literature 21) Washington 1950. For the connection between Angelo and Simon, see Angeli Clareni, *Opera*, vol. 1: Epistole, ed. L. von Auw, Rome, 1980, and P. Bellini, *Blessed Simon Fidati of Cascia*, The Augustinian Series, vol. 13, Villanova, 1988.

11. The pioneering study, and still the classic work on the "Great Union" and its background, is by F. Roth, "Cardinal Richard Annibaldi, first protector of the Augustinian Order, 1243-1276," *Augustiniana* 2 (1952) 26-60; 3 (1953) 21-34, 283-313; 4 (1954) 5-24.

12. K. Elm, *Die Anfänge des Ordens der Augustiner-Eremiten im 13. Jahrhundert*, Diss. phil. Münster 1957; *idem*, "Neue Beiträge zur Geschichte des Augustiner-Eremitenordens im 13. und 14. Jahrhundert. Ein Forschungsbericht," *Archiv für Kulturgeschichte* 42 (1960) 357-387; *idem*, "Italienische Eremitengemeinschaften des 12. und 13. Jahrhunderts. Studien zur Vorgeschichte des Augustiner-Eremitenordens," in *L'Eremitismo in Occidente nei secoli XI e XII*, Atti della Seconda Settimana internazionale di studio, Mendola 30.VIII.— 6.IX.1962, Milan, 1964, pages 491-559.

13. The view that these sermons were written for propaganda purposes by an Augustinian friar was given authority in the sixteenth century when Erasmus

made the assertion. It was repeatedly stated that the author was the Augustinian, Jordan of Saxony (c.1370). In fact the author was a medieval Benedictine monk; R. Arbesmann-W. Hümpfner (ed.), *Liber Vitasfratrum Jordani de Saxonia* (Cassiciacum Studies in St. Augustine and the Augustinian Order I) New York, 1943, xxiv-xxxix.

14. Katherine Walsh, *The Observant Congregations of the Augustinian Friars in Italy*, Phil.-Diss. Oxford, 1972; *eadem*, "The Observance: sources for a history of the Observant reform movement in the Order of Augustinian Friars in the fourteenth and fifteenth centuries," *Rivista di Storia della Chiesa in Italia* 31 (1977) 40-67; *eadem*, "Papal policy and local reform I: The beginning of the Augustinian Observance in Tuscany," *Römische Historische Mitteilungen* 21 (1979) 35-57; *eadem*, "Papal policy and local reform II: Congregatio Ilicetana. The Augustinian Observant movement in Tuscany and the humanist ideal," *ibid.* 22 (1980) 105-145.

15. L. Álvarez Gutíerrez, *El movimiento "observante" agustiniano en España y su culminación en tiempo de los Reyes Católicos* (Studia Augustiniana Historia 6) Rome, 1978.

16. F. X. Martin, "The Irish Augustinian reform movement in the fifteenth century," *Medieval studies presented to Aubrey Gwynn*, ed. J. A. Watt, J. B. Morrall, and F. X. Martin, Dublin, 1961, 230-264.

17. See the studies of Elm, in particular his contribution in: *L'Eremitismo in Occidente*, note 12 above.

18. J. W. O'Malley, *Praise and blame in Renaissance Rome: rhetoric, doctrine, and reform in the sacred orators of the papal court, c.1450-1521* (Duke Monographs in Medieval and Renaissance Studies 3) Durham, NC, 1979. The orators included the Augustinians, Aurelio Lippo Brandolini, Raphael Brandolini, Mariano da Genazzano, Giles of Viterbo, Ambrose Massari of Cori, Nicolò Palmeri, Paolo da Roma, Giovanni Battista Signori, and Dionisio Vázquez.

19. C. O'Reilly, "*Maximus Caesar et Pontifex Maximus.* Giles of Viterbo proclaims the alliance between Emperor Maximilian and Pope Julius II," *Augustiniana* 22 (1972) 80-117; *idem*, "'Without Councils we cannot be saved.' Giles of Viterbo addresses the Fifth Lateran Council," *ibid.* 27 (1977) 166-204.

20. E. Ypma, *La formation des professeurs chez les ermites de Saint Augustin de 1256 à 1354*, Paris, 1956.

21. The essential works on this subject are U. Mariani, *Il Petrarca e gli Agostiniani*, Rome 1959; R. Arbesmann, *Der Augustiner-Eremitenorden und der Beginn der humanistischen Bewegung* (Cassiciacum 29) Würzburg, 1965. J.E. Wrigley, "Petrarch, St. Augustine, and the Augustinians," *Augustinian Studies* 8 (1977) 71-89; E. Luciani, *Les "Confessions" de Saint Augustin dans les lettres de Petrarque*, Paris, 1982.

22. Nothing substantial on Marsigli has been published in recent years, but see the brief and valuable assessments of him in his Augustinian and cultural context by Arbesmann (see note 21). Well worthy of attention and publication is the dissertation by P. Gallagher, *Luigi Marsigli, the Florentine Humanist, 1342-1394*, University College, Dublin, 1972.

23. See the references to Biglia (especially under the name Schnaubelt) in A. de Meijer, "Bibliographie historique de l'ordre de Saint Augustin, 1945-1975," *Augustiniana* 26 (1976), notes 1611-1614, and for the years 1975-1989, *ibid.* 31 (1981), notes 3807-3813.

24. For Legrand: *ibid.* 26 (1976), notes 1569-1578; 31 (1981), notes 3794- 3795. Evrencio Beltran, *L'Idéal de Sagesse d'après Jacques Legrand*, Paris, 1989.

25. For Capgrave and Bokenham, *Augustiniana* 26 (1976), notes 1639-1655; 31 (1981), notes 3818-3823.

Chapter 5

Prior General and Reformer

Giles is of particular interest and importance not simply as general of the Order at a crucial period of its history, but because he represented to a striking degree two qualities, the humanism of the Renaissance and an urgent sense of the need for religious reform, which were manifest in so many of the Augustinians who played an active part as either Catholic or Protestant reformers. In that sense he is a key to an understanding of the condition of the Augustinian Order in the early sixteenth century.

This is not the occasion to treat of the humanist tradition in the Augustinian Order. It is sufficient to refer to the background in which the outstanding figures were Dionigi da Borgo San Sepolcro (d. 1342), friend of Petrarch, Jean Coci (d. 1364) at Avignon, Cardinal Bonaventura da Peraga (d. 1389), Luigi Marsigli (d. 1394), Martino da Signa (d. 1387), friend of Boccaccio, and Jacques Legrand (d. 1414/5) at Paris.[1]

Giles was a product of this background and a child of the Renaissance. But he was primarily a reformer, and here it is well to remember that he was not a pioneer nor did he create the reform movement in the Augustinian Order, but was a product of it.

What was the task awaiting Giles? At that time the Augustinian Order numbered about 22,000 friars in 1,000 friaries. There were twenty-six provinces — thirteen for Italy, Dalmatia, and the Grecian Islands, four for France, four for the Germanic lands, Poland, and the Low Countries, two for Spain, one each for England, Portugal, and Hungary. In addition to the provinces there were the observant congregations within the body of the Order. They had created an intricate situation.

The Observant Movement

The observant reform had been formally instituted by the prior general, Bartholomew of Venice, when in the year 1385 as a means of rejuvenating the Order he selected the monastery at Lecceto near Siena as the light to shine before Augustinians.[2] Lecceto was at that time already famous for its spiritual radiance, associated with Saint Catherine of Siena and the English mystic, William Flete.

The reform movement spread vigorously throughout the Order. The houses of the observants began to form units, entitled "congregations," distinct from the provinces. These congregations, enriched with privileges and exemptions from both the priors general and the Holy See, gradually acquired a measure of independence, though this varied according to each congregation. The powerful Lombard congregation was united to the Order by no more than tenuous connections, and in January 1498 had secured a papal declaration which for all practical purposes exempted it from the jurisdiction of the prior general. The congregation of Saxony, to which Luther belonged, was hardly less insistent on its claims to semi-autonomy, and in April 1505 the Saxon and Lombard congregations agreed to a union. Other congregations, such as that of Lecceto, acknowledged their subjection to the prior general, but with reservations. The observant problem was in this advanced stage when Giles became prior general in 1507.

There were then ten congregations: six in Italy, two in Spain, one in Germany, and another in Ireland. The members of the congregations were styled "observants," while those of the parent stock were called "conventuals." Thus within the same country, state, or region there were two bodies of Augustinians, distinct from and sometimes hostile to one another though both owed allegiance to the one prior general.

The troubled history of some of the congregations during Giles' period of office should not obscure the fact that they were founded to satisfy the heartfelt need for Church reform. It is significant that three of the most notable reformers of this period — Savonarola in Italy, Cardinal Ximenes in Spain, and Luther in Germany — were members of the observant reform in their orders. The movement was so successful among the Augustinians that it captured the leadership of the Order during the fifteenth century. The notable priors general, Giuliano Falciglia (1443-1458) and Alessandro Oliva (1458-1498), were observants. Giles himself was a member of the Congregation of Lecceto. However, the idealism which originally brought the Augustinian observant movement to birth had in many cases spent itself by the beginning of the sixteenth century. Success frequently banishes the vivifying spirit of a spiritual revival. The observants' zeal to extend the reform gradually became infected with grasping ambition. Their concern to uphold high spiritual standards tended to become a righteous condemnation of the conventuals, and in some instances it manifested itself as defiance of the priors general who would not see fit to canonize every new step of the congregations.

The Augustinian situation was not unique. The Dominicans were painfully aware of the problem from the case of Savonarola and his championship of the congregation of San Marco. The Franciscans were at this time in a state of profound crisis due to the division between observants and conventuals. The division was given a permanent canonical status in 1517.

The Augustinian Order in Decay?

It should not be imagined that the observants were the only main cause of anxiety for Giles. The conventuals were also a source of uneasiness. Since the year 1485 the Order had lacked a firm hand continuously at the helm. A series of five ill-starred priors general had been unable to prevent the growing relaxation of religious discipline. The vigorous Ambrose da Cori (1476-1485) was arrested and jailed in the Castel Sant'Angelo because of his alleged criticism of Innocent VIII. His successor, Anselmo da Montefalco (1485-1495), though a shining example of virtue, was an old man when elected and became so crippled with rheumatism that he had to resign in favor of Mariano da Genazzano (1495-1498). Mariano had all the qualities needed in a reformer, except good health. The courageous program which he published for reform was first thwarted by the Lombard congregation, then cut short by his premature death near Naples in December 1498. He was succeeded by Graziano Ventura (1498-1504), whose piety was not matched by his competence and whose death in 1504 was a benefit rather than a loss to his Order. Agostino Faccioni (1504-1506) became vicar general on Ventura's death and was unanimously elected prior general in September 1505, but his career of promise ended abruptly with his death on 26 June 1506. Giles was then summoned to rule the Order.

Considering the worldly and even disreputable standards set by the Roman curia from the time of Sixtus IV (1471-1484) it was a wonder that a general rot did not set in among the Augustinians during the troubled twenty-one years between 1485 and 1506. The quality of the priors general elected from the time of Giuliano Falciglia (1443-1459) to Giles of Viterbo proves that the general condition of the Augustinian body was healthy and that the majority of its members still held fast to the ideals of the religious life. Several of these generals were observants and their primary concern was the spiritual improvement of the Order. Indeed, a valid criticism is that the Augustinians more than once made the mistake of electing men who were holy rather than capable. However, it would appear that too often the generals were admired rather than imitated. Because of the unsteady and interrupted government of the Order after Ambrose's deposition in 1485, the Augustinians suffered from a growing relaxation and indiscipline. Nevertheless, one must be cautious in accepting any generalization about the decayed condition of the Order at the beginning of the sixteenth century. Such an opinion is part of an exaggerated view which certain Protestant and Catholic historians have adopted about the state of the Church on the eve of the Reformation.

It justifies the religious revolt for Protestant writers, whereas Roman Catholics believe it a proof of the divine nature of their Church that it could endure such corruption yet display an extraordinary vitality in response to the challenge of the Reformation.

If Giles and his fellow reformers are summoned as witnesses their words seem conclusive proof that the Order was tottering on the brink of dissolution. One could quote *ad nauseam* to this effect from Giles' registers, letters, and instructions; for example, in a letter of 20 May 1508, he graphically stated that for a hundred years the Order had been in a state of decay, its former glory and good example all but perished.[3] One of his principal supporters, Gabriele della Volta, in his preface to the Augustinian constitutions published in 1508, described the Order previous to Giles' election as in a moribund condition, hopelessly awaiting its own death. When the Augustinian, Ambrogio Calepino, dedicated the second edition of his famous dictionary to Giles in 1509 he praised him for healing and restoring the Order.[4]

All such statements must be seen in their context. Giles allowed himself the license of exaggeration which is a characteristic tendency of preachers and reformers, and which at least in pre-Reformation days could openly express itself in uninhibited denunciation of weakness, folly, and vice within the Church. Augustinians like Gabriele della Volta and Ambrogio Calepino exaggerated the decadent state of the Order so that they might magnify Giles' achievements as reformer. The more accurate assessment of the condition of the Order would seem to be that it was in a state of laxity rather than of corruption.

The Program for Reform

Giles had already set about the work of reform even during his eleven months as vicar general, as we know from a brief of Julius II, but no systematic progress could be made until the general chapter of May 1507 had placed him safely in control of the Order for six years. His program for reform was formulated in thirty decrees issued at the general chapter.[5] It was a bold program, yet the basic notion was not any revolutionary plan but an insistence that there must be a return to the letter and spirit of the *Rule* of Saint Augustine. Giles, a true son of the Renaissance, looked back not forward. Just as poverty was the hallmark of the Franciscans so for Giles the *vita communis,* or common life, was to be the Augustinian means of spiritual perfection. He unhesitatingly stated that on the observance of the common life depended the health of the Order. The "common life" meant renunciation of private property, participation in communal religious exercises, attendance at common meals, observance of the cloister, a careful administration of the common property, limited intercourse with lay people, and, finally, a greater degree of mutual charity and an intensification of the spiritual life.

He gave particular attention to studies. Since degrees and teaching posts were always rungs on the ladder leading to positions of authority in the Order, he sought to rally all the young talent and brightest promise in the Order to his program by introducing a rule that nobody was to be accepted for higher studies unless he declared for reform.

If Giles were to enforce his program of reform he would of necessity have to tread on the corns not only of his own friars but of secular and ecclesiastical authorities throughout Europe. To do so with impunity he needed the wholehearted support of the papacy. Here his friendship with Julius II stood him in good stead. On 25 June 1507 he was granted the *Bulla Aurea,* which confirmed all the privileges granted by previous popes to the Augustinians. The Franciscans and Dominicans had secured such a bull in 1497, but the curialists and bishops in Rome had prevented a similar concession to the Augustinians. It required somebody of Giles' influence to win the prize, and even the strong-minded Julius was for some time deterred by the storm of opposition raised by the curialists on hearing of the proposed grant to the Augustinians. But having once taken the decision in favor of the Augustinians Julius supported Giles to the hilt.

The *Bulla Aurea* was followed on 30 June 1508 by a papal brief which in some ways was an even greater concession than the *Bulla Aurea* since its main message was the communication of the *Mare Magnum* of privileges hitherto the proud possession of the Franciscans and Dominicans. Another brief was issued on 24 September excommunicating lay people who refused to yield up property belonging to the Order. A further brief, *Breve Apostolorum*, was published on 7 October, granting Giles permission to imprison and punish any Augustinian living outside his monastery on the strength of a papal dispensation gained on false or insufficient grounds. This was intended to close an obvious loophole still open to shifty friars trying to escape the searching hand of reform. The purpose of this series of papal documents was indicated in yet another brief, issued on 7 October, confirming Giles' election as prior general. It stated that his objective should be reform and whatever was conducive to the common good of the Order.

A fitting climax to the papal concessions was the publication of the first printed version of the constitutions of the Order in November 1508. The body of the constitutions dated back to the year 1290, but as long as they were available only in manuscript copies it was inevitable that subtractions and interpolations were made by different provinces and congregations over the course of two centuries. Giles wanted an authentic printed version in each house of the Order. It was therefore an event of considerable importance when the constitutions came off the printing presses at Venice in November. The constitutions were not the only item in the volume but they formed the main part of a tidy book which was devised to give within two covers all that was necessary for a friar to attain to spiritual perfection according to the Augustinian mode of life.

The book began appropriately and logically with the *Rule* of Saint Augustine, followed by the classic commentary on the rule by Hugo of Saint Victor. While the commentary was a mystical exhortation on Augustinian spirituality, it was followed in contrast by the constitutions which formulated the canonical structure of the Order and the legislation for its government. The second part of the volume began with the *Caeremoniale* where ample provision was made for the official devotional life of the Augustinians at Mass, divine office, and other liturgical services. The printing of this section with music is an admirable example of the perfection attained by typography at Venice early in the sixteenth century. The remainder of the volume comprised a series of papal documents listing the notable privileges and exemptions won by the

Order since the Great Union of 1256. It was indicative of Giles' policy toward the observants that the privileges of the Lombard congregation were printed as a distinct sub-section but in company with the papal grants to the Order. Giles would respect the rights of the congregation but he was defining the limits of its position within the Order and was also making obvious that it was the Lombards alone and not the other observants who were entitled to these privileges.

This section of the book was rounded off with copies of the Golden Bull and of the briefs granted by Julius II. The volume concluded with a letter from Giles to all members of the Order. He reminded them of the pope's beneficence and of the duty which was now incumbent on them to justify such generosity, and he exhorted them to live as befitted the spiritual children of Saint Augustine. He stated that he had sought these privileges from the pope on the explicit understanding that the friars would in return set about a reform of the Order. This view of Julius as a patron of religious reform deserves notice since it is an aspect of his life which rarely receives attention.

The volume taken in conjunction with the thirty decrees of the general chapter of May 1507 represented Giles' program for reform. The next eleven years were to show to what extent it would be realized.

Enforcing the Reform

Giles was elected prior general at Naples in May 1507, was reelected at Viterbo in May 1511, and was confirmed in office for a further term at Rimini in May 1515. He was created a cardinal in July 1517, but continued as prior general until January 1518. His years of government may be conveniently regarded in two periods, with the Lateran Council which opened in May 1512 as the dividing line. This is not an arbitrary division. The Lateran Council, and the attacks made on the rights of the friars by the bishops during its sessions, gave a new impetus to the reform movement.

Giles wrote on 3 October 1508 as if in a fever:

> Day and night we are busy with reform. All our concern, thoughts, and actions have this one aim: that we obey the pope and cardinal protector by restoring the Order from its present state of decay to its former glory. Otherwise we cannot satisfy God, man, or our own conscience.[6]

What in fact did he attempt for reform? How persistent were his efforts? Was his program announced at the general chapter of 1507 followed by practical measures? If his efforts were effective how account for the readiness with which a noticeable number of Augustinians joined the Protestant revolt?

Six characteristics may be distinguished in Giles' method of promoting reform throughout the Order: more attention was given to the Italian provinces and congregations than to those beyond the Alps; in Italy he concentrated on the colleges and big houses; in all provinces the major superiors — the provincials, regents of study, and in many cases the priors — were either men of his own choice or, if not, were confirmed in office only on condition that they would join in the effort for reform; he kept up a constant output of letters in order to stimulate the friars and to keep himself well-informed on the progress of the reform; whenever possible he visited houses and provinces, or sent visitators with full powers in his own name; the strength of the reform came from Italy.

It was only to be expected that the Order in Italy would receive the lion's share of Giles' attention. Ever since the thirteenth century the preponderant influence in the Order had been Italian. The greatest concentration of Augustinians was in Italy — thirteen Italian provinces to balance another thirteen beyond the Alps, and eight congregations of observants in Italy as against the four congregations for Spain, Germany, and Ireland. Inevitably then the greatest press of business in the Augustinian curia came from the Italian houses and friars. By contrast the non-Italian countries tended in their nascent nationalism to resent intervention from a prior general in Rome. And there was the plain geographic difficulty of trying to supervise reform in parts of the Order far distant from Rome.

The surprising fact is that despite these reasons for the slackening of bonds with Rome the provinces beyond the Alps received proportionately, as provinces, almost as much supervision from Giles as did those in Italy. An analysis of his first register, Dd 11, which covers from March 1509 to December 1510 and from June 1512 to June 1513, is illuminating on this point.[7] And his other registers are of a like pattern. In the first register the highest numbers of entries are for the provinces of Ancona and Romagna, which are dealt with fifty-four and forty-five times respectively. There are thirty entries for the important province of Lombardy, but twenty-nine for Bavaria, the same number as, in each case, for the provinces of Siena and Sicily. While the province of Florence, which was near and dear to Giles, claims eighteen entries, an equal amount exists for the province of Saxony. The province of the Low Countries, styled "of Cologne," for all its distance from Rome, merited seventeen entries as against fifteen for the province of Naples.

Hungary, considered to be one of the remote provinces of the Order, is dealt with on eleven occasions in the register, the province of Venice receiving no greater attention. England, also regarded as a remote part of the Order, has ten entries, apart from those which treat of the Irish vicariate, a subdivision of the English province. The province of Puglia had likewise ten entries. France and Spain were comparatively well treated. Fifteen entries for the province of Toulouse, sixteen for Paris, fourteen for Aragon and fifteen for Castile form a favorable comparison with the numbers for the Italian provinces. It was likewise with the observants; for example in this register there are sixteen entries for the Congregation of Genoa and eleven for the Congregation of Saxony.

At first sight it appears baffling that the provinces and congregations — the main administrative units of the Order — received no more than a few or a half a dozen communications a year from Giles. The vast majority of the entries in the register deal with individual friars and friaries. This goes to prove, what is also evident in his letters, that Giles had not full faith in the effectiveness of circular letters but believed that real reform would come through the cooperation of individual friars and single houses until it embraced each province and congregation. He concentrated on the important houses and relied on the support of a number of chosen friars.

An analysis of Giles' first register is instructive concerning the houses of the Order. Altogether two hundred and twenty-one are Italian. The remaining forty-one friaries were beyond the Alps — in thirteen provinces and four congregations. There was an obvious disproportion between the attention given to the Italian friaries and those beyond the Alps. This does not contradict what has previously been stated about the balance of interest which Giles held between the Italian and non-Italian provinces. It was comparatively easy to have sufficient global knowledge about each province in order to direct its progress. It would have been almost impossible to have known the condition of each house beyond the Alps, whereas Giles in his preaching tours up and down the length of Italy had been able to make the personal acquaintance of many of the Italian houses and friars.

Promotion of Studies

An important part of Giles' program was his dealings with the colleges. It was his right to confirm the appointment of students and professors in the houses of higher studies in the different provinces. Paris, still theoretically the principal college in the Order, does not figure even once in his register for the nomination of friars to higher studies, though it does on other scores. This corroborates Giles' complaint to the cardinal protector, Riario, that the college had lost its original character and become national instead of remaining international.[8] Oxford, which formerly was second only to Paris in the intellectual program of the Order, is mentioned once for the nomination of students to the college. There is no mention of Cambridge as a house of studies though the early years of the Lutheran movement were to reveal that the Augustinian friary at Cambridge was a focus for keen and unorthodox theological discussion.

The lack or paucity of entries for the other ultramontane colleges such as Cologne, Erfurt, Toulouse, Cahors, Gran in Hungary, Álcala, and Salamanca shows that the practice of nominating to these houses of higher studies was exercised by the provincials rather than by the general. However, within the confines of Italy where the priors general had retained their grip on the disposition of students and professors Giles exploited the opportunity to insist on a high standard of studies and fidelity to the program of reform. Perugia, Bologna, Naples, Siena, Florence, Milan, Padua, Genoa, Rome, and Venice all received his attention. These were colleges for both Italian and ultramontane provinces, and an appreciable number of students came from abroad. Italy still attracted German students, particularly from the province of Bavaria.

Giles' hope was that these young men, destined by ability and education to be the future leaders of their respective provinces, would receive such a thorough spiritual and intellectual training in the Italian colleges that they would return as the spearheads of the reform in their respective countries. He expounded his view in a letter of 24 July 1507 to Paolo da Genazzano, regent of studies at Naples:

> We shall expel the lazy and the slothful and exclude the drones and dishonest bees from the hive. Nor shall we permit, insofar as it lies in our power, that those obtain degrees who make no progress at studies. In no circumstances will the laurels of victory be awarded to those who have not seriously and strenuously fought in the intellectual arena. It is impossible to say how much the Order has

suffered, how greatly it has declined because of those who are eager to share the honors but unequal to the labor, to study, to learning. Who will burn the midnight oil when he believes that another will be treated as his equal who spends not only the night but a goodly part of the day in bed?[9]

Giles had little compunction in rejecting any student who was judged to be unsuitable in character or intellect. He wrote from Orvieto in July 1508 that a Portuguese friar, Francisco, who was a stumbling block for his fellow students in the college of Sant'Agostino at Rome was to be expelled from Italy and deprived forever of the opportunity of higher studies. Thus, he sharply remarked, would an example be set of what was to befall delinquents.[10] A Bavarian student who was not proving satisfactory was ordered back to Germany in June 1509; curt notice was served in the same month on two German friars, a source of scandal at Bologna, who were to be expelled from the college and sent packing out of Italy; two Spanish students returning to Castile in November 1509 were granted permission to receive holy orders on condition that they proved their ability in the examinations.

Leaders for the Reform

Giles' efforts for reform were to a certain extent hampered by the very democratic constitutions of the Order which did not allow him to change superiors without most serious reasons, even when he believed that they were not sincerely bent on cooperating with his program. He had seen the problem at the time of his election in May 1507, and he forearmed himself and forewarned the brethren by decreeing that only those who declared for reform and proved within eight days that they were living accordingly would be promoted to the houses of study. As those with degrees were the most likely to be appointed superiors Giles was preparing a generation of superiors who would be committed to reform. We have already seen him enforcing his program in the colleges in Italy.

There remained the difficulty of dealing with the older age group, friars already superiors or likely to be appointed to positions of authority at provincial chapters. He could not, except for the gravest of causes, depose superiors already in office, but he had an effective weapon at hand with which to safeguard the future. He was entitled to refuse confirmation of any or all the appointments made at the provincial chapters unless he was confident that the superiors chosen were of his own mind on reform. As provincial chapters were held annually in Italy, and every three years in the ultramontane provinces, he had good reason to hope that within about six years the priors of at least the important houses and the provincials would belong to the reformers.

The system of conditional confirmation in office became a regular feature of Giles' policy and not just a rule which he applied in exceptional cases. Among his letters is the directive which he composed for newly elected provincials.[11] Therein he laid down the principle that the provincial and the acts of the chapter would be confirmed only on condition that reform was seriously undertaken. Agreement to a general principle was not sufficient in Giles' eyes, and he formulated eight rules to be observed. These dealt with prayer, discipline, and the vow of poverty. The eighth rule obliged each provincial to send a monthly report to Giles on the progress of reform. As a final clause it was stipulated that before the provincial was confirmed in office he was to read out these eight rules in front of the capitulars and swear to observe them.

Giles showed that he meant business. In October 1509 he warned the provincial of the Toulouse Augustinians that unless he undertook a reform of the province another friar would be sent in his place. A few days later, on 4 November 1509, a similar warning was sent to Martin of Pecs, newly elected provincial of the Hungarian province. During the previous week, on 28 October 1509, Siegfried von Speyer, provincial elect of Rheno-Swabia, was confirmed in office on condition that he would reform the province. Giles did not hesitate to depose the vicar general of the observant Congregation of Puglia in May 1509 on the score that he was a character of evil repute and had been elected at a chapter held without Giles' permission; instead Giles appointed his own vicar, Simone da Rocca Monteragone. Even a provincial once confirmed in office was not safe unless he fulfilled his promises; thus in October 1513 Giles brusquely ordered the provincial of Narbonne-Burgundy to resign from office.

The system of conditional approval of newly elected provincials was also applied to the appointment of priors of those colleges and houses which were, at least nominally, under the direct jurisdiction of the prior general. Giles was far from pleased with the condition of the monastery at Paris, and when confirming the new prior, Pierre Gérard, in office on 7 September 1507, he did so on condition that the reform would be introduced within two months.[12] He specified that this meant fidelity to the rule, constitutions, and the decrees of the general chapter, the care of studies, the observance of silence, of the common life, and of all other regulations of the

Order. He commanded the senior members of the community to inform him within two months if his instructions were being followed and warned them that if not he himself or a representative of his would go to supervise affairs at Paris.

Vigilance by Letters and Reports

Giles cultivated letter writing as a form of literary art, but he also turned it to good account as a means to stimulate provinces, friaries, and individual Augustinians in the campaign for reform. Shortly after his appointment as vicar general of the Order in 1506 he wrote to Evangelista, prior of the house of Naples, asking for frequent and detailed reports on the spiritual revival expected at Sant'Agostino.[13] A circular letter issued about the year 1510 on the important issues of the Order asked that daily reports on the improvement of religious observance be sent to him.[14] About the same time he instructed each new provincial to send monthly reports on the state of his province.[15] He also depended on selected friars to keep him informed on conditions in the different provinces. Thus on 9 April 1509 he requested an English friar, Stephen Curtes, to send immediately an account of the Order in England and commissioned him to write frequently. Giles maintained this effort throughout his years in office. He wrote, for example, on 7 July 1516 to Agostino Fivizzano whom he had sent as his special agent to Paris, thanking him for three letters on the condition of the Augustinians in that city.[16]

Visitators: The Agents of Reform

The mention of Fivizzano at Paris is a reminder of the system of visitators, one of the most effective instruments adopted by Giles to establish and direct the reform both in Italy and beyond its confines. The ideal course might seem to be a personal visitation by Giles of all provinces, but it could be convincingly argued that the lengthy absence of the general from Rome which this would involve might well create more problems than it would solve. He seems to have begun his term of office with the intention of making a personal visitation of the ultramontane provinces but his uncertain health, the accumulation of Augustinian problems in Italy, and the demands made upon his time by Julius II and Leo X rendered this impossible. He attempted a visitation of the German provinces early in 1516, but this was incomplete because it had to be fitted in while he was on a mission from Leo X to the Emperor Maximilian.

Whenever opportunity allowed he visited the friaries in Italy. In a letter of January 1509 he mentioned that up to that time he had inspected the friaries at Siena, Florence, and "many other places."[17] However, most of the visitations were conducted by his chosen agents.

A month after being appointed vicar general he was employing visitators. The community at Milan had become bitterly divided, words led to blows, eventually swords were drawn and blood spilled. Giles wrote in distress to the provincial of Lombardy, Bartholomew Valmach, on 23 July 1506, appointing him visitator at Milan. A second letter is of special interest because it includes instructions on how the visitation was to be conducted.[18] Bartholomew was first to hold a thorough examination of those concerned, then sift all the facts, come to clear-cut decisions, and promulgate them. He was given power to reprove, punish, transfer, or expel any member of the community. All those belonging to the house at Milan were ordered to submit to him in virtue of their vow of obedience.

Visitators were sent to other houses not because of any flagrant breach of discipline as at Milan, but to raise the standard of religious observance. With this purpose in view he summoned five of the Leccetan friars after his election in 1507 to help him in the administration of the Order.[19] One of them, his friend Serafino Ferri, was appointed reformer of the Augustinians in Tuscany, became prior of Sant'Agostino at Rome in July 1509, and was sent as visitator to the house at Siena in September 1509.

Just as Giles made it a principle when appointing a prior not to select a friar who was a native of that locality, so his visitators were almost always members of a different province from that to which they were sent on their mission. For example, Mariano da Cave of the Roman province was appointed visitator of Bologna in September 1509, and a Lombard, Innocenzo Balbo, was sent to Sicily in June 1513.

It was comparatively easy to put pressure on the brethren in Italy, but a greater effort was needed to promote reform among the friars beyond the Alps. There were three stages in Giles' program for the ultramontane provinces: first, letters of exhortation and warning, combined with the confirmation of each provincial's election made conditional on his support of the reform; secondly, the appointment of a member of the province to act as reformer within that region; finally, when circumstances demanded it, the introduction of a foreign friar with wide powers, who supervised the reform on the spot. Sometimes he was a "visitator," staying for a limited amount of time, with certain defined objects; sometimes he was a "reformer," who remained on indefinitely, acting as the eyes and ears of the prior general.

Usually the agents were Italians; for example, Agostino Vincentino was sent as regent of studies to Hungary in July 1512, and Teofilo Romano as visitator to Aragon and Catalonia in April 1513. But for the reform of Rheno-Swabia Giles selected a German friar, Johann Parvus, in April 1514; for two Anglo-Irish houses an Irishman, Gerard, in March 1517; and Pieter Fine, a Flemish Augustinian, as reformer of the Cologne province in June 1517.

A glance at Giles' efforts in Paris, Spain, and Saxony will illustrate the progress of reform.

Reform at Paris

Giles set great value on the condition of the monastery at Paris, and although his belief in Paris as the intellectual center of Europe was outmoded there was no denying that the standards set by the Paris community had a profound effect on the four French provinces. Shortly after his election as prior general Giles made a stirring appeal to the friars at Paris, exhorting them to recover the intellectual leadership of the Order.[20] He wrote again on 7 September 1507 giving precise directions on how the religious life was to be strictly observed, and reminding the friars of the importance of study.[21] It was on this occasion that he confirmed in office the prior, Pierre Gérard, on condition that he introduce the reform within two months. The following day Giles wrote to the cardinal protector, Riario, asking that the cardinal himself write to Gérard stressing in the first place the need for strict religious observance, secondly the grave obligation of a thorough training for the students, and thirdly to remind the prior how important was the example of Paris for the entire Order.[22] Some months later Giles sent a snappy letter to Gérard reminding him that the reform decrees must be put into practice.

How much Gérard undertook is unknown but when Giles wrote on 22 June 1509 to confirm Roger de Porte as provincial of the Paris province he insisted on the need for reform and on the particular care to be given to the monastery at Paris. Five months later he had to remind the provincial of the urgency for reform at Paris and throughout the province. Giles waited for a further six months and when he saw no tangible results forthcoming he appointed a member of the province, Etienne Conservans, to be visitator and reformer of Paris and other houses.[23] Conservans for one reason or another did not rise to expectations, perhaps because the task was too much for one man. In 1511 Giles chose Antoine Pulcher as chief reformer of the province and gave him three assistants, Pierre Gervase, Jean Parentis, and Conservans.[24]

Giles informed Pulcher that this province was his greatest worry and asked him to concentrate his attention on the monastery at Paris. He sent a further letter to Pulcher about this time, explaining what reform meant in practice.[25] There was to be a devout attendance at office in choir, silence in the cloisters, dormitories, and refectory, all were to wear the habit of the Order and to be present at night prayers. Giles wanted no half-measures and demanded of Pulcher that he aim at a total reformation of the province, advising him to work in cooperation with Gervase, Parentis, and Conservans. Twice in the same letter Pulcher was instructed to act firmly, even severely if necessary.

It was unfortunate that Giles' intervention in the affairs of the Paris province could not have been undertaken before the year 1510. Up to that time he could have counted on the ready cooperation of the dynamic and pious Cardinal Georges d'Amboise (1460-1510) who had the approval of the French monarchy and the support of Rome in his reforms of the secular and regular clergy. The bitter, and at times ludicrous, opposition which d'Amboise met from the Dominicans and Franciscans is proof that the history of the Augustinians was symptomatic of the decayed condition of the mendicant orders as a whole in Paris.

When Giles found that the hopes which he reposed in Pulcher and the other three French friars bore little fruit he selected an Italian, Moncetto, in June 1514 as visitator of the provinces of Paris and Narbonne-Burgundy. But Moncetto was being taxed beyond his powers since he was also reformer of the English province, and in February 1515 his task was made still more difficult when he was appointed reformer of the province of Toulouse-Aquitaine. The attempts at reform in the French provinces and particularly at Paris, but directed from Rome and depending on Italian agents, were gravely hampered by the political tension between Francis I of France and Pope Leo X during these years.

After May 1516 when king and pope were on amicable terms it was possible for Giles to take more direct action with the French brethren. It was also to his advantage that Louis Chantereau was elected provincial of the Paris province in June 1516. Chantereau was confessor to Claudia, wife of Francis I, and it was doubtless hoped that he would use royal influence for the benefit of the Order. Giles wrote to express his delight that a complete reform could now be undertaken and asked Chantereau to ensure the appointment of a prior at Paris who would encourage strict religious observance.[26] Giles judged that the time was ripe for direct intervention, and on 7 July 1516 he informed the Augustinians at Paris that he was sending a reformer of high quality, Agostino Fivizzano, who had already proved his worth as a reformer at Rome, Siena, Florence, and Bologna.[27]

The low ebb of religious life in the French provinces is painfully evident from what is perhaps the blackest page in Giles' register. On 4 September 1516 he admonished the friars at Paris to observe the regulations already made by Moncetto concerning the chanting of office, the wearing of the tonsure, meals in common, the ban on the frequentation of taverns, and the expulsion of brethren implicated with prostitutes. He deplored the disobedience of those who criticized his policy and spurned the reformers he had previously sent to Paris.

Other entries on the same page of Giles' register show that the monastery at Lyons, head house of the Narbonne-Burgundy province, was if anything in a worse condition. Giles forbade the Augustinians to allow the suffragan bishop of Lyons any jurisdiction over the friary, or to permit him to retain the keys of the house or to dispose of its property, and most of all to bring his mistress into the friary. The rot had set in among the community; Giles deprived the procurator of his office and of the right to say Mass "because of his vile life, and the nun who is his acknowledged mistress, and because of his colossal ignorance."

Nevertheless the outlook in France was not completely somber, for the provincial at Paris was proving his worth. Chantereau came to Rome in July 1517 and Giles felt so satisfied with his progress that he appointed him reformer of the Paris college and province for two years. It had taken Giles ten years to establish the reform at Paris, but it was ten years too late, and even then it was on a shaky basis. Three months later Luther was to make his defiant protest at Wittenberg, and the whirlwind he loosed was to affect France as well as Germany.

Reform in Spain

Giles, for all his insistence on detailed regulations about the internal life in the monastery concerning matters such as silence, poverty, dress, and behavior, realized that the real crisis in his Order and in the Church in general was not essentially a matter of morals and behavior but of doctrine and discipline. For this reason he strove primarily for unity in the Order; he believed that if this were attained, reform in morals and behavior would follow. It is here that his dealings with the Spanish and German friars had particular significance. The main problem facing Giles was to restore the international unity of the Order, for without unity there was little hope of enforcing the reform program. The first requisite for this unity was obedience to the prior general. Paradoxically, the friars in Spain, taken as a whole, were the most reformed in the Order, but they also proved, in the case of the Castilian and Toledan observants, to be the most disobedient. Likewise, a group of the German observants resisted Giles' plan for greater unity in organization.

When Giles became prior general the observant Augustinians so dominated the Spanish scene that the conventuals were a negligible factor. The recalcitrant stance of the Spanish brethren was due in large part to their rising Spanish nationalism and the consciousness that on the score of religious observance they could challenge any province or congregation in the Order.

It is significant that the Spanish observants looked to the Congregation of Lombardy and not to that of Lecceto. We have already noted that in the beginning of the sixteenth century the Lombard congregation was a serious danger to the unity of the Order. Before 1505 the Spanish Augustinians were grouped into five administrative units — the province of Castile and Toledo, the Congregation of Toledo, the Congregation of Castile, the province of Aragon and Catalonia, and the province of Sardinia then in the process of formation, with its center at Valencia. The driving force was the Congregation of Castile which was supported by the authority of Queen Isabella (d. 1504) and King Ferdinand (d. 1516) and which absorbed the province of Castile and Toledo in 1505. During 1508 Juan de Moradillo, vicar general of the Castilian observants, defied Giles so impertinently in his letters that Giles bitterly commented that Saint Augustine would certainly not expect to receive such letters from his sons and hardly even from his enemies.[28] Moradillo and his followers found they were not dealing with a weak-kneed general, and when they refused to submit to Giles he placed them under ecclesiastical censures which were not lifted until March 1510.

Giles had also to join issue with the Toledan observants who were attempting to take over houses of the Sardinian province at Valencia. This province which was not fully established until 1511 had a special place in Giles' plans, because though it was composed of observants it accepted the canonical status of a conventual province instead of claiming the rights of a congregation. In Giles' eyes this was the ideal solution for the reform of the Order. It meant that the friars would have the discipline and spiritual standards of the observants but would be as subject to the prior general as were the conventuals. Giles himself, it must be remembered, was an observant of the Congregation of Lecceto.

The Sardinian province had been founded by a Spanish noble-man Juan Exarch (d. 1512) who under the inspiration of the Nea-politan observants began to form a new province from Augustin-ian houses in Sardinia, the Balearic Islands, and at Valencia. The Toledan observants coveted the principal house of the Sardinian province, at Valencia, but Giles took a firm stand in 1509 and thwarted their plans.

Giles had an ambitious plan for the majority of the Augustinians in Spain. He aimed to form a union between the observant congre-gation of Castile and that of Toledo, and, with this once completed, to transform the body of united observants into "the province of Castile." He wished it to adopt the character of the province of Sardinia — preserving the religious standards of the observants but remaining subject to the prior general like any conventual province of the Order.

Giles set his master plan in operation on 5 May 1510 when he appointed a loyal Castilian observant, Francisco della Parra, as his vicar and visitator for Castile and Toledo. Giles in his instructions to della Parra stated that the prior general's authority had been flouted in Spain, even by the superiors, that dissensions and in-trigues were rife there, and that in order to put an end to this intolerable state of affairs della Parra was to introduce uniformity and obedience.[29] Della Parra's commission aroused a wave of opposition from the Spanish observants, and though they ap-pealed at first successfully to Rome it was Giles who eventually secured the support of Julius II. Nevertheless, rather than have the Spanish observants in a ferment of indignation Giles withdrew della Parra's commission, taking care to remark that this compromise was only to tide over the crisis until the situation could be reviewed at the next general chapter.[30]

Giles' restraint was rewarded when the general chapter at Viterbo in 1511 unanimously reelected him general and arranged, with the consent of the Spanish observants, that the congregations of Castile and Toledo should unite to form the province of Castile. This province was to write a glorious chapter in the history of the Augustinian Order and the Spanish Church throughout the remainder of the sixteenth century.

Reform in Germany

At the time when the dispute with the Spanish observants was at its height a similar crisis was causing an upheaval among the friars in Germany. There, as in Italy and Spain, the observant movement was the most significant development of the Augustinian Order in the fifteenth century.[31] Because Martin Luther was a member of the Congregation of Saxony the history of the German observants in the early sixteenth century has usually been either misunderstood or misrepresented. Historians have been unaware of the policy pursued by Giles during the decade before the Reformation. If we bear in mind Giles' program for reform we shall see that the course of events in Germany was part of the same pattern which was taking shape in Spain during those years.

The dominant figure in the history of the German observants was Andreas Proles (1429-1503), a zealot of implacable resolve. By the time of his death in 1503 there was a thriving congregation of twenty-seven monasteries under the care of Johann von Staupitz, his talented successor. Staupitz aimed to make the Congregation of Saxony as independent of the general as was the Congregation of Lombardy. He was within an ace of success, and had even secured a papal bull on 21 June 1505 in favor of his scheme, followed by a papal directive of 15 March 1506 entrusting the archbishops of Mainz, Magdeburg, and Salzburg with the execution of the bull. At this late stage the Augustinian general at Rome, Faccioni, woke up to the situation, and after he had remonstrated with Julius the bull and directive were both withdrawn on 24 March 1506. When Faccioni died on 26 June the problem was still at a crucial stage, unresolved, with the German observants for their part thwarted and dissatisfied, while the Augustinian authorities at Rome sorely resented what they regarded as the backstairs intrigues of the observants with venal officials in the papal curia.

Giles inherited the problem and quickly set himself to solve it. Since he had the backing of Julius II he might well have adopted an unrelenting line toward the discomfited observants. Instead he set himself to win them over. By good fortune Staupitz came to visit the papal court at Bologna in the spring of 1507 as agent of the elector of Saxony for the University of Wittenberg. Giles was at the papal court and his presence there may well have been the primary though unofficial reason for Staupitz' journey to Italy. There was also a representative of the German observants, Nicholas Besler, staying at Rome since the spring of 1505, whom Giles summoned to Bologna. The German observants were in an awkward position now that their scheme for independence had been quashed by the papal brief of 24 March 1506. Staupitz therefore responded gratefully when Giles promoted a peaceful policy which would not only save face for the congregation but would satisfy its expansionist desires. The procedure was to be the same as with the province of Castile — union between the conventuals and observants so that while the province would become observant in character and control, canonically it would be a conventual province subject fully to the prior general.

On 15 December 1507 Cardinal Bernardino Carvajal, papal legate in Germany, signed the bull of union at Memmingen in Swabia. According to this document the provincial and conventuals of the Saxon province had in agreement with the observants petitioned the legate for the union. Although the agreement was bilateral most of the advantages were in favor of the observants. A chapter was to be held at which an observant would be elected as common superior for both conventuals and observants. Staupitz judged it impolitic to publish the bull at that juncture, but busied himself taking over conventual houses in two other German provinces, Rheno-Swabia and Cologne. Giles knew that Staupitz' triumphant progress would arouse opposition, and to silence the critics he issued a declaration on 26 June 1510 praising Staupitz for all he was doing to foster unity among the German brethren and recognizing him as both provincial of the Saxon province and vicar general of the congregation. Rumblings of dissent could already be heard from a group of the observants, and to prevent any open defiance of Staupitz' authority Giles commanded the members of the congregation on 29 July to accept their vicar general under pain of incurring the penalties of rebellion.

Giles' order was in itself a victory for the central government of the Order since he was declaring in effect, with Staupitz' consent, that the prior general had full rights over observants as well as conventuals. Armed with Giles' support Staupitz returned to Germany and summoned representatives of the observants to Neustadt on the Orla in September 1510. Here he secured a majority for his policy and issued a letter on 30 September announcing that he was hereby publishing the bull of Cardinal Carvajal and that the proposed union between observants and conventuals had the approval of the prior general. This deference to Giles was a notable change from the strained relations which had existed between the German observants and previous priors general. Seven of the German observant friaries resolutely opposed the union, despite exhortations to obedience from Staupitz and Giles. Martin Luther now appeared on the scene. The spearhead of the dissident observants was the monastery at Erfurt, and the leading figures in the community were a distinguished professor of theology, Johann Nathin, and the young, vigorous, and idealistic Martin Luther. There is no doubt that their opposition to Staupitz' plan arose principally from a genuine zeal for reform and from a conviction that union with the conventuals would mean a lowering of religious standards in the congregation. The prior general seemed to be the one powerful authority who might lend an impartial ear to their case. Luther and a companion made their way to Rome during the winter of 1510 and lodged their complaint with Giles.

This is not the place to discuss Luther's visit to Rome except insofar as it relates to the general problem of reform at that time in the Augustinian Order. The delegation failed in its purpose. The plan for a union between observants and conventuals was upheld by Giles, who ordered the dissident observants to accept the decisions already made between himself and Staupitz. The change which came over Luther at this point is of great significance. He was won over to the idea of the union and returned to Germany a supporter of Staupitz. Jedin suggests that this can have been due only to the influence of Giles with whom Luther and his companion discussed the petition of the seven dissident observant friaries.[32] It has been either overlooked or forgotten by Catholic historians that Luther at this stage made a difficult decision in favor of unity and authority; in consequence, on his return to Germany he had to leave the community at Erfurt who now looked upon him as a traitor to their cause. It is tempting to speculate what might have happened if Luther, at another great crisis in his life, in 1517, had been handled by some papal agent as understanding and persuasive as Giles.

Jedin makes a further provocative observation, pointing out that the evidence indicates that in the winter of 1510 the monastery of Sant'Agostino was at the one time host to three friars, each of whom was eminently representative of a great movement — Giles of the Renaissance and Catholic reform, Luther of the Reformation, and Seripando of the Counter-Reformation.[33] What a wealth of talent they bore between them!

Giles at this stage was determined to push ahead with his plan. He got an assurance of support from the Emperor Maximilian and he also wrote on Staupitz' behalf to a number of the German rulers. Feelings were running high among the German Augustinians, and Luther, now in the vanguard of those who stood for unity and obedience to the general at Rome, was inveighing against the dissident observants whom he sarcastically styled "the little saints." They continued to oppose the union and finally Giles issued an excommunication of the seven friaries on 1 October 1511, but wisely committed its publication to Staupitz. Even with this thunderbolt in reserve Staupitz failed to shake the resolve of the dissident observants when he met their representatives at Nuremberg.

At that stage Staupitz lost heart and sent a messenger, Johann von Mecheln, to Rome to confer with Giles. The outcome was victory for the dissident observants. A chapter of the German observants was held at Cologne in May 1512, the attempt to form a union of observants and conventuals was dropped, and as a sign that peace was restored Staupitz was reelected vicar general of the congregation. So, the unity which Giles sought was not achieved, but unity between the observants and the general at Rome was preserved.

Why did Giles give way before a minority group of the German observants? On his side he had a solid phalanx — papal authority, the Emperor Maximilian and the Elector of Saxony, the conventuals in Germany, and an absolute majority of the observants. Giles' overriding principle was the need to preserve charity; without it he believed there would be no real unity. Rather than disrupt the peace of the German Augustinian world he was willing to abandon, at least temporarily, the plan for union of observants and conventuals in Germany. We have seen that Giles was faced with the same problem and opposition in Spain, but by postponing the plan and biding his time he witnessed eventually the voluntary acceptance by the Spanish observants of union with the conventuals. He may have hoped for a similar development in Germany and the prospects were encouraging when he had succeeded in winning over to his side promising young friars such as Martin Luther.

From Reform to Reformation and Counter-Reformation

It is only in reading, folio by folio, through Giles' registers that one realizes how dominated he was in his policy as prior general by the idea of reform. His first register, Dd 11, may be chosen as evidence. A random selection of ten pages for each of the years 1509, 1510, 1511, 1512, and 1513, reveals that in these fifty pages there are only eight on which the words *reformatio* or *vita communis* are not explicitly mentioned. Many of the other entries are different expressions of the need for reform and the common life. These commands and exhortations on the pages mentioned were sent to provinces, houses, and individual friars in Italy, France, Germany, Hungary, Spain, England, and Crete. Thus on 16 October 1512 he sent a series of lengthy letters on the urgency of reform to the provinces of England, Aragon-Catalonia, Bavaria, Cologne, Paris, Narbonne-Burgundy, Portugal, Rheno-Swabia, Saxony-Thuringia, Toulouse, and Sicily. He furthermore instructed the provincials to have copies of these letters forwarded to all houses under their jurisdiction. In the somewhat cynical and calloused Europe of that day the Augustinians would be pardoned for believing that Giles was a man with a bee about reform in his bonnet.

It is not surprising that this constant insistence on the need for reform, this repetition of the word *reformatio*, should have made both the notion and the word a part of the conversation and outlook of the average Augustinian. It was little wonder then that so many of the friars in different provinces were receptive to the latest winds of change, be they Protestant or Catholic, which blew across a Europe eager for a reform in head and members of the Church. The fact that an appreciable number of Augustinians took the side of the Protestant reformers has hitherto often been interpreted by Catholic historians as a proof of the decadence of the Augustinian Order. In this present age the problem is now seen in a different light. In 1547 Cardinal Ercole Gonzaga wrote of certain monks at Mantua that there was no danger of their becoming Lutherans since "they have no other interest but to drink, eat, and sleep."[34] The observant movement in the Augustinian Order, and in particular the twelve year rule of Giles of Viterbo, had made the Augustinians aware that their purpose in life was other than to "drink, eat, and sleep." This is not to lay the blame for the Augustinian defections to Protestantism at the door of Giles of Viterbo, but it does draw attention to an important aspect of the problem which has been overlooked or misrepresented. There were many other factors, personal, local, and national, which have to be taken into account in dealing with individuals such as Luther, Robert Barnes, and Agostino Mainardi. Such men were numerically a fraction rather than even a minority of the Order, but they were nevertheless a significant representation. However, they in no way represented the ideals of Giles of Viterbo who had epitomized his program for reform in that arresting sentence in his speech at the opening of the Lateran Council: "Men must be changed by religion, not religion by men."

Notes

1. See the admirable study by R. Arbesmann, *Der Augustiner-Eremiten orden und der Beginn der humanistischen Bewegung,* Würzburg, 1965.

2. D. Gutiérrez, *The Augustinians in the Middle Ages 1315-1517,* History of the Order of St. Augustine, volume I, part II, Villanova, 1983.

3. Angelica, MS 1170, fol. 23v-24r.

4. A. Calepinus, *Dictionarium,* Trino 1521.

5. See *Analecta Augustiniana* IX (1921), 64-68.

6. Angelica, MS 1170, fol. 21v.

7. A. de Meijer, *Aegidii Viterbiensis O.S.A. Resgestae Generalatus* I, 1506-1514; II, 1514-1518, Fontes Historiae Ordinis Sancti Augustini, prima series, volumes 17-18.

8. See Appendix 2.

9. *Ibid.*

10. *Ibid.*

11. *Ibid.*

12. Siena MS G.X.26, page 83.

13. *Ibid.,* page 5.

14. *Ibid.,* page 294.

15. *Ibid.,* pages 209-211.

16. *Ibid.,* pages 311-313.

17. Angelica, MS 1170, fol. 25r.

18. Siena MS G.X.26, pages 13-14, 15-17.

19. A. Landucci, *Sacra Ilicetana Sylva, sive origo et chronicon breve coenobii et Congregationis de Iliceto,* Siena, 1653, page 30.

20. Siena MS G.X.26, pages 22-23; Signorelli, *Egidio,* pages 228-229.

21. Siena MS G.X.26, pages 81-84.

22. *Ibid.,* page 86. Signorelli, *Egidio,* page 229.

23. Augustinian General Archives, Dd II, fol. 37v (7 March 1510); de Meijer, *Aegidii*; I, no. 532, page 185.

24. Siena MS G.X.26, pages 263-265.

25. *Ibid.*, pages 259-263.

26. *Ibid.*, pages 296-297.

27. *Ibid.*, pages 327-328; see *Lettere Familiari* II, pages 204-209.

28. Siena MS G.X.26, pages 107-112. Signorelli, *Egidio*, pages 231-232.

29. Siena MS G.X.26, pages 223-225. Signorelli, *Egidio*, pages 238-239.

30. Siena MS G.X.26, pages 239-244.

31. A. V. Müller, "Der Augustiner-Observantismus und die Kritik und Psychologie Luthers," in *Archiv für Reformationsgeschichte* XVIII (1921) 1-34; R. Weijenborg, "Neuentdeckte Dokumente in Zusammenhang mit Luthers Romreise," in *Antonianum* XXXII (1957) 147-202, is of exceptional value for its understanding of the dispute among the German observants.

32. H. Jedin, "Die römischen Augustiner-Quellen zu Luthers Frühzeit," in *Archiv für Reformationsgeschichte* XXV (1928) 266-269.

33. *Ibid.*, 269.

34. Cuthbert, *The Capuchins*, London 1928, page 127, note 15.

Chapter 6

Renaissance Person

Giles of Viterbo has remained an elusive figure for historians. This is at first sight puzzling, as there is a considerable amount of information available concerning his activities, although much of it is in manuscript. Furthermore, the external facts of his life suggest that he was a man of some importance. He was general of the Augustinian Order for twelve years, 1506-1518, during a momentous period of its history and a cardinal enjoying the confidence of the popes during the tumultuous events of the early Reformation.

He has come under the spotlight of history in published works because of certain facts which do not necessarily indicate his real significance. His *Historia XX Saeculorum* has supplied historians with valuable facts and comments on late Renaissance popes; his reputation as a humanist was secure ever since Giovanni Pontano (1462-1503) composed the dialogue *Aegidius* in his honor; he is known as the prior general with whom Luther treated during his visit to Rome in 1511; his incisive oration at the opening of the Fifth Lateran Council in May 1512, with its pithy epigram, "Men should be changed by religion, not religion by men," is often quoted as one of the last public appeals for reform in the Church before the storm was loosed in Germany; he made a brief appearance in martial character when he gathered a force of 2,000 soldiers at Isola near Rome in 1527, to free Clement VII then besieged by imperial troops in the Castel Sant'Angelo.

Historians have on the whole dealt kindly but not accurately with Giles. He suffered his share from critics during his lifetime, but they did his reputation no serious damage. He could not protect himself from his friends the humanists, and it was their presentation of him as the beau ideal of Renaissance clerics which persisted up to 1960. Historians had concluded that he was no more than a typical part of the frivolous hollow world of Leo X.[1] It is paradoxical that Giles, with the example of Pope Paul II (1464-1471) in mind, made the salutary observation that one should not risk offending men of letters.[2]

Giles of the Humanists

Pontano, the genial Umbrian, crowned Giles with immortality, acknowledging him as the inspiration and central character of the *Aegidius*.[3] Therein we are shown a delicate figure, the gilded cleric of the Renaissance, a favorite member of the Pontanian Academy of Naples. Pontano, not content to see in Giles the qualities desired of churchmen by enthusiastic admirers of Rome and Greece, put into the Augustinian's mouth a sermon which has too readily been accepted as authentic. In the course of the sermon Giles is made to draw a comparison between the death of Christ and the sacrificial death of Decius; in discussing the supernatural birth of the Savior there is reference to the birth of Minerva from the head of Jupiter and to the belief of the Egyptians that women can conceive from the wind. Though in fact these classical references are fitted adroitly into a Christian context there is no convincing evidence that Giles was author of the sermon. When we compare it with any of his authentic sermons we are left with the suspicion that it is Pontano speaking through the mouth of Giles.[4]

The impression of Giles as a polished priest of Renaissance circles was strengthened by the publication of his *Caccia bellissima de amore*. This was first printed anonymously in a collection with other poetry in 1523, was published separately in 1537, and was reprinted during the seventeenth and eighteenth centuries. While. the theme was undoubtedly religious, and no sacrifice of Christian principles was made to pagan mythology, it gave no sense of that unvarnished Christianity which came back into vogue with the Reformation and by whose standards Giles is even still being judged.

Sannazzaro (c. 1456-1530) thought to repay a debt to Giles when he wrote the well-known *De Partu Virginis*. A quotation in a sermon preached by Giles was the seed from which this epic poem followed.[5]

The *De Partu Virginis* relates with a wealth of illustration from pagan mythology about the coming of Christ on earth. The angels and the muses alike are summoned to hail the birth of the Redeemer; heaven is styled Olympus, God the Father is called the Thunderer, the ruler of Olympus and the King of the gods. When the poem was first published in 1526 it was prefaced with a letter of exultant commendation from Giles. Though the letter drew a favorable comment even from the sharp-tongued Erasmus[6] the association with Sannazzaro meant that Giles was regarded as belonging to those "Ciceronians" whose medley of paganism and Christianity the same Erasmus assailed so bitingly in the *Dialogus Ciceronianus*.[7]

Pietro Bembo (1470-1535) and Jacopo Sadoleto (1477-1522), considered with some justice to have been the high priests of Ciceronianism in the early sixteenth century, made public their affection and respect for Giles.[8] Sadoleto may have been conscientious and pious but the witty and immoral Bembo was in popular estimation a more typical representative of the prelates in Renaissance literary circles. The publication of Bembo's letters in 1548 and of Sadoleto's letters in 1554 showed that the friar was accepted by them as a literary equal and was lauded as a model to be followed.[9]

So it came about that by the middle of the sixteenth century an image of Giles was being created for posterity. It was primarily as a man of letters that he was commemorated by Lelio Gregorio Giraldi in *De poetis nostrorum temporum*, published in 1551, but even during his lifetime this was the aspect of his life which earned the readiest plaudits of his literary friends. In 1515 when the erudite Jewish printer, Girolamo Soncino, and a group of citizens at Fano decided to publish Cleofilo Ottavio's *Anthropotheomachia* they dedicated it to Giles in recognition of the impression which his humanism, piety, and versatile learning had made during his visits to the city. There were two other talents which were taken to be characteristic of Giles — his eloquence and his mastery of oriental languages. Paolo Giovio (1483-1552), whose sketches of Renaissance personalities have influenced all subsequent literature on the subject, presented Giles as a man with the triple gifts of literary style, a golden tongue, and an unequaled knowledge of biblical lore.

Giles and Jewish Literature

The attention drawn by Giovio and others to Giles' oratorical ability and scriptural knowledge accurately reflect two of the qualities which gained him contemporary fame. In 1510, even before he had come to the height of his oratorical powers, he was described by Paolo Cortese in *De Cardinalatu* as worthy to rank with the most renowned Italian preachers, Saint Bernardine of Siena, Saint John Capistrano, Roberto da Lecce, Mariano da Genazzano, and Girolamo Savanarola. Nor was this the mere fulsome exaggeration of a Renaissance writer. It was later stated that so fierce was the rivalry between various cities demanding the services of Giles as preacher that Pope Julius II reserved to himself the right to decide in which cities the friar might preach.[10]

The highest compliment was paid to Giles as a preacher when he was selected to deliver the discourse at the opening of the Fifth Lateran Council on 3 April 1512. His moving oration was immediately printed and was acclaimed by both humanists and reformers. It has caused his name to be remembered when more important incidents of his life are forgotten. Catholics and anti-Catholics have quoted it to suit their different purposes. Luther referred to it in the year 1531 as a proof of the corruption of Rome.[11] Pastor has chosen one phrase of it to express the reform movement at Rome in the early sixteenth century.[12] A notable feature of Giles' oration was its catena of biblical texts. This indicated an intellectual interest which assumed increasing proportions throughout the last twenty years of his life.

By the time that the bitter dispute about Reuchlin's *Augenspiegel* was brought to Rome in 1513 Giles was already deep in his study of holy scripture and of rabbinical literature. Unhesitatingly he threw his influence on the side of Reuchlin. Giles, like Reuchlin, was then devoted to a study of Jewish mysticism, particularly of the cabala. He believed that the philistines of religion, in attacking Reuchlin, were endangering something of immeasurable value to theology and the spiritual life of Christians. The vitriolic *Epistolae obscurorum virorum* were published in Germany during the years 1515-1517, lampooning the alleged ignorance of Reuchlin's adversaries, and a more positive presentation of Reuchlin's case was made in 1519 with the second edition of *Illustrium virorum epistolae, hebraicae, graecae et latinae*. Among these letters, addressed to Reuchlin from leading humanists in Europe, were three written by Giles.[13] His reputation at this period is made evident in the polemical work of a Franciscan, Pietro Galatino, *De arcanis Catholicae veritatis, contra obstinatissimam Iudaeorum nostrae tempestatis perfidiam*, published in 1518. Though Galatino did not spare the Jews he took care to pay warm tribute to Giles' biblical and cabalistic knowledge.

The outbreak of the Lutheran revolt, and the support given to it by the younger German humanists who had applauded Reuchlin's stand, brought cabalism and its supporters into disfavor with Rome. On 23 June 1520 Leo X forbade the circulation of *Augenspiegel* as a book offensive, scandalous, and unlawfully favorable to the Jews. Fortunately it was recognized that Giles' scriptural interests were not confined to the cabala, and he was known as the principal patron of Elijah Levita, the founder of modern Hebrew grammar. Elijah's *Bachur* which was printed at Rome in 1518 was dedicated to Giles, as was Elijah's Chaldee lexicon completed in 1529. There is a more striking indication of Giles' part in scriptural studies, but it was overlooked by his biographers. The first complete Greek edition of the Bible to be published was issued at Venice in 1518 from the house of Andrea Torresano and Aldo Manuzio. The volume was dedicated to Giles. Manuzio had died three years previously, but in the dedicatory letter Andrea told of the literary interests which brought Giles and the prince of publishers together in close friendship.

Further evidence of the friar's biblical interests was brought to public notice almost forty years later when Widmanstetter published his Syriac version of the New Testament. This renowned orientalist ranked Giles among the memorable figures in the history of biblical studies. He acknowledged the debt which he owed to the Augustinian since the days when Giles encouraged him to persevere in the study of Arabic and he recalled with pleasure that he had access to Giles' valuable library of oriental manuscripts. Widmanstetter made the extraordinary claim that at one period the friar was in effect the only European scholar with a knowledge of Arabic.

It had doubtless redounded to Giles' cultural reputation in 1503 when Aldo Manuzio dedicated to him the first printed edition of Origen's homilies on the Old Testament, but the association of Giles' name with the heterodox Origen was unlikely to escape notice during post-Reformation days when the watchdogs of orthodoxy at Rome were quick to pounce on anybody who showed sympathy with those who deviated from the traditional teachings of the Church.

Distorted Image

So, by the time that the generation which had known Giles passed away, an attractive but distorted image of the Augustinian had been created for posterity. Giles was presented as a cultured though virtuous Renaissance prelate, the polished orator, the Ciceronian stylist, and accomplished poet, a pioneer biblical scholar astray in cabalistic literature. On such evidence alone, and for many generations it was the only printed evidence available, it was pardonable to ask — was Giles any more than an intellectual jackdaw, more interested in the glitter of new discoveries than in their real value? Had he any central purpose in all his intellectual ramifications? Furthermore, while the liberal-minded might pardon his association with worldly prelates such as Bembo and Cortese, there were undoubted misgivings about his friendship with men of suspect orthodoxy such as Pontano and Reuchlin. The damning aspect of this picture was not that it was untrue, but that it was half-true. Giles' image was presented totally out of focus. Subsequent writers for long did little to adjust the historical lenses so that the image might correspond with reality.

Giles' spiritual personality and religious convictions received practically no attention. Among his friends and intimates there was unanimous agreement that he was a priest of exemplary virtue. Yet, Giovio could not restrain his malignant pen from mentioning some spicy tidbits of gossip. Having dealt out praise with a generous hand to Giles he remarked that certain malicious critics believed that the friar's ascetical pallor was artificially produced by inhaling the smoke of wet straw and that his denunciation of vice was to divert attention from his own loose living. Giovio hastened to add, with his tongue in his cheek, that these stories were due to venomous rumor rather than to any "certain evidence" of illegitimate children.[14]

Giovio's gossip, though wide of the mark, did draw attention to the neglected aspect of Giles' life. In assessing the man and his work there is an obvious need to consider primarily his membership in the Augustinian Order. This was the body to which, while still in his teens, he made religious profession. His spiritual and intellectual development was made under Augustinian guidance. The Augustinians believed him so worthy a representative of their ideals that he was elected prior general at three successive general chapters — 1507, 1511, 1515. His main energies during twelve years of constant activity were directed to a reform of the Order. Indeed, his preaching and literary interests can be properly understood only in the light of his unwavering desire for reform. Yet he was judged almost exclusively on his oratorical and intellectual abilities. In fact, these were subsidiary aspects of his life, at least until he was created cardinal in 1517 at the age of forty-eight. It would be equally unjust to judge Disraeli, prime minister in Great Britain (1868, 1874-1880), with whom Giles had many resemblances, on his novels, with little reference to his parliamentary and political career.

Giles of the Augustinians

During his lifetime Giles received his mead of praise in works written by Augustinians. When Paolo da Genazzano published his edition of Gregory of Rimini at Venice in 1503 he dedicated it to Giles, whom he described in extravagant Renaissance terms as a Platonist, a notable preacher, and an ornament of the Augustinian Order.[15] Five years later — Giles being then prior general of the Augustinians — the Venetian provincial, Gabriele della Volta, edited the first printed version of the Constitutions of the Order,[16] and in the dedication to Giles exhorted him to effect a thorough reform of discipline and learning among the friars. A thousand copies of the work were printed, and although it also contained records of several precious privileges obtained for the Order by Giles from Julius II, it failed to leave posterity with any impression of Giles in the role of ecclesiastical reformer. Yet, it was his success as a reformer, no less than his impressive range of learning, which formed the principal theme of the letter with which Ambrogio Calepino dedicated the second edition of his famous dictionary to Giles in October 1509.[17] Ambrogio Flandino, a bishop and a leading light among the Augustinians, in a work published in the year 1523, treated Giles as an exemplar of the learning and virtues desired in a son of Saint Augustine.[18]

Sixteenth Century

One would have expected, therefore, that as prior general and reformer he would receive adequate attention from the historians of the Order. Unfortunately, historical studies found no great figure among the Augustinians in the sixteenth century. The Spaniard, Alonso de Orozco, published a chronicle of Saint Augustine and the Augustinian Order at Seville in 1551.[19] Its purpose was to edify, and Giles' term of office, which had seen the advent of Luther, was diplomatically skirted. Another Spanish Augustinian, Jerónimo Román, published a further chronicle of the Order at Salamanca in 1569.[20] Román showed historical ability, but his interest was mainly in the Augustinians of the Iberian peninsula, and Giles received scant attention. A comprehensive history of the Order was attempted by the Italian Augustinian, Giuseppe Panfilo, bishop of Segni. His work was published at Rome in 1581.[21] It was largely based on secondary sources, and for that reason his treatment of Giles added little to what was already available in the writings of the humanists. So the sixteenth century passed without any substantial change in the accepted picture of Giles.

Seventeenth Century

The seventeenth century was the golden era of Augustinian historiography.[22] There one would expect an accurate assessment of Giles' life and work, or at least of his years as prior general of the Order. Two major causes combined to defeat any original investigation or new interpretation.

The main source of information about the program and activities of the priors general are the Dd registers in the Augustinian General Archives, Rome. One of the two registers covering Giles' years as prior general had disappeared from the archives by the sixteenth century. There were, however, copies of Giles' registers then in existence. One historian, Torelli, used them, but only to a very limited degree. Subsequently these copies also disappeared. Supplementary to Giles' registers were the letter-books containing copies of the letters he sent out and received. The letter-books are also missing, and were not at the disposal of the historians in the seventeenth century. Nowadays, due to copies which have come to light in other archives and libraries, we can make good to an appreciable degree the lack of the original registers and letter-books.

Apart from the fundamental difficulty of lack of primary source material the Augustinians labored under a serious psychological difficulty when wishing to treat of Giles as a member of their Order. They were conscious, over-conscious, that Luther, the man who rent in twain the unity of the Western Church, had been an Augustinian, and that Giles was prior general of the Order when Luther first raised the standard of revolt. Giles himself was taunted by Cardinal Corneto with the fact that Luther was an Augustinian.[23]

In 1520, two years after Giles resigned from the prior generalship, his successor, della Volta, wrote to Staupitz, vicar general of the Saxon Congregation to which Luther belonged, telling in earnest sorrow of the disrepute which had come on the Order due to Luther's defiance of Rome.[24] The same chagrin is evident in the history of the Augustinians by Nikolaus Kreusen, published at Munich in 1623.[25]

Kreusen, having lauded Saint Augustine as founder and glory of the Order, turns to deal with Luther whom he treats as the supreme disgrace on the good name of the Augustinians. Side by side with a traditional hymn in honor of Saint Augustine he printed another version execrating Luther.[26] Torelli, writing during the last quarter of the seventeenth century, could hardly find words expressive enough with which to denounce Luther.[27]

In view of such an attitude common among the Augustinians, and in the absence of satisfactory documentation on Giles' years as prior general, it is understandable that the historians of the Order should have accepted the picture of Giles drawn by the humanists of the sixteenth century. But while this interpretation was still accepted as authentic in the post-Tridentine era it was then no longer regarded with favor. Giovio had etched an engaging picture of Giles while a student at Padua, strumming the lyre as he sang to accompany his own verse.[28] The Augustinian historians, who knew in retrospect that Luther even as a student had grappled with the crucial problems of grace, free will, and man's redemption, cannot but have felt that Giovio's picture suggested Nero fiddling while Rome burned. Felice Milensio wrote a history of the German Augustinians which was published at Prague in 1613.[29] He gave special attention to the Saxon congregation and implied that a pusillanimous policy pursued by Giles allowed the dissident elements, including Luther, in the congregation to initiate successfully a policy of opposition to Roman authorities. The same year as Milensio's work appeared Thomas Gratien, provincial of the Low Countries, published a general very brief survey of Augustinian writers.[30] Gratien's work by its set limits treated only the literary aspect of Giles' life, and even then attempted no new assessment of his writings.

Another friar from the Low Countries, Corneille de Corte, published at Antwerp in 1636 a series of biographical sketches of outstanding members of the Order.[31] The very title of the work, *Virorum illustrium elogia*, made evident the laudatory spirit in which de Corte approached his subject. He was interested almost exclusively in Giles' public activities as a preacher, diplomat, and cardinal, and did not attempt to probe his character and motives. Nothing new was added to our knowledge of Giles by Kreusen's annals of the Order published in 1623,[32] or by Simplicien de Saint Martin's folio volume of biographical sketches printed at Toulouse in 1641,[33] or in Elsen's ambitious dictionary of Augustinian notables which appeared at Brussels in 1654.[34]

A welcome step forward was taken by Lorenzo da Empoli in 1628, when he edited the *Bullarium* of the Augustinian Order.[35]

Empoli's purpose was practical: to supply a compendium of the rights and privileges of the Order. For that reason he omitted far more papal documents than he included. Nevertheless, the collection includes several important papal briefs and bulls addressed to Giles by Popes Julius II (1503-1513) and Leo X (1513-1521). Their publication indicated, though to a very limited degree, a view of Giles as prior general and ecclesiastical reformer. The documents were capable of another interpretation. Since they showed Giles to have been a trusted agent of two popes who typified the Renaissance spirit they could be, and in fact were, made to fit in with the existing interpretation which had been created by the humanists in the sixteenth century. This is what happened in 1677 when the Jesuit, Agostino Oldoini, issued his edition of Chacon's history of the popes and cardinals.[36] The Giles who emerged from his pages was the court preacher, diplomat, and man of letters. There was no reassessment of the standard opinion.

One would have expected otherwise from Tomás de Herrera (1585-1654), a Spanish Augustinian, whose *Alphabetum Augustinianum*, published at Madrid in 1644, is still a most satisfactory reference work on Augustinian history.[37] The absence of most of the original sources about Giles in the Augustinian General Archives during Herrera's years of research in Rome may explain his superficial treatment of this subject. Still, little use was made of Giles' second register, then available in Rome. Herrera's estimation of Giles was summed up in the opening sentence: "Giles of Viterbo ... a celebrated writer, and the most famous preacher of his day."[38]

Special attention was given to the diplomatic missions on which Giles was sent by Popes Julius II and Leo X to Venice, Naples, and Germany. All this was no real advance on previous biographers.

However, three Italian Augustinians writing in the second half of the seventeenth century helped toward a greater knowledge of Giles' life and work. In 1653 Ambrogio Landucci published a history of the Augustinian Congregation of Lecceto.[39] The congregation, centered on Lecceto, "the seminary of saints" near Siena, was the oldest and the most famous of the reforms in the Augustinian Order. Landucci related that Giles was an exemplary member of the congregation and how he used the Lecceto friars to spread the reform throughout the Order. Landucci's work, like so many of its kind, suffers from being pitched on a eulogistic note.

Luigi Torelli of Bologna (1609-1683) attempted, with a fair measure of success, a discursive history of the Augustinians.[40] When treating of Giles he enjoyed the advantage, denied to preceding historians, of consulting copies of the registers covering Giles' period as prior general. He was thus in a position to present Giles the Augustinian, the reformer of his Order. Nevertheless, two factors weakened Torelli's treatment of the subject. He tried to deal with all aspects and personalities of the Order. In consequence, Giles receives little systematic study, but appears, disappears, and reappears on innumerable occasions throughout the seventh and eighth volumes of the work. In addition, Torelli lacked the detachment of the critical historian. The pity is that somebody with the caliber of Herrera did not have the opportunity to examine the copies of Giles' registers.

Domenico Antonio Gandolfo (1653-1707), an Augustinian of the Genoese congregation, was interested principally in literature. In his *Fiori poetici dell'eremo agostiniano* (Genoa, 1682) he presented a brief life of Giles and reprinted four of his published poems. He again treated Giles as a writer in *Dissertatio historica de ducentis celeberrimis Augustinianis scriptoribus* (Rome, 1704). His *Le porpore agostiniane* (Genoa, 1696), designed to treat of various Augustinians as cardinals, contains the best of the three accounts which he wrote of Giles. Gandolfo deserves credit for collecting and arranging in these works much of the information already in print about Giles, but his only original research on the subject was a labored attempt to prove that Giles was of noble parentage. A few new facts about Giles were added by Agostino Arpe, also of the Genoese congregation, in a volume of biographical sketches published in 1709.[41]

Eighteenth Century

The eighteenth century saw the publication of sections of Giles' letters. As far back as October 1685 two famous figures of the Saint Maur Benedictine Congregation, Jean Mabillon and Michael Germain, located a number of his manuscripts at Naples.[42]

The letters which they then transcribed were published in 1742 by two other monks of the Saint Maur Congregation, Edmond Martène and Ursin Durand.[43] These twenty-five letters contain precious autobiographical facts about Giles and reveal neglected aspects of his character as well as his concern for ecclesiastical reform. Subsequent writers overlooked one important fact about these letters. They came from a collection which had been compiled to demonstrate the felicity of Giles' Latin style.[44] Bernard Montfaucon, another Benedictine of the Saint Maur Congregation, in

publishing a catalogue of manuscript collections in various European libraries listed sixty-four manuscripts which had passed from
Giles' library to the royal library at Paris.[45] Although the manuscripts are a valuable indication of Giles' intellectual equipment
they could easily be mistaken as mirroring the whole man. It is
needful to bear in mind that they were only part of the library he
possessed in his later years.

Three German publications attempted a more balanced presentation of his intellectual interests. The *Fortgesetzte Sammlung von
alten und neuen theologischen Sachen* of 1748 included a brief anon-
ymous study of Giles. This summary, based solely on published
material, was necessarily incomplete. However, it had the merit of
being a critical appraisal of the printed sources. Johann Albert
Fabricius of Leipzig was perhaps too ambitious in attempting to
compile in his day a comprehensive list of late medieval and
Renaissance authors and their works.[46] He added nothing new
about Giles, but recognized his place in Renaissance literature and
mentioned several of his works which were known from published
sources. Johann Felix Ossinger (1694-1767), a German Augustinian, undertook and completed the herculean task of producing a
bibliography of Augustinian authors since the thirteenth century
and added useful biographical notes on each writer.[47] He depended mainly on published sources, but gave a more complete
list of Giles' works than did Fabricius. For almost a hundred and
fifty years it remained the most satisfactory bibliography of Giles.

The last quarter of the eighteenth century witnessed the tardy
publication of the funeral oration preached on Giles in 1532 by
Lorenzo Grana, bishop of Segni.[48] A later critic stated tartly, although with some exaggeration, that the panegyric dealt with
everything except the dead man.[49] Giovanni Amadutio, who edited Grana's oration, included useful footnotes, particularly one in
which he mentioned Giles' works then preserved in the Angelica
Library, Rome.[50]

A solid contribution toward an understanding of Giles was
made by Girolamo Tiraboschi in his monumental history of Italian
literature.[51] He was the first to attempt a survey of the friar's life as
a whole. Much of his information was drawn from Gandolfo and
Ossinger, but he also availed himself of notes put at his disposal
by his friend, the Augustinian Giacinto della Torre (1747-1841),
who was deeply versed in Italian literature — hence his friendship
with Tiraboschi. His own then unrivaled knowledge of Italian
literature allowed him to assemble information from printed

sources hitherto overlooked. The comprehensive nature of his general history gave authority to his estimate of Giles' place in Italian literature. He considered Giles to have been the most famous orator of his day. It was principally under this aspect and as a Renaissance scholar and poet that he viewed him. Tiraboschi's biographical notice remained for one hundred and thirty years the most satisfactory account of Giles.

These then were four of the major contributions to Egidian studies in the eighteenth century: the letters published by Martène and Durand, the list of manuscripts printed by Montfaucon, the bibliography compiled by Ossinger, and the biographical notice written by Tiraboschi. None of these essayed or provoked a reassessment of the picture of Giles drawn by the humanists in the sixteenth century. Indeed, they seemed to corroborate the established opinion. Ossinger's bibliography systematized what already existed in print; Tiraboschi's study concentrated on Giles' literary and humanistic achievements; the catalogue of Giles' library represented the intellectual interests of his later years as cardinal; the letters published by Martène and Durand were from a collection designed to produce an appreciation of Giles' Latin prose.

One work published in the eighteenth century threw light on the neglected side of Giles' life. Anton Hoehn, a German Augustinian, wrote a compact history of the Rheno-Swabian Augustinian province. His study was based to a great degree on the archives of the province.[52] Though this limited the range of the book, it gave it a satisfying documentary foundation. The test of objectivity for any German Augustinian historian is the period concerning Luther. Here Hoehn showed himself critical and as fair-minded as the circumstances of his surroundings allowed. His attitude was a welcome contrast with that of Milensio, who had written on the same subject a hundred and thirty years earlier. Hoehn traced the history of the observant movement among the German Augustinians, the development of the Saxon Congregation to which Luther belonged, and the attitude adopted to it by Giles. Hoehn's study, like Landucci's history of the Lecceto congregation, allows us to see Giles encouraging the reform movement among the friars.

Nineteenth Century

Almost half of the nineteenth century passed before any serious contribution was made to Egidian studies. Even then it was a mistake, but a *felix culpa,* which reawakened interest in Giles. Konstantin Höfler, a member of the Munich historical school, edited the *Pro memoria ad Hadrianum Papam VI, de depravato statu Romanae Ecclesiae et quomodo reformari possit atque debeat* in 1846 and attributed it to Giles. This hard-hitting criticism dealt with the evils of the Roman curia and of ecclesiastical administration. In truth the author was Cardinal Campeggio, but this was not known until Friendensburg published an article on the subject fifty years later. Meantime interest was aroused in Giles the reformer. In 1854 Höfler published that part of Giles' *Historia XX Saeculorum* in which he treated of the pontificates of Popes Alexander VI and Julius II.[53] There Giles showed his distaste for the worldly commitments of these popes. Another German scholar, Hugo Laemner, having investigated various libraries and archives in Italy as sources for Church history, stressed the fact that the Angelica library in Rome had a rich collection of documents dealing with Giles as a reformer in practice.[54]

From that time forward four factors in historiography helped toward an understanding of Giles. The animated discussions on reform, pre-reform, and Counter-Reformation turned attention to the Augustinian Order. Closely connected with these discussions, yet distinct from them, was the rapidly increasing body of literature about Luther. A hardly less controverted problem, and one of no little importance for an appreciation of Giles, was that of the nature of the Renaissance. Finally, and with some relation to this problem, there was the research into Jewish history of the late middle ages and Renaissance.

In the year 1879 Theodore Kolde, a fair-minded admirer of Luther, produced a monograph on the Augustinian Congregation of Saxony.[55] Of necessity he had to consider Giles and his attitude toward the vigorous but not always prudent policy of the congregation. In Kolde's work Giles emerged as an ecclesiastic eager to promote reform but equally anxious to preserve unity of spirit and administration. The Catholic viewpoint of events in the Saxon congregation and among the German Augustinians was set out by Nikolaus Paulus in a study of Johann Hoffmeister, an Augustinian opponent of Luther. Two years later, in 1893, Paulus published a biography of Bartholomaeus Arnoldi von Usingen, an Augustinian who first figured as one of Luther's favorite professors at Erfurt but who later sharply crossed swords with him. These two works, despite certain limitations, are important as showing Luther in his

Augustinian setting. Some attention was paid to Giles but he remained no more than a shadowy figure in the background.[56]

The scenes through which he moved and the men with whom he mixed became alive once again with the publication, which began in 1879, of the diaries of Marino Sanudo, a Venetian public figure whose diaries cover the years 1496-1533.[57] Sanudo's information and comments are invaluable, but they allow no more than occasional glimpses of Giles the popular preacher, the papal diplomat.

An Italian savant, Antonio Magliabecchi (1633-1714), had remarked that Giles' fame diminished after his death because his works lay unpublished. It is obvious that no fair estimate of the man could be formed until his writings and letters were examined. Ever since the sixteenth century he had been judged almost entirely on second-hand evidence. The credit for again going to the sources which showed Giles' own mind belongs to Léon-Gabriel Pélissier, later dean of the Faculty of Letters at Montpellier University. In the year 1892 he published an article describing the Egidian Latin manuscripts in the Angelica library, Rome.[58] It was a coincidence that at the time when Pélissier was examining Giles' works in Rome the chief librarian of the Angelica, Enrico Narducci, was compiling a catalogue of manuscripts, including all those described by Pélissier. Narducci's catalogue appeared in 1893, and gave in some respects a more detailed, although necessarily a more bloodless, treatment than Pélissier.[59] A description of Giles' Greek manuscripts in the Angelica library was edited by Muccio and Franchi de' Cavalieri in 1896. This study has been updated by John Whittaker's remarkable contribution in 1977.[60]

Pélissier's interest in Giles bore fruit in a doctoral thesis printed in 1896.[61] This was a specialized piece of work, a study of Giles' historical composition, *Historia XX Saeculorum*. Pélissier's investigation was keen and concentrated, but it suffered from the defects not uncommon to certain doctoral theses. He was over-critical, a quality understandable in a man anxious to prove his ability and objectivity. Less excusable from an academic viewpoint was Pélissier's assessment of Giles, based as it was on this one historical composition and a mere external acquaintance with a number of other works.

Six years later Pélissier implicitly passed judgment on his own doctoral thesis. In 1903 he published a manuscript, the original of which was composed during Giles' years as prior general of the Augustinian Order.[62] Giles was now revealed as one who had been

devoted to the religious life and to ecclesiastical reform. The contents of the manuscript came as a revelation to Pélissier. But it was
a revelation which he could not comprehend. How little he appreciated the significance of the manuscript may be judged from his
regret that the first editor, Noris, was interested in Giles as a
religious rather than as a humanist and diplomat.[63] The introduction which he wrote for his edition of the manuscript demonstrated
his inability to resolve the historiographical problem of Giles.

Comparison between the Giles of whom he wrote in 1903 and
the Giles he described in 1896 leaves the curious impression that
Pélissier was dealing with two different persons. The clearest
example is where Pélissier in 1896 dismissed Giles as an historian,
but in 1903 paid tribute to his qualities as an historian. In 1896
Pélissier accused Giles of preening himself on his achievements, of
being a place-hunter and of flattering the reigning popes so that he
might gain a cardinal's hat. In 1903 he commented on Giles' humility and modesty, his reluctance to accept ecclesiastical office, his
independent stance in the face of the popes. In 1896 he described
Giles as ineffectual though sincere, a reformer on paper. In 1903 he
wrote of Giles' successful efforts for reform.

It would be hard to exaggerate the influence of Pélissier's *De
opere historico Aegidii Cardinalis Viterbiensis* on all those who subsequently wrote about Giles. Pélissier's work was the first monograph to deal with the subject, and his conclusions were accepted
as those of the authority on the subject. Unfortunately his revisions
in *Miscellanea di studi critici edita in onore di Arturo Graf* were
generally unknown or as often not available for scholars.

One would excuse the mistakes which Pélissier made in 1896
when he assessed Giles on incomplete and misleading evidence.
Although it was a tribute to the French scholar that six years later
he should have completely changed his opinion he made no attempt to reconcile the two contrary pictures he had presented. All
unknowingly he posed in a vivid manner the central problem of
Giles' life and character. How reconcile the friar's undoubted
reforming zeal with his ease in the classical world and his unaf-
fected friendship with humanists, several of them of loose morals
and suspect orthodoxy?

Some light was thrown on the problem in the year 1847 by a
publication which had escaped Pélissier's notice. Francesco
Trucchi edited a collection of unpublished poems, among them six
madrigals attributed to Giles.[64] They were addressed to Vittoria
Colonna (1490-1547), marchioness of Pesaro, one of the remarkable

figures of the reform movement in Italy. The madrigals show how Giles sublimated what could have been simply a human affection. The greater test was for Giles to mix with and treat as equals the men of the Renaissance, yet not compromise his religious ideals. Several of his friends did not set a high standard for private morals, and their interpretation of Christian beliefs was hardly orthodox. Giles in such a setting, the Pontanian Academy of Naples, was the subject of a valuable article by Francesco Fiorentino, which appeared in 1884.[65] An equally important contribution, but one overlooked by Pélissier, was contained in Gothein's study of the Renaissance in southern Italy, published in 1886.[66] Both Fiorentino and Gothein used original material and showed that Giles was a man of moral influence among the humanists in the mezzogiorno. Giles, as we have seen, was renowned during his lifetime as a scriptural and oriental scholar. He continued to be remembered under this aspect during the seventeenth and eighteenth centuries. The Jewish literary revival in the nineteenth century reawakened interest in his rabbinical and cabalistic erudition. Moritz Steinschneider (1816-1907), who was the first to make a systematic survey of Jewish literature, and who remains probably the greatest of Jewish bibliographers, set Giles against the background of sixteenth century Jewish studies. Giles for him was not merely one of the most cultured Christian hebraists of his time, but was the patron of Jewish scholars and the defender of the Jews in their hour of need.

Steinschneider's praise of Giles was repeated in the specialized works of Ginsburg, Grieger, Perles, Graetz, and Reiger.[67]

The catalogues of Hebrew manuscripts at Munich and London, published at the end of the nineteenth and in the early twentieth centuries, gave accurate information on some of Giles' research into Semitic studies.

However, it takes a long time for the findings of specialized research to percolate into general works of reference. How far Giles had sunk into oblivion may be seen from two works of survey on the literature of the middle ages. The first edition of Potthast's bibliography of the middle ages, published in 1862, did not mention Giles; the second edition, published in 1896, gave him notice solely due to the Egidian and pseudo-Egidian works edited by Höfler.[68] Chevalier's comprehensive bibliography of the middle ages summed up Giles' importance in one bare line — an Italian poet of the fifteenth century.[69] Up to the second decade of the present century encyclopedias and general works of reference gave Giles short shrift.

Twentieth Century

Recognition came for Giles in 1906, when Ludwig von Pastor produced the first part of the fourth volume of his history of the papacy.[70] Pastor's extensive examination of manuscript and printed sources made him aware that in Giles he had to deal with a seemingly complex character. How explain the man who had hitherto been presented under three different guises — Giles the orator, papal diplomat and humanist, Giles the cabalist and scriptural scholar, Giles the ecclesiastical reformer? Pastor's difficulty was increased beyond measure by his own interpretation of the Renaissance, the division into pagan and Christian Renaissance. Giles was the friend of Pontano and Sannazzaro, of whom Pastor markedly disapproved. Was Giles then to be classed with the sheep or the goats? Pastor did not attempt to reconcile the different aspects of the Augustinian's life and character. He placed him on his right hand, as a reformer at least in theory. He commended Giles warmly: "If ever a man deserved the red hat it was this distinguished man, who combined a classical education and general learning with a great capacity for business and a profound piety." Pastor expressed a fervent hope that somebody would attempt a biography of the friar.

The opportunity to assess Giles which Pélissier and Pastor let go by default was taken in 1914 by Heinrich Böhmer, a well-known historian of the Reformation period. Böhmer was strongly Lutheran in his sympathies, but in his biography of Saint Ignatius of Loyola displayed an ability to appreciate the Catholic viewpoint. In his book on Luther's journey to Rome he devoted a chapter to Giles.[71] Although brief it was no superficial study, but an investigation based on manuscript material and on a wide range of printed sources. Böhmer more than anybody before then came within an ace of understanding Giles. He realized that the dynamic urge in Giles' life came from his zest for reform — reform in studies, reform in morals, reform in ecclesiastical discipline. It was thus that the apparently conflicting aspects of his character could be reconciled. Yet, in the last analysis Böhmer failed to evaluate Giles accurately. The failure was due to a double-defect, of interpretation, and of source material. Böhmer, as might be expected in an admirer of Luther, saw the Renaissance as sharply divided into pagan and Christian. In this he was at one with Pastor. Giles' friendship with the classical humanists was interpreted as a sign that he had unconsciously compromised his reform ideals. Böhmer, under the influence of Pélissier's earlier study, weighed Giles in the balance as an effective reformer and found him wanting. Böhmer's defect of interpretation would have been rectified if he had consulted Pélissier's edition of Giles' register and had been thus aware of the reassessment it demanded of previous judgments on the friar. Giles' registers show him as the reformer in practice. Böhmer's interest in Giles' reforming activities had been whetted by Kawerau, who in 1911 published the extracts of Giles' registers from a manuscript copy in the Berlin Staatsbibliothek.[72] Böhmer, on a visit to Rome, examined one Egidian register in the Augustinian general archives, but circumstances allowed him no more than a hurried and unsatisfactory investigation. Böhmer had only six hours at his disposal, he had to work in an ill-lighted room on a dark day, and his eyes were tired from reading the Vatican registers. The Egidian register is in a difficult script.

A year after Böhmer's book appeared, a selection of Giles' letters concerning reform was published by Fovio Pazzaglia at Rome.[73] This jejeune work was announced as a sample of the complete collection of Giles' letters which was stated to be then with the printers. Pazzaglia's plan was a stillborn project. Other documents of great importance for an understanding of Giles were published during 1921-1922 in the *Analecta Augustiniana*. Eustasio Esteban, the Augustinian archivist general, edited a collection of the unpublished briefs and bulls from Popes Julius II and Leo X to Giles. Equally important but more illuminating was Esteban's edition of the reform decrees issued by Giles when he was elected prior general of the Augustinian Order at Naples in 1507.[74]

Had Esteban published these documents a year earlier they could have been used to considerable advantage by Alphons Müller in a valuable study which appeared in 1921.[75] Müller an ex-Dominican and an outspoken admirer of Luther, was interested primarily in the theological sources of Luther's theology. In order to understand Luther's attitude to reform Müller turned his attention to the Augustinian Order. He showed penetration in his comments. His judgments would have carried greater weight had he not been led astray, as had Böhmer before him, by a series of misdated entries in one of the Egidian registers at Rome. The mistake was corrected seven years later by Hubert Jedin in one of his early probings into Reformation history.[76] Jedin's article, with its minute examination of two registers in the central Augustinian archives, is a landmark for those interested in Giles.

Up to this time Giles' theology was a closed book, though he was known as the author of a major theological work and had been referred to in his lifetime as a *teologo grandissimo*. Alphons Müller attempted in a number of studies to prove that the unorthodox ideas which distinguished Lutheranism from the traditional teachings of the Church were to be found in the writings of Augustinian theologians of the fourteenth and fifteenth centuries.[77] A French theologian, Jules Paquier, following out this line of thought, set himself the task of comparing Luther's theological principles with those of Giles. His conclusions, published in 1923, showed that there was no convergence of ideas between the two Augustinians.[78] Paquier, in the process of his lucid demonstration, expounded how Giles' neoplatonic treatment of the *Sentences* was in the manner of Marsilio Ficino. The study would have gained in value had Paquier been aware of the evolution in Giles' philosophical beliefs. Nobody had taken note of the fact, or the significance of the fact, that in his younger days Giles edited three works by Giles of Rome (c. 1247-1316), a brilliant pupil of Saint Thomas Aquinas, and founder of the school of the Augustinian friars.

General works of reference finally began to show the results of research on Giles. In 1915 Aurelio Palmieri, an Italian Augustinian, contributed an article on Giles to the *Dictionnaire de Théologie Catholique*. It was a remarkable advance on any general account up to that date. It is surprising that Palmieri overlooked the incisive study of Giles which Böhmer had included in his *Luthers Romfahrt*. Fourteen years later David Perini incorporated Palmieri's account, without acknowledgment, in his *Bibliographia Augustiniana*. In addition to at least two mistakes of Palmieri, Perini added some errors of his own. Nevertheless, Perini's compilation on seven hundred years of Italian Augustinian literature is indispensable as a reference work for any study of Giles and his times.

Recognition for Giles

The biography which had been called for by Tiraboschi, Hergenröther, Steinschneider, Pélissier, Pastor, Böhmer, and Paquier was finally attempted by Giuseppe Signorelli in 1929.[79] This was not a full-scale biography, but a rapid survey of Giles' life and writings. It is here opportune to consider the merits and defects of Signorelli's work.

Signorelli, as chief librarian of the Biblioteca Comunale at Viterbo, had the time and the opportunity to acquire a thorough knowledge of Italian printed works dealing with Giles and the events of his period. This advantage tended to become a defect. Signorelli had a marked inclination to display a ragbag collection of information about minor characters and side issues.

One of the merits of his work is its detailed knowledge of Viterbese history. His thorough grasp of local history enabled him to elucidate problems which are often only fully understood by local historians and antiquarians. Giles' birthplace, and even his family name, were disputed matters. For an understanding of Italian figures of the Renaissance such local knowledge is almost an essential. Each city cultivated an independence and self-consciousness all its own. This mentality persists to the present day, though to a diminished degree: Signorelli's approach to his subject was a demonstration of the fact. His interest in Viterbese history was allowed to dominate the book. The preface opens with the ringing reminder that Viterbo should recognize its own heroes — *heroes agnoscite vestros* — and the last chapter pulsates to a close on the proud note of "illustre concittadino."

Signorelli, methodic and painstaking, has written an attractive biography. Though it would be scathing, and even unjust, to label his work as superficial it is manifest that it displays no profound analysis of character or of events. Signorelli states the "what" not the "why." It was unfortunate that he was not abreast of international scholarship. He was unacquainted with the studies by Böhmer, Paquier, and Jedin, but one can readily forgive his oversight. It was compensated for when he drew attention to a volume of Giles' letters in the Biblioteca Comunale of Siena.[80] This precious collection reveals not Giles the fine phrasing humanist but the ecclesiastical reformer with a whiplash in his words and an almost ruthless power of decision. The letters confirm and illumine what are often only bare entries in his registers. Signorelli made only a very limited use of the letters: his interest was mainly in Giles the humanist and papal diplomat. Despite the shortcomings of his biography Signorelli has cleared the ground in a thorough fashion. All students of Giles are in his debt.

In 1937 Jedin published his magisterial study of the Augustinian, Girolamo Seripando (1492-1563), cardinal legate at the Council of Trent, 1561-1563.[81] Though he dealt but briefly and in passing with Giles, he showed that Seripando as a Platonist, scriptural scholar, and ecclesiastical reformer was profoundly affected by Giles. The same question of the relationship between religious reform and the new learning was discussed by Professor Toffanin of Naples in a study of Pontano.[82] The book contains two chapters on Giles' fusion of classical learning and Christian piety. Toffanin's comments are valuable but he would have been on surer ground had he argued from Giles' writings rather than from Pontano's version of what Giles said. Toffanin argued mostly from the *Dialogus Aegidius* of Pontano, though he also consulted the studies by Fiorentino, Gothein, and Signorelli.

Another Italian scholar, Eugenio Massa, had made Giles the object of special study.[83] He went directly to original sources, Egidian manuscripts at Rome, Naples, and Paris, and edited a representative section of one of Giles' compositions. By then, with the exception of Signorelli, Massa had published more than any other author on Giles. However, the quality of the work may be questioned. Massa owed most of his fundamental ideas about Giles and the Augustinian school of theology to Müller and Paquier, and gave no sign of knowing that research over the previous twenty years had disproved these notions. His interest was in Giles as a Renaissance thinker, and he paid little attention to him as a reformer of the Augustinian Order. When he did discuss him as a reformer he conveyed a totally wrong impression. He described him as dominated by the idea of a Church, spiritual and interior, in contrast with the institutional organization of the Roman Catholic Church.

Massa's work is not without merit however. Apart from the original sources he draws attention to Giles as a Renaissance thinker. He propounds at some length a theory that Giles' object in his writings was to defend theology by a new critical and historical method. Massa also contends that Giles was a pioneer in his philological approach to scripture. Provocative comments are made on the development in Giles' thought under the stimulus of Plato, the classics, the cabala, and the Talmud.

There have been other contributions on Giles. The biographical notice by Ugo Mariani in the *Enciclopedia Cattolica* carries no weight: it adds nothing new to our knowledge of Giles and repeats a few stock factual errors. One of the more difficult problems of Giles' life for a biographer is that of the cabala, which only a specialist can treat adequately. Fortunately Professor François Secret, an acknowledged authority on the Christian cabalists, has studied Giles.[84] A Swiss scriptural scholar, George Schelbert, has completed an examination of Jerusalem Targum which was copied for Giles in the early sixteenth century. Lutheran studies continue to excite research on the Saxon Congregation and Giles. Reinhold Weijenborg, a Dutch Franciscan, published an important article which brings into relief the efforts made by Giles to strike a golden mean between encouragement of the reform movement among the German Augustinians and the maintenance of unity in the Augustinian Order.[85]

By the late 1960s a veritable stream of publications on Giles had begun to appear in many different countries on diverse aspects of his life and his intellectual activities. This stream increased during the 1970s and 1980s, so that by the early 1990s it was proving to be a flood-tide. It would be very difficult to keep track of these publications were it not for the painstaking bibliographical surveys on the Augustinians edited regularly by the Dutch scholar, Alberic de Meijer, in *Augustiniana* of Louvain.[86]

Here it is practicable to mention only a personal selection of the many publications which have appeared since the early 1960s right up to the early 1990s. The outstanding work — a watershed in Egidian studies — is the book of the American Jesuit scholar, John W. O'Malley, which appeared at Leiden, Holland, in 1968. This was basically his doctoral thesis presented at the University of Harvard in 1966.

O'Malley gave generous credit to the author of this book, an Irish Augustinian, who had pursued the subject of Giles of Viterbo since 1950 and presented his conclusions in a doctoral thesis at the University of Cambridge, England, in 1959. This work was made available to O'Malley, who broadened the subject by a series of enlightening articles on Giles even before his book was published in 1968.[87]

Egidian studies came to a high point in 1982 when an entire session of the Augustinian International Historical Institute at Rome and Viterbo, 20-23 October 1982, was devoted to Giles of Viterbo under the title, *Egidio da Viterbo e il suo tempo*.[88] It was a delayed but much deserved appreciation for Giles of Viterbo and the Augustinian reform movement which he embodied in his person. Significantly this reform movement preceded, almost by a century, the Protestant Reformation of Martin Luther, who undoubtedly was influenced, as he himself acknowledged, by Giles.

Historians today have not yet clearly disentangled these intricate essential connections between the Catholic Reform of the fifteenth century, the Protestant Reformation of the early sixteenth century, and the doctrinal Roman Catholic Counter-Reformation of the Council of Trent, 1545-1547, 1551-1552, 1562-1563.

In 1960 the author of this book published at Louvain his compact seminal survey, *The Problem of Giles of Viterbo*.[89] Since then there has been increasing evidence, not merely each year but sometimes in several months of the one year, articles and books, in which Giles figures as a dominant or major phenomenon. They revealed some of the manuscript treasures which Giles accumulated, and the fruitful ideas which he disseminated to friends, and from the pulpit, or tossed off in letters and in his own unpublished works, as well as in his marginalia of the manuscripts he was assiduously studying.

Besides, he maintained a string of Jewish, Arabic, and Christian scribes who delved at his expense and under his direction into rare sources. His overall object was a quest for evidence to explain God's message pointing to Jesus Christ, the Redeemer.

Giles saw the pre-Christian classical authors in Greece and Rome as welcome (even if unconscious) forerunners of the Messiah, in the same vein but at a different level to the Jewish prophets and scribes of the Old Testament. All of them, pagans, sophisticated Greeks and Romans, scholarly Moslems, were part of an intricate dazzling tapestry of the plan for Divine Redemption of the whole human race.

Giles was here the true *uomo universale* of the Italian Renaissance, combining literature, art, architecture, science and technology into an integrated unity. For him there was no need to force humanity into a confrontation of pagan and Christian. He composed pastoral eclogues about the birth of Jesus, the Resurrection, and the Ascension into Heaven, in which he stressed the Renaissance joy at the ultimate victory of Christ and the Church rather than the medieval sorrow at the sufferings and death of the Savior in Jerusalem and on the hill at Calvary.[90] In this context, too, he was no respecter of persons in a religious sense. His Jewish teacher was Eliah Levita, the greatest Hebrew scholar of his day in western Europe,[91] just as the Spanish-born Leo Africanus, the most notable Moslem scholar, in western Europe, was his instructor in Arabic.[92] Both became members of his household at different times. For him Leo Africanus was not an infidel and Levita was not a Jew, an outcast. Giles was a protector of the Jews and secured papal approbation for a Jewish printing press at Rome.

One of the biblical manuscripts which Giles acquired and studied, now in the Vatican Library as Neofiti I, has set off a train of volumes and articles. It is a Palestinian Targum of which a polyglot edition has been edited in four volumes at Barcelona by Professor Alejandro Diez-Macho.[93]

A main collection of Giles' Greek manuscripts in the Angelica Library, Rome, has received detailed attention from Professor John Whittaker, an internationally recognized expert in classical studies.[94] Another manuscript, this time in Syriac, has come to light in the University library at Innsbruck, Austria, and shows that Giles was following the Maronite developments with the Vatican in the early sixteenth century.[95]

Much of the basic material for an understanding of Giles and his activities was still unpublished in the 1960s, but this has now been put right to a large degree. In 1962 the question of the unpublished registers of Giles as prior general of the Augustinian Order was raised by the author of this book.[96] The demanding task of editing the registers, which are scattered in parts at various libraries in Europe was undertaken by the Dutch Augustinian, Alberic de Meijer, and magnificently completed in 1988.[97]

Another basic source is the public orations of Giles. Dr. Clare O'Reilly of University College, Dublin successfully tackled the difficult problems of two famous orations by Giles.[98] She has grappled with an even more important area — the letters on reform of the Augustinian Order which exist in a unique manuscript at the Biblioteca Communale, Siena. Her edition has been completed and is published by the Augustinian Historical Institute at Rome.[99]

The formidable task of editing the *Lettere Familiari* of Giles was undertaken by Dr. Anna Maria Voci Roth of Rome and successfully accomplished in two volumes, published by the Augustinian Historical Institute, Rome, in 1990.

Another very important source, the sermons of Giles of Viterbo as bishop, was studied by Professor John Monfasani of the State University of New York. He published three of these sermons from the Vatican Library in 1983,[100] has located some more, and is now preparing them for publication.

Research on Giles is still full of pleasant surprises. The erudite Father Benedict Hackett, of the English Augustinian Province, discovered and edited a precious "lost" treatise of Giles on the famous Augustinian monastery at Lecceto.[101] There is no doubt that the future will see many more such gratifying surprises from Giles.

Giles the Reformer

This chapter is a witness to the truth that first impressions die hard. Any student of Giles' life will find difficulty in ridding himself or herself of the picture drawn by the humanists of the sixteenth century. Giles' registers and letters, written during his years as general of the Order, convey a different impression from that left by the humanists. He emerges as a man dedicated to a spiritual revival. Nevertheless, it must be borne in mind that he was a Renaissance man, intensely interested in all the developments of the new learning. Two main aspects of his life thus suggest themselves for study, his place and thought as a humanist, his program and activity as an ecclesiastical reformer.

On closer examination it will be seen that these two aspects cannot be separated if he is to be properly understood. There was no separation of "pagan" and "Christian" elements in his thought. His ideals found practical expression in reform — reform which he preached for the daily lives of the people in so many Italian cities, reform of discipline which he formulated when prior general of the Augustinians, reform in theology which was to be presented in Platonic terms, and reform in biblical studies so that the living word of God might be heard in all its keenness. But he expressed himself frequently in classical terms, in the language of the humanists. For Giles reform was not revolution. He was no Renaissance man in revolt against medieval gothic. He saw reform as identical with revival, and in that he was a true product of the Renaissance. He was an enthusiast for the revival of classical studies, but also fostered the study of scholasticism. Similarly, reform of the Augustinian Order meant for him a return to what he conceived had been the primitive fervor of the Augustinian hermits in the fifth century and of the Augustinian friars in the thirteenth.

It is salutary, when reconsidering the impression of Giles created by the humanists, to realize the extent to which scholars, with a misplaced confidence, accepted the conclusions of previous writers. However illuminating are the reflections of historians there is no substitute for original sources.

Notes

1. H. Böhmer, *Luthers Romfarht*, Leipzig, 1914, pages 41-47.

2. *Historia XX Saeculorum*, Biblioteca Angelica, Rome MS 502, fol. 243r. I am indebted to M.B. Hackett, O.S.A., for this reference.

3. See Summonte's edition of "Aegidius" in *Opera omnia Johannis Joviani Pontani*, II, Venice, 1518, fol. 154v-173v.

4. "Sermo Aegidii ad populum," *ibid.*, fol. 156v-158r; G. Tiraboschi, *Storia della letteratura italiana*, VII, part 4, Modena, 1792, page 1592, suggested that Pontano had strung his own words on Giles' ideas. The sermon is built around the saying of Christ, *I am the way, the truth, and the life* (John 14:6), and although Pontano probably touched up the sermon in the style of the humanists, it has a christological character which has no parallel in any of Pontano's authentic works, and which very likely derives from a sermon preached by Giles.

5. J. A. Vulpius, in *Opera Sannazari*, ed. Jan Broukhus, Amsterdam, 1728, page 514. Before publishing the poem, Sannazzaro gave the manuscript to Giles for his comments.

6. Erasmus to Budé, Basle 22 June 1527, in *Opus epistolarum Des. Erasmi Roterodami*, ed. P.S. Allen, VII, Oxford 1928, pages 94-95.

7. In Erasmus, *Opera Omnia*, I, Leyden, 1703, pages 973-1026. Though Erasmus criticized *De Partu Virginis* for its amalgam of pagan and Christian sentiments, he paid compliment to the prefatory letter by Giles, see page 1020 A.

8. Giles' oration at the opening of the Fifth Lateran Council on 3 May 1512 was printed at Rome, prefaced with a letter from Sadoleto to Bembo. There were two printings at Rome in 1512 (?), of which there are copies in the Cambridge University Library; there was another printing by Stuchs at Nuremberg, see Signorelli, *Egidio*, page 169, note 83; it was reprinted in P. Labbé and G. Cossart, *Acta Conciliorum*, ed. J. Harduin, IX, Paris, 1714, pages 1576-1581. The official oration by Giles on the occasion of the treaty between Julius II and the Emperor Maximilian in November 1512 was printed at Rome in 1512 (?), with a prefatory letter from Sadoleto to Sannazaro; the letter was reprinted in Sadoleto, *Epistolae Familiares*, I, Rome, 1760, pages 16-17.

9. See the six letters from Bembo to Giles during the years 1523-1531, in Bembo, *Lettere*, I, Rome, 1548, pages 115-124. See also Bembo to della Volta, Padua, 23 November 1532, on the death of Giles, "nostro Signor Cardinal Egidio, il quale era e dotto e amico dei dotti e letterati, e grato e gentile, e sopra tutto pieno di soavissima facundia che addolciva gli animi di chiunque usava con lui," *ibid.*, pages 382-383. See Sadoleto to Giles, Carpentras, undated but after 1517, in Sadoleto, *Epistolarum libri sexdecim*, Lyons, 1554, pages 115-117. In particular see Sadoleto to Bembo May 1512 (?), "Sumus enim experti pluries illam huius viri mulcentem omnium aures atque animos eximiam eloquentiam vernacula quidem lingua hetruscorum quae illi patria est abundantem sed ex uberrimis et graecae et latinae eruditionis fontibus deductam: magno enim hic studio theologiae ac philosophiae altissimis artibus comites litterae politiores adiunxit," in Sadoleto, *Epistolae Familiares*, Rome, 1760, pages 18-20.

10. L. Torelli, *Secoli Agostiniani*, VII, Bologna, 1682, page 557; VIII, Bologna, 1686, page 175.

11. D. Martini, *Luthers Werke: Tischreden*, II, Weimar, 1913, page 348; see *ibid.*, the editorial notes and corrections. Luther during 1536 again referred to Giles' outspoken sermon, see *ibid.*, III, Weimar, 1914, page 345.

12. "Homines per sacra immutari fas est, non sacra per homines," in *History of the Popes*, VII, facing title page and page 10; see *ibid.*, X, page 389.

13. Giles to Reuchlin, May 1516, fol. 49r-50r; Giles to Reuchlin, Denis Reuchlin his brother, and Elizabeth his sister, 20 October 1516, fol. 50r-51r; Giles to Reuchlin, 24 May 1517 (?), fol. 51r.

14. Paolo Giovio, *Elogia virorum doctorum*, Basle, 1546, fol. 54r.

15. *Commentaria Gregorii Ariminensis in Primum et Secundum Sententiarum*, ed. Paulus de Genazzano, O.S.A., Venice, 1503. The dedicatory letter is dated from Padua, 1 April 1502. This edition was reprinted at Venice in 1518 and again in 1532. See D. Trapp, O.S.A., "Gregory of Rimini manuscripts, editions and additions," in *Augustiniana* VIII (1958) 430-436.

16. Printed at Venice in November 1508. Eustasio Esteban gave a detailed description of the volume in *Analecta Augustiniana* II (1907-1908) 30-31, 35-41, and reprinted the dedicatory letter by della Volta, as well as a letter of approbation from Giles dated Rome, 1 November 1508.

17. Ambrosius Calepinus, O.S.A., *Dictionarium*, Trino, 1521. Calepino died in 1511, but he had prepared a second edition with a dedicatory letter to Giles dated from Bergamo, 1 October 1509. This edition did not see print until 1521, when it was published by the Augustinians of Bergamo. They dedicated the publication anew to Giles, from Bergamo 13 January 1519, but at the rear of the volume included the original dedicatory letter from Calepino to Giles. The 1521 edition is extremely rare. I located copies in the Biblioteca Marciana, Venice, and the Biblioteca Civica, Bergamo, but the edition is not in the British Museum, the Bodleian, Cambridge University Library, the Bibliothèque Nationale at Paris, or the Biblioteca Nazionale at Rome.

18. Ambrosius [Flandinus], *Quadragesimalium concionum liber*, Venice, 1523, fol. 481v-482r. This is a rare work of which copies are in the Biblioteca Angelica, Rome, and the Bibliothèque Nationale, Paris. Flandino deals with Giles in the course of a sermon on Saint Augustine, and having as its topic the fusion of the active with the contemplative life.

19. Alonso de Orozco, *Cronica del glorioso Padre y Doctor dela Yglesia Sant Augustin: y de los sanctos y beatos: y de los doctores de su orden*, Seville, 1551.

20. J. Román, *Chronica de la Orden de los Eremitanos del glorioso Padre Sancto Augustin*, Salamanca, 1569.

21. Joseph Pamphilius, *Chronica Ordinis Fratrum Eremitarum Sancti Augustini*, Rome, 1581.

22. See F. Roth, "Augustinian historians of the XVIIth century," in *Augustiniana* VI (1956) 635-658.

23. For the cardinal's taunt and Giles' pithy reply, see Torelli, *Secoli Agostiniani*, VII, page 503; VIII, page 29.

24. Della Volta to Staupitz, 15 March 1520, ed. T. Kolde, in *Zeitschrift für Kirchengeschichte* II (1877) page 480.

25. Nicholas Crusenius, *Monasticon Augustinianum*, Munich, 1623.

26. The two versions begin and end thus, in *op. cit.*, pages 190-191:

De S. Augustino	De Luthero
De profundis tenebrarum	De profundis tenebrarum
Lumen mundo exit clarum	Praedo surgit animarum
Et scintillat hodie	Et punitur hodie
Olim quidem vas erroris	Olim quidem vas honoris
Augustinus vas honoris	Luther erat, mox erroris
Datus est Ecclesiae . . .	Hostis inde Ecclesiae . . .
Salve gemma confessorum	Procul caece, dux caecorum
Lumen Christi, vox coelorum	Umbra foetor inferorum
Tuba vitae, lux Doctorum	Tuba mortis, vox bellorum
Praesul beatissime.	Exul perfidissime.
Qui te Patrem venerantur,	Qui te Patrem venerantur
Te ductore consequantur	Te ductore condemnantur
Vitam in qua gloriantur,	Igni, in quo cruciantur
Beatorum animae.	Damnatorum animae.

27. *Secoli Agostiniani*, VII, Bologna 1682, page 333; VIII, Bologna 1686, pages 28, 30, 39, 42, 66, 69, 180.

28. See *Elogia virorum doctorum*, fol. 54r.

29. Felix Milensius, *Alphabetum de monachis et monasteriis Germaniae ac Sarmatiae citerioris Ordinis Eremitarum Sancti Augustini*, Prague, 1613.

30. Thomas Gratianus, *Anastasis Augustiniana in qua scriptores Ordinis Eremitarum S. Augustini qui abhinc saeculis aliquot vixerunt, una cum neotericis, in seriem digesti sunt*, Antwerp, 1613. Giles is treated on pages 9-10.

31. Cornelius Curtius, *Virorum illustrium ex Ordine Eremitarum S. Augustini elogia cum singulorum expressis ad vivum iconibus* Antwerp, 1636. Giles is treated on pages 92-107. The particular value of De Corte's work is its fine series of engravings.

32. *Monasticon Augustinianum*, Munich, 1623. Pages 189-193 concern Giles.

33. Simplicien de Saint-Martin, *Histoire de la vie du glorieux Père S. Augustin, religieux, docteur de l'Eglise, evesque d'Hippone, et de plusieurs SS. BB. Saints, bienheureux et autres hommes illustres de son ordre des hermites*, Toulouse, 1641. Giles is treated on pages 743-744.

34. Philippus Elssius, *Encomiasticon Augustinianum*, Brussels, 1654. Giles is discussed on page 14.

35. Laurentius Empoli, *Bullarium Ordinis Fratrum Eremitarum Sancti Augustini . . . ab Innocentio III usque ad Urbanum VIII*, Rome, 1628. The editor is generally referred to as "Empoli," though his surname was Orsacchi; Empoli was his place of origin.

36. Alfonsus Ciacconius, O.P., *Vitae et res gestae Pontificum Romanorum et Sanctae Romanae Ecclesiae cardinalium*, ed. Augustinus Oldoinus, III, Rome, 1677, 395-397. The first edition by Chacón at Rome in 1601 had no more than bare mention of Giles.

37. See Herrera's autobiographical account in *Alphabetum Augustinianum*, II, pages 462-463, and the bibliographical study by Gregorio de Santiago Vela in

Ensayo de una biblioteca Ibero-Americana de la Orden de San Agustín, III, Madrid, 1917, pages 590-631.

38. In *Alphabetum Augustinianum,* I, page 42. Giles is treated on pages 42-45.

39. Ambrosius Landucci, *Sacra Ilicetana Sylva, sive origo et chronicon breve coenobii, et congregationis de Iliceto in Hetruria Ord. Erem. S. P. Augustini in Tuscia,* Siena, 1653.

40. Luigi Torelli, *Secoli Agostiniani ovvero historia generale del sagro ordine eremintano del gran dottore S. Aurelio Agostino vescovo, divisa in tredicii secoli,* 8 vols., Bologna, 1659-1686. The last volume was posthumous. Torelli's earlier work, *Ristretto delle vite de gli huomini e delle donne illustri . . . dell'ordine Agostiniano,* Bologna, 1647, was written before he consulted the general archives in Rome, and has nothing original about Giles.

41. A. Arpe, *Pantheon Augustinianum, sive elogia virorum illustrium Ordinis Eremitarum S. P. Augustini,* Genoa, 1709. It includes, pages 263-266, a brief life and poem in honor of Giles; page 269 supplies a list of Giles' works which Arpe saw in Rome.

42. J. Mabillon and M. Germain, *Iter italicum litterarium Dom Johannis Mabillon et Dom Michaelis Germain,* Paris, 1687, pages 110-111, tell of examining the Egidian letters in the library of San Giovanni in Carbonara. Their research there was cut short by the unaccountable change in attitude of the librarian. See *ibid.,* 111.

43. E. Martène and U. Durand, *Veterum scriptorum et monumentorum historicorum, dogmaticorum, moralium, amplissima collectio,* III, Paris, 1724, cols. 1233-1268.

44. See the letter of Fra Serafino, the compiler of the collection, to Fra Deodato, Lecceto, 25 October 1507, in Martène and Durand, III, cols. 1238-1239, and Fra Deodato to Fra. Serafino, Siena 15 January 1508, *ibid.,* cols. 1242-1243.

45. B. de Montfaucon, *Bibliotheca bibliothecarum manuscriptorum nova,* II, Paris, 1793, pages 778-779. A number of the manuscripts were identified in the *Catalogus codicum manuscriptorum Bibliothecae Regiae,* 4 vols., Paris, 1739-1744; see numbers 527 (1-2) 596-598, 3363, 3367, 6589.

46. J. A. Fabricius, *Bibliotheca latina mediae et infimae aetatis,* I, Hamburg, 1734, pages 62-63.

47. Johannes Felix Ossinger, *Bibliotheca Augustiniana, historica, critica, et chronologica in qua mille quadringenti Augustiniani Ordinis scriptores eorumque opera tam scripta, quam typis edita inveniuntur,* Ingolstadt-Augsburg, 1768.

48. L. Grana, *Oratio in funere Aegidii Canisii Cardinalis Viterbiensis ex MS cod. membranaceo Bibliothecae Marii Compagnonii Marefuscii S. R. E. Card. amplissimi eruta, et a Johanne Christophoro Amadutio nunc primum in lucem edita,* Rome, 1781. See Appendix 1.

49. "Il romano Lorenzo della Grana vescovo di Segni gli tesse l'elogio funebre, dove di ogni cosa discorre, salvo che del povero defunto," F. Fiorentino in *Archivio storico per le province Napoletane* IX (1884) 452.

50. *Op. cit.,* pages 5-6. Among the Egidian manuscripts he mentioned was a copy, now lost, of the invaluable "Acta Ordinis," also lost. This volume of the "Acta Ordinis" covered Giles' years as prior general, May 1507-1511.

51. G. Tiraboschi, *Storia della letteratura italiana,* VII, part 4, Modena, 1792, pages 1592-1597.

52. Antonius Hoehn, *Chronologia provinciae Rheno-Suevicae ordinis FF. Eremitarum S. P. Augustini*, Würzburg, 1744. The work is imprinted 1744 on the title page, but page 178 deals with events of the year 1745.

53. "Die Lebenschreibungen der Päpste in Zeitalter K. Maximilian's I vom dem Cardinal Aegidius," in *Archiv für Kunde oesterreichischer Geschichts-Quellen* XII (1854) 378-387. A substantial section of the *Historia XX Saeculorum* was printed as an appendix by M. Creighton, *History of the papacy during the period of the Reformation* IV, London, 1887, pages 279-287.

54. H. Laemner, *Zur Kirchengeschichte des sechszehnten und siebenzehnten Jahrhunderts*, Freiburg, 1863, pages 64-67.

55. T. Kolde, *Die deutsche Augustiner-Congregation und Johann von Staupitz*, Gotha, 1879, pages 460-472.

56. Nikolaus Paulus, *Der Augustinermönch Johannes Hoffmeister*, Freiburg, 1891. See in particular pages 120-164, "Die deutschen Augustiner in der Reformationszeit."

57. Published in 58 volumes at Venice, 1879-1902.

58. L.-G. Pélissier, "Manuscrits de Gilles de Viterbe à la Bibliothèque Angélique," in *Rev. biblioth.* II (1892) 228-240.

59. H. Narducci, *Catalogus codicum manuscriptorum praeter graccas et orientales in Bibliotheca Angelica, olim coenobii Sancti Augustini de Urbe*, I, Rome 1893. Giles' manuscripts are described on pages 1, 177-178, 223, 281, 292, 316, 416-418, 487, 489-490, 526-527, 529.

60. In G. Muccio and P.F. de Cavalieri, "Index codicum graecorum Bibliothecae Angelicae," in *Studi italiani di filologia classica* IV (1896) 10, 125-127, 131-132, 139, 141. See John Whittaker, "Greek Manuscripts from the Library of Giles of Viterbo at the Biblioteca Angelica in Roma," in *Scriptorium* 31 (1977) 212-239.

61. L.-G. Pélissier, *De opere historico Aegidii Cardinalis Viterbiensis*, Montpellier, 1896.

62. L.-G. Pélissier, "Pour la biographie du Cardinal Gilles de Viterbe," in *Miscellanea di studi critici edita in onore di Arturo Graf*, Bergamo, 1903, pages 789-815. The manuscript in question, "Vita et epistolae Aegidii Cardinalis Viterbiensis," was compiled by another Augustinian cardinal, Enrico Noris (1631-1704), and is now in the Biblioteca Laurenziana, Florence, MS 219. Noris' manuscript is a synopsis of Giles' first Dd register, now missing.

63. See above, note 62, *Miscellanea*, page 794.

64. F. Trucchi, *Poesie italiane inedite di dugento autori*, III, Prato, 1874, pages 124-129. The madrigals are in a manuscript of the Magliabecchi collection in the Biblioteca Nazionale, Florence. Trucchi inaccurately described it as Cod. 720; it is Cl. VII. 720. The madrigals are on fol. 99v, 122r (also on 278r), 116r, 123r, 122r, 122v (also on 278v).

65. F. Fiorentino, "Egidio da Viterbo ed i Pontaniani di Napoli," in *Archivio storico per le province Napoletane* IX (1884) 430-452; republished posthumously in *idem, Risorgimento filosofico nel Quattrocento*, Naples, 1885, pages 251-274.

66. E. Gothein, *Die Kulturentwicklung Süd-italiens in Einzel-Darstellung*, Breslau, 1886, pages 449-459.

67. C. D. Ginsburg, *The Massoreth Ha-Massoreth of Elias Levita*, London, 1867, pages 12, 14-20, 71, 96-97, 130; L. Geiger, *Das Studium der hebräischen Sprache in Deutschland*, Breslau, 1870, pages 56-64; *idem, Johann Reuchlin, sein Leben und seine Werke*, Leipzig, 1871, pages 306, 399, 404, 437, 450; J. Perles, *Beiträge zur Geschichte der hebräischen und aramäischen Studien*, Munich, 1884, pages 155-158, 163, 179-180, 200-203; H. H. Graetz, *Geschichte der Juden*, IX, 2nd ed., Leipzig, 1877, pages 44, 90-91, 155, 214, 266; P. Reiger, *Geschichte der Juden in Rom, 1420-1870*, Berlin, 1895, pages 86-92.

68. A. Potthast, *Bibliotheca historica medii aevi: Wegweiser durch die Geschichtswerke des europäischen Mittelalters bis 1500*, 2nd ed., Berlin, 1896, page 18.

69. U. Chevalier, *Répertoire des sources historiques du moyen âge: bio-bibliographie*, Paris, 1877-1886, page 385. The second edition, Paris, 1905, had nothing further about Giles.

70. L. Pastor, *Geschichte der Päpste*, IV, part I, Freiburg, 1906, page 141.

71. "Egidio Canisio und der Unionstreit," in H. Böhmer, *Luthers Romfahrt*, Leipzig, 1914, pages 36-75.

72. D. G. Kawerau, "Aus den Actis Generalatus Aegidii Viterbiensis," in *Zeitschrift für Dirchengeschichte* XXXII (1911) 603-606. Kawerau did not give a precise reference for the manuscript, then newly acquired by the Berlin library, and as yet uncatalogued. It is Deutsche Staatsbibliothek, Berlin, Ital. Fol. 173, see *Mitteilungen aus der königlichen Bibliothek* IV, Berlin, 1918, page 77.

73. F. G. Pazzaglia, *Lettere inedite del Card. Egidio Canisio Viterbese*, Rome, 1915, pages vii-23.

74. *Analecta Augustiniana* IX (1921) 17-28, 64-66. The decrees are known only indirectly, from their repetition in the decrees of the general chapter held at Naples in 1539.

75. A. V. Müller, "Der Augustiner-Observantismus und die Kritik und Psychologie Luthers," in *Archiv für Reformationsgeschichte* XVIII (1921) pages 1-34.

76. H. Jedin, "Die römischen Augustiner-Quellen zu Luthers Frühzeit," *ibid.* XXV (1928) 256-270.

77. A. V. Müller, *Luthers theologische Quellen*, Giessen, 1912; *idem*, "Agostino Favaroni e la teologia di Lutero," in *Bilychnis* III (1914) 373-387; "Zur Verteidigung Luthers und meines Buches 'Luthers theologische Quellen,'" in *Theologische Studien und Kritiken* LXXXVIII (1914) 131-172; "Giacomo Perez di Valenza, O.S.A., vescovo di Chrysopoli e la teologia di Lutero," in *Bilychnis* IX (1920) 391-403; *Una fonte ignota del sistema di Lutero: il Beato Fidati da Cassia e la sua teologia*, Rome, 1921; "Il Dr. Paulus di Monaco, il Beato Fidati, e Lutero," in *Bilychnis* XIX (1922) 247-257; *Lutero e l'Agostinianismo medioevale*, Rome, 1929.

78. J. Paquier, "Un essai de théologie platonicienne à la Renaissance: le Commentaire de Gilles de Viterbe sur le premier livre de Sentences," in *Recherches de science religieuse* XIII (1923) 293-312, 419-436.

79. G. Signorelli, *Il Cardinale Egidio da Viterbo, agostiniano, umanista e riformatore, 1469-1532*, Florence, 1929.

80. MS G. X. 26. The confusing character of Lorenzo da Ilari's catalogue, *La biblioteca pubblica di Siena* VI, Siena 1847, explains why the manuscript was overlooked.

81. H. Jedin, *Giolamo Seripando, sein Leben und Denken im Geisteskampf de 16. Jahrhunderts,* 2 vols., Würzburg, 1937. An English translation by F. C. Eckhoff was published at St. Louis, MO, 1947. It omits many of the footnotes and the valuable appendices.

82. Giuseppe Toffanin, *Giovanni Pontano, fra l'uomo e la natura; in appendice il dialogo "Aegidius" tradotto da Vincenzo Grillo,* Bologna, 1938.

83. E. Massa, "Egidio da Viterbo, Machiavelli, Lutero e il pessimismo cristiano," in *Archivio di Filosofia* (1949) 75-123; *idem,* "Egidio da Viterbo e la metodologia del sapere nel cinquencento," in *Pensée humaniste et tradition chrétienne aux XVᵉ et XVIᵉ siècles,* ed. H. Bédarida (Paris, 1950) 185-239; *idem,* "L'anima e l'uomo in Egidio da Viterbo e nelle fonti classiche e medioevali," in *Archivio di Filosofia* (1951) 37-138; *idem, I fondamenti metafisici della "dignitas hominis," e testi inediti di Egidio da Viterbo,* Turin, 1954. Professor Massa was a member of the Faculty of Letters, University of Pisa.

84. "Les Dominicains et la kabbale chrétienne à la Renaissance," in *Archivium Fratrum Praedicatorum* XXVII (1957) 319-336; "Pico della Mirandola e gli inizi della cabala cristiana," in *Convivium,* N. S., I (1957) 31-47; and in a specific way in *Le Zôhar chez les kabbalistes chrétiens de la Renaissance,* Paris, 1958, pages 34-42. A major advance toward an understanding of Giles has been made by Professor Secret's *Egidio da Viterbo: Scechina e libellus de litteris hebraicis,* 2 vols., Rome, 1959: Edizione Nazionale dei Classici del Pensiero Italiano, an attractive edition of two of Giles' cabalistic works hitherto unpublished.

85. R. Weijenborg, "Neuentdeckte Dokumente im Zusammenhang mit Luthers Romreise," in *Antonianum* XXXII (1957) 147-202. This is a study of exceptional value.

86. A. de Meijer, O.S.A., "Bibliographie Historique de l'Ordre de Saint Augustin, 1980-1984; avec quelques complements d'années anterieures," in *Augustiniana* 35 (1985) 192; *ibid.* 39 (1989): "avec des complements des années anterieures," page 392.

87. John W. O'Malley, "A Note on Gregory of Rimini: Church, Scripture, Tradition," in *Augustinianum* 5 (1965) 365-378; "Giles of Viterbo: a sixteenth-century text on doctrinal development," in *Traditio* XXII (1966) 445-450; "Historical thought and the Reform crisis of the early sixteenth century," in *Theological Studies* 28 (1967) 531-548; "Giles of Viterbo: a Reformer's thought on Renaissance Rome," in *Renaissance Quarterly* 20 (1967) 1-11.

88. The proceedings of the conference were published with remarkable speed in 1983 by the Augustinian Historical Institute at Rome, simply under the title, *Egidio da Viterbo, O.S.A., e il suo tempo,* but exasperatingly (for bibliographers) without the name of an editor. In fact the demanding editorial work was anonymously undertaken by Carlos Alonso, O.S.A., the patient Spanish editor of *Analecta Augustiniana* (Rome).

89. Charles Astruc and Jacques Monfrin described *The problem of Giles of Viterbo* as *"remarquable étude,"* in their edition of the catalogue of Giles' manuscripts now in the Bibliothèque Nationale, Paris. See C. Astruc and J. Monfrin, "Livres latins et hebreux du Cardinal Gilles de Viterbe," in *Bibliothèque d'Humanisme et Renaissance* XXIII (1961) 551-554, at page 554, n. 1.

90. An edition and felicitous rhyming English translation of the eclogues were prepared by an American Jesuit professor of classics, Edmund F. Miller, who died on 6 December 1989. See Appendix V for English translation.

91. Gérard E. Weil, *Elie Levita, humaniste et massorète, 1469-1549*, Leiden 1963, especially chap. IV.

92. For Leo Africanus, see *Encyclopédie de l'Islam*, vol. V (1983) 728-729.

93. For Egidio, see in particular vol. I (1968) and vol. II (1970).

94. "Greek manuscripts from the library of Giles of Viterbo at the Biblioteca Angelica in Rome," in *Scriptorium* 31 (1977) 212-239.

95. Severin Grill describes this Syriac MS, which he located at Innsbruck, see "Eine unbekannte syrische Handschrift in Innsbruck, cod. 401, Bibl. Univ.," in *Oriens Christianus* 52 (1968) 151-155, but he was unable to identify its original owner. This was achieved by Jean Gribomont, see "Gilles de Viterbe, le moine Elie, et l'influence de la littérature maronite sur la Rome érudite de 1515," in *Oriens Christianus* 54 (1970) 125-129.

96. "The registers of Giles of Viterbo. A source on the reform before the Reformation, 1506-1518," in *Augustiniana* 12 (1962) 142-160.

97. *Aegidii Viterbiensis, O.S.A., Resgestae Generalatus, I, 1506-1514* published at Rome, 1988; *Aegidii Viterbiensis, O.S.A., Registrum Generalatus, II, 1514-1518*, published at Rome, 1984.

98. "'Maximus Caesar et Pontifex Maximus.' Giles of Viterbo proclaims the alliance between Emperor Maximilian I and Pope Julius II," in *Augustiniana* 22 (1972) 80-117; "'Without Councils we cannot be saved.' Giles of Viterbo addresses the Fifth Lateran Council," in *Augustiniana* 27 (1977) 166-204.

99. Giles of Viterbo, *Letters as Augustinian General*, Rome, 1992.

100. "Sermons of Giles of Viterbo as Bishop" in *Egidio da Viterbo, O.S.A., e il suo tempo*, Rome, 1983, pages 137-189.

101. "A 'lost' work of Giles of Viterbo," *ibid.*, pages 117-127.

Chapter 7

Scripture Scholar

No book on Giles should be published without an account of Giles as a scripture scholar. He was a gifted individual in so many different fields — classical Latin and classical Greek, he composed Italian poetry, he began a novel in Italian, he edited the scholastic philosophy of Giles of Rome, he wrote a theological commentary on Peter Lombard (but in the spirit of Plato) and a spiritual commentary on the history of the papacy. He was not merely a man with an inventive pen; he had a golden tongue and the practical ability to negotiate in political affairs. For these reasons, he was a renowned preacher and an able papal diplomat. As prior general of the Augustinians for twelve years he was an apostle of reform, but he applied his high ideals with common sense. However, all these interests and activities fall into second place beside his fascination with biblical studies. As a young friar in his thirties he was seized with a vision of truth in holy writ, and this became the pillar of fire guiding him through many difficulties and vicissitudes for the rest of his earthly pilgrimage. It became the dominant interest in his life.

In 1497 Giles took the examination for the much-coveted magisterium in theology. The experience was not a mere formality, as he recorded in a letter to Ficino.[1] Giles expounded the whole course of theology in the light of Platonic thought, though with due deference to Aristotle. More than one of the examiners assailed his exposition so vehemently that he might have succumbed were it not for the intervention of some of the cardinals who were present. He was awarded the laurels and was appointed to teach theology at Florence. So, he found himself back in a congenial atmosphere, near Ficino, in a city which paid honor to Plato.

His stay at Florence was short, but it was of decisive importance in his intellectual and spiritual development. Some of his manuscripts which have survived from this period reveal his growing interest in Greek learning.[2] They show his love for Greek classics and indicate a reverence for Plato. A copy of Jamblichus is evidence of his neoplatonism and is an early sign of the overpowering attraction which mysticism, especially that of the cabala and Jewish mysticism, was to exercise over him in his later years.[3] Florence was a city associated with Pico della Mirandola (d. 1494), who was the first to seek in the cabala a clue to Christian mysteries. Giles was later to acknowledge his debt to Pico.[4] It is very likely that during his stay at Florence Giles began to learn Hebrew.

However, it would be a mistake to believe that Giles, by residing at Florence, was living in the splendid isolation of the ivory tower of the academic. Florence at this very time was the center of a religious storm largely created by the electric personality of the Dominican, Girolamo Savonarola. One of Savonarola's notable opponents was the Augustinian prior general, Mariano da Genazzano, and it was he who summoned Giles to Rome in the autumn of 1497 to preach before Pope Alexander VI, who in his turn was the principal target for much of Savonarola's denunciations. Giles was in Rome by October 1497 and thus escaped the worst effects of the storm which began to burst over Florence in November and swept away Savonarola to his public execution in the Piazza della Signoria in May 1498. Giles, though obedient to Alexander as pope, had no sympathy with the corrupt practices of the papal court, which he denounced in one memorable sentence: "There was then no regard for human or divine justice. All was ruled by gold, violence, and lust."[5]

Giles was never again to live in Florence, though he visited it on several occasions in later years. About Easter 1498, he was taken to Naples, as a companion, by Mariano da Genazzano, for a visitation of the Augustinian houses in that province. It was literally a fatal tour for Mariano, who died during the return journey, in December 1498 at Sessa. Giles was also stricken with illness at the same time, but recovered, and after a visit to his native Viterbo, he returned to Naples. The two years which he was to spend there represent a separate chapter in his life.

According to Giles' own words he withdrew to Naples, to give himself for two years to contemplation of divine things.[6] This is corroborated by the fact that he went to live, not with the conventual Augustinians at Sant'Agostino, but with the observants at San Giovanni in Carbonara where there was a higher ideal and practice of Augustinian life. That was of considerable importance in his role as an Augustinian and may be seen as the first clear manifestation that he was committing himself to the reform movement and to a policy which was to carry him, much against his will, to becoming general of the Order.

Important as was the time at San Giovanni in Carbonara for his own spiritual life, and for the history of the reform movement, it sheds only an indirect light on the making of Giles as a scripture scholar. While his conversion to the reform movement may thus be said to have begun with his return to Naples in the spring of 1499, his conversion, with the same intensity, to scriptural studies did not take place for another eight years, until 1507, with his election as prior general and did not gain full force until 1515, with the arrival of the Jewish scholar, Elijah Levita, in Rome. Nevertheless, it would be wrong to assume that during his two years at Naples Giles was insensitive to holy scripture. Even then he was involved in a process attuning him to the golden hour which struck in 1515 with the appearance of Levita on the scene. Already in 1502 there was substantial evidence to that effect, as we shall see. His immersion in Jewish studies was a gradual, not an instantaneous, process.

The Naples Experience

Our appreciation of how Giles developed at Naples has been distorted, unintentionally, by three admirable scholars, Fiorentino writing in 1885, Gothein in 1886, and Toffanin in 1938. They treated Giles only insofar as he formed part of the literary circle at Naples dominated by that great Renaissance figure, Giovanni Pontano. Even the fine Neapolitan scholar, Pèrcopo, who published, in 1936 and 1937, such enlightening studies on the life and writings of Pontano, failed to take due note of what Pontano wrote to, and about, Giles of Viterbo. Though Pontano had inherited and continued a bitter Neapolitan tradition of hostility to clerics, and even to the Christian religion in the fields of both morals and doctrine, he frankly admitted in his letters and later works that the gentle arguments of Giles had changed his views on this life and the hereafter. Pontano abandoned his astrological determinism in favor of faith in God's providence. In his moral tract *De immanitate* he stated that Giles was there as a living witness to fortitude and the Christian truths. In response to a suggestion by Giles, he studied Augustine's *The Immortality of the Soul*, and, to the astonishment of his friends, wrote a hymn in honor of Saint Augustine in January 1501, sending it to Giles. His highest tribute to the friar was to compose a work in his honor, entitled simply *Aegidius.*

It was not only Pontano who succumbed to the charm and Christian arguments of Giles. A host of people at Naples, and not simply the literary figures, were anxious to ensure that Giles would remain with them. His reputation as a preacher was gaining momentum. But Giles showed common sense when he remarked to a friend that at Naples you were assured of success as long as the words were wrapped in the elegant phrases of the humanists, and he capped that statement when he wrote to a fellow Augustinian humanist, Raffaele Brandolini, at Florence, commenting that at Naples he expounded doctrine in Platonic terms so that his audience might lift their eyes to life beyond the grave.[7] His knowledge of Plato was not second-hand. He wrote in October 1501 to a friend at Lecceto, asking as if on a matter of life and death that he procure him a copy of Plato in the Greek text. Search for it, he pleaded, so that I may buy it, or have it on loan, or even have it copied.[8]

Where does this get us to understanding Giles as a scripture scholar? Plato is not holy writ. We must continue to follow the logical sequence of his development if we are to appreciate how he became an outstanding student of the scriptures.

In the same spirit in which he had written to Brandolini, Giles exhorted Pontano to reflect on immortality and on the fact that he was numbered among "the sons of God."[9] Pontano took the point and in replying to Giles developed the concept of divine sonship. This inner life, Pontano argued, is gradually frittered away during our passage through this world, until in our old age we turn once more to God as we prepare to rejoin him in heaven.[10] The Platonic concept of the return of the soul to God was one which Pontano freely acknowledged he had received from Giles. This Christian interpretation of Plato by Giles did not mean that he was disregarding the other Greek classical authors. In 1501 he was being sent from Rome copies of Homer, Hesiod, and the eclogues of Theocritus.[11]

While we know that Giles in his sermons at Naples also included references from the New Testament, the main body of evidence is to citations and illustrations from classical authors. However, we must remember that Giles, according to himself, sought to present Christian truths in a form acceptable to his sophisticated listeners at Naples. Still more important is the fact that the evidence has come down to us almost entirely through the letters and works of the literary set at Naples. It is therefore selective and not necessarily fully representative of the form in which Giles delivered his sermons. A more accurate impression of how Giles was able to deliver the Christian message to the people at large, and not just to the select few, comes from Florence where he was preaching in the following year, 1502. A layman, Piero Parenti, who had heard both

Mariano da Genazzano and Savonarola, recorded in his chronicle of Florence the impression made upon him by Giles:

> I shall deal with the Augustinian friar, Giles of Viterbo, who is so like Fra Mariano da Genazzano that you would not believe it possible. Their resemblances are as follows: the same stature, the same pronunciation, the same method when introducing the sermon, the same vehemence in developing the theme, the same eloquence and erudition. Indeed, in learning, Giles surpasses Mariano. He is skilled in Greek, Hebrew, and Latin. He is a philosopher and a profound theologian, a Platonist and an Aristotelian, and is versed in profane and sacred history. All this is accompanied with a perfect knowledge of, and dexterity with, the scriptures.[12]

For our purposes the mention of Giles' expertise in Hebrew and his familiarity with the scriptures are the most valuable references in Parenti's commentary. It shows that Giles, during his stay at Naples, must have continued his study of Hebrew, however little attraction that branch of learning had for the literati there, and that his sermons were well-grounded in holy scripture. These were qualities which were of secondary importance at Naples, at least for his learned audience.

One might be inclined to take Parenti's tribute in 1502 to Giles' expertise in Hebrew with a grain of salt, as an example of Renaissance literary exaggeration, were it not for substantial evidence from the year 1504, as we shall see later, showing him by that time to be already deep in Hebrew studies, delving into the Jerusalem Targum. There is another valuable piece of evidence for Giles' study of Hebrew, namely his copy of a printed rabbinic lexicon, now in the Angelica library, Rome.[13] Unfortunately, the volume is not dated nor do we know the year in which it came into Giles' possession, but the fact that the extensive marginalia by Giles throughout the volume are all in Latin, and not in Hebrew as was often his practice in later years, suggests that this book was one of the basic works which went into the making of Giles as a scripture scholar. It may even date from his years at Florence, in the 1490s, when Pico della Mirandola was a recent bright memory and Savonarola the center of violent controversy.

Vibrant Preacher

It is obvious from Parenti's comments that Giles, by his character, education, and beliefs, was cast in a mold totally different from that of revivalist preachers such as Bernardine of Siena and Savonarola. They were prophetic figures, consumed by an inner flame, casting fire on the earth. It is difficult to decide how lasting was the effect of the emotional turbulence they excited by their religious preaching. On the other hand, it would be a mistake to underestimate the effect of preachers such as Giles, whose appeal was at least as much to the mind as to the heart, since there is abundant evidence that he enjoyed widespread popularity, even among unlikely classes of the people. Perhaps the most striking example was in the year 1508, when he preached a special sermon to the prostitutes of Rome.

Giles was so highly thought of by King Frederick of Naples that the friar could describe the monarch as "mihi coniunctissimum."[14] Frederick sent him to preach in Puglia, that picturesque area in the southeast of the kingdom of Naples. Even though the mission had a purely spiritual purpose, it ended quite abruptly when Giles was summoned to Rome. The reason for the summons is not given but it was almost certainly political. King Louis XII of France, by secret arrangement with King Ferdinand of Aragon and with the consent of Pope Alexander VI, seized the kingdom of Naples, and King Frederick had to leave the country. The presence of Giles, a friend of Frederick, in Puglia would be an embarrassment, and so he was called to Rome. That ended his close association with Naples.

The time spent at Naples, most of it in the peace of the monastery of San Giovanni in Carbonara, led him to three resolutions which he saw as forming the pattern of his future life. First, he would join the observant branch of the Augustinian Order, to which the friars in Carbonara belonged. Secondly, thus withdrawn from the world he would have the opportunity for a life of prayer and asceticism, in which he would seek union with God by meditation on the Crucified Savior. This meant a study of the gospels and holy writ. Thirdly, and arising out of the two previous resolutions, he would, when called upon, preach the word of God to all and sundry. He fulfilled that program during the years 1502-1506, but was then by papal decree placed in charge of the Augustinian Order and had to assume a different role from the ideal he had in mind.

After Giles had preached the Lenten sermons at Siena in 1502, he went to stay at the nearby Augustinian observant monastery of Lecceto and took the opportunity to become a member of that congregation in April 1503.[15] The house at Lecceto had been for more than a century the official model for the observant movement in the Order. The ideals and lifestyle in the monastery seemed the answer to what Giles was seeking. He now embarked on a series of preaching assignments which satisfied his desire to communicate the gospel message. However, much of his thought process and imagery still belonged to the classical world, particularly of Greece. At this stage, he was more the Christian humanist than the scripture scholar. Let me illustrate with three examples from this period of his life. As noted earlier, on 8 October 1503, at the request of the city council of Siena, he delivered a sermon in the piazza before an exultant crowd celebrating the coronation of Francesco Piccolomini, cardinal of Siena, as Pope Pius III. Giles took for his text a verse from Psalm 103: *He has made the moon for seasons: the sun knows the time of its going down.* Though he constantly returned to that verse in his discourse, he also quoted liberally from Saint Augustine, Boethius, Ptolemy, and the *Timaeus* of Plato.

The second example is from the following year when he was living in the solitude of a hermitage on the isle of Martana, in Lake Bolsena. We still have two of the books he had with him on that occasion, June 1504.[16] They are heavily annotated copies of Bessarion's *In calumniatorem Platonis*, and Valla's Latin translation of the *Iliad* of Homer. Plato and Homer continued to be two of his favorite authors.

The third example is a striking illustration of how he fused Christian thought and classical learning in three eclogues which are his longest excursion into Latin poetry. They are to be found in manuscripts in the Angelica library, Rome, and the Biblioteca Nazionale, Naples. The first eclogue *Paramellus et Aegon* is autobiographical (with Giles as Aegon) and stands as an introduction to the other two eclogues. It clearly owes its form to Vergil, with the two shepherds, Paramellus and Aegon, discussing the troubled world in which they are living. The second eclogue, on the birth of Christ (*De ortu Domini*), is self-explanatory, as is the third, *De resurrectione Domini*. The eclogues have value on literary grounds, as Renaissance Latin, but also merit attention for their theological content. Giles, a true son of the Renaissance, returns to a classical model, to the pastoral, for a suitable setting and series of images. He concentrates on two doctrines, so prominent in the early Christian Church, the incarnation and the resurrection. He, as it were, skips the passion and crucifixion of Christ, as well as so many other devotions which were typical of the medieval world. Giles appears as an optimist, convinced of the redemption of humankind and consequently of one's dignity as a child of God. Nature is once more harmonious, and the very animals manifest themselves as God's creatures. All this stems from Christ, the Redeemer, who took flesh, died, but rose again, victorious. Now there is no room for despair. Man has been made the measure of all things.[17]

These three examples show Giles to have been at this stage a man firmly committed to expounding the Christian message, but who wished to express himself through classical images and language. He saw no conflict between the ideals of the moral teachers of Greece and Rome, such as Plato, Homer, and Vergil, and those of Christianity. He expressed his view vividly in 1504, with a marginal note in his copy of Bessarion's *In calumniatorem Platonis:* "Si Plato damnatur religio patitur."

Biblical Studies

There is clear proof of his increasing concentration on biblical studies from this same year 1504. It is evident in one of the most important manuscripts surviving from Giles' collection, and now in the Vatican Library, as *Codex Neofiti 1*. It is unique, the only known copy of the Jerusalem (or Palestinian) Targum. When its discovery was announced in 1954 by the Spanish scholar, Alejandro Diez Macho, it caused a thrill of excitement throughout the circles of biblical scholars. An erudite edition of the manuscript in six volumes was published at Madrid during 1968-1979, under the direction of Diez Macho, and a flood of minor studies of various aspects of the manuscript has continued to flow since 1954 to the present day. The manuscript was copied at Rome by Menahem, "the most junior of scribes, son of the honorable rabbi, Mordekai . . . and I have copied this here in Rome, in the year 1504, for the great scholar, Master Giles — may his glory be extolled" (fol. 446b). Marginal notes by Giles show that by this time he had a competent knowledge of Hebrew and that he was already probing for leads into cabalist literature.

A major change, almost a revolution, in his ordered existence and in his development as a scholar took place in June 1506, with his appointment as vicar general of the Augustinians by Pope Julius II, who had come to know him as a preacher and as a zealot for the reform movement. The initial reaction of Giles to his appointment was to regard it as a disaster for his secluded life and precious studies. In fact, it proved to be a landmark in his progress as a scripture scholar. Undoubtedly, he was for the next twelve years heavily involved in administration and public affairs, but his position as general of the Order conferred three benefits on him which he was able to turn to the advantage of scholarship, particularly of his own scripture studies. First, he had the status to influence people of wealth and position in favor of scholarship. Publishers and printers listened to him. He was sought as a sponsor, and he could find sponsors. Secondly, through the Augustinian Order, he had an international network of communication, particularly when he was seeking for rare works in the field of biblical studies. Thirdly, he had money at his disposal. Hebrew works, both in manuscript and print, were rare and expensive, and previously, as an individual mendicant friar, he had very little money to acquire them. Now all that was changed.

He wrote to the friars of Lecceto in July 1506, lamenting his appointment as vicar general, and mentioned, as one cause for regret, that he might find it impossible to complete a large-scale work on which he was engaged, and which he described as a composition to rebut the poisonous weapons of certain anti-Christian philosophers.[18] He was referring to his commentary on the *Sentences* of Peter Lombard. This work, as yet unpublished, was discussed in 1927 by Professor Jules Paquier of Paris and later by Professor Eugenio Massa. It is a sizable composition, running to over 400 folios in manuscript. The greater part was written by the year 1510. By that date, he had progressed to page 373, but it took a further two years to add another five pages. In the commentary he refers to the incessant distractions which prevented study and peace. In a letter of 3 October 1508 he had written: "Day and night we are busy with reform. All our concern, thoughts and actions have this one aim. Otherwise we cannot satisfy God, man, or our own conscience."

He was busily occupied as prior general, preacher, and papal agent. Nothing but his instinctive love for learning could have sustained his continued activity as a scholar.

The work on Lombard is only nominally a commentary on the *Sentences*. Giles used Lombard's scheme as a means to discourse in a Platonic manner on God, the Trinity, creation, baptism, and the missions of the Holy Spirit. In the process he condemned what he believed was the impiety of Padua and of the Averroists. He cites freely from the Christian scriptures and from Homer, Vergil, Aristotle, and, of course, Plato.

Yet, he did not persevere and finish the commentary. Instead, he turned to another major work, now entitled *Historia Viginti Saeculorum*, and significantly the subtitle states that it is built on an interpretation of the psalms. The role of Giles as a student of the scriptures now begins to gain clearer definition. The work was an

ambitious undertaking and was intended to be a Christian interpretation of the story of humankind.[19] If anything, it was an attempted history of the popes, but falls far short of even that limited
mark. Nevertheless, quantitatively, it is a massive work, running
to about 700 folios, written to some extent in the style of Cicero and
Seneca, studded with aphorisms and pithy observations. It contains a wealth of scriptural, philological, and accidental historical
knowledge. It is a fascinating ragbag of information. Giles was not
scientific in his exposition, nor critical (by our standards) in his use
of sources. His general argument was that the Church, as the
mystical body of Christ, should be considered historically and that
each psalm revealed a stage of God's providence in dealing with
humanity. Usually, he did not draw on documentary sources for
his facts, and he added little to our knowledge of the patristic and
medieval centuries. His enthusiasm for the classical world was
tempered by his convictions as a Christian. He rejoiced in the
change which, as he expressed it, brought Christian churches
where there had been pagan temples, devotion to the Blessed
Virgin instead of to Venus, sanctity in place of impurity, chastity
instead of lust.[20]

The composition has a twofold value for the historian. Giles'
recollections of contemporary popes and events are illuminating
and informative. The work, taken as a whole, is the literary expression of a Christian humanist who saw God's providence in everything and could quote as easily from Homer and Vergil as from the
Old and New Testament. The work is unfinished and Giles never
grappled with the arduous task of finally preparing it for publication. There are five copies of this work, but none is an autograph.
However, the copy in the Biblioteca Nazionale, Naples, VII. F. 8.,
is the one to be followed. It was transcribed by Scutelli, scribe and
literary coadjutor of Giles in the 1520s. This copy has the notes and
corrections by Seripando, who prepared it for printing. He inserted
chapter headings and subtitles for chapters. More than twenty
years ago it was announced that Professor Massa had prepared a
critical edition of the whole work for publication at Zurich, a
promise as yet unfulfilled.

Jewish Literature

Instead of concentrating on completing his *Historia*, the Platonic
commentary on Peter Lombard, Giles switched his energies to an
ardent study of Jewish literature. We have no certainty about his

first steps in Hebrew, but it is very likely that these were taken during his stay at Florence in 1497. The knowledge of Hebrew had almost died out among Christians in late medieval and early Renaissance Europe. Pico della Mirandola, that versatile genius, was the person who, more than anybody else, led to its revival. He died in 1494, but the impetus which he gave to Hebrew studies was a living heritage with the Florentine neoplatonists when Giles studied there. We have already seen that in April 1502, a Florentine chronicler, Piero Parenti, described Giles as skilled in Hebrew, but Hebrew studies were still in a rudimentary condition, even in Renaissance Italy. There were two main difficulties which hindered Giles from delving into Hebrew and its allied branches. Hebrew works, either in manuscript or print, were rare and expensive. Secondly, even when he became prior general and had funds to draw upon, he had to find some expert to act as his tutor if he was to make substantial progress.

Giles began his pursuit of Hebrew learning not simply as a scholar; it was not learning for its own sake. His purpose was to penetrate into the hidden meaning of the scriptures. In his *Historia*, written between 1513 and 1518, he declared that the growth of biblical studies was one of the five greatest events of his own day. He was scientific in his approach to the problem. He stated that the means to do so were, first, a precise knowledge of the language, and, secondly, a study of the mystical commentaries on the Old Testament.[21] Pride of place among these mystical works was given to the cabala, that corpus of medieval Jewish literature.[22] The remarkable parallels between the theological doctrines of the Florentine neoplatonists and of the cabala go far to explain how readily Giles committed himself to an exaggerated belief in the worth of the cabala. In 1901 Enelow was able to declare about Giles, "There is scarcely a classic of Jewish medieval mysticism that he has not translated, annotated, or commented upon."[23]

The study of Hebrew, of the cabala, and of rabbinical commentaries became henceforth the great passion of his intellectual life. Venice was one of the great printing centers in Italy, and besides was a meeting place for Jews coming from and going to the Near East. Again and again, Giles wrote to his friend, the Venetian Augustinian, Gabriele della Volta, asking that he buy him Greek and Hebrew works.[24] But della Volta was not his only agent in this field. Giles wrote from Rome on 15 December 1513 to a fellow friar, the German Hebraist, Kasper Amman, for various versions of the Targum and for a catalogue of Reuchlin's library. His hunger for

Hebrew learning was evident in a postscript to Amman where he declared that he valued Hebrew manuscripts above treasures, riches, and kingdoms, and that he would be forever in Amman's debt if he secured such works for him.[25]

In May 1514, Giles requested della Volta to arrange that if any friar were journeying to Damascus, he would seek out a full copy of the Zohar, the most famous of the commentaries on the cabala.[26]

According to Widmanstetter (1506-1557), a leading biblical scholar in the sixteenth century, it was due to Giles that the Zohar was made available for Christians. Giles had gone to considerable expense to have a copy of the massive Zohar transcribed in 1513 by Issac ben Abraham at Tivoli, and had then himself made extensive extracts from it in translation, which he had prefaced with the triumphant, if somewhat weary, statement, "Incipit liber Zohar super liber Mosis: labore magno quaesitus: maiore inventus: maximo rescriptus: longe ac multo cumulatiore in latinum raptim cursimque excerptus. f. Egidio Viterbiensi Eremita."[27]

Shortly afterward, to his dismay, he discovered that Isaac ben Abraham's copy was taken from an incomplete manuscript of the Zohar, but, undeterred by the information, he set about procuring a full copy of the work from Damascus, through the good offices of della Volta, as we have seen.

In December 1513, he protested to della Volta that he was being unjustly accused of extravagant expenditure on Hebrew manuscripts, but in the same breath he asked della Volta to seek him out further Hebrew works,[28] and within five months he was urging della Volta to hunt for a copy of the Zohar at Damascus. Two years later his Hebrew teacher, Elijah Levita, enthusiastically, though perhaps not wisely, disclosed that Giles had already spent a great deal of money on Hebrew works and was prepared to spend more.

Giles had no hesitation, as prior general, in his insistence that the Augustinian friars under his rule must observe strictly the vow of personal and communal poverty, but equally he did not hesitate to give free rein to expense when his object was the quest for the truth in sacred scripture. He was not just a Renaissance scholar, a bibliophile hunting out manuscripts for their own sake. The ideal which impelled him in these studies was expressed in a beautiful prayer which he included with his exposition of a cabalist text in May 1513:

> Lord, I have penetrated the enemy camp. Give me light to find my way; give me light to understand whatever will unlock the mys-

teries of your law and to refute whatever is contrary to it. So may it be granted to me, Lord, girded as I am with arms seized from the enemy, to contemplate those depths of your law, those wonders of your revelation, which not even Christian eye has seen nor ear heard.[29]

It shows that while he was aware of the shifting sands on which he was treading in cabalist studies, he had no doubt that he was on the right religious track.

It was the same conviction about the sacred quality of the cabala and talmudic literature which drove him to enter the arena on behalf of Reuchlin's *Augenspiegel*. The publication of Reuchlin's work exploded into a controversy which divided even churchmen on both sides of the Alps into hostile camps. Giles declared himself a firm advocate on behalf of the German scholar.[30] Lefèvre d'Étaples wrote to Rome in defense of Reuchlin and earned the commendation of Giles who was a member of the commission of bishops and theologians adjudicating on the dispute.[31] The prior general nailed his colors to the mast by publicly announcing that Reuchlin had been made an affiliated member of the Augustinian Order.[32] Giles wrote to him officially in 1516 declaring: "We are defending not you but the law, not the Talmud but the Church."

Giles employed a series of Jewish scribes in his pursuit of Hebrew learning. His most famous Jewish association was with Elijah Levita.[33] Their partnership has enriched enormously the literature of Hebrew studies in western Europe. Levita, born in Germany, had settled in Padua, but was driven from that city when it was sacked in 1509 by the imperial forces. He spent some years at Venice, but was unable to find a Jewish or Christian patron who would make it possible for him to continue as a full-time scholar. Finally, in 1515, he made his way to Rome with his family, and it is a clear indication of Giles' reputation as a Hebrew scholar that Levita sought him out and confidently petitioned him for support. The meeting between the homeless scholar and the Augustinian prior general has been immortalized by Levita in his *Massoreth Ha-Massoreth*. He tells in delightful rhythmic prose how he called upon Giles and introduced himself:

> When the prince heard my statement he came to me and kissed me with the kisses of his mouth, saying "Art thou, my lord, Elijah, whose fame has traveled over all countries, and whose books are to be found in every corner? Blessed be the God of the Universe who brought thee hither and bade thee come to me. Now stay with me and be my teacher, and I shall be to thee as a father and shall

support thee and thy house, and give thee thy corn, thy wine, and thy olives, and fill thy purse and bear all thy wants." And we took sweet counsel together, iron sharpening iron. I imparted my spirit to him, and learned from him excellent and valuable things.[34]

Giles was faithful to his word. As prior general, he could afford to support Levita, who unraveled for him the intricacies of Hebrew, while Giles in his turn instructed the Jew in Greek.

Even before the advent of Levita to Rome, Giles had been well aware of his own limited knowledge of Hebrew and of the imperfect manuscripts and books with which he was studying Hebrew language and literature. On the first folio of the copy of his Hebrew dictionary, now in the Angelica library, Rome, he had penned shrewd comments:

> Curavit Frater Egidius Viterbiensis Eremita haec haberi, tamenetsi inepta, insula et minus latina. Maluit tum haec usui esse suis quam contempnere. Usui vero possunt esse non mediocri si quis cum hebraeo codice conferat; sine quo, conferre possunt nihil.[35]

He was adamant, as those comments show, that it was necessary to go to the sources, to the original Hebrew text, and not to depend on translators and interpreters. Under the expert tutelage of Levita, he could now pursue his ambition with assurance. The study of Hebrew, and in particular of the cabala and of rabbinical commentaries, became henceforth the great passion of his intellectual life. It received the consent and the encouragement of Levita, one of whose first tasks in 1515 was to transcribe certain mystical writings of the twelfth century Jew, Eleazar of Worms. When Levita finished the work in 1516, he added a colophon:

> I wrote this book for one of the pious men among the Gentiles, a perfect and upright man, a priest of the Hermits of Saint Augustine. His name is Master Giles, the head and master of all the priests mentioned above in all countries of the lands of Christians. The Lord grant him the grace to study this book and to understand what is written in it, as well as in the other precious books which he bought or ordered to be copied, for he spent an enormous amount of money on it, and his hand is still stretched out to spend it until he is possessed of all the books we have.[36]

Printing

When Giles became a cardinal in 1517, he took Levita and his family into his household. It was under such orthodox patronage that the first Jewish printing press was established in Rome, and in 1518 Levita's *Séphèr ha-Bahur* appeared as its first product. Levita had been assured of financial support from three Jewish brothers, Isaac, Yomtob, and Jacob, printers and sons of Abigdor Levi. They had fled from Padua in 1509, at the same time as Levita, and settled in Rome. The problem, however, was not financial but ecclesiastical suspicion of Jewish scholarship. In 1516, due to the influence of the Dominicans who had shown their opposition to the Jews by their attack on the *Augenspiegel* of Reuchlin, Pope Leo X issued a bull requiring printers to submit Jewish works for scrutiny and approbation before publication. The personal intervention of Giles with Pope Leo X resolved the problem. A Hebrew press was set up on the premises of a Christian printer, Giovanni Giocomo Fagiot da Montecchio, at the Piazza Montanara, beside the Jewish quarter. Printing of *ha-Bahur* by the three sons of Abigdor Levi began on 1 April and was completed after sixteen days, with Levita visiting the premises three times daily, anxiously checking the work. The final product was not impressive, particularly by the superb standards of Italian printing in this period. The paper was of poor quality, the type was not clear-cut, nor was it helped by a heavy ink. Nevertheless, the publication was a landmark in its own sphere. It was officially issued in August 1518, fortified by the approbation of Leo X. The printers apologized for the typographical imperfections of their product and assured the public that their next publications would be of better quality.

The content of *ha-Bahur* dealt with abnormal form of words in the Old Testament, words which were irregular, hybrid, or unusual. The work was a by-product of Levita's preparation of a Hebrew grammar, *Séphèr ha-Harkabah*, which appeared some months later, the second fruit of the Jewish press in Rome. Levita's *ha-Bahur* had been fortified by a papal approbation, and *ha-Harkabah* carried in addition an approbation signed by three rabbis, Israel ben Yehiel, Sabbatai ben Mordekhai, and Joseph Hagri ben Abraham, who formed the rabbinic tribunal of Rome. This approbation authorized, by Jewish direction, not only *ha-Harkabah*, but *ha-Bahur* already printed. It also provided for the publication of a table of paradigms of verbs and nominal forms. This was composed at Rome in 1519 and published at Pesaro in 1520, under the title, *Pirqey Elijahu* (The Chapters of Elijah). The approbation of the rabbinic tribunal of Rome, dated 10 September 1518, was granted for ten years to Elijah Levita and the three sons of Abigdor Levi.

It will be noted that *Pirqey Elijahu* was printed by the Jewish Soncino press at Pesaro, not by the Hebrew press in the Piazza Montanara at Rome. This is a significant indication of Giles' role as protector of Hebrew learning. The first two publications of the Hebrew press at Rome had been issued under the patronage of Giles, who was literally near at hand, in his cardinal's residence at the corner of the Via della Scrofa and the Via dei Portoghesi, with Levita and his family as part of the household. Giles left Rome on 16 March 1518 as papal legate to Spain, and did not return to Italy for a year. In his absence, the Hebrew press at Rome languished, and Levita arranged that his *Pirqey Elijahu* be published by the Soncino firm at Pesaro. This Jewish press had close connections with Giles, having published the official Augustinian *Privilegia fratrum heremitarum S. Augustini* in 1516, and also the *Anthropotheomachia* of Cleophilus Octavius, dedicated to Giles, from its office at Fano in 1516.

Languages

In 1516, two years before Giles left for Spain, he had already committed Levita to a study of the Aramaic language insofar as it concerned the Old Testament. Five years later, when the Jewish scholar had completed the project, he added a note on the last page of the manuscript on 9 June 1521:

> Finally finished with the help of the Lord of the World. It is dedicated to a Prince of the Church, a man beloved and highly valued, and of whose merits, in my Introduction, I have mentioned of no more than a mere part. This important work was finished today, Sunday 4 Tammuz 5281, which is the year 1520, according to the calendar of the Christians. The work was composed at Rome, the great city which rules empires. May the Lord God be blessed for ever, the God of our Fathers.[37]

This note is followed by another in Latin, in Giles' hand:

> We have gathered together, in this order, items which hitherto have never been assembled in this fashion, and to which we have added annotations and concordances.
> By Elijah [Levita]   Friar Giles, Cardinal

The original manuscript in two volumes, and bearing the title *Zikhronot*, now reposes in the Bayerische Staatsbibliothek at Munich. It comprises three works directly concerned with the study of the Massorah, that body of post-Christian Jewish scholarship, based on tradition, which aimed at establishing an accurate text of the Old Testament: 1) an introduction to the works of the masters of the Massorah and to their methods; 2) 167 massoretic lists; 3) a great massoretic concordance. Though Levita made a copy of the third part of *Zikhronot* at Venice in 1536 for a new patron, Georges de Selve, bishop of Lavaur and French ambassador to the Republic of Venice, even that was never printed. Nevertheless, *Zikhronot* was a seminal work which led to the composition and publication of two of Levita's memorable studies, the *Meturgeman* and the *Massoreth ha-Massoreth*.

Levita himself has left on record the story of how *Meturgeman* came to be written:

> After I had finished my important work on the roots of our holy language, and which I named *Séphèr ha-Bahur*, dedicated to the very revered Cardinal Giles of Viterbo, he then demanded of me, in order to slake his thirst for knowledge, that I produce a study of the Aramaic language. He exhorted me, his servant, and encouraged me to compile a lexicon of the roots of the Aramaic language, all its verbs, nouns, and particles as were to be found in the paraphrase of the Bible, without adding or omitting anything. I commenced to compile this work at Rome, that great city, in the year 1526, but in 1527 the city was captured. I was deprived of my worldly possessions and all my books were stolen. By that time, I had already finished more than half of the work, but all that remained with me after the Sack of Rome were notebooks and jottings, which I recovered, soiled and torn, in the middle of the street. I brought these literary remains with me on my exile from city to city, from state to state, until I finally arrived at Venice, that magnificent city, which I reached in 1529.
>
> The cardinal asked me why I had not finished the work which he had commissioned me to produce, and I explained all that had happened to me. He directed me to complete the project, and, as in the past, he attended to my needs. I bent my energies to the task, and I finished the work today, Wednesday, the eve of the moon feast of Schebat, in the year 5291 that is, 19 January 1531 here at Venice, with gratitude of the Living God.[38]

A Spanish biblical scholar of our own time, Raimundo Griño, who has devoted much attention to the *Meturgeman*, believes that it has a unique importance for biblical Aramaic, and that it is a treasure trove embodying more than 3,300 root words.[39] He describes it as the equivalent of an Aramaic-Hebrew dictionary, but as superior to any other dictionary in the field, since it can be regarded as having a dual purpose, Aramaic-Hebrew, and Hebrew-Aramaic. It has special value because of its quotations from the Targums.

Levita's introduction to the *Meturgeman* has further information on the stimulus which Giles continued to give his former tutor. Levita relates: "The cardinal maintained his patronage, and cooperated with me in editing another work which I had begun, a scriptural commentary concerning grammar and exegesis."[40] This last project to which Levita refers is his *Massoreth Ha-Massoreth*, another landmark in the history of Hebrew orthography and grammar.

Though Levita composed six other works after his *Massoreth Ha-Massoreth* and saw four of them in print, it was the crown of his scholarly labors. Its very title *Massoreth Ha-Massoreth* (Tradition of the Tradition), using "tradition" in the biblical sense, is an indication of that fact. Levita fled from Rome after the sack of the city in 1527 and made his way to Venice. More than ten years later, most probably during the winter of 1540-1541, he traveled over the Alps and settled for his final years at Isny, on the Danube, in southern Germany. Neither at Venice nor at Isny did he forget his debt to Giles, to whom he looked back with nostalgia and gratitude. He expressed it with feeling in the introduction to his *Zikhronot*. He relates that in 1516, he had made his way as a refugee from Padua to Rome, the city of the pope, "the noble one among nobles. . . . There also live, in great numbers, princes, lords, cardinals, bishops, wise and intelligent." He continues:

> At this time there lived among them a very distinguished cardinal, a personage of great importance, wise as Solomon, whose name was Giles, the magnificent. He was a wise man, and sought God; he behaved with integrity, a just man among the just men of nations which have a part to play in the future world. He was without peer, understanding not only our language and knowing our literature, but also the scriptures, as well as tradition. He was conversant with all the works of the cabala. He had been initiated into the mysteries of that field of knowledge and was possessed of exceptional wisdom.[41]

The Massorah was the attempt to establish the traditional text of the Old Testament, and *Massoreth Ha-Massoreth* was the result, according to Levita, of twenty years' study of the problem. It represented his conclusions about the difficult grammatical system used for the Aramaic (alternatively called Armenian or Chaldean) texts of the Bible, in contrast with the smooth cohesion of the Hebrew texts. Hebrew had been the classical language of Israel, and all of the Old Testament (except for certain chapters of Ezra, Daniel, Nehemiah, and Jeremiah, written in Aramaic) was cast in Hebrew. However, it ceased to be a spoken language about the fourth century B.C., and Aramaic (a Semitic language closely related to Hebrew) became the vernacular of Palestine and was the language which Christ used. To satisfy the religious needs of the Jewish people, in those circumstances, the Hebrew scriptures were translated into Aramaic paraphrases, known as Targums.

Even before Levita arrived at Rome in 1515, Giles was keenly aware of the importance of the Targums. He had written in January 1515 to his close associate, the Venetian Augustinian, Gabriele della Volta:

> On the subject of the Targums, it would please me that you do not relax your efforts on behalf of this matter which is so close to my heart. Indeed, here in Rome, a man had died, who was a great authority in this field, and the pope Leo X has ordered that his books are to be preserved in the Pontifical Library. Furthermore, His Holiness has in his great generosity given me a copy of the Targum and several other books. Little wonder then that his name is a happy omen for me.[42]

The avid interest which Giles showed in acquiring copies of the Targums, of the Talmud, of the cabala, and of any text or commentary on the Old Testament has been widely known ever since his own day but the precise reason which motivated Giles has only too rarely been appreciated.

Hebrew, for him, was the language in which God spoke to humanity, or as he put it vividly it was the only language transmitted to humanity by the Holy Spirit. It was truly a sacred language, and his ultimate quest was for the inner meaning of the language, the precious "veritas hebraica." The nearer he could come to it, the clearer would be the message of God to man and woman. Every jot and tittle of Hebrew was therefore important, as were all languages and branches of knowledge related directly or indirectly to it.

Because of the colorful variety of his interests and activities, Giles is seen as a representative of the Renaissance *uomo universale*, pursuing knowledge for its own sake. Undoubtedly, Giles has a considerable amount of the *uomo universale* in his range of interests, but his scriptural studies must be seen as his increasing central interest. He wanted to know and understand the word of God, using every available intellectual tool and discipline. It is in this context that we must see his efforts to learn Syriac and Arabic and acquire manuscripts in those languages. It can be too easily assumed that he was the gifted Renaissance scholar, anxious to conquer another two kingdoms of knowledge in this Age of Discoveries.

It had been widely known in Giles' own day not only that he was an assiduous scholar of Hebrew, but that he had ventured into Aramaic. Doubtless he was tutored in Aramaic by Elijah Levita. While Giles' knowledge of Aramaic is well known to modern scholars, only recently did they become aware that he had also branched out into Syriac. The fact was overlooked that within less than a generation of Giles' death the renowned German biblical scholar Widmanstetter (1506-1557) had given public notice of Giles' active interest in Syriac. Widmanstetter, in the introduction to his Syriac version of the New Testament, ranked Giles among the memorable figures in the history of biblical studies, and he recalled with gratitude the permission to have access to Giles' oriental manuscripts.

In our own day a revealing shaft of light has been thrown on Giles' excursion into Syriac studies by the discovery of a manuscript in the University Library at Innsbruck. The manuscript, according to the colophon, "was written in the city of Rome for our reverend and holy Father, the monk Giles, from the city of Viterbo, in the province of Rome, who belongs to the order of monks of Saint Augustine."[43]

It is a copy of the Psalter, transcribed by Elias bar Abraham, and finished on 17 February 1517 at Rome. Elias was one of three delegates from the Maronite community in the Lebanon, sent to Rome in February 1515 by the Patriarch Simon Peter ibn Hassân and by Elias, the civil governor of Bécharri, to attend the Fifth Lateran Council, at which Giles had delivered a widely-acclaimed discourse on 3 May 1512. Elias, the copyist of the manuscript, was a subdeacon, a monk, and a disciple of the Patriarch Simon Peter. His fellow delegates were a priest, Joseph Khoury, and a deacon, Moses. Elias, though the most junior in rank as a subdeacon and only twenty years old on arrival in Italy, made the most permanent contribution of the trio. His considerable literary activity is witnessed by the Syriac manuscripts he copied, which are now in the Vatican, at Modena, and in Paris. He was the first professor of Syriac in Europe of the Renaissance, having a strong influence on Teseo Ambrogio and Andrea Maes. Giles of Viterbo was one of his patrons, as the Innsbruck manuscript shows, and was probably also one of his pupils. The Innsbruck Syriac Psalter has a special importance in the liturgical history of the Maronite rite because of the inclusion of certain doctrinal items, notably the Ave Maria and the Nicene Creed. The Psalter is one other example of the biblical treasures which Giles was gathering in his untiring search for the word of God in all branches of knowledge.

It was later stated by the Austrian Augustinian historian, Xystus Schier (1727-1772), that Giles had also embarked on a study of Turkish and Persian, but, while this is quite possible in view of Giles' insatiable appetite for any branch of learning related to scriptural studies, I have found no evidence to substantiate the claim. It is otherwise with Giles' reputation as a foremost scholar in Arabic studies. According to Widmanstetter in 1555, Giles was at one stage the only scholar in Europe with a competent knowledge of Arabic; he had encouraged Widmanstetter to persevere in the study of Arabic.[44] In 1954 I was fortunate enough to locate in the Angelica library, Rome, a sheaf of notes on the basics of the Arabic language, compiled in 1519 for Giles.[45] In fact Giles was already beyond the rudiments of Arabic studies by that time. When he was in Spain as cardinal legate during 1518-1519 he used the opportunity to have a copy made of the Koran. Such was Giles' reputation for Arabic studies by this time that in 1520 he was presented by Pope Leo X with a Tunisian Arabic scholar, known to European scholars as "Leo Africanus," who had been captured in the Mediterranean by Sicilian corsairs. These hard-eyed Sicilians undoubtedly had a dry sense of humor in the gift they presented to His Holiness, but Giles turned their gift to advantage by accepting Leo Africanus as his tutor in Arabic studies, as he had Elijah Levita in 1515 for Hebrew studies.

His interest in Arabic studies continued, as is shown by a presentation copy of the elements of Arabic grammar sent to him by Bishop Agostino Giustiniani from Fiorenzo, Corsica, in November 1524.[46] Giustiniani, a Dominican and bishop of Nebbio, was the scribe. He introduces the work with a laudatory letter of dedication to Giles. The bulk of the composition is in Latin, peppered throughout with Arabic words; the main part ends with the *Ave Maria* and the *Pater Noster* in Arabic.

Even when Giles was abroad on papal missions he utilized the opportunities to add weapons to his biblical armory. While he was cardinal legate in Spain in 1518 he had a copy made, in two tomes, of the Koran, the Arabic text with a Latin translation.[47] A catalogue of part of his library, when cardinal, lists an alphabetical index of the Koran, in Spanish, and also notes that there were four other works in Arabic in the library, but tantalizingly does not disclose the contents, presumably because the cataloguer did not know Arabic.

Giles was not a mere patron of learning, avidly acquiring Greek, Hebrew, Aramaic, Syriac, and Arabic manuscripts for their own sakes. He was first and foremost a diligent student of holy scripture, with its many branches and allied disciplines. His personal manuscripts and the copies of them in the Bibliothèque Nationale, Paris, and the Staatsbibliothek at Munich are witness to his limpet-like study of what were then new treasures of learning. As a representative example one may take his *Vocabula diversorum librorum Hebraicorum,* a formidable volume of 722 folios, with each page consisting of four to five cramped columns written in his delicate script. When Erasmus visited Rome in 1509 he made it his business to meet Giles as one of the learned figures in the city,[48] and ten years later when Celio Calcagnini returned to Italy from Hungary he wrote of Giles as a scholar in a class of his own by reason of his profound knowledge of the ancient world.[49] The de' Medici family had for many years looked on Giles as a favorite son. Pope Leo X (1513-1521) presented him with several manuscripts, including a Targum and a richly-illustrated Hebrew Bible.[50]

The small study of the cabala, which Giles completed for Cardinal Giulio de' Medici in 1517, is now in the Vatican Library, while the more intensive and extensive survey of the subject which he wrote during the years 1528-1531, for the same Giulio de' Medici then reigning as Pope Clement VII, is in the Bibliothèque Nationale, Paris. Both were edited excellently by Professor F. Secret in 1959.[51]

Yet, it is a sad fact that Giles never committed his vast biblical knowledge to print. He continued to collect manuscripts, to study and annotate them. He composed several works on philological and cabalist topics, but he did not submit himself to the discipline of halting at some stage to prepare any of his works for the printing press. This is doubly curious in view of the fact that he had launched into print on an ambitious scale in 1493, at the early scholarly age of twenty-four, with his edition of three of the works of Giles of Rome.[52]

Thereafter Giles continued to study, to amass learning, to plan, and even to prepare various works for publication. But there was always some new subject or topic which acted as an *ignis fatuus,* beckoning him on to what he fondly hoped would be a new revelation. Increasingly the scriptures became his major preoccupation. His letters, sermons, and literary works demonstrate how completely the Bible grew into the very texture of his thought. As a true son of the Renaissance he believed that even the word of God could be illumined by the learning of the Graeco-Roman world, and he saw Plato, like John the Baptist, as a forerunner of the Christian message.[53] To Plato were added the neoplatonists, then Iamblichus, Porphry, and Proclus, whose metaphysical and mystical teachings prepared Giles himself for the cabala.

Out of his encyclopedic scriptural knowledge, extending to Hebrew, Aramaic, Syriac, Arabic, and the cabala, Giles bequeathed nothing in print to posterity. There is however one striking tribute to the esteem in which he was held by scriptural scholars. The first published version of the Bible in Greek issued from the Aldine press in 1518 was dedicated to Giles by the editor, Andrea Asculano. In his dedication Asculano commented how apt it was that this unique edition of the inspired work describing the origin of the human race, the promulgation of God's message, and the history of the chosen people should be dedicated to Giles, whom he styled as a "most energetic defender of the Catholic faith."[54]

Conclusion

As you might expect I consulted a number of Jewish scholars and rabbinical authorities about Giles. They were unanimous in agreeing that he was not merely a highly important but a prophetic figure in the history of Judaeo-Christian relations. They believe, rightly or wrongly, that Christian biblical scholars are still on the wrong track, that they have closed their minds to the Jewish heritage of Christianity. As one impatient but well-disposed rabbi said to me, "Was your Jesus Christ not a Jew, trained in Jewish lore and traditions? Were the twelve apostles and early disciples not Jews? How can you understand them and their message unless you delve into the Jewish background from which they came? Was your Blessed Virgin Mary not a Jewess? How can you understand the *Magnificat* unless you appreciate the religion in which she was trained?" My rabbi friend then added: "That is where your Giles of Viterbo was ahead of his time, ahead of the twentieth century Catholic and Protestant churches. He tried to penetrate into the riches of Jewish religion, of the chosen people. And he went a great distance in his understanding. But the Reformation and the Council of Trent reversed all that progress. You Christians have withdrawn to mutually hostile and embattled positions. Forget your squabbles! Bury your common enmities. Turn again to what Giles of Viterbo was investigating, the common ground between the chosen people and the early Christians."

It is a piquant coincidence that the same year, 1518, which saw the publication of the Greek edition of the Bible at Venice dedicated to Giles of Viterbo, also witnessed the assault launched against the Church of Rome by Luther in the name of holy writ, gaining dangerous momentum in Germany. A glib critic might contrive to draw a contrast between the two Augustinians, picturing Giles as the humanist scholar, divorced from everyday reality, engrossed in the philology and purely academic aspects of the scriptures, while Luther was the man of personal religious feeling, seeking the living word of God in holy writ. This would do Giles a grave injustice. We know that he pursued, energetically and realistically, a systematic reform program in the Augustinian Order while he was general. The wonder is that he could contribute so much, even during those difficult years, in two very different fields of activity, as reformer of the Augustinian Order and as a scripture scholar.

Notes

1. Giles to Ficino, Siena, Spring 1497, in *Supplementum Ficinianum*, ed. P. O. Kristeller, II, Florence, 1937, pages 315-316; see *Lettere Familiari*, I, pages 101-104.

2. J. Whittaker, "Greek manuscripts from the library of Giles of Viterbo, at the Biblioteca Angelica in Rome," in *Scriptorium* 31 (1977) 212-239; see pages 216-218, 237.

3. *Ibid.*, pages 223-225.

4. J. W. O'Malley, *Giles of Viterbo on Church and Reform*, Leiden, 1968, page 8. Giles, in his Hebrew grammar, now Vat. Lat. 5808, fol. 2r, acknowledged his debt to Pico.

5. Giles in his *Historia XX Saeculorum*, in the section edited by K. Höfler, in *Archiv für Kunde osterreicher Geschichte-Quellen* 12 (1854) 379-382, see page 381.

6. Giles to Mannio, in Martène and Durand, III, cols. 1249-1250, see col. 1249; see also *Lettere Familiari*, I, pages 104-105.

7. Giles to Brandolini, Lecceto 23 April 1502, in Biblioteca Angelica MS 1001, fol. 218v; see *Lettere Familiari*, I, pages 145-146. Giles to Serafino, 6 January 1503, in G. Signorelli, *Egidio*, page 219 (V); *Lettere Familiari*, I, pages 180-181.

8. Giles to Adeodato, Naples 29 October 1501, MS 1001, Biblioteca Angelica fol. 196v; see *Lettere Familiari*, I, pages 128-129.

9. Giles to Pontano, Rome 3 November 1500, ed. E. Pèrcopo, in *Lettere di Giovanni Pontano a principi ed amici*, Naples, 1907, page 77; see *Lettere Familiari*, I, pages 111-113.

10. Pontano to Giles, Naples 13 December 1500, *ibid.*, page 61; see *Lettere Familiari*, I, pages 113-115.

11. Cariteo to Giles, in Biblioteca Angelica MS 1001, fol. 172v; *Lettere Familiari*, I, pages 133-134.

12. Cited by J. Schnitzer, *Savonarola nach dem Aufzeichnungen des Florentiners Piero Parenti*, Leipzig, 1910, page 299, from P. Parenti, "Istorie Fiorentine," in Florence, Biblioteca Nazionale, MS II. LL., fol. 133.

13. Rome, Biblioteca Angelica, Aut. 7. 2. The volume is printed in Hebrew, in folio, unnumbered, no date or place of publication. Giles' notes run throughout the volume; his signature is on the first and last pages.

14. Giles to Constantino Areniti, prince of Macedonia, Cimino, July-August 1507, in Martène and Durand, III, col. 1246.

15. A. Landucci, *Sacra Ilicetana Sylva*, Siena, 1653, pages 30, 59, 135, quoting from the Lecceto archives now dispersed elsewhere.

16. Both are now in the Biblioteca Casanatense, Rome. Bessarion is Incunabulum 1261; Homer is Incunabulum 1261a.

17. See Appendix 5.

18. Giles to the friars of Lecceto, Cimino, July 1506 in Martène and Durand, III, cols. 1235-1238.

19. L.-G. Pélissier, *De opere historico Aegidii Cardinalis Viterbiensis*, Montpellier, 1986.

20. Giles, in his *Historia XX Saeculorum*, cited by Pélissier, page 31. See the excellent chapter IV, "The Church in time and place," in O'Malley, *op. cit.*, pages 100-138.

21. Giles in his *Dictionarium sive liber radicum*, Biblioteca Angelica (Rome) MS 3, fol. 1r. In his *Historia XX Saeculorum*, Giles praised the Septuagint translation of the Bible but declared that a critical revision of it was necessary; see Pélissier, *De opere historico*, page 48.

22. On Giles and the cabala, see O'Malley, pages 84-89, and the authoritative study of the Christian cabalists, F. Secret, *Les kabbalistes chrétiens de la Renaissance*, Paris, 1964, with particular treatment of Giles, pages 106-126.

23. H. G. Enelow, in *Jewish Encyclopedia* 1 (1901) 219. Scriptural studies since 1901 have reinforced Enelow's statement about Giles.

24. See the letters cited by D. Gutiérrez, "De antiquis Ordinis Eremitarum S. Augustini bibliothecis," in *Analecta Augustiniana* 23 (1954) 163-174, especially page 172.

25. Giles to Amman, Rome, 15 December 1513, in H. P. C. Henke and P. J. Bruns, *Annales literarii*, I, Helmstadt, 1782, pages 195-196.

26. Giles to della Volta, Rome, 8 May 1514, cited by Gutiérrez, page 172; *Lettere Familiari*, II, page 183.

27. Paris, Bibliothèque Nationale, MS Lat. 527 (1), fol. 5r. It is a substantial manuscript of 566 folios, both text and marginalia in Giles' hand. It is described in *Bibliothèque Nationale: catalogue générale des manuscrits latins*, ed. P. Lauer and others, I (Paris, 1939), page 184. For the relationship between it and the Hebrew text, Rome, Bibl. Casanatense 2791, from which it was translated, see F. Secret, *Le Zôhar chez les kabbalistes chrétiens de la Renaissance*, Paris, 1958, pages 34-42.

28. Giles to della Volta, Rome, 14 December 1513, in Biblioteca Angelica MS 688, fol. 48r-49r; *Lettere Familiari*, II, pages 179-180.

29. Paris, Bibliothèque Nationale, MS Lat. 598, fol. 65r. The prayer is printed by Secret, see note 27.

30. See L. Geiger, *Johann Reuchlin, sein Leben und seine Werke*, Leipzig, 1871, pages 306, 399, 404, 437, 450; O'Malley, *Giles of Viterbo*, pages 75-76.

31. Giles to Lefèvre d'Étaples, 11 July 1516, ed. F. Giacone and G. Bedouelle, "Une lettre de Gilles de Viterbe (1469-1532) à Jacques Lefèvre d'Étaples (c. 1460-1536) au sujet de l'affaire Reuchlin," in *Bibliothèque d'humanisme et renaissance* 36 (1974) 335-345; see *Lettere Familiari*, II, pages 209-210.

32. Giles to Reuchlin, his brother Denis, and his sister Elizabeth, Rome, 22 October 1516, in *Illustrium virorum epostolae, hebraicae, graecae et latinae ad Ioannem Reuchlin*, Haguenau, 1519, fol. 50r-51.

33. See G. E. Weil, *Élie Lévita, humaniste et massorète, 1469-1549*, Leiden, 1963, chapters IV, IX-XII.

34. E. Levita, *Massoreth Ha-Massoreth*, ed. and trans. C. D. Ginsburg, London, 1867, page 97. The English translation catches something of Levita's poetic style.

35. Biblioteca Angelica (Rome) MS 3, fol. 1r. This work, entitled *Dictionarium sive liber radicum*, is a translation by Giles of the *Book of Roots*, by the famed medieval Jewish scholar, David Kimhi.

36. British Library, Add. MS 27199, fol. 601r.

37. Munich, Staatsbibliothek, MS Heb. 74 (2), fol. 596r. Surprisingly, the scribe, Levita, misdates his colophon to 1520.

38. Levita's comments are to be found in the introduction to the original manuscript of *Meturgeman*, now in the MS Orient 84, Biblioteca Angelica, Rome.

39. R. Griño, "Importancia del *Meturgeman* de Elias Levita y del MS Angelica 6-6 para el estudio del mismo," in *Sefarad*, 31 (1971) 353-361; *idem*, "Un nuevo manuscrito del *Meturgeman* de Elias Levita," in *Homenajea Juan Prado* (1975) 571-583; *idem*, "El *Meturgeman* y Neofiti (I)," in *Biblica* 58 (1977) 153-188.

40. Levita's comments were at the end of his introduction, and are cited by Weil in *Revue d'histoire et philosophie* 41 (1961) 152.

41. This excerpt from the first page of *Zikhronot*, Munich, Staatsbibliothek, MS Heb. 74, is given in translation by Weil, *Élie Lévita*, page 85.

42. Giles to della Volta, Rome, January 1515, MS Biblioteca Angelica, Rome 688, fol. 53r-v; see *Lettere Familiari*, II, pages 186-187.

43. J. Gribomont, "Gilles de Viterbe, le moine Élie, et l'influence de la littérature maronite sur la Rome érudite de 1515," *Oriens Christianus* 54 (1970) 125-129. While it is the merit of Grill to have discovered the manuscript (see S. Grill, "Eine unbekannte syrische Handschrift in Innsbruck, cod. 401, Bibl. Univ." in *Oriens Christianus* 52 [1968] 151-155), the credit of identifying Giles as its owner and of explaining its significance belongs to Gribomont. For further information on the Maronite delegates at the Council, see N. H. Minnich, "The participants at the Fifth Lateran Council," in *Archivum Historiae Pontificae* 12 (1974) 157-206, especially 166-167.

44. Widmanstetter, *Liber Sacrosancti Evangelii*, Vienna, 1555, fol. [10]. Widmanstetter's statement has been repeated by K. H. Dannenfeldt, "The Renaissance humanists and the knowledge of Arabic," in *Studies in the Renaissance* II (1955) 103.

45. The notes are part of a volume of mixed manuscript and printed items, with the location number, Bibl. Angelica, SS. 11. 11; the notes are item 4. On fol. 26r is

the enlightening comment, "Rudimenta Linguae Arabicae, excerpta per me Fratrem Franciscum Gambassiensem, anno 1519, sic volente ac iubente Reverendissimo D. Egidio Cardinali meo patrono, qui Latinae, Grecae, Hebraicae, necnon Arabicae linguae scientissimus fuit, et mecum multos discipulos his linguis initiavit." Notes on fol. 27v-28r, in Latin and Arabic, are in Giles' hand.

46. Munich, Staatsbibliothek, Cod. Arab. 920. For this manuscript, see J. Aumer, *Die arabischen Handschriften der K. Hof-und Staatsbibliothek*, Munich 1866, page 149, note 920, formerly Cod. Or. 100. Aumer mistakenly dates the dedicatory letter from Florence in Italy; it is from "S. Florent.," that is, Fiorenzo, on the north coast of Corsica.

47. Milan, Biblioteca Ambrosiana, MS Ambrosiana 100 Inf. is a copy of the Koran, Arabic text and Latin translation, copied in 1621 by a Scot, David Colville, from two tomes compiled for Giles when he was cardinal legate to Spain in 1518, and corrected at Viterbo in 1525 by Leo Africanus.

48. Erasmus, *Responsio ad Petri Cursii Defensionem*, in *Opera Omnia*, I, Leiden, 1706, page 1751A.

49. See *Opera Omnia Calcagnini*, I (Basle, 1554), page 101.

50. Giles to della Volta, Rome January 1515, in MS Biblioteca Angelica, Rome 688, fol. 53r-v (see note 42 above). A massive Hebrew Bible, richly illustrated, was a donation from Leo X to Giles, as recorded by Giles on page 1, "Fratris Aegidii Viterbiensis Leonis X munus," and is now in the Biblioteca Angelica, Rome MS Orient. 72.

51. *Scechina e Libellus de litteris hebraicis*, ed. F. Secret, 2 vols., Rome, 1959.

52. *Egidii Romani Eremite de materia celi questio. Egidii Romani de intellectu possibili contra Averoym, questio aurea.* F. Egidius Eremita Viterbiensis castigavit et dedit. Padua, September 1493. *Egidii Romani Comentaria in VIII libros physicorum Aristotelis*, ediderunt Magister Bernardus Granellus Ianuensis et f. Egidius Viterbiensis Eremitanus Sancti Augustini, Padua October 1493.

53. In his commentary on the Sentences of Peter Lombard, Giles propounded the theory that Plato had arrived at a knowledge of the Trinity by reason alone, see Paquier, in *Recherches de science religieuse* 13 (1923) 424-425.

54. For this edition see T. H. Darlow and H. F. Moule, *Historical catalogue of the printed editions of Holy Scripture in the library of the British and Foreign Bible Society* II, London, 1911, pages 576-577.

Chapter 8

Death and Legacy

At the final session of the Lateran Council which closed on 16 March 1517 it was resolved that a general crusade would be proclaimed, and protracted preparations for this purpose were conducted during the following twelve months.[1]

Alarming news about the activities and intentions of the Ottoman Sultan, Selim I, finally galvanized Leo X to action in the spring of 1518. Four cardinals were nominated to the principal courts of Europe, Farnese to Germany, Giles to Spain, Bibbiena to France, and Campeggio to England. Giles reached Barcelona on 13 June and won the admiration of King Charles and the Spaniards as much by his affability as by his preaching. A correspondent writing from Saragossa to Venice on 31 July 1518 commented that "all Spain runs after him to hear his preaching."[2] The legates at Augsburg, Paris, and London fared badly, but to the pope's relief King Charles pledged himself to wholehearted participation in a crusade. Giles returned in a glow of optimism to Italy in May 1519, and on his way to Rome turned aside for the general chapter of the Augustinians at Venice.

General Chapter

The election was nominally an open contest, but in fact it was all but predetermined by Giles. With a view to ensuring the election of della Volta as prior general he had arranged before leaving for Spain in April 1518 that the Signoria of Venice would act as hosts to the general chapter. The diarist Sanudo stated as an accepted fact that the cardinal was coming to Venice on behalf of della Volta.[3] Giles was received "like a Roman emperor,"[4] partly because the Venetians considered him as one of their own, partly because they judged him to be a likely candidate for the papal tiara.[5] Giles, with an accurate eye for artistic effect, joined the magnificent reception not in his cardinal's robes but in the plain black habit of an Augustinian friar. Three days later the general chapter assembled with eleven hundred members of the Order present and della Volta presiding by papal nomination.[6]

The following day he was unanimously elected prior general, and on 13 June forty-one decrees were issued for the spiritual and disciplinary improvement of the Order. They embodied the thirty decrees promulgated at the general chapter of 1507 and were thus an assurance for Giles that his reform program would be continued.

Giles was received by the pope in public consistory on 6 July, amid congratulations on the apparent success of his mission in Spain.[7]

The crusade project faded into the background due to a variety of reasons, not the least of which was the explosive question of the imperial succession. Giles had written from Barcelona on 19 February 1518 in support of Charles' candidature, and although Leo tried every means in his power to withhold the imperial crown from the young monarch he had eventually to accept what seemed unavoidable.

Almost Pope

The friendly relations between Giles and Charles, as also the esteem in which the cardinal was held by Venice, were two of the reasons why he was considered to be *papabilis* after the death of Leo X on 1 December 1521. A fortnight before the conclave opened on 27 December his chances were already highly rated.[8]

At first it appeared that Giulio de' Medici would be elected, but the opposition of the French party and of some of the imperialists ruined his chances.[9] The de' Medici bloc then laid their hopes on Alessandro Farnese but the scrutinies of 1-4 January showed that he could not gain the necessary two-thirds majority. Some observers in Rome asserted that it was Giles' vote and influence which thwarted Farnese, but it is impossible to check the truth of these statements.[10]

The number of votes for Giles rose from two to nine during the first six scrutinies, and the wagers laid on his name at the banks increased.[11] A deadlock had ensued by 4 January when Clerk, the English envoy, wrote to Wolsey that the two most talked of candidates were Cardinal Piccolomini and Giles. He commented that Giles was exceedingly learned, skilled in Latin, Greek, Hebrew, and Aramaic; "he is a wise man and of no faction . . . is of no great kindred, and hath few kinsfolks, and finally amongst us hath no spot, saving that he is a friar."[12]

Theoretically Giles' chances stood high as he was by reputation of unblemished life, noted as a reformer and politically acceptable to almost all parties. Yet, his very detachment from civil and ecclesiastical politics meant that he lacked any one hard-pressure group to push his nomination. Furthermore, his championship of the religious orders at the Lateran Council had alienated the curial cardinals who almost without exception were members of the secular clergy.

The outcome after a further five days was the unexpected election of Adrian of Utrecht. The chagrin of the Roman populace knew no bounds on hearing the result, and Giles was blamed by some for the election of a "barbarian." One satiric sketch circulating in Rome showed Giles' coat-of-arms, three crosses on three hillocks, with Giulio de' Medici hanging from the central cross, Cardinals Armellini and Pucci who were de' Medici's most vocal supporters at the conclave suspended from the other crosses, and kneeling beneath the three figures was Giles exclaiming "It is right and just."[13] Giles, in contrast with many of the other cardinals, was well-treated by the new pope but he never became one of his confidants.[14]

To the relief of all but a handful, Adrian died on 14 September 1523 and was succeeded by Giulio de' Medici as Clement VII on 18 November. During this intensely contested election Giles was one of sixteen cardinals who held out firmly for de' Medici against Farnese.[15]

After the conclave Giles received in common with all the cardinals a benefice of 1,000 ducats, and was granted the see of Viterbo in December 1523.[16] Unfortunately the diocesan archives for his years as pastor of Viterbo have disappeared, but sufficient evidence can be gleaned from other sources to indicate that he exercised his episcopal duties with diligence.[17]

Last Years

The religious revolt in Germany had a painful personal interest for Giles. It was he as prior general who had conferred with Luther when the young German friar came to Rome in 1511 on behalf of the seven dissident friaries. One might suppose from Giles' biographers that he went to his grave without having come to grips with the current momentous problems of grace, faith, justification, and spiritual authority. Certain evidence which has been overlooked conveys a different impression. Clerk, the English envoy at Rome, writing to Wolsey in January 1522 remarked that Giles was loud in his praise of King Henry's book against Luther, which he knew by heart and of which he had made a digest.[18]

The Biblioteca Angelica in Rome has a copy of a polemical work against Luther written by Archbishop Johann Faber of Vienna, and published at Rome in 1522. The frontispiece has an autograph dedication by Faber in which he describes Giles as a doughty defender of the Christian religion.[19]

Since the year 1739 when Montfaucon published a catalogue of one section of the Royal Library at Paris it has been known that Giles possessed three manuscript works dealing with aspects of the Lutheran controversies.[20] This is not the place to discuss their contents except to note that one appears to have come from Giles' pen and the other two are also proof of his interest in the burning questions of the hour.

Montfaucon's catalogue demonstrates that Giles as cardinal retained his interest in the classics, Plato and Aristotle, and scriptural studies. It is well to bear in mind that sixty-four manuscripts listed by Montfaucon represent only a section of Giles' library. A considerable number of his books and manuscripts perished during the sack of Rome in 1527.[21]

The disastrous capture of the city by imperial troops involved him in a curious episode, the only occasion on which he had recourse to arms. Rome was stormed and taken on 6 May, and Pope Clement sought refuge in the Castel Sant'Angelo. He was on the point of surrendering when news arrived that an army of the League, 15,000 strong, which was coming to his relief was at Isola, nine miles from Rome. At the same time Giles collected together a force of 2,000 mercenaries and led them to Isola with the avowal that he wished to be in the forefront of the troops.[22] The indecision of the duke of Urbino took all fighting spirit out of the Leaguers, the army broke camp and dispersed, and Giles made his way back to Viterbo. The fates were unkind to him. Artistically his life should have ended with a flourish as he led the 2,000 soldiers in a hopeless attempt to rescue the pope, but he was not a fighting man and his mercenaries were not of the stuff of martyrs.

During his oration at the opening of the Lateran Council in 1512 Giles declared that reform would come only through a general council. In 1530 when the Emperor Charles pressed for a council the pope reluctantly summoned a secret consistory to discuss the matter. Giles was one of three cardinals who spoke so warmly on its behalf that all twenty-six cardinals present gave their assent to the proposal.[23] However, he did not live to see the council which he so much desired, and in several other ways his final years were tinged with disappointment. In 1531 he and Cardinal Ghinucci got the pope to intercede for the Jews of Portugal threatened with persecution by King Juan III, but the king gave no ear to Clement's appeals.[24]

Augustinian affairs brought him little solace. Della Volta was his choice as prior general in 1519, and Giles himself was nominated cardinal protector of the Order in 1521 after the death of Riario.[25] Such a combination augured well for the spiritual vitality of the Order, but these hopes were not fulfilled. Della Volta began energetically but by 1522 his pace had begun to lag. He proved unequal to the task of coping with the disorganization caused by war, pestilence, and the spread of Lutheranism.[26] Giles had no more than a nominal say in Augustinian affairs and had to witness much of his work being undone. He felt this as a personal disappointment, and wrote sadly in April 1531 that despite all that he had done for the Order he was remembered by no more than four of the friars.[27] He comforted himself with the reminder that Christ had to be content with Peter, James, and John. Among the four friars Giles named Seripando, and it was significant that he was silent about della Volta. The reform program was not resumed until Seripando became general of the Order in December 1538.

The last entry which Giles made in the registers of the Order was an unintentional commentary on his own career as reformer and on his hopes for the future. In that entry of 11 April 1518 Seripando was awarded the baccalaureate in theology. He and six other Augustinians received their degrees and swore in return to do their utmost on behalf of the common life.[28] Giles shortly before his election as prior general at Naples in May 1507 had received Seripando into the Order. At the general chapter he decreed that only those dedicated to reform were to receive degrees. Seripando's career in the Order and at the Council of Trent may be regarded as a fulfillment of Giles' hopes. Seripando died on 17 March 1563 while cardinal legate at the Council of Trent. In his will he referred to the example set for him by Giles.[29]

Giles had died on 12 November 1532.

Notes

1. See *History of the Popes*, VIII, pages 219-231.

2. Sanudo, *Diarii*, XXV, col. 600. For Giles' time in Spain, see the over-enthusiastic account in Signorelli, *Egidio*, pages 70-76. Signorelli indicates a rich series of sources to which should be added the reports of English agents in *Letters and*

Papers, Henry VIII, II, part 2, 1247-1248, pages 1247-1248, 1308-1309, 1325, 1327, 1332.

3. Sanudo, *Diarii,* XXVII, cols. 338-339, May 1519; page 358, June 1519.

4. Rome, Augustinian General Archives, Dd Register 13, fol. 73r, 7 June 1519.

5. For the reasons which decided the Venetian authorities to give a splendid reception, see Sanudo, XXVII, cols. 338-339, May 1519; col. 358, June; for a description of the lavish celebrations, see *ibid.,* cols. 363-368.

6. See documents edited in *Analecta Augustiniana* IX (1921) 29-39. Della Volta in a letter to Giles, Venice, 13 June 1519, stated that it was solely due to Giles' interest that he was elected prior general, *ibid.,* 249.

7. *Il Diario di Leone X di Paride de Grassis,* ed. P. Delicati and M. Armellini, Rome 1884, page 74; Sanudo, *Diarii,* XXVII, col. 473, 9 July 1519.

8. Sanudo, *Diarii,* XXXII, col. 262, 16 December 1521.

9. For an account of the conclave, see Pastor, IX, pages 1-25, and the sources he mentions. Pastor, in his account, concentrates on Giulio de' Medici and Alessandro Farnese, and gives little indication of the way the voters swayed in favor of Giles.

10. Undated and unsigned document from papal archives. The editor in *Cal. S. P. Spanish, 1509-1525,* page 392, states that Giles had been confessor to Farnese for many years and went around to the cardinals relating stories of Farnese's evil past life. One cannot place much credence in this story. See also the reports of Gradenigo, the Venetian ambassador, in Sanudo, XXXII, cols. 385, 413, 416, 433, January 1522.

11. *Cal. S. P. Spanish, 1509-1525,* pages 389-393; Sanudo, XXXII, cols. 384.

12. Clerk to Wolsey, Rome 4 January 1522, in *Letters and Papers, Henry VIII,* III, part 2, pages 86-89.

13. Sanudo, *Diarii,* XXXII, col. 416, 19 January 1522.

14. Giles as one of the poor cardinals was granted an annual pension of 600 ducats, *ibid.,* XXXIII, col. 449, 10 September 1522; all the cardinals were made to shave off their beards, except Giles, *ibid.,* col. 444, 5-6 September 1522. Pastor, IX, page 94, mistranslates Sanudo to mean that Giles was also obliged to shave off his beard.

15. See report of the Florentine ambassador at Rome, 23 November 1523, ed. P. Berti, in *Giornale storico degli archivi Toscani,* II, 1858, pages 122-123.

16. G. van Guilik and C. Eubel, *Hierarchia Catholica Medii Aevi,* III, Munich, 1910, page 335.

17. Signorelli, *Egidio,* pages 88-90; *idem, Viterbo,* III, pages 24-27.

18. In *Letters and Papers, Henry VIII,* III, part 2, page 829.

19. "R.mo in Christo Patri ac Domino Egidio Viterbien. latinae, hebraicae ac graecae doctissimo utriusque philosophiae professori meritissimo, religionis christianae propagnatori fortissimo suo ex animo selectissimo patrono ad candidam censuram Faber dono dedit." The work is entitled *Opus adversus nova quaedam et a christiana religione prorsus aliena dogmata Martini Lutheri,* Rome, 1522. The reference number of this volume in the Angelica Library (Rome) is Aut. 6. 3.

20. B. de Montfaucon, *Bibliotheca bibliothecarum manuscriptorum nova,* II, Paris, 1739, page 779, numbers 14, 28, 29. Number 14 is "Informatio contra Lutheranam

sectam, pro Sedis Apostolicae auctoritate. Puto esse opus Aegidii Cardinalis Viterbiensis," but is now not available. Numbers 28 and 29 I located in Bibliothèque Nationale, Paris.

21. Lucillo Filalteo to Contarini, 8 August 1527, told of the loss of Giles' library at Rome, in *Philaltei libri tres epistolarum*, Pavia, 1564, fol. 41r-42v. The manuscripts catalogued by Montfaucon were from the episcopal library at Viterbo.

22. For this martial episode in Giles' life, see Signorelli, *Egidio*, pages 92-96, and the important reference in Pastor, IX, page 420, overlooked by Signorelli.

23. Jedin, *History of the Council of Trent*, I, page 265; Pastor, X, page 149.

24. H. Graetz, *Geschichte der Juden*, IX, 2nd ed., Leipzig 1877, page 248; Pastor, X, pages 371-372.

25. By papal brief of 9 July 1521, *Analecta Augustiniana* IX (1921) 230-232.

26. Jedin, *Girolamo Seripando*, I, pages 161-165.

27. Giles to Sebastiano di Rimini, Rome 3 April 1531, in Angelica, MS 762, fol. 7v.

28. "11 Aprilis 1518: Fratrem Nicolaum de Tridentino et Fratrem Hieronymum Seripandum lectores, bacchalarios in sacra theologia publicavimus . . . [the other names follow] . . . qui omnes iuraverunt communem vitam se innaturos et eam pro viribus prosecuturos," Dd 12, fol. 157v.

29. See Jedin, *Girolamo Seripando*, II, page 231.

1. Editor of *Egidii Romani de materia celi questio.*
2. Editor of *Egidii Romani de intellectu possibili: contra Averiom questio aurea.*
3. Co-editor of *Egidii Romani Commentaria in VIII libros physicorum Aristotelis.*
4. *Oratio de aurea aetate.*
5. *Oratio prima Synodi Lateranensis.*
6. *Oratio post Tertiam Sacri Lateranensis Concilii.*
7. *Dialogus in honorem Sanctissimi Cesaris Charoli Regis.*
8. *De Ilicetana familia.*
9. *Aegidius Antonio Zocholo et Romanis.*
10. *Libellus de litteris sanctis.*
11. *Scechina.*
12. Occasional Latin poems:
    a) *Aeterne studium laudis et inseri.*
    b) *Ecce opus antistes quod iam celeberrimus egit.*
    c) *Domino Petro memoriae Magistro.*
    d) *Quid vitam studio insanam exercemus inani?*
13. *Caccia de amore bellissima.*
14. Six madrigals to Vittoria Colonna.
15. Tabula propositionum in via Aristotelis ac Temestii.
16. Monumenta et index de Aristotelis erroribus.
17. Sententiarum liber primus usque ad XVII distinctionem ad mentem Platonis.
18. Historia XX Saeculorum.
19. Historiae Heremitarum synopsis.
20. Panegyricus Ilicetanus.
21. De mirabilibus Bononiae (poem).
22. Epigrammata tria.
23. Eclogues:
    a) Paramellus et Aegon.
    b) De ortu Domini.
    c) In Resurrectione Domini.
24. Latin translation of Petrarch's poem, *Canzone alla Vergine.*
25. Cyminia (an Italian novel).
26. Dictionarium sive liber radicum (Hebrew).
27. Tagin (Hebrew lexical work).
28. Traductio et expositio librorum Cabalae et Talmudis (I).
29. Traductio et expositio librorum Cabalae et Talmudis (II).
30. Glossarium Chaldicae linguae et Cabalae vocabula.
31. Vocabula diversorum librorum hebraicorum exposita.
32. Interpretatio et annotationes in librum decem Sephirot et in libros Cabalae.
33. Ben Hacane liber qui Pelia dicitur.
34. Nonnulla opera cabalistica.
35. Liber de revolutione 27 litterarum hebraicarum secundum viam theologicam, in lingua hebrea.
36. De moribus Turcarum.

Appendixes

Editor's Note

The appendixes were compiled by the editor with a view to offering and preserving the richness and diversity of Giles of Viterbo's thought in English translations. Each appendix contains an introduction which gives the background to the selections.

Appendix I contains the funeral oration for Giles of Viterbo by Lorenzo Grana of Roma, bishop of Segni, Italy.

Appendix II offers a collection of sermons:

1) a letter to Antonio Zoccoli and the Roman people which in reality is a sermon and thus placed here;

2) Fulfillment of the Christian Golden Age under Pope Julius II, probably the best example of Giles' erudite scholarship;

3) The Inaugural Oration of the Fifth Lateran Council, in which Giles demonstrates the meaning of councils;

4) a sermon preached in the basilica of Santa Maria del Popolo, Rome, which is a masterful blending of religion and politics;

5) three pastoral sermons.

Appendix III contains a selection of Giles' letters to various people and groups. These letters depict the private life of Giles with his friends, the scholarly life of Giles with his colleagues, and the official life of Giles as prior general of the Order of Saint Augustine.

Appendix IV is Giles' treatise on the monastery of Lecceto.

Appendix V contains the Eclogues written by Giles of Viterbo. These eclogues demonstrate Giles as a renaissance person of his era.

Appendix I

Funeral Oration for Cardinal Giles of Viterbo, O.S.A.

by Lorenzo Grana of Rome,
canon of the Lateran Basilica and bishop of Segni

Most Reverend Fathers, if there should be anyone who perhaps believes that in undertaking this engagement to speak today I am relying upon the practice I have had in those studies at which, in many and varied assignments, I have spent almost all my time, or that relying upon the authority of this outstanding honor, far in excess of any that I have ever deserved, which the Supreme Pontiff Clement VII, with your kind approval, has paid me, or that my motive is the desire for some reward or promotion or fame, I wish that any such person would consider in wisdom and in fairness that I have always adopted a limited and modest lifestyle. If anybody thinks otherwise of me, with an honest and unprejudiced appraisal, he should sweep such a preconceived opinion entirely from his mind.

Can there be anyone so utterly silly, with such self-interest, so unaware of the general opinion and the life of this city, as not to acknowledge the outstanding spiritual and intellectual gifts credited to Cardinal Giles? Honesty, integrity, piety are to be reckoned; his incomparable eloquence is to be proclaimed; his scholarship in all the branches of learning, languages, and disciplines is to be mentioned; the remarkable and fruitful work undertaken in keeping with your honor, authority, and majesty is to be adduced; and finally (to summarize it all in a word) who is there, I say, who cannot see that for due praise of Giles, it would need Giles himself to sing his own praises!

However, there is associated with this onerous undertaking much sadness, commitment, and personal loyalty. I approach it prompted by due reverence. While I wish to avoid the reproach of being ungrateful, I do not deny that it is a thankless challenge I am facing, since I neither wished nor thought it proper that Giles, who quite often in your circle commended highly my slight ability to speak, who counted me among his most dear and close friends, whose spiritual legacy to me, even as he was dying, survives, now that his life is over, should be denied the benefit of this broken and fragile voice. In celebrating his praises I should employ any talent and skill I possess. As far as I am able I shall do so, encouraged by your kindness in being prepared to hear me with calm attention.

Giles was born in the city of Viterbo of parents notable not so much for the distinction of their family name as for their goodness, honor, and piety. Through their labor and effort it came about that their son even from the cradle became accustomed to words and behavior that tended toward the worship and praise and fear of God. Moreover, when he had completed his early education he was handed over to respectable teachers of literature.

There flourished at that time in Viterbo, as in several cities in Italy, academies of *belles lettres* and of the arts where not only the most outstanding local teachers exercised their profession, but outsiders also, distinguished in every branch of learning, who had been drawn there by the qualities of the place, the beauty of the city, the general affluence, and the blossoming of literature. However, it is not my intention to enlarge at all on the antiquity, the eminence, the nobility of that city; for to start with I would have to pay tribute to the whole race, the past ages, and the power of the Etruscans, how they divided the control of the whole of Italy between twelve "colonies" and forever gave their names to the Tyrrhenian and Adriatic seas. From them the Roman Republic derived its ceremonial celebration of triumphs, its sacred rites, its soothsayer, its wartrumpet, and theatrical plays.

Without giving offense I should not omit to mention so many famous fathers of our own time and by silence to consign to oblivion the testimony of King Desiderius about the inhabitants of Viterbo inscribed on a marble tablet in Lombardic script. All of this indeed, even if it is in the common run of praise, also relates to the fame of Giles. His distinction shines forth, however, due to his own good reputation, so that, as antiquity has left as testimony of the famous Marcus Cato the Elder, whatever may have been his birthplace, he seemed destined to make his fortune. He willingly left for others such inscriptions and citations. He was simply content to be counted among those who by their own virtue and industry opened the way for themselves to the highest ranks and offices. It is proved by the evidence of almost all mortal men that in some sense greater commendation and universal acclaim is given to those who succeed in arriving at the highest honors by the hard and narrow path of virtue. This is seen to be the view always of those in this city, always of those of the Christian religion, always of those in your senate, and always, Fathers, this is the same view which you and your associates, renowned for this same reason, have held in the highest esteem.

Although, Most Reverend Fathers, I have always regarded your position not as merely human, but also as truly divine, although we observe in it different levels of virtues, ranks, and talents, yet we feel that not one of you is chosen without heavenly counsel, authority, and intentions, then is placed in the highest position as if by a heavenly hand. People are mistaken if they believe that you whose power closely approaches that of the immortal God himself and is so closely connected with the Vicar of Christ on earth, are in charge of the divine aspect of men, that is, the mind, and that you have by chance, or fortuitously, assumed this massive burden of responsibility. Your authority is from God, established by God, and everything that you are we look up to and admire as of divine origin.

But to return to Giles: amidst his abundance of teachers, with his great talent and by continual study he turned his attention to poetry as well as to prose and even to antiquity itself. In addition he cast his mind toward the religious life, and its vows. Deciding to make those most sacred vows to God, he at the age of twenty-two, under a favoring star and with the happiest auspices, entered the Order of Friars Hermits of Saint Augustine in which, in addition to Christian holiness, he continued to develop all the virtues of a clerical student.

Next he set out for Padua and, O good God, what profit he derived from his studies; how broadly, how high did his voice resound, like that of an eagle in flight! For when he was discussing problems of logic, physics, or theology, sometimes himself replying to difficult questions, sometimes criticizing the opinions of others, he rarely found people who dared to meet him, so to speak, on equal terms. This is not surprising, since he was strongly and abundantly equipped with eloquence. He could clearly, elegantly, and gracefully express the perceptions of his mind and explain them, as it were, down to the finest detail. So that he would not in any way neglect whatever could enhance his style, he also studied Greek literature, adding that as a splendid and necessary basis for his studies.

At that time the superior of the Augustinian Order was Mariano, who came from Genazzano in Lazio and who, without contradiction, would be ranked in the first place as a public speaker. He invited Giles to come from Padua to Rome, and under him Giles' reputation grew and surpassed all that was thought and might be expected of him. Indeed, here in this very place, Rome, with a large number of you in attendance, he debated on new and unfamiliar problems — first in the manner and from the point of view of Plato, followed by that of Aristotle, and in a subtle and forceful speech, now in defense of one view, now of the other — and was decorated by the same Mariano with the doctorate in theology and was appointed as an Augustinian Magister in perpetuity.

Afterward, when Mariano was dead, Giles, drawn by an idea long since conceived in his mind and by the attraction of much-desired solitude for contemplation, chose a retreat on Monte Cimino in the district of Suriano not far from Viterbo, a very secure dwelling-place and very pleasing to him. There he turned his whole attention and thought to the deepest examination of the literature and chronicles of the Jews. How often Giles, when instructed by those who were his religious superiors, would at the earnest request of certain rulers in Italy go and deliver an oration, but yet would groan at being torn away from his tranquil and most praiseworthy kind of life. Nevertheless, realizing that the souls of the good are tested by obedience and patience, he yielded to the command of others rather than to his own comfort and desire.

What is there, Most Reverend Fathers, that I can tell you of his public speaking that you would wish to hear? You yourselves have seen him in a great many places, but especially in this church of Sant'Agostino; you were always present and attended in great numbers when the people of Rome thronged to hear Giles speak on the most sublime questions of the Christian religion, on the mysteries and secrets of the faith, on all the liberal arts; when secular leaders and men of letters thought it shameful, despite their other most important preoccupations, to forego any public appearance of Giles, who spoke with such authority, such elegant fluency and learning, when he moved them to sadness and tears with such gravity and sharpness and severity, when he inveighed against the vices of the age, when vehemently and with an awesome sweep with the sword of his tongue he cut to pieces the monstrosities of heretics. I shall not speak of the hidden realm accessible to Giles alone in his panegyrics.

I shall not mention the grace of his oral delivery, as well as of his voice and finally of his whole body, when he could stimulate all sorts of emotions in kings, princes, and the common people alike, when all his words were drawn from the store of his eminently good judgment, never anything worthless, nothing common, nothing vile. So we were made to realize that a truly godlike man in whom not so much the honeyed streams from the mouth, as they say, of Apollo, or the thunders and lightning so much admired by the Greeks, but the very concept of truth and of the perfect orator, had come down on earth to mortals from that divine mind. In truth, Most Excellent and Virtuous Holy Fathers, I do you a great wrong, and most unfittingly in this place especially, as I review so sparingly and so slightly those matters which should rather be left to silence and unspoken meditation and thought.

Throughout all of Italy when Giles' reputation was flourishing no less for his dignity, his spirituality, his integrity, than for his learning and eloquence, there arose the urgent problem as to who should succeed as prior general of the Augustinian Order after the death of Mariano. A great number who could be candidates for the office of prior general were hungry for it, but Pope Julius II sent a reliable messenger to invite Giles, whose thoughts were far removed from high office, calling him out of his retirement at Suriano, and because of his well-known virtue and prudence, placing upon him the charge of this great Augustinian Order. Do I need to recall how, despite the dignity of his office, he showed such kind respect for his elders; he invited them to meetings; he rewarded with due honors and gave suitable positions of responsibility to those with scholarly talents; he held in veneration those who were outstandingly pious and holy; for the rest he encouraged not just one but all the virtues, with the result that through his unceasing scholarship and nightly studies he enhanced the entire Order of Augustinians, adding to its greatness. The friars, recognizing a leader who was upright, learned, and modest, in whom avarice could not induce greed, nor hatred induce anger, nor the love of pleasure induce sloth, nor ambition induce unworthy hope, were greatly affected by his actions and his principles.

It is useless for rulers to lie awake at night; they labor in vain to restrain by regulations those of modest and perfect virtue who believe they are subject to force, threats, intimidation, or torture. It is difficult to maintain control over men: their minds are not easily subjugated. The person in authority should be good, just, strong, temperate; he should regard it as a worthy object to mould to his own nature and behavior those who are under his power and command.

Pope Julius II saw that these qualities were clearly and constantly exemplified in Giles. Judging him most suitable for the conduct of major negotiations, he appointed him legate to the illustrious Venetian Republic to confer with the most august members of their senate on the question of the Flaminian territories, which he was duly reclaiming for the Church of Rome in accordance with ancient legislation. If in that place — and let me say nothing too severe lest by now peeling back the skin I may seem again to be tearing open Italy's wounds — if those political leaders had agreed to the requests, the persuasion, the advice of Giles, the Adriatic would not have been flooded with the mortal blood of all those killed in that atrocious conflict.

After the death of Pope Julius II and when Leo X de' Medici, to the joy of his contemporaries, was borne to the chair of Peter, when Francis II, the most Christian and powerful king, had led his legions into Italy, and laying low the opposing forces had recovered Milan and all the cities of the Insubrians,[1] and there were fresh moves toward war afoot, that Supreme Pontiff, Leo X, having regard for public calm, sent Giles to Germany to negotiate with the Emperor Maximilian for a concordat among the Christian leaders and the pacification of the Italian states. Giles there judiciously and ingeniously succeeded in soothing and assuaging the anger of Maximilian. On his return to Rome Giles sketched out the words, the wishes, and the views of the Emperor and German princes, as though painting them on a votive tablet for the pope. Leo X, therefore, at that great assembly of cardinals which he held in 1517, with admirable prudence and magnanimity believed that the fate of a man of such virtue, Giles in whom nature had gathered together the culmination of all the virtues, should no longer be left to chance but that he should be picked out for the highest honor. Indeed I seem to see and to hold in my mind's eye that day upon which, on a surprise instruction from Pope Leo, John Matthew Ghiberti, now the most virtuous and excellent bishop of Verona, the splendor of the Augustinian Order and the firm protector and patron of all good men, called Giles to the Vatican.

How great was the joy among men of letters at that time! What great hope and credit accrued to men of virtue when they saw that it was not by odious canvassing of someone else's favor, not through power or arrogance, not by time-serving and servility, but through his own just desserts and his gift for conciliation that Giles had attained to that office — the cardinalate — from which for so long men of literature and science had been excluded, and which was regarded by many as being closed off not by locks that were in any way weak, but by strong bolts and bars, when for many years the minds of great rulers have been filled with the conviction that, because of their merit, men of letters should be provided with heat, food, and encouragement, but that within the limits of their rank they should be confined to certain grades of office so that they might live neither in a totally contemptible state of poverty nor amidst an abundance of riches and power, but should console themselves with a certain whiff and reputation of distinction rather than with the fruit and reward thereof. Only through extreme pressure from rulers are men endowed with the utmost learning and eloquence promoted to the highest honors, and even they are in very small numbers.

No precedent could be found that was more detestable, more abominable, more cruel in its ability to silence such talents. Are persons manifestly devoid of scholarship, destitute of virtue, to be promoted and elevated to the highest ranks, as if some kind of statesmanship can be expected of them, and as a consequence in these critical times for the secular state, are long hours of hard work to be set at nought, is literary merit to be despised, are the other virtues to be confined to squalor, obscurity, and desperation? This Pope Leo would not tolerate, that scion of the de' Medici family crowned by heaven, who also by a renewed sowing of all the heavenly virtues did not fail to enhance that crown. He, I say, would not permit that his own reign should be polluted by such infamous shame, should be corrupted by such a scandalous blemish and disorder.

So he selected men of your Augustinian Order who were notable for every kind of virtue, and honored them with dignity and distinction, so that there remained none among the great number of priests who was not regarded as worthy of such rank, worthy of such a great honor, worthy of the gift and generosity of so great a prince. Just as when we gaze at the sky on a calm night we find delight in the brilliance and profusion and variety of the many stars, so in this gathering,[2] wherever we turned our eyes, the distinguished virtues of Leo X presented themselves to us in their remarkable bounty.

But I realize that my present duty is to speak only of Giles. While he set out to conduct himself in his high-ranking office with all dignity and virtue, paying attention to the mind and opinion and work of the cardinals for the general advantage of the Christian faith as well as dispensing relief for the worthy poor, yet there was no curtailment of his customary gentleness and kindliness, no diminution of his life of toil or of the nature and pursuit of his studies. For all through the day and night as he meditated upon the law of the Lord, he continued his studious and careful researches into secret and obscure volumes of the Jews, which he had heard were kept as a mystery by the scholars of that race.

So valuable was his unwearying toil and generosity — he spared no labor or expense, and sometimes would pay up to 300 gold coins in order to examine and have transcribed even a small volume — in order that countless propositions which that stiff- necked race had the audacity to dispute with us were, through the evidence of their own writings, demonstrated to prove the truth of Christian belief, with enduring benefit to the Christian commonwealth, thanks to Giles. What greater and more profitable day will dawn for us than that on which the records of his genius, and the testimony to his scholarship, all those books on recondite subjects that he wrote with consummate fluency, will be published, read, and admired.

Although it was in this scholarly field that Giles' greatest effort was exerted, yet he never failed to provide practical support for any writer; on the contrary, he habitually welcomed in his home a great many Italians, French, Spanish, and British of small means but rich in knowledge, and he would literally have them fed, give them financial assistance, commend them to the pope, and would endeavor to introduce them to influential people. Indeed he also bestowed upon the university of this city of Rome and on so many outstanding luminaries, the most learned men in Italy, such love and such favor, and invited them with so much kindness to make use of his own work! For he showed himself ready always to provide them with both the useful and the ornamental. In this connection, Reverend Fathers, I shall speak openly, as I feel, for there is nothing that is more likely to create a bond between the minds of good men than courtesy, clemency, the gracious response and liberality in giving.

What if people feel that your work is half-hearted or find you irascible and difficult? They judge ill of your attitude to themselves, and if at times they receive presents, they do not accept them in a kindly and joyful spirit. To these people Giles poured out thanks profusely while they made use of his writings and his patronage; indeed he would wisely say that on their account he was duly offered an opportunity to exercise the functions of his office, and duly to make investments, when, in acting as patron to good men, he invested his own endeavors which, as befitted the nobility of his rank, he could deny to none who sought them.

Through the performance of such duties under Pope Leo the authority of Giles increased, and among yourselves, very Reverend Fathers, his service was no less whenever he delivered an opinion with gravity and honesty, his attention not distracted in either direction, and what he considered was for the good of the Christian commonwealth he would assert with the greatest candor and freedom of spirit.

All of you he venerated as imperishable authorities, he praised, and heaped every honor upon you. Therefore when envoys were to be chosen from among your number to draw up an accord among the rulers of Christendom, it was your wish that, with the authority of the same Pope

Leo, Giles should go to Spain to the then King Charles, now most auspiciously Emperor. That prince welcomed Giles with kindness as befitted his rank, full of admiration for his mind, his wisdom, and his eloquence. Deeply moved also by Giles' piety and holiness, he earnestly requested of him, since he had never heard anything more pleasing and agreeable than the Augustinian's everyday natural way of speaking, that he stimulate an audience on some public occasion.

Giles kindly agreed, and on a stated day, after first having extolled the virtue of Charles and the eminence of his royal ancestors, Giles then spoke of the needs of a Christian state, that is, the complete uprooting of foul heresy by treading on the asp and the basilisk, and eagerly going to war against the Turks. With such fire and fervor of spirit he urged peace and friendship and agreement, that his utterances seemed more than human, and he had a remarkable effect on the mind of Charles and of all the nobles who were present.[3] O happy soul, by whose gravity and eloquence princes were bowled over and could come to a clear judgment of the Roman church, seeing that it sent senators of such virtue to foreign nations with the ability to convert not just the minds of private individuals but whole kingdoms and provinces to the true religion, faith, and worship of God.

Here I am deliberately passing over his return to Rome, his business duly concluded, laden with gifts from Charles, when he experienced the kindness and liberality of Leo, and on the untimely flight of that pontiff from this city,[4] how well Pope Adrian VI acknowledged and proclaimed Giles' virtues; and how at the papal consistory held after the death of Adrian Giles consistently gave the view that the cardinal vice-chancellor Giulio de' Medici, whom we now venerate as Clement VII, was worthy of supreme power and sovereignty on earth. Although Giles supported his view with the utmost effort, zeal, and authority, there were still many of you who looked to Giles, not only thinking that he should be promoted in rank, but you were even making remarkable efforts in that direction, with the complete agreement of Cardinal Giulio de' Medici himself, who seemed not at all averse to that idea.

I also forbear to describe his achievements amidst the calamitous and pitiful destruction of this city. For although due to ill-health Giles had retired to the region of Piceno, where he was immersed in ceaseless study, vigil, and toil, when information reached him that by the activities of an impious and abominable patricidal gang churches and altars were being desecrated, corpses snatched out of tombs, the bones of the saints trampled underfoot and thrown around, houses plundered, homes set on fire, fathers of families killed, infants slaughtered before their parents' eyes, venerable leaders burned and butchered, nobles bound in chains, priests on all sides murdered, all the nobility subjected to horrible torture, and the supreme pontiff and cardinals besieged in Castel Sant'Angelo, he said: "Shall I, Giles, oblivious of my position, continue to enjoy the safety of this place while the most holy vicar of Christ is under siege? Can I under such circumstances spend my time here at liberty while my most earnest and prudent colleagues continue under attack? I will not tolerate or endure it."

So without any delay, not only through messengers but in his own person, he called together the people of that most loyal and excellent province. He speedily assembled forthwith two whole legions of the bravest men of the Firmani, the Aesinati and the Esculani, and the flower of all Italy, which once long ago had taken up arms to liberate this same city during the consulship of Marcus Tullius Cicero. Giles himself with incredible swiftness set out by a side road to the meeting of leaders, whom he had heard were intending to discuss the crisis on a particular day. When he discovered that they were deeply divided by conflicting opinions, some considering that the right thing to do was to head for Rome and make an outright bid to save the supreme pontiff, others that they should stay put, he urged them in forcible terms not to waste time in consultation and hesitation in such a grave crisis which demanded swift and immediate resolution. If they were unwilling to commit their entire army, they should allow him personally to go ahead with the soldiers. His intention was to mount an assault on the city, and, since he knew that his own men were eager for battle, to attack the enemy with great force and risk their luck. It was a unique opportunity for which all brave men could encounter death with the highest commendation. If he should perish with his two legions, their forces would not for that reason be reduced, or their authority at all shaken. But if, as was his hope, he succeeded in breaking in and, with God's good help and with good luck, set the battle in motion, then if they agreed they should send forward their reinforcements and move rapidly to certain victory.

Notwithstanding this proposal, they clearly expressed their objections to Giles' proposals and to concerning themselves either with the fate of the city or with the plans of people who, not for Italy's advantage, thought it wise to attack from an unfavorable position and put themselves at such risk. They ordered their troops to advance no further. Giles returned sadly to his own people, raising his eyes and hands to heaven, saying with tearful entreaty, "You, Peter and Paul, great patrons, I call upon you as witnesses today that with these decurions and chief centurions and centurions, for the sake of your city, your altars and churches, for the sake of Christ's Vicar and most Reverend Fathers subjected to iniquitous and undeserved dangers, I have not taken flight, I have avoided no risks, I have sought out death freely and avidly when it was necessary and not offered to me. I beseech you, whose authority prevails in heaven, guard, protect, and defend Clement VII, in whose life and wisdom rests the only hope of the Church, together with those excellent Fathers, and by a mighty miracle of yours, rescue them from the hordes of the impious." After that, in many splendid words he commended the loyalty, bravery, piety, and diligence of the soldiers and ordered them back to their home territories, each to protect his own city and buildings.

With what acclaim then shall we celebrate, with what words shall we honor, with what token of gratitude shall we extol this immense virtue and marvelous breadth of mind? For it was not in prosperous and safe times, but amidst affliction and despair, not by great sums of money or any hope of booty, but by his eloquence alone that Giles had drawn together those legions and with such force of mind and courage that he prevailed on them to follow him to battle and to possible death.

In limiting my speech to this one remarkable instance of his magnanimity, I shall only add this thought — that out of all the moral virtues, none is to be found of which Giles does not provide many outstanding examples. Certainly in those that relate to the sacredness of the Christian religion, who were more diligent, who more vigilant than he? For amidst such important activities he never neglected the sacred ministry, and to the Almighty God toward whom alone he had directed his whole mind, he never ceased to offer the perpetual sacrifice of the Mass. On the contrary, when experiencing the bouts of sickness that affected and almost wore him out, he was not beguiled by the vain hope of living, by which almost all mortal men are captivated, but was ever watchful and prepared and ready with his lamp lit to meet Christ approaching as he went into the wedding feast.

So that he would not be held back by any thoughts of human affairs, he drew up a will two years before his death, making over his whole property to three friars of your Order most deserving of every commendation, in whose probity, justice, and integrity he trusted. The property consisted of no great or very splendid household effects and a small amount of money, for he lived in an extremely frugal manner with his well-behaved household servants, while sparing no expense in acquiring books and in helping the poor, in furnishing a suitable pleasure garden in the Campo Marzio for the learned conferences of his friends, and in restoring the dilapidated church of San Matteo,[5] under whose patronage he was named a cardinal. But he did pass on to the care of those three friars his treasures of learning — those famous writings — and the care of his dear sister and of his beloved servants. So, rather late in his own estimation (for he had reached the age of sixty-three), but too early for the Christian commonwealth or for your Order, and too soon for the needs of our times, he was overcome by a burning fever and commending himself to Christ with his whole mind, he breathed forth that godlike spirit.

This, Most Reverend Fathers, is what I have, as it were, compressed into a small space and squeezed in and kneaded down concerning your sublime and magnificent Giles, whose achievements you can judge to be all the greater and more splendid in that from such an amount that is worthy of praise you know that in my address much has been left out and abridged, for I am barely carrying out my sad and pious duty.

Very rightly in every state, commonwealth, empire, and especially in those of our religious orders, the perpetual and abiding memory is cherished of those who through their spiritual and intellectual gifts have shone forth brilliantly by their skill in letters, scholarship, and language. Those who have combined honor, probity, and holiness with great learning and eloquence, who have behaved humanely, liberally, and generously toward all good men, who through their personal virtue have been held dear by kings, peoples, and nations, opening the way for themselves to the highest honors, who have not hesitated to put their life in serious danger for the liberty and safety of all, who throughout whole days and nights have pored over, preserved, and preached the law of the Lord, then Cardinal Giles, in whom we beheld all these virtues gathered together in one man, will be venerated by all posterity, and cherished eternally.

Your Order, the Augustinians, together with the whole Christian commonwealth, will extol him, and never in any age or time growing old will he be celebrated as other than an undying, ever- present, auspicious, and propitious inspiration for all good and learned people.

Translated by Mary Brennan

Notes

1. Insubrians — the most powerful Celtic peoples of Gallia Cisalpia in Northern Italy; allies of Hannibal (218-201 B.C.). The Insubrians were finally subdued in 196 B.C. but were granted Latin rights in 89 B.C. and full Roman citizenship forty years later. See Encyclopedia Britannica, micropaedia, vol. V (1982) 372.

2. Lateran Council V.

3. This oration was published as *Dialogus Reverendissimi in Christo Patris Domini Aegidii S.R.E. presbyteri cardinalis in honorem sanctissimi Cesaris Charoli regis catholici Hispaniarum utriusque Sicilie dominini nostri* at Barcelona, 1518-1519. A copy listed by G. W. Panzer, *Annales typographici* 9 (Nuremberg, 1801) 300 (10) as being then in the Scheurl Library, Nuremberg. Much of the Scheurl collection has been sold or dispersed since 1801, some of it going to the Stadtbibliothek Nuremberg, but the Giles oration is not now in the Scheurl Library — see F. X. Martin, "The Writings of Giles of Viterbo," in *Augustiniana*, 29 (1979) 159.

4. In 1527.

5. San Matteo in Merulana.

Appendix II

Sermons

A Letter to Antonio Zoccoli and the Roman People

This text of Giles of Viterbo (written between 1503-1508) is edited from what seem to be the only two extant versions. Found in manuscript in the Biblioteca Nazionale (MS V.F.20, fols. 256r-281r), Naples, and in the Biblioteca Angelica (MS lat. 1001, fols. 11r-23v), Rome. The Naples and Angelica codices are collections of Giles' correspondence, and the discourse on man's dignity is presented in the form of a letter, addressed "to Antonio Zoccoli and the Roman People." In its structure and content, however, the discourse much more closely resembles a formal discourse or sermon than it does the other "epistolae familiares" among which it is found. What is particularly distinctive about the present text is that it relates the theme of man's dignity to the dignity and destiny of the city of Rome.

The present discourse falls into three rather distinct parts. The first part treats of man's divinization through the power of divine love, his responsibility to respond to God's love especially with love for his neighbor, and the evil consequences of living without love. The second part of the discourse is a long transition from the theme of man's divinization to that of the destiny of Rome; Elisha is here presented as indicating man's divinization in his very name and as being a type of Saint Peter. The last part deals with the destiny of Rome, particularly as this was providentially mediated by Peter and his successors, including Julius II. Giles relates the last part to the first by recalling that Rome was chosen by God in love and that Rome must respond with love. This last part is animated by a bold rhetoric, as the nuptials between humanity and divinity are specified in the form of the nuptials between Rome and Christ.

The religious message of this "letter" to Zoccoli and the Roman people coincides with Giles' general viewpoint on Christian reform. The purpose of reform is not to change religion in any of its practices or beliefs, but to transform the individual Christian. "People must be changed by religion, not religion by people." Charity effects the transformation which Giles saw as central to reform.

Giles seems specifically to relate this present "letter" to the question of reform in his final apostrophe to Julius II. The discourse ends with a brief appeal to Julius II to fulfill the exalted duties of his office. This appeal can be interpreted as an early expression of Giles' concern for the reform of the Church under papal leadership. It also seems to indicate that Giles hoped the discourse would be brought to Julius' attention by Zoccoli. If this is the case, it helps explain why the discourse contains nothing personal to Zoccoli beyond the first two sentences, in contrast with Giles' other letters to Zoccoli, which are very personal and direct.

For more background on this "letter" and for the critical text, see John W. O'Malley, S.J., "Man's Dignity, God's Love, and the Destiny of Rome. A Text of Giles of Viterbo," Viator 3 (1972) 389-416.

203

Divinization through the Power of Divine Love

I received your two letters, which I have read over often because, even though they are brief, they exhibit great love. I myself am accustomed to call such love, maybe somewhat ineptly, the salt of all, since everything is tasteless without it. It is this love that our Lord gave his heroic disciples and, unless I am mistaken, this was all he gave them. He came *to dwell with us in Kedar and other lands* (Ps 120:5) for no other purpose than to bring us this love from heaven. This great power of love, a power meant for heavenly beings, is it not marvelous that it comes to humans? *God led forth the Lord from Olympus*, that is, he made him human and thus humans became gods in this same love. And they were all children of the most high, *as many as received him*, precisely because they received him through this love. *They were born not from the will of the flesh* (like the Aristippians and their children born of marriage[1]), *nor yet from human will* (like the Stoics and those who were established in power by eminent men), *but from God.* They were born of love, reborn *by water and the Holy Spirit* (Jn 1:12-13), cleansed in a living stream, whereby they are filled with the life of God: of the Spirit and in the Spirit, who is divine love, and of the Son and Father.   •

You may wonder how it can be that people are children of God. But just as what is born of a human being is human, of deer, deer, and of peacock, peacock, in the same way what is born of God is also God. What, then, becomes of the human nature, the flesh and blood, as they say, when it changes into God? In other words, does it become God and is God produced? But why do you marvel that humanity becomes God? Was not God made human and *the Word made flesh*? For if God, who has in himself the highest existence, becomes human, why then should not humanity, whose final resting place is in God, be changed into God?[2] Imperfect things are drawn to perfection by something in nature that stimulates them. But they are born of God through love, not nature. And why not nature? Because *the Word was made flesh and dwelt among us* (Jn 1:14), and he begot us when he was conceived in our hearts in a way very different from how children are generally begotten. For children are conceived to be born, while Christ dwells within us that he might beget us even before he is conceived by us. Lying hidden within us, Christ draws out of his very self seeds of fire. For he is stone and flint; and, as you know, "seeds of fire are hidden in the veins of flint."[3] Thus when Christ knocks out sparks, he kindles the soul and fans the heart into flames. *How our hearts burned within us on the way*, said those journeying to Emmaus.

Those who are led by the Spirit of God, says the Apostle, *these are God's children* (Rom 8:14), that is, those born of divine love *are born of God.* But how so? Because *the Word was made flesh*. He was made such, you see, so that by dwelling in us, he might enkindle fire and love within us, and so that by Christ's assumption of mortal nature, we might be born again immortal. But the cause of all this is love, which is the very reason God became man, as I said. A young woman seeks the kiss of this love in a wedding song,[4] not a Hymenian or Talassian song of a Sabine's rape,[5] but the kiss of the eternal Father. And she calls the eternal Word to a human marriage, hoping and imploring that, after our parents were banished by God because of their guilt,[6] God might one day allow their exiled human descendants to be joined to this spouse.

God promised this marriage to our father Adam when he said the woman would crush the serpent's head.[7] This is understood of the Virgin Mary whom Jeremiah sees encircling a man with the Hebrew letter Mem,[8] closed, as it were, against nature, saying by this that she is the gate closed to the east, through which we approach the one Lord. Ezekiel saw this young woman who conceives.[9] Isaiah saw her. For when she delivered, *a child was born and a son was given to us* (Is 9:6). He promised this marriage to Noah after the destruction of the world; to Abraham, and to his son and grandson; to Moses after crossing the Eritrean sea; finally to David, that shepherd called from his sheep and pen to the kingship and governance of a people; to David who composed the loveliest songs of his language, singing of the glory of this marriage and bridegroom.[10]

David's son, however, played more sweetly, inasmuch as he, more freely than anyone, was allowed to be at leisure. Solomon sang his Canticle, a fully divine and secret work, and has a much sweeter vision of holy and chaste love than does Catullus, with his obscene and sordid love. In the Canticle, courting games of groom and bride are celebrated, as well as their marriage, which was promised by the highest God and desired by people from the creation of the world. In the Canticle are found the pleasures of husband and wife, the kisses, the sighs, the embraces, and the most chaste and ardent love of young women. In sum, everything that occurs in it occurs through love, because love is the source of all passion.

Always moved by love, then, the divine goodness *created heaven and earth* (Gn 1:1): pure intellects in heaven and intellects enclosed and covered with flesh on earth. By love, the supreme God reconciled the fathers with himself, considering them worthy of divine friendship, comforting and embracing them. To some, God revealed the future, to some he gave the law. But he never rested until he sent down his own Son, whom he made mortal. He decreed that he should die a cruel and wretched death, nailed to a cross, so that enlightened mortals might understand for once just how great was the love of the supreme God. He gave his immortal Son to be killed in order that mortals might find life. Witness the extent to which love holds sway in heaven! One remembers only rarely when a person suffered death for another; nevertheless, no one doubts that people love. But divine love is so much greater than human love because it compels God to endure more things and more unworthy things for mortals than mortals are accustomed to endure for each other. In love he descended to us and in love we must ascend to him. In love he died and was cut off from the living that we might live, joined to that love.

Since God endured so much for our sake, what repayment is required? That we, perhaps, should die in turn for his sake? Actually no. Indeed God is satisfied with an easy repayment and requires only one thing.[11] He does not command many things; there are not many commands in the gospel, not many things people must do. *Only one thing is necessary* (Lk 10:42) according to God's word. Thus there are not many things, but one. And what is that one? I do not understand the one thing you command. I do not want a mortal interpreter. "I pray *you* to sing":[12] Tell me the one thing you command. For your easy law commands only one thing. Speak, then, and I will listen to what it is. There is none so impotent that he cannot do this one thing. What, then, is this command?

Hear the voice of the Lord, if you are (as we believe) his sheep.[13] It is his voice from heaven, by Jove! So hear the following! *This is my command, that you love one another as I have loved you.* Therefore, if you are grateful to God, if you wish to pay back the debt, if you do not despise his wounds, his cross, and his death, then take care to manifest love. Yet not just any love: but *love one another as I have loved you* (Jn 15:12). The meaning of divine love is now revealed; wherefore, by emulation, let us love one another and the divine goodness itself!

The Lord gave this command twice to his long-time companions, and when they loved, when he made them inflamed with love, he said at once, *Now I no longer call you servants, but friends* (Jn 15:15); and again, *You are the salt of the earth* (Mt 5:13), as if to say, "The love inside of you will serve and preserve all things." The entire world, already rotting for many centuries from vices and errors, will now smell sweet through you. Your salt will not only keep all things from rotting, but will cause to appear the sweetest and tastiest things of our creator. And by the supreme law, what hatred had made detestable, love will make pleasant and delightful. Those who had fallen from heaven when hatred took their wings away, now rise again to heaven because love has restored their wings. Finally, all things that had perished by hatred's robbery will be restored by love's renovation.

Certainly, just as some say that salt causes souls to crave pleasure, so I affirm, not without some sense, that through salt, love is bestowed upon those called to divine hope. For if sumptuous meals, elegant meals and even, if you will, pontifical meals lack salt, nothing is more unsavory, nothing more unpleasant, nothing, in short, more tasteless than these meals.[14] By Hercules! The Apostle affirms the same thing about love: *If I should have all virtue, enough faith to move mountains, enough kindness to give all my goods to the needy, enough patience and fortitude to give my body to be burnt in flames, but have not love, I am still nothing* (1 Cor 13:1-3). This love can do all things. When it is absent, mortals are nothing; but when it is present it makes them immortal gods. For the sons of God are called gods since like arises from like.

Receive this oracle: *Love your enemies that you might be children of your Father* (Mt 5:44-45). Behold, you are made a god! And lest you suppose Christ meant children of a mortal or terrestrial father, he added, *who is in heaven*, as if to say: "Take up each wing of love." These twin wings would be yours, if "twin doves should by chance appear."[15] If she were the Father's daughter, she would recognize these birds as God and immortal love, which lead her "to the ethereal heavens."[16] Further, this salt was what gave so much power to the last supper, so that the mortals who reclined at table arose immortal and *will taste*, to use the Lord's words, *death no more* (Jn 8:52).

Do these preserved and remaining seeds drive away death from those who return to love and grace through the Eucharist? Scripture is not silent, for when the meal was removed, the Lord explained that seeds were scattered and that foundations arose, and so new crops and new buildings — *a new heaven and new earth* (Rv 21:1), as he says. I will love the seed he cast out. When some Greek commanded salt to be cast into ditches, he wished to be thought foolish, although he was not foolish at all.[17] Thus the Lord is to be made known by foolishness, as the Apostle writes.[18] But really nothing is less foolish. The *salt of the earth* began and thus crops soon appeared in the whole world and the heavenly granaries burst with the abundance of harvest. Never lay the earth so rested that the reaper could not fill up his carts and chests;[19] he waited for the name of this seed, so fertile, this newly discovered seed for new crops. And so when the meal was served, as John recounts,[20] it happened. I tell you just as he said it: *Let the earth listen and hear, O heavens, what I speak: You once were earth* (Dt 32:1), *but now are salt of the earth* (Mt 5:13), *and you, heavens, will be called the glory of God* (Ps 19:2).

It continues in the Gospel, *I give you a new commandment*, that is, the salt, that new seed, which I sow in you, my furrows. But why this seed? *That you might love one another. And this will show that you are my disciples* (Jn 13:34), if you keep the love I planted. All the volumes of Holy Scripture extol this love on every page, so that they seem to be written for no other reason than for this love. *Love*, says Solomon, *covers all sins* (Prv 10:12), and again, *Better to be invited to a meal of cabbage with love than of fatted calf with hatred* (Prv 15:17). In the book of Wisdom also, it is written by Philo, *Oh how sweet is the pure generation with love!* (Wis 4:1).

Speak, young woman, of the greatest gift of marriage. *He set*, she says, *love within me* (Sg 2:4). On the inside she had nought of civil virtues, but the bridegroom, the wisest maker of the world, *filled her with love* (Sg 3:10). But you, most fortunate woman, what ring did you receive? Jeremiah spoke only of *the love of your wedding* (Jer 2:2). But for how long does this ring endure? Jeremiah again: *I have loved you with an everlasting love* (Jer 31:3). O love, much more powerful than a magnet! By such great rings, this hidden love draws six other rings. From every area of the world, this love snatches reluctant souls into heaven with divine chains. *I have drawn them*, says the Lord through Hosea, *with the chains of love* (Hos 11:4). Why are these chains unable to be broken? For the experienced wife tests every power, and even *great floods could not extinguish this love* (Sg 8:7). By this love, the apostles became like gods!

Paul writes to you in Romans when he proclaims, *The love of God was poured out into our hearts* (Rom 5:5). He also asserts that *God commends his love to us* (Rom 5:8). Later Paul shows that this love is not weakened by any fortune. *What, then*, he says, O Romans, *will separate us from the love of Christ?* (Rom 8:35). Wherefore he closes his letter with this admonition, *that they should love one another in fraternal charity* (1 Tm 6:11). He says the same thing to Timothy: *Pursue love*, for he had written earlier that *love alone is the end of the commandment* (1 Tm 1:5). He encouraged the Philippians: *Let your love grow more and more* (Phil 1:9). He told the Colossians: *Above all, put on love* (Col 3:14). He commanded the Ephesians *to be rooted in love* (Eph 3:17) and (it is right to add) to be always growing in love. He demonstrated the reason to the uncomprehending Galatians, saying that the Holy Spirit is love.[21] He urged this love upon the Hebrews.[22] He prayed that the Thessalonians might embrace it.[23] Finally, he showed the Corinthians that love is the one thing compared with which there is nothing better, nothing more desirable, nothing, in the end, more divine bestowed by God upon mortals.[24] When love is taken away, everything is lost; when it is present, everything is gained.

Should I mention Peter, who was asked thrice by the Lord whether he loved, and thrice claimed that he did.[25] Although a simple fisherman, did Peter not write that *continual love ought to be maintained because love alone covers a multitude of sins* (1 Pt 4:8)? I pass over briefly the First Letter of John, where it can be seen that he praised love again and again, and investigated all the things commendable about it. Is it not in this epistle that John dares to call love not simply divine, but God? — *God is love* (1 Jn 4:16). Other virtues lead to God, but this virtue, through which the other virtues tend toward God, is God himself. Thus nothing sadder can happen than when this one virtue is lost, about which even God mourns: *You have abandoned your first love* (Rv 2:4). He mourns again in Matthew. And in Luke, the Lord himself mourns, *You neglect justice and love* (Lk 11:42). In Matthew, foreseeing the misery of our time, Christ says, *Alas, alas for those times, when the love of many shall grow cold* (Mt 24:12).

Am I tediously drawing out this letter by redundant superfluity? No, for while this love remains, the world will remain; when it departs, the world will perish. *Heaven and earth will pass away* (Mt 24:35), as Matthew, Mark and, many centuries earlier, Haggai wrote and prophesied.[26] The preservative salt arose over time from the sea, and the sea corresponds to love. For as the Gentiles say, "Venus arose from the sea."[27]

Sacrifices that love does not render acceptable offend rather than placate God, who considers the soul. Indeed, first the soul is considered by heaven, to see whether it is loving, and only then are the sacrifices placed on the altar. *The Lord regarded Abel and his offerings, but did not regard Cain* (Gn 4:4-5). First he regarded Abel and then his offerings. That is, if offerings move God at all, they do not move him of themselves, but only when they are joined to flames of love. You good priests who rise early in the morning to perform prayers and rites to our God — the flame of love should first burn in your soul. If this is not the case when you prepare the flour and headbands, you are performing a useless work. *It is useless for you to rise before daybreak* (Ps 127:2). You obtain salty flour without salt, a tasteless sacrifice. As Job asks, *Who can eat a tasteless meal?* (Jb 6:6).

You say you make bread with salt and grain. But *your salt is tasteless* (Mk 9:49), as Mark mentions, derived from that statue into which Lot's wife was turned. This is the salt of those whose knowledge is bright, but whose life is dark. They understand very well, but live very poorly. Surely they have a certain salt, full of flavor in their many writings and disputations. With the wisest teachings they encourage many "to live well and blessedly."[28] But since they are never moved by their own teachings, their salt is an unmovable statue. Holy Moses and Aaron cursed them thus in their song: *May they become unmovable as stone* (Ex 15:16).

For every action of mortals lies still and stiff and cannot raise itself to the blessed life unless love adds wings. But with this love they fashion twin wings, one that carries the prayers of mortals to heaven, another that carries gifts from above to mortals. Jacob saw *angels ascending and descending a ladder* (Gn 28:12). Why did he have so clear a dream except to reveal to people that the road to heaven is only by the steps of love? For while the soul is exiled on earth, human holiness is brought to God and divine goodness to man, as if by messengers sent to and fro. By these messengers, then, our action is taken to heaven, and by them celestial gifts are transmitted to us.

If someone grows stiff in a faded love, even though he may have some salt, it is frozen, hard and unmovable and is thus unable to rise up. Turned back into the heaviest statue, it cannot be moved from its place and be lifted up or forward by any power. It can no more be moved than a huge quantity of iron. One finds this in Sirach. For when that which cannot be done is explained, he says that *it is easier to carry salt and a piece of iron* (Sir 22:18). Here clear mention is made about the heaviness of salt and how unsuitable it is to carry into the heights. This is also expressed in Wisdom: *The dryness of thorns and a pile of salt* (Zep 2:9), where he means the frozen thirst for riches, a thirst connected to an empty notion of love. It is shown there in a marvelous way how this thirst presses and weighs down the person held and possessed by these diseases.

But in Colossians, the Apostle speaks of another kind of salt that should be possessed in every action. Is this not the salt of love, friendship and grace? *Let your speech*, he says, *be always in grace, seasoned with salt* (Col 4:6). This means that whatever you shall say, charity and love ought never to be lacking in your conversation; and thus it will be pleasing to both God and men. Matthew calls this holy salt the *salt of the earth*, while he calls the other kind useless. *If salt becomes flat, what will restore its saltiness?* (Mt 5:13) he asks. Similarly, the philosophy and teaching that people gained from research was called empty and useless by the Apostle, your fellow Roman citizen, for whom it is inconsistent that you who enjoy greater things should envy Roman glory. In Colossians, he writes something I want you to consider. For he says in an earlier chapter that *we have been taken from darkness and brought into the kingdom of the Son of God's love* (Col 1:13). And in the following chapter, he discusses what opposes this holy love. Earlier he had spoken of the first salt. Now he considers the second salt, which is unfit for the altar, inimical to God and contrary to religion: *See that no one deceives you by philosophy and empty deceits according to the tradition of men, according to the elements of this world, and not according to Christ* (Col 2:8).

Thus far the Apostle. The Lord had said, *If salt becomes flat, what will restore its saltiness?* Therefore there is a certain salt that becomes flat and useless. Now the Apostle says that philosophy is empty, that every study which does not attain the human end is empty.[29] This end is God, *the Alpha and Omega* (Rv 1:8), Christ Jesus. Therefore that wisdom that does not savor Christ is empty salt and unfit for any use, but must be thrown out, rejected and *trampled by men* (Mt 5:13). Those who trample it truly deserve to be called human since they do not believe everything from the deceitful senses, like those philosophers who barely lift themselves above beasts in their judgment. For this reason, I do not see how they can be called human, when, with the divine power of reason set aside, they accept nothing other than what brutish sense suggests to them. We, however, seek *the things that are above and not the things on the earth* (Col 3:1-2) Nor do we wish to be so addicted to sense that we consider non-existent whatever the eye does not see nor the ear hear. But that is just how they consider it who desire portions of irrational sense. They seem not to want to be rational, nor to be human, but rather relatives of the beasts and sheep. It is only right that their brutish and empty salt is trampled by people. And may it also be driven away with boos and hisses by those who listen to reason!

Both kinds of salt are found in Mark, the good and the tasteless. *Salt is good*, he says, *but what if it becomes tasteless, how will you season it?* (Mk 9:49). For every sacrifice is seasoned by salt. Mark has only these words, but Luke adds more. Since there are two kinds of sinners, some have guilt in the body and others have guilt outside the body. The former rot from pleasure and lust, the latter are slaves to honor and power. Both despise the Spirit and holiness; both are joined to things that waste away and die, to flesh and blood, as Jesus says. By salt, nevertheless, flesh is usually preserved from both corruptions of the body, within and without. They call the one our earthly corruption, the other, the corruption of the dunghill (I am not ashamed to use the words of my gospel text).[30] Thus Luke says: *Salt is good. But if it becomes flat, what will restore its saltiness* (Lk 14:34), or, as another text has it, *how will it be seasoned?* (Mt 5:13).

Now notice the two kinds of flesh to be seasoned with apostolic salt. For he continues: *Neither is it useful for the earth, nor for the dunghill* (Lk 14:35). By the latter should be understood the filthy sins of the body, which turn their practitioners into brutes. Thus Joel ridicules them: *Mules rotted in their own dung* (Jl 1:17). By the former should be understood those others who forget heaven and follow after the wealth and pride of the earth, wherefore it is not unjustly called earth. *Why are you proud, earth and ashes?* (Sir 10:9). But the divine word everywhere detests flesh that lacks salt as abhorrent to holy things. Thus Ezekiel admonishes: *You were not washed with water unto health, nor were you salted with salt* (Ez 16:4). And the book of Judges affirms the same: *It was destroyed that he might sprinkle salt in it* (Jgs 9:45). Also Job complained that *it was not seasoned with salt* (Jb 6:6).

And in Sirach, one reads that *he poured out frost like salt* (Sir 43:21). Things without salt and love are fittingly compared to frost, for what is far removed from fire becomes frozen. Therefore, everything separated from love is completely frozen, since love is called a flame and a fire: "It is a soft flame at the core,"[31] he says. And again: "I recognize the remnants of an ancient flame."[32] And once more in the same work: "And he is weakened by a blind fire"[33] and "My fire, Amynthas."[34] Further, is not "burning," which is the action of fire, very often used for "loving"? "Corydon burned for Alexis"[35] and "Dido burns with love,"[36] and such expressions are often read in many places. But why should we accept shadows? Let us approach the light or fire, that we might understand the fire lighting up and burning in the soul. What do you say, Paul? *The love of God was poured out into their hearts* (Rom 5:5). In other words, the Holy Spirit, the love of Father and Son, flowed into their hearts. But in what image? In the form of which element? Tell us of its nature, Luke, the most skilled physician: *allotted tongues as of fire appeared to them* (Acts 2:3). What clearer testimony do you expect? The Spirit appeared first as dove, the bird of love.[37] The Spirit assumes the nature of fire, as had been promised, when he is sent to the assembly of the heavenly republic.[38] Finally, the Lord said in Luke, *I have come to send fire upon the earth* (Lk 12:49), speaking of that very Spirit whom the assembly was to receive in the future.

So far we have said that love is called fire. But now, read the book of Mark: *All will be salted with fire* (Mk 9:48). What a mystery this seems! The holy fire is called love, and thus fire is love. *The victim will be salted with fire*, and so will be salted with love. Therefore, after the holy evangelist said that *every fire will be salted*, he continues by explaining himself: *And every victim will be salted with salt.* Is not everything that is salted salted with salt? But victims are salted with fire. Besides, fire was called love above, and Chrysostom agrees,[39] considering both to be salt. If he came, then, *to send fire upon the earth*, he came to send salt upon the earth.

I believe we have so far established this: that love is of so much worth (love, which the Lord sometimes called salt and sometimes fire) that God came to earth for the purpose of sending, bestowing, and kindling love, and by it, as if by salt, to protect the dying from death. The old law surely foreshadowed this. Leviticus warns: *Do not take away the salt of your covenant* (Lv 2:13). And Numbers speaks of *the eternal covenant of salt* (Nm 18:19). Surely the sending of the Messiah and the Spirit is meant, I say, at which time his people are fed like a nursing child. The perfect salt was given late in the law. Both laws have come from God: one law is weak, like a youth, the other is mature and stable. Milk is in one, necessary salt in the other. The one provides a food gentle enough for tender children, the other provides the food proper for already robust men. Read Sirach: *The principal and necessary things are salt and milk.* In the second place, he named the purpose, placing first that which is made for the other's sake. And lest you should misunderstand him, he adds, *bread and honey* (Sir 39:26). Surely, God promised honey and milk to be useful for those children. I will give, he says, *and I will bring you into a land flowing with milk and honey* (Ex 3:17).

From our Lord, we know the word he spoke to his successor, Peter, and others, *You are a priest forever according to the order of Melchizedek* (Ps 110:4; Heb 5:6; 7:17) This order of Melchizedek, since it performed holy duties, offered bread, and not honey or milk. Therefore, honey belongs to the earlier law, bread to the later. Both milk and bread are necessary for man's health. For it is right that one be provided with circumcision or faith who would reach divine vision. If you are wise, be careful not to comply with any service to God where salt is absent. You shall offer a calf and other things. Ezekiel says, *Let the priest put salt on them* (Ex 43:24). It also says in Leviticus, *You should offer salt in every sacrifice* (Lv 2:13).

It still remains for me to review what Elisha[40] did since, by his wonders and portents, he was predicting those things about which we have spoken. The last day had come in which Elijah was to be seen among mortals. He was seeking to part from his friend Elisha, so that when he should be taken into the air no one would see him going. For he did not want to be seen while he was lifted up. His good friend, violently crushed, as he indicated, at the departing of the highest conductor and charioteer, did not want his dear master to be torn away from him. Elijah went along and made up many reasons, now here, now there, hoping to finally leave human things behind and be lifted up to heaven without witnesses. And so he proceeded to Bethel; he proceeded to the Jordan, he proceeded to Jericho. But the other, with a stubborn determination, stayed by his side, and clinging to his cloak, confessed with tears and sobs, *As the Lord lives and as your soul lives* (which was a custom of swearing for the Hebrew people) *I will not leave you* (2 Kgs 2:2.4.6). All Elijah's attempts proved useless, and he tried every artifice in vain. After he had cut off the flow of the river Jordan, after he had left behind the sons of the prophets in Bethel and Jericho, and after he had granted the sign of his double spirit, he stopped for a while and was even then snatched away from his friend and from the ground. And behold *a fiery chariot* (2 Kgs 2:11) suddenly fell from the skies and landed between them, and before the eyes of a stunned and shouting Elisha, the chariot immediately carried off the seized one through the air.

What did Elisha do then? He did not want to let him go, but he could no longer follow him. He returned to the prophets, hardly holding back his feeling of loss. The prophets urge him to be of good cheer and promise to do all they can: they appoint fifty men and order everything to be explored by them; all mountains, valleys and places to be searched, examined and inspected, to see if the one taken up by God had been placed down anywhere. Finally, they encourage him to stay with them, for then he will find countless sons in place of the one father; every necessity will be present and nothing lacking. They finally encourage him to become father of the country and of that city, which is not displeasing. And besides, it is a famous and illustrious city, very suitable for human endeavors, and adorned besides with an assembly of fathers who can hardly be despised. Strictly speaking, there are one or two things lacking for the full happiness of the people: in fact the water is not very wholesome, and the ground not very fertile. But the remaining things are such that he would lack nothing of the life of mortals. Elisha was weighed down with grief, but although he had decided not to accept their consolation or terms, he was, nevertheless, pleased by the kindness of the people, so that he appeared to have accepted everything with gratitude. He also applied his mind to add what was lacking for the happiness of the place, saying, *Bring me a new vessel and put salt into it* (2 Kgs 2:20). They immediately obeyed. Then, lifting the vessel in his hand, he stood next to the edge of the spring and spoke to the water in a loud voice, saying, *Thus says the Lord God: I order these waters to be sound* (2 Kgs 2:21), and let every infection and infertility depart, and let the waters be in the future wholesome, pleasant, and fertile. Immediately, and from then on, these waters were the best and healthiest in the area.

This matter, although it happened as we have related it, surely holds a great significance, and one not at all obscure, for Christian realities. I will approach it, however, in the hope that he will be present with us, he who willed that this matter be done and recorded, so that he could make himself manifest to us through the actions of his friends, the prophets. At the beginning the names present themselves which must be interpreted for us. For Cratilus teaches that names are not imposed without reason, and the Lord says to his prophet, *I call your name* (Is 45:3). And again he says to Isaiah, *I have called you by your name* ((Is 43:1), and once more, *The*

Lord called me from the womb (Is 49:1). And the apostle Paul: *He calls things that are not as though they were* (Rom 4:17). And it was said to God's friends: *All the hairs of your head have been counted* (Mt 10:30), that is, all the occurrences that befall you happen with me arranging them. It should bring joy and exaltation *that your names are written in heaven* (Lk 10:20). These names are written with a new pen, but *before the foundation of the world* (Eph 1:4), as the Apostle says, they were called and written. Therefore we do not impose names for people at their birth who are elected to the highest place, but we call them names that were determined before the birth of the world.

Elijah was the teacher, Elisha the disciple. Elijah means god, lord, or ruler. Elisha means lord, salvation,[41] ruler. Although it can be said that the complete and entire Trinity created, still it especially befits reason, that is, the Son, first because all things were made and created by the Word, as by a pattern and idea of things, second because he was given the charge to defeat and banish the unjust occupier of the world. Our commander said he was certain of power and victory, since he encouraged his soldiers to fight strenuously and do battle with a sure hope; a voice was heard from heaven and his beatitude in face and clothing was seen on the mountain, where the testimony of Moses and Elijah was received.[42] *It comes,* says our illustrious commander, *that hour comes when the ruler of the world will be overcome and cast out* (Jn 12:23). Therefore he who is Lord by right both created the world and regained it from occupation by an unjust invader. He was formerly called by the prophets lord, king, and commander. *Send the lamb, Lord, who is ruler of the earth* (Is 16:1), prayed Isaiah. He further says, *A child is born to us and a son, whose government is upon his shoulders* (Is 9:6). And again: *The moon will turn red and the sun will be astonished when the Lord of hosts shall rule in Zion* (Is 24:23), that is, when he shall receive his kingdom on the cross. For he was crowned with thorns, and even acknowledged a king by the testimony of the ungodly, who inscribed this title on the chariot of the triumphant one: *Jesus the Nazarean, King of the Jews* (Jn 19:19).

Since there are *many gods and many lords* (1 Cor 8:5), as Paul wrote to the Corinthians, why is there only one God above all gods, one Lord of lords, King of kings and Ruler of rulers? He is one since he is Lord but has no lord. For just as numerically nothing comes before unity, and nothing comes before the beginning point of a finite line, and just as within troops and divisions nothing surpasses the commander and chief, so generally in the ordained nature of things nothing is prior to the first. Others indeed are called gods or lords, but are neither lords nor gods. Only this one both is called and is God and Lord.

Now Elijah signifies these two. Therefore, by that name, he seems to be understood much more truly than before. Elisha was the salvation of God, while Elijah was God. Elisha was not God, but the salvation of God himself. There is a certain salvation that is the same as God. And there is another salvation that follows Christ, which is not God but only of God. Salvation was accustomed to be used for savior, and Latin authors allow this. We, however, are not inventors of names but faithful imitators of Scripture. It is more detestable, and we run a greater risk, when we deviate from divine rather than from Latin authors. I have applied the name of savior and salvation not only to God, but also to the companions of God, who believed in him when he lived, were present with him when he died and finally followed him when he departed from the earth. Isaiah says, *The remnant will go forth from Jerusalem* (that is, those whom the Lord left as his successors) *and salvation from Mount Zion* (Is 37:32). And in Psalm 28, David speaks about *the protector of the salvation of his Christ* (Ps 28:8). And this is not different from what is said by Isaiah, Joel, and Obadiah. For when Habakkuk writes, *Your four-horse chariot is salvation* (Hb 3:8), what else did he mean by this expression than the four writers of the gospel?

Some interpret the name of savior in one way and some in another. Some speak of a savior as God and cause, while others speak of saviors as living instruments of God. Hosea has the first usage: *There is no savior besides me* (Hos 13:4). Obadiah employs the other: *The saviors went up to Mount Zion* (Ob 21), although it is not unknown to me that also Joseph was called savior because he freed his people from famine, enriched and enlightened them.[43] Because Elisha is called the salvation of God, and not God, his name should be taken for God's instruments, ministers, and disciples — those twelve among all, and especially Simon Peter, the ruler among the twelve. When you hear Elijah, understand God dwelling on earth and Peter establishing the assembly. When you hear Elisha spoken, that disciple who so diligently followed in the footsteps of his teacher Elijah, understand Peter and the holy assembly who followed Christ, their teacher, and who forsook all so they could follow him. When Elijah is being lifted into the air, he holds his disciple who clings to his side; the Lord holds his Elishas who do not bear his celestial departure with a calm spirit. Elijah was snatched into the air while his disciple looked on. Our second Elijah *was lifted into heaven while they watched* (Acts 1:9). The former left behind his cloak for Elisha; the latter also left behind his cloak, the pontificate, for his disciples and especially for Peter.

The returning Elisha strikes the corruptions of water and earth. We explained the corruption of the earth above when we recounted the two kinds of sins; the other corruption is of the body, which was called dungheap in that place, but is called water here. Both signify corruption of a weak soul and filth in the body. *You were poured out as water* (Gn 49:4), Jacob said to his unclean son, who dared to defile the paternal bed. Both discovered wickedness in Jerusalem, both that which is performed in the body and that which is performed outside the body, that is lust and desire for power with riches and honors. But we said what Elisha did before the restoration, that he ordered a new vessel with salt to be brought to him.

Listen, Romans! Hear, O seven hills. Listen especially you, most holy Peter. You, I say, you, the great Julius. For Elisha and Simon Peter made the effort for you. Each knocked down the rank of Aaron and stripped away its sacred ephod and sacred underpinnings; each commanded Aaron to leave the temple and yield it to my Julius. But let us see what Elisha did. *Bring me a new vessel* (2 Kgs 2:20), he said. And my Elisha, head of the disciples, Simon Peter, does the same. For anointed by the Lord into the greatest priesthood, since Jacob had anointed the rock, he was ordered by the Lord to be called Peter, as if he were the firm and unmovable foundation of the new church. First *the ointment ran down the head* (Ps 133:2) (the fullness of grace in Christ), *then down the beard, the beard of Aaron* (inwardly into Peter, the highest priest), and finally *into the border* of his vestments, as into last vessels of grace. Peter is *the vessel of solid gold, the great priest, the vase adorned with every precious stone* (Sir 50:1.10), which we read in Sirach about the high priest!

But overflowing with the power of great faith, Peter seeks the people who seem able to be made a vessel worthy of receiving such a thing. He walks about, he preaches, he disputes, he exhorts, he relies on every resource, if somehow he might show that Jerusalem, the home of the old law, was constituted the seat of the new law; that just as the ancient vessel had received the incense of shadows, so might it now receive the poured out oil of his name, which is above every name, and of true light. But the Hebrew people, *hard of heart* (Ex 32:9), as Moses said, and stubborn, in an amazing way not only do not receive Peter, nor the other chosen fathers, but persecute him with cruel hatred, banish him from the Synagogue, order him to keep silent about Christ, and threaten him with punishments, prison and death if he should not keep silent.[44]

What did the ruler of the divine company do? He had twelve fountains with him to flood the souls of mortals with living waters and to change mortals into gods. He certainly had water, but did not have vessels worthy of such wealth. He says to the fathers, Hear, happy souls, of what the Spirit warns: unholy ground receives not sacred rain — ground from which God receives disgrace instead of honor, shame instead of praise, hatred instead of love, death instead of gifts, the ground, I say, of murder and irreligion, partaking ungodliness and sacrilege — but God hears the voices of blood, guilt, and murder, crying out for vengeance. That ground is the reason the prophet, foreseeing the future, forbade his son to take a wife from among the girls or young women of Canaan.[45] Noah said, *Cursed be Canaan* (Gn 9:25), who uncovered his lord and father; but God affixed his naked Son to the cross and destroyed him with punishments and a most horrible death. Therefore let us move to this other place as soon as possible. Let us leave behind these ominous regions and travel to better lands. Do we pour out pearls and blessed dishes into a pen of pigs? A sacrilege so immense or foul has now departed. *Bring me a new vessel!*

Who would put new wine in rotting skins? Precious liquid requires precious goblets and vessels. Find me new realms!

Behold the Spirit speaks: Christ is head of heaven, Rome head of the world; Rome is ruler, Christ is ruler. If this celestial bridegroom seeks a bride in the world, let ruler marry ruler, king marry queen, the emperor of heaven and earth marry the empress of the world. You are mine, mine, O seven mountains of Rome! Hail, O happy bride! Hail, Tarpeian Cliffs! Hail sacred hills! Hail, Aventine Hill! For you, this new Romulus is as much greater than Romulus as God is greater than man! The old Romulus welcomed twelve birds into you so that he could call you Rome; the new Romulus welcomed twelve doves for you that they might call you Christian. They brought an olive branch to the sacred forum so that the city, fully anointed with the peace-making ointment, might close the temple of Janus forever. Hail, O seat of Janus, now truly Janiculum — "the great door"! There is now a door in you whence begins the road to the heavens! Hail Etruscan Hill, you that are connected to Janiculum Hill. Janus lifted up Italy, which was crying in you as if in a cradle. I shall lift up the religion which is crying in you. The Etruscan religion desired this for itself, the temple of Volturna desired this, the Etruscan priests, interpreters of divine things, desired this: Immediately after the flood and destruction of the world, they produced again the best seed, cast among those who serve false gods. The temples, the altars, the sacred groves, the rites, and the ceremonies from your Etruria all predicted and foretold this for themselves.

You, Tiber River, gliding past my Vatican, you will be a vessel for a religious stream. I carry up new waters. So spread out your breast and become a vessel for me; I beg you, be made new! Therefore I take you by the hand, I claim you for myself, for my sons, grandsons and all my posterity, and I change you back to Albula-Tiber, "the White River," whence we may become *whiter than snow* (Ps 51:9). I give, appoint, dedicate you to Christ and to the ministers of heaven, and I hand over to you the strength, majesty and power of the Jordan River. But I also command you to receive salt and to taste of the fruits of God, which are always salty. In love, God was drawn forth that he might be made human, in love that he might hand over himself, in love that dying he might pour out blood and water, so that I might consecrate you and your right bank. Therefore I consecrate you and three times designate, call, and name you the River of Love; and I command you to be a safe preserver and protector and teacher of holy mortals, my beloved blessed ones.

Heavenly bodies, you are witnesses! You, moon! You, sun! You, ethereal spheres, observers of all! I, governor of eternal kingdoms, having obtained my bride, shall have made her eternal. May she live forever! But let me die now, and with me the divine heroes and my thirty-four heirs. The creator killed his brother that he might embrace you, my bride;[46] we will die to atone for you. He made you guilty of death that he might rule;

we shall make you ours that, when your death sentence has been pardoned, you might rule. Therefore, receive the keys and you shall rule not only earth and sea, but also heaven.[47] Open heaven when you wish and close it again when you wish.

Your other young women will fall. You, as their ruler, will outlive them all. Now be faithful, be in good faith, be innocent, just, pure, and godly; now be not another's, but mine; be complete, be simple, be without evil intent, without luxury, without ostentation, without desire for gold; be loving of the bridegroom, your bridegroom, and of all your beloved ones. And thus suited to enjoy a royal wedding, you are now to wash yourself in the twelve rivers. Receive, then, the name Washed.

Rome, a name derived from Romulus, Rome, for the future you should trace your name from the same root whence also love derives it. None of the ancients designate you as Rome, but Valentia (Strength), called this long before the children of Amulius. Sometimes designated Strength, sometimes Power, you were joined in fellowship with God. For only Jerusalem is equal to Rome but has fallen forever in Asia. When I seek you, I make you a vessel of divine authority, I put into you *the salt of the earth*, by love I restore you as ruler of heaven and earth. Surely there was a great power of Romulus, of kings and emperors and there still is a great power in the whole world. Yet it continually sets. You, however, shall be the power of our kingdom and of the kingdom of all ages, whose "ages and end I do not establish."[48] You would surely have a certain end if you were going to dwell on earth, but not if you were going to dwell among the stars!

I have said this that you might love and love with the strongest love. That name was given to you not by the divination of a vulture but by the care and providence of God. Your name is Rome. "You may be called Rome from the word 'power'," Platonicus Phaedrus explains.[49] In your name you have both powers for bringing things back again; you should embrace both love and fortitude as the bride you will love, or should love more ardently in this life.

Listen, fathers. Our young woman has made up her mind and forsakes his rivals. She adorns herself, she combs her hair, she bathes and puts on perfume. She runs rejoicing to meet him. She sings the wedding song. She already burns for embraces. Listen, she is present, I recognize her voice. *May he kiss me with the kiss of his mouth, for your love is as strong as death* (Sg 1:1; 8:6). She gives kisses, most happy man, to us. Our love cannot bear to live without you. Farewell, O Augusti! Farewell, Claudii, Flavii and Neros! You are adulterers, not men. I [am betrothed] to a man, but one who is also God in his own nature.

When I was a neglected country, he established me as his country. After the gods of the peoples were repelled, I gave myself to the God of gods. Declining the people who were proud of their Israelite name, he substituted us as the true Israelites. We in turn, with the darkness of our errors rejected, receive God born of God. He leads the remnant of Israel out of the east. In the western lands of this people, we open the temples of Julia. The seed is God's, the field Julia's. Julia shall receive the one dwelling in a divine house.

You are already "under a shady tree. I sat in the shade,"[50] for which I had been longing. I sit surely not as a widow, but a divine angel sits beside me: the angel of Gideon was seen under the tree. He orders me to be saved, he admonishes me to be Rome and consequently to be fit and suitable enough to concentrate on love and power, to proclaim the battle of Midian, to gather an army, pour out troops, and seize the spoils from the plundered camps. Surely with the enemy conquered, victory and triumph are assured.[51]

But I who was once Rome am now Romula, and there are no troops, no companies, no divisions for battles. *I will be with you*, he says, *and you will strike down Midian as one man* (Jgs 6:16). Hear, Gideon, who separates the chaff from the grain. O you, whom the Lord of Israel chose and appointed. Hear the angel urging you "under the oak tree: The enemy has walls"[52] to ravage the bride. On both sides an enemy threatens: sin within the house, and a savage tyrant on the outside. Each enemy frightens me, but the domestic enemy much more. He enters temples and altars. He invades the entrance, the sanctuary, the holy double-doors, the hearts, minds, and souls. He brings destruction upon the holy flock and erects his trophies.

The young woman weeps, her cheeks cut with fingernails. She appeals to the man with a tearful voice. She implores heaven and all the gods. She pounds upon her guardians, Peter and Paul, with cries. Yes, she asks you to be available from whatever place. She is not heard by mortals. If she is deserted by immortals, nothing remains for her except despair and ruin. There is already enough of these things and more than enough scandal has been given!

He invokes you, most blessed Julius, he orders you to look at the angel, to comply with his command, to acknowledge your own tree. Everyone demands that ground, all mortals and all divine beings demand it. The air, sky, stars and God himself, whose heir you are, admonishes you to undertake a work worthy of your soul. You should apply salt and preserve things that are decaying; you should build back up what has collapsed, correct what is faulty, reform the distorted, revoke the antiquated and, as much as you are able, move against both of these enemies. Elisha, Peter and the bride urge this to be done; likewise, finally, urged the Lord himself in Matthew, when he says, *I have not come to put peace on the earth, but a sword* (Mt 10:34). But do these things in such a way that it would be proper to enjoy that *peace which surpasses all understanding* (Phil 4:7). God, our heavenly pastor, wills that you bear arms under this general and most happily bring back victory to the house of our Lord God, who lives forever. Amen.

Translated by Michael Woodward

Notes

1. See Cicero, *Fin*. 2.6.18.
2. See Augustine, Sermon 192, 1; 342, 5.
3. Vergil, *Aeneid* 6.6-7.
4. See Sg 1:11.
5. See Livy 1.9.
6. See Gn 3:24.44-45; 3:15.
7. See Gn 3:15.
8. See Jer 31:22.
9. See Ez 43:1-2; 44:1-2; 46:12.
10. See Gn 9:1-17; 17:15-22; 22:15-18; 35:1-12; Ex 32:13; 19:3-6; 2 Kgs 7:8-16.
11. The text adds: *that we love one another*, but I omit this clause because Giles appears to want to hold the answer in suspense. See Jn 13:34; 15:12; 1 Jn 3:23.
12. Vergil, *Aeneid* 6.76.
13. See Ps 95:7-8; Jn 10:3.
14. See Horace, *Carmina* 2.14.28.
15. Vergil, *Aeneid* 6.190.
16. *Ibid*. 6.193.
17. See Vergil, *Aeneid* 2.81.
18. See 1 Cor 1:17-25; 3:18-19.
19. Vergil, *Aeneid* 6.655.
20. See Jn 13:2.
21. See Gal 3:1; 5:22.
22. See Heb 13:1.
23. See 1 Thes 3:12; 4:9.
24. See 1 Cor 13.
25. See Jn 21:15-17.
26. See Mk 13:31; Lk 21:33; Hag 2:7.22.
27. Ovid, *Ep. Sapphus* 213 (bis).
28. Cicero, *De Officiis* 1.6.19.
29. See Col 2:8.
30. See Lk 14:35.
31. Vergil, *Aeneid* 4.66.
32. *Ibid*. 4, 23.
33. *Ibid*. 4.2.
34. Vergil, *Ecl*. 3.66.
35. *Ibid*., Ecl. 2.1.

36. Vergil, *Aeneid* 4.101.

37. See Mt 3:16; Mk 1:10; Lk 3:22; Jn 1:32.

38. See Sg 2:10; Ovid, M. 15.386.

39. See John Chrysostom, *Homilies on Matthew* (incomplete work) 10: PG 56, 685; also *Homilies on Matthew* 15, 7; 32, 7; 33, 7: PG 57, 232.386.

40. See 2 Kgs 2.

41. Text adds *deus*, but later Giles says Elisha does not include this meaning.

42. See Mt 17:1-13; Mk 9:1-12; Lk 9:28-36; 2 Pt 1:17-18.

43. See Gn 41.45.

44. See Acts 4:5-22.

45. See Gn 4:10; 28:1.

46. Thirty-four refers to the number of popes from Peter to Sylvester.

47. See Mt 16:19.

48. Vergil, *Aeneid* 1.278.

49. Plato, *Phaedrus* 238c.

50. Vergil, *Aeneid* 6.136.

51. See Jgs 6:11.

52. Vergil, *Aeneid* 2.290.

Fulfillment of the Christian Golden Age under Pope Julius II

The discourse of Giles of Viterbo on the Golden Age is edited from what seems to be the only extant version, found in manuscript (CXVI/1-30) in the Biblioteca Pública e Arquivo Distrital de Évora, Portugal. The discourse was delivered by Giles in a somewhat different form in Saint Peter's basilica in Rome on 21 December 1507, at the request of Pope Julius II and in his presence. The king of Portugal, Manuel I (1495-1521), had written to Julius from Abrantes under the date of 25 September 1507, to announce to him some great news. The king, recently informed of three important events regarding his interests in the Far East, now wanted to communicate his information to the pope: the Portuguese, under the leadership of Lourenço de Almeida (†1508), had landed in Ceylon and obtained from the most powerful ruler there an agreement to pay an annual tribute to the Portuguese crown; on 18 March 1506, de Almeida won an important naval victory over the Zamorin of Calicut; and in the same year another Portuguese fleet discovered the island of Madagascar.

Julius responded to this news by declaring three days of thanksgiving in Rome, which were to culminate in a solemn celebration in Saint Peter's on 21 December, the feast of Saint Thomas the Apostle. This celebration consisted of a procession of the pope, cardinals, and prelates to Saint Peter's, a Mass offered by one of the cardinals, the exposition of relics to veneration, the publication of a plenary indulgence, and a sermon preached by the "solemnis praedicator," Giles of Viterbo. After the event the pope requested Giles to put his sermon into writing.

The first part of the sermon consists principally in philosophical and theological arguments on the nature of the Golden Age or the "golden life." The second half deals directly with the accomplishments of Manuel of Portugal, as seen in the total context of the pontificate of Julius II. Giles views these accomplishments as fulfillments of the predictions of scripture and as fulfillment of the Golden Age initiated by Christ.

For more details on the event and for the critical text of this sermon see John W. O'Malley, S.J., "Fulfillment of the Christian Golden Age under Pope Julius II: Text of a Discourse of Giles of Viterbo, 1507," Traditio *XXV (1969) 265-338.*

The following is an outline of the discourse:
I
1. *Introduction: The Origin of the Libellus*
2. *The First Two Golden Ages: Lucifer and Adam*
3. *The Third Golden Age: Janus and the Etruscans*
4. *The Fourth Golden Age: Christ*
5. *The Significance of the Number Twelve*

II
1. *The Excellence of the Christian Golden Age and Its Prospects under Julius II*
2. *Manuel's Achievements under Julius II*
3. *Julius' Achievements and His Future Tasks*
4. *Manuel's Destiny and Role*
5. *Peroration*

Brother Giles of Viterbo, Augustinian, to King Manuel, greeting in Jesus Christ.

At long last I am sending you, most excellent and happy king, the little book I composed about your exploits. Feeble and uncouth in style it may be, but I send it in the firm hope and expectation that you are the king to whom the prophecies of the fathers pointed in far-off, turbulent ages, the king who would restore religion. I did not send it earlier because I hoped it would be dispatched to you by Pope Julius II, and so the importance of the content would be enhanced by the importance and authority of the sender. However, he who stirs the minds of mortals from within urges me now to send you the little book myself. In this way the divine will, if hitherto unrecognized, may now become plain to you; or, if plain already, may knock once more at the door of an elect ruler, and solicit afresh the ears of one who bears the name Emmanuel.

For your part, then, you must read this little book repeatedly, acknowledge God's gifts and render thanks to him, listen to his promptings and gird yourself to carry out the rest of your tasks. Never forget Saul, Israel's first king, who listened to Samuel and was called to rule, but was later cast down from the kingship for his carelessness. You have absolutely certain pledges of God's love toward you, for he has willed you to seek out, explore, discover, and civilize all those regions of the sea which lie to the south, from the sun's rising-place to its setting. As king of the south, you are thus to become the latest in a line of "kings of the south," that is, kings washed in the baptismal waters of the Holy Spirit who have waged the wars of justice against the wicked "kings of the north," as Daniel has written in the ninth chapter of his book. As such you will be supported by the help of the Archangel Michael, as Daniel also teaches, so that you may reach those islands, conquer them on behalf of believers and, to use the prophet's words, inaugurate an age of which the like has never been seen before. If in this new age you listen and obey, persevering in zeal and loyalty, then the entire people whose names are in the Book of Life will be set free; those who have fallen asleep in the dust of the earth or are oppressed by the tyranny of unbelievers will awaken and rise up, while the unbelievers will be *blown away like dust from the face of the earth, as it is written at the head of the book* (Ps 40:3; Heb 10:7).

To work then: forsake merely human affairs, forget the easy life, recognize that you were born to accomplish God's work. Give your mind to it, ponder it, strive to bring it to perfection. We have watched a king running swiftly as he entered on his course, and beating others by God's help; let us now watch this same king attaining his goal and carrying off the prize.

Either I will come to you at the earliest opportunity; or, if this proves impossible and you prefer it so, I will declare to listening ears *what the Spirit is saying* (Rv 2:8) to the Church, as John bids us — or rather as the

Holy Spirit himself commands, he who calls us in the psalm *to tell of his salvation day in, day out* (Ps 96:2).

Farewell.

From Rome

I

Introduction: The Origin of the Libellus

. . . had shown, he promised. This he did to the young Joseph, whom he set up like a god for Pharaoh, as Genesis recounts.[1] So also he did for Moses, under whose leadership his people shook off the yoke of slavery: Moses split the sea and made a way through it, received the law from God, and beheld wonders without number.[2] So too God did for Joshua, under whose command the Hebrew people took possession of the promised land.[3] Thus God dealt with the young David too, calling him from the sheepfold and conferring on him immense glory both as king and as prophet.[4] It was the same with Peter, with Paul, with the apostles and with others whom God embraced with special love, and into whose hands he delivered races, peoples, and nations; to them he entrusted the government of affairs, and the city and empire of Rome.

Finally he has dealt in like manner with you, Holy Father, for to your faith and to the power of the keys you wield the most distant people of the Indian Ocean has this year submitted, even that greatest of islands, Ceylon. Before your reign it lay hidden and inaccessible to Christians, just as it was itself ignorant of the Christian name.

Yet God willed to give to Your Holiness a gift of which not even the possibility could have been apprehended by any of your predecessors, and to this end he raised up Manuel as king in Portugal, endowing him with righteousness, prudence, moderation, and, above all, intense piety. He had to contend with many opponents to gain the kingdom; but, once called to it, he dedicated himself, his abilities and the resources of his realm to the service of God. He sent out vessels to search the oceans for races and peoples to whom he might bring the name of Christ. For many years he pursued this task, with great effort and at vast expense. Eventually his ships sailed round that entire African coast which is washed by the great Ocean, from the Straits of Gibraltar and the Pillars of Hercules right around to Arabia and Ethiopia, They wrought great deeds in India, conquered rulers and peoples there, seized the trade in spices from the King of Egypt and Syria, and at last invaded Ceylon, the island Pliny called a "different world."[5] Upheld by Christ's help rather than the might of men, the conqueror of Ceylon defeated a powerful Indian fleet and forced a paramount ruler with authority over six kings to pay an annual tribute. Under those skies he was the first to make known the Christian message; in that land he first laid the foundations of your faith, and was the first to extend even to those races the boundaries of your sacred empire.

As soon as you received the news of an event so fortunate both for Christendom and for yourself you acknowledged your debt to God, ordered prayers to be offered, and decreed solemn thanksgiving. You summoned the senate and people of Rome and went in procession to Saint Peter's, where you prostrated yourself before the high altar in humble thanksgiving to God, and this on the very festival day of Saint Thomas of India, whom we rightly believe to have been present with us in all that was done in India. You further ordered that in the presence of Your Holiness and the College of Cardinals I should preach about the immense blessing received from our almighty and loving God by the flock of which you are shepherd, in that the King of Portugal had, under your auspices, enlarged the bounds of your most sacred empire even to India, so ushering in a golden age in that newly-discovered land. After I had obeyed, suggesting from the pulpit some thoughts on that golden age which India had received from a golden king, you further commanded that I should put my remarks into writing and make them available to readers.

So then, I have complied with your direction, and reproduced in pamphlet form the sermon I preached that day on the golden age and its four parts, and on the King of Portugal's most auspicious victory; but I scarcely know if I have come up to your expectations. However, I would point out that in my work as prior general of the Augustinian Order, a position you yourself wished me to occupy,[6] I am so heavily engaged that I would not think myself able to please even a person of mean understanding or a private individual, let alone Pope Julius, to satisfy whose judgment one would need to be exquisitely gifted and enjoy unlimited competence.

Since I am to speak of the "golden life" which the King of Portugal has, under your authority, introduced among the peoples of India, I must begin somewhat further back; for our subject is the destiny of good men and that human happiness on earth which approaches as nearly as possible the happiness of heaven. There can be no theme of contemplation more beneficial to humankind than this. It was this that the priests of Egypt were seeking when they traced the origin of all things to the Nile. Among the Bectrians and Persians the Brahmins sought it; the Tyrrhenians sought it at the Tiber, and the Ionians in Greece. The Italian philosophers searched for it in Italy under the guidance of Pythagoras; and the scholars of the ten sects sought it with enormous toil, pilgrimage, and contempt for all other things. Longing above all for happiness, as we all do, we must exert ourselves to the utmost to find the gateway to it. Hence our sermon will take as its starting point the beginnings of sacred history itself.

The First Two Golden Ages: Lucifer and Adam

At the very beginning a golden age was inaugurated in heaven, when the incorporeal intelligences were created. These creatures were pure forms, it is said, and endowed from the outset with heavenly wisdom. When, however, the golden age declined through the pride of those princes who fell away from God, he resolved to repair the damage; and he formed man from the earth, ordering him to be happy, insofar as what is of earth is capable of happiness. In addition to the beneficence of skies, plants, and animals, all of which were readily available to our first parents in that golden age, far more valuable seeds were implanted in their own minds, seeds of the golden life. It will perhaps be worth our while to examine these, so that we may realize what kind of people we ought to be in our blessed Christian condition.

God, says Moses, engendered *both heaven and earth* (Gn 1:1). A particular form of speech is used in the opening words of Genesis, to make us understand that the work was done with supreme power, wisdom, and goodness. *In the beginning*, it says, *God created heaven and earth*. Greek grammar later accepted the same mode of speaking, for in Greek neuter nouns signifying a plurality govern a singular verb. Thus when Genesis says *Elohim*, a plural, it does not mean several gods (for as Aristotle and Plato, drawing on Homer, declare, "There must be only one ruler");[7] but it teaches that there are several hypostases, if I may use the Greek expression. It thus hints at the truth that whatever is done outside the Trinity is the work of all the hypostases, the action of the whole Trinity.

Thus heaven and earth were created by the supremely wise generative work of God. By the two words "heaven" and "earth" we should understand that two classes of beings were created, corporeal and incorporeal. In fact the natural order is divided into three parts: some things, such as the elements, are entirely corporeal; others, like the heavenly intelligences, are completely unencumbered by bodies; others again, such as human beings, have been given a nature midway between the two, and are made up of both.

The soul is almost divine, yet being wedded to the gross body it has been contaminated with the first touches of disease, as it were, through contagion by the body, in the shape of certain disturbances and passions. Now corporeal nature, of which we consist, is fourfold. The first principle of matter is a unity, to be sure, being like the formless container of all forms; but it finds expression and is initially clothed in four forms. According to Plato,[8] when it is distinguished into great and small the following divisions occur: when the greatest possible quantity is present, matter bursts forth as fire; when the smallest, it becomes earth; when fairly large, it becomes air; when fairly small, it becomes water. Or, to adopt the Peripatetic scheme, when it becomes hot and dry, it turns into fire; when it mingles damp with heat, it becomes air; when cold and damp, water; and when cold and dry, earth. Matter, as people say, is very like the sea-god Proteus: "it transforms itself into all kinds of uncanny shapes, into a fire, or a horrible wild beast, or a flowing river."[9]

These four kinds of matter, however, are continually at loggerheads and warring among themselves; and this is why souls confined in human bodies composed of mutually hostile elements are continually tossed hither and thither. The four passions and disordered affections derive the seeds of all evils from these four warring elements. From chill, compressed earth arises fear; from water, which thirsty animals long for, arises concupiscence; at gusts of wind we dissolve into sickly melancholy; and from fires, that most liquid of elements, we melt into pleasure. The poet testified that these plagues flow from the body and its members when he sang, "Hence come fear and desire, pain and pleasure."[10] The first two depend on future prospects, the last two are elicited by present conditions. Two are prompted by extreme adversity, the other two by an abundance of favorable circumstances.

We have demonstrated the sources of all human evils: they are like four hellish fountains from which our immortal race is flooded with troubles, diseases, shameful acts, death — in fact, every kind of poisonous slime. Nothing evil ever happens that is not caused by passion. Yet our great and good God who, as David sang, made human beings *a little lower than the angels* (Ps 8:6) not only engendered in heaven those incorporeal spirits who should have lived the golden life at once, had they not acted foolishly; he likewise created humans who, bodily beings though they were, would possess heaven one day if they acted wisely, for he willed that they too should share the golden destiny, and be, though inferior to the angels by nature, yet in no way inferior to them in happiness. He therefore imposed peaceful order on those warring elements in the bodies of our first parents, so that they were absolutely free from disease and death, and had the power to quiet their impulses without difficulty and easily conquer them.

Under God's guidance they eventually "arrived at joyful places, pleasant meadows and happy dwellings amid blessed groves."[11] I will pass over all the other provisions made for their golden life, and mention only that there they discovered a most pure fountain flowing into four rivers, in which they could both drink and bathe. Any who had drunk or washed here would be overcome by no burning passion, soiled by no contamination from the four plagues. *God settled them in a paradise of delight* (Gn 2:15), says Moses. All fear was absent here and all sorrow, for life without evil has no place for sorrow either. Evil desire and lust were alike absent. The foul pleasures of the vulgar found no place. Chaste and rightful joy alone reigned, accompanied by reason, and from such sovereignty the place derived its name; it was called a paradise of delight.

I will pass over in silence the fair climate, the fertile soil, the abundance of trees and fruits, the perennial greenness of the grass and the garlands of blossoming flowers, the alliance of autumn's bounty with perpetual spring. I will not dwell on the delight of beasts, birds, and fishes. Since none of these could harm man, each one of them would have considered itself wretched and unhappy if it were not doing its utmost to be useful to him or at least to give him pleasure. They would run to meet him, put themselves in his path, greet him, keep him company, and render him all kinds of service. I will also pass over in silence the life of the mind as it exercised itself in the search for truth; for, in the words of my holy father Augustine, our first parents conversed with the natures of things, which is to say that with intelligence free from all constraint they beheld the natures, the innermost qualities, and the tendencies of all creatures. Their minds were not, like ours, clouded by ignorance and unable to discern the meaning of things, but clear, endowed with the innate brightness of wisdom, and able to contemplate not only other objects but the light of God himself with a kind of familiar understanding.

Ah, but how true it is that the human soul cannot bear very much happiness! At the instigation of the devil our first parents fell from this golden way of life. The author of discord, ejected from his own golden inheritance, could not but envy one who now possessed it. He resented the transfer to a bodily human of those joys which he, an incorporeal spirit, had lost, and the ability of one sprung from the earth to keep hold on earth of what he, a heavenly being, had been unable to retain in heaven. Often, indeed, the wretched are as much chagrined by the happiness of others as by their own misfortune. So he offered Adam an apple which, as Moses tells us, was of very beautiful appearance; and he promised that if Adam were to eat it he would gain an understanding of good and evil and be like the immortal gods.[12] Every human being is by nature avid for knowledge, as Aristotle testifies;[13] and according to Cicero the Sirens, of whom Homer wrote, enticed sailors, ensnared them with songs and put them to sleep by no other allurement than the prospect of knowledge.[14] Lured, therefore, by the same Siren voice, the first man, father of all humankind, devoured the beautiful apple and so suffered everlasting shipwreck, forfeited that golden delight for himself and all his posterity, and sank us into the final, all-devouring abyss of woe.

So then, golden life was lived in twofold form: one on earth by humans, the other in heaven by angels. Both were very beautiful, both very brief. In neither case was the golden life perfect and definitive, for this is reserved for those who enjoy the vision of God's beauty in heaven. Throughout a period of 1,656 years after Adam's fall, as the Hebrew author reckons it, a weakened human race befouled itself with every kind of vice, like a roller spinning downhill, departing so far from the golden life that not only were there no longer any traces of gold, but all memory of it was blotted out in the black night of oblivion.

The Third Golden Age: Janus and the Etruscans

In the measure that our just God tolerates evildoers mercifully, so does he at long last punish them heavily. He called Noah, a just man, and revealed to him his plan.[15] Once the ark was built, God sent the flood to submerge everything, so that, warned by the wrecking of the whole world and the enormous slaughter of the human race, we should sin less gravely and less often, unless we are entirely bereft of sense. Noah emerged from the ark and admonished his descendants to live justly, to banish avarice, to be content with the produce of trees and fields, and to preserve decency, sobriety, and good fellowship among themselves. He taught them the sacred rituals and exhorted them to fidelity and religious observance, telling them that if they were careful in these matters they would be safe and happy, whereas if they neglected them they would be unhappy and wretched. According to many writers the third golden age began now, inaugurated by Noah, although it did not match the earlier age in holiness, for we cannot compare the maimed and degenerate nature of the children with the perfect, unspoiled nature of their parents.

Nonetheless some semblance of that golden splendor was established by holy Noah, a man most pleasing to God; and it endured among mortals for some years. Trogus and Justin, who begin their history at the end of this period, assert that its golden glory continued to radiate until the time of Ninus, who was the first to take up arms against his neighbors, prompted by greed for power. In earlier days kings had been appointed so that peoples under their rule might be free from harm and enjoy golden peace; but Ninus, unmindful of that holy partnership and lusting for domination and gold, took arms and drove golden holiness from those lands by the sword. His father had been Belus, who in Eusebius' view was called Saturn; after him the Capitoline Hill was later called Saturnia.

The historians tell us, however, that before the arrival of Saturn Janus ruled with golden laws over Etruria on the other side of the Tiber. I may be able to examine his government more fully on some other occasion; now, when a new world has been discovered by the effort and zeal of golden King Manuel, I will confine myself to what is relevant to the appointed sermon. The very happy victory won by a happy king promises us future happiness in no small measure. Why did divine providence arrange that a bronze model of a ship should be hidden in Janus' temple, if not because the Etruscan throne of Janus, which Your Holiness now occupies, already accustomed as it was to rule benevolently, was to be dedicated to the benevolent laws of the barque of Christ? Why was that bronze model of a ship hidden with Janus, if not because the Etruscan hill of the Vatican was to send the most holy laws of Christ to the end of the earth through the ships of a noble king, and in alliance with the standards of Portugal to win an outstanding victory over those Indies which the Roman Mars never touched?

In order to help our golden King Manuel to contemplate the golden
pattern left by kings of old, let us imagine the tree which typified the
golden age. Human beings used to eat acorns in those days, according to
Pliny, Aquinas, and Vergil. Plato, unique among all philosophers, commanded acorns to be served to the citizens of his republic in order to
encourage them to golden conduct.[16] Let us then consider the acorn-bear-
ing oak, which appears most appropriately on the standards of the richly
blessed King Manuel. Let us picture four branches springing from its
trunk, representing the four constituents of the universe. The first stands
for the foundation (*fundamento*) or the earth; for the earth deserves the
name "foundation," both because it alone remains unmoved and is the
basis of all things, and because it is so styled by Wisdom who said, *When
I weighed the foundations of the earth* (Prv 8:29). The second branch stands
for water (*aquae*), the third represents the play of wind (*venti*) and air, the
fourth light (*lucis*) and heavenly fire.[17]

By their interaction these four elements in the human body bring forth
four plagues, and the names of these [in Latin] begin with the same letters
as do the elements from which they derive. Thus the foundation (*funda-
mentum*) or earth begets fear (*formidinem*), water (*aqua*), weariness (*aegritu-
dinem*), the play of wind (*ventus*) and air pleasure (*voluptatem*), and the
confused light (*lux*) of mortal fire lust (*libidinem*). The frigid, contracted
character of the earth can be fittingly compared to the fear which freezes
and contracts the soul. Sickness and weariness, occasioned by ill fortune,
resemble tempestuous water; so in the Song of Songs the bride proclaims
her fortitude under this image: *Many waters have not been able to quench
love* (Sg 8:7). We associate pleasure with the play of wind and air because
the seed which is ejaculated after the climax of pleasure is very much like
air. Finally it is obvious that burning lust resembles the burning light of
fire.

We have mentioned the four elements which, like four bodies, make
up our human frame; we have also spoken of those four sources of all
evils which sprout like four heads from the four bodies. Let us now speak
of the means by which human beings have learned to defeat the plagues
and triumphantly gain a golden victory. In the works of Plato it is stated
that the rulers of Persia were customarily trained by four teachers.[18] The
first inculcated fortitude (*fortitudinem*), the second temperance (*armoniam*) which controls the movements of appetite, the third right reason
(*veritatem*) which gives rise to wisdom and prudence, and the fourth
enlightened judgment (*luciferum*) and justice, which, as Aristotle avers, is
more luminous than the evening and morning stars.[19]

After the flood the Persians and Armenians were the first to receive
golden teachings from the man who had survived the devastating waters.
According to Josephus the Babylonian Berosus recorded that as the flood
waters receded Noah disembarked in their country, and taught them the
principles of a more upright life. Not long afterward these principles

seeped into Egypt and Etruria, if we are to trust contemporary observers; they relate that at this early period a golden age flowered among these three nations, and that subsequently the tokens of virtue, learning, mystical rites, and sacred knowledge were long preserved among them. Thus these nations cultivated almost the same arts and ways of life, since they had been privileged to derive the principles of their belief and conduct from the same teacher and at the same period.

We will demonstrate this fact from Etruscan history more fully and clearly at some other time; for the present suffice it to say that humankind was nevertheless born amid warfare, for human beings consist of hostile elements at war among themselves, whence spring those four plagues which are the greatest enemies of human reason. Plainly, mortals enter upon their life amid warfare and the clash of weapons. Why, then, is our nature not content with one kind of battle — that which is always raging between the elements, whereby disease, old age, and death itself assail us — but must give occasion to another kind of struggle as well, in which the plagues contend fiercely against the dominion of reason? Etruria, however, remembering the flood, subdued the passions derived from humankind's origin and also its warlike tendency. Against the earthly foundation (*fundamento*), water (*aquae*), wind (*vento*), and the light of fire (*luci*), and against the other four enemies fear (*formidini*), sick weariness (*aegritudini*), pleasure (*voluptati*) and lust (*libidini*), Etruria pitted fortitude (*fortitudinem*), temperance (*armoniam*), truthful prudence (*veritatem*) and enlightened justice (*luciferum*). Thus it raised an impregnable defense against them.

It is, however, a slight matter merely to overcome the enemy in war. The peace which follows can be much more harmful than war, unless the leisured times of peace are directed by both good laws and good arts; for just as nothing can be better than leisure if we use it rightly, so nothing can be more abominable if we abuse it. Hitherto we have been discussing wars, victories, triumphs, the peace they won, and the banishment of the sword. Now let us consider the works of peace and the gold peace brought with it. To make this clearer, I think it necessary to look back a little.

When all those things of which the world consists first came into existence, some beings were allotted a superior, noble nature, participant in divinity; others received an earthly, common nature, far removed from the divine. The latter were clotted and molded together as they lay in the dregs of their bodily mass; the former are completely free from bodily organs and possess a simple, immortal nature. One kind are sunk in mud and matter, and are perceived by the senses; the other could be described as endowed with an intelligible nature, since they are known not by eyes or ears, but by the intelligence alone.

Hence the Hermetic writings, as also Plato in his *Philebus* and in the sixth book of the *Republic*, think in terms of two worlds: one is the ordinary world perceived by the senses, and subject to death; the other is divine, open to the intelligence and immortal.[20] Although these doctrines are the product of human analysis and opinions, they seem nonetheless consonant with divine wisdom; for when God lived among mortals he denied that he was of this world,[21] thus plainly indicating that there is another world in which he is Lord, where he who is blessed confers blessedness on his subjects.

This superior world consists of three parts. The principal part is that on which heaven and the whole of created being depend; the middle part is that of heavenly angelic intelligences; the third is the realm of human souls. This last, being created in association with bodies and matter, has been injured by its earthly partner. The middle realm, although entirely free from any defilement or burden of the body, consists nevertheless of a union of essence and existence, and hence is in a certain sense mixed, including a tinge of imperfection in its perfection, and thus has not been endowed with absolutely simple purity.

As for the Supreme Being who dwells at the summit of all things, he is pure simplicity, golden radiance and radiant gold; he is God, and is best compared to the sun and the sun's light shining in highest heaven. The middle realm is like the air, and the lower is like our eye. The Godhead possesses light of himself, or rather is light. The second and third realms, being far distant from the nature of light, can fittingly be called night and darkness; Saint John proclaimed that *they did not comprehend* (Jn 1:5) the light. Both of them, angels as well as human souls, had been allotted natures which lacked light, and so they were content with their own darkness, failing to turn to that sun which is *the true light* (Jn 1:9), or to believe in the light or walk in it, as Light himself testifies. Instead they lie in blackest night and are eternally exiled from the light of which the sublime eagle sang, *The darkness did not comprehend it* (Jn 1:5).

The sun, however, does illuminate clear air and the clear eye; and the Sun of Righteousness (by which I mean not that luminous body, the ordinary sun, but *the true light*) likewise illumines both the angels and also *every human being who comes into this world* (Jn 1:9), enabling them to become children of God although born on earth, and to fly together toward the world which knows no dark shadow but glows with golden light. The King who, as Plato taught in the sixth book of the *Republic*,[22] shines in the intelligible world as the ordinary sun does in the world of sense, has engendered angels in heaven and human souls on earth so that there should be creatures who would recognize the golden riches of the light for which they were born, should love them, seek them, attain them, and eventually enjoy their possession.

Not all are wise, though, and it is very easy for anyone to slip from the reasonable course; so not all the heavenly intelligences or all the human souls turn toward the light. A large portion of the former were unfaithful to that primal light and are exiled to hell and the nethermost regions. They drag with them into their infernal exile the majority of those blind human souls who are ensnared by the dark temptations of riches, honors, and pleasures as by the three jaws of Cerberus. Yet the wiser group of them, weighing itself well and recognizing its inferior quality and its kinship with silver and bronze, does seek after gold and the light, so that although of itself it is dark and fashioned of mere silver, it may be clothed in light and in gold. Thus it can happily attain the highest good, and *stand as queen at* God's *right hand in a golden robe, clad in light as in a garment* (Ps 45:10).

Three things are needed for the blessing of life. First there is the earth or the field, in whose furrows the seeds of life are to be sown; then there is the seed of light which fills and weds the earth, brings forth vegetation and flowers and thus clothes the naked ground; finally, since common light is insufficient to give the bountiful day of which we speak, the light from that Sun which irradiates the intelligible world must rise upon it.[23] We can see these three in the gospel parable, where we are told that the seed which *fell into good earth* (Mt 13:8) was sown by him of whom his Son declared, *My Father is the farmer* (Jn 15:1). Plato says the same in the sixth book of his *Republic*,[24] and so also does that Platonist Vergil in his sixth book, singing, "Here the ampler air clothes fields with radiant light; they know their own sun and their own stars."[25]

Now the head or capital part of all happiness is that Sun which, so far from borrowing his golden light from elsewhere, is light itself by his very nature; and is pure gold, as his bride testifies in the Song of Songs: *his head is finest gold* (Sg 5:11). *The head of Christ is God* (1 Cor 11:3), according to the Apostle's interpretation. It is obvious, I maintain, that any share in this divine gold is more resplendent than light, and such a share those fortunate ages enjoyed. In view of this it is easy to see that the people "whose happy fortune it was to travel toward their beloved Father and behold his countenance"[26] lived a truly golden life. Yet this second form of it had declined a little from the original form with which our first parents were endowed.

It is not difficult now to see the justification for calling that period in Etruria under Janus a golden age. The primordial life of the heavenly beings was rendered golden by the vision of their golden Father, the second, on earth, not by the vision of the Father, which no one can enjoy in this life, but by their very penetrating intelligence and perfect righteousness. Under Janus in Etruria education made use of these two powers to teach the path to the supreme good, opening sacred doors with these two keys; for indeed the twin powers of understanding and will are inborn in our rational nature. That is why revelation attests that two Persons only proceed from the unbegotten Father. The activity of these two powers, intellect and will, as long as they proceed from the golden head, make for a blessed life.

In Etruria the two powers were distinguished into a twofold understanding and a twofold righteousness. The first stage of Etruscan education taught philosophy to children not yet ready for the study of divine things, instructing them in the nature of the skies and the elements, metals, plants, animals, and other matters accessible to the senses. Once reason had grown stronger a second stage ensued, in which minds were lifted out of the wood and introduced to the study of the golden branches and the golden nature of God. So far, these two disciplines are concerned with the intelligence. But now, since knowledge of beauty in the intellect comes first, and love or desire for beauty in the will follows, the third stage of education was instruction in love. It warned and taught the students of the need to rise above all human attachments in high-souled contempt, and not merely to subdue and control greedy cravings (which, as we mentioned earlier, is the object of warfare) but to root them out completely and throw them right away by heroic virtue. The fourth stage of teaching was the discipline of the Tyrrhenians, whereby the mind, now spurning human preoccupations, was enkindled with divine love. Thus the first stage taught philosophy, the second theology, the third human love, the fourth heavenly and divine love.

The purpose of these disciplines was to develop a soul living in friendship with God, to win his favor, and to receive with eager mind golden rays of light from the divine fount. When these ends had been achieved, a happy life was lived on earth. There were no quarrels, seditions, or wars, because love of those things which furnish pretext for wars was absent. People suffered no grief or fear because, since they did not covet human things, but felt for such things only a high-minded indifference, they could have no reason for fear or grief. If we do not desire a thing, we are neither afraid of losing it nor upset when it is lost.

Their entire life was a joy, a joy that surpassed ordinary pleasure inasmuch as the object of their love was more dependable, closer to God and more enduring. Everywhere there was faith and concord, everywhere peace flourished. By their fourfold navigation they hoped to reach a harbor beyond human tempests; and so greatly did they love their studies — or, rather, such was their zeal and energy for the attainment of their goal, the highest good — that with minds aspiring to the stars they despised and spurned everything that lies beneath the stars. The whole work of Etruria was directed to this one end: that the soul should come to know itself, and should grow accustomed to dwelling in the groves of light; that it should think of nothing else, bend its efforts and exertions to nothing else, but to render itself blessed by unceasing meditation, mindfulness and vigilance.

The stages of Etruscan education gave promise of this. True, they dealt with material facts, transient matters, and fluid things perceived by the senses, but in so doing they elevated toward heaven, by four steps, minds hitherto buried in bodily existence. After all, our knowledge always begins from the senses. The second discipline freed itself from the flux and fog of matter, and from the dregs and dross defiling material things.

Leaving sense behind, it led its students to the vision of that golden reality, entirely free from any defilement, which can be glimpsed and contemplated only by the gaze of the mind. Accordingly the Etruscans named the second discipline "wisdom" or "dawn," for it seemed to reveal the sun to them and let sunshine into their minds.

Love of what is honorable and right gives rise to heroic virtue, and so "heroic virtue" was the title they gave to the third phase. Love springs from what is beautiful, for it is characteristic of beauty to arouse love. There are two kinds of beauty, however, and only two: everything that makes use of reason, and that which Plato and Dionysius[27] declare to be above reason. As beauty is twofold, so also is love. The first kind is love of reason itself, for nothing that God has made is better or closer to the divine than reason. Thus love of reason preserves us from forsaking reason and changing into beasts, or into *bristling boars* through drinking Circe's draught of debauchery, or into *bears in cages;*[28] it saves us from the fate which David feared, that we should degenerate into horses or mules *which have no understanding* (Ps 32:9) or any intelligent faculty or use of reason. Anyone who is abandoned to vices and debauchery and makes no use of reason forfeits the right to be called rational. What is commonly styled "virtue" opens to us the right-hand path; when we follow it we are adorned with constancy, temperance, prudence, and justice, to such a point that we not merely avoid acting in a way opposed to reason (for that is achieved by the four virtues proper to battle) but with high-souled virtue disdain whatever is repugnant to reason. Since this love of reason both teaches and brings to perfection in us all the virtues relating to conduct, the name "heroic virtue" rightly belongs to it.

The fourth stage was concerned not with human reason, which is more or less cloudy and obscure, but with the supereminent reality which glows above all reason with divine light and glory. When the soul approaches this it flings itself into the burning light; and just as a piece of iron thrust into fire becomes fire itself, so the soul, plunged into the flames of that light, burns and glows. It drinks deeply of the sacred radiance until, completely filled and inebriated, it is wholly changed into light. It ceases to be a soul, for it has become glowing light. The first of the four disciplines is called the "fount," because searching humans find it in their path and it is the first to instruct them on the fluid world. The second is named "dawn," for it ushers in the golden sun. The third is referred to as the virtue of heroic power, or the "heroine of virtues," inasmuch as it lifts all other virtues to the loftier glory of heroes. The fourth, on account of its purpose and its action, claims for itself the very name of "light," for it is not a mere pointer to light, as the dawn is, but unites itself completely to our souls and takes possession of them.

From all this we can clearly discern the nature of Etruscan teaching, before it was corrupted by the superstition of later seers. It consisted of the fountain (*fons*), the dawn (*aurora*), virtue (*virtus*), and light (*lux*). The fountain searched out the traces of the highest good, and taught people to glimpse it from afar. The dawn revealed that what had been distantly glimpsed was near at hand. Heroic virtues, or the heroine of the virtues, loved deeply what had been revealed. Finally the light entered into possession of the beloved.

There are two kinds of good things, human and divine. By human I mean here anything that is brought forth; I call divine him by whom everything other than himself is brought forth. The one is finite offspring, subject to change; the other is God, the immutable Father, infinite. Moreover, just as there are in the universe these two kinds of good, one in the parts of the universe and the other in its Creator, so also it is granted to man to reach out to them with two hands — intellect and will — so that nothing may be wanting to his felicity. By these two powers he among all the creatures of the universe is most akin to his Creator and most closely resembles him. Man apprehends both kinds of good with his intelligence, and embraces both with his love. The human things we come to apprehend are called science or knowledge, the divine things we glimpse are called wisdom. Similarly the love whereby we pursue human objects is called heroic virtue or the heroine of the virtues, while the love by which we mount to the divine bears the name of light. When we have worked through the sequence of six days to the end love will rest with God on the seventh day, in possession of that absolute and supreme God, which fashioned every keenest faculty of the soul for this fulfillment. The world has this twofold character of itself. Through contemplation we win the twofold understanding, by loving we attain the two loves. The Lord's two Testaments could be given these two names: the Old represents knowledge or science inasmuch as it promises human rewards, a *land* widely *flowing with milk and honey* (Bar 1:20), while the New stands for wisdom, since it promises divine gold and heavenly treasures. He who promulgated the perfect law urged us to seek unfading treasures in heaven.

Plato's Latin disciple drew the same distinction, teaching that mortals should aspire to gold and strive for a blessed life.[29] Our duty, he showed, is to be guided first by the science of the Sibyl, and then by the wisdom that comes from divine inspiration. Diodorus in his sixth book asserts that the Etruscans took care to do precisely this, devoting most of their time to the investigation of nature and to theology.[30] Vergil, after speaking of the twofold object of the intellect, goes on to speak of the twofold love of the will: "twin doves," Aeneas calls them when he "recognizes his mother's birds."[31]

The psalmist, like a Christian Pindar, tuned his lyre to a most beautiful song about the same four activities. *If you sleep among the sheepfolds* (Ps 68:14) . . . he sang. By "sheepfolds" he meant our inheritances, that is, the two Testaments we inherit, one of which offers human happiness and science or knowledge, while the other promises divine rewards and wisdom. Minds which find their repose in these become, in the psalmist's words, *the silvered wings of a dove* (Ps 68:14); this means that they receive the wings of both kinds of love as the gift of the Holy Spirit of love who descended by the Jordan in the form of a dove,[32] he who of old had inspired those *pure words of the Lord* (Ps 12:7) which were *like silver refined in a furnace* (Ps 18:31). The same Spirit was preparing to give *pinions of pale gold* (Ps 68:14), for he was to fill the hard hearts of the apostles with a fire of love powerful enough to lift the human race to possession of divine, eternal gold. This was the purpose of that third golden age which succeeded the flood; it was built on the four disciplines through which people might come to possess the light of divine gold, insofar as this was granted to mortals before the coming of the Light itself.

Let us pause now and gather together all the features of this third golden age, and look at it under our symbol of the oak tree with four branches.

First we must write in the names of the four elements: on the first branch the foundation (*fundamenta*) or earth, on the second water (*aqua*), on the third wind (*ventus*) or air, on the fourth fiery light (*lux*). Next we must insert in due order the four passions which give birth to all our affective states; these begin with the same four initial letters: fear (*formido*), sick weariness (*aegritudo*), pleasure (*voluptas*), and lust (*libido*). These four passions arouse the two kinds of warfare in which mortals are engaged; and so after them we must add a third kind of picture to represent the four standards of victory and triumph. These fit the same pattern of initial letters: they are fortitude (*fortitudo*), temperance or moderation (*armonia*), right reason or truth (*veritas*) which gives rise to prudence, and enlightened (*lucifer*) justice. After these four champions which banish war and weapons we must add the golden disciplines of Etruria, and these too maintain the pattern of initial letters. First we have the fount (*fons*) of science and philosophy, then the dawn (*aurora*) of divine wisdom, next the heroic virtue or the heroine of virtues (*virago virtusque*), and finally the very light (*lux*) of the Godhead. Plunged into this light souls are filled with divine gold; they can be called golden, such is their proper name.

In order to ensure that the Etruscans should be continually aware of these four letters, Janus dedicated them to Etruria in a special way. He founded a four-part royal city in the foothills of Mount Ciminus and used to name its quarters in accordance with the four initials. The citizens who dwelt in one part he would call Faluceres, those in another Arbani, the third group Vatulonii and the inhabitants of the fourth Longolani. In the center of these quarters he planted a grove, which he declared sacred to Vulturna, an ancient Tyrrhenian deity. There the Lucumones, or Etruscan priests, vigorously studied the four disciplines. This is why even today the grove is often called FAVL by the local people. From the same letters was derived the name of the maiden whom the Etruscans gave of old to

Hercules, according to Verrius; and our own Lactantius later mentions this too.[33] In that city very ancient rocks are sometimes to be seen; they are regarded as sacred and are inscribed thus

FA

VL

So, then, we have first of all the four elements, secondly the principal passions, thirdly the virtues, fourthly the disciplines, fifthly the quarters of the Tyrrhenian metropolis, and sixthly the name of that grove which, according to the Mantuan seer who was to spring from Etruria, was called a wide "space of consecrated ground"[34] in the religion of our fathers, because there dwelt the Lucumones who delved into the secrets of sacred learning.

Now, however, we find a seventh instance of the same initials in the superstitious disciplines which flourished in a later age of far different complexion: those concerned with lightning (*fulguralis*), divination (*auspiciorum*), prophecy (*vaticinantium*), and soothsaying (*litantium*). People skilled in the first art foretold the future from study of those things which Aristotle sets out in his *Meteorology*,[35] that is from thunderbolts, thunder and lightning, comets, showers, winds, water, earth tremors, and similar phenomena of nature, which are so far from conclusive that we could rather call them miscarriages. Practitioners of divination gathered their omens from human speech, and their auspices from the song, flight or species of birds. Prophets waxed wise about future events on the basis of either external portents or internal inspiration from their gods. Soothsayers declared that good or evil fortune could be signified in advance by the entrails, droppings, or sinews of sacrificial victims.

All things flow forth from good sources, but all are easily corrupted, and there is nothing so excellent at its beginning that it cannot be ruined after a short time. It is in the nature of things to deteriorate. Etruria flourished in earlier days with the glory of its mysterious disciplines when its citizens focused their chaste and pure endeavors on divine learning; at this early period they were held to be very powerful and close to God, by reason not of any profane and detestable sorcery but of a kind of holy, secret magic. The nature of this magic of theirs is suggested by Plato, who declares that Zoroaster's magic was nothing else but divine worship.[36] The Etrurians, however, after winning great fame throughout the world by their good and mysterious arts, saw the honor of their name dwindling daily as these good arts declined, and tried to bolster their sinking reputation. Having lost the noble contemplation attained through their education, they brought in deceitful and cheating superstitions; nonetheless they were, according to Diodorus, universally admired for it.[37]

I have dwelt somewhat fully on the third age, under Janus, in order to make it clear that although that era, content with the very simple fare of acorns, came near to blessedness, the Portuguese king has established a far more blessed life in the Indies. He has carried the golden acorns from your oak to the lands of sunrise and the remotest peoples, and like some new Janus has opened for them the gate to a golden age. We have considered the first golden age, of Lucifer in heaven; the second, of our first parents in the garden of delight; and the third, that of King Janus in Etruria. The last golden age on earth is well worth our attention, for under the rule of Your Holiness the fourth golden age now shines out from the same sanctuary whence the third, under Janus, shone forth of old. In his reign, though, the gold lay hidden, for it was locked in by two keys, the rivers Tiber and Magra; whereas now that you hold the Vatican Hill, your messenger Manuel, more bountiful than Janus, has carried the sacred fruits of your golden tree across the world's oceans from the place of sunset toward the sunrise. So now, as I approach this fourth golden age, I will relate what philosophy surmised about it, what were the premonitions of the Old Testament prophets, who was the founder of this truly golden age and what is the nature of the gold itself.

The Fourth Golden Age: Christ

Plato, principal of the Academy, gives an instance of the golden life being lived by the human race in its early days in the city of Critia.[38] In his *Cratylus* he relates that Hesiod testified similarly concerning that period, and that a decline ensued in which it fell to silver, then to bronze, and then to base iron.[39] He left us in no doubt as to the meaning of gold. In his first book on *The Laws*, however, he wrote that there are two kinds of gold, one within ourselves and the other originating and existing outside us. The former, he taught, was to be sought, embraced and cultivated, the latter to be shunned, feared and cast aside.[40] He had given the same instruction in the sixth book of his *Republic*: we should make use of the gold which shines in our minds, but not even touch the gold outside the mind. It is very clear what he understood by this gold within our minds, for, as he says in the sixth book of the *Republic*, it is nothing else but knowledge of the Good, recognition of the true, supreme Good, and the best possible instruction of the mind. He therefore declared all good and wise people to be rich, truly rich, for they possess true wealth and gold that cannot fade.[41] In his *Gorgias* Plato wishes the soul to be tested with a touchstone to see if it is golden.[42] In the third book of the *Republic* he recommends that such a golden person be sought and the administration of public affairs be entrusted to him; in the eighth book he says that only golden minds should govern, while others should obey and submit to the king. Before this he had clearly warned in the sixth book that unless the one who reigns and rules is made of gold, states will be overturned and ruined.[43]

In case any of us might delude ourselves that this gold in the mind could be acquired either from the bounty of nature or by adroit dealing,

Plato testifies in the third book of the *Republic*[44] that it is given to human beings by God, who is its source. It is like the quest for the Golden Bough:

> it will easily follow your touch of itself
> if the Fates so will; but if not
> then by no strength of your own, nor by the harshest weapon,
> will you conquer it or wrest it from its place.[45]

In these texts the philosophers tried to teach us that while human gold may be acquired without divine favor, divine gold can never be.

So, then, I think we have tracked down the true gold. It is what Lucifer glimpsed in heaven (for if he had not, he would not have fallen), what our first parents reached out for in the garden of delights, and what later in Etruria Janus tried in vain to give his people. As Plato recognizes,[46] mortals can be endowed with an immortal gift only by Almighty God himself, and no single one of the people we have named was God. No man ever was, except Christ Jesus. He is the King of kings. Contemplating his advent, the Sibyl sang, "Now the maiden Justice comes again, and Saturn's reign returns."[47] Plato, who had warned us in his *Gorgias* that gold of this kind is carried by a son of God, corroborated the fables of the poets, who believed that the scepter borne by Minos, the son of Zeus, was made of gold.[48] Yet it was not from the poets that Plato derived this, but from the very fountain of truth, for a golden scepter is indeed to be sought in the hand of him who is the Son of God.

Plato's disciple Vergil also noticed this point, for just as he had borrowed from the Sybil in declaring "throughout the world a golden race will arise,"[49] so also he borrowed from Plato the conviction that it would be no product of human reason but a gift sent down from heaven by God: "Now is a new race sent from highest heaven," and "a progeny beloved of the gods, great stock of Jove."[50]

Nor should I omit the witness of Trismegistus in the Hermetic works: in reply to an inquirer he said that regeneration would be accomplished by a man who would be Son of God.

How loathsome, then, was the faithlessness of the Jews who, although so closely bound to God, refused to grasp what peoples far removed from him made their own! How could they fail to understand that gold would be restored to humankind by none other than immortal God, when even their own books were not silent? We may leave aside the passages in Exodus and the book of Kings where God decreed that in the golden temple all the appurtenances should be golden or gold-adorned, and recall how he himself often promised that he would give them gold. First he rebuked the Hebrew people for having despised in their worship and heedless rites, and profaned by their sins and irreverence, that appearance of gold which they had received from God centuries earlier. So Jeremiah lamented, *How has your gold grown dim?* (Lam 4:1). He meant that their religion had been despised and corrupted and their gold had deteriorated into base metal.

Yet God promised that he would bring back the golden centuries, and scarcely a prophet failed to write of this. I will pass over others, for fear of prolonging our search for witnesses to immoderate length; but let anyone read the sixtieth chapter of Isaiah, and the subsequent ones to the end of the book. There it can be seen that the prophet fully, openly and distinctly pointed to ages when darkness, war and all evils would be removed, and light, gold and all good things restored. *Arise, be enlightened, Jerusalem*, he says, *for your light has come* (Is 60:1). They will bring *their gold with them* (Is 60:9), he adds; and a little later, *In place of bronze* I will give *gold* (Is 60:17). Consistent with this is the promise in the book of blessed Job, where God pledged himself to give *torrents of gold instead of flint* (Jb 22:24); it was as though he was shaming the impious Hebrews by foretelling the future piety of believers. David too spoke of the Messiah who was to inaugurate the new age, and when singing of the Messiah's royal coming he inserted the line, *Gold from Arabia shall be given to him* (Ps 72:15): this means, he will receive the light and happiness of a blessed country.

No one on earth has ever been allotted this gift except the soul which has united itself to God on earth. Lest we should be so foolish as to expect heavenly gold from anyone else than God in heaven, he declared himself to be its source in the prophecy of Joel: "The gold is mine." Accusing those who arrogated to themselves a reputation for wisdom he said, *You have carried off the gold which belongs to me* (Jl 3:5). When Pythagoras in Egypt heard this, he denied that he was a wise man, and preferred his doctrine to be called not wisdom but philosophy; that is, love of wisdom. Apart from the Peripatetics, all philosophers disclaimed the odious, conceited name of wisdom, agreeing with Plato that wisdom and gold must be sought from God alone.

At last, when peace and tranquillity reigned widely among mortals, the predictions of prophets and Sibyls came true. God appeared on earth. *Kings of Tarshish and the islands* offer him *gifts* (Ps 72:10); envoys *from Sheba* (Is 60:6) come, bringing him incense and gold. He summons the dismayed tyrants. He casts out the *prince of this world* (Jn 12:31); he expels war, weapons, and warlike ways. In the waters of the Jordan he washes away the traces of our ancient sin. When his sun sets in death, death and guilt die with him. The serpent dies too. When he rises from the dead, light, life, and a new day rise with him. His mighty heroes are secretly gathered. They are to be strong and noblehearted, he tells them, for noble hearts are needed for glorious enterprises. They are to *go out to the whole world* (Mk 16:15); they are destined to be *princes over all the earth* (Ps 45:17); they are to travel to every land and region throughout the world, to banish warlike ways and establish golden customs, and to awaken humankind to divine realities.

The Apocalypse speaks of God giving *gold refined by fire* (Rv 3:18), and it was indeed gold in the form of fire sent by God which they received in their souls when at the coming of God's Spirit *charity was poured into their hearts* (Rom 5:5). Now the twelve leaders were truly full of that divine gold which, as the Apostle declares, is the artificer of all things and possesses all power.[51] Fearful men, men unskilled and uneducated, speak in a variety of tongues.[52] After drinking in the gold of the Holy Spirit they become fearless, very wise and fluent of speech. They give sight to the blind, hearing to the deaf, and speech to the dumb. By a gesture or a command they drive out diseases, vices, and demons. They restore the sick to health not simply by a touch or a word, but — what is even more wonderful — even by the shadow of their bodies. Why need I elaborate further? People are astounded, and they forsake their sins, their wealth, their estates, their homes, and their wives; they leave behind everything which derives from the earth and fall in love with gold from heaven, seeking it, longing for it. In the end they are so intoxicated with this heavenly gold that they joyfully abandon all human things. They strive for heaven alone. Meanwhile, satisfied with the gold they have already been given, they lead a golden life on earth.

I said earlier that this golden age was the fourth in our series, but in fact it is the only one which truly deserves to be called golden. The others bore golden traces or shadows, but were not truly gold. Never did that golden presence of God fill Lucifer, or our first parents, or Janus; never did it confer all kinds of virtue on anyone before this time; never did it send men out equipped with knowledge of all tongues to all nations, all languages, all races. Now at last the apostles were filled with gold, and so imbued were they with contempt for worldly things and desire for heaven that they vied with each other in confronting tyrants, overcoming them by their constancy, and provoking them to fury. With minds aflame with love they flung themselves on swords or into water, joyfully certain of the blessed life that awaited them as soon as they should free themselves from their mortal bodies and take flight heavenward for the stars. They had drunk from rivers of gold, and were no longer able to take their ease or slacken their efforts until they came to the primal fountain, where they have now become golden themselves and, as John tells us, live golden lives in a city of pure gold.[53]

The same four letters which of old were held sacred in Etruria were foreseen also by Ezekiel with reference to this fourth age, for in his vision he saw first a human face (*faciem*), then an eagle (*aquilam*), then a calf (*vitulum*), and finally a lion (*leonem*).[54] Later, in the new age, these same four symbols were appropriated to the evangelists. This is why I hold that it was by divine providence that Etruria consecrated those four letters, for they were to stand for the four animals later adopted by the four gospels. Judea had in its wicked foolishness rejected the gospels, but the four capital letters were honored in Etruria because in God's providence the capital of all the churches, that church which was to teach other churches the four gospels, was to be situated on the Etrurian Hill of the Vatican.

Further, just as the animals have four different faces, and there were four men who bore these symbols in their writings about the life of our golden Prince, so also did they seek out and write about four different aspects of our Lord, namely his bodily condition (*faciem corporis*), his appetitive urge (*appetitum*), his will (*voluntatem*) and the Logos. In Matthew we read of his bodily condition and his genealogy.[55] Luke, who testifies that Jesus in his agony sweated drops of blood, shows us the appetitive urge of the lower part of his soul, the part which did not enjoy beatitude. Mark's account reaches that higher part of our Lord's will, which even while he was still on his earthly pilgrimage was inebriated with a *flood of delight* (Ps 36:9) and happiness, *drinking from the torrent by the wayside* (Ps 110:7). Mark points to this not only in our Lord's risen life but also earlier at the Transfiguration, for while Matthew had told us that Jesus' *clothes became white* (Mt 17:2), Mark added that they seemed to glisten, suggesting that the light of his inward beatitude had broken through even to his clothing. John, whom Jesus specially loved, was the only one to reach the Logos or Word, for as he rested on the breast of his loving Lord he saw that same Word resting in the secret intimacy of the Father's bosom.[56]

Since these four living creatures had soared higher than we could reach either by the work of contemplation or by our weak human speculation, it was necessary that four intelligences should later be lifted up in pursuit of them, and thus explain, expound, and demonstrate to us the flight of the four creatures. Jerome, therefore, assumed the face (*faciem*) of a man, for he was highly educated in human literature and made the Hebrew and Greek books accessible to Roman readers. Augustine imitated the eagle (*aquilam*) by a sublimity of mind not unlike its own; the higher the eagle soared, the more happily did he follow. Pope Gregory guided and followed a pontifical ox-calf (*vitulum*), for although he had himself spurned profane and wayfaring disciplines, he was given the sacred fields of divine mysteries to plow and cultivate. Who, finally, could fear to associate Ambrose with the lion (*leoni*)? Unarmed, and crowned only with a miter, he did not hesitate boldly to attack armed emperors surrounded by armed men, openly to accuse them, and to forbid them access to altars and churches.

It is evident, then, that he who inaugurated the new age embraced more truly and more fully the mysteries of those letters which the Etruscans held sacred. He alone represented both the fountain (*fontem*) of natural science and the dawn (*auroram*) of divine wisdom, as the Apostle clearly testifies when he exclaims in wonder, *Oh, how deep are the riches of God's wisdom and knowledge!* (Rom 11:33). In this way Christ showed forth the first two disciplines. The two remaining parts, concerned with the twin loves, were indicated when he laid the double foundation of godly life and spoke of the two wings needed for flight to heaven; for when questioned about the way to eternal life he replied, *You shall love the Lord your God, and your neighbor even as yourself* (Mt 22:37-39).

This charity, flying with its two wings, as we might say, ranks so high in the Apostle's estimation that it alone would suffice without any other virtue, whereas without it all the rest together would fall short. *Charity is poured out in* the *hearts* (Rom 5:5) of Christ's disciples. I speak of none other than the Spirit who in the beginning was the artificer of all things, and was said to hover *over the waters* (Gn 1:2), brooding over the incipient creation.

Thereafter he surveyed all that came to be; for he who created all things, both human and divine — I mean corporeal and incorporeal beings — himself enters their minds and makes himself their mental pair of eyes: one for seeing human objects, the other for divine. Finally he possesses every virtue, for he it is who gives the two wings of love, as Plato explains in the *Phaedo*.[57] These twin loves surpass and embrace all virtue, according to the teaching of the Apostle which we have just noted.[58]

We have now examined the disciplines of this fourth age, an age as far superior to the three that went before as true and solid gold outshines a gilded plate. In his *Meno* Plato handed on the tradition that Jove's golden scepter,[59] which according to Homer was borne by King Minos, symbolized divine instruction and doctrine;[60] but if this is the case, how could Lucifer's age be adjudged golden, when he spurned the golden fount of light? Or the age of the first humans, who gave their allegiance to Lucifer, the scorner and deserter? Or yet the age of Janus, born among those who, in the psalmist's words, made bold to *rise before the light* (Ps 127:2)?

That golden light which renders a period of history golden, and brings a blessed spiritual life into being for us, cannot be attained unless it be most ardently loved and zealously sought; for it is not chance that renders us blessed. Only what is first known can be loved, however, and the infinite light could not be known until it revealed itself and gave itself to men and women to be seen and contemplated, clothing itself in a body like ours and sharing life on earth with human beings.

When Homer assigned Minerva as a companion to Ulysses, to instruct him, to foretell the future, and to show him the way home to his native land,[61] the spot was indicating that it was from heaven that the light would come to earth, bringing salvation to humankind. Plato makes the same point in various parts of his works, particularly in the *Alcibiades*, where Socrates warns us that we should not offer sacrifice until someone appears to lift the veil from our eyes and show us how to distinguish between God and man, and to teach us how we should bear ourselves with regard to things both human and divine. Plato in his *Epinomis* believes that this could be accomplished only by God or a son of the gods.[62]

It was God himself, in the person of Jesus, the Son of God, who brought us this very light, for in giving himself as its fountain (*fontem*) he revealed the goal of all human searching. Dawn (*aurora*) broke when he made known to us that his birth was effected by the Father's power, through an outpouring of the fostering Spirit.[63] He manifested every depth of human love, for he neither disdained our life nor shrank from death for the sake of the human race. He manifested divine love, for he willed to have nothing, in order to love the divine beauty with his whole heart.

These, then, are the four disciplines of the golden age. Jesus did not learn them from Etruria; rather it was he who handed them down to be transmitted to Etruria. As he prepared to send the four holy disciplines, by means of the four gospels, to Etruria initially and then to the entire world, he gathered certain heroic men, so that he might use their Spirit-filled hearts as channels and conduits to distribute rivers of gold. We must now say a few words about the number of these heroes, in order to show the supreme wisdom of every disposition made at the opening of the new age.

The Significance of the Number Twelve

It is beyond doubt that the golden fountain, the Son of God, willed to offer himself as a mortal man among mortals in order to turn us who were made of iron into immortal, golden beings. *If anyone is thirsty*, he said, *let that person come to me and drink. Out of his heart will flow streams of water* (Jn 7:37-38), living water leaping up to eternal life. The moment people had drunk, they at once put off their iron nature and their mortality and, in the power of the Spirit who *makes all things new* (Rv 21:5), were clothed in golden life.

There is in every human being a triple soul, however; Plato in his *Timaeus*[64] and Plato's disciple, Vergil, left us their witness that to all newborn humans "Feronia their mother has given three souls."[65] In its substance the soul is a unity, to be sure, but in its parts and its powers it is complex. With the part which nourishes us we feel pleasure, with the irascible part we fear, and with the part which unites us to divine truth we contemplate and savor wisely the things of God. A person who yields to the dominion of sensual pleasures has but one soul; a person who loves immoderately what is less lovable and fears what is less fearful has only two souls. That person, however, in whom golden reason is not mixed with the lead or iron of the untamed parts will be conqueror of both himself and others; he is suited to royal tasks, as Plato asserts, and most fit for golden company.[66] He has appetite, but he rules it with moderation; he has the capacity to be angry, but he holds it firmly in check. Above all he has a citadel of reason, which he guards under the sway of contemplation. The two former powers drag us down to the brutes, whereas the third lifts us to divine things. So powerful is reason that it can make itself a receptive vessel, open to the divine fountain, drinking in floods of golden light; thus reason establishes within itself a very clear, peaceful, divine spring, and the strength of that divine tranquillity suffices to ward off any kind of disturbance.

Now, there are two kinds of disturbance. On the one hand lies the soft lead of cupidity, on the other rages the iron fury of anger. I am using the word "cupidity" now to refer to the appetitive part of the soul and "anger" to mean the passion which prompts us to be either more rash or more timid than is warranted by reason. The impulses of cupidity arise from the imagination of either good or evil. Imagination of good things is distinguished into three phases. At first the good object offered to us by the imagination strikes us as pleasing, and it arouses love, which is the source and origin of all disturbance. Once love has awakened the good object is seen as a goal, and hence there is agitation, for it attracts the soul and moves it to seek what it loves. This movement or impulse is usually called desire by moderns, but the ancients called it lust or concupiscence. Finally we attain the object and rest in our goal like travelers in repose after a journey; but then there is an upsurge of delight, because that thing which we first loved, then longed for while we did not have it, is now in our possession to enjoy. So the object is first recognized as agreeable, then longed for, and at last possessed. First we love, then we long, then we enjoy. Thus it is that three kinds of disturbance are aroused by imagination of the good: love, cupidity, and pleasure.

Similarly three opposite effects ensue from the imagination of evil, for it is obvious that from different causes different effects will flow. When we perceive the existence of something evil we first hate it, then we turn away from it and avert it as far as we can. When at last it does come and the evil is upon us, we are sorrowful.

Let us take as an example the story of Paris as related by Homer, for there is no human being who is not at some time in Paris' quandary. Within him are leaden cupidity, iron anger, and golden reason; and these three powers encounter three beautiful beings, representing pleasure, advantage, and honor.

Venus, Juno, and Pallas — each has her own beauty to allure the shepherd. Each of them tries to draw him away from the others by her arts, to present herself as more attractive then the other two, and to entice him into her own camp. When the youth recognizes the beauty of these three, three loves immediately spring up in his mind, for all three please him once he has looked at them carefully. He thinks about them and considers what sustains and attracts him, and realizes that one choice must be preferred to the other two. Indeed, two must be completely rejected so that the third may be chosen (for while it is possible to love all of them simultaneously, they cannot all be sought and gained). Nature has established the same rule in the breeding habits of the eagle, for, as the poet would have it, as recorded by Aristotle, the eagle hatches three squabs, but pushes out two of them and rears one only.[67] Human beings have to do the same.

At first Paris simply loves Helen, as presented to him by the seductive Venus. Then, once Venus has conquered the languid, effeminate youth, she who had been loved equally with her two rivals begins to be preferred to them and more ardently desired. This was the occasion of Paris' sin which proved to be the source and origin of all evils. Once the longing is aroused in his mind there arise also determination and resolve to gain its object, and this continues until the beloved and longed-for Helen is possessed. She awakens love in him when she is seen as pleasing, lust when she is longed for, and finally pleasure when she is abducted from Mycenae.

Just as this threefold sequence occurs in pleasant things, so does it also in misfortune. Hatred arises as the Greeks seek to get Helen back; then aversion lest intercourse with Paris render Helen an adulteress. To prevent this they wage war for ten years. The third phase occurs when the supreme evil has happened: the city is burnt, the country ruined, Helen is gone, and the sequel is bitterness of mind and much sorrow.

Such are the disturbances that beset the leaden part of the soul; but the iron part too has its troubles deriving from the imagination of good or evil — similar disturbances or even worse. Both parts of the soul are attracted by what is good, but whereas a soft, easy good draws the leaden part, it is a hard, difficult good which attracts the iron. When, therefore, an arduous good is presented to us we either hope to attain it or despair of the possibility of doing so. On the one hand hope coaxes us, on the other despair is ready to give up the desired object. As for the apprehension of evil, when we have reason to think that danger threatens we either sink down in spirit and are then paralyzed by fear, or we struggle wildly for life and bold recklessness drives us. If our blood grows hot with desire for revenge, anger burns within us; but if it does not, then no unjust injury can move us and we are always listless. No other passion is mentioned by Aristotle or other philosophers.[68]

For our own part we cannot be persuaded that a person who puts up with every injury without becoming upset is any the less to be censured than one who is seized with angry desire to avenge them all. It is generally agreed that princes, at least, act very justly when they are angered by wrongdoing and take measures to punish it. Even if reason were not sufficient to prove this, we would have the witness of the scriptures to support it. It is not the anger of princes alone, however, that is meant when we are warned, *Be angry and do not sin* (Ps 4:5); in other words, "Be angry with sinners and evildoers." Unquestionably anger, and even fury, are attributed to God himself: *O Lord, do not rebuke me in your anger* (so runs the Hebrew), *nor correct me in your fury* (Ps 6:2).

Let us return now to the example of Paris. This same man who had been impelled by the urges of the leaden soul was now troubled by the impulses of the iron as well. He had hoped to gain a mistress; now he despaired of regaining a reputation. Boldness fired him to set fire to his native land, but a different passion frightened him away from extinguishing the flames. Anger surged up in him against Antenor who counseled him to restore Helen to the Greeks, but listlessness held him back from repelling the two Ajaxes who raged against Ilium and the Trojans.

We ourselves are no better than he was, for we too are made of iron and lead. Our golden citadel of reason is beset on the one side by love, cupidity, and pleasure, and by their opposites, hatred, aversion, and sadness; on the other it is attacked by hope, boldness, and anger, together with their opposites, despair, fear, and listlessness. These twelve plagues are within mortals, and although they are unable of themselves to enter or overthrow the sacred temple of reason, yet through the enticements of habit they can win their way in.

The dwelling of reason is situated in the highest part of the soul, but these plagues haunt the vestibule below in the sentient region, and there they lie in ambush for Queen Reason and her laws and instructions. They wait for her to be deceived and open the gate, like Tarpeia, so that they may gain control of the capital, lay waste the golden region with their iron weapons, and drive away their plunder of wretched souls from the paths of heaven down the road to hell. As an Academic philosopher has it, drawing on ancient tradition, "At the very porch, at the outermost door of Orcus, there have grief and the pangs of conscience made their bed."[69]

The Stoics and the Peripatetic philosophers inquire whether any passion can disturb a wise man. It is worth asking whom, in the last analysis, they hold to be wise. The spirits who lived in heaven in the first golden age might surely have been considered wise; their leader possessed a nature more glorious and exquisite than any other, apart from God himself. They suffered no bodily disturbances, for they were incorporeal, but they had their own disturbances all the same. The golden life of our first ancestors was characterized by disturbances, but only such as were subject to reason; and had not reason itself turned away from God, these impulses would never have revolted against reason.

The efforts of Janus and Etruria were directed to the recovery, insofar as this was possible, of that golden way of life which had decayed; by patient reflection and prolonged research they strove to discover what had initially driven out the golden lifestyle and what hindered its re-establishment. If that golden treasure had been unknown or hidden it could indeed have been dismissed as unimportant, but once recognized and examined it could not. Hence virtue and the golden life have found no more pernicious enemy than ignorance. By the guidance of both God and nature Etruria came to understand that nothing could be more godlike than this divine gold, and that therefore the people called "gods" in the psalmist's phrase, *You are gods* (Ps 82:6), and indeed all human souls, are born for no other destiny than to contemplate the radiance of divine gold and come to possess it. They further realized that once someone had recognized it, such a person could be held back from possessing it only by the onslaught of the twelve passions. These present twin objects to our gaze: the one they persuade us to avoid, the other to seek; prosperity on the one hand, adversity on the other; right and left; "on the right proud Scylla, on the left insatiable Charybdis."[70]

Wherever we turn, if we yield to the winds of passion we are overcome by the storm and we sink. Our golden mind is mired, submerged, and buried in the filth of its waves. A golden life (insofar as we can describe it) is nothing else than a life in which golden reason is kept clear of both the harm and the ugliness of the passions, a life in which the sway of reason is sovereign and the passions are its obedient subjects. The kingdom is governed not by force or arrogance or arms, but by quiet, gentleness, and peace. There are two aspects to this: on the one hand the subjects of reason, free from disturbance, keep themselves within the bounds of obedience and peace, while on the other the rule of reason is supreme. The activities of such a kingdom are no other than the pursuit of the four disciplines and reflection upon them.

Let a very shrewd observer provide us with a definition of the two parts of the Etruscan teaching in a poetic couplet:

Under that king, men say, the times were golden,
with such sweet peace he ruled his people.[71]

The first line describes the rule and activity of reason; the second the obedience and peace of the subject passions. Why was this written, if not to ensure that later generations should always remember it, and safeguard that golden glory to the utmost of their ability? This is possible only if the twelve passions that rebel against reason be conquered and subdued.

In order that the number of these enemies should be kept habitually before their eyes, they divided the whole of Etruria into twelve regions. According to Vergil the same arrangement was built up in Mantua, on the model of Etruria: he avers that

Threefold were her races,
four the peoples within each race.[72]

The Etruscans appointed one priest from each of these regions to serve at the shrine of Vulturna. These priests lived in the grove called in ancestral religion "a wide space of consecrated ground";[73] it was in the foothills of Mount Ciminus. There the twelve men strove with most vigilant care to ensure that their Italian empire (for empire it was; according to Livy it stretched from sea to sea)[74] should be governed with golden administration. With this in view they encouraged their people to victory over the twelve enemies. For the same reason they appointed twelve lictors, equipped with rods for keeping the crowds who flocked to Vulturna under golden restraint.

In his great wisdom Almighty God approved of this arrangement, for when he laid the foundations of his new people in the beginning, he too observed the pattern of three and twelve. He had willed that in Etruria there should be a threefold race, and within each race a fourfold division of peoples, making twelve. Nonetheless he also provided for three fountainheads — Abraham, whom he called *father of many nations* (Gn 17:4), Isaac and Jacob; and as soon as possible he added to these three patriarchs twelve leaders, whom he gave as sons to the patriarch Jacob, and to these again twelve tribes, and as many other benefits as possible to this number of twelve. Furthermore he appointed these twelve heavenly leaders over the whole world, as twelve shepherds who by spiritual guidance were to teach, persuade and coerce the flock of humankind to golden probity. Plato in his fifth, sixth and eighth books on *The Laws* divides the city into twelve districts or streets, and in order not to depart too far from Moses he even sets up and names twelve tribes there.[75]

An observance which was thus carefully preserved in ages which were not truly golden, but only gilt or imitation gold, was respected also by him who was in truth the Lord of the golden restoration. He did not hide the fact that he had twelve legions of angels at his command, yet he chose twelve leaders on earth. We may ask whether he chose them for peace or to wage war, for he who daily urged people to peace also said that he had brought to earth not peace but the sword. Perhaps, then, he who invited people to both also called his apostles to both: first to take up arms against rebellious passions until they conquered them, but then to be merciful to the vanquished and endow them with peace? *Be valiant in warfare* (Heb 11:34), he told them, and do battle against the ancient serpent. That serpent bit our first parents and inflicted on them the twelve wounding passions. So now when the Lord ordered his followers to do battle with the serpent he commanded them to defeat the twelve poisons which had been left in human bodies by the serpent's bite.

The Apostle observed *a different law imposed on his members* (Rom 7:23), which *conflicted with* the divine law within. This alien law can in no way be subdued and overcome unless its twelve heads be cut off, like the heads of Hydra. That person wages war who lays low some Geryon with its fourfold body; that person also wages valiant war who puts to death the whole Geryon and Hydra. The Apostle exults in his victory over them, claiming, *I have fought the good fight*; and lest it be supposed that he like some Roman and Christian Horatius had slain twelve Curatii, he added, *I have finished the race* (2 Tm 4:7). He did not omit to mention the reward, declaring that he would lead his triumphal procession and win his crown of righteousness. No one should doubt that the insignia of victory would correspond in number to the conquered enemies, for another apostle shows us the crown of the victorious Church aglow with *twelve stars* (Rv 12:1).

A person who is conquered by the passions allows twelve habits to grow up in his spirit ("habits" is what philosophers call them when contrary to right reason). When these have grown strong the "chariot gets out of control,"[76] no longer responding to reason, the charioteer. The person who overcomes and subdues them, however, acquires habits in harmony with reason, and lives on earth a life scarcely different from that of heaven.

In the book of Genesis Moses suggests the different natures of two families: the twelve descendants of Ishmael and the twelve sons of the patriarch Jacob.[77] Similarly in Exodus and Numbers he refers to the twelve powers which precede the formation of habits, under the image of *twelve fountains of water* (Nm 33:9). These were in Elim, that is, in the defective part of the soul. He speaks of habits which have solidified in opposition to reason as twelve stones from the lowest part of the Jordan's bed; he even called these stones "very hard," since habits are not easily broken. Indeed they are never dug out from their deep watery bed except by Jesus, who comes to choose twelve men and bring the ark of the Church *into the fortified city* (Ps 108:11), that city of which David sang, *Of you are told glorious things, O city of God* (Ps 87:3).

In this city the ark of Jesus is established, and so also is the authority of the twelve men by which the resistance of the twelve stones is worn down. What is the authority of the Roman See but that divine authority which the twelve chosen heroes long ago received from our Lord Jesus? Day by day they tame the wild oxen of inward warfare, not by the sorcery of Medea but by piety and holiness. Once tamed, the twelve oxen become like those which Solomon ordered to be placed beneath his bronze sea, or again they become the young lions which he set on the steps of his great throne; for the same passions which are first called "tame oxen" because they have forsaken human lusts can later be named young lions, once they have grown vigorous in hunting and defending the things of God.

II

The Excellence of the Christian Golden Age and Its Prospects under Julius II

We have passed in review the four ages to which the epithet "golden" has been attached — those of Lucifer, our first parents, Janus, and Christ; but it can easily be inferred from our exposition how far the fourth age is superior to the rest. As our Lord's words in Matthew's gospel suggest,[78] the condition of mind and soul of people not yet in heaven can be assessed in a threefold manner. One cup may be stained and dirty. Another may be presented which is clean but empty. Finally a third may be produced, polished bright and full.

An age which is ruined by iron and lead has people whose souls are like dirty vessels. Isaiah admonishes them in the words, Cleanse your-selves, *you who bear the vessels of the Lord* (Is 52:11). Since at such a period souls are given over to the passions, they derive their name from the most turbulent of the passions, and are called "vessels of wrath." *Israel has been devoured*, says Hosea, *and has become like an unclean vessel among the nations* (Hos 8:8). The sacred writers often referred to Israel as an *earthenware vessel* (Jer 22:8), a *potter's vessel*, a vessel of *wrath* or a vessel of *death*.

Then there is a second kind, that of souls who keep clear of the passions as far as possible by the exercise of reason; as Vergil has it, they "burn with a pure flame."[79] These people do indeed keep their cups clean insofar as human frailty permits, and so although in truth they are empty, they were yet called golden by our forefathers, who believed that a simple mode of life was best. Such a judgment might have been correct if our minds were capable of attaining the supreme good by our own efforts; but, as even Aristotle states, all minds who seek after the first cause have their ultimate good not in themselves but in the first cause.[80] It does not matter therefore how free they are from every passionate defilement, how clean, peaceful, and singleminded: if they are not filled by the golden light of God they are empty and ghostlike. Since they have fallen short of their supreme destiny they cannot truly be called golden, but only silver, inasmuch as they are second-best; or if they claim the epithet golden it is applied to them improperly.

In a manner not unlike that of the twelve forces we discussed earlier, these people do deserve to be called silver in the measure that they have caught the light of reason. Moses speaks in the book of Numbers of twelve silver bowls;[81] and the four virtues, which our own writers call the cardinal virtues, as being the pivotal points and pillars of right conduct, are called silver, because they are developed for the most part by human reason. Thus we read in the Song of Songs, *He made its posts of silver* (Sg 3:10). The ages of Lucifer, of our first parents and of Janus were of this lower rank. They did not attain the supreme radiance of God but were satisfied with the light of created reason, and therefore deserved the name of silver. Since, however, they believed that there could be nothing better for the mind than reason, they ascribed the great name of gold to every-thing which accorded with the reason of this world.

Finally there is a third group of souls who are not merely clean but also open to the light of the divine sun. Brim-full and inebriated with it, they are themselves changed from silver to gold and at last live a truly golden life. Just as we saw Moses, author of the Old Law, fashioning silver bowls,[81] so also did Solomon, who typified the giver of the New Law, place bowls on the tables in the temple, as the books of Chronicles record;

but his bowls were not of silver but of gold. Similarly Moses filleted the pillars with silver, according to the book of Exodus; but in the third book of Kings we find Solomon covering the pillars and all other parts of the temple with gold, so that nothing except gold would show. This was a sign that the King of Peace (which is what the name "Solomon" means), the Son of God, would found the Church of the apostles, and that this Church, spurning and casting off worldly things, would shine with the golden light of God alone. The apostles would forsake all things to gain this light, to be filled with it, and like precious vessels to carry it throughout the world.

The first age was that of nature decaying and turning foul; the second that of an aged and imperfect law. The third is the age of the New Law, absolute, perfect, entirely good, the age which alone throws away everything else to find the heavenly treasure and the precious pearl of the Lord. We know that Solomon *built himself a palanquin* (Sg 3:9), and that this was a type of the Blessed Virgin, of the Church, or of the soul living by faith, for in it Almighty God sits and is at rest. Yet in order to give an indication of the age of the New Law, the author added that Solomon *covered its back with gold* (Sg 3:10).

The conditions we have described prevailed at different periods, but it seems that today they all occur together. Moreover, even among those who are enclosed within the fold of the Church there are some who have so dedicated themselves to God that their whole toil is for nothing else but to be filled with God; others who rely on the resources of human reason and embrace what seems honorable; others again who concentrate entirely on material things. Of these last some bear themselves haughtily and with conceit, while others act basely and meanly. Thus the first group live an age of gold, the second an age of silver, the third an age of iron or wood, imitating the cedars of Lebanon, and the last a leaden or earthenware age, seeking only what is convenient or pleasurable. These different types are mentioned by Paul in his letter to Timothy. *In a great house,* he says, *there are not only gold and silver vessels, but wooden and earthenware ones as well* (2 Tm 2:20). Yes, why not, since on Paul himself God bestowed no more apt and appropriate name than *vessel of election* (Acts 9:15), a vessel which was to bear the divine name and the flood of divine light throughout the whole world?

So then, we have described the three kinds of age, of which only the one which attains what is best can be called golden; but Christ alone brings the best, for he is God and the Son of God. He brings it because he himself is the best, as he is also the greatest of all. To transport this gold far and wide throughout the world twelve heroes were chosen, who were to be like twelve vessels holding the heavenly ambrosia. Since the truth which was contained in that light filled and satisfied the intellect, it can rightly be called ambrosia, while the goodness in it delighted and inebriated the will, as though with nectar. Lest anyone should be debarred from such happiness those twelve vessels carried it over almost all the world and gave light and gold to peoples living in darkness and under an iron yoke. They had summed up their gold in twelve articles, so that there are twelve parts to the light whereby we believe and see the twelve hidden mysteries. These men were few indeed, but so dear were they to God that they were sent to peoples and nations who had no faith, to preach and give the faith to them. To men of iron they brought a golden life, and so deserved the name "apostles."

Today, in your reign, Pope Julius II, these same things are happening. Peoples hitherto unknown are being discovered, Christ is being preached to ignorant and wondering folk, a new world lying toward the sunrise is being won, wretched iron which was a stranger to faith is being turned into your faith's blessed gold. Before you were called to your high office Jeremiah and Joel wept and wailed. You have taken *my gold* (Jl 3:5) away, said one; *How the gold is tarnished!* (Lam 4:1) exclaimed the other. One lamented the capture of faithful cities; the other mourned over the profanation by vices and impiety of those not captured but in far worse case than the captured, as a familiar enemy acting by stealth is more to be hated than an open foe.

Consider how much more God has loved, adorned, and enriched you than other pontiffs, and how specially he has acted on your behalf in order to win your love! While it was his will to take away flocks of believers from other shepherds, to you he has given peoples who have never even heard the name "believers." Pope Eugene[82] wept that the gold had been taken away when he heard that so many thousands of faithful Christians, including Giuliano Cesarini and King Vladislav, had been killed in a fierce battle. Pope Nicholas[83] wept over the grievous wound he sustained when the glory and the guardianship of a Christian civilization was snatched from him, at the destruction of the Empire of Byzantium, Greece, and the East. Pope Calistus[84] wept at the loss of Lower Mysia and the overthrow of Corinth, which commanded a view of two seas. Pius of Siena[85] wept, for in trying to regain lost territories he lost not only the Peloponnesus, the Mediterranean and the island of Mytileni, but even the two eastern kingdoms of Trabizond and Upper Mysia, when Thomas Palaeologus was driven out and the kings of Mysia and Trebizond met with cruel deaths. These two were the last imperial survivors of my own noble Tyrrhenian stock. Paul of Venice[86] wept at the loss of the very useful island of Euboea, and in the very year that he lost the island he lost his life as well. No less did your uncle Sixtus[87] weep when a savage foe conquered Cafa, Kroia in Macedonia, Drisht, Lesh, Leukas which people call Santa Maura, Cephalonia, and Zante. Finally Pope Alexander[88] wept over the ports of the Peloponnesus and the occupation of its maritime coasts after an incredible slaughter of Christians.

I pass over in silence the events which preceded the reign of Pope Martin.[89] Those years had greater cause for mourning than the ones already enumerated, for no kind of strife is more detestable than civil war. It would be shameful to relate what the Church suffered through many years on account of smoldering schism; such is the name given to a state of affairs in which several popes are elected.

All these pontiffs were advanced to the highest office, yet they seem to have been promoted only to tears and grief. You, by contrast, must thank God not only that no part of the sacred flock has been lost while you have been shepherd, but also that a great region of the East has been added to it. You alone, in this our age, should be thankful, for when the golden branches of your oak tree made their appearance, kingdoms yielded as though they were longing to be conquered, attracted by the gold of its branches and hoping to cull from it a golden life.

The guardian angels of those kingdoms were familiar with the patently clear prophecy of Isaiah, whereby it was foretold that a land from which religion had taken flight would return to religion and imitate an oak tree *spreading out its branches* (Is 6:13). In his sixth chapter Isaiah had revealed the glory with which the Church would be invested under the Emperor Constantine. He had shown the mouths of priests cleansed by a burning coal, especially those of priests who would play a part in the early spread of the faith. Then he had predicted that there would later be priests who, though they read out the law and beheld the mysteries, would understand neither the one nor the other. He had foretold that the holy city, Jerusalem, would be overthrown, and other kingdoms wrenched away from the Christian faith. Throughout many centuries and down to our own times, this is what has been happening.

Yet having bewailed the calamities, Isaiah also sang of the victories. *Left desolate in the midst of the land, it will be multiplied* (Is 6:12), he said, hinting at the recovery of Jerusalem. Still, he went on, *there will remain but a tenth* (Is 6:13), warning us that Christianity would regain possession of the Holy Land only after long effort and not without blood. *It will be converted and will stand like a terebinth,* he continued, speaking of a nation which knows not the Christian faith, promising that it will embrace Christianity and that, as religion flourishes there, it will increase mightily.

After describing the happiness of these events, Isaiah indicated the time at which the happiness could be expected. *It will be like an oak tree,* he said, giving us a premonition of the kingdoms which would seek the faith from an oak; but, he added, an oak which would *spread out its branches.* By this expression he suggested that we shall not merely recover what was ours, but even extend our territories. The mention of the oak directs us to the time of Pope Sixtus, when King Ferdinand of Spain, together with his wife of rare virtues, Isabella, attempted the reconquest of Granada, still occupied by the infidels, which they overthrew after ten years of war. You may understand Isaiah's assertion that the oak will *spread out its branches* as a reference to yourself, for your oak tree not only delights to spread its shadow over these Catholic monarchs, but also extends its branches to those who have never heard of our religion.

Manuel's Achievements under Julius II

It remains for us to recognize what King Manuel of Portugal has given these people in bringing them the branches of your tree. Vergil has taught us that the golden bough is not carried into the abode of the blessed, but "set up on the threshold."[90] The Apostle suggests an interpretation of this: when we reach the perfect gold of the blessed, what is imperfect will be left behind. He shows that faith can be regarded as imperfect inasmuch as it hopes for the supreme good as something future, but does not possess it as present. Now if faith is symbolized by a branch, it is fitting that the fruits on the branch should be matched in number by the different articles of faith. Manuel, conqueror of Ceylon and the Bay of Bengal, is wreathed with oak leaves, for together with the golden oak he brings them a golden age. Let us now consider in what this consists.

He who gives the branch is the first to appear wearing the Christian and pontifical oak. The happiness we are considering was signified long ago in the prophecy of Isaiah, which can be interpreted in the following manner. In his forty-ninth chapter Isaiah addresses Ceylon and another neighboring island: *Hear, O islands . . .* ; and to make it clear that he is speaking also of India, a country very distant from the Western Church, he continues, *And listen, you peoples who are far off. The Lord has called me from the womb* (Is 49:1). In chapter seven he had pointed to two enemies, naming them "the son of Remaliah and the King of Syria," and asserting that they would no longer arouse fear when someone appeared who would be called Emmanuel. Can we not see, then, what a blow has been struck at the King of Syria now that our King Manuel has snatched from him the trade in spices?

We must now examine in turn the foundations of the golden age laid among the conquered peoples by King Manuel, showing how they are strengthened by the prophecies of Isaiah. Such prophecies are obviously concerned with these islands and the recent victory, as can be plainly read in his forty-ninth chapter. So, then, the victor gives the vanquished the first branch, on which grow three golden acorns, so that the vanquished may be nourished on the victuals of the golden age; for the *just man lives on faith* (Rom 1:17).

The first acorn embraces and conceals beneath its gold what Peter, the first pope, placed in a basket from the collected scraps, namely faith in God as the almighty Creator of the world and the whole of nature. By such faith the first of the passions is healed in the golden life, for when that supreme good which no other good can equal is accepted as lovable, holy love springs up. This holy love is named by Isaiah a chosen arrow. Indeed, people use this term for love both sacred and profane; Solomon says in the book of Proverbs that a young man looks at a girl until an arrow pierces his heart,[91] and Vergil writes of a "lethal dart"[92] finding its mark.

The second acorn was fashioned by John, who strove to make us recognize Jesus as the Son of God, so that to him our second passion should aspire, that passion called concupiscence by earlier writers, but desire by ours. According to the Apostle, he *on whom the angels desire to gaze* (1 Pt 1:12) is Jesus; and a second prophecy also points to him, for Isaiah says in the same chapter, *My God has become my strength* (Is 49:5). He is plainly testifying that King Manuel won his victory through the help of Emmanuel, Jesus.

James, son of Zebedee, provides the third acorn, asserting that Jesus was conceived through the Holy Spirit and born of a virgin mother. Our third passion, pleasure, is excluded when a virgin becomes pregnant without intercourse with a husband. This is the teaching of the prophecy: *I have sent you as light to the nations* (Is 49:6), for Christ's light rose with none of the attendant darkness of Venus, and Christ has been preached by the Portuguese king to nations and regions where he was never proclaimed before that king's coming.

So far we have been examining a happy branch, but next comes a somewhat sadder one. It is reasonable that the second and the fourth should have this character, for Pythagoras by no means approved of these divisible numbers. Andrew is in charge of the first bud on this second branch, Philip of the second and Thomas of the third. Andrew nailed to a cross adored his crucified Lord who by his death appeased the Father's hatred and reconciled mortals to the Father, thus healing our fourth passion, hatred. So the prophet sings, *I have preserved you to raise up the desolate heritages* (Is 49:8), a task achieved by both Emmanuels; for the Emmanuel of Nazareth raised up those of Syria and Judea, and the Emmanuel of Portugal those of India and Ceylon.

Philip declares that Christ went down to hell, in order that people plucked by his power from those light-shunning prisons might be led to the stars *clad in light as in a garment* (Ps 104:2), according to David's prediction. Then too did our fifth passion fall away, the passion called flight or aversion, clearly in reference to the misery of hell which is to be avoided more than all else. Moreover Isaiah foretold that Christ would recover all the spoils which had been lost, in the words, *By my own life, says the Lord, you shall clothe yourself in all these* (Is 49:18). The prophet thus promised Portugal that it would occupy and take possession of lands hitherto strangers to God.

The sixth passion of the soul is understood to be sickness or sadness, and this was assuaged by Thomas when with exploring hands he recognized the Risen One returned from the underworld. The same thought occurs in Isaiah: *Rejoice, O heavens*, he says, *for the Lord has comforted his people* (Is 49:13). He was promising those triumphs of a victorious king which have both rendered your days happy, Pope Julius, and also ensured that Christendom, so inured to misery and affliction after centuries of slaughter, should cease weeping at last and rejoice to find itself laden with sumptuous spoils.

The acorns on the third branch belong to Bartholomew, Matthew, and James of Alphaeus. By testifying that the risen body of Christ has ascended on high Bartholomew arouses hope, the seventh human passion, hope that not our souls only but even our bodies will ascend to the heavenly dwelling places. The prophet hinted at this too with his words, *Your ruined land* will be too *narrow* (Is 49:19). This means that the endowments of our bodies will be too great to be contained within our earthly frame; it predicts also that the ruins of the city of Rome will be too cramped on account of the arrival of conquered peoples. The prophet sensed too that Portugal would be overcrowded; and indeed so great a quantity of oriental goods and spices is being imported there that it exceeds Portuguese requirements and must be sent from an overflowing Portugal to other shores.

Matthew crushes boldness, the eighth passion of the soul, by declaring that the Son of God will judge all things. Hence the enemy will be disappointed, he who makes bold to hope that our King will lose what he has once grasped; for either none of them will ever be lost or, if they are, the King will win them back. The prophetic oracle confirms this: *Shall booty be stolen from the strong?* (Is 49:24). Human machinations do not gain the mastery over divine works; and just as all human things are perishing, so are divine things unchanging and eternal.

James of Alphaeus brings order into the ninth agitation of the soul, which is called anger, for he brings before us that divine Disturber, the Holy Spirit of God, by whom the kings of the four quarters of the earth have been stirred up in our days. If one drew a line from the eastern sunrise to the western ocean passing through your holy feet, Julius II, and you were to turn toward the east, you would see in front of you the forces of your enemies fighting among themselves. Behind your back you would hear mighty France preparing for war; to your left the King of the Romans, valiant in battle; to your right, southward, the ruler of Egypt uttering every possible threat because he cannot endure with equanimity the success and happiness of Portugal. In the midst of it all your own tree towers,

> . . . as when in mighty strength
> winds from the Alpine north buffet an oak,
> vie to uproot the tree with savage blasts
> on every side; the battered tree trunk groans,
> its leafy branches deeply strew the earth.
> But fast it holds its rocky crag, and strikes
> toward Tartarus with plunging roots as far
> as with its summit to the airs of heaven.[93]

As we read in the gospel, it is well established on solid rock.[94] Isaiah foresaw these four upheavals of our day: *Behold,* he says, *these shall come from afar, others from the north, from the sea, or from the southern land* (Is 49:12). He knew that the countries of the East are indeed far from you, that France is bounded by two seas — the Mediterranean and the Atlantic, that Germany is toward the north, and that Egypt lies to the south. If anyone were to peruse the histories of bygone events, no epoch would be found upon which the wars of these four nations have fallen simultaneously, so the prophet's oracle can refer to no other age.

Finally Simon Peter plucked the first acorn of the last branch when he introduced the Catholic Church, queen of all things, and the communion of saints, as the creed affirms. These two are of so much worth to God that there is no one whom they cannot render dear to God. So when both are intervening, every reason for despair is taken away. Despair, then, which holds the tenth place in the order, should not be feared. Many, however, have despaired whether it would ever be that the Church could grow to its ancient fullness, since a fierce enemy snatched away everything except a corner of Europe. But Isaiah rightly encourages hope when he predicts that kings will nourish the Church and lead it to its ancient greatness: *Kings and queens will be your nurturers* (Is 49:23). This reveals that Queen Isabella and King Ferdinand began, under Pope Sixtus, to see to it that Granada ate the fruit of the apostolic oak, and that the seed of religion, already long extinct, sprouted again there. And now also our king of Portugal has planted this seed under the Indian sky, has worked zealously for it to sprout, and has become a most careful nurturer of the young plant.

Fear, eleventh among the motions, devours souls that are conscious of sin and it makes us unable to keep from fearing greatly an enemy that has grown in such a marvelous way. But coming to our aid is Jude, who exhorts us to be of good cheer when he proves, if I may use his words, the forgiveness of our sins.[95] For it is easier for God to be appeased than for a person even to wish that he be appeased. But how can the multitude of our enemies be conquered by so few? Listen to Isaiah urging all fear to be completely laid aside: *I will feed your enemies with their flesh* (Is 49:26). This is clearly fulfilled in your own time when the ruler of the Turks and another who initiated a new heresy, whom they call Sophin in the vernacular, battle each other with savage and cruel weapons. Each fights against an enemy of religion; each acts without knowing your own purpose; and while each believes he wages war for himself, he actually wages war, with God so decreeing, for your republic. Victory may never be hoped for with greater certainty and ease than when enemies suffer internal war.

Stupor, as I have mentioned, holds the final place. Because they were torn by so many wounds they had received, stupor descended upon our former rulers and they were not eager to bestir themselves. But our king has not only bestirred himself, indeed he causes stupor among the people he has defeated, accomplishing what Isaiah revealed would be done: *I will lift up a sign and they will offer sons* (Is 49:22). For when he was about to do battle, King Manuel exhibited a standard with a golden cross. This sign benefited those sacrificing their lives by opening up an entrance into heaven and eternal life. But when the enemy saw this sign, they collapsed, stunned in mind and body. Seizing upon their fear, King Manuel immediately slew a countless horde and many more perished in the sea. He graciously allowed others to live, those who sought mercy and peace, in order that there might be some who, having received the sign of the cross, would hear and receive Matthew's gospel, which claims that the dead will one day live again and have eternal life.

These, then, are the twelve golden acorns, the twelve foundations of religion, which King Manuel brought to the Indians and which they received from the conquering king. This king was fortunate because he arose as the founder of a golden age among the Indians. And they, in turn, were no less fortunate. In their need they received salvation, and this even from a conquering enemy. They found themselves in a state which usually happens to those of us who desire things that do not agree with reason. For when someone's desire is victorious in its fight against reason, this is the same as being shamefully conquered. Like a cow, this person refuses to listen to reason. When those who desire evil things are conquered, this should be taken as their victory. Thus, while Manuel conquered India, India's infernal weapons were conquered. Other peoples, when they were conquered, lost their homeland; but the Indians would not have found their homeland had they not been conquered.

The captured island and its neighboring peoples were exiled from the heavenly Jerusalem and the land of divine promise, as they call our homeland, not only for forty years, like the Hebrews from the country of their fathers, but from the creation of the world, through many thousands of years. They were exiled up to the present when, under your sovereignty over the Christian world, Manuel, king of the peoples, brought in the name and faith of Christ. They were completely without God and the knowledge of God until Prince Julius and General Manuel began their rule and the peoples began to know and receive God. And David sang of this: *The Lord reigned. Let the earth rejoice and the many islands be glad. Blessed is he who comes in the name of the Lord* (Ps 97:1; 118:26). To our joy, this is fulfilled in the conqueror Manuel, whose name means *God with us* (Mt 1:23), as Matthew interpreted it. For if Manuel had not been received, no one in Ceylon would have received God and the divine gold.

Further, this name that was celebrated in the prophecy of Isaiah and confirmed in Matthew was understood as Jesus the protector. The old and the new law both acknowledged Jesus the protector, that friend of God, that God born of God, that man of the Hebrew race, that defender of the entire human race. These peoples who were once exiled from Jesus in their country are now led back by him into their heavenly homeland.

Now Manuel of Portugal, by whose leadership God and victory were with us, manifested at the same time the power of both Jesuses. He imitated God's Son to the extent that, under his tutelage, *a people who dwelt in darkness have seen a great light* (Is 9:2), as was foretold in prophecy. He opened the eyes of the blind, revealed the way of truth, gave the waters of Siloam and baptism, raised the sign of the cross to be venerated. And although nothing is harder to conquer than custom, and there is no stronger custom than that established by religion, he nevertheless easily taught the peoples, steeped as they were in strange superstitions for generations, to strip off the darkness of error and put on the light of truth.

He is considered no less like Joshua, that ancient Jesus, unless perhaps something more seems to be allotted to our king than to Joshua. For Joshua brought a people to a human and hostile country while Manuel brought a people to a celestial and divine country. Both robbed from the Egyptians, in the one case, humble things that the Hebrews could carry in their hands, in the other case, precious riches of the Orient. When the sun stood still, Joshua fought in the golden age's shadows; carrying the sun, Manuel drove away the shadows and introduced a golden age.

But I do not wish to explain everything of each conqueror, how similarly yet dissimilarly they triumphed in victory (for something should always be left to the discovery of others!). Nevertheless, I have decided here, at the end of my discourse, not to omit one thing, so that in that Jesus you might recognize your pontifical happiness and Manuel might recognize his victory. We read in the first book of sacred history that the leader, Joshua, had worked long in the favor of the divine name and had subdued the people and crushed their kings in battle.[96] Hear, however, highest pontiff, and you too, King Manuel, listen to these prophecies and victories, and respond to God by inspiring happiness, godliness, virtue, and thanksgiving. I will now recite the words of history: When that Jesus, whom, with the letters of his name changed, we call Joshua, had completed everything, *on that day he made this covenant: he took a great stone and set it under the oak that was in the Lord's sanctuary* (Jos 24:25-26). Remember the words I have just recited to you, since it would seem right to suspect nothing in them about the Portuguese victory. But God never did anything great for his people which he had not previously signified to them or their rulers. In fact, God promised through the prophet Amos that he would always do this very thing: *The Lord God will not accomplish his word unless he has previously revealed his hidden plan to his servants through the prophets* (Am 3:7).

When God foresaw that grand and new victory of the sea where no Christian had ever conquered, it was rightly signified beforehand in the divine books and foretold to you, the pastor of his people. Unless he wishes, God does not give foreknowledge of coming events in such a way that the future is known before it comes to pass. But Augustine taught that our times were predicted in the holy scriptures.

Since this is so, who can fail to see what was shown above, that Joshua signifies King Manuel? In an amazingly short period, and in many places, Manuel, like Joshua before, worked for the cause of divine honor. He helped his enemies by pouring out and extending holy signs. He triumphed in victory over enemy forces. He brought back spoils and carried riches into Rome.

But to God, the Savior, whose seat you occupy on the hill of the Etruscan Vatican, he brought a stone. This metaphor is a customary usage of the prophets: it names stone any island with cliffs and stone sides against which the waves and swells break. And so that the meaning might be even plainer and clearer, and lest anyone consider that the rock or stone alluded to is small, he added that this stone was not only large but very large. And because he thought that the name, stone, was not clear enough, he called it very large. Wherefore he was attempting to describe the island, the largest of islands, as far as the inspiring divinity allowed. This description, then, when he portrays the island as the largest, clearly cannot signify anything but Ceylon, because this one island could not only surpass in magnitude the other islands, but is even believed to nearly equal a continent by those who called it "the other world of lands."[97]

Our Joshua won this island, he acquired it by the labor, study, and investigation of many years, in navigation through many ports, many seas, as far as the world reaches; with many riches, ships, and crew members sent out, finally with pain and difficulty he discovered it, he conquered what he discovered, and he subjected what he conquered to the Christian empire. But to whom did he subject it? These words of prophetic history show that he subjected it to Pope Julius. *He placed it,* he says, *under the oak* (Jos 24:26). Undoubtedly, this is as clear as if he had said: He forced it to pay tribute to the Christians under Julius II. What I have just said would be enough. But the prophet wished the matter to be grasped more fully, more clearly, and more openly, so that one might understand how it speaks of the pontifical tree and the prince of holy things. Thus he says, *He placed it under the oak which was in the sanctuary* (Jos 24:26), whereby is explained not only the oak, but also the office of the holiest and most blessed high priest.

If one speaks about the priest or sanctuary, the Jews, green with envy, cry out that this is Jerusalem, which the Jew Moses gave to the Jewish people to rule nothing but the Jewish Holy Land, and is not the city of Rome. But we read of two prophets who propose laws, Moses and the Messiah (by which they meant the anointed king) whom God foretold would be like Moses. The Apostle Paul, most knowledgeable of Hebrew traditions, calls Moses a servant and the Messiah Lord, because the psalm's heading speaks of the one: *A hymn of Moses, God's servant* (Ps 90:1), while the beginning verse speaks of the other: *The Lord said to my lord* (Ps

110:1). From this it is established that Moses must be called servant and the Messiah Lord. Therefore the sanctuary of Moses (I use an expression familiar to them) is the sanctuary of the servant, but he desires that of the Messiah to be understood and called the sanctuary of the Lord, not of the servant. And these are the words: *He placed it under the oak, which was in the sanctuary of the Lord*, which is to say almost the same as if he had said: under Julius, pastor of the Roman Church.

You see now, most divine pastor, how much you owe to God. For when you had fallen into the most ruinous times with so many disasters, you were given King Manuel for your happiness and peace of mind. By this king you perceive that a new world of lands is discovered for the sacraments of your religion, an enemy conquered, laws given to the conquered, the empire extended, and a golden age produced; not an age of Lucifer, nor of Adam, nor of Janus, but of Christian and apostolic holiness. O happy Pope Julius! O fortunate King Manuel! Your age was not only not shaken from hostile injury, but even merited distinguished and eternal praise for a wondrous victory over enemies.

What honor, what praise, what rewards can be given to the victor Manuel to equal the greatness of his deeds? Surely his is a virtue so bright and divine that it should not obtain inferior rewards, although it cannot find equal rewards. We are now considering human rewards that are all so deficient and meager that by their defect they detract from his virtue. But perhaps the virtue God gives to humans is bestowed by the same God for immortal rewards, which, as the Apostle reveals, *so exceed all understanding that they do not even arise in the heart of man* (Phil 4:7). Indeed this is that virtue from God that comes to the fathers who, since they cannot receive the rewards that are owed, receive what they can, content with a great, but only partial, honor. If we are right to call apostles those who carried our golden faith to distant peoples, then the king of Portugal, if not an apostle (for that is strictly speaking an ancient title), surely deserves to be called apostolic.

Julius' Achievements and His Future Tasks

But you, Pope Julius, must convince yourself of this, you must believe this, that there are two enemies of your empire, who the prophet Isaiah, in the seventh and eighth chapter (what I will say I wish to be easily located), says will fight against the Romans. And here he foretells that they will be conquered by the Roman Mars — our translation has *the fly of Egypt and the bee that is in the land of Assyria* (Is 7:18). One is the king of Syria and Damascus, the other makes himself emperor of Asia and Greece. But before these things are told I see that your oak is revealed and immediately at the victory the name Emmanuel, although the translator wrote *God with us*, is read twice.

For when a prophet is going to signify our age, he prophesied about things he had seen himself. And if you begin from Peter and follow the succession throughout history until your own pontificate, these things never appear except under Julius II. Surely Isaiah predicted that the Roman See and throne, which the prince of the apostles founded and dedicated in the Roman temple for the high priests, would be lifted up in two ways, first in the vast structure of its buildings, and second in the new extension of its empire.

In the year, he says, *that king Ozias died* (Is 6:1), whose name means the vision and strength of God. We understand him to be Pope Pius II, who was thought to be called, like Aaron, to restore the divine religion. Therefore he says, *in the year that he died* (Is 6:1), not the year that he was elected, because it did not seem that the elected pope would live but, strictly speaking, die and be succeeded by you, from whom the structure of the temple and the extent of the empire would receive marvelous increase. *I saw,* he says, *the Lord sitting* (Is 6:1). He wished to say, I saw Julius II, pontifex maximus, succeeding Ozias at his death and sitting down on the throne of our religion that was about to increase. The prophet continues, *sitting upon a high and lofty throne.* When he says *high throne* he is referring to the high restoration of the temple; when he adds *lofty* he is alluding to the empire increased by the Portuguese armies.

But lest anyone should say these are very obscure interpretations, in the book they call Sirach God wanted us to read words that are clearer than light. For in the fiftieth chapter we find written, *Simon, son of Onias, high priest* (Sir 50:1). Of course Simon is usually interpreted as obedient, and Onias as grief of the Lord. But what else does being obedient to God mean than to follow Peter, to whom, as the Lord says, *flesh and blood did not reveal the divine truth, but the Father who is in heaven* (Mt 16:17)? But that priest whom flesh and blood render most indulgent, who bestows the heredity of Peter on his own sons, family, and relations, is not being obedient to God who reveals and instructs. Therefore he calls you obedient, whom sons do not seduce, whom grandsons do not plunder, whom relations do not influence to the dishonor of the Church. For you the Church is wife, children, and the entire family. You love her alone; you ponder and work to render her wealthy, growing, and shining in her own majesty. For this reason, I understand you are called Simon, which is also known to be the name of the first pope. And just as a Roman has his Caesars and an Egyptian his Ptolemies, so a Christian calls his high priests Peter, and he names Simons those who comply with the law and are zealous for holy things.

But in order to portray you distinctly, the holy author calls you the son of Onias, because Saint Jerome and Origen interpret this name correctly as the grief of the Lord. How could the holy prophecy indicate your situation more clearly? For among those elected to that rank, who ever suffered more rebellions, calamities, exiles, and adverse circumstances than you? Good God, how many were the years you were put to flight, how many the dangers you escaped, how many the times you suffered in Italy and among foreigners, how many the swords, poisons, and plots you survived, how many the plans of death you overcame, with God's aid, so that when you were called to that seat, and after you renewed both temple and empire, you obtained an eternal glory for religion.

After Simon's obedience and zeal for the holy place and Onias' former deeds of life are recorded, then he immediately turns to your actions, saying, *the high priest propped up the house, and in his days he strengthened the temple; also the height of the temple was established by him* (Sir 50:1-2). You propped up the house when you restored the cities ruled by the popes, which were filled with blood and were almost collapsed on account of feuds, sedition, and murder. Having abolished the factions, you brought an end to the terrible destruction of the cities, so that (it was like a miracle!) you immediately gained control of things, and afterward nothing was heard of murders, which before you were very frequent, both in the seditious cities and on the besieged roads. Blood was never shed, sword never drawn, in that cause. And if you had not resisted so much bloodshed with prudence and zeal, the house of Peter, which they call his patrimony, would have been threatened. Therefore not unjustly does this holy passage say that as high priest you propped up the house, for the flock, which was sinking from the rampage of sedition and robbery, you saved from violence.

Finally when he says you strengthened the temple, he speaks of the restoration of those cities that had departed from the faith of the Church, and where the powers of the Church had been weakened from this defection. Approaching this matter with a courageous spirit, you did not stop until you restored the ancient strength of the Church. Bologna, in particular, was brought back with much trouble, many difficulties and great danger to your safety. Is the strengthening of the temple anything other than the appearance of your strong oak, by whose fortitude the broken Church was restored and reinforced? When we pray for a priest to be holy, we sing, *Remember David, O Lord*, where, on behalf of the righteousness of priests, these words are uttered so the one may progress in special virtue and salvation. But concerning David, both king and priest, we read in 1 Samuel 16:18, *the son of Isai, mightiest in strength,* where the divine narrative judged that this king and priest should be portrayed only in a picture of strength. Therefore I understand these as prophecies for the future, when the Christian temple had to be strengthened by someone both king and priest, since priestly strength appeared in the temple. I understand this, then, as the temple strengthened by you, for I see that the rebel cities did not want to obey your predecessors, and for a long time they despised the precepts of priests, while God recorded for your reign: *David, and all his meekness. He brought forth the horn of David* (Ps 132:1.17) and ordered them to place their necks under your feet and to receive their strength.

A third point is added in Sirach. For after the house was propped up and the temple strengthened, it continues, *also the height of the temple was established by him* (Sir 50:2). It does not say the temple was founded by you. Others were responsible for this: Solomon, Zorobabel among the ancients, Sylvester, Constantine and others among us. But who is it that, finding the temple already built, thought to enlarge it and began to lift it into so high a structure? Surely no one did this but you, Julius, pontifex maximus, who, with your great mind that cannot be content with common things, applied your spirit to restore Saint Peter's temple and to raise it up to heaven in a wondrous building. You will leave to posterity an eternal monument of the greatness of your mind, the magnificence of your devotion. You will make descendants more certain about what kind of person and how great a person Julius was, and what the difference was between yourself and other princes. You alone should think that you command the Romans and are the highest prince, that you despise all present things as about to crumble, that you meditate on the fitting publication of coming events, on the future ages, on eternity itself, especially in those matters that pertain to the honoring of holy rites, divine worship, the splendor of religion, and the adornment of piety, that is, to the temple's restoration which you have accomplished.

Thus everyone is convinced, having seen the structure of foundations already built, that Rome, even though it was always the greatest displayer of enormous works, will have nothing, Italy nothing, finally the whole world will have nothing more lofty in height, more magnificent in cost, greater in excellence, more esteemed and admired than your temple. Therefore just as the prophecies of the old law predict a future Solomon, who would construct the fallen temple, surely it was much more fitting that the prophecies should foretell of you, who built the temple of the immortal and eternal priesthood.

So you should not marvel that they do not respond to the calling and inviting divinity, because God, the highest and greatest, wished that you and your matters be written about beforehand and ordered me to reveal them to you. And thus the Lord said you would prop up the house (I gladly repeat the divine words) because you would resist the bloodshed of your people. He said you would strengthen the temple because the rebellious cities would be restored when you alone overcame them. He said you would establish the height of the temple, which after more than twenty-five ruling popes, after 1,500 years, after countless Christian emperors and kings, only you, Julius II, lifted up. You so loved and cherished our sacred faith that you struggled to lift and raise the roof of the most holy temple up to heaven. You would concentrate the wonder of all buildings and miracles into that single work of religion.

But it was not enough for the Holy Spirit to have predicted these three things through humans so many centuries ago unless he had foretold a fourth thing by a most clear and open prophecy: that you would extend the Church, not only in the height of its walls, but also in the length of its empire, as was said above. For when you were pastor, the Portuguese king added to the Christian flock territories unknown to Christians. The holy prophecy surely sang about this double increase of the Church given by you alone among all others: *He also established the height of the temple, a double building* (Sir 50:2). I do not remember ever reading anything more direct, more clear and manifest than this prediction of your accomplishments.

The four parts of this prophecy are so consistent with the things accomplished by you that they cannot be adapted in all respects to the actions of any other person. I think the passage from Sirach sufficiently clarifies those words of Isaiah, *the high and lofty seat* (Is 6:4), by which nothing else could be rightly signified (if we wish to interpret them with regard to a visible throne) than that double building. We learn very clearly from the other prophecy that this pertains to your times and deeds.

But although these four prophecies I have just explained ought to suffice completely to show the shape and prophecy, which is not vague, of your pontificate, yet in the same place in Isaiah where the high and lofty seat is described there is no doubt that a fifth thing can be added to the above four. For when he said that the whole earth would be filled with divine glory, which will happen when the enemies of the faith are conquered, *the lintels of the doors will be moved* (Is 6:4), by which he understands the great changes of principles: that the lips of a priest will be cleansed; that a great king will be seen, who will lead victorious armies; that a certain upright man will be seen, who will interpret the divine will to princes and will be sent to accomplish a grand work; that men will see and hear but not understand or believe the divine plan and the magnitude of the changes and mysteries, even after the conquering of certain cities and the splendid victory of our people, after the increase and extension of your kingdom, and after the multiplication, as the prophet says, of faith, which was certainly seen to have weakened and diminished before you came. Since, I say, he said all these things, Isaiah, the clearest of all the prophets, did not allow himself to set down something vague, but signified you alone in such a way that surely only a stubborn person could understand him to be speaking of someone other than Julius. For when he told all these things and taught lastly that religion would be enlarged, he devised the metaphor of a tree to indicate the times and the pastor. He says that the peoples would be converted to holiness in the future just as *the oak that extends its branches* (Is 6:13), by which he signified that the authority of your pontificate would reach to the territories of your enemies.

The prophecies I have reviewed desire this for you, Isaiah seeks it, the provident Spirit demands it through Isaiah: You must despise all human things. Summoned by these divine words, you must set your heart on divine things, cultivate them, meditate on them. Feeding the flock that you shepherd with justice, generosity, and charity, you must lead it from the zeal for human to the zeal for divine things. You must take pains to uphold law, faith, and piety with devotion, constancy, and purity, so that penalties for vices and rewards for virtue are not lacking. You must decree, persuade, and command that princes and kings of the Christian republics give up their hatreds; that they not wage war among themselves; that the children within the bosom of their parent not do violence with arms against their brothers contrary to their mother religion and contrary to the holy and divine will. Our entire discourse is directed to this, not that we may commend your virtues, although virtue should always be commended, not that we may recount your honors and praises, but that we may move your mind, that we may arouse your heart, that we may enkindle your soul to undertake and complete these things; that you might do what the prophecies once sang of, now that your most happy deeds have fulfilled the prophecies in almost all their parts.

Only this remains, only this is left of what the prophet added concerning all your deeds: *What had been forsaken in the middle of the earth will be multiplied* (Is 6:12), where he predicts that the holy city Jerusalem, occupied by filthy enemies, would be recovered in our day. Isaiah, Job, and David call Africa and Europe *the ends of the earth* (Is 41:5; Jb 38:13; Ps 135:7) because they are washed by the ocean along much of their boundary. But Judea, situated on the border of Asia, by which it is separated far from the ocean and finds itself in the middle of the habitable world, they call with good reason perhaps the center of the earth. In Psalm 74, the land that God gave birth to is given the same description. This psalm had the title, *Understanding for Asaph unto the End*. Asaph is interpreted as collecting and gathering. The head of the Church will be at the end of time, because, understanding that he was called by God to recover both Judea and Mount Sion, in which the Lord had once dwelt, he will gather the people, prepare an army, and with the Lord as general will regain the city captured by the enemy.

Five psalms are joined together.[98] The first is the psalm we have just spoken of. In it the pope mourns over the sanctuary that was burned, the tabernacle that was defiled, and the inherited land that was taken away; and he prays for the Lord to vindicate his cause, lest the enemy boast of his stolen country. The following psalm renders thanks to God because he had won the victory, removed rulers, and taken away troubles; because no one fought against the divine will in deed or word; because God the Judge, who is the Son that will appear as an enemy, decided that he would be humbled and then exalted. Then the third psalm celebrates and sings of victory because, after the enemies who did not know God or divine truths were driven out, he *destroyed the powers of the ungodly, their bow, shield, sword, and stronghold*. The fourth psalm tells of the high priest Aaron who led his people in the second place into the captured city, just as formerly Moses had first led them after he defeated Pharaoh. And the psalm gives thanks to God, as much because he will restore what he took away from Jerusalem, as because, with God's help, he will treat with favor what he restored, calling both *a change of the right hand of the most high* (Ps 77:11). Finally in the fifth psalm it is taught that the priest and the Christian people, having acknowledged divine assistance in conquering the enemy, in repairing the city, in obtaining victory and happiness, should hear the divine law and promise to keep it; that they should love it, observe it, work on it, so that they might pay back to God what was received; that they might be zealous for God; that they might be united with God and cling to him.

In the first psalm, when Asaph prays God the Father to show mercy to his lost and defiled heritage, he recounts the service of the Son. Although the Son was eternally with his Father before time and heaven began, he nevertheless was made ours and assumed human form. *He made salvation*, he says, *in the middle of the earth* (Ps 74:12). You have done other things, Pope Julius. You destroyed the plotters, you subdued the rebellious, you laid the foundation on the renewed temple, you gave a double enlargement to the Church when you increased the extension of the Church and increased the number of believers through the Portuguese success. You lack nothing to be considered the most fortunate of all except that you become like Asaph, that is, that you bring together the rulers after peace is restored; that you gather an army, send them against the enemies of Christ, and restore to your mourning bride the heritage of Christ, and the country, home and tomb of Christ.

Oh how fortunate, how happy you would be, Julius, if the words of the prophets would be listened to, if you would not resist God when he blesses, if the gifts God has offered would be accepted, if you would become Asaph, the assembler and gatherer of believers, the tamer and conqueror of ungodly peoples! For this God snatched you from so many misfortunes; for this he preserved you; for this he decreed that you be called Julius and that you govern Rome; for this the prophecies cry out that you, having fulfilled their other aspects, might undertake to fulfill this also. God pledges himself as commander. He promises that he will give counsel, that he will give troops, that he will give victory. Nothing is lacking now to win an eternal triumph unless you fail to take up the campaign.

Why then do you wait in hesitation? But, you say, our own people must first come to peace, and afterward the enormous enemy can be fought, so that the discord of our people may not be our ruin before the weapons of the enemy are seen. But understand that there is no other reason for our people to make peace except this alone: that you may send the souls, the troops, and the strength of arms of our great rulers against the public enemy of our republic and of our religion. For "lively courage"[99] cannot rest until it descends unto the field, where it exercises its powers and presents itself to be tested. Command our weapons to be turned toward the East, command the passion of your people to break out against the ungodly tyrant.

If there was ever any hope of being victorious, these things now promise it to you: the enemy's fear, the power of your rulers, the huge preparation of the German war, the good fortune of King Manuel, Julius' success, and the words, predictions, and judgments of the prophets. I am silent about the sudden and prodigious growth of Sophin, ruler of the Persians and author of new heresies, whom the peoples of the East follow after as a man sent to earth by God to repair the ruins of collapsed religion. It is already known that the Byzantine tyrant received a considerable wound from him; that he sent forth a huge army; that he led his European force across into Asia; that he feared if he were attacked in an Eastern war, the Christian force moving from the West might rise up and overwhelm him.

I keep silent about the people of Greece after Byzantium was captured, who, being defeated and conquered, could be forced to obey the tyrant, but so far have not been induced to depart from their faith and religion. There is no surer road to victory than the zeal and faith of the people. It is very necessary, then, to attend to this, because the same hope that we entertain at this time for the Greek people, the enemy will entertain in the next generation. For the old people who still remember the old religion will die out, while the youths who are ignorant and unaware of it will arise.

I omit the flower of Christian men, whose greatness easily lasts longer than anything else. Indeed we have, to begin from the East, the people of Bohemia and the Danube, who are nearest to our enemies' territories and have become accustomed to continuous wars with them. They do not consider anything more ancient, nor do they desire anything more eagerly, than to be allowed to take up arms against them. We have the hard and aggressive Germany, to which, if perhaps it needed anything above the native power of its people and the laws of the empire, was added the most famous might of the emperor, for whom it is harder to assemble all his troops than for the enemy to pour out its forces. We have the men of warlike France, who, even omitting their ancient triumph in the East and passing over their most Christian king, are more powerful, I do not doubt, than others, whether in their great passion of soul, in their practice of warfare, or in the great amount of their gold and wealth. We have the king of the British Isles, who is eager for Christian expansion and has always been ready to take up arms against the ungodly. Is he too far away to obey you when you call and to offer himself to the one calling?

We have our Italy, although when it is ruled by greed we may not rightly call it ours nor Italy. A happiness perfect in every way has not been given to any place on earth. For whatever God and Mother Nature adorned, vice and greed have corrupted. Yet rulers survive in it, no matter what kind of Italy it is. Republics survive. The Council of Venetians survives, whose power and opulence surpasses the others. Through many centuries, many wars, many disasters the Venetians exposed their bodies against a people opposed to the Christian name. They were the rampart and *protecting wall* (Is 26:1), to use the expression of the prophet, of the Christian republic.

Between the Ocean and the Pyrenees we have Spain, most similar in temperament, speech, dignity, and glory to the valor of the Roman army and religion. Ferdinand, the Catholic King, rules Spain throughout its borders. Rather than describing all his exploits, let us just say that he is neither inexperienced nor a newcomer in the fight against the ungodly. For through General Consalvo Fernandez, who won the Neapolitan kingdom with incredible force, the king took Cephalonia in the Aegean Sea from a most stubborn people, and he won the port of Africa with great effort. At the heel of Europe he defeated and expelled the ungodly enemy of our faith from the kingdom of Granada, which he overcame in a war that lasted almost twelve years.

Manuel's Destiny and Role

Finally we have that king of Portugal, on whose account this present discourse was made. But concerning him, that you might acknowledge him to be the person God gave to your joy for the salvation of Christian things, I believe I must speak a little more fully. I must show you, Pope Julius, that the deeds of this king make manifest that in your times, if you are willing and agree with how I see it, you may extinguish ungodliness, renew religion, and restore the most esteemed, most reverend, most auspicious majesty of the Holy See. I will present the testimonies of the same prophet, when he prophesied in a connected speech about the actions of both you and this king. For he spoke about you and about your throne and temple, which became so lofty as it was elevated under your guidance. And in the same place he said that religion would be multiplied under your oak. Then, when he was going to show how this king will be of use to you, he stated his name in the next two chapters, where, not in a concealed expression but in a clear designation, he called him Emmanuel.

It is well known that it was customary to interpret the revelations of a holy text in a two-fold manner, either by the hidden signification of a more removed meaning, or by the bare narration of truth. The words Isaiah recorded concerning Emmanuel contain both kinds of meaning, an obscure one concerning Christ, and a clear one concerning King Manuel. For example, when God speaks to King David, he says that his offspring would build the temple, whose eternal covenants were going to be established. You will find the text is about Christ if you look into more penetrating truths, but if you observe the surface light, you will find that it is about Solomon. Since it is understood of a mortal king, who built the temple of marble and stone, much more should it be understood of the immortal God, who underwent death and erected his Church.

As much as he could, Isaiah signified your accomplishments. Then he signified the name of your king. In the third place, he signifies the new way of creating this king. *His empire will be multiplied*, he says, *on the throne of David* (Is 9:7), which foretold that religion would be enlarged and extended broadly in the East. When he spoke of *the burdened way of the sea across the Jordan*, he also added that *a people who walked in darkness have seen a great light* (Is 9:2). Everyone now sees that this event has occurred to the peoples of the Indian Sea, whose way, although known to no other humans and very burdensome to penetrate, King Manuel, the first of all people, has made known and accessible.

But that he might reveal the way, established by divine providence, of creating this king, the prophet purposely referred to the throne of King David, that is, to his ascension to the throne of the kingdom. For when God wanted his first kingdom in the East, he set up King David. At this new and unusual rite of instituting a king, he orders one of Isai's sons to be anointed, who at that time, as we read in the book,[100] were seven in number. The six older sons were considered famous in feats of arms and competence. But the seventh, the youngest of all, was still a boy who shepherded his father's sheep, living a pastoral life out in the open with the flock. Human occupations have nothing more firm in strength, more safe in innocence, more quiet, tranquil, or sweet, with troubles and worries far removed, than this kind of life.

Who was there that did not believe the firstborn, or those nearest the firstborn, would be called to the highest dignity of the empire? But God has never been accustomed to undertake new things without calling a man to do them by a new signification of things. This is so that his providential setting up of a man might portend a providential result of deeds to be accomplished. For this reason the son of Isai was summoned to enlarge the kingdom, to conquer peoples, to lay the foundation of a holy empire, a son who was not older by birth, but considered the least of the seven. For things that happen in human affairs by divine will, happen beyond the order of human affairs, so that the human mind might acknowledge that God is the author of the things that seem to be done beyond the customs of men.

Since we have said how David was created king for the fulfillment of the old law, that God offered the kingdom to the youngest of seven sons, now we must say how our Emmanuel acquired his kingdom, who you will realize was called to the renewal of the new law. You will understand that he was made king with the greatest similarity to David. Because God was about to give a most splendid victory in the East and in the Indian Sea, he decided that one of the Christian kings should be chosen who did not surpass the others in wealth and power.

The seven kings presented themselves to the divine mind (I do not speak now of him to whom pertain both the rule of the Roman Empire and far better titles in the kingdom). In naming them I will use the names of their people: there were the kings of Hungary, Poland, France, Spain, Britain, Naples, and Portugal, who, joined by allegiance to the Roman pontiff, could force all the people the pope ruled to obey the papal authority. From these kings, after the richer and more powerful were passed over, God chose him who did not have great strength of resources and who lived at the furthest limits of the whole earth.

David sang of himself and of men dear to God in that line that is often cited from the holy scriptures, *raising up the poor from the earth* (Ps 113:7). He spoke of himself, who had been lifted up to rule the kingdom and win many victories for the kingdom. But what David handed down about himself as king is also surely that of which the divine maiden sang, she who, having arisen from the offspring of King David, bore the king of kings while still remaining a virgin. She says, *He has put down the mighty from their thrones and has exalted the humble* (Lk 1:52). And again this same Hebrew and Christian muse (thus I have dared to name the author of this song) agrees with the Hebrew prophet. For when he sang in Psalm 113:6 and also in Psalm 138:6 that *God regards the humble*, the Virgin replied many centuries later: *Because he has regarded the humility of his maidservant* (Lk 4:48). David spoke of the king of the Hebrews, while the maiden spoke of *the king of all ages*, as Paul calls our God in his letter addressed to Timothy.

Therefore, in order to raise up someone humble and content with a small kingdom to obtain the richest and brightest trophies of the Orient, rather than a king of the most powerful and wealthy kingdom, he decided in his divine judgment that this province should be set aside for a king of Portugal. Good kings, then, aroused by divine impulses within, began to sail with many men through the Atlantic Ocean, in order to explore and learn about the entire coast of Africa, which is pounded by this ocean, and to record their many discoveries on the journeys undertaken. Kings sent out ships for as many as twenty years. The sailors in them were very knowledgeable in the art of navigation and prepared with a readiness of spirit to undergo for long periods whatever adverse things should occur. Nor were they sent with any other counsel than to seek new places toward the rising of the sun, to sketch islands, harbors, and promontories, to keep on in navigation and research until they should penetrate the Indian coasts and make known to humans the route of navigation that extends this far.

If this endeavor should actually succeed, it would come to be regarded among the deeds that are as much divine as human. For it was meant to be that the blessed name of our God should also be manifested to the ignorant nations; that the people who inhabited the small area of this continent of earth and were forced to be cut off from the ocean, as if by a wall in a tight prison, now, finally having come out of prison, should learn and become accustomed to enjoying a more open sky, when their world is at last opened wider.

They sailed until the times of Alexander VI, and on the way so many ships and sailors perished in sailing that, had not God strengthened their souls, they would have often stopped, as if by a most pernicious counsel, at the beginning of their journey. Oh how many times they regretted sailing! How many times they were weary of the difficulties, troubles and dangers! How often they determined to retrace their steps and to sound the retreat! But the more they despaired of going on, the more they were at once stirred up by God to go on and persevere.

But every endeavor is taken up to no purpose unless it is taken up according to God's will. For *there is one who sows*, as my Christ handed down, *and another who harvests* (Jn 4:37). King John ruled Portugal under Pope Alexander VI. After his further study on this matter, after the attempt of Henry, after the effort of his father, Alonso, after his own diligence for so many years, John could never succeed in passing beyond the promontory they call the Cape of Good Hope, and the Indian harbor was never seen by his sailors. It was King John's fate to reach this far, but beyond it God and nature, with the continually adverse winds, never allowed him to pass, because another time and other rulers had been appointed for this glorious victory in the Indies.

Edward, former king of Portugal, had fathered three children: Alonso, Isabella, and Ferdinand. From King Alonso was born King John, from Isabella, Joanna, and from Ferdinand, another John, Edward, Diego, and lastly our Manuel. And from King John was born his son, Alonso. When John came to the Cape of Good Hope, King Edward I had already died. His three children, whom I said he had fathered, namely King Alonso, Isabella, and Ferdinand would also die after him. This left King John, his son, Alonso the Younger, Joanna, daughter of Isabella, and, in addition to these three, the four sons of Ferdinand: John, Edward, Diego, and Manuel.

God was about to reveal the Indian world; he was about to make known a passage through the open sea from Tajo to the Ganges; he was about to give the search for wealth of the Orient first, and then the abundant spoils of a famous triumph. He was considering in his divine counsel who of these seven that we have named seemed most worthy of such splendor and such glory of deeds. It is right at this point to ponder both the fortunes of human affairs and the strength of divine judgments. *Who has helped the spirit of the Lord*, exclaimed Isaiah, *or who has been his counselor?* The lyric poet of the Hebrews said as well, *God's judgments are a great abyss* (Ps 36:7).

It is this God himself who produced the world and the people in it; who willed that Noah and his family should survive from the immersed race of humans; who began an image of the golden age in the same location, from the Janus in Etruria to the right bank of the Tiber, where, after many Etruscan kings, he established the eternal empire of true gold; who united Abraham to himself, led him from his homeland, and encouraged him in the hope of an eternal inheritance; who put Joseph, the youngest of the brothers, in charge in Egypt and willed that he be the deliverance of his father and brothers; who spoke to Moses out of a burning bush, calling him from the sheepfold of Jethro his father-in-law to the rulership and liberation of his people; who gave Prince Joshua, after the tribes were subdued, the land he had once promised to Abraham and the patriarchs; who made Saul, when he was searching for his father's three missing asses, the ruler of the holy people of Judah; who raised up David, the last and least of Isai's seven sons; and in like manner he chose Manuel, the final and last of the seven to whom Portugal belonged. *Oh how incomprehensible*, says the Apostle, *are the judgments of God, and how unsearchable his ways* (Rom 11:33).

It is this God who predicted Cyrus, king of the Persians, calling him by name in the prophecy of Isaiah before he had become king; and he fulfilled what was foretold for his reign by inducing Cyrus to lead the Hebrews back from Babylon; who moved Darius, his successor, not only to permit, but even to support, the return of the Hebrews and the restoration of their city and temple; who exiled Dardanus from Etruria that he might found the Trojans in Asia; who brought Aeneas, the Etruscan who set out from Troy on a long course of travels, back to the Tiber to become founder of Alba and the Alban kings, from whom, after thirty years, the virgin Ilia bore the founders of Rome. And when they were to be thrown out to the crowd, although unjustly, he decreed that God, the son of a virgin and of God, should give a beginning to this city's kingdom that was about to perish. For it is known that later he truly consecrated God, born of God and virgin, by his blood unto an eternal empire. (For what Sibylla foretold about our God, Christ, posterity fastened upon the man, Romulus; and what was read about the mother of the Lord, that a virgin was going to conceive and give birth, they wrongly attributed to Ilia, the vestal virgin; and the things said about Christ's priesthood, which would exist at Rome forever, were interpreted of Romulus' kingdom, which was to fall after a few centuries.) It was this God, I say, who preserved unharmed from out of the water those twins that Amulius had exposed; who arranged for them to be raised by Faustulos and impelled them to found a city by a ditch. This city was later enlarged by seven kings, and it grew to such magnitude, now under consuls, now under Caesars, that as queen of almost the whole earth it at last received the king of all. It is this God who decreed that the empire of all should belong to this city alone, in which the perpetual throne of the emperor was to be established; who once raised up David (that we might return to our theme), the last and least of Isai's seven sons. This same God, by whom all these things were done so long ago, finally in our age has chosen Manuel, the final and last of all from among those seven to whom, as we said, belonged the kingdom of Portugal.

No one could have ever believed or suspected, when seven suitable heirs to the throne remained, that six who were prior by law were going to die before the death of King John, and that Manuel, the last, was going to succeed John at his death. Alonso, son of King John, died an adolescent of admirable character. Joanna died, to whom the inheritance of rulership rightfully belonged by the law of this kingdom. Manuel's three older brothers died. Finally, King John died and Manuel received the reins of the kingdom. People have understood that kings are called to their reign by God, but that those are especially raised up by a conspicuous signification who are called to an extraordinary glory of accomplishing great deeds.

Surely Isaiah did not intend his revelation, *His empire will be multiplied on the throne of David* (Is 9:7), to mean anything but this: that just as the kingdom of the Hebrews once grew up in the East, so now for a second time God would create a Christian empire in the East. One was through King David and the other through King Manuel. The fate of each king was the same. The way each obtained his kingdom and the success of each in conquering his enemy and enlarging his kingdom were the same. It was proper that each be called from the family of one man, Isai for one and Edward for the other. There were seven in Isai's family when Samuel, the high priest, sought the one on whom to bestow the diadem of the kingdom. There appeared again seven in the family of Edward under Alexander, the high priest, when God sought someone who could merit by his piety, take hold of by his courage, and sustain by his power, the great fortune of this kingdom. Surely it is thought an equal calamity when a prince rules whose character is either ungodly or mean-spirited. David was the last of seven Hebrews while Manuel was the last of seven Christians. Samuel preferred David alone to six of his elders while God preferred Manuel alone to six of his elders.

Each was a child, each the last, and surely each received his kingdom unsuspectingly and beyond the expectation of everyone. For this reason Isaiah, since he related the name of Manuel often in the seventh and eighth chapters, was going to describe his throne in the ninth chapter, and calls it *the throne of David* because each, while he was youngest, merited to be preferred to six elders. Did the prophet remain silent about this? No, in fact he writes in the same place that *unto us a child is born* (Is 9:6). In the same chapter this is shown to mean both Davids; and both extensions of the empire are meant when he says, *His empire will be multiplied on the throne of David.* Here the likeness of both Davids is acknowledged: their smallness, their election out of seven, their triumph over the enemy, and the growth of their empire.

Finally after all this follow two very clear prophecies concerning the things of faith to be restored. For in the ninth chapter it is written that by his actions *the remnant will be converted* (Is 10:21.22); that those of the people who did not yet accept the true religion will now accept it; that the ungodly will embrace with all their might the religion of their godly adversary.

But there is a time of autumn and another time of spring. The exuberance of flowers first reveals the richness of fruits. *When the fig tree puts out leaves*, says the Lord, *you know that summer is already near* (Mt 24:32). We have seen leafing branches; we have seen the swollen buds of full spring; we have seen sunny gardens blossoming in an array of painted colors. Can one expect anything other than the abundance of autumn?

We have seen what was written in the sixth chapter, that in the time of Julius' oak *the throne was exalted and lifted up*, by which two kinds of building were signified. In the seventh and eighth chapters we have seen the name of Manuel, which the prophet made known without any mystery. In the ninth chapter we have seen the establishment of King Manuel, another David, who was called as a child from out of seven to accomplish these mighty deeds.

Now it only remains for us to see what the tenth chapter tells us to expect: *The remnant will be converted*, and the entire world will accept faith and religion; and finally to see what things are read in the eleventh chapter: *In that day the nations will beseech this root of Jesse, which remains for a sign to the peoples* (Is 11:10). Here is portrayed the faith and cross of Christ, which were brought to the people of the Indian Ocean by the Portuguese David, and which must be brought as soon as possible to other peoples.

Because the beginnings of campaigns are usually the most difficult, while what follows after is easier, the prophet adds, *and it will come to pass in that day that the Lord will direct his hand for a second time to possess the remnant of his people* (Is 11:11). Surely this prophecy means that, in the time when the things we have enumerated shall come to pass, the Roman pontiff and the Roman Church will for a second time possess the Churches of Asia.

He also added something that has been so much looked for in the prayers of all Christians, something that is usually not recited without great emotion nor without an abundance of pious tears: *His tomb will be glorious* (Is 11:10). Oh that holy, Oh that happy day on which the most blessed tomb, neglected by the apathy of so many rulers, will be received by the godliness of one pope and rescued from the enemy and from decay and neglect! Be on guard, Pope Julius, against believing that any glory can be greater than that a prince should satisfy the prayers of the entire republic. *His tomb*, he says, *will be glorious.* See how great is the glory that will result from this victory that will make divine religion glorious!

I see in the same place, where the words concern the recovery of his tomb, that mention is made of our Manuel, who would strike down the tyrant possessing the tomb and compel the islands that were ignorant of the faith to accept *the faith by hearing* (Rom 10:17), as the Apostle says. *He will direct his hand,* says the prophet, *to possess what remains, from Assyria to Egypt, from Ethiopia to the islands of the sea; and he will raise up a sign for the nations* (Is 11:11-12). Is it not as clear as day that Manuel was called by God to discover and conquer the islands of that impassable sea?

Surely it was more difficult to discover by our travels those most remote places than it was to conquer them. Therefore, as the prophet concludes, we will rule Asia for a second time, since we will capture what shall remain from Egypt to the islands of the sea. Thus in our age we have already taken what Egypt was forced to leave behind. We have captured the enormous wealth of the Egyptian tyrant. We have captured the tribute that the ruler of all the islands offered of his own accord. What is there in this prophecy that lacks fulfillment except this: that, if sin and cowardice do not interfere, we shall capture Asia and that the Lord's *tomb shall be glorious?*

Furthermore, on this second David, King Manuel, the provident Spirit left this verse: *I have found David, my servant. I have anointed him with my holy oil* (Ps 89:20). Since he wished this verse to be understood of either David, later he said something about the second David which could not be said of the first: *I will place his hand in the sea* (Ps 89:25). Let the monuments of the ancients be read, let their histories be recited; none of the Tyrians, none of the Cilicians, none of the Romans, lastly none of those who were powerful in the glory of maritime activity ever traveled over so much of the sea, ever made so many harbors accessible, ever manifested to humans so many seashores and nations as the Portuguese David. For perhaps it was more fitting that among all sailors, he was preferred above any other. And thus this is truly that David of whom God uniquely foretold when said, *I will place his hand in the sea,* and whom he had called *David, my servant* (Ps 88:20).

Who this is that can be called a servant of God we are clearly shown in another psalm. Speaking of justice and judgments, it immediately says, *for your servant guards these* (Ps 19:11). The servant of God is defined as someone who does not depart from the commandments. *God found David, his servant,* that is, he found Manuel to be obedient to his law and divine precepts. Manuel would say that he would rather be without a kingdom than allow injury to be brought against anyone in his kingdom. They are unjust rulers who, although they say they love justice, do not listen to or meet with those who seek justice. They would hear only their own concerns, and in all these matters are unable to maintain a justice removed from injury. Therefore Manuel comes out to the public on appointed days, and he offers himself to be looked upon and approached. He listens to each one in the crowd, nor was this king ever approached by any little woman whom he would not listen to or who herself, having been heard, would not prevail upon the king. I am speaking of those who implored the justice or mercy of the king, which he says is no less of an adornment in rulers than are the sun and moon, the brightest lights, in heaven.

It was usual to say that what pertains to his other virtues must be interrupted often. Just as nothing in the kingdom is greater than the king, so no one should be more moderate, more constant and better. Manuel has continually detested the pleasures of the body in his speech no less than in his life, so that by example he has guided even the weakest men of the kingdom to chastity and temperance. For it is easier to follow the habits of rulers than their commands, nor does any law become so quickly persuasive to those to whom it is commanded than by the life of the one commanding. Furthermore his soul, which is not lifted up in prosperity, does not sink or collapse in adversity. He also asserts that they who do not bear patiently the adverse events of fortune could certainly be called people, but not men. With Plato, he thinks that the republic that has many poor must itself be poor. Therefore he works diligently to help and sustain the needy with royal assistance and generosity.

Finally he is especially studious of divine things. For besides the temples, altars, holy vessels, vestments of priests, and other ornaments of religion, which he has restored, enlarged, and embellished with royal splendor, he makes sure that he is not outdone by any priest in the psalms and prayers that priests pray to God seven times daily. It would take too long to enumerate everything. Let it suffice to know that God rightly said of him, *I have found David, my servant, and I will place his hand in the sea* (Ps 89:20.25).

I will make an end of my discourse. But I would not omit what Isaiah, the portrayer of our age, said to show our king more clearly. He had said that the king would lift up a sign among the nations. He had indicated that the king should particularly use the cross in his standards. And lest he fail to point out all things as with a finger, he writes in chapter twenty-nine about Alexandria, which was once the city and Church of Mark, the divine lion and evangelist. This city was named Ariel, that is, the lion of God, in honor of its first and best pastor. In our age this city is all but ruins. But it continued to maintain one thing, that from it, as from a unique spring, an abundance of spices and fragrant herbs were carried to all the harbors of the Mediterranean Sea and to every part of the world that lies from Egypt and Syria to the western sun. The most celebrated market in that city, after it began to attract crowds, not only never departed, but no reason ever arose to end or change it.

Looking at the astronomers' instrument they call the globe, we see that our king, who was led, as we have taught, by the divine hand, encircled the land of Alexandria and Africa by the ocean that faces south. Having followed the globe, and intending to go around the land by the ocean, he proceeded to that place where the riches of those spices arise; and taking them away, he sailed through the ocean to Portugal. These were the spices which had for many centuries been sent to Alexandria from the Indies, and which we obtained from Alexandria. Nothing remained of Alexandria and Lion but the trade of spices. But he removed this trade that had been so constant in it through the centuries. Having followed the globe, King Manuel also conquered the city of Alexandria, when he took away the one thing left in that city.

I have recounted the history. Now I will explain the prophecy that Isaiah recorded in that place which was written for us, as we showed above. *Woe*, he says, *Ariel, the city of Ariel that David conquered* (Is 29:1). Here God certainly decreed this final ruin of Alexandria by the Portuguese David. It continues, *I will encircle Ariel*, because while it earlier faced ships from the north, only this king circled with his fleet from the south to conquer its wealth. *And it will be*, he says, *sorrowful and full of grief* (Is 29:2), when the city understands that its reason for glory and wealth has been taken away.

Finally the prophet adds that the coming king claimed so much glory for himself because he added an eternal monument of such great and so unusual a glory on his standards. For Isaiah says, *I will encircle as a globe in its orbit* (Is 29:3), by which words I do not know whether anything clearer could be expected in any prophecy. For our king has two signs, the cross and the globe. In the eleventh chapter he showed the one, and in the twenty-ninth chapter the other.

I could gather innumerable other words from holy prophecies that agree with our theme, but it was enough to write this much in a rough and confused style. If we listen diligently and not with a deaf ear, we must be greatly moved to expect the things that we have seen are attached to these prophetic words, and to give thanks to the supreme God by our piety and manner of life. For you, Pope Julius, pastor and protector, God has accomplished these great deeds through the Portuguese David, and he has promised that he will accomplish even greater things.

Peroration

We have spoken of the golden age. We have spoken of your happiness. We have spoken of the victory and virtue of King Manuel. It remains to bring this discourse to an end. But at least I will have pointed out that these things, so clear and so favorable, have occurred in your time in order that you may be aroused to complete the happiness of your flock. So then, most blessed father, see how many words, how many prophecies, how many fine deeds God calls you to. Surely he freely bestowed these great things upon you so that you might freely undertake even greater things. Since there are three categories of people to be governed—for some always obey their rulers, some seek mercy because they do not always obey, and some do not obey nor ever seek mercy—the best rulers surely give peace to the first category, mercy to the second, and subdue the rest with warlike necessity. You, having attained these three, decreed three days of public thanksgiving. You called and ordered me three times to compose a discourse for the people.

We began our first discourse in honor of Perugia. For when no one at the time wanted you to depart from the city, and when you had removed the armies, subdued the internal wars, put an end to the shedding of blood, murders and feuds, then you confirmed all things in a most tranquil peace. Therefore the words you ordered me to compose, I arranged concerning peace and your peaceful oak. Then, when Bologna was hardly accepting your approach, was refusing or delaying it, you, after winning the city, offered mercy to those asking for it. When I composed a discourse concerning this mercy given, I encouraged you to listen to the cries of Rachel and to attack the Eastern enemies of the faith with war and troops. Now the king of Portugal has conquered their Indian seas, subdued their proud and stubborn souls, and ordered them to follow the golden life. Now called to speak for a third time, I have spoken about your three victories which the apostolic king brought forth for you.

I see that these three policies, which you have employed most beneficially toward these three groups of people, were set down by a Latin writer. In his words about the practices of the best ruler you will recognize the deeds excellently accomplished by you. For to Perugia, Bologna, and Ceylon, as it was right and just, you brought peace, mercy, and war. You gave peace to the easy, showed mercy to the difficult, and conquered the proud with war and arms. Accept now these lines that are well-known to the people:

> In governing the peoples of the empire, remember the Roman peace, and (these will become arts to you) while imposing your rule, remember to show mercy to the submissive and to subdue the proud.[101]

I have willingly commended your happiness, Julius, most reverend pope. I have commended your courage, I have commended the deeds you splendidly accomplished with hope and wisdom so that you might realize that the memory of deeds well-done is not lost; so that you might be aroused to perform those things that remain; so that you might do what the name of Julius, and the reputation of your courage, character, and power, ought to move you to do.

You should be moved by the armies of your kings, which, with a great hope of reward, were turned against the people opposed to your faith. Consider at times your own authority. Consider the great men of Christianity. Consider the two kinds of rewards, those God gives to the one dying and those people give to the one who lives. What we sow in our labors is very brief, what we gather at harvest is eternal. If you contemplate these things often, accurately and skillfully, I doubt not that it will come to pass that, whatever our rulers have lost over the past thousand years, you will in a brief time of seeking restore and establish. And you will renew for a rejoicing flock the golden fruits of your oak and the golden ages in your Etruria.

Translated by Maria Boulding, O.S.B. and Michael Woodward

Notes

1. See Gn 41:41.

2. See Ex 3-40.

3. See Jos 1-12.

4. See 1 and 2 Sm.

5. Pliny, *Natural History* 6.2.

6. See Chapter 3 of this book.

7. Homer, *Iliad* 2.204; see Aristotle, *Politics* 1292a.

8. See Plato, *Timaeus* 49c.

9. Vergil, *Georgics* 4.441-442.

10. Vergil, *Aeneid* 6.733.

11. *Ibid.* 6.638-639.

12. See Gn 3:6.

13. See Aristotle, *Metaphysics* 980a.

14. See Cicero, *Fin.* 5.18.49.

15. See Gn 6:9.

16. See Pliny, *Natural History* 16.1; Vergil, *Georgics* I.148; Plato, *The Republic* 372c-d.

17. Here and in the next pages Giles makes an elaborate play on the letters FAVL, which cannot be reproduced in English (translator).

18. See Plato, *Alcibiabes I* 121e-122a.

19. See Aristotle, *Nicomachean Ethics* 1129b.

20. See Herm., *Asclepius* 3.34b; Plato, *Philebus* 23c; Plato, *The Republic* 509d.

21. See Jn 8:23.

22. See Plato, *The Republic* 508a.

23. See Vergil, *Aeneid* 1.306; 3.311; 5.64; 8.455; see also Sir 8:17.

24. See Plato, *The Republic* 508a.

25. Vergil, *Aeneid* 640-641.

26. *Ibid.* 6.108-109.

27. See Plato, *The Republic* 509b; Dionysius the Areopagite, *The Divine Names* 2.2.637d.

28. Vergil, *Aeneid* 7.17.

29. *Ibid.* 5.735; 6.98.

30. See Diodorus, S 5.40.1-5.

31. Vergil, *Aeneid* 6.190,193.

32. See Mt 3:16; Mk 1:10; Lk 3:22; Jn 1:32.

33. See Lactantius, *Institutes* 1, 20.

34. See Vergil, *Aeneid* 5.761.

35. See Aristotle, *Metaphysics* 338a-339a.341b-342a.

36. See Plato, *Alcibiabes I* 122a.

37. See Diodorus, S 5.40.2.

38. See Plato, *Critias* 109b.

39. See Plato, *Cratylus* 397e-398a.

40. See Plato, *The Laws* 631b-d.

41. See Plato, *The Republic* 484c-487a.496a-497a.508e.

42. See Plato, *Gorgias* 486d.

43. See Plato, *The Republic* 413c-414b.543a-547b.495a-b.

44. *Ibid.* 416e-417a.

45. Vergil, *Aeneid* 6.146-148.

46. Plato, *The Republic* 379a-e.

47. Vergil, *Ecl.* 4.6.

48. Plato, *Gorgias* 526c-d.

49. Vergil, *Ecl.* 4.9.

50. *Ibid.* 4.7.49.

51. See 1 Cor 13.

52. See Acts 2:1-5.16.

53. See Rv 21:18-21.

54. See Ez 1:10.

55. *Genituram* could also mean the star of his nativity (translator).

56. See Jn 13:25.

57. See Plato, *Phaedrus* 246a.

58. See 1 Cor 13.

59. See Plato, *Min.* 319b-320d.

60. See Homer, *Odyssey* 11.569.

61. *Ibid.* 5.5.

62. See Plato, *Alcibiades I*; Epin. 976e-977b.988a-b.989d.

63. Alternatively this sentence could be understood as a reference to intratrinitarian relationships, in which case it could be translated: "Dawn . . . when he made known to us the power of the Father from whom he derived his own being, and the procession of the loving Spirit" (translator).

64. See Plato, *Timaeus* 69d-70a.

65. Vergil, *Aeneid* 8.564-565.

66. See Plato, *The Republic* 519a-b.

67. See Aristotle, *The History of Animals* 563a.

68. See Aristotle, *Nicomachean Ethics* 1125b.1126a.

69. Vergil, *Aeneid* 6.273-274.

70. *Ibid.* 4.20.

71. *Ibid.* 8.324-325.

72. *Ibid.* 10.202.

73. *Ibid.* 5.761.

74. See Livy 5.54.

75. See Plato, *The Laws* 745b-e.760b-c.848c-e.

76. Vergil, *Georgics* 1.514.

77. See Gn 25:30.

78. See Mt. 23:25.

79. Vergil, *Aeneid* 6.747.

80. See Aristotle, *Nicomachean Ethics* 1177b.

81. See Nm 7:84.

82. Eugene IV (1431-1447).

83. Nicholas V (1447-1455).

84. Calistus III (1455-1458).

85. Pius II (1458-1464).

86. Paul II (1464-1471).

87. Sixtus IV (1471-1484).

88. Alexander VI (1492-1503).

89. Martin V (1417-1431).

90. Vergil, *Aeneid* 6.636.

91. See Prv 7:23.

92. Vergil, *Aeneid* 4.73.

93. *Ibid.* 4.441-446.

94. See Mt 16:18.

95. See Jude 20-21.

96. See Jos 1-12.

97. See Pliny, *Natural History* 6.24.

98. Psalms 74-78.

99. See Vergil, *Aeneid* 5.754.

100. See 1 Sm 16:10-12.

101. Vergil, *Aeneid* 6.851-853.

The Inaugural Oration of the Fifth Lateran Council

delivered by Giles of Viterbo,
prior general of the Augustinian Order

Giles of Viterbo delivered this address in the Lateran basilica on 3 May 1512 in the presence of the pope, the cardinals, and the bishops who composed the council. As Hubert Jedin stated in his classical work on the history of the Council of Trent, Lateran V was the last attempt at a papal reform of the Church before the breakup of Christian unity.

Pope Julius II (1503-1511) convoked the council in July of 1511 in the midst of his war with Louis XII of France. The council directed its attention to a reaffirmation of papal authority within the Church in contrast to the problem of conciliarism and, more importantly, to the need of reform.

With the defeat of the papal forces at Ravenna, Italy, panic and fear grasped the people of Rome. Giles in his address sees the defeat as "an act of divine providence, intended to show us that we should not rely on mercenaries, but yield to the arms of the Church." For this reason Giles insists on the need for reform. His famous quote is contained in this sermon: "Man is to be changed by the sacred, not the sacred by man."

For a critical edition of the oration, see Clare O'Reilly, "'Without Councils we cannot be saved.' Giles of Viterbo addresses the Fifth Lateran Council," Augustiniana 27 (1977) 166-204.

Considering that so many notable speakers are available in the city, I suppose everyone here present is wondering why someone like me, who can in no way be compared with these luminaries, should appear before this august assembly to address the weighty issues that confront the Christian world. I might rightly say that something intervened to place me before others — not any virtue of my own, but a certain rationale of prior times and events, by which the issue itself invited me to hurl the first weapon in this conflict and to take the auspices of the Holy Lateran Council.

About twenty years ago — when insofar as I had it in me and my meager talents availed — successively I explained the gospels to the people, interpreted the prophets, and expounded the Apocalypse concerning the destiny of the Church to virtually all Italy. I affirmed again and again that my auditors would see both disturbances and disasters of the Church and would perceive at some time or other a reform of the Church. Now it has become apparent that this was correct, that the one who said this *would* come to pass is now testifying that this *has* come to pass, that the one who so often exclaimed: *My eyes will see the days of salvation* (Lk 2:30), now at length exclaims: My eyes have seen salvation and the holy beginning of the expected restoration.[1]

Now you are present, O restorer of the world, offspring of God the Father, savior and redeemer of mortals. You give me the power to speak; you endow my oration with the power to move; and you afford the Council fathers the power to celebrate a true, holy, and judicious Council (not in words, but in reality) and to extirpate vice, to foster virtue, to trap the foxes swarming to destroy the holy vineyard in this raging storm. And you grant the restoration of our fallen religion to its former purity, its ancient light, its native splendor, and its sources.

And so I might offer insights concerning the Council which are always advantageous to the Church, and others which are fundamental to our times, noting that I would not dare to invert the style of the prophecies but would adopt the speeches and whole phraseology, as it is commonly received, both because it is proper for man to be changed by the sacred, not the sacred by man, and because it is a simple statement of truth.[2]

And the division immediately comes to mind that some matters are divine, some heavenly, and some human. Since the divine are movements devoid of change, they do not need reform. But the heavenly and the human require reformation, inasmuch as they are subject to modification. For example, when the moon has come into correspondence with the sun, and the sun has descended from Cancer to the winter solstice, creation, in a manner of speaking, suffers a great loss. The heavenly bodies then make complete compensation, because natural law requires their reascent. Thus they restore to creation all the daylight they took away in their descent. But if the passage of these bodies through the heavens, although perpetual, ceaseless, and everlasting, nevertheless is cyclical and restorative, what happens in the third category which consists of fluid, frail, and ephemeral entities? Such entities necessarily must either undergo quick annihilation or receive continual reformation.

Consequently, self-reformation, culture, and discipline bring to the human spirit what food furnishes to maintain life, and generation supplies to perpetuate species. Just as animals cannot live very long without nutritious food — so human beings, so the Church, cannot act properly without the care of Councils. If rain is denied to meadows, water to gardens, cultivation to fields, pruning to vineyards, or if nourishment is refused to living organisms, in a brief time the former dry up and go wild, while the latter fail and die. So, for the most part, changes made after the reign of Constantine (which added a great deal of splendor and embellishment to religion) weakened the rigor of Christian morality and ascetical practices in no small measure.

As often as we have failed to hold Councils, we have seen the Bride of Christ abandoned by her Bridegroom, and yesterday's gospel passage fulfilled: *A little while, and now you shall not see me* (Jn 16:16).

We have seen Christ asleep in the boat and the force of the gale,[3] which is the fury of heretics, tearing at the white sails of truth.

We have witnessed the evil of cupidity, that dreadful craving for gold and possessions.

We have observed the brazen boldness of evil men raging against the rights, authority, and majesty of the Church.

We have seen, I repeat, force, rapine, adultery, immorality, and every evil plague so confuse the sacred and profane, so assail the barque of the Church, that it almost gave its side to the flood of wickedness, almost foundered and sank.

Today, petitions to the Holy Spirit were decreed by the Council fathers. After the fathers again took refuge in the Council at his admonition, they emended and composed everything as quickly as possible. After they mastered the winds and gales, they were carried, so to speak, into the safest of harbors, where they compelled violence to yield to reason, outrage to justice, vice to virtue, tempest and flood to peace and tranquillity.

To the Holy Spirit, the God of fishermen, sea, and waters, they sang the hymn: *Many waters cannot quench charity* (Sg 8:6), and the hymn: *Winter is now past, the rain is over and gone. . . . Arise, my love* (Sg 2:11.13). For the Bride lies sleeping, like trees in winter.

Through the efforts of Councils, she rises and grows green again, just as woodlands put forth leaves in springtime when the sun returns. As sunlight waxes, fruitful zephyrs blow, and productive plantations germinate. Through the illumination of Councils and the Holy Spirit, breezes blow, and the dead eyes of the Church revive and receive light, as the second part of the prophecy is fulfilled: *and again a little while, and you shall see me* (Jn 16:16). And this certainly means nothing else but that the light of the Holy Spirit, which is extinguished when Councils are omitted, is kindled anew and recovered in Councils, like new fire struck from flint.

To this, Paul, the glory of the apostles, said, as he pointed out the source of salvation:

Without faith it is impossible to please God (Heb 11:6).

But without Councils faith cannot stand.

Therefore, we cannot be saved without Councils.

But to prove empirically what we have demonstrated by reason, we must consider that what we are to believe has three roots from which the whole faith of the Church flows: first, the unity of the divine nature; second, all-creative Trinity in the one nature of Father, Offspring, and Love; and third, the conception of the divine progeny in the Virgin's womb. On these, as on the loftiest summits and holiest mountains, both the nine remaining divisions of faith and all piety are founded. For *the foundations thereof are in the holy mountains* (Ps 87:1). Certainly, unity is called a mountain of God, because in the one essence of God there is also precisely one nature, and for us to realize that unity is not solitary nor sterile, but possessed of the utmost fecundity, *a fat mountain is added* (Ps 68:16). But the prophet calls the body in the Virgin united to the Word *a curdled mountain* (Ps 68:16).

And so this is that tripartite vine established on the lofty mountains, which the prophet spoke of as future and the gospel verifies as present.[4] But the vine had already perished, for, as David testified, *the boar out of the wood had laid it waste* (Ps 80:14), and the ferment of philosophy had devastated it. Arius attempted to remove the first mountain by destroying the unity; Sabellius, the second by confusing the persons; and Photinus, the third by rashly overthrowing the virgin birth. The three of them were seduced by a desire for glory and an eagerness for new things. Like ungodly giants, they dared to move the mountains out of place to make a way for themselves to attack and demolish heaven. And they had already realized their purpose, for what they were proposing in their philosophy the princes were imposing by force of arms. Philosophy was plying us with argumentation; armed force was assailing us with confrontation. The former was trying to overthrow the faith with deception; the latter, with violence. The former was striving to overturn *what* was believed; the latter, to destroy *those* who believed. The former raged against piety and souls; the latter, against bodies and life. On the brink of extinction:

What was the divine Bride to do?

Where was she to turn?

Where was she to flee?

Whose protection, whose assistance, whose support was she to implore?

The tempest was frightful.

The ship was sinking.

Finally (not to delay) she found no way to get away and escape except the Council of Nicaea, where God showed himself from heaven to Pope Sylvester, who was sitting at the helm and on the point of abandoning ship.

And God said: *O you of little faith, why did you doubt?* (Mt 14:31).

And immediately by his divine power, God restored the mountains of faith and defeated the audacity of the giants.

Having escaped this way, the Maiden has learned by experience, inasmuch as she perceives, no matter how her foes threatened her, that no institution has the capacity to protect her more securely, deliver her more opportunely, or vindicate her more effectively than a Council. In this way, it comes about that nothing extinguishes the charity of the Church;[5] and God the Holy Spirit makes his dwelling in our souls.[6] He alone, as Moses testifies, moves over the waters as conqueror of the deep and master of tempests.[7]

But now, what I have said about faith, which would certainly be in vain if the Council had not been convoked, I would generally wish to have the same understood about temperance, justice, wisdom, and the other virtues. For we all look for idleness instead of labor, leisure instead of employment, and pleasure instead of anxiety. However, if we turn our attention to the concerns of Councils and ask when they will be realized — to take a census, to explore the rationale of life and morality, to apprehend, judge, and punish the reprobate, and the contrary, to attract, foster, and improve the upright — then incredible incentives to appreciate and acquire virtue take hold: men assemble, discuss excellence, root out vice, pursue perfection, undertake nothing dishonorable, nothing ignoble. That was the distinction of that Council, from which, as from the Trojan horse, so many brilliant lights of genius flashed.

That approbation of virtue, that detestation of vice gave birth to the Basils, Chrysostoms, and Damascenes of Greece, the Jeromes, Ambroses, and Augustines of Italy, who with a great company of similar champions, O good God, filled the Christian treasury with books, writings, and monuments, the heavenly gold and silver of learning and discipline.

I will pass over a matter that really should not be neglected (unless time is opposed), which concerns the rulers of the Church and pastors of the people, on whom the whole authority and security of Christianity has been established. For as this lower world is directed by the movement and light of the heavens, so the Christian nations are governed by their rulers as heavenly pastors. For the pastors to be good two things are necessary. First, they must shine with the light of discipline, as they teach others. And second, as they practice the holy actions they teach, they must be especially eminent, particularly in action. These are the two things which Christ, the prince of pastors, taught, when he ordered his disciples to carry burning torches, so as to organize clearly; and to be girded, so as to act morally.[8] At the same time he applied himself marvelously, because he was both *the light of the world* (Jn 8:12), and the wisdom of God the Father,[9] and he was called the holy of all holies,[10] and because he surpassed all righteous men in holiness of life. And for these reasons, he said: *I am the Good Shepherd* (Jn 10:11.14).

But the evangelist who writes that he *began to do and to teach* testifies that he said he was good for both reasons.[11] Indeed, after God the Holy Spirit breathed on and filled those twelve leaders, who were *made princes over all the earth* (Ps 45:17), they so attained the two heavenly powers that they even merited to be called "the heavens,"[12] as the most commonly known oracle is described: *The heavens show forth the glory of God* (Ps 19:2). By this we are advised we should celebrate the glory of those rulers who have imitated and acquired both the wisdom of heavenly enlightenment and the sanctity of moral conversion. This concern is by far the most important of all; and history reminds us of the consideration the Council expended on it. For men who joined a holy way of life to outstanding learning were sought out, conveyed, and equipped from the whole Mediterranean world by the Council fathers, to the great praise of the electors, the profit of the Church, and the advantage, joy, and applause of the people.

What should I say about the gravest and most dangerous issue of all, which is so deplorable in our time? I am speaking about the injustices of princes, the insolence of armies, the threats of soldiers. For what expression or viewpoint could be more disconsolate than for the Church, the queen of heaven and earth, to be considered as devoted to violence, or given to assistance, or apprehensive of the weapons of rascals! Indeed, this pestilence is spreading,[13] advancing, and waxing so strong at this time, that the whole authority of the Church and the liberty with which God endowed her seems overturned, crushed, and virtually destroyed.

For this reason, beware, Julius II, Supreme Pontiff, beware lest you believe any mortal man has ever envisaged something better or more beneficial than the convocation of the Council, which you yourself conceived through the inspiration of the Holy Spirit.

Certainly no king, no prince can disdain its decrees, or neglect its dictates, or deny its authority. For if any of them have dared perchance to take little account of the Pontiff himself, who is of himself defenseless, they have grown accustomed to fear and revere him if he is invested with the authority of the Council and the consensus and goodwill of princes and nations.

For if we review the achievements of Councils, we will understand there is nothing more powerful, consequential, and secure than they. For it was in a Council that Gregory X designated Rudolph as emperor against John of Spain and Alonso of Portugal. It was in a Council that Martin IV excommunicated Peter of Aragon. It was in a Council that Boniface VIII decided against King Philip. It was in a Council that Gregory X at one time, and Eugene IV in the memory of the fathers, united the Greek to the Latin Church. It was in Councils that Innocent IV and Gregory IX acted against Emperor Frederick II.

Indeed, it was in this very building, the most eminent of all edifices, which is wont always to overcome its foes and never to be overcome, and in a Council, that Innocent II deposed his adversaries, and Alexander III defeated Victor IV and his associates, and Innocent III deposed Otto IV from the emperorship, and Martin V dispersed the hostile arms of tyrants.

And (not to cover everything) whatever worthy of praise and glory was accomplished in the Church from the age of Melchiades, either to fend off the enemy, or to unite the commonwealth, it all took its origin from Councils — and the practice of dealing with issues in Councils was accepted.

For what else bespeaks a holy Council, except fear of evil men, hope for righteous men, rejection of error, cultivation and restoration of virtue? Thereby, the devil's deception is defeated, sensual temptations are banished, reason regains its lost defense, justice is restored from heaven to earth — if only God returns to his creatures. For if he said: *Where there are two or three gathered together in my name,* I come to them and *I am in the midst of them* (Mt 18:20) — how much more willingly does he betake himself to where, not just two or three, but so many leaders of the Church are assembling. For if John calls pastors of churches angels,[14] what is it that such a great assembly of angels cannot seek with pledges and secure from God with prayers?

Here, Eve is recalled from exile.

Here, the head of the serpent is crushed by the heel of a holier Maiden.[15] Abraham is led from the land of the Chaldees.[16] Hagar, the handmaid, obeys her mistress.[17] Once again a covenant is struck with God.[18] The circumcision of hearts is introduced.[19]

Here, the father of the patriarchs, securing a ladder, opens a way into heaven.[20] He is clasped to God in a wrestling match, and for listening to God receives a name.[21]

Here, the people, as if oppressed by hunger in the wilderness, beseech God for sustenance, receive the bread of heaven and angels,[22] and savor the sweetness of the heavenly banquet.

Here, when men's hearts have become like stone, they are struck by Moses' staff and pour out fountains of water.[23]

Here, the treasure hidden in the field is uncovered,[24] the pearl is purchased,[25] the lamps are lit,[26] the seed is sown in the good ground,[27] the grain of mustard seed grows into a tree,[28] the olive tree is grafted into the wild olive.[29]

Blessed, therefore, are those times which have supported Councils; foolish are these times if they do not acknowledge the Council, and miserable, if they neglect it. We have touched on the ancient advantages of Councils as cursorily as possible; now we will taste our own as briefly as possible.

I, therefore, call upon you, Julius II, Supreme Pontiff; that almighty God who wills for you to take his place on earth calls on you, the God who has already chosen you from such a great college, the God who has defended you for the ninth year as the spouse of his Church, the God who has endowed you with both a good mind for reflection and such a great faculty for action, as he never granted to any of your predecessors, specifically so that you would drive away robbers, cleanse the roads, suppress sedition, raise up the most magnificent temple of all that has ever been seen, make of the militia an army of the Church to be feared by great kings (which no one was able to do before this), so that at length you may produce an empire, that you may recover Rimini, Favi, Ravenna, and many other places. Even though the enemy was able to take these places from you, the enemy was not able to disable the Supreme Pontiff from accomplishing all these things. For the courage of great princes is not to be judged from one instance or one event, but from their plans and actions.

Now, these two things were lacking from your accomplishments, that you would convoke a Council, and would declare war on the common enemy of Christians. And what you have considered, sponsored, and decreed from the beginning, you are now offering to God, to the Christian flock, to your own, and thereupon to piety and faith. And you should know that you have raised great expectations in all good men, for, if you were for a certainty forced by troublesome wars and evil times to defer these goals, you could not be moved by threats, or weaponry, or disasters to neglect or abandon them. Rather you fortified your heart with such resolution that these floods, these inundations, no matter how many, could not extinguish your staunch charity.[30] In addition to all these imperishable favors I have enumerated to delight your heart, twice in former years God called you back to life, once at Bologna and once in Rome, when you were considered as good as dead in your chamber.

And so that same God kept you alive to carry out these great works. By a manifest miracle, God himself would restore life to a near-dead Pontiff, and through a holy Council, the Pontiff would restore life to a near-dead Church. Thus, in union with its reviving Pontiff, the Church would also revive in its morals. That God, I say, requires and commands you to turn these two things over in your heart, to tend and complete them, and (as the prophet orders) to overthrow, eradicate, and destroy error, debauchery, and vice, and to plant, cultivate, and raise moderation, virtue, and holiness.[31]

But many other things, especially the loss of our army, ought to excite us to do these things. I think the disaster with the army was an act of divine providence, intended to show us that we should not rely on mercenaries, but yield to the arms of the Church. If we would return to our own arms, we would emerge victorious. Our arms, however, are piety, religion, probity, supplication, vows, "the breastplate of faith," and "the armor of light," to use the words of the apostle.[32] If we will return to these works of the Council, just as we were inferior to an enemy in arms that were not our own, so we will be superior to every enemy in arms that are our own. If you recall the war Moses fought against Amalec, you will see that the people dear to God were always conquered when they trusted in the sword, and always triumphed when they supplicated God in prayer. Joshua was leading the army into battle; the priest Aaron, and Hur, and Moses were climbing the mountain. The former were attacking the enemy in an armed body; the latter were beseeching God with purged hearts. The former were using swords; the latter were employing prayers. The former were fighting with steel; the latter were resisting with piety. We saw the weaponry of both, namely, military and religious, but now we recognize which is ours, because God has shown us the reality. When Moses, Exodus says, held up his hands, the Israelite army conquered; when he lowered his hands, the army fell back.[33] And (not to call it into question) at the end of that account it is written: *The hand and war of the Lord shall be against Amalec*, that is, against the enemy of the Church, *from generation to generation* (Ex 17:16). By these words God is certainly warning us that both generations, and both the Churches, that is, of Moses and of Christ, are conquered by military weaponry, but triumph by pious practices.

They are overcome in armed struggle.

In sacred conflict they are victorious.

Relying in the beginning on its own arms, the Church took Africa, acquired Europe, and occupied Asia. It carried Christian symbols all around the Mediterranean, neither by force, nor war, nor steel — but through religious endeavor and moral excellence. But when the Spouse *in gilded clothing* (Ps 45:10), who at that time was invoked, summoned, and sought after on all sides, insanely exchanged the golden cloak of ardent spirituality for the steel weaponry of Ajax, she lost the dominion born of the blood of the twelve apostles. She forfeited Asia and Jerusalem. She was forced to abandon Africa and Egypt. Along with the Byzantine Empire and Greece, she saw a good part of Europe snatched away from her. It was the voice of God saying: "When Moses' arms are weary, and prayers and vows cease, Joshua is conquered and Amalec triumphs."[34] So we ourselves have seen, when religion has exchanged the weapons of prayer for those of steel, the Church has been driven, ejected, and expelled from almost the entire rim of the Mediterranean. Muhammed has grown into a behemoth. Unless we abandon steel and return in the bosom of piety to the altars and worship of God, he will increase day by day, will subject everything to his authority, and will occupy the whole Mediterranean basin as the most impious avenger of our impiety.

I perceive . . . yes, I perceive that, unless we impose restrictions on our morals, either at this Council, or by some other arrangement, unless we compel our avidity for human things, the source of all evils, to yield to love of divine things, we have finished with the Christian commonwealth, we are done with religion, it is all over with piety, we have squandered the very riches our fathers garnered from the increase in divine worship — which we, on the contrary, are about to lose by neglect. For these possessions have grown so much from extreme poverty to extreme wealth that it seems they will perish not so very much later. And, unless we signal a retreat, unless we settle our accounts, that very rich fillet, which has been used as a decoration for priestly functions, will hardly be found for use as a garment.

Hear the divine voices sounding on all sides, the voices on all sides demanding the Council, peace, and that holy crusade.

For when will our life be more agreeable?

When will ambition be more forward?

When will avarice be more inflamed?

When will the licentiousness of sin be more brazen?

When will the audacity of speaking, disputing, and writing against piety be either more frequent or more secure?

When will not only negligence, but contempt of sacred things among the people, of the sacraments, of both keys and sacred precepts, be greater?

When will our faith and religion be more open to ridicule (or common abuse)?

When — alas! — will schism in the Church be more pernicious?

When will the enemy be more powerful?

When will the army be more truculent?

When in passing have signs, portents, and prodigies of both the threatening heavens and the trembling earth seemed more frequent and horrible?

When — alas! weeping hinders me — when has the slaughter and the disaster, either previously at Brescia, or later at Ravenna, been more bloody?

When, I say, has any dawn shone more sorrowful and calamitous among the unpropitious days than the most holy light of Christ's Resurrection Day?

Indeed, what are all these things (unless we are made of iron), what else but utterances sent from heaven? For they have truly been made the utterances of God (as Proclus says). They say concerning this particular prophetic pronouncement that *he spoke, and they were made* (Ps 148:5). And in the Hebrew mysteries we learn that the whole world was founded by ten sayings, which we read in Genesis.[35] The events we perceive taking place are therefore utterances of God, utterances of God admonishing and instructing you to have the Council in order to reform the Church, to abrogate the war of both men, to restore a twofold peace to your Spouse sadly assailed on all sides, to avert the swords threatening the jugulars of the city and of Italy, to restrain our licentious living, which is gravely wounding the heart of the Church.

For it does not matter much how much land we possess, but how just, how pious, how zealous we are for divine things, so that finally after so many evils, so many troubles, so many calamities, you hear our sovereign Christ pointing out the Council to Peter and his descendants as the only remedy for all evils, the solitary harbor for the imperilled ship, the sole strategy to strengthen the commonweal. O Peter, he said, *being once converted, confirm your brethren* (Lk 22:32).

Do you hear, O Peter?

Do you hear, O Paul?

Do you hear, O ever august heads of the Church, bulwark and defense of the city of Rome?

Do you hear what a mass of adversity the Church founded in your blood was led into?

Do you see the battle lines slaughtered on both sides?

Do you see the carnage?

Do you see the disasters?

Do you see the fields covered with heaps of slain men?

Do you see how the earth has absorbed more gore this year than rain, that it drank less moisture than blood?

Do you see that Christian strength has declined as much as was once sufficient to combat the enemy of the faith? Nothing remains for us except desolation — nothing but annihilation. Give aid, help, and assistance;

snatch our foundering Church from domestic disasters, as you once delivered it from the malice of unbelievers and tyrants.

The people are praying — men and women, every age group, both sexes, the whole world. The fathers implore; the senate beseeches. Finally, the Holy Father himself suppliantly entreats you to preserve his person, the Church, the city of Rome, these churches, these altars, these sacred things, and these leaders of your cause, and through the guidance of the Holy Spirit to affirm and care for the Lateran Council convoked before you today by Julius II, the Supreme Pontiff, which will become auspicious, productive, and propitious for us, your Church, and for the entire Christian commonweal, unto the salvation of the whole world.

He also implores the pacification of Christian princes and the direction of their arms against Muhammed, the public enemy of Christ.

He further beseeches you that the charity of the Church not only will not be extinguished by these floods, these tempests, these waters, but rather will be cleansed of all the stains it has incurred and restored to its pristine purity and splendor through the merits of the cross and the guidance of the Holy Spirit, through which it is being sanctified today.

I have spoken.

This oration was delivered in the Lateran Palace on May 3, 1512.

Translated by Joseph C. Schnaubelt, O.S.A.
Edited by Joseph Reino

Notes

1. See Sg 2:15.
2. Euripides, *Phoenissae*, 469.
3. See Lk 8:23.
4. See Mt 21:33-41.
5. See Sg 8:7.
6. See Jn 14:23.
7. See Gn 1:2.
8. See Lk 12:35.
9. See Mt 13:54; Mk 6:2.
10. See 2 Mc 14:36.
11. See Acts 1:1.
12. See Mt 19:28; Lk 22:29-30.
13. See 2 Tm 2:17.
14. See Rv 1:3.
15. See Gn 3:15.
16. See Gn 11:31; 15:7.
17. See Gn 16:1-16.
18. See Dt 29:1.
19. See Dt 30:6.
20. See Gn 28:12-13.

21. See Gn 32:24-30.
22. See Dt 8:16; Ps 78:24-25.
23. See Ex 17:6; Nm 20:7-11; Ps 78:16.
24. See Mt 13:44.
25. See Mt 13:45-46.
26. See Mt 25:1-13.
27. See Mt 13:3-9; Mk 4:3-9; Lk 8:5-8.
28. See Mt 13:31-32; Mk 4:31-32; Lk 13:19.
29. See Rom 11:17.
30. See Sg 8:7.
31. See Jer 1:10.
32. See Eph 6:13-17; Rom 13:12.
33. See Ex 17:8-13.
34. See Ex 17:11.
35. See Gn 1.

A Sermon Preached in the Basilica of Santa Maria del Popolo

On the feast of Saint Catherine, 25 November 1512, an anxiously awaited and long negotiated treaty between the Emperor Maximilian and Pope Julius II received public proclamation in the church of Santa Maria del Popolo at Rome.

The importance to the papacy of the occasion, the personal satisfaction felt by Julius on achieving his objective, the determination on his part to lose no opportunity of forwarding his aims or consolidating his success, and the strategic use to which he put the diplomatic gesture were all reflected in the setting for the proclamation and the ceremony surrounding it. Santa Maria del Popolo had become the jewel of the della Rovere family and their dearest loved church in Rome. It was originally erected on the site of a huge walnut tree popularly supposed to have been rooted in the tomb of Nero and to have sheltered the demons that haunted the place. Restored and enlarged in the thirteenth century by Gregory IX, who transferred to it from the Sancta Sanctorum of the Lateran the painting of the Virgin once attributed to Saint Luke, it was entirely rebuilt by Sixtus IV della Rovere, probably between 1472 and 1478. In the following years, and particularly during the pontificate of Sixtus' nephew Julius II, the church became a veritable treasure house of renaissance art.

The monastery attached to Santa Maria del Popolo belonged — as it still does — to the Augustinian friars who were the custodians of the church. It was the prior general of this Order, an influential member of the Church, a renaissance humanist, and an outstanding preacher — Giles of Viterbo — who was chosen to deliver the sermon at the solemn sung Mass that marked the proclamation of the treaty.

When Mass was ended Giles began his discourse. It was a long one. It must also, for all its length, have been of interest to his listeners, for it brought no criticism from de Grassis, who was quick to record the reactions of the assembly and to remark on any sermon he considered long-winded. After the discourse the ceremonies were concluded with the reading of the terms of the treaty. The Pope intoned the Te Deum and, after the usual prayers, gave his blessing. Then, following the ceremonies which had taken almost four hours, a dinner was held in the adjoining Augustinian monastery to bring the day's celebrations to a close.

For a description of the scene for this sermon and for the Latin text, see Clare O'Reilly, "'Maximus Caesar et Pontifex Maximus': Giles of Viterbo proclaims the alliance between Emperor Maximilian I and Pope Julius II," Augustiniana 22 (1972) 80-117.

Prefatory Letter

Jacopo Sadoleto to Actius Sincerus Sannazaro[1]

From the way in which my friend Giles of Viterbo, prior general of the Order of Saint Augustine, is accustomed to sing your praises, I am well aware how high you stand in his esteem. You have figured very often in our conversations. Indeed, your talents and erudition (to which I too can bear witness), as also your humanity and elegant way of life, have been so unceasingly commended by him as to make it evident that you enjoy both his utmost confidence and his unmatched affection.

At the promulgation of the treaty with the Emperor Maximilian entered into by Pope Julius II, the sermon was preached by Giles of Viterbo, and it seemed right to me that this sermon should be made generally available. For the aforementioned reasons, therefore, I decided to dedicate it above all to you, that you may read it as an outstanding piece of work by a man most dear to you, sent to you by another who is also your friend. In this way you will not only continue to be famous for your taste in good literature, but also indulge it in such a way that you will not cease to love us both. Farewell.

A Sermon Preached in the Basilica of Santa Maria del Popolo

by Friar Giles of Viterbo, Prior General of the Order
of the Hermits of Saint Augustine, Concerning the Treaty
between Pope Julius and the Emperor Maximilian
after the Third Session of the Lateran Council

If divine blessings have ever been granted so unmistakably that humans seemed to be aware of the very presence of God, I believe that it falls to my lot today to commemorate such benefits in this sacred assembly, benefits most glorious and renowned. In this very year we had reached such a pitch of calamity in our affairs that we dared not hope for deliverance, dared not even wish for it. Yet God has made his presence felt not simply to deliver your country by the flight of a most powerful enemy, but also to strengthen it by the friendship of the august Emperor. So marvelous is this event that we seem to have seen God's active help with our own eyes — nay, his very presence.

I am to speak then, honorable fathers, of God's wondrous kindness and Caesar's wondrous good will toward your state, and I deplore the fact that both skill and time commensurate to the opportunity are lacking. I am ashamed to deal in meager fashion with so rich a theme, but the scanty time available compels me to do so.

As you well know, a detestable schism had arisen,[2] and was now attempting to secure by armed force what it could not gain by any authority. In central Italy armies were massed which, had they been united in a common good purpose, would certainly have been powerful enough to recover Christian lands, and indeed to increase them worldwide, for the Church, in great fear of the invader's arms, had had recourse to the Catholic King of Aragon. Even though the latter had already drawn up and equipped a great fleet for a devout expedition to Africa, he was obliged, eager as he is to extend and protect all sacred possessions, to change his plans and come to the Church's aid.[3] He therefore dispatched a Spanish army to Bologna, there to defend and regain the possessions of the Church.[4] At Ravenna battle was joined, and although casualties were heavy on both sides, it was the enemy who won the day.[5] Such panic spread in Rome that it could hardly have been greater if the city walls themselves had fallen. Some people suspected that God did not care about the affairs of mortals, for, they repeatedly asserted, a good father makes it his business to preserve his own, not destroy them.

I must, then, indicate briefly how well hitherto and how wisely today God has taken care of your interests, so that it may be plainly understood that he is not only concerned with human affairs, but close to his own with unbelievable intimacy, and cannot forsake them in their troubles.[6] I will not recall now the Stoics' doctrine of "fate," or the "chance" of Democritus or Epicurus; I will not open up deep questions about divine providence, though our subject might perhaps call for that, if time permitted. Rather it will be sufficient if I touch on those matters which will prove that this year's disasters, terrible as they have been, and all others that have befallen us, were sent by God not to destroy the human race but to restore it.

Now, when things are to be restored, this has to be done on the same principles whereby they were set up in the first place; and since Moses described the creation of the world in a series of days, it is customary to think of the restoration of human affairs under the figure of successive days, similar to those which saw the world's birth. By the common consent of the Academy,[7] the Old Testament and the New, every restoration of human souls by which life is granted to men is represented as a movement whereby they struggle out of darkness and rise up with all their might to seek and gaze upon the sun.

According to the Platonists, darkness is that ignorance with which the body infects the soul, and the disposition or inclination of the soul as it turns toward the world of the senses. However, if the horizons of human experience are lifted far above this darkness, to be found rather in the most sublime light of the true Sun, as both Plato's *Republic* and John's gospel testify,[8] we must go straight to that fourth day on which, as we read, the sun first shone upon the earth.[9] The first day saw the creation of light, the second the division of the waters; on the third all growing things sprang up from the earth, and on the fourth day the sun beamed from the sky.[10]

We shall now recount that same sequence of days which followed the night of this year's disaster. Just as after eternal night the created order welcomed those primal days, so has the Church this year seen a succession of days dawn upon her after the darkness of the catastrophe at Ravenna. On the receipt of those most grievous tidings, indeed, night fell upon the minds of all, casting them into turmoil beyond belief, and prostrating them with fear. Yet there was one man who stood firm and unyielding, mindful of the oak tree[11] that was his family's symbol, one man who was not cast down — Pope Julius. Following the example of Almighty God, whom he represents, Pope Julius said, "*Let there be light*" (Gn 1:3). Forthwith the priests were summoned, prayers appointed to be said, the principal apostles venerated, and now this discourse is preached by me.

On the first day, then, the day which saw the opening of the Lateran Council, such light shone in our minds, such hope was born in us that we seemed to have routed the enemy more surely than we had approached the altars. On the second day the Fathers took their places according to custom, and the papal letters were read. Thus a separation was made between the upper and the lower waters, whereby the Lateran Council was as though fixed firmly in the heavens, while the Council of Pisa had to recognize its true parent and was ordered to yield and submit at last.[12] Thereupon the third day broke, the gladdest, brightest, most beautiful day of those that had so far dawned, the day which has brought forth for you the richest fruits of a Council so inauspiciously begun. The dawn of this day encouraged ships in harbor to sail forth, never doubting that there would be complete safety for those in whose hearts was the divine presence; this day assured them that human dangers were not to be feared by those who have recourse to divine worship, and that the strength of holy Church consists not in weapons or wealth, but in holiness alone.

At a moment when scarcely a man remained who could take up arms to defend the approaches to the city gates, some news broke in Rome. (Here I must pause to lift my voice in prayer: O holy, supreme God, Father of all creation, how wise are they who worship you, how foolish they who do not! How happy those whom you love, and how wretched those whose actions estrange them from your love; for as you are most mighty in your acts and wise in your government of the world, so also are you very gentle in loving and forgiving, and generous in helping and serving us.) As I was saying, news spread in Rome that the enemy were withdrawing of their own accord. They were retreating by the Flaminian Way, they were leaving your territory! A text was tossed from one citizen to another, never more apt to any day or doing: "The wicked flees though there is no pursuit."[13] Indeed, the enemy forces had been put to flight not by armed men, for these they had conquered, but by the unconquered Godhead whom they had despised.

Oh, the goodness of God! How much joy, delight, and laughter did this third day bring, this day when your state, your property, rank, goods, and personal safety were snatched from destruction and restored to you! Not by arms or legions or the engines of war, nor by any human defenses, but solely by the help of our gracious God were we saved.

Long ago Abraham defeated his foes, but he was armed, as also were his followers.[14] Moses was victorious, but then Joshua led the army.[15] Saul conquered thousands and his son-in-law David ten thousands,[16] yet both wore battle gear and both were skilled in the arts of war. God's people won marvelous victories, first when pharaoh of Egypt was overwhelmed,[17] and later when the Assyrian Holofernes was beheaded;[18] yes indeed, but on the shore of the Red Sea stood a mighty host of Hebrew youths who could bear arms, while Holofernes was killed by the hand of a Hebrew woman with sword-stroke and plunging dagger. When the Church and Pope Julius won this victory there was no battle-line drawn up on your Flaminian Way, no arms, no defensive garrison, not a man, not a woman, to make a stand against the taunting enemy. Accordingly, this victory — by far the greatest of all victories — must be attributed to faith and not weapons, to religion and not military power, to God and not man. No victory has ever been won more worthy to be held in everlasting memory and celebrated for all time to come. Even the most depraved openly confessed that God alone had fought for them; all agreed that nothing could be worse, more hateful, and more disastrous than unbelief, while nothing could be better, safer, or more trustworthy than faith. Divine power had been so clearly manifested to mortals that, unless we were bent on obstinate denial of what was plain to see, we had to admit that after this no place could remain for doubting divine providence.

Thus far we have touched upon the three days which preceded; consider now the fourth day, in honor of which this sermon was appointed. It could be thought that the fourth day was chosen in the beginning as the sun's birthday so that you, after spending three days in the Basilica of John,[19] the guardian disciple, could quite rightly transfer your sessions to that of the Blessed Virgin[20] whom he revered; for in this way you pass this fourth day, the day of the sun's birth, in the Basilica of her from whom the far greater Sun arose. As the scripture testifies, *He pitched his tent in the sun*, or, more correctly as the Hebrew text has it, *Solely in her did he pitch his tent* (Ps 19:6).

Some people declare that no living thing can bear to gaze unflinchingly at the sun except the eagle,[21] which alone has strength enough in its eyes. Accordingly on this fourth day let us contemplate a noble and lofty eagle, well acquainted with the sun's rays and powerful of sight: I mean the Emperor Maximilian, who today wishes to achieve universal renown as the one who shuns the darkness of discord, hates schisms in the Church, and revokes whatever support he formerly gave to the Pisan intrigue, in order to find, acknowledge, and worship his true Sun in the Lateran Council.

We read also that the philosopher quoted a verse from an ancient poet concerning the eagle's young: she hatches three chicks, but then drives two away and brings up only one.[22] What else is this bird's instinct with her brood but a kind of image of God, if one may so speak? God issued three laws: one implanted in Adam's nature, one on tablets for Moses, and one in the divine person of Christ. However, he himself bears witness that he threw away two and confirmed one only when, having repudiated the earlier movement, he asserts, *One alone is my beloved*. The devout eagle, then, emulates God in loving one chick only; she hates and rejects what is double and divided, since, as learned men have it, such plurality is associated with imperfection rather than perfection, with evil rather than good, with things which drag on endlessly rather than what is conclusive.

The Emperor,[23] then, was asked to favor the Council; and he could not refuse once he had heard that name "sacred council" by which the unity of the Church, insofar as it has been harmed, is customarily restored and reestablished. He held that no course of action was more worthy of a Christian prince than to strive for the reform of the Christian Church, and nothing more unworthy than to neglect the task. He knew that all the authority to effect such reform resided solely in the work of the Council, where discords are appeased, where enmity, wars, and violence are banished from the heart of the Church's lands, where princes and kings are reconciled, and where the public enemies of Christians are vanquished. If any false opinions are extant, they are there examined: any who hold positions at variance with the faith are gravely punished, any who do not merely hold such positions but also teach their errors are punished more severely still, while the strictest penalties of all are meted out to those who not only teach false doctrines but also commit them to writing.[24] Injustice is put down and rights duly restored to rulers, pomp and display are restrained, what is honorable and seemly reinstated; shameless arrogance declines, modesty and temperance of life are encouraged. Generous people are preferred to the avaricious, the enterprising to the slothful, the respectful to the impudent, the innocent to the criminal, the honorable to the vile. A youthful bride is sought for the aging King David;[25] and the Church, shedding the squalid garments of worn-out customs like a snake sloughing off its skin, is renewed in joyful youth.

How happy this our age, if in the fear of God it carries through the Council as it should, how blind if it fails to understand, how wretched if it turns aside in disdain! Great Caesar, pondering these things, indicated that he was not simply willing to convene a council, but positively desired to do so. However, when he was informed that the Pisan movement was in revolt against the head of the Church, so that the one thing it should have been careful to keep undivided and intact was not merely at risk but was being rent and torn to pieces, then, said the Emperor, "I marveled that the city of Pisa, which for so many years had preferred to suffer extreme evils rather than submit, did not call out the mob." He therefore withdrew immediately. As he had previously deemed it right to consent to the council, so now he deemed it right to disengage himself from the faction. In this he imitated God, whose champion he is, for God earlier embraced the Hebrew people when they were receptive to divine revelation, but later deserted them when they scorned it.[26] We should not think on this account that God was fickle, for he could never forsake anyone who dealt honorably. No, rather it was they who broke away from him, by continually refusing to walk in his ways.

I have spoken of your attitude, mighty Caesar, but have said nothing of your actions; I have touched on what you thought, but passed over what you did. Who indeed could compass in speech the constancy, steadfastness of mind, and courage with which you held firm and defended that decision which you had reached after inward reflection, attacked though you were from every side? Assuredly it is very easy to conceive great plans, but always very difficult to execute them.

The most esteemed bishop of Gurk, illustrious prince of the Empire,[27] has testified to me how great were the difficulties and labors he incurred as he strove to outwit the evil men whose schemes would have corrupted that noble purpose. Both your own glorious estate and the unity of the Church owe to this prelate's virtue a debt which will be the subject of preaching forevermore. What stratagems did not those schemers employ, directed toward him, to be sure, but designed to sway you, Caesar, from your decision? What rewards, what gifts, what dignities, what greater things still have they not promised? Yet you show yourself deaf to their persuasions, unaware of their pleas, untouched by their promises, uncorrupted by their bribes; you issue a statement entirely worthy of any emperor, but especially fitting to Maximilian: that it is Caesar's glory to reckon nothing great except God, and that, having learned from infancy to despise gold and human possessions, you would hardly at your time of life prefer them to him.

Oh, how happy is this day if we make holy and proper use of it, if we allow God to confirm these treaties by his divine will, if we regard what is done today as ratified, firm, and sacred; and if, finally, we ensure by our longings and prayers that this friendship of Caesar may continue, and may be extended to the other princes gathered here!

I called this fourth day the birthday of your sun, holy Fathers, but it may be called in the future the birthday of your country, for today your council, your decrees, sanctions, and laws are rendered valid; today they are confirmed in perpetuity. Today fear fades away and confidence returns. Suspicion, alarm, and confusion are banished; strength, steadfastness and security are established. This day brings hope to friends, terror to enemies, joy to the well-disposed, grief to the wicked, dread to evil people, and courage to the good. This day uplifts your allies, strengthens them, and gives them new heart; but it weakens, batters, and terrifies your foes. On this day, as the proverb has it, a tiny divine shoot has sprung up for you. May our success in fostering it match the anxiety with which we longed for it and our happiness now that it has come! God is the author of these great gifts; may he grant that the hearts of the people who receive them may appreciate the generosity of the donor. May he grant that as he so readily heard our pleas, we may not be ungrateful for the undying benefit we have received.

Astrologers write that when important planets are in conjunction, great and unprecedented events are usually to be expected. What then are we to expect with regard to the unity of the Church, when, as is proper to the fourth day,[28] no common luminaries but the very greatest have come together, and this not to serve as a demarcation for a month or some brief space of time, but in perpetual friendship? Surely this is a portent of some great good fortune? What are we to expect, I ask, seeing that by the most profound laws of nature kindred things are always united? Thus water is found with earth, air with water, and fire with air, linked in constant and abiding fellowship. It is otherwise in the affairs of kings and other princes: each has his own sphere of authority in some particular kingdom or region, and for this reason there are many kings and many princes. The Emperor Maximus, however, is unique, and the Supreme Pontiff is unique, in this one world. Each of them holds supreme sway not over a solitary province or a single kingdom as others do, but over the whole. Each of them is supreme lord of the human race and of the entire world: the one as Emperor, the other as Pope; the one by armed force, the other by authority; the one equipped with human strength, the other with that which is divine. One is empowered to crush the impious, the other to reinstate them in piety; one to enforce the return of those who fall away from religion, the other to welcome them when they return. What can be more reliable, constant, and enduring, what better, more profitable or holier, than the conjunction of these sacred planets, a conjunction which effects not an alliance between a part and another part, a kingdom and another kingdom, but the union of the undivided with the undivided, the whole with the whole, the greatest with the greatest? It is inevitable that as individual kingdoms are separated by position and space, so also they may be at variance in outlook and interests; but when the whole is in question, that whole which exists everywhere, there is no place for division, for all things are held together not by some extrinsic and precarious bond, but by the unifying force of nature itself.

To work, then, O most glorious luminaries![29] By your sovereign will you command the world; rescue then a world snatched from you! Give orders to your subjects to take up arms, save a commonwealth ready to collapse! It is beyond dispute that this friendship of yours is devout in origin, most fortunate with regard to the rank of those it reconciles, and supremely necessary in view of contemporary upheavals, for two kinds of foe oppose us, either of which would suffice alone to harass and ruin the Christian cause — nay, more, to overthrow and destroy it altogether.

Battle threatens us within and without, I say, but there is one source only: that evil demon, the monstrous enemy of public weal. In one place he stirs up the fierce Muslim people, in another he foments vice and crime. Abroad he fills the land with infantry and cavalry, and the seas with ships and navies beyond belief. At home he entices some to lust and greed, others to sedition and grievous schism. Hell seemed hitherto content to fight us on a single front, in one simple battle at a time, but now it gathers all its forces, attacks us at every point, and hurls all its weapons at once.

The Barbary corsairs are massing in Africa, the Turks are afire in Thrace by land and sea, in Italy many oppose you, and beyond the Alps whole kingdoms are pitted against you; on all sides is the fury of war and the clash of arms. Yet both spheres of power are concerned, for on every side force usurps the place of justice, disgraceful conduct ousts decency, ambition flouts moderation, dishonorable and impious deeds keep carnival where holiness and religion should reign.

Arise, then, and do battle with both enemies! Assuage domestic strife, banish civil war. Bind all Christian kings and princes to your cause. Root out hatreds, dissensions, and quarrels. Grant pardon to anyone who has gone astray, and a helping hand to any who has fallen. Remember that you are Romans, one as Pontiff, the other as Emperor. It is the Pontiff's task to bring peace at home by means of religion, the Emperor's to subdue enemies abroad. Both of you are Romans, and as such your duty is to be merciful to all your Christian subjects, but to vanquish the rising pride of the Muslims.[30]

Look at the Byzantine tyrant[31]: I mean not that old man unfit for war, who for many years now has been so enfeebled by luxury that we have been able to wander freely without danger,[32] but that young man of savage and bitter disposition, in the ardent prime of his life, vigorous in combat, afire with greed, renowned for cruelty, exceptionally strong, well-equipped with both land and sea forces, and already invading your territory in an irresistible onslaught. If in earlier days the Turks took Otranto with a small company of troops — a company, moreover, not even under the leadership of any great commander — and so held it that only after the death of that commander could we recover it; if the father of the present ruler, though an effeminate and soft old man, always more eager for pleasure and luxury than for warfare and glory, yet snatched Methoni, Koroni, Lepanto, and almost the whole Peloponnese from your rule; if later through the courage of a few men he smashed the enormous fleets approaching Mytilene, what will the son do with his youth, strength, determination, and ferocity? What will he do who has at his disposal so huge a horde of armed men on land and sea that he openly boasts he will not merely destroy Christendom, but gain control of Europe, Africa, and eventually the whole world? He is motivated not only by desire for glory, but also by religion, by fear, and by the great injury inflicted on his terrible sect on the occupied seaboard of Africa by the efforts of King Ferdinand of Aragon. The Turkish ruler is aware of Ferdinand's fidelity of spirit and the growth of his forces during recent events. He knows that he must either crush those forces at once or see them under the very walls of Byzantium. Of what, then, is he not capable, spurred on as he is both by the hope of seizing another's empire and by the fear of losing his own?

We stand amazed at his success in inflaming the minds of those barbarians to war, as he persuades them that the resources of a single

Christian king have increased to such a point that, unless they oppose him with all their might, they risk losing the rest of their empire, their homes, households, wives, children, and eventually their very lives. Seized with madness, they willingly abandon everything; eagerly they rush to arms with the ferocity of tigers and sweep down upon us athirst for our blood. See for yourselves, while we are delaying with frivolous matters, while we are preoccupied with internal enmity and dissension, they are amassing such forces that, unless you send help with the utmost speed, the Christian cause will be finished.

Persuade your rulers to settle their differences, then, quiet rivalries, recall your peoples to peace and concord. It is time for consultation to take the place of anger, reason to replace impetuosity, and necessity to quell resentment. No memory of quarrels or injuries must be harbored now. No one's individual grudge must be indulged to the detriment of the common good. No private feuds must be preferred to the public weal, for this often brings states to disaster. Rather let internal peace be restored, crime rooted out, conduct kept honorable, and prayers offered. Then muster, deploy your dedicated weapons, and confront the savage foe! Fight for your dwellings, your churches and holy places, your property, and your own safety. Subdue the impious brute at last; recover the domains snatched from you, win freedom for oppressed peoples, and eternal glory and stable peace for Christendom!

Do you realize, Pope Julius II, do you realize what this day demands of you? Do you realize what is demanded by this treaty with mighty Caesar, by the turn of events, and by today's most holy and supremely necessary meeting? I rehearse your past achievements very willingly, so that your satisfaction in remembering what you have done already may urge you to address yourself to what you have not done yet. Everyone has watched you undertaking mighty tasks, and mighty tasks only: hounding swindlers, thieves, and tyrants, constructing buildings that will last forever, raising up a magnificent church, bringing vast lands, many peoples, and beautiful cities under your sacred sovereignty. These great and splendid works can be seen for what they are, but greater yet are the privileges which Almighty God has conferred on you this year, in enabling you to subdue those twin monsters which have widely devastated Italy and all but destroyed the Church. I speak of schism and war.

David called schism a deaf adder, and war a dangerous basilisk.[33] They had unleashed against your ship such winds and waves, so many storms and tempests, as almost to sink her. No mortal man could have believed that, tossed about and nearly overwhelmed as she was, she could ever have escaped from such peril. What words, then, what eloquence, what gift of speech could describe how suddenly God heard your prayer in this crisis, how graciously he came to aid you with great miracles, and how he delivered you, to the wonder of all? Who is sufficient to relate how, fortified by divine help, you overcame those monsters, prudently wore them down, and endured until the blessed victory? Beyond all hope and all belief, beyond what anyone could have conceived possible, you extricated yourself and your ship and brought her safely into harbor. At one and the same time, and with amazing speed, you delivered Italy from the burden of war and the Church from schism!

This is an unprecedented happening, one greatly longed for, one which our forebears never saw and posterity will not credit. It is obvious to all that God has never granted to any Pope but yourself to achieve such things as these. Yet amid all our happiness I will, by your leave, say what I really think, for it is fitting that a true pontiff should listen to the truth and that I as a priest should speak it. No one can fail to see that what you have achieved is very great and glorious; but somehow humankind is a little greedy, and wants more still. Two plagues remain for you to defeat, one at home, the other abroad: at home a contempt for religion that grows by our tolerance, and abroad that insolence which attacks and oppresses the Christian faith.

Here in the heart of Christendom the one commits all manner of crimes and disgraceful acts; on the Bosphorus and in Thrace the other is amassing arms and preparing an invincible fleet against us. The one inflames the minds of our citizens with greed and seduces them from the truth with deceitful doctrines; the other, its greedy imagination fixed on Rome, your wealth and your treasures, musters a ferocious army. One undermines faith and morals, while the other threatens slaughter and bloodshed. In the words of Augustine, the great patron of this Church,[34] the former is a dragon plotting insidiously,[35] while the latter is a savage raging lion, spurting flame from its eyes and nostrils and openly stirring up war. Both are set to robbing us: the lion of earthly possessions, and the dragon of heavenly rewards. The lion would snatch this mortal, failing life from us, the dragon life eternal. One attacks bodies, the other souls. The lion seeks to get rid of God's representative, while the dragon would get rid of God himself; and both evil deeds spell mischief, ruin, and disaster for your most sacred bride. To such a point have the resources of these enemies grown, such a peak have they reached (as you seemed to indicate yourself when reading out the dispatches — from Rhodes, I think), that we must either decide now to win a glorious victory over them or, if we refuse this opportunity, miserably perish. Could the wickedness of our ways or the power of our enemies be greater? Our own vices oppress us so grievously, and the Muslims invade us with such force, that there remains for us no hope of survival, but only the certainty of speedy defeat, unless you oppose them with the utmost of your strength.

Do you wish to make permanent the victory you have won by God's gift, the achievements of this day, and the treaty concluded with mighty Caesar? Do you want your suppliant state, your own memory, your deeds, this soaring church, your successors, Rome's monuments and trophies of victory, and all that is yours, to be ever stable, safe, and blessed with peace? Then unite us all at home; root out domestic evils; purify public morals; banish from the state all debauchery, licentious behavior, vices, long-running feuds, quarrels and weapons. Bring these affairs to order, and rulers into harmony in a true and holy peace; and then muster every resource that Christendom can provide and proceed to the destruction of that imminent peril, that fearful scourge, the invading Turk. If you have at heart God's cause and the love of true glory, you will leave everything else aside and attack these twin plagues. You will overcome and expel them, just as you have already mastered those other twin evils in valor of spirit and with like success. Thus there will be a victory over four conquered beasts corresponding to the four days of this Council already celebrated; for just as you have trodden on the adder and the basilisk, so you will also trample on the lion and the dragon.

Such a happy outcome is presaged by this day, this friendship, and this treaty with august Caesar; for here are united the minds, the power, and the resources of the two greatest rulers in the entire world. One of them has the means to banish domestic evils by his authority, the other is able to defeat the impious foe by force of arms. Both together, under the guidance of God, can free Christendom from all misfortune and endow it with everlasting peace. That is all I have to say.

Translated by Maria Boulding, O.S.B.

Notes

1. Jacopo Sadoleto (1477-1547), classical scholar, accomplished Latinist, poet, prominent member of the Roman Academy, bishop of Carpentras (1517), cardinal (1536). Jacopo Sannazaro (Actius Sincerus) (1455-1530), Italian humanist poet and central figure in the Pontanian Academy. Like many members of these renaissance academies, he took a Latin name, Actius Sincerus.

2. The anti-papal, schismatic, Council of Pisa assembled by Louis XII in 1511.

3. In June 1511, after the loss of Bologna to the French and when the papal and Venetian troops had been completely dispersed, leaving the papal states and Rome open to the enemy, Julius turned to Ferdinand for help. The Spanish king decided to suspend military operations in Africa and send the army to Italy to assist in the reconquest of Bologna.

4. On 26 January 1512 the combined Spanish and papal army invested Bologna. However, on hearing that Gaston de Foix had managed to slip past with his troops on the night of 4-5 February and was actually within the walls of the city, the besiegers broke camp.

5. Ravenna was taken by the French in an exceedingly bloody battle on Easter Sunday, 11 April 1512.

6. See Jn 14:8.

7. The Platonic Academy.

8. See Plato VII, 514-520; Jn 1:9.

9. See Gn 1:16-19.

10. See Gn 1:3-19

11. The oak tree, symbol of the della Rovere family.

12. At the second session of the Lateran Council, 17 May 1517, the Council of Pisa was pronounced null and void.

13. See Lv 26:17.

14. See Gn 14:15.

15. See Ex 17:9-13.

16. See 1 Sm 18:7.

17. See Ex 14:1-29.

18. See Jdt 13:8-11.

19. Saint John Lateran.

20. Santa Maria del Popolo.

21. Emperor Maximilian.

22. See Aristotle, *Historia Animalium* VI, 6:563a.

23. Emperor Maximilian.

24. With this graduated scale of culpability Giles has perhaps in mind in a special way the Paduan Peripatetics whom he accused not only of believing and teaching false doctrine but even of committing it to paper, thus ensuring survival of the errors and their transmission to vast numbers of people. See J.W. O'Malley, *Giles of Viterbo on Church and Reform: A Study in Renaissance Thought,* Leiden, 1968, pages 33, 46.

25. See 1 Kgs 1:1-4.

26. See Ps 106:40-41.

27. Matthäus Lang (1468-1540). Provost of the Augsburg chapter (1500), bishop of Gurk (1501), cardinal (1512), archbishop of Salzburg (1519); it was only in 1519, however, that he was ordained and consecrated bishop. Having entered the imperial service as a secretary, he quickly rose to a position of power and influence. The emperor designated him as representative at the negotiations leading to the League of Cambrai (1508) and to the treaty with Julius II (1512).

28. See Gn 1:16.

29. Pope Julius and Emperor Maximilian.

30. See Vergil, *Aeneid* 6:853.

31. Selim I (the Grim), son of Bajazet II. Born 1467, he dethroned his father, 25 April 1512, and, it was said, caused him to be put to death. As a ruler he was warlike, energetic, ruthless, and fanatical. He died in 1520.

32. Bajazet II, son of Mohammed II. Born 1447; reigned 1481-1512. When dethroned by his son, Selim, he died before he could reach the place of his voluntary exile and the rumor was spread that he had been poisoned by an emissary of his son. Bajazet was more fond of pomp and splendor than of fighting battles and he made no great conquests except for the acquisition of the cities of Lepanto, Methoni, and Koroni. His reign was clouded at its beginning and at its end by insurrection and military mutiny.

33. See Ps 91:13.

34. The Augustinian friars, whose monastery was attached to the church of Santa Maria del Popolo, were the custodians of the church.

35. See *Confessions* VII, 21, 27.

Pastoral Sermons

Three sermons, preached by Giles while he was bishop of Viterbo, were discovered by Professor John Monfasani (see Vatican Apostolic Library, Vat. lat. 6320, fol. 123ʳ - 146ᵛ) and edited in Latin by him (see John Monfasani, "Sermons of Giles of Viterbo as Bishop," *Egidio da Viterbo, O.S.A. e il suo Tempo*, Rome, 1983, 137-189).

I

A Sermon Delivered by the Most Reverend Giles of Viterbo, O.S.A. in Tuscania on 1 October of the Year of Salvation 1525.

God communicates by signs.

Our great and good Lord uses symbolic things, persons, and events to reveal the secret ordering of his will. I have found a great number of such signs as I peruse the holy scriptures; but that sign, in my opinion, seems to be first and foremost which serves as a criterion for discernment. Through this sign, God has separated the baptized from the unbaptized, and the children of the kingdom from the sons of perdition, and made us victorious and triumphant over our most fearsome enemy.

There was, if you remember, a huge giant in the camp of the Philistines — a colossal, most insolent giant. He was so enormous that the whole army of the chosen people fled in terror at the very sight of him.[1] What was king Saul to do, when he saw his cause failing, his forces turning tail, and no one daring to confront that dreadful tower of a man — much less engage him in hand to hand combat? Goliath meanwhile was shouting abuse and insult at the people of God, provoking and challenging them to battle. Everyone was shrinking back; no one dared to come to quarters with him. He flaunted like a basilisk on the desert waste, as he ranged between the battlelines.[2]

But the champion of whom the psalm sings: *Behold he shall neither slumber nor sleep, that keeps Israel* (Ps 121:4) — he would not allow the humiliation of Israel to continue. For David, son of Isai — *ruddy and curly-haired, unarmed but anointed by God* (1 Sm 16:12-13) — had heard of his people's opprobrium. Taking his shepherd's crook and sling, he left the sheepfold to seek king Saul's permission to stand against Goliath.[3] After he had selected three smooth stones from the stream,[4] he confidently sallied forth against the enemy, relying only on the name of the Lord. A stripling was advancing on a giant; a fly, armed with a sling, was stalking an elephant. But the impact of one stone from David's strong hand felled Goliath. Triumphant, David used the giant's own sword to lop off his head. The stone was still embedded there — in the brow. And so David held up the severed head and pointed to the forehead to signal his victory. Today, I am pleased to say something about this sign, especially to you who will soon be signed on your foreheads.

It certainly embarrasses and grieves me to have to say it. No matter how often we would assemble in this place, no word about it would ever have come to my lips, nor would it have even occurred to me — if only you were mindful of your own salvation, and would seek the sacrament without which you are only half-Christian, whichever of you have not been signed. Nay, rather, whoever disdains to be signed is on the verge of perdition. For I understand there are not a few adults and even older persons among you who are not ashamed to come into the temple and court of Christ our king without his royal seal. You should blush to serve under the standard of so great a sovereign without bearing his emblem! Is the person who dares to enter military service without a patron not subject to capital punishment? Does a man not tempt fate in the battleline if he cannot be distinguished from the enemy? Citizens! Recognize the disaster threatening you, unless your city endorses and receives this great sacrament.

Learn from Exodus, I beseech you, how the Old Testament was handed down to teach us about this world. There you will discover that God used portents and a series of ten plagues to deliver his people from the tyranny of pharoah.[5] The same night the Israelites were to leave Egypt, he ordered them to smear the lintels of their houses with the blood of the paschal lamb. Because of this sign, the angel of death would pass by. He would leave unharmed these houses where he found the lintels marked with blood. The other unsigned dwellings he would reap with Pluto's scythe.

Acknowledge what has happened, I adjure you! Up to now, you have migrated from Egypt. You have shaken the servile yoke from your shoulders. At this point, you will perhaps protest that you have been *baptized*. I ask you, where is the mark on your lintels, the sign of Christ on your foreheads? If you have not received it, you cannot make a satisfactory response. Then woe to you, because the angel is going to deliver the unsigned to death! The Lord wills it. Yes, he wills it. Our lawgiver commands it. Our king orders us to mark his soldiers with his sign in order to distinguish and protect them.

You ask how I know this? Because we find this command in Exodus. Is it found anywhere else? Yes, it is. The prophet Ezekiel certainly writes: "It is necessary to mark everyone with the tav sign, as many as wish to escape death and destruction."[6] Do you want to avoid imminent disaster? Then show me the tav written on your forehead. Anyone who does not wear the tav will not escape. Tav is the sign of Christ. The sign of the cross is traced in chrism on the brow. Woe to those whose foreheads do not bear this kind of tav!

Is there any other mention of this great mystery? There certainly is. Read the prophecy of the flying eagle.[7] Does the cry of that magnificent spirit not thunder everywhere as it soars on high: *Behold, behold, I, John, saw another angel ascending from the rising of the sun, having the sign of the living God; and he cried with a loud voice to the four angels, to whom it was given to hurt the earth and the sea, saying: "Hurt not the earth, nor the sea, nor the trees, till we sign the servants of our God in their foreheads"* (Rv 7:2-3). I see four angels girded to hurt the earth and the sea, that is, the whole world. But you, do you have the sign of the living God on your foreheads? John makes those who have the sign safe and secure from the destroying angels. But they have reason to worry who do not bear the sign of the living God. What sort of sign? The cross of Christ traced on the forehead. Who traces it there? Only the bishop puts the sign there when he performs the anointing. He is the very angel with *the sign of the living God* in his hand (Rv 7:2).

Therefore, draw near (for when dinner is over, we will enter the church for the signing). Bring the boys in your arms, the infants, and the little girls. Lead the adults in, and let them kneel in ranks before the bishop. Realize that you sponsors are about to incur an affinity with the parents of those about to be signed, a bond so strong that it can dissolve even contracted marriages, to say nothing of the impediment it creates. Bring no more than two, and be sober at least, if you are (not) wont to abstain after dinner. When you approach, be free of every stain of sin, so that the dove will not find any impediment in you and fly away. For the Holy Spirit does not abide with sin.

However, so that you may understand how important this matter is and be able to appreciate the grandeur of the sacrament of chrism, listen, and I will certainly tell you what no living Christian of my acquaintance can relate, something drawn from the fonts of secret Aramean theology.

But, as a matter of fact, no gospel in the yearly cycle could be more fitting for our work today than the pericope where our savior asks about the Christ, *whose son is he* (Mt 22:42). So that you may perceive this more fully, I think we should begin a little higher, that is, further up in the text, on which our reading depends. Before the Lord interrogated the Pharisees, he was himself interrogated twice: first, by the Sadducees, concerning the resurrection, then, by the Pharisees, regarding the greatest commandment in the law.[8]

The Sadducees generally accepted Jewish teaching, with the exception of the doctrine of the resurrection.[9] This they opposed. As to the rest, there was no notable difference at all between them and other Jews. And so they were the first to attack the Savior, and, as they would to any Jew acknowledging the resurrection, they presented to him for explication an enigma which concerned a wife who had been married, one after another, to each of seven brothers, who successively died. "If the wife rose again, and the brothers likewise rose again, tell us, Master, to which of those brothers would the wife belong, inasmuch as she was wife to all of them."[10] But the wise Master most humanely — as if they were most humane! — brought forth from his treasure of supernal wisdom two prophetic responses. By the first, he confounded the scriptural naiveté of the Sadducees. "Does one not read in the books of Moses: *And God said: I am the God of your fathers, the God of Abraham, the God of Isaac, and the God of Jacob* (Ex 3:6)? Those three patriarchs have already died, and they will not rise again according to your unspeakable doctrine. Is he therefore to be called the God of the dead? What could be more inept than this? So God would be inferior to a worm? But if he is not the God of the dead, then at some time or other Abraham, Isaac, and Jacob will rise. *He is, therefore, not the God of the dead, but of the living*" (Mt 22:29.31-32). By the other response, he refuted the very fat Minerva of those who said that marriage and the procreation of children would continue after the resurrection. "You are completely in error," he said; "there will be no weddings in the kingdom of heaven"; thereafter, no marriage partners will be celebrated except Christ and his one bride, the Church. Then the whole Church, like one being, one virgin, will enter the marriage chamber of her man, enjoy his embraces, and be made happy at the very sight of him. In the fatherland, therefore, *they shall neither marry nor* — to use his own words — *be married; but shall be as the angels without any bodily impediment* (Mt 22:30). Affronted by these responses, the Sadducees withdrew.

Then the Pharisees drew near, that other sect of the Jews, who, like religious, were separated from crowd and people by their way of life, their morality, and their customs. After the Pharisees had taken note that the Sadducees had been confused because of their inexperience with the law of Moses, they were inflated with empty pride and proceeded to boldly question the Lord Jesus about the teaching of Moses and the preeminent commandment in the law.[11] "The law contains many commandments, some six hundred and more. Which of these, in your opinion, is the greatest and most excellent of all?" Then, by Divine Providence, the Word of the Father replied,[12] taking the Pharisees to task for their overconfidence in their own knowledge. From Exodus,[13] he quoted the greatest commandment of the law, and said: *You shall love the Lord your God with your whole heart.* Your *whole* heart, you ask? — yes! your *whole* heart, and *all* your strength. The second is like it: *and your neighbor as yourself. On these two commandments depend the whole law and the prophets.* When they heard this, the Pharisees were overawed and reduced to silence.

Then — now we are dealing with our present concern — the Lord put a twofold question to the Jews which required a single answer: *What think you of Christ? Whose son is he?* (Mt 22:42). You who are about to be anointed, listen! I am asking you about Christ. What does "Christ" mean to you? The Greeks derived this title from the holy Hebrew tongue. For the Greeks call the Messiah the "Christ," while the Latins call him the "Anointed." Anointed with what? Peter tells us: *how God anointed him with the Holy Spirit* (Acts 10:38). This is the very purpose of the sacrament we will administer today: namely, to confer the Holy Spirit. Why are we called Christs and Christians except for our anointing with this very chrism? So the psalm reads: *Touch not my anointed* (Ps 105:15). For this reason, the whole Mystical Body of Christ, that is, the whole Christian assembly is called Christ, as Solomon attests in the Song of Songs: *Your name is as oil poured out* (Sg 1:2). Who, therefore, would dare call himself a Christian, if he has not been anointed with the chrism of Christ? Do you perceive then that the power, dignity, and authority of this sacrament is so extraordinary, that the baptized can hardly be called proper Christians, unless they have also been anointed. In today's gospel, the Savior very judiciously examined the power of the Christ title, to which the Pharisees were blind. He asked: *What think you of Christ? Whose son is he?* (Mt 22:42). He was saying: "What import does this word 'Christ' have for you, inasmuch as the whole perception of your law depends on its meaning?" But taking his question in a carnal sense, they replied with the name of his forefather, "David's." Through such reference, the Lord was striking and nourishing the spark of faith — however abortively! And to explain the essential elements of Christian faith to them, he pressed on by asking: *How then does David in spirit call him Lord, saying: "The Lord said to my lord, sit at my right hand?"* The eyes of the Pharisees were overwhelmed by this burst of light — they could not bear the divine sun. Found deficient in their secular, mortal wisdom, they withdrew.

But you can in no wise understand the name and nature of Christ unless you apprehend the great and the small: God and man, Word and flesh, anointed and anointing. You who are about to be anointed, give this point your full attention, so that you may appreciate the magnitude of the sacrament of Christ, true God and true man. Without it you will remain semi-Christian — that is, unless we mark you with unguent.

Do not think that baptism and chrism were lacking in Old Testament times — if not as equal sacraments, at least as corresponding rites. For, in place of ritual washing, the Hebrews practiced circumcision of the foreskin on the eighth day. Then, at puberty, the circumcised was required to submit to *priat*, that is, the reopening of the circumcised member.[14] If a man failed to undergo *priat*, he was considered uncircumcised. Therefore, just as *priat* was at one time the affirmation of circumcision, so chrism is the affirmation of baptism. For in baptism you are bound by the sacrament of Christian service; through chrism you are confirmed in it. In baptism, you choose a new life; in chrism, you ratify your commitment. Baptism is the beginning of virtuous and blessed existence, that is, truly Christian life; chrism puts the finishing touch on this work. Further, by baptism you are made Christian; by chrism you are marked with the sign of the cross and admonished with a slap to remember to profess your Christianity, not just in words, but in reality and deeds. What deeds? That *you shall love the Lord your God with your whole heart and soul and mind, and your neighbor as yourself* (Mt 22:37.38). Finally, the effect of baptism is to put on Christ,[15] inasmuch as it unites you to the body of Christ, in which you become and perdure a Christian. But the effect of chrism is to demonstrate by deed that, as the apostle avers today, *you are walking in a way worthy of the vocation in which you are called* (Eph 4:1), that is, you are persevering in Christ by abiding in the Christian life — nothing greater or superior to this can be conceived or expressed.

Now, from the secrets of ancient Aramean sages, a quasi-prophetic source, I am pleased to present superior wisdom particularly pertinent to our concern here today, which so far as I know no one has garnered from even the principal authorities. It will help you to understand the antiquity of the sacraments established in the gospel. The greatest of the Hebrew prophets, Moses, writes that the fabric of the world was completed by the creator in six days. He sings of works and days. What was produced on each of the days? On the first day nourishing light burst forth, and *God saw the light was good, and there was evening and morning one day* (Gn 1:3-5). And it was properly one, for good involves one and unity. The first division of one is a separation from good, and entails evil.

In this regard, consider the work of the second day: the creation of the firmament for the separation of superior and inferior waters. Because of this division of one into *dyad* and *dion*, which, among the Pythagoreans, is also a separation into infamous and unfortunate,[16] this entity causes the prophet to omit the declaration of goodness over this work. For nowhere on the second day will you find it called good, because *dion* is never good, inasmuch as it is removed from one, which consists of unity. Consider antiquity. How many evils, how many disasters one reads about — all the ruined cities, provinces, kingdoms, and empires! What caused it all? *Dion*! In our time too, *dion* has disrupted even the strongest houses — nay, rather almost the whole of Italy! The example of the neighboring city of Viterbo gives more than sufficient witness that *dion* never involves good. The account of the work of the second day, therefore, properly omits all mention of good, although it is mentioned twice on the third day. For it says twice: *God saw that it was good* (Gn 1:5): when the dry land had appeared, and after he had clothed the dry land with varicolored grass and foliage.

On the fourth day, he created the ornaments of heaven, the sun, moon, and stars. Here good is also mentioned. On the fifth day, he filled the waters with living beings, namely, fish that swim. Here is another allusion to goodness. So light was good, and fish, reptiles, and birds were good. Each work of five days was certainly good. Moses therefore said, *God saw that it was good* (Gn 1:25) — but something was lacking. And so, on the sixth day, man, king of the universe, was formed out of mud. Into him God, the true Prometheus, infused a soul and mind of such great dignity, of such great excellence, that the angels marveled and expressed their indignation: "because you have set a sparkling jewel in filthy muck. You have made man from mud, and he lacks the light of your law." The angels were astonished, and the powers of heaven marveled, when man was created.

What more should I say?

All the animals were brought to their sovereign, man, for him to impose names on each of them. Consequently, so great was his mental acumen, so excellent was his knowledge of all things, that man, Adam, was able to give everything its name. For names are not established by an arbitrary or extraordinary inclination of mind, but, as Plato attests in the *Cratylus*, correspond to the nature of things and depend on comprehension of reality.[17] Therefore, because no one can envisage anything more sublime than the foreknowledge of Adam, the sage rightly exclaims in the secret theology: "At that time Adam touched heaven with the crown of his head," that is, with the pinnacle of his intellect. Consequently, when the Creator had called his children to himself, that is, the minor gods or angels, he said: "Henceforward, do not disdain man because he was formed from mud." Behold, you perceive his sublime state and his lofty intelligence, a faculty so powerful that he can designate each thing with its proper name, which is a feat within the ken of only the wisest philosophers.

What need is there for words?

Reality itself bears witness to and bespeaks the dignity of man. When light burst forth, God saw it was good. When the dry land — the adornment of the land — the stars in the sky — the fish of the sea were all good, and in the rest of creation, besides man, there was nothing except good. But, when man was created, it was as if God had put the supreme and final touch to his work, and scripture no longer pronounced the work good, but *very good*: *And God saw all the things that he had made, and they were very good* (Gn 1:31). In Syriac, one says *Thob Meod* for *very good*, and it is rightly said, because man is the sovereign end of the whole sensible created universe. And so, when he had declared man the king and culmination of the universe, God was delighted with his work, as Plato very clearly states.[18] And, when God considered everything he had made, he saw it was very good because of its end, which was oriented to perfection.[19] But if anyone persists in denying this is so and asserts that we have dreamed it, let him read the ancient examples in secret Aramean theology, let him search the scriptures, as our Savior admonishes.[20] He will discover truth in this very place. The sages have a special interpretation of the words *Tod Meod*, which is Hebrew for *very good*, because Meod (very) consists of three letters: *Me*, *Aleph*, and *Daled*. These letters can be shifted around to spell "Adam," which is the good of man, inasmuch as man is the end and common boundary of the microcosm-macrocosm.

These dazzling considerations, which cause us to marvel by their novelty and beauty, also bolster our faith. But those concepts are much more important and wonderful which lie hidden below the surface —

insights garnered from the inmost resources of the superior wisdom revealed to our holy fathers. Or do you think holy scripture is joking and invented so many great things about Adam, the first man, just to praise and raise him to the stars? This arrow is aimed much higher. Why was it necessary for the Holy Spirit to commend the first Adam to such a degree, if the creature would soon rebel against his Creator, would thereafter be exiled from paradise, live in sweat and sorrow, and finally die and descend into hell?[21] Let us therefore believe that Moses sang of the divine mysteries of things to come and of our salvation in his account of the six days of creation. What is the meaning of man's origin from the slime of the earth on the sixth day? Brought into existence, the potential latent in man was declared *very good* (Gn 2:31).

Certainly in the sixth age — on the sixth day, as it were, of the foundation of the world — Christ was born in flesh and from flesh as true man, the second Adam — far better than the first, stauncher, and much more excellent. His persona is truly congruous with all former privileges. This man is Prince of the Universe — also Father, and King, and End, and God. This man is rightly said to tower up into the sky, and every other thing that can be said in praise of him is rightly said. If we compare the first Adam with the second, our remarks never seem judicious. And if we make a partial or common reference to the second, he always remains greater and superior. And so, born on the sixth day, Adam is the type of the One born in the sixth age and sixth generation, the "Anointed," the Messiah, the One promised in the law and prophets as restorer of a failed world. The exceedingly great goodness of God become man is meritorious beyond all thought and expression.

At this point, let us reef our billowing sails. I have revealed this new concept to you — something never heard before and, so far as we know and our inquiry has determined, something never comprehended — a perception by which you will know that Christians must be anointed by Christ: that he is eternal with the Father, that in this, the sixth age, he became man for our sake, that the Father has given him *a name above all names* (Phil 2:9, Eph 1:20), that is, not the name of a faultless man, but of the divine essence: the tetragrammaton, which is expanded and, like precious unguent, flows into three sacred numbers: 12, 25, and 72. Christ was the Man of Salvation, the unguent to be poured over the whole world. But because unguent is carried in jars, he immediately chose twelve vessels, 12 apostles. But they were insufficient. So he filled 72 others with the *oil of gladness* (Ps 45:8), which is the unguent of the Holy Spirit. Through these vessels, the sweet smell of the priceless ointment of Christ[22] is wafted far and wide.

Now you understand, and you clearly recognize the "Holy Anointed One." You know God's "Anointed" not only from the gospel passages that deal with Christ, but from the ancient Hebrew prophets. May you likewise hear and carry out the precept in the letter of Paul: *to walk worthy*

of the vocation (as anointed Christs) *in which you are called* (Eph 4:1) —
Christians, about to receive the chrism of Christ, in order to be *perfect*
Christians.

Translated by Joseph C. Schnaubelt, O.S.A.
Edited by Joseph Reino •

Notes

1. See 1 Kgs 17:4-54.
2. See Lucan, *Pharsalia* IX, 726.
3. See 1 Sm 17:31.
4. See 1 Sm 17:40.
5. See Ex 12:21.
6. See Ez 9:4. The Hebrew letter "tav" had the form of a cross.
7. See Rv 8:3; 14:6.
8. See Mt 22:23.
9. See Mt 22:23; Mk 12:18; Acts 23:8.
10. See Mt 22:24-29.
11. See Mt 22:34-37.
12. See Mt 22:37-40.
13. See Dt 6:5.
14. There is no such rite in Judaism. The closest parallel is the cutting of the bar mitzvah boy's hair. The word Giles seems to have in mind is *Peri'ah*, a part of the circumcision ceremony, which involved rolling back the foreskin after the incision. *Peri'ah* was part of circumcision soon after birth and not a separate rite at puberty.
15. See Gal 3:27; Rom 13:14.
16. See Plut. Plac. I, 7 (881E).
17. See Plato, *Cratylus* 387D, 338E-390E, 423D-E, 436A-C, 438A.
18. See Plato, *Timaeus* 37C.
19. See Aristotle, *Physica* II, 194a33.
20. See Jn 5:39.
21. See Gn 3:16.19.
22. See Sg 4:10.

II

A Sermon Delivered by the Most Reverend Giles of Viterbo, O.S.A. at
Bagnaia (Balnearia) on 8 October of the Year of Salvation 1525. Sunday of
the Paralytic.

In the beginning, when man was sent forth from the hand of God, the
palm of God's hand was wide open and full of every good. For man was
a most extraordinary creation, the summit and culmination, as it were, of
all God's works. Such art and force and wisdom and enlightenment were
manifest in man that he seemed to be a kind of miracle: the marvelous
recipient of all the perfections scattered through creation.

When the children of God, the angels, perceived that man would be
fashioned from earth and chosen unto such a height of dignity, they
conceived a great envy of the new creature, to say nothing of their
admiration for him. Gathering in council to address this issue, they said
to the Creator:

Since you made us incorporeal and independent of matter like yourself, and we therefore share your immortality, being simple acts and
intelligences such as you are, and since you have not created us out of the
slime of the earth like men, but rather in the resplendent empyrean of
heaven, why are you choosing to elevate packed mud to such prominence
and hiding the treasure of your light, wisdom, and glory in such a
repository?

Why are you setting so precious a jewel in clay?

Why are you making our condition mean and our lot ignoble?

Why are you repudiating a golden vessel and putting your nectar in
an earthen bowl?

It is not fair to exchange gold for brass. If you are seeking intelligence
and mental acumen that penetrates even to the depths of the abyss, we
are so powerful in intellect that we are called intelligences and minds. If
you desire purity, what is more pure than abstract forms?

Finally, where is it more agreeable to find your law, which is the
fullness of light, than in us, who are called light itself? For in the testimony
of Moses, it says: *Be light made. And light was made* (Gn 1:3).

So spoke the angels.

But, when man had been created, all the animals were brought to
Adam for him to impose names on them — its own name for each
according to its nature — and he bestowed a fitting designation on every
single one.[1] God then said to the angels:

Why do you disdain the man fashioned from mud?

See how much he excels, how wise he is. He has so much of our
intelligence that he knows how to match each thing with its proper name.

Unless he grasped the very nature of things, and were it not for man's
marvelous perspicacity, he would be unable to do this.

Oh how fortunate man would have been, had he retained his elevated state! But man always goes to extremes. Alas! how changed he is from what he formerly was! How briefly he kept the enlightenment and happy life bestowed on him! For he exchanged a paradise of delights for tribulation and misery, the tree of knowledge for crass ignorance, the tree of life for death, pleasure for sorrow and sweat of the brow.[2] Man plunged from exultation to anguish.

In such a context as this, the gospel very fittingly speaks of the paralytic.[3] For, just as man incurs paralysis and falls from rank and status, so his lapse from grace leaves man wounded and destitute in his members "from the admission of sin" (to use the theological idiom). Although only purely natural things remained for man (for when grace was lost, man was left in purely natural circumstances), even natural things sustained hurt, vitiation, and corruption. Thenceforward, reason was infirm; free will was weakened. Thus, though man was free to fall and languish, he lacked the integrity to recover and recoup. He remained destitute, deprived of the potential to function well. For this reason, today, under the type of a paralytic suffering from an incurable ailment, Adam is offered a cure by a physician who is not only human, but divine.

Nevertheless, I am afraid this paralytic from the past has much significance for the present. Note how long this paralysis, this illness, has gripped the human race — right up to the year 1525. The prophecy of Daniel is very appropriate for our time, for where is prophecy now? Where is sanctity? We have neither sanctity, nor prophecy. There is, moreover, no devotion, no faith, no charity. I fear Daniel's Abomination of Desolation has arrived.[4] The devotion of men has definitely ceased.

Like us, the primitive church put much hope in the devotion of women. "Intercede," it said, "on behalf of the devout feminine sex." For the world would be on the way to extinction except for the prayers of women. No matter how often the ship has tossed on the waves and almost foundered, the devotion of women has always been an anchor of hope for it. The distinction we otherwise ascribe to the "just man" — that he is the foundation of the world, the column that keeps it from toppling: men like Noah and Abraham — that attribute we sometimes impute to the devout feminine sex, because that sex is the underpinning which forestalls the collapse of the world. For women are better disposed toward the church, toward prayer, toward tears than men. Men tend to be hardened. By nature, women are more inclined to religion. Now religion is gravely ill. How do we recognize a life-threatening malaise? When a sick person's pulse is too faint to be felt, we know his condition is critical.

Take the church's pulse right now.

There is no pulse.

Where can we find the hint of a pulse to give us hope? The devotion of women!

Take the pulse again.

There is none. There is none, I tell you, or it is very weak.

Then what hope is left? The anchor is lost; the foundation has collapsed; no pulse can be found; the patient is near death.

Hope of recovery is fading.

The Physician came some time ago, and he brought help for the destitute, miserable creature, now left half alive, and it is already 1525. For it takes no less strength to restore a collapsed palace than it did to construct it. God constructed man, but a little later man fell. The Good Physician, who is much more learned and powerful than Podalirios, Machaon, and Aesculapius, came to seek and restore what had perished. God, covered over with this tunic of death, came to apply his remedy to our wounds.

I said Bagnaia (Balnearia) is ailing. I said we want to find a remedy. But first we have to examine the lesions, to diagnose what they require. But even before that, we have to determine their location. Therefore, pay attention. The hurt is restricted to three sites in the mind. There are no more than three lesions. But the remarkable presence of the mind is not apparent to the eyes. It lies hidden within. But we discern it by extrinsic judgments of its effects. For, whenever we wish to read small handwriting, we use eyeglasses, that is, artificial glass eyes, which enlarge the letters for our natural eyes. But what pertains to the mind is even more minute and tenuous. Let us therefore put on our spectacles. Let us use glass eyes.

When we read Plato, we discover that the populace of his *Republic* is divided into three orders: the king, the people, and the magistrates. The king resides in the lofty citadel; the people live on the lowest level; and the magistrates hold the middle. The king rules; the people are ruled; the magistrates are ruled in part, and in part they also rule. Laws, judgments, penalties, and rewards descend from the king to the people through the mediation of the magistrates. Nor does the decorum of the royal persona allow the king to look down; instead he uses magistrates as intermediaries. The king issues decrees; the magistrates carry them out. And this is especially pertinent to the order of the well organized republic, because it is the function of the king to rule, of the people to obey, and of the magistrates to expedite.

The same is true of the republic of the mind. The king reigns in the castle; the people await his commands; and the magistrates carry them out. In the kingdom and city of the mind, the intellect holds the scepter, and reason is its queen. She orders, commands, and rules. Situated below are the commons and people, which are appetite himself (or the faculty of desire) and a multitude of passions. Although it is accustomed to be uproarious — to excite winds and storms — appetite nevertheless calms the horse and ties it to the manger when the king commands. And, submitting itself to its sovereign, which is queenly reason, appetite says:

"Your task, O queen, is to search out your desire; my duty is to do your bidding."[5]

And on the middle level there is a magistrate whom the passions address as force or ardor. The Greeks call him courage. The king gives his command to his consort or executrix. The queen executes the order. Appetite acts on it. But sometimes appetite contrives to go his own way, against the wishes of the king and contrary to his commands. Somewhat aroused, the force of anger represses the onset of the rebellious populace and does what Maro sings about Neptune: "With speech he sways their passion and soothes their breasts."[6]

Whenever the commons rebel and desire to ravage, murder, and plunder, the magistrate of the mind is aroused and grows angry. How good this anger is! In this regard, the Psalmist says: *Be angry, and sin not* (Ps 4:5).

The whole infection or wound of sin is restricted to these areas. We find one area in the sovereignty of reason: pride and ambition, vice of the spirit, not of the flesh, for a demon cannot sin by gluttony; it sins, not by avarice, not by excess, but by pride. But in the magistracy of anger we find two areas stemming from the magistrate's failure to curb the passions of the people, who then rebel through twofold concupiscence: either desire of gold or riches, that is, of external goods in the category of fortune (which is concupiscence of the eyes), or craving for sensation and pleasure of the flesh, that is, for goods of the body (which is concupiscence of the flesh). The apostle John explains these three wounds with brevity and wisdom: *For all that is in the world is the concupiscence of the flesh, and the concupiscence of the eyes, and the pride of life* (1 Jn 2:16).

You will ask: "Why do you limit the number of wounds to only three? Does the serpent not have seven horns, that is, seven capital sins?" Generally, we employ only these three categories, because every other consideration has reference to them as genera, principles, or fonts.

Oh how fortunate man once was, inasmuch as sovereign reason was in command, since appetite obeyed its master, because magisterial force executed the royal mandates. Then man was living precisely as "man." For man consists of nothing other than reason and mind. But the order was immediately reversed. The king obeyed the people; and man was subject to woman; reason followed feeling; mind responded to appetite, and spirit conformed to flesh. The republic, kingdom, and authority of the mind was perverted into tyranny. Man was then perceived as a beast or brute, rather than a man, as the psalm attests: *Man when he was in honor did not understand: he has been compared to senseless beasts, and made like to them* (Ps 49:21). He was in a paradise of delight. He enjoyed the food, nectar, and ambrosia of the gods. But he did not count his blessings. In exile, he learned to sigh for love of his lost fatherland.

The cautious and wise person who wishes to remain in a paradise of pleasure — but who would not wish it? — ought to take measures to insure that what happens to many does not happen to himself. For it is written in the books of ancient wise men, especially in the collection of Hebrew wisdom called the *Gemara* (to use the vernacular) that four men, enthralled by the concept of paradise, undertook a great journey to the East.

Legend told of a most fertile garden found on those shores which was more beautiful by far than the garden of the Hesperides (to say nothing of Adonis) — lovelier than the blissful isles of the pious, or even the fabulous Elysian fields, so admired and celebrated among the Greeks. Finally, after crossing an enormous expanse of ocean and land, as it pleased God, they found the seat of the blessed or, in other words, paradise itself. But because the cherub with the flaming sword, turning every way, was standing guard, like Argus or the ever watchful serpent, to keep anyone from entering there — they were by no means ignorant of this — with certain medicaments (to use the parlance of the sages) they assuaged the effects of the angel's sword just enough for them to enter the garden safe and sound.

When they had made their way in, they were bathed in a fragrance so sweet that any dead person exposed to it would come back to life. They saw every kind of tree bearing fruit all year long; they spied the tree of life and knowledge. Whatever can bring joy, attract the eye, please the ear, delight taste and touch, in fine, every kind of refined delectation and earthly satisfaction conceivable was theirs in abundance. There was no place for sorrow, or grief, or mourning. Everything was charming and pleasing. Everything therefore smiled on those who had entered; branches heavy with wondrous fruit stretched down to them. Everywhere they were invited to partake of Good.

The first man was wasteful, or would it be truer to say he became extravagant because of the great abundance of good things? He completely lost his sense of proportion. When his foolishness became apparent, he was immediately ejected. The second man was overwhelmed by avarice. The third man became melancholy. The fourth man, because he ate as much honey as there was, left the garden in peace and blessing, just as he had entered it.

What do these things signify? With an angel guarding it, could anyone even see paradise, let alone enter it? Are they fables? They are certainly not fables, but rather parables for our consideration, like the instruction of Solomon on small folk and the wise man.[7] So what does the garden of delights signify? Paradise in Hebrew is *Gan Eden. Gan,* or garden — it is treated in the arcane books of the ancient theologians — signifies a rank in relation to God, or one of the ten most sacred lights reserved for the chosen. It abides with us in latter days, dwells among us, and is concerned with our affairs; we otherwise call it the Holy Spirit, or rather the church, the mother of all. All the points considered above which derive from the teaching of arcane theology devolve on this consideration, and it is called the harbor light and storehouse of divine illuminations. Wherefore, Solomon sang about *a garden enclosed, a fountain sealed up, and fruits of paradise* (Sg 4:12-13). Eden, moreover, as we have learned from the prophetic voice, is the first light issuing from the dawn of creation. The same is the spoken Wisdom — *Dibur* — "Word," which subsists absolutely there on high, but looks down on us here, and proffers its healing hand to us (for it is characteristic of wisdom, not fortune, to heal and cure). This is the nature of the paradise of delights. Plato very clearly depicts it as the fountainhead of truth and wisdom.[8]

Indeed, inasmuch as this wisdom is communicated to us here in four levels — certainly, as it is customary to promise in fables, Marsilius handed down the crutch he had pilfered — and four categories of those who receive and drink from this ocean or immense fountain of light, certain individuals incur folly therefrom, because their minds are weak. But thereafter priests and scholars dismiss folly just as backward children reject erudition. Yes, they take offense and scandal at this and come to shipwreck in port. The third group reacts badly to honey and dies. But those who make moderate use of honey, so as not to upset or bloat their stomachs, but rather soothe them, such wise men not only enter paradise in peace, but leave it in peace.

Holy scripture affords four examples: Adam, Noah, the sons of Aaron, and Abraham. They all enter paradise, that is, they all drink from the font of divine wisdom. Thereafter, Adam becomes foolish on account of the little woman and is expelled. Noah loses his wits.[9] The sons of Aaron perish in flames and fire from heaven.[10] Abraham enters the garden of wisdom with prudence and leaves it in peace, because he is as sparing as necessary, and eats what and as much as he should, that is, according to the capacity of his stomach. The others sinned three times in a threefold manner: Adam within, Noah in the middle area, and the sons of Aaron without. Adam sinned in his heart, since he was unwilling to cast gloom on any of his pleasures. Hence, he depressed the fate of the world. Noah stifled the expression of his mind, and never moved his lips on behalf of the liberation of man. Thereby he showed his heart was hard, and lost his reputation as a just man. But the sons of Aaron sinned by deed, when they failed to abstain from forbidden food. Abraham, however, was fortunate, because he never erred in thought, word, deed, or heart. He believed, and it was reputed to him unto mercy.[11] He opened his mouth in the presence of the Lord to prevent the destruction of Sodom and Gomorrah.[12] By deed, he played host to angels.[13] By deed, he would not spare his only son, so that he could obey God.[14] Therefore, he entered paradise in righteousness, and left it in peace.

I mentioned the sickness of Bagnaia (Balnearia). Does Bagnaia (Balnearia) not daily sin within? Would that it were not filled with vain cures! Or — woe is me! — would that Bagnaia (Balnearia) did not sin at all! For hardly have they been born when its children spout blasphemies! When

angered, they curse their enemies with cancer. Perhaps Bagnaia (Balnearia) has holy deeds. Reality says no. Does Bagnaia (Balnearia) have no
need of a doctor? Would that it did not need one! I fear very much that
Isaiah's prophecy fits this town exactly: *From the sole of the foot unto the top
of the head, there is no soundness therein* (Is 1:6). See how much it needs a
physician. We have not promised a remedy. But because we have divided
your land into two parts, namely, adults and children, and the children
again into those younger than seven and those older than seven, we have
provided the remedy of discipline for the older children (children on
whom cities, not teachers, base their hope) and ordered the instructor to
come. Send the boys to a school where you can train them and develop
suitable men, who will recoup the republic. We have diagnosed three
kinds of lesions.

What sort of remedy is required?
What kind of hurt is involved?
Have you washed yourself inside?
Or is your heart like Adam's?

Then cleanse your heart. Make your conscience glisten. Do not imitate
the old Adam. Instead, be a new man, a new creature.[15] Make yourself
beautiful within, because it is written: *Blessed are the clean of heart* (Mt 5:8).
Your face will reflect holiness, or does Noah oppress your mind? Apply
the medicament of prayer and divine hymnody. Express yourself on
behalf of good or, perhaps, like the sons of Aaron, your lesions are
external? Then do some good right away! We have applied a healing hand
to children, the tender young, because, if they are inclined to excellence,
there is great hope they will accept the counsels and customs of a better
life. You see how readily the supple little seedling is bent. But when it has
grown into a hoary oak, what force it takes to sway it! It would sooner
break. So we hope your little shoots, with the help of God, will receive a
measure of salubrious husbandry from their teacher. For a recent infection is cured rather easily. But if it becomes chronic and saps the strength,
then the physician despairs of curing it.

I perceive that the cure of the other division, the adults, is far more
serious and difficult, inasmuch as it suffers from the paralysis of age.
Consequently, their malignancy perdures. All three lesions prevail; and,
worn by their years, they can scarcely endure the physician's hand. At
this stage, they sin within, in the median zone, and without. Their
paralysis has grown because of long deferral of treatment. Who but God
will cure them? But the Lord has sent his representative.

Therefore, O almighty God, you who created Adam and then expelled
him when he sinned, you who castigate the sinner, you who preserved
Noah when the deluge destroyed the world, you who burned and consumed the delinquent sons of Aaron — if you cast Adam out of the garden
of delights to struggle and die with all his posterity, because of his one
sin — if you rightly forbade Noah to be called "the just" and over-

whelmed the world with the flood, because Noah kept silence when he should have prayed for those who were perishing — if you annihilated the sons of Aaron with fire from heaven, because they once partook of forbidden food, just as the comrades of Ulysses devoured the cattle of the sun[16] — we, your people, are here before you.

We have sinned, not once, but over and over again.

We have remained in sin for hours, for days, and even for years.

We have grown worse, more base, more depraved, within and without, in our middle, and in every part — even though you threatened us with exile and death, flood and fire — in spite of your consummate mildness to the worst of us. You spare us, notwithstanding. I believe you stay your hand because of your all-wise patience, and allow severity to compensate for tardy punishment. In the end, you reap all things with the sickle of justice. You are indulgent now, so that you can completely overthrow an impenitent and hardened people later.[17] Today you heal the incurable paralytic. But I, the unworthy pastor and head of this people, refer this paralytic on his pallet to you, the best of physicians.

We lack faith. Give us faith.

We lack devotion. Give us devotion.

As you once spoke the word of life and salvation to the paralytic, speak now and say: *Rise, take up your pallet, and walk* (Mk 2:9).

Translated by Joseph C. Schnaubelt, O.S.A.
Edited by Joseph Reino

Notes

1. See Gn 2:19-20.

2. See Gn 3:19.

3. See Mt 9:1-8.

4. See Dn 9:27.

5. See Vergil, *Aeneid* I, 76-77.

6. *Ibid.*, 153.

7. See Prv 1:1-6.

8. See Plato, *The Republic* X, 614B; VII, 540B.

9. See Gn 9:20-21.

10. See Lv 10:1-2.

11. See Gn 15:6.

12. See Gn 18:23-33.

13. See Gn 18:1-8.

14. See Gn 22:1-14.

15. See Gal 6:15; 2 Cor 5:17; Eph 2:15; 4:24; 1 Cor 15:45.

16. See Homer, *Odyssey* XII, 294-415.

17. See Rom 2:5; Bar 2:30.

III

A Sermon Delivered by the Most Reverend Giles of Viterbo, O.S.A. at Bagnaia (Balnearia) on 15 October of the Year of Salvation 1525.

The world is sundered into two cities. One is called the City of God. It confers exceptional light and peace on its citizens. The other, Babylon, is hostile to God. It gives its citizens night, darkness, turmoil, and misery. In that city, utter chaos reigns, with all hope of good and salvation forsaken. The first is formed from love of God; the other from hatred of God. And although the division of these two cities is apparent to God, nevertheless, while we make our pilgrim way here in this world — my father Augustine is the author of this concept — they do not seem separate to us, but intermingled, the one with the other, just as the grain is trampled on the threshing floor together with the chaff, until the day of winnowing and separation appears. "And amid the smiling corn the luckless darnel and barren oats hold sway."[1]

Then the chaff is removed from the wheat, the stalk and straw from the grain, in order to save the wheat and discard the straw, to gather the wheat in the granary and give the straw to the flames. For the Apostle says: *The fire shall try every man's work, of what sort it is* (1 Cor 3:13). For, like gold and the purest silver, the furnace will not consume the citizens of the City of God, but render them lustrous. It will not destroy, but purge them. It will not, like alchemy, devour true citizens. Moreover, before this destruction and separation takes place, both cities remain mixed together without any certain distinction. For we do not discern who are true citizens of the Good City, or denizens of the other.

Nevertheless, the king of the heavenly city wished to decorate his soldiers, citizens, and friends, even in this world, with certain insignia which would distinguish them from the enemy, and would cause the enemy to flee in terror at the very sight of them. For by day and by night we have princes of the evil city lying in wait for us, the spirits of darkness, who leave no stone unturned, as the saying goes, in their efforts to make us citizens of their city. To prevent this, our commander has given us a garment adorned with his insignia. Thus, his faithful servants are separated from the unfaithful, the citizens of his city from the citizens of impious Babylon.

And so this garment is the symbol of a Christian. This garment is the baptismal robe of Christ which today's gospel[2] discusses so plainly and clearly. There it is made apparent how God rejects those not dressed in that garment, and the number of them that lack it.[3]

The occasion is the marriage of the king's son. A splendid and sumptuous banquet is prepared in the royal hall. The tables are filled with guests. The poor enjoy the royal bounty. The king enters the hall to meet his subjects. He looks around. He recognizes a multitude of his people. He rejoices. Wherever he turns his eyes, he sees tables filled with his guests.

But look!

As he observes more closely, he catches sight of a man at table not wearing the garment, his insignia, the drapery of the wedding feast. A shadow passes over the king's countenance. His eyebrows contract. His brow is furrowed. His eyes burn. Terribly angry, not to say astonished, at the audacity and indignity of the act, he says: "Friend, why did you come into our palace hall not wearing our insignia, that is, without a wedding garment?"[4] Thereupon, he indignantly orders the attendants: *Tie him up, hand and foot, and throw him into the darkness outside* (Mt 22:11-13).

You perceive the great shame and suffering of the man who was ejected from the wedding feast, because he dared to enter the king's celebration without a garment marked with the royal seal. He is cast from the bright hall into darkness, from bounty to distress, from rejoicing to wailing, from pleasure to gnashing of teeth.

What a dreadful change! Why did it happen?

Because he approached the royal presence and table without the royal insignia! Thus the first Adam was exiled from paradise. The ejection was almost the same, but the cause was somewhat different. Adam was expelled from paradise, the guest from the wedding; Adam from delight, the guest from the banquet. The latter was sitting at table; the former was enjoying the company of his wife. The latter was cast into exterior darkness; the former was forced into labor, sorrow, and struggle. The cause, however, was somewhat different, but almost equal. The latter was banished from the wedding, because he did not bring the proper garment with him; the former, because he lost his. Both, nonetheless, were enjoying themselves, the former, because he had entered paradise; the latter, because he had joined the marriage feast. The latter was expelled; the former fled, when the cherub, the sentinel with a flaming sword, turning every way, barred paradise to him.[5] For Adam was driven from the blessed abode of our fortunate brethren, because he had lost the insignia which God had bestowed on him at the very beginning, that is, the regal robe of original justice. The guest was expelled, because he did not bring the indispensable wedding garment with him.

Be careful, Bagnaia (Balnearia), not to go on living without the royal seal. And do not lose your seal, or you may be exiled from paradise, like Adam, who lost his seal.

You will ask why Adam's children and all his posterity were penalized with the guilt their father incurred by his solitary sin. What did his children merit, if he alone sinned? Do you not perceive that, if a father squanders his property and sells the family's farm, its home, and all its clothing, his innocent children will also suffer from the lack of the goods he has sold? Just this way, Adam forfeited to the enemy the regal robe bestowed on him by the king. Therefore, all his posterity have remained ignominiously bereft.

Baptism, moreover, in washing away the stain of original sin, restores to the soul its lost beauty of justice. The man who has baptism, as we said elsewhere, has the certain principle which ascribes us to the heavenly city, but he is not complete. He does not have the fullness or refinement which the anointing of confirmation confers. We will have to say something more about this sacrament a little further on, just as we discussed it previously in another place.

Please give me your strict attention, as I describe how this sacrament is derived from the five barley loaves,[6] that is, from the old law — from under the "bark," as it were.

Since Israel, as you know, was the people of God and, in the inheritance of the Lord, his chosen possession, God wanted the Israelites to be different from all the rest of mankind, especially from the city of Babylon — separated from the impious by a clearly discernible sign — so that the children of Israel would be distinguished from other nations, as the savior indicated in the gospel, when he said: *Behold a true Israelite* (Jn 1:47).

After the first man had lost his regalia, that regal robe of original justice, he was succeeded by Noah. God then gave Noah the sign by which he would understand the covenant interdicting forever all future deluges.

I will set my bow, he said, *in the clouds of heaven as a sign between you and me* (Gn 9:13), a three-colored iris, white, red, and green, with sapphire above.

By this sign, eight clearly signified souls were saved on the ark.

Not much later, God called Abraham, and promised him many great things: *I will make of you a great nation* (Gn 12:2).

Abraham was silent.

Blessing, I will bless you (Gn 12:2).

Abraham remained silent.

I will multiply your seed like the stars of the sky, and like the sand on the shore of the sea (Gn 22:17).

Abraham still kept silent.

But when he said: "I will give this land to your seed," Abraham stirred.

Of course, the issue was a kingdom, where his seed would be king. For God gave his people no small gifts. Laws. What else? A priesthood. Some third thing? A kingdom. When God mentioned law, Abraham was silent. The same, when God spoke of priesthood. But when God alluded to a kingdom, Abraham responded: "Will you promise a kingdom to my seed?"

"I will give this land to your seed."

"To whose seed? Could it be to a servant born in my house? Obviously not to my own seed, for Sarah and I have reached an age when we have no hope left of ever having a child. Since this is so, how should I know for certain?"[7]

Observe!

Somewhat credulous, Abraham asked for a sign. It was as if he were saying, "By the sign you will show that what you promise is virtually impossible."

Then God ordered Abraham to sacrifice a cow, a ram, a she-goat, and a turtle-dove or pigeon. These are taken to refer to four kingdoms of the Hebrews, but in no wise pertain to our concern. Edom, that is, the Roman kingdom, is considered last. They call Scechina, that is, Israel, the dominant force guiding these considerations of ours. Abraham sacrificed the animals. He sought a sign. God gave a marvelous sign, for Abraham saw a furnace descend from the sky over the victims. Flames of fire were issuing from the bronze.[8] When he witnessed this miracle, Abraham was astonished, and he remembered the omnipotence of God. Abraham believed God, and it was reputed to him, not unto merit (for it was as if his belief was compelled by the sign), but unto the mercy and grace of God, which is called *Zedaca*, not *Zedech*. In this place, the interpreters are completely in error, since they interpret the passage: "It was reputed to him unto justice."[9] It should rather be interpreted completely to the contrary. Then Abraham received from God the sign for the separation of the faithful from the unfaithful, concerning which God spoke.[10] Circumcision, certainly a seal of the flesh, separates Israel, which represents the City of God, from Babylon, which represents the *Goi*, or Gentiles.

But notice that this was a double sign among the ancient Hebrews. For although boys received the seal of circumcision in their flesh on the eighth day, nevertheless, the Hebrews did not yet deem the infant or boy completely circumcised. Rather, he was considered uncircumcised unless the *priat*, that is, his member, received circumcision again. Note, therefore, how Father Abraham received many signs, because he was not content with one: fire from heaven, conflagration of the holocaust, circumcision, and *priat*.

It is written, nonetheless, that Abraham, despairing of having posterity from his wife, entered at Sarah's urging unto Sarah's handmaid, Hagar, in order to have offspring by her. But when Sarah saw Abraham honor her handmaid, she was overcome by jealousy and cast the handmaid out. Carrying a skin of water, the handmaid roamed aimlessly.

As Hagar sat weeping and her boy wandered about, an angel came to console her.

"Do not be afraid," said he. "I will make you into a great nation."

Hagar called the son born to her Ishmael, that is, "the hearkening of God," because the prayer of the afflicted had been heard.[11]

Who was this Ishmael born of the Egyptian handmaid? It is a marvelous thing. From Ishmael come the Turks and the Moslems, who smite the Hebrews. With grievous afflictions, the Ishmaelites took away the temple, the priesthood, the kingdom, and Jerusalem itself. They commit the Jews to perpetual servitude. Because of the sin against the Egyptian handmaid, the Hebrews suffer retribution from the Egyptians, that is, the Moslems; and we ourselves sustain much greater hardships from them. Since they use force to snatch even children from their cradles in spite of wailing mothers, since they occupy the Holy Sepulchre and other holy places, that which the angel said to Hagar the handmaid has been fulfilled: "I will make you into a great nation."

Alas! Consider how great: they have almost the whole Mediterranean under their sway!

Who holds Asia? Moslems!

Who occupies Africa? Moslems!

Who has conquered a fine and notable part of Europe? Moslems!

Our forces have been restricted to such a narrow area! We hold only this corner and slender tail of Europe. And how long Hagar and Ishmael have reigned far and wide! They have reigned a long time — 900 years!

Why? you ask.

Because of their acceptance of the sign of circumcision, even though it is imperfect without *priat*. What do we say about those who accept the perfect sign? We say they will prosper very much indeed, since acceptance of the imperfect sign has caused Islam to spread so much by land and by sea. Islam does not have *priat*. Therefore, in place of *priat*, it holds the kingdom of Priam in Asia, that is to say, the head of the land. Nevertheless, because it does not have *priat*, it is said to be the boot of the dog, and a wild beast, because it lacks the perfect sign of man.

We read these things in the old law, which is the mother of the new law. There all things are found depicted and represented which are described as accomplished in the gospel. For the Hebrew sages say the law and prophets foreshadow nothing other than the times and deeds of the Messiah, who, according to the testimony of his adversaries, has the power and authority to change and renew the law and everything stemming from antiquity.

The Messiah therefore has come. He has renewed everything coming from antiquity. He has changed the old man, which is circumcision. Just as he set up the rock of waters,[12] that is, baptism, he established the sacrament much more easily, and, if he had to change all rituals, he accepted the culmination of anointing in place of the old *priat*. And just as the Roman Church, in emulation of its parent, accepted the baptism instituted by its Lord in place of circumcision, so it accepted confirmation in lieu of *priat*.

You will observe: *He that believes and is baptized shall be saved* (Mk 16:16). We believe a child is certainly saved, and not damned, in spite of not being anointed with chrism, although the negligence of the parents who omitted it is condemned and punished. Take note that baptism was instituted to effect the restoration, renewal, and salvation of mankind. It is from baptism that we assume the garment, the pure insignia, of a new creature.

Indeed, in harmony with the gospel, the Apostle speaks magnificently in today's epistle concerning this garment of renovation, when he says: *Stripping yourselves of the old man*, that is, the errors, the vices, and the particular blemish of the old life, the stain of original sin, *put on the new man* (Col 3:9-10) through baptism, that is, the new life of the heavenly Adam. But baptism is imperfect without the anointing.

Do you wish to fulfill those who are imperfect and magnify their Spirit and supreme dignity?

Then bring the little children today to be anointed with chrism. Thereupon, they will pertain perfectly to the City of God, inasmuch as they will have received the complete insignia of the King.

It is a sign to God to the extent indicated by the gospel reading[13] and the epistle of the apostle,[14] and both Testaments are in agreement. This certainly includes lofty considerations. We are not greatly concerned if you have already forgotten what I said above, provided you pay strict attention to what I am about to say.

May I say why?

Monks of Bagnaia (Balnearia), you should accept what I say today as a sign and portent sent by God. Thus far we have addressed you three times: first, when we impressed you with the sickness of your land; second, when we qualified that sickness; and third, when we proposed a remedy. And because we distributed your populace into two equal categories and, using the analogy of the body, into two principal groups of members (into seniors and juniors, and major and minor), we likewise separated the minor members into infants and children. For the older children who are ready for education, we suggested a remedy, namely, a teacher. Today, we are extending our hand to the infants, proffering the remedy of confirmation. We still have to find a remedy for the grown children, but, because we think today's sermon would be too long, we will commit all else to God. He will himself send an angel to supply it. You meanwhile listen to what pertains only to your city of Bagnaia (Balnearia).

For we find the name of Bagnaia (Balnearia) commemorated three times in sacred scripture. Perhaps, you ask, how did the Holy Spirit place any consideration of this little city or town in the mouths of the prophets? I do not know what the prophets thought. I only know this: God cares for every single man, to say nothing of towns and cities, republics and kingdoms, and scripture does mention Bethlehem, and places like Capernaum and Nazareth, which are in no wise cities. For this reason, stop marveling that God takes care of Bagnaia (Balnearia). So, I find this sort of name twice in the Song of Songs, and once in the Psalms. Give your full attention to the prophetic words that pertain to you. You will understand that you have been afforded the sign of the sun, and it is marvelous and new. Now I will recount these for you in a brief oration, so that you will not tire of hearing the word of life concerning your salvation, and the oration will be over immediately.

Note that, just as *stabularia* (things belonging to a stable) is derived from *stabulum* (stable), so *Bagnaia* (Balnearia) — the place of the bath — is derived from *balneum* (bath), whether because this place of yours was once a bath, or because (and this seems more likely) it had custody of neighboring baths. In any case, the place of a bath is a balnearia. Scripture employs a substantive of this connotation, *balneum* (bath) or, if you prefer, lavacrum (bath), twice in the Song of Songs, as elsewhere. For the Holy Spirit intentionally or, as it were, by design caused our Pindar to compose the whole of Psalm 60 on his harp from the place of the bath.

The Psalm begins: *O God, you have cast us off.*

If I ever spoke truth, God has cast us off, that is to say, he has cast off these places. My reckoning is from the middle of the pontificate of Leo X (1513-1522). For such a plague was not sent in the time of Saul, so that Israel would not be exposed at the same time to plague and an unrighteous king, who was worse than plague, but waited for good king David. In the same way, the plague began to invade these shores during the reign of a good pope, and we do not yet see any limit to it.

We therefore rightfully say: *O God, you have cast us off.*

And so the first citation in the Song of Songs employs the connotation of Bagnaia (Balnearia) thus: *Your teeth as flocks of sheep, that are shorn, which come up from the washing (balneum)* (Sg 4:2). It was the time of shearing, when the shepherds were more concerned with fleece than sheep. It will not be so now. Do not be fearful as long as we preside over the sheepfold and cattlepen. We want to pass over the first citation referring to the shorn sheep and replace it with the second citation from the Song of Songs which reads: *Your teeth as a flock of sheep, which come up from the washing (balneum)* (Sg 6:6). Let your woolens remain with you in your chambers. We are not looking for your wool, but your salvation.

Up to this point we have cited from scripture randomly, that is, wherever we found an expression referring to the bath (*balneare*). Now give your attention to Psalm 60 which is specially dedicated to Bagnaia (Balnearia).

It begins: *O God, you have cast us off.*

Oh that God has not abandoned Bagnaia (Balnearia)!

Is there any hope?

Yes, there is.

Listen to the song of hope pertaining to you: *Moab is the bowl of my hope* (Ps 59:10). Truth does not speak this way; but thus: *Moab is the basin of my bath* (Ps 60:10). You hear that God values you so much that he said: *Moab is the basin of my bath*, as if he were to say: "Bagnaia (Balnearia) is mine." How enviable!

What about other places? Are other country towns not his? Is only Bagnaia (Balnearia) his? Is this hardly credible? Do you not want to believe that Bagnaia (Balnearia) is his daughter of the white hen? Accept the sign as absolutely certain.

For as to the sign of Noah, there is the rainbow; as to Abraham, there is a declaration. If your mind is so stubborn, or rather so obtuse and injudicious, that you do not see it, or believe it, accept the sign. For in regard to you the psalmist says: "You have shown a sign to your people."[15]

What sign, pray?

The sign of Gideon.

Gideon could not otherwise be brought to faith except through this sign. At night a trickling dew wet the area around the fleece, but the the fleece itself was completely dry.[16] See the miracle. The same has happened to you. Is not war being waged not far off? The whole vineyard has experienced this rain, or rather the hard arm of war. Viterbo experienced it. For it sent and lost very many. Tuscany experienced it. Soriano experienced it. They were attacked and overwhelmed by force. Only Bagnaia (Balnearia) did not experience it.

Why were you immune?

Why should you be so free?

Where did you acquire these great privileges?

How did you merit it?

The prophet has certainly sung: "You have shown a sign to your people." Recognize the sign of divine charity, clemency, and goodness toward you. All your neighbors are weeping. Only you are laughing.

He has shown a sign, so that you will turn toward it, a sign by which you may understand that you are called from Babylon to the City of God. If you understand this sign, blessed are you! Cursed are you, until you have grasped its meaning! Otherwise, although you alone may be laughing now, while your neighbors are weeping, I fear the time may come when only you will be weeping, while everyone else will be laughing.

Translated by Joseph C. Schnaubelt, O.S.A.
Edited by Joseph Reino

Notes

1. Vergil, *Georgics* I, 154. ·
2. See Mt 22:1-14.
3. See Mt 22:14.
4. See Mt 22:12.
5. See Gn 3:24.
6. See Jn 6:9; Mt 14:17; Mk 6:38; Lk 9:13.
7. See Gn 15:1-21.
8. See Gn 15:17.

9. See Gn 15:6.
10. See Gn 17:9-14.
11. See Gn 16:11; 21:9-18.
12. See Ex 17.
13. Mt 22:1-14.
14. Eph 4:23-28.
15. See Ps 60:5. The psalm says: *You have made your people feel hardships.*
16. See Jgs 6:39-40.

Appendix III

Letters

References to letters are made to
Anna Maria Voci Roth, *Egidio da Viterbo, O.S.A. Lettere Familiari*, Rome, 1990
Clare O'Reilly, *Giles of Viterbo, O.S.A. Letters as Augustinian General*, Rome, 1992
E. Martène – U. Durand, *Veterum Scriptorum et monumentorum historicorum, dogmaticorum, moralium amplissima collectio . . .* , III, Paris, 1724
G. Signorelli, *Il cardinale Egidio da Viterbo agostiniano, umanista e riformatore 1469-1532*, Florence, 1929.

In these editions the authors give the various sources of the letters, which are:
Roma, Biblioteca Angelica, MS. Lat. 1001
Roma, Biblioteca Angelica, MS. Lat. 688
Roma, Biblioteca Angelica, MS. Lat. 1156
Biblioteca Apostolica Vaticana, MS. Chigi N.III.77
Firenze, Biblioteca Mediceo-Laurenziana, MS. Ashburn. 287
Napoli, Biblioteca Nazionale Centrale, MS. V.F.20
Siena, Biblioteca Comunale degli Intronati, MS. G.X.26
Siena, Biblioteca Comunale degli Intronati, MS. B.IX.18
Biblioteca Apostolica Vaticana, MS. Vat.Lat. 3146.

The editor is indebted to Dr. Clare O'Reilly for her help in editing these letters of Giles of Viterbo, and to the translators: Maria Boulding, O.S.B, Mary Brennan, and Gerard Deighan, for their labors.

1. To Marsilio Ficino

I was about to set out for the city of learned men and the ruler of almost all the world, and to embrace the teaching of the divine Plato, a doctrine almost wiped out through the indolence of listless times and become a novelty, yet still a doctrine most divine. I feared however that on my own I would not be able to resist sufficiently the poisoned teeth of the sacrilegious Peripatetics, and so I left Padua and betook myself to you, the great restorer and illuminator of the Academy, and I decided that your terse work on Parmenides would not be enough for me unless I heard you face to face discoursing on the lofty subject of the forms. Having done so I departed from you in great joy. So great was my admiration for your teaching, your eloquence, your competence, and your zeal that my impression was not that I had visited Marsilio Ficino, professor of the noble arts and high priest of the muses, but that I had consulted the oracle of Ammon, of Dodona, of Delphi, or whatever more authoritative oracle there may be. The speaker's presence was of such power that I considered myself as Alcibiades at the side of the disputing Socrates, so full was I of Socratic inspiration.

337

Therefore, with ardent longing for holy contests I completed my journey as quickly as possible and entered Rome full of zeal. Then I set forth Platonic propositions for defense against the Peripatetics, and announced the day of combat. The fiercest of soldiers came together, seething with envy and resentment; they arranged their camp, putting the stronger in charge of the left and right wings, while the light-armed men undertook the lighter battle — or so it seemed at first. But when they had routed the whole line . . . [lacuna in text] . . . one could behold Hector making a murderous attack on Plato's breast with a Thracian spear, Memnon striking his groin with a bloodstained sword, Amazons rushing in with battle axes and Paris fighting craftily. The rage of the assailants! The sight of them in their anger! How great the noise of the whole army! You would have said that the heavens and every building were collapsing. I listened to the din of the clashing arms and the falling woods: with such force and effort did they fight that it seemed they were about to abolish the name of Plato entirely, and it would indeed have died had it not received the favor of the holy priests whom they call cardinals. However, a doctrine which is divine could not be shaken by the madness of wicked men, and with the aid of God and of Plato's good and helpful guarding spirits we came safe: and in such a way that our enemies blushed before the immense greatness of Plato.

I was about to come to you immediately, so that you who encouraged the horse to go forth from the starting box might see it also rejoicing in the wondrous happiness of victory. However, when I came to Siena I was warned of a sinister plot and ordered to delay there. I decided to do my business by letter, since there was no other way. I await with great longing to receive back a letter from you through this messenger — I could desire nothing else as much. I wish to know whether the new works of Porphyry and the others have been printed. I expect that in this matter you will do more for the republic of letters than those commonly thought to be its most distinguished members. This indeed was all that was lacking to the high praise of your studies; for by your exposition of Plato you converted every noble mind to the Academy. You made them conversant with the works of Plotinus, introduced them to the heavenly realms with your theology, made them secure with your triple life, sanctified them with your religion and made them shine forth with the rays of your sun; through your commentary on the *Timaeus* they became versed in natural philosophy, through your explanation of the *Symposium* they became lovers of beauty; you made them accurate in every aspect of Platonic teaching, and caused them to be so saturated with your most noble labors, toils, and many writings that they called you the father of their studies — though it is uncertain which group we should consider in your debt, the soldiers of the Greek or of the Latin Academy.

In very truth, the latter are greatly in your debt; you cast aside all concern for an empty and common teaching and imbued them with the study of a true and holy philosophy, raising their eyes to the light of divine contemplation. Nor indeed are the Greeks any less in debt to you: forgotten through decay and isolation they lay in the black and shady night of Lethe, but you rescued them from this most obscure darkness and exalted them in their own wonderful glory. Hence it is that we should consider that Marsilio Ficino has been sent to us by divine providence, to make clear to us that the mystical theology of Plato is highly consonant with our sacred teachings and indeed anticipates them. This, my Marsilio, is the reign of Saturn, the golden age so often sung of by the Sibyl and the prophets; this is that age of Plato, in which he foretold that his works would become especially known.

Farewell.

Lettere Familiari I, 101-104   (Siena, Summer 1499)

2. To Serafino

I would come to visit you had I not lost my mule: it died at Ferrara, having brought me to its master's abode. Greetings once again, my most loving father! That good angel of mine led me out and led me back again, under the guidance of my Crucified Lord. See how late fate decreed that I should return to this delightful God-filled grove. How much time, how many undertakings have been lost! People complain that I have written nothing, but in fact it is a miracle that I am alive at all!

It is now eight months since I left Cimino. The Lord knows how many labors, how much talking, how many journeys have filled that time! What "region of the earth," what part of Italy, what sea, what shore have I not visited? Having completed my duties in that most proud city of the Venetians I traveled right around the coast of the Adriatic: Cividale, Chioggia, Ravenna, Rimini, Pesaro, Fano, and, on the elbow of Italy, the town of Ancona, well defended within a very safe port, and the coastland of Loreto. Then I visited the arms of Saint Nicholas of Tolentino, and finally that unique source of certitude for our faith, the almost divine virgin of Montefalco, the sole glory of my Order and clear proof of the truth of Christianity. I shed tears at the house of Loreto and at the shrine of Saint Nicholas, but on seeing the wonders of the virgin Clare I almost passed away. O great God! How great was her power with God when alive, how great even in death! When we meet you will learn of wondrous things. The image of the Crucified, the three hairs and the blood still fresh and knowing of the future not only draw forth tears but snatch away the heart and soul. I say nothing of the beauty of her body — there is nothing more gracious, more spotless or more fresh in the whole world. You would sooner say she was just closing her eyes in sleep. All who look on her are terrified, fearing that she is about to give some warning; she gives prior notice to the people of all that is to happen, and often she rushes through the city by night and has been seen by a great number of people. I shall tell you more when I see you.

Lettere Familiari I, 266-267   (Cimino, 2 July 1505)

3. To Serafino

Greetings. If ever I have desired to write to you it is now. I hear you have performed a task for me in Viterbo and in Florence: no one could have done a greater favor for his best friend. However, since our conversations and the late sailing of your ship promised that you would come to Rome in September, I have not written for a month now. I was afraid that when you were entering Rome my letter would be seeking you out in the woods. The great Lorenzo, your friend and mine, has returned to Rome, though from now on we must no longer address him merely as great but as most illustrious and duke of Urbino. The pontiff went off to Viterbo to refresh his spirits, and is now expected in Rome.

Now at last you are at the point of setting sail and untying the cable of your reluctant boat: I do not understand why you still delay. "I would not take the milk of birds," as Aristophanes says, nor indeed would I accept even the milk of cocks in place of a boat; that is to say, I would not exchange it for almost any riches or power. A boat in Rome is a great status symbol — it signifies that one has power in heaven and on earth. Paul by his example advises you to hurry here with all your might: he sailed in that boat, and in order to make its image the summit of things human and divine and consecrate it to eternal memory, he undertook not only to steal away the club of Hercules and the bolt of Jove, but the complete overthrow of Hercules himself and of Jove himself. See now with what spirit you ought to take to the boat, for the sake of which the prince of the apostles boldly undertook so many things and brought them to a happy issue. Beware lest you delay: the wind may call the sailors elsewhere or the arrival of many merchants may increase the price of merchandise. Rather seize the profit right away, as the saying goes, from sunset, from the ship's entry into port; for in matters of great importance, if the opportunity is not taken immediately it is easily impeded or indeed lost altogether.

Therefore leave the ninety-nine in the desert and seek the one sheep: unless you begin the search immediately it will perish.

Farewell.

Lettere Familiari II, 213-215   (Rome, 24 October, 1516)

4. To Mariano of Genazzano, Prior General of the Augustinian Order

You have banished me to the wretched shores of the Lucrine Lago d'Averno. We have a view of both Cumae and Baiae, but the place is of worse repute than any Cyprus or Sardinia. However, we can spend our idle moments investigating the miracles of nature about us, the

Phlegraean fields where perpetual fires are to be seen, and a thousand treacherous boiling springs. The onlooker is seized with terror as he hears what seems more the groaning of the damned than the hissing of flames. We go down to Miseno, of all mountains the most aerated, for inside it is full of hollow vaults. We go down to the thousand underground caves, hidden ways long and magnificent leading to the realms of Pluto, dwellings which know of neither sun or light. Finally we enter into the sanctuary of the Sibyl and stand in that small cavern richly adorned with shells and mosaic — so often I have beheld there something which surpasses all comprehension and expression. We once dragged you away from your desk to bring you there, but I almost died when I saw that the stuffiness of the enclosed air so impeded your breathing that you emerged panting and perspiring, almost lifeless. However, when you come back, I have for you some great and very noteworthy items.

I think that you shall have King Frederick as a most zealous devotee. By the exceptional and royal gifts which he has bestowed on you, much to the amazement of Naples, he had indicated that your friendship will not bring him any less glory than it will you. He understands the man you are, and the high esteem in which you have been held for a long time now by peoples, states, leaders, and indeed by all of Italy: this age has seen no greater example of refinement, of elegance, of strength.

You spoke of relinquishing your office of general. Amidst all that you have done I see much that is distinguished, but in truth there could be nothing more outstanding than this. Pittacus did so, as did Solon, and many others; none however did so as honorably as you, for in a private capacity you will be able to do more than other men when in office. Indeed, I know that the taking on of this office deprived you of a great deal, more perhaps than its renunciation will restore. When you had power you were considered great, but now that it has been removed your status will surely be much reduced. Already I see myself speaking in our council, praising your greatness, relating your deeds, explaining how you arrived at your decision both to take on and to lay down your office, giving back the seal and renouncing the purple in your name; the fathers are astounded, and the whole senate begs that you do not do it, voices are heard among the common fold saying that the order is finished, that the times are unworthy of so great a man; they approach me and beg me to tell them if I think there is any way to make you change your mind. Finally, when I am steadfast in maintaining that there is no way I can persuade you, I see myself prophesying many other things, things which will bring glory both to God and to yourself: what every Christian desires shall come to pass, and they who have heard the eloquent speaker will also know the eloquent and wise writer, while those races whose remoteness or backwardness prevented them from enjoying the eloquence of the speaker will enjoy that of the writer. There shall be no reason why ages to come should envy us for having you — that arrow will fly on forever, faster than the wind, as if driven from a bow. You ask for faith as pure as glass; but if glass is not enough, accept, if you will, crystal, and this of the unadulterated and excellent kind. In our crystal there is no corrosion, no roughness, no dark cloudiness, no hairy streaks, no knottiness. It is crystal such as not even Nero broke before his death.

You have therefore your crystal which I send you like morsels, not hard but more malleable than wax. This is what is spoken of in the Psalm (147:17), in Ecclesiasticus (43:22), in Ezekiel (1:22), and in the book of Revelation (4:6; 21:11; 22:1), where I think we are shown much of the purest and most constant faith. However, your goodness prevents me from doing other than wishing what you wish and what is in the interests of your greatness. My own work on Plato will be done when and such as God permits. I choose Plato for no other reason than that he departs from God less than any other philosopher has seemed to do, a fact that not even our Augustine, the most learned of all learned men, was able to ignore.

My wish is for your health. Your friend Serafino of Cremona wrote to me saying that you were well. I beg you to make every effort to preserve this condition, for your good health is of great importance for Christianity.

Lettere Familiari I, 98–100   (From the banks of the Lago d'Averno, late 1498)

5. *To an unidentified young friend*

Greetings. My assistant on his return has told me that all is well with our ladies, and this has given me enormous pleasure. Over and over again I wish that with you too things are going well, so much so that this is an increasing source of joy and hope as the days go by. You, my son, have indeed an incentive to great virtue in the example of your home. For your father's virtue as well as the extreme care he took with your education had the result that there was no one who would not guarantee that you would grow to be a most learned as well as a virtuous man. Come then, young man of great hope, and with all zeal, and effort, and diligence, see to it that now as a man you realize your promise as a boy. Expectation is certainly a dangerous matter, most difficult to live up to and equally shameful not to. It would be regarded as a breach of trust on your part if you applied yourself to anything else but the study of literature.

Work hard at those studies, then, and love them; be in love with them and greedy for them, so that nothing can draw you away from them. You should realize too that there is no more grievous loss than the loss of time: for while this is so at every age, yet it is much more truly so in the flower of youth in which you now are when, as it were, the time for planting is pressing on, and if it slips past the noble seeds may not be sown in the furrows. There will be no hope of a harvest if cockle, or wild oats, or burrs spring up, resulting in hunger in the home, and ridicule from others. For there is nothing more wretched than the farmer who has a great reputation for plowing and sowing, and yet reaps no harvest and produces nothing.

Your interest in the lyre and the cithara does not please me very much: that kind of study of popular music (I mean for the Latins, not for the Greeks who are somewhat soft) always entails a waste of time and a loss of reputation. Alcibiades preferred to be regarded by the Greeks as somewhat ignorant rather than put his hand to a musical instrument. Do not, therefore, persuade yourself that as someone who for many years now has been teaching all over Italy, the educator of cities, of princes and of kings, not alone the professor of the Augustinian Order but also, by God's will, their leader, I will allow lyre-players to live under the same roof as I do. Change your mind now, my son, and take heed of the words of Aristotle in his *Politics* and of Plato in his *Republic*, that there is no sweeter harmony than when there is accord between a well instructed mind and a pleasant disposition and way of life, and when the highly educated mind under the rule of reason can moderate the conduct of one's life.

I speak to you freely and I shall never do otherwise. For as you are very dear to me, so I would wish you to be worthy of the highest esteem, and then you will become all the more dear to me the more I see you detach yourself from anything blameworthy. And I wish that there is no one to whom you are not equally dear as you are to me.

I am sorry that at present there is a huge number of my own community here every day, and the house can scarcely hold us; but if you cannot come to us, there is nothing that will prevent us from going to you.

Farewell, most sweet son, and take care that you fulfill the great expectations that all have of you.

(Cimino, 9 July 1507)

Letters as Augustinian General, 141-143

6. To Serafino

When the letter I received had made it clear that I had to go into the woods and make my way speedily into the mountains, I had begun to make preparations for the journey, and since in the course of it I saw the Virgin, I believed that she would accompany me on my way, and rejoiced to have such a leader. Today I now see that she has finished her entire journey and arrived at her intended destination. For this reason I must find another companion. You promised that I would have news of everything in four days, but now eight have passed. For the sake of our friendship, send someone immediately to tell me what has taken place and what you have decided we must do. I know that our affairs and our comfort are of great concern to you. That good young fellow is for the most part providing for our needs.

(Isola Martana, 9 July 1504)

Lettere Familiari I, 233

7. To Serafino

Last summer the whole of France, the Romagna, and the Veneto made me out to be dead and mourned my death. When I was back again conducting the December ceremonies at Ferrara and fulminating against vice and immorality in the presence of the people and princes, Rome had it that I was dead once more and the people of Venice were informed by my father and lord, the bishop of Caiazzo, that I had died of poison. Indeed I could have been quite frightened, if Christian philosophy had not persuaded me that death is a good thing, and that there is nothing more completely removed from evil things than the death of the saints, or, to express it more truly and more properly, of the servants of God. For it very swiftly rescues us from the toils, the hatred, the envy, and the disloyalty of men, and sets us down in a place of safety; and it promises us the joy of the happy life such as in this miserable life here we cannot even guess at. Though most unworthy, I received by God's generosity a very favorable omen: a sure pledge was given me of that journey to the stars which only death may grant us. Would that death would carry me off tomorrow, or at this very moment as I write, or in the night that follows, or when the sun sets today, or even today at midday, or at this very hour. Let death, I say, carry me off, and take away my senses and every evil, promising me in return everything that is good. Why do I drag my limbs on any longer into these dying hours? Why do I add sin to sin? Why do I hold myself in check amidst the weapons of malicious enemies? There is no fight without blood, no struggle without slaughter. Rare are those who do not fight to the death or at least fall severely wounded. Oh how happy indeed, in the first place, is the man who with all the members of his body intact, that is with the powers of his mind untainted, goes in beauty to the beautiful. Again happy too the man who though stained a little can easily purify himself from sin and leave his bondage, like a captive who has been washed and anointed.

Finally, I shall recommend all that is good, and, roused to undertake my journey by the voices of all, shall consider myself the disdain of the Syrian, who rules all things by his power. Your goodness and charity will be able to temper the situation, and I ask you not to allow anything to be done there if not in a holy and honorable manner. The Venetians received me with great applause, since they had feared the attempt at Ferrara to hold on to me. If you give any money to our Syrians, I promise to make full and immediate repayment.

Farewell, and remember your friend (as I hope you do), especially when you offer Mass.

Lettere Familiari I, 256-257   (Venice, 15 January 1505)

8. To Serafino

Even if your kindness toward us was very great and the mules remained with us for several days, nonetheless everything went against us and prevented them from doing much to assist us: two feast days, a scarcity of bricks, a scarcity of nets, and the fact that work is little pleasing to men. Still they brought along as many bricks as were found — they would have carried more if there had been more — and some planks, and did some other things of use to this little place. I send them back so that the driver may do there whatever must be done, hoping that if I send them back readily and without delay you may likewise be ready to let us have them for two or three days next week.

Otherwise I wish you health and blessing, and if there is anything you want me to do, just give the order and I shall be most willing to carry it out. My witness shall be my whole life, and I shall only be able to forget you when the weak vessel of this body is destroyed: here my little soul sleeps in unwelcome exile, *my residence is prolonged* and *I dwell with the inhabitants of Cedar* (Ps 119:5). I do not know whether I will be able to forget you even then, when we are led into the tabernacles of the Lord and behold in wonder the camp of the Lord, *the tents of Israel* (Ex 19:2) and the *curtains of Solomon* (Sg 1:4).

But even if I am not grateful to you (something you may never expect), God cannot but be grateful: those works of yours are full of splendor and light.

That church of the Holy Trinity at Viterbo, believe me, will not collapse tomorrow, for it has been restored and enlarged and brightened up through your careful efforts, that place of prayer where you sing praise to God, with the painted arches, the shining ceiling and white walls, the magnificent altar, the forecourt and vaulting all refurbished, the open space in front of the entrance fenced in and planted, and covered walks erected here and there in the gardens. And not to mention everything (for not everything can easily be mentioned), the two best monuments to your own excellence: within the monastery you have restored good conduct, and holiness of life has been re-established by your word and example; outside it is acknowledged by the City and Republic of Viterbo that, while you are among them, as they say, they have no fear of any adversity. On the contrary, they are so attached to you, and have such regard for you, and care for you so much that they not merely believe, but even declare, that you are filled with some divine power. All these things, I say, are so splendid and magnificent and illustrious that they will survive the corruption of every age, and though they render all men silent, yet these achievements will forever speak of you.

As to myself, if ever you do not have my aid, consider me, indeed call me, most ungrateful. However, I shall not omit to mention that of all mortals you are the dearest to me, and to hope that I shall be similarly dear to you after these few days.

Lettere Familiari I, 270-271   (Cimino, 15 July 1505)

9. To Serafino

You write to say that you want to be among your own people before taking yourself off elsewhere. You are a person unmatched by any in honesty and prudence, since through your outstanding achievements everywhere, but especially in Siena, you have placed us more greatly in your debt than either I myself or the Order should ever be to anyone. On that account, in order that the blessing which God has bestowed on you alone may be shared by many, and that you may also preach the gospel to other nations, you may, therefore, go wherever you wish, but you should go with such a disposition that what you have accomplished there you will do also in other places where you will find circumstances far less difficult and far more favorable. I long to see you! Meanwhile you may leave Master John Benedictus to deputize for you, unless you have other views on the matter.

For it is my wish that a pearl of great price, that is your *lamp*, should not *be hidden under a bushel* (Mt 5:15; Mk 4:21), and that Augustine's "whole house should be filled with the odor of the ointment" with which that city has been filled by you, as I believe; and this opinion has come to me from all far and wide, including our dear Jerome Ptolemy who is so very dear to me precisely because you are very dear to him. Farewell.

Lettere Familiari II, 138   (Rome, 21 April 1509)

10. Giles to Mannio Capenati

Will you never cease your complaints that I do not write to you, to Mario, to Botonti, to Almadiani and even, if it were possible, to your children? I would ask you to listen to me, Nicholas my friend.

When I was eighteen I entered the Augustinian Order, and was ordained to the priesthood. I then read for a year at Amelia, directed by Hippolyto Crucigerula. In the following year I went to Padua, and studied hard to understand, as best I could, what Aristotle and other wise men thought about our mortal life, about divine things, and finally about the soul itself.

Thereafter I sailed to Adria and spent two years reading in Istria, poring over Plato night and day with the help of a famous man, Domitio Gavardo. I was recalled to Rome by the Cardinal of Saint George and Friar Mariano, and there I expounded and defended the whole of Plato to the best of my ability. I gained my degree and was then sent to Florence to teach dogmatic theology.

Soon I was recalled to Rome to speak before Pope Alexander, and having done this with some clarity I was forbidden to leave. Mariano, who at that time governed the Order, chose me as his associate, making me lavish promises, but uttering dire threats against me should I refuse. Very reluctantly I obeyed. Another oration had to be delivered before the pope, and shortly afterward we made for Naples. There Mariano died; I escaped death, but had lost the zest for life. Close to death as I was, many things became clear to me, and I resolved to forget human affairs entirely and renounce everything except God. He himself is my witness how I did this, and with what holy and devout intention.

Then I was sent to Apulia by King Frederick, by whom I have always been more highly esteemed than one mortal man should be by another. I was recalled to Rome, preached the gospel at Siena and in Etruria, and came back to Rome. From there I went to admonish the people of Florence, Bologna, and Ferrara; I put the fear of God into them and exhorted them as the situation required. I then made my way to Venice, where I tried by my warnings to set the people on another road to the same God; they coerced me into promising my services for the following year.

I went to live on an island in the Lago di Bolsena, but papal letters once more dragged me away from there and back to Rome. I tackled the business of spreading the gospel to Rome, and once this was finished returned to my island. Under strong pressure from the letters, protests, and threats of my friends, however, I was forced to emerge, willy-nilly. I came away so that I might not seem either to resist my friends too much or to listen to them too little, but I shed many tears over this departure.

I came to Cimino, to the church granted by the Cardinal of Saint George at the instance of Almadiani and his family, Zoccoli, Botonti, and all my friends. Yet even here I found but a very unsafe refuge, for there is never a village, never a rural estate, where I am not needed to preach.

Look at all my wanderings; see how I have to be running around; consider the endless vexations of my journeys. If I, then, can for so long endure to go without the peace I crave, surely you and my other friends can endure to go without my letters?

I have thought it best to tell you this whole tale, in the hope of somehow cooling the ardor of your demands. Farewell then, and grant me just a little breathing-space amid all my troubles and hardship.

Lettere Familiari I, 234-236   (Cimino, August 1504)

11. To Gabriel of Venice

Greetings. I had no letters from you in Rome; I wonder whether to expect them in the heel of Italy.

We have seen Cori, Terracina, Sessa, and Capua. We toured Naples, and the strongholds which even now remember barbarian ferocity; or, I should perhaps more truly say, we wept over them. If you saw the countryside between Gaeta and Naples you would think that the rest of

Italy and of the world had often been left to run wild, and yet the Sardinians think the whole coastline dull. To sum up my own impressions I would say that this whole region is a fair garden, wonderfully cultivated, full of marvelous fragrances, and glowing with golden fruit.

If you love me, write and tell me how things have been with you, and whether Deodatus still soothes everyone with his lute or flute or pipe. He shows signs of having forgotten us, but I have not forgotten him. I should be writing to him, but will do so at another time more fully.

In earlier years I was uplifted to heaven; but now, condemned for some offense unknown to me, I am thrust down to hell. I go in daily terror of the Sibyl's cave, the Acherusian lake, and Charon's boat. Yet there awaits us a happier destiny, that mystery of which the same Cumaean Sibyl prophesied; let us continually prostrate ourselves in adoration before it. Farewell.

Lettere Familiari I, 97   (Lake Pozzuoli, 21 May 1498)

12. To Giovanni Botonti

In a way typical of your conscientious piety you made out your case with great labor and zeal when you urged us not to disdain our monastery at Viterbo, but rather to seek out holy men from every quarter and bring them there like a new swarm to colonize the house, so that they may restore and care for it, and build up the community. You declared that love for our own native province and kindred ought to move us, and that we owe this service to the age-old kindness of our Lady, who long ago defended the city against the darkness of Deucalion and long-lasting night. You further asserted that the desires and feelings of the citizens and of nearly all good men demand this, and that they frequently threaten those who falsely claim the title of religious, for they long to see the place occupied by men worthy of it. Moreover you stated that you personally attach the utmost importance to your request, and that if we are in any way indebted to your faithfulness, your goodwill, and your service, we ought to grant it out of love for you.

Well then, I have yielded to your persuasion, and I have turned my eyes toward the tutelary gods of my homeland. The whole matter is to be arranged without delay, but on this condition: that he who blew the trumpet to signal the advance will himself lead with spear and sword in the battle.

Yes, you have played a major role in the consultations and decisions, and you must be in charge of implementing them and making a success of the enterprise. Listen, then, to what I have settled, relying on you.

With Serafino beside me I discussed the matter with the Leccetans. They put pressure on the senate, and eventually all the senators came to promulgate their decrees with great joy, although they declared that they would take no action unless I am present myself when the work of building begins. They also entrusted the province to Serafino as consul-designate, and so strong was the consensus in his favor on the part of both old men and young that the consul's very name seemed a pledge of victory.

It now remains for you to prepare everything that will be needed for the campaign, including an authorization from the Holy Father, such as, for instance, we are writing to the Lord Antonio Zoccoli, gently encouraging the city fathers to make progress, and attempting to arouse in the citizens a willingness to help with resources.

We are awaiting a papal brief as a matter of urgency, however, lest an enemy sow tares and ruin the crop even as it begins to show.

Farewell to you in the Lord. Be sure to let us know what you decide and what you achieve in all these matters.

Lettere Familiari I, 155-156   (Siena, 7 May 1502)

13. To Master Jerome of Genazzano

You have already reached home, I hear, and are fully prepared to apply yourself to the serious pursuit of good and holy studies. This news brought me no little satisfaction and pleasure, and I cannot tell which gives me more gratification of spirit — your love for me or your own spirited determination to help our Order. This is because I particularly hoped that it would be through your efforts that the intellectual attitude of the Academy of Naples would be eradicated and banished, for it gives rise not only to all stupidity but to the din of falsehood and every evil as well. Naples, called after Parthenope, was born to leisure; but the greater the leisure, the more ardently studies ought also to be cultivated: they ought and they must, and such has been my hope.

Make it your business, then, to see that the young devote themselves to dialectic, the middle students to philosophy, and the seniors to theology; that they work with care, diligence, and dedication; and, incidentally, that the teachings of Giles are adhered to, read, and defended. If we neglect him, we could be failing the Order.

Farewell now. It is right for you and your companions to enjoy that quiet leisure, for although Campania usually resounds with the clash of arms, at the present time, as I see it, only Campania is at peace, while all the rest of Italy is staggering. News reached Rome that on 14 May 80,000 Venetians were slain by the French at the River Adda, and in that slaughter the courage, strength, and flower of all Italy perished. The reaction to this in Rome was mixed: in some quarters the city gave open signs of joy beyond belief, in others it was smitten with incredible fear. No hope is left for Italy except the goodness of Almighty God and the saving, unconquered strength of Prosper Colonna. In my name, commend ruined Italy to him again and yet again; tell him that we need the support of God, who cannot fail us, and of Camillus, whom he can send us. The salvation of all Italy depends on it.

Letters as Augustinian General, 209-210   (Rome, 20 May 1509)

14. To Gabriel of Venice

Reading about the activities of the enemies of the faith has brought tears to my eyes, for they seem as eager for victory as we are sluggish about our affairs and about winning.

I have been to the Pope and set forth the matter. I gave him a full and detailed account and made it clear how easily he could be the champion of the Christian cause. He was extremely concerned, but the situation is difficult. He referred us to Germanus and showed the strength of the case against Christ's enemies; he did his best to prevent his coming to Italy, especially at this time when he realizes that such an arrival could have unfortunate consequences. Germanus replied that he has friendly relations with Sophis, and knows his way of life and how easily he could accept our law, although he differs from us in some small degree. Moreover he was born of a Christian mother, Germanus says. To the request that he cancel his visit to Italy he made no response.

Nonetheless the Pope promises to do all he can to persuade him to cease his activities; I know he is keeping this promise and so do all in Rome. There is great anxiety in all minds lest, if he be victorious, everything may yield to him. Whatever happens, I will write. I am sorry not to be giving you more hopeful news. I long for nothing more earnestly in this life than to be of service to those in whose debt I stand: you are in the best position to know this.

Signorelli, *Egidio,* 245

15. To Stephen of Genazzano

Your letters have reached me. They deal constantly with the same topics, and I resolved to comply with your wishes as duty bids me, though desire no less. I have been sent to Germany, and the only thing I can do is write to you, and to him who is your appointed companion, urging you to use your judgment and assuring you that I will confirm by any letters that may be required whatever course you decide to take.

Now, however, as I prepare to return to Italy my first thought is to send this letter to you, my most beloved father, and to greet you before anyone else, as is my bounden duty. The war is now reaching its climax: may God look mercifully upon his Church, and may you ask prayers for the Church and for us. The end must come within a few days — or if not the very end, at least the beginning of the end. Then a fuller hearing and more accurate adjudication of your case will be opportune.

As we begin the new year after Easter, according to custom, I hope that you will begin with yet more strenuous effort to carry out the reform in the common life, in the office, in the observance of silence and enclosure, and in the rule about not entering one another's cells; apply it to journeys outside, to unauthorized customs and conversations, to clothing and a more appropriate type of footwear, and to any other matters which we believe need to be dealt with by your prudence and integrity. I pray, beg, and entreat you to exert yourself wholeheartedly in this task, devoting to it all your attention and understanding. If, as I hope, you will do this, then although many people are dear to me, none shall be as dear as my one and only father, M. Stephen. Your tears will never fade from my mind or my remembrance, for they are clear signs and proofs of your tender love for me.

Signorelli, *Egidio*, 246   (Verona, 22 March 1516)

Official Letters

16. *To His Holiness, Pope Leo X*

Both the age and circumstances demand, most holy Father, that the gift I send you should be no other than an olive branch. For a time dedicated to the olive branch is at hand and nothing else is to be seen throughout the city and the world than olive branches being borne aloft. That the oil of the olive is the most appropriate symbol of the high priest, as being by far the closest of all to the divine light, is indicated in this testimony from Leviticus which says: *This is the anointing of Aaron*. Indeed for that reason also it was the custom for kings to be consecrated with olive oil: *With holy oil I have anointed him*, God says in the psalm; and to the Messiah, his Son who was both the greatest king and high priest, it was said: *God, your God, has anointed you*. There lies concealed in the writings of the Hebrews a hidden reason for the anointing which deserves to be sought by all, and especially by the one who without reliance on force, or guile, or bribery, but because he is endowed with honesty, learning, innocence, and piety above all other mortals, is called, as it were, Aaron. Add to this the fact that when they were to make some statement that was important, or holy, or sure, or especially sacred, the ancients regarded it as impossible to do so suitably without the use of the olive. Homer, most learned in secret things, would not have the steadfast and sacred bed of Penelope, a future witness to her chastity, made of anything else but olive wood. Though the raven did not come back, the dove bearing an olive branch was received back by Noah, the priest of the sacrifice. In the book of Judges, the wretched blessing of dominion, which the trees offered to an olive tree because it gives light to both gods and men, is dismissed and rejected. When God was to ride in triumph into his own city he was supported by the people waving branches of this tree. And if some monstrous giant or cyclops should ever make an assault on your heaven-sent authority, his eye must be pierced by the trunk of an olive tree like that of Polyphemus, and Minerva, disregarding vexations, has taught us that a wise man should be presented to the Phaeacians only between two olive branches.

So for these reasons I send you olive branches that you should realize that you have succeeded Julius, as Numa warring Romulus, to restore peace in these blessed times and cultivate the sacred rites in happy ease, fostering the higher arts with wisdom and liberality, in which you are most godlike. You should strive from now on to give back the peace of Numa to your people, to restore the sacred ceremonies to the churches, and to rescue from darkness the disciplines which offer themselves to you alone, so that you may rightly be believed and acclaimed as given by Almighty God to mortals to help them in their human affairs, and alone of all the pontiffs you may be represented with branches of the illustrious olive, bearing the sacred symbols, knowing that you have in mind those kingdoms which, unless you wish it, no force of arms or no attack may overthrow. The divine gift of the olive, of which Theophrastus writes: it is by far the most long-lived and enduring of plants.

Yours. . .   (Rome, 19 March 1513)

Lettere Familiari II, 175-177

17. To the Emperor Maximilian

To His Most Serene Highness Maximilian, Roman Emperor

The whole Church and all faithful Christians regard your sovereign majesty as an excellent and very powerful bulwark against the enemies of religion; it follows, then, that they cannot fail to place their chief reliance upon your favor and good will. My own Augustinian Order in particular promises itself such benefits from your Highness as may confidently be expected from a monarch so firmly devoted to Saint Augustine. It is encouraged in this persuasion partly by the eminently religious attitude of your Highness, and partly by the incredible benevolence shown to our Order by your ever-revered father of blessed memory. My fathers reverenced your father with the utmost loyalty, and we today reverence you, his son, with no less loyalty but even greater hope, for we believe that we already see your invincible forces about to win rich booty from the conquered enemy of Christ. I hope later to explain more fully our grounds for this prediction and our certainty in it, when I kiss your sacred and victorious hands.

For the present I am sending Reverend Father James Baptist of Ravenna, a man known to your Majesty and a beloved son to me. I have entrusted him with the task of promulgating and circulating the indulgences granted to our Order. With the greatest humility I therefore commend him and his office to your Majesty; and I give, surrender, and dedicate to you my entire Order, together with myself who hold high hopes of your victories.

Lettere Familiari II, 8-9   (Venice, 24 January 1507)

18. To His Eminence the Cardinal of Saint George, our protector

Most Reverend Father in Christ and Most Reverend Lord.

The fathers in Paris made many requests of me. Some I granted, though perhaps not altogether rightly, for the prior, who has been in charge of that house for many years, is responsible for dire losses to the Order both in matters of scholarship and in observance of the rules. In earlier days our young men would be sent there, and a stream of thoroughly learned men would flow from that house, as from a Trojan horse or from the best schools of Athens. Yet nowadays hardly anyone is sent there; or, if anyone is sent, either they do not admit him, or after admitting him they force him to leave. When that monastery was well governed, no religious order surpassed us in sacred studies; but when we fall into the power of tyrants with a thirst that not even the sea can quench, swimmers are scarce. Where scholars in every kind of discipline formerly flourished, hardly one, alas, can be found today. Moreover we had about forty very learned doctors who wrote books on sacred subjects, every one of whom was educated at the Paris University. It is obvious that the ruin of that monastery has brought ruin on the whole Order.

Send letters, I beg you, to deal with this situation. The prior's name is Peter Girardi. The letters would need to point out two things: they must be instructed to reform their observance and way of life in accordance with the norms laid down by the fathers in the chapter definitions, as the senate and people of our Augustinian Order decreed in the assembly at Naples; and they must pay heed to the reception and training of young men of ability, for unless this is done, the Order will need to be concerned for the salvation of its members, and be hard put to prevent great harm befalling both that monastery and the Order as a whole. Finally, they must make strenuous efforts to amend their lives and improve their studies. They must be told that this is the wish of the Holy Father and of your Eminence, and that you will spare no pains to ensure that these instructions are complied with.

To turn now to other matters, I take this opportunity to thank you for granting a letter of recommendation to my kinsman, which will, I hope, be of considerable assistance to him as he seeks to keep his cargo ship out of the hands of pirates. I wish to mention also the letter sent to our Assessor. While dealing with the case in hand he submitted to the letter, accepted the senate's decision, came to me joyfully and informed me that you, excellent prince, most zealous for every virtue as you are, had with some warmth given your support to Friar Juliano. The senate would have concurred, and even eagerly concurred, with this judgment, had they not murmured somewhat about a small house; but the question can easily be settled. I would thank you, did I not hope that you would thank me, since indeed I am confident that he is a man who, more than any others who now speak publicly, will satisfy your most exacting standards. I wish I could say this more readily of the Augustinians. There is indeed nothing which should more readily be said, for if the mind is nourished by searching for truth, and happy when it discovers the true causes of events (as a writer says, "Happy is the person who has succeeded in recognizing the causes of things") then speech, which is the tool of reason, which explains and lays bare before its hearers the inner secrets of the mind, fails in the very duty for which it was created if it falls away from rational truth.

All goes well at Rome apart from the movements of their eminences the cardinals: some of these are close to death, others have even advanced to meet it, others again take measures to save their lives, while others are incapable even of this; many do not dare to return. And — good heavens! — there are people who envy them! What star will be deemed so inauspicious by the astrologers, that the scattered fathers will be reckoned under its influence?

I trust that through the wisdom and kindness of His Holiness all these things will be settled, and that matters which seemed so difficult at the beginning will have an easier outcome, or at any rate a more profitable one.

Finally, since the business of brethren who forsake the Order and the habit is growing daily more urgent and causing me immense distress, I need an audience with His Holiness as soon as possible. I would therefore think it best that the Order should be commended by your letters to one of the cardinals, so that in your absence we could rely on his attention, especially in these matters where the Order is seriously imperiled.

Farewell. May Almighty God preserve your Eminence unharmed for my sake and that of the Church, and, as we hope, increase his favor toward you.

Letters as Augustinian General, 168-170   (Rome, 8 September 1507)

19. To His Eminence the Cardinal of Saint George, our protector

It is necessary for me to have frequent recourse to you, Your Eminence, because a variety of problems arises daily in the Order. I hear that a certain Brother Germanus has solicited letters whereby he is seeking to get a prior appointed by you in a certain monastery, contrary to the decision of the Order. Although your attitude is very well known to me from long acquaintance, I have nonetheless deemed it expedient to write and tell you that the man in question is considered unsuitable not merely for this office but for religious life itself. His villainies have led to his condemnation and expulsion by his congregation. I want you to know what kind of man he is, in case anything is written to you in support of his claim. In my view it is sufficient for a noble ruler to know his own people. I can no longer endure my longing to see you. May Your Eminence enjoy good health. I hope to watch your right hand planting tall trees one day.

(Rome, 18 September 1507)

20. A Letter from Pope Leo X to Giles of Viterbo, Cardinal Legate

To Giles, Cardinal Legate

Beloved son, we think it better that Your Eminence should guess, rather than that we ourselves should describe in writing, the joy and gladness which uplifted our spirit when we received Your Eminence's letter. Our joy was occasioned by the unique and outstanding faith, industry, and diligence wherewith you have served God and ourselves, and enhanced your own virtue. With no slight pleasure — indeed with a pleasure that can scarcely be conveyed in a letter — we marked the result of your hard work, as we learned of the magnificent and noble decree of the Catholic King and of his valiant nation, issued for the defense and safeguarding of Christendom. This decree serves as a basis for our own actions, and by it the saving of our religion seems almost assured. We have therefore thanked God, and continue to thank him, that through your cooperation he has opened a passage into harbor for our holy and wholesome plans and exhortations, which not long ago seemed to be tossed to and fro by the waves.

With all our heart we promise and assure Your Eminence that we have amply and abundantly found in you all that we had a right to expect from a most prudent person, a man of great learning and integrity, a most distinguished legate of this Holy See and a highly deserving Cardinal of the Roman Church. The hope we had earlier placed in you has proved in no way deceptive. We were aware of your talents and efficiency; yet we should first and foremost render to God praise and glory for the fact that they have been able to accomplish so much, for without him all our efforts would be absolutely useless.

Now that we have formed brave and noble plans, beloved son, it remains for us to work steadily and with due care to insure that they are translated into deeds, such deeds as have been determined with burning zeal by the great King of France, and by the devoutly loyal and unconquered leaders of Spain and Belgium. They have issued orders concerning the equipping of fleets and the mustering of armies, so that their forces may be ready for action. These measures are of the highest importance, both for the safety of Christian people and as a terrifying signal to the enemy. The savage Turks must understand that our kings do not lack stomach for the cause, as they perhaps suppose, but that Turkish ferocity and greed confront mighty opposing forces, and in particular those of the Catholic King. His ancestors fought the infidels and championed the cause of Christ, and although the present king is but on the threshold of his maturity, he strives not merely to emulate the exploits of his forbears but to outstrip them. We pray that God may look favorably on his excellent intention and resolve; and we hope that the king will vindicate his family name, the distinction of his rank and his nobility of soul by some illustrious and memorable victory. We trust that this will happen; indeed, we prophesy that it will, in virtue of our own burning desire for the salvation of Christendom and for his glory and honor.

Your Eminence will learn from the letter of our beloved son Julius what matters remain for you to deal with, and how earnestly we are urging all kings and princes to join an alliance of such fame and high renown. Your Eminence can trust this letter.

Rome, 12 December 1518, the sixth of our pontificate

See Signorelli, *Egidio*, 252-253

Augustinian Order Letters

21. *To the whole Order*

Thus far we have toiled for four years. For when the supreme pontiff Julius II passed away and Leo X became pope, of all mortals the mildest, most humane, most merciful, the hope was enkindled in the most reverend lord prelates of falling upon the religious orders and depriving them of their privileges. This they had for a long time wished to do with all their hearts, and though Julius had stubbornly prevented them, the gentleness and mildness of Leo was an invitation to them to do so.

The assignment was given by the Orders to the very reverend lord General of the Order of Preachers, a man of exceptional learning and authority, and to me as well. For these four years by day and night we have pursued cardinal protectors, cardinals, bishops, ambassadors of kings and princes, and finally the Pope himself, but especially the three commissioners of the Holy See; we have defended our position and, as far as was permitted, we have protected it. The Council's wish was to do away with everything that they alleged had been wrested from the popes by us by means of circumvention, deceit, fraud, importunity, or force. They said that episcopal dignity had not only been damaged but indeed had been dishonored, shattered, and almost overthrown. Therefore, as we pointed out in the chapter of Rimini, so as not to criticize everything, as they reiterated, they formulated eighty articles by which they strove to whittle away at our privileges. For example: concerning the paying of a quarter of all goods, confessions, burials, preaching, the administration of justice — if we ourselves did not act within the course of a month we would pass into the jurisdiction of the bishops — and other such things.

I wrote about this crisis to the whole Order, so that in the danger that beset us all we would be supported by the assent and the prayers of all. They were demanding these eighty points and left us all to our own counsels. The Pope ordered us to concede some of the points, reporting that they would not agree to terminating the Council unless, as they wished, they could remove some of our privileges. When it was not given to us to retain them all, we tried our best to keep those which seemed, as it were, of special importance and essential to the Order. The most reverend Father General of the Order of Preachers was of great assistance, constantly adducing many scholarly and impressive arguments. I compared the Order to a city under siege, which has two basic needs, provisions to sustain life inside the walls, and defensive fortifications outside; each of these is necessary for the city, the one to protect it from hunger, the other from the enemy, either of them alone scarcely offering safety; for if one is missing it will perish. What use are city walls if one dies of starvation? What use are food supplies, if the enemy lays it waste? So it is, I said, with a religious order: within we are sustained by alms; outside we are defended by legal control; one will perish if we are deprived of a quarter, the other will collapse if our business is to be settled by the judgment of prelates. And accordingly we would undergo every kind of torture rather than allow ourselves to be damaged on these two counts.

With the help of your prayers, therefore, and by our own efforts we prevailed upon our most holy and clement lord Leo X to leave them untouched, and certain other concessions were made to the bishops which do not in any way affect the life of the brethren. The largest concession made was concerning the religious sisters whom they wanted to be subject to the ordinaries. After our protestations the final outcome was that this should not hold for those who lived in community but only for those who lived in their own homes. The other orders acquiesced, and I alone obtained permission to extend the privileges of the communities to even the private virgins — this was in the previous summer. Last summer I asked that widows too should be included. Concerning married people no discussion was allowed.

This is what has been accomplished so far, which we think should be indicated to you so that you may know what has been secured through your prayers. And we certainly never hoped for this beforehand. Now give thanks to God who guards us, and pray for our most holy Lord who has left nothing undone on our behalf, and with greatest reverence pay attention to the reverend prelates, for this is required by their position as well as by our own situation, and indeed because to a great extent our safety depends on it. I have described the purpose of our cross on which the Lord cried out to the Father: *Why have you forsaken me?* (Mk 15:34). So also we have long seen ourselves abandoned by God because of our sins, when we were rejected, when we were subjected to abuse, and insults, and ignominy, when we were terrified by shouting and threats. As regards favors, our fathers *called out* to God *and were saved; they hoped in him and were not confounded.* Each of us was *a worm and not a man, open to* derision and *contempt, reproached by men and cast off by the people.* Presently they opened their mouths and perhaps *would have swallowed us up*; but *blessed is the Lord, who did not put us within reach of their teeth. The locust* has laid hold of *what the caterpillar left behind,* and delivered from one tempest we are caught up in another hurricane. And indeed since another trouble is approaching and there is no one to help us, I have thought it right to inform you fully about it.

The Council and those who hold all power of action with the the Pope have resolved to reorganize the mendicant orders, and have already begun to do so; already documents approving this have been signed and promulgated. They have begun with the Friars Minor, who seem to be more undisciplined and vulnerable, and they have been ordered to hold a meeting of the chapter this year, although they held one last year; and it is to be held not in one of their more undisciplined monasteries, but in one where there has been reform, so that by their good advice, effort, and endeavors that whole order may be united in a uniformity of life and conduct: the acceptance of young boys, the possession of money, and laxity are to be eliminated, and the *Rule* is to be rigorously introduced. The prior general has gone from here to the monastery of Assisi, as if to the source, to direct the whole matter from there and confront the task of restoration and repair, believing that all that is in store for the order is great confusion, bringing with it much disruption, grief, and calamity. The general of the Order of Preachers is handing over to his people in Lombardy whatever monasteries he can, hoping by that procedure to escape from danger himself; and he states that none are more obedient to the order or more scholarly than those reformed members. As our own Lombards are not so, I do not know how we could contemplate such a procedure, for if we were to surrender our monasteries to strangers, we would see our fathers in perpetual banishment in their own homes.

There is still some time left to us to consider the problem even if it is a very short time indeed. Nevertheless while this interval remains, while this short while is given to us, while it is possible to form a plan, pray; give notice of your prayers and order all to pray unceasingly; and then gather all the fathers together and decide what needs to be done, before the time comes when there will be no opportunity for discussion or consideration, but only the necessity to obey and to submit. It has come to the point where either in deference to the decree of the Apostolic See our Order must be reorganized with great vehemence and clamor, as is happening now to the Friars Minor; or our monasteries must be handed over to reformed friars, as the Order of Preachers have surrendered theirs; or a third option is that we must organize ourselves and revert to the undiminished form of the *Rule*. That this will be most difficult to achieve, I fully realize.

I felt that I should write to my father superiors about these matters and draw your attention to them immediately, so that I can have your response and know what your desires are, and take measures in consultation with you in our common interest; and so that (even if I had to die for your sake) I should never be wanting in my duty to you; for the sake of your safety and peace I would give up not only everything else but even my very life, advanced as I am in years.

Gather all together; order prayers, intercessions, fasts. Then, trusting in God, take counsel with one another, summoning the wisest of the fathers of the province, and promptly write to me a report of what takes place. For the situation is at boiling point, so that whatever is to be done must combine speed and wisdom.

Full of tears I bid farewell to my beloved vine and wish it safety, lest *the wild boar* rush *out of the forest* (Ps 80:14) and destroy it; and lest, in the place where I see so many shoots springing up, instead of the expected grapes, the harvest be one of *wild grapes and thorns* (Is 5:2.4). No adversity is fearful to me, for my age is such that (if I survive) these troubles will be relieved by freedom from commitments; if I do not survive they will be relieved forever by my death. But either to see my fathers and children under attack or to leave them to the fight would be more painful, more grievous and more bitter to me not only than death but even more bitter than the cross.

I await your decisions and will accept your arrangements with the greatest possible attention, and whatever way you approve I will follow as far as is permissible. You yourselves, meanwhile, gather yourselves together; get your affairs in order and read over the laws carefully; establish a way of life for the community that is clearly in keeping with them, so that when the question arises as to sending outsiders to us and expelling us, you can reply that you have already put everything to rights; show yourselves ready for inspection, and place in a safe haven yourselves, your house, your household, your land and its produce.

Lettere Familiari II, 216-220   (Rome, 13 January 1517)

22. To his brethren in Lecceto

Giles the hermit greets the fathers in Lecceto.

Greetings to the assembly that was once my own most shining light. Troubled in spirit, shaken in mind, and almost demented, I am writing to you so that you, happy souls, may weep with me. My most bitter bitterness compels me to write. You must hear of the calamity that has befallen your friend Giles, and of his extreme affliction, and come to his aid with your pious prayers, so that my great bitterness may be in some way alleviated.

Realizing that there are three levels of good, of the body, of the mind, and of external things, I have long since persuaded myself, in my ignorance of the future, to offer these in sacrifice to the Lord; and all of these, in whatever small measure I possessed them, I would not bestow upon God — for what do I have which I did not receive? — but would return to him. And the more easily to achieve this, I held fast to the reins of my religious order. I had done very little: I went up to Carbonara; and that was not even enough: tearfully I made my way to the holy place of the ilex trees (Lecceto) to devote myself to that holy way of life among the groves. Everything was marvelously pleasant and captivated my mind in a wonderful way. But so that I would neither be far off from there nor caught up with human company, under the auspices of the holy ilex trees I restored the monastery of Viterbo. Having restored it, I went on up to the wooded retreat of Cimino where I had the hope that I would offer to God those three gifts in perpetuity.

As best I could, I surrendered my puny half-alive body, which could scarcely endure toil or hot weather, to its cross, to fasts, to vigils, and to acceptance, not indeed either as I would have wished or as I ought, but as far as the frailty of my weak senses allowed. In a much truer sense I also gave away material things, having no care for opulence, holding everything in common, lavishing on the brethren and the household whatever was brought there. I was not ashamed about the second cross, that of poverty, causing wonder among the guests that I did not fend off poverty, but only misery and indigence and hunger. I took up a third cross, not in common with the others but peculiar to myself, to clear my mind of every other preoccupation and base all my study and effort on investigating and meditating upon spiritual matters and the law of the Lord.

The first of these, I confess, I was scarcely able to pursue, for my own sin is always against me; but the other two I took so far, with God's help, that, as far as I know, I was second to none. But if I had in any way offended in the first two, I thought and hoped that I would compensate by the great effort of the third, which with incredible eagerness I determined to embrace, for it was not shared with others, but intrinsic to me, and personal, and my very own. This I espoused in a stable union and declared it mine, thinking that I would walk with the Lord, for he it was who said: *He who will come after me, let him take up his cross* (Mt 16:24). He did not say a shared cross, or another's, but *his* cross. Therefore I took up mine, intending to meditate on the law of the Lord by day and by night.

There still remain those hurried writings of mine which, while the wooded retreat still held me, increased wonderfully in volume, when I caught the missiles of the philosophers upon the shield of truth and set myself to thrusting and flinging them back upon the impious enemy. Whether I succeeded in doing so or not I do not know. This I do know: that very often I felt a wonderful pleasure when, though a mere man, I cast back the weapons, which seemed to be aimed at the cross of Christ, upon their originators, the monstrous enemies of the cross of Christ.

This kind of life was a delight to me: this alone seemed to be the best and happiest, for I had entered upon the best part which was not to be taken away even by death's reaping hook. I led a life of my own:

whenever occasion demanded it I would instruct the towns of Italy, so that I would not be completely free and, my time being my own, would not be devoid of all activity. The remainder of the year was spent in meditation: there was nothing that I wished for; I was not shaken or disturbed by any desire or any fear. Imprudently I compared my state to heaven; I believed that I had stamped out all human considerations, supposing that I had won an envious destiny and that there was no life on earth — I do not say better, for I was never quite that foolish — but none more tranquil, more restful, more free of care or more happy. But see how the Lord demonstrated how vain are the thoughts of men, and that man is not God but an exile in Egypt.

Take heed, beloved fathers, and realize that nothing is more mistaken and capricious than human fancy. That same Giles who recently seemed to himself to be happy, in his folly dreaded no adversity and boasted that he would not, under any condition, change his way of life, asserting that he was not inferior to any Attalus or to any Augustus. I have spoken of happiness: now I speak of disaster.

I was in the garden of the Cimino grotto, reciting one of the psalms, on 27 June, when the sun was already close to its Spanish dwelling. And, lo and behold, a junior brother, whom we had sent to the town a little earlier to buy food of some kind, came back very soon, in a lather of sweat from his rushing. When we asked him the reason, he announced the arrival of Anthony Zoccoli. Soon everyone was leaping for joy. We asked where he was and quickly went to meet him, greeted him, surrounded him, embraced him. We asked the reason for his sudden and unexpected arrival. For my mind already knew and had a foreboding of something bad and sinister, and my heart was beating fast. Secretly I prayed to God that things would turn out well and that my friend's arrival was a happy omen. He told us to be of good cheer and declared that he was the bearer of only friendly intentions. Besides he had wanted for a long time to come to us and to become familiar with the wooded retreat and visit the chapel, the shade, the springs, which he had so often heard me praise. In his company were Mannio Capenas and Jerome Augustinianus, the assistant to the archbishop of Durazzo. Although I suspected the ill-matched companions, nevertheless I trusted my friend who told me to have no such suspicion.

We spent that part of the day joyfully and a good part of the night; and although we were fasting for the vigil of the apostles, I ordered him to dine because he was exhausted by the great heat and the traveling. When the meal was over, he came into my cell; he called for a chair, and, when the door was closed, he said: "My dear Giles, you must bear this! Your friends could do no more." And with that he presented the pope's letter, committing to me the reins of government of the Order. Immediately I jumped up in a state of terror (I would not write this if I did not have witnesses) and the tears burst forth in a stream as never before. Stretched out on the ground, I called on God and men to witness as I cursed my lot, my words mingled with vehement groaning. These, I said, were the machinations of enemies who envy a carefree man his happiness and lie in wait for us with the lure of high office. I wept with broken sobbing; Anthony wept, already regretting his action. The whole community wept, for they had come running to the door. I declared then that I would rather undergo every suffering, that I would endure any misfortune, any fate, even the harshest, and that I would leave the realms of Christendom rather than enter upon this office.

Next I set forth the many reasons why it was impossible for me to undertake it: That as well as not being physically very strong, I was unfit for and unequal to such a great task; that the whole situation was too confused for me to retrieve it; that it presented a threat to my soul and my salvation; that I could not allow the work of thirty years to be wasted; that I was not going to cast away in one moment of insanity my reputation for public speaking which after so many years had spread over the length and breadth of Italy; that I was not unaware of my age, my inexperience, my ignorance, or my weakness; that the malice of many powerful enemies was not concealed from me. And when I had enumerated a great many other factors, our dear Zoccoli was greatly moved and so was Capenas. They seemed to show sympathy and began to beg me not to refuse them one thing: that was to go to Rome with them, for they had little doubt that for the reasons I had given I would be set free and would succeed in my appeal with the princes of the Church who were neither unreasonable nor inhuman.

I wanted to come to you. They replied that time was pressing for their return. The prior of Viterbo came to mind; I sent to him to come to us immediately. He came with all speed and was informed of the matter. He advised me to go to Rome and present my case, pleading that it was a difficult matter, and that when I had done all this, whatever might befall I should regard it as the work of God. Finally I felt compelled and hastened on my way. I met the Protector, and so many tears sprang up that I could not speak. When I was at liberty to draw my breath, I pleaded my case, mentioning the reasons that I have listed above and many others, and then prostrated myself on the ground as the bishop of Caiazzo arrived. Finally, although I had done and said and tested everything possible, it was all in vain. The Protector told me to depart with these concluding words: he enjoined me to bear it with equanimity and no longer to offer resistance to God and to the princes of the Church. He declared a little angrily that if I obstinately continued to hold my ground, everyone would say that never had anyone deceived people more than Giles, for he preached good conduct to others but wished to make no effort to do good himself. Or he would be called very ambitious in wanting to be superior not over his religious brethren but over the whole world. In that way I, unhappiest of all men, was obliged to be silent, and

I returned home. It was necessary to go to the Pope. He directed me to accept it all, and he would lighten my burden. For the first few days I wanted to die, as I wandered around Rome in the company of Ambrose of Naples, the theologian, whom I have as witness to my tears and mourning and my unhappy outpourings.

I have accepted the first cross and will make my body and my life available for these short days on earth, which I must not speak of (for I hope to merit an honorable discharge). I have accepted the second and will endure all exterior suffering and bear all calumny, infamy, all complaints and finally all conspiracy against me. Lastly, I will in every way bear the third cross, which is peculiarly my own, forsaking all mental and intellectual activity and will devote myself to the concerns of my brethren, a harsh and difficult matter indeed for me fostered, as I have been, among books. I have taken the hills of your Lecceto and planted on them those three crosses to appear before my eyes at all times as the three monuments of my unhappiness. Desire will be felt as a cross for the body; anger will experience the cross of patience, which will be very toilsome. The mind will be aware that it must accept the cross of abandoning its pursuits, and this especially wounds and hurts me. And because of those crosses I will constantly repeat, again and again: *My most bitter bitterness.* Bitterness will always torment my senses and my body and my appetites; *most bitter*, for I must tolerate anger, *mine*, for my mind is desolate and unhappy. I hope soon to talk to you and embrace you, and trust that from you I shall receive much comfort.

Martène and Durand, cols 1235-1238

23. To the brethren at Siena

We have suffered a great loss, an immense loss, in the death of our Master General Augustine, who on 26 June departed this life, or, as we should more truly believe, made his way to a life which is much better. The constant and unflagging integrity of his life gave promise of no outcome but this; for from his earliest youth, it is said, until his last days he lived with such fidelity and devotion that he could not but die a most holy death.

For our own part, then, we must sorely grieve at losing so great and valued a father; but for his sake we deem it right to rejoice. Even though, in the eyes of the foolish, holy men may seem to die, they are established in peace; and though by human reckoning death is always held to be harsh, yet, as we repeat daily, *the death of his saints is precious in the sight of the Lord.*

We would beg you, then, to follow him with your prayers, the office of the dead, and the solemn rites demanded by custom. Let no honorable or loving service be left undone in your suffrages for one who was a father to us all.

So far I have spoken of him, but now I turn to the consequences for ourselves. We judge it important to write in some detail to you on our situation and to hear of yours. Through no merit whatever of our own we, who lag so far behind our forbears, have been called to this weighty service; but we also believe that we must take heed that at least we incur no reproach for the way we carry it out. We must do all that has been thought proper to such high office by men who, if not holy or wise, were nonetheless careful and conscientious.

However, what is the use of the heavenly firmament unless it is moved by a higher cause, and in its turn finds earthly causes receptive to the motions it is to impart to them? We have taken the reins of government reluctantly, and would certainly relinquish them readily did we not hope for both divine grace and the help of your good will. We entreat you, therefore, as most beloved brethren, to see that we have no cause to rue our acceptance of the burden.

You will ensure this if you reform the conduct of our monasteries and of all our friars; for it was in this hope that the Holy Father and our Lord Protector summoned us, with this stipulation: that they entrusted to us the responsibility for the Order, that we should take every measure, employ every means, leave no approach untried, and even, if necessary, risk our own life to restore the ancient dignity of the Order and, insofar as it rests with us, recover the sacred beauty of our laws. Our task is to ensure that Saint Augustine's family shall diverge as little as possible from the rules Saint Augustine gave us.

Provincials, you are our fellow workers. Use the authority you have to see that a beginning is made in the reform and adjustment and good arrangement of all things, so that standards of behavior and the rule of religious life are observed through your help, industry, and zeal, insofar as your competence extends. We have touched only lightly on these matters, but we shall deal with them more fully when we learn that through your efforts the foundations of the holy building have been laid.

Our reverend Protector had decided that the general chapter was to be convened next year, at Pentecost, but he has as yet given no firm indication. The best thing therefore will be for you to choose a definitor, and hold yourselves in readiness in case he keeps to his original decision. We will let you know immediately when anything is settled about this.

Farewell in the Lord, and pray for us.

Lettere Familiari I, 329-330   (Viterbo, 15 July 1506)

24. *To the whole Order, concerning the forthcoming Chapter*

Our general chapter was celebrated last year, and too frequent a repetition of this event would probably be harmful; however, as circumstances alter it is necessary to change our plans and actions too. This is especially true in view of the fact that in his administration and government of public affairs it is of the greatest importance that the head and ruler of the whole Order should have been appointed and endowed with authority in a holy and lawful manner, by the consent of the fathers, according to custom. Since the head is the most important part of the body, it certainly deserves special care.

In accordance, therefore, with the wishes of His Holiness the Pope and our most reverend Protector the chapter will take place next year, at the solemn feast of Pentecost; and, God willing, it will be celebrated in the region of Etruria. You must, then, insure that the delegates who are to be sent, according to our laws, to record their votes and wishes, are prepared and ready. We are expecting you, and we will make every effort to see that you are lodged as comfortably as possible.

We also wish that men of eminent erudition should come to the chapter, if there be any such among you. They would do honor to our illustrious theologians and lend dignity to the Order. Indeed, we earnestly desire you to make sure that the most learned attend and take part in the chapter; for it is our hope that very distinguished disputations may be held on this occasion, not only to the glory of the Order but also to its profit. When lively intelligences see how greatly we honor any outstanding scholars, they will themselves kindle with enthusiasm for study and zealous desire to gain knowledge and virtues, and the more they apply themselves to study the keener they will become. It is clear from the gospel how powerful an influence example can bring to bear on people's minds, for when the example of our Lord and of the holy apostles was shown to the world, almost everyone followed in these most holy footsteps.

As soon as a definite place has been decided upon by our most reverend Protector you will be notified.

Farewell.   (Cimino Soriano, before September 1506)

Letters as Augustinian General, 116-118

25. To the whole Order

We are to celebrate this year our Order's general chapter, and we have been at pains to insure that it will serve not only to unite and strengthen the Order, but also to profit all Christians. We have therefore obtained rich and far-reaching indulgences from His Holiness Pope Julius; and we have secured also a faculty which was not generally granted to us, namely the authority to absolve penitents not only from all other sins, however grave (a concession frequently granted), but also from those reserved to the Apostolic See. This faculty has not ordinarily been granted to us.

Since, however, we should not hide our light under a bushel, but allow it to illumine everyone in Christ's household, we earnestly desire that so splendid a light may be diffused and shine out far and wide among the faithful, so that we may bring home an abundant harvest of souls growing in grace, and may, as far as is permitted to us, open the way of salvation to all. By such gentle leading we may draw very many toward salvation.

It is vital, therefore, that this news be widely promulgated, so that on hearing it all may arouse and prepare themselves. *But how will they hear, unless someone preaches to them? And who will preach, unless they are sent?* We are therefore choosing you [*Although the letter is addressed to the whole Order, Giles abruptly switches here to the second person singular, as though something had dropped out, or to use this as a form letter for reform and perhaps insert a name here.*], a man most zealous for your own salvation and that of others, a man capable of sowing the divine seed and reaping plentiful fruit in souls to be saved: we appoint you in this respect as a spiritual farmer; we give and grant to you the right to represent us and the entire authority we have ourselves received from the Apostolic See, as can be ascertained from the apostolic letters, and as you will verify in the copy sent to you.

Since one man alone cannot be everywhere, we further empower you to choose and appoint in your province suitable envoys, preachers, and confessors, and to make all such arrangements for the furtherance of this work as the Apostolic See has empowered us to make here. In the name of the Father . . . etc. We beg you to make the salvation of souls your first and principal concern; and then also to insure that whatever offerings are to be made toward the celebration of the chapter be attended to with careful precision.

Letters as Augustinian General, 129-130   (Venice, 19 January 1507)

26. *To the community in Paris*

(To the letter we have already written we now add a few points as follows) We must not omit to point out that in the past your monastery was unrivalled in turning out illustrious men; from this unique source were justly derived the many lofty prescriptions in chapter 36 of our Constitutions. Yet now incredible pain and immense distress overwhelm us, for we grieve to see that not a single province has received any eminent man these many years past, whereas in former days not only provinces but even individual monasteries had someone equipped with excellent learning acquired in your monastery.

We therefore beg and most earnestly demand that every effort be made to insure that we do not suffer such grave loss in respect of scholarship. Let us be ready to try every approach, explore every avenue, and use all means to restore in their entirety the great benefits of learning and the opportunity for sound studies. To achieve this end we need the advice, help, and cooperation of you all.

Letters as Augustinian General, 93-94   (Cimino Soriano)

27. To the Vicar of the Spanish Congregation

Saint Augustine stood out as an unconquered defender of the Christian faith. He was by far the most learned of all learned men, and on account of the threefold light of his teaching he has with good reason been compared to the morning star, to the full moon, and to the very source of light, the sun. He taught his family and posterity so faithfully to reflect this great light that, so far from the darkness of night engulfing it, not even a hint of darkness should ever be found among them.

With this in mind we wrote to that province of yours in the farthest west, the place of sunset. We decreed that persons suspected of infidelity should be excluded from our most faithful flock. We took it for granted that you who are natives of Spain would respond with faith and dutiful piety to the kings of Spain; but now we see that you have spurned us, dashed our high hopes, and played false to our trust in a way we could never have anticipated. You write me letters which Saint Augustine would hardly expect from his enemies, let alone from his sons. In the first place you have the impertinence to instruct us, in a manner as ignorant as it is insolent, on the meaning of the word "neophyte," on the time and circumstances in which the suspected persons arose in Spain, and under which monarchs they originated. Your ignorant rashness, manifest in your letters — your repeated letters — astonishes me more and more by the day. Now it leads you to the reckless and unheard of course of not simply disobeying orders, but even, in your pride and insolence, scorning obedience. This is the most detestable of all conduct; or, rather, the supremely detestable of all detestable things is your attempt to marshal foolish, cowardly and self-contradictory arguments, to defend your obstinate opinion, and finally to pierce me to the very heart by comparing these savage enemies of Christ to Christ himself, the Blessed Virgin, and the apostles. You claim that, being of Jewish descent, these men who hold false views on the faith should not be accused — as though my Lord Jesus, the spotless lamb in whom no guile or sin was found, had not been accused!

I did not write that all persons very recently converted to the faith are evil; I have never said or even thought that such was the case. What I did say, and continue to say, is that those of suspect opinions and ill repute are bad. Yet you maintain that the Augustinian Order ought to follow the guidelines laid down by Augustine in the matter of oaths. Upright men do swear sometimes, and incur no guilt in so doing; the patriarchs swear in the Pentateuch and the angels swear in the Apocalypse. Melchizedek served the Lord, and the Lord swore irrevocably concerning his future high priest, swore that the true religion should be established not according to the law of the circumcised, but according to the order of the uncircumcised Melchizedek. It is thus very often possible to swear without sin. Nonetheless we are warned never to swear an oath, because for the most part it is sinful. Similarly there are a good many dreams which are not merely truthful but sent by angels or even by God: such were the dreams of the two Josephs, one in the Old Testament and the other in the New. Yet all the same we are forbidden to lend credence to dreams. Demons sometimes prophesy accurately, yet they mingle falsehood with truth, and so it is not right to believe demons. All such unreliable things are to be kept away from the certitude of our faith; and in the important matter which concerns us here we must take the greatest care that the body and blood of my Lord Jesus should not carelessly and irreverently be put into the hands of his enemies, hands stained by that very blood of the Lord.

In this present crisis I was wary of the dangers which the Order had to face. For your part, you have fallen prey to some unimaginable delusion, and you are championing the cause of the suspected persons against Christ, against the gospel, against the orders of your religious superiors. I do not know who in that faction put such ideas into your head; all I know — and all too well do I know it — is your ignorance, and I would you knew it too! Not content with professing such notions you have gone further; you dare to threaten me and the Order, declaring that if we hold to our decision you will take steps to insure that someone rues it! What appalling arrogance! This is impudence unheard of even in enemies of the Christian cause! The King of Spain has persecuted that sect, condemning some of them to death and others to exile; but you set yourself up as the opponent both of the king and of religion, daring to accuse both and asserting that any who persecute that evil sect are guilty of grave sin!

I have written these few lines to you, my son; may they be received as a son should receive them, for they are written by a father. He who spares the rod spoils his child; yet I love you so much that I have resolved to spare the rod all the same. I will not, however, spare the pen. I want you to accept what I have written, a little harshly perhaps, so that by this one letter I may correct my son and brother in private between ourselves, and so that you may listen and come to your senses, acknowledge your fault, and seek pardon. If you will do this, not only will we refrain from invoking the authority of the Church; we are even ready to welcome you as a most beloved and obedient son, and we shall see to it that neither Brother Francis de la Parra nor anything else shall harm you or your brethren in any way whatever. By the sacred communion of Christ's blood, by holy charity, by our hope of glory to come, we lay you under obligation to recant and submit to the obedience you have vowed; and if need be we command you in virtue of holy obedience, and on pain of degradation and imprisonment as a rebel, that you depart no more from your obedience.

If, as we hope, you comply with our wishes, we shall refrain from invoking any further papal or royal assistance. If you were to act otherwise, we should eagerly and zealously seek it, in order to save you, who are personally a man of faith, from forsaking a most faithful religious

Order in the cause of infidelity. Rather you will walk confidently in God's house, and strive to insure that between yourself and us there may be but one mind and one heart in God. Since we share one faith and one head, you will be most dear to us if you take care to avoid any schism among us, and any danger that the members of Christ and of the Order be sundered or fragmented into factions, for Christ is not divided.

Farewell.

Letters as Augustinian General, 190-194

28. To the Congregation of Lecceto

Your congregation has always been close to our heart, on account of both its venerable age and its admirable standards of observance. So truly is this the case that, as you know, we prefer it to any other province of the whole Order, and have chosen it as our own residence, regarding it as a sure way to heaven. When we first entered the shade of those sacred oaks we exclaimed, in the words of the holy patriarch, *Truly this is a holy place! It is nothing else but a house of God and a gate of heaven!* Since you elected me to rule the Order I can conceive no good thoughts without the memory of your place and your province first coming to mind.

Now, therefore, that we have to deal with the matter of Saint Augustine's monastery, we have resolved to refer it to no other kind of men than yourselves. You have pride of place in our life, and so it is fitting that you profit our monasteries too in a manner consonant with your dignity. We have compelled your Father Vicar to undertake the task of reforming that community, in spite of his initial refusal and reluctance. To the limits of our power we urgently beg you, and by the obligations of charitable fellowship we bind you, to collaborate in this undertaking. If you will do so, you will not only glorify God and satisfy our wishes; you will also enhance the dignity and distinction of your own noble congregation.

(Rome, 13 September 1509)

Letters as Augustinian General, 239-240

29. Letter to be sent out to the Order announcing the General Chapter and appointing commissioners for the indulgence

In accordance with the wishes of our Holy Father Pope Julius II and our Most Reverend Cardinal Protector, the general chapter of our Order will be held in Rome, God willing, this year at Pentecost, for the purpose of examining the Order's affairs and safeguarding the traditions of our fathers.

The poverty of the Order makes it impossible, however, for us to support the great number of brethren who will come, and for this reason the Holy Father has granted us indulgences, and has sent us a brief in which the concession of these is set out as fully as possible.

Since we cannot be everywhere in our own person, we appoint you commissioner for the indulgence in your province and wherever else you may happen to be, provided that you do not get in the way of any other of our commissioners, should you chance to meet them. We also give you authority and faculty to absolve, and to appoint confessors, preachers, and, if need be, other commissioners. We wish these to enjoy as much authority as you shall grant them. We hope that you will always keep in mind the resources and needs of the Order, and so work with the utmost zeal, care, and diligence, though always according to your conscience. You must, however, warn everyone of whose services you make use in this cause to exercise the greatest caution, lest they ensnare the souls of others or their own. This is especially the case in the matter to which the Holy Father has attached the penalty of excommunication, as you can read in detail in the brief; for while attempting to earn nourishment for the body we must not forget to take care of the soul.

We hope that everything will be handled with both prudence and diligence, and this is why we have chosen you in particular, a man whose charity, prudence, love, and faith have always been very well known to us, attested as they are by ample evidence.

Farewell in the Lord. Keep us fully and frequently informed on all these matters. Make it your business to insure that alms are recorded in detail by those who receive them and carefully kept by those who collect them until you either bring them to the chapter or, if that is quicker, send them.

Letters as Augustinian General, 247-249

30. To a provincial on behalf of Pope Julius II

Greetings in the Lord, venerable Brother.

He who is not with me is against me, and anyone who does not gather is scattering. Those dangerous times are upon us of which the apostle, filled with the Holy Spirit, often warned us, times in which men love themselves, yield to their passions, and forsake religion and piety. When the affairs of the Church are in such a flux, when part of the sacred college has abandoned the pope, and set up a council at Pisa to undermine the pontiff and the whole Church, when Pope Julius II has called them back and threatened to expel them from the sacred college if they do not return, when he has convoked a council to be held next Pentecost in the Lateran Basilica — with the affairs of Christianity in such turmoil, I say, if you do not stand fast by the head, you will be taking up arms against Christ. For my own part, if I were not gathering you together I should be scattering you, and should consider myself not the shepherd of my flock but its disperser and destroyer.

You, then, must prepare yourself to travel, if need be, and issue orders to all priors, regents, vicars, masters, students, preachers, and all other brethren of whatever rank, forbidding them to attend, to countenance or to pay heed to any council other than that of the Lateran, and this on pain of excommunication. By this letter, though reluctantly, we excommunicate any who so offend.

If among the friars in your province there be any outstanding scholars, you must order them to go to Rome at the appropriate time, prepared to engage in disputation in favor of the Apostolic See and the Pope. You know what kind of pontiff occupies the throne of Peter, and how great a pope Julius II has shown himself to be. You know too how much he has achieved for both the Church and our country. Living up to his name, Julius, he has rid the city of murderers and criminals, the woods of robbers, and the roads of footpads; he has brought peace to the patrimony of Saint Peter and the cities of the Papal States; he has adorned Rome with magnificent buildings and undertaken the construction of Saint Peter's Basilica on a vast and wonderful scale. He has recovered Faenza, Rimini, Ravenna, and Cervia for the Church, and many other towns along the Flaminian Way; with enormous effort he has retaken and held Bologna, more than once gravely risking his life. Others have been called pontiffs and acknowledged as supreme princes among all bishops, but he can be called "supreme" for a different reason: he can and ought to be, for he has achieved more, and regained more, than any other; he has held possessions never held by any other who bore the title "Supreme Pontiff"; and so he has a right to be called not merely supreme among bishops but supreme among Supreme Pontiffs!

To turn now to your own situation: you should reflect on the great privileges and gifts which Pope Julius has conferred on your Order. He issued that Golden Bull by which he threw heaven open, confirmed all your rights, and added to them. Besides this he has issued many a brief conferring most useful faculties in liturgical matters. While he has treated the Order with great kindness and continues to do so daily, he promises to do for it greater things still.

In view of all this you must attend to the execution of our commands with the utmost diligence, shrewdness, and zeal. Instruct everyone to be ready for these tasks, so that we may be united to Christ through his vicar, who is our head, and may prove that the benefits we have received from the Head of the Church have been conferred not on the unfeeling and thankless, but on the grateful people who are mindful of them. See that the traveling expenses of the friars who come are met by the province; this may seem to many an onerous imposition, but assure them that it is worthwhile, both because they can thereby serve the public weal, and because we might be acting unjustly if they basely deserted him to whom they are so greatly indebted.

Letters as Augustinian General, 317-319

31. *To the friars of the monastery at Naples*

Greetings to you in Christ, venerable Brothers, and consolation in these hard and wretched times. Ah, my sons, what we now experience are those most dreadful days which Christ foretold in the gospel and Paul in his letters, and not without tears. The crown is fallen from my head; the might and the flower of Spain and France lie slain. As a Catholic I mourn the Spaniards and Italians, as a Christian I mourn the French, and as a man I cannot but weep over all the slaughter. The fields are choked with corpses; so many thousands are killed, so many leaders captured, so much strength broken, that the dead would have been enough to defeat Christ's enemies. Let us then weep before the Lord who made us, let us pray and beseech him, so unhappy is Brescia, so grievous the suffering that wretched Ravenna has endured. Let us reflect and amend our lives, for perhaps God will turn to us once more and forgive.

Our most Holy Father the pope has summoned a Council at the Lateran and ordered a complete reform. We therefore command the provincial and the prior to turn their attention to the matter in a spirit of fear and trembling, so that an extensive and thorough reform may be effected. In these disastrous circumstances, when armies are annihilated, legions destroyed, garrisons overthrown and cities ravaged, when rivers are awash with Christian blood and no slightest hope of escape remains, may it please God to allow us to save our souls. No longer is there any prospect of salvation for Italy, but let us at least attend to our souls' salvation.

We must effect both an inward reform of the soul and an outward reform in bodily matters. The common life must be established, for on this our salvation depends; there must be a pooling of goods without any deception; wandering out of the monastery and any unholy customs must be banned. With regard to clothing, footwear, beds, food, and all similar matters everything is to be reformed and regulated according to our laws.

Besides all this we exhort you to keep peace, particularly with your provincial. At Rome his virtue was seen to be outstanding, greater than anything we have heard of in our day. All the more, then, do we marvel that some people pit themselves against so great a man, and this especially over decisions which, since they were made by us, cannot be rescinded by the brethren without our authorization. Think well on this, you who are making trouble for the foremost man in my Order, and consider what people will think of you, if at a time when the world is terrified after so great a massacre, and on all sides people are suffering from the devastations of war, the monastery at Naples is alone so irreligious and inhuman as to be still thirsting for warfare and blood.

If, as we hope, you forsake your strife and your errors and accept peace and reform, you will please God, gain our favor, and improve both the reputation and the prospects of your most unhappy community. At a time when soldiers are worn out and exhausted and longing for quiet rest, how disgraceful it is that your unquiet house alone should seem daily more eager for war, and intent on anything but peace!

We wish this letter to be given to the Provincial; its provisions are to be read out in the province and implemented.

Farewell. May peace, and Christ, and salvation find a home in you.

(Rome, 17 April 1512)

P.S. We hope to visit you before the dangers of summer, in order to encourage good men, and strive to win the others back for Christ by any available means, and set them on the way to salvation.

Letters as Augustinian General, 332-334

32. To an unidentified provincial

In this wonderful year the Lord has given a new impetus to our affairs: he has sent the Church a new and holy bridegroom, who is the great hope of Italy and of the world, to be the guardian of her doctrines and the one under whose guidance the Bride-Church will grow young again. She will throw off the outworn garments of evil and be made new once more. The holy council of the Lateran is working for this, promises it to us, and directs our minds to it: this holy council which was inaugurated under the Spirit of God and is now to be brought to a splendid conclusion under the mighty leadership of Pope Leo, for the reformation of Christendom. Let us at last descry, and recognize, and contemplate the light of the rising sun, a light which I would even call the birth of God. Let us acknowledge it, I say, as a visitation from the Lord, who is calling and admonishing us to return to him at last after long exile, wide wandering, and deep darkness, to come to a better mind, and to be reformed and regenerated by a holy renewal of our lives.

For our part, as we have been the first to receive gifts from blessed Pope Leo, so too, by his orders and by the command of Almighty God and the sacred council, we must be the first to undertake the holy and heavenly task of reform. Permissions which we obtained from others only with difficulty and over many years Pope Leo has in a few months confirmed and greatly extended, for the purpose of stimulating, enkindling, and inflaming us by these gifts to a fresh reform of our life.

In view of this let new hope be born in you, new plans and a new outlook. With unshakable constancy of mind and equal effort set yourself to the great and holy work of the reform of the Order. See to it that in your province the system of visitation flourishes, that the laws and ceremonies are observed, that silence is kept and due attention given to seemliness of dress, evening prayer, and the divine office. Scapulars are not to reach to the ground, but to be suitably short. Novice masters shall nurture their charges with good observance and appropriate instruction, and novices shall not wear the black habit until profession. Let us see you taking thought for these matters and others laid down in our laws: you must insure that they are observed. Be certain of this, that there is no way in which you can do your duty to God and to us, no way in which you can further your own salvation and honor together with that of the sheep in your charge, except by giving this reformation priority over all other concerns.

Letters as Augustinian General, 341-342

33. To an unidentified friar

So highly have you deserved of our Order that neither we nor the Order itself can, we believe, offer you proper recompense. It is a grief to us that in desiring to load you with honors we overload you with work, for you ought to be resting in honorable leisure rather than be troubled by so many labors and cares; however, it is neither fitting nor safe to entrust the charge of the province to any other person than yourself, for it is falling into ruin and we believe you are the only one who can regenerate it.

Continue, then, to bear with your usual wisdom the burden we have assigned to you until the chapter, and when the right and proper time for this arrives, do your best to insure that it takes place.

Letters as Augustinian General, 343

34. To the Order

The Holy Father has put the whole Christian people in his debt, and our Order in particular. It is right, therefore, that when he demands of us a holy, thorough, much needed, and unusual reform within our flock, we should comply with his wishes and obey wholeheartedly. He has always been a most prudent man and entirely dedicated to God's service, and he seems to long for nothing more vehemently, and to hope for nothing more steadfastly, than to open the way through this holy Lateran Synod for the universal restoration of the whole world.

In obedience to the Pope's wishes and the rules laid down by our fathers, and mindful of our salvation, let us too make fitting preparations for reform. The first and most necessary provision is to insure that there be no body without a head, but that a shepherd be in charge of every flock. Such a person must, as Plato advises, show himself to be skilled in healing wounds, in purifying what is unclean, and in rebuilding ruins. Yet at the Viterbo chapter you elected only three priors to hold the annual office, and now here we are at the fourth year and you have no superior. We therefore command you, within ten days of receiving this letter, to elect in due canonical form and according to custom a man of integrity capable of introducing measures for reform. We hereby grant him the authority customarily delegated to other priors, and we exhort him to foster the common life and to bring back into force the neglected precepts of our laws. We also command M. H., on pain of being held a rebel, to relinquish to the community the post he holds; and, if he is found to owe

the community anything, he is to be compelled under the same penalty
to make it good.

Signorelli, *Egidio*, 245   (30 May 1514)

35. To the whole Order

A powerful, terrifying storm has burst upon us. For three years now
the attack by the bishops in the Lateran Council has been raging against
us and the other mendicants. They have been trying to render obsolete,
withdraw, and cancel the privileges, indults, concessions, exemptions,
indulgences, faculties, authorizations, and powers which have been
granted to us by so many illustrious pontiffs; they have been unwearying
in their attempt and tackled it with all their might and main.

All these three years there has been no respite for us; no peace has been
granted. Day after day we have been summoned and dragged in; day
after day we have been arraigned either to listen to our enemies or to
plead our own cause. We have been scurrying to the Pope, to our
Protector, to other cardinals, to the orators employed by monarchs, to this
one or that, to beg for support, help, and aid. We have often had to go
before the commissioners, usually to dispute about particular points;
rarely has a day gone by on which we were not forced to do battle with
great effort in this field.

We were hoping that the affair would end in this month of July, but
now the case is deferred until next winter, and this means great danger
of shipwreck for us on turbulent seas. It is not safe for poverty to try
conclusions with the rich and powerful, nor is it good for a nightingale
to contend with a hawk or a vulture.

For this reason, when they were alleging that we extorted these privileges and then abused them wantonly and frivolously, and that in any
case such privileges are regularly granted only for a lifetime, we left
Rome, not wishing to watch the final ruin of the Order. We struck out
across Italy, traveled across the Alps and through the snow, arriving in
Germany in mid-winter and thereby exposing our age and health to great
hardship and mortal danger. We visited as many provinces, monasteries,
and brethren as possible, and summoned those we were unable to visit;
we took care to send instructions, letters, and messengers to those who
were too far away. Our object was to arouse the concern of all at this time
of extreme crisis, and to find out if there is any way of avoiding the
danger.

So now we are writing to you, buffeted as we are by these stormy
waves. We beg you to support your tottering Order with your faith, your
loyalty, and your labor; we ask you to resist its destruction by every
means in your power.

All our hope is in God, for men love themselves more than they love
us. We therefore command that you, the provincial, in virtue of obedience

and on pain of deprivation of office, should, either alone or by co-opting assistants, focus and concentrate your entire mind, attention, intelligence, and effort on the reform. If we thus improve we may hope to win divine help and a shield against those who are attacking us, so that God's anger may not blaze out against us nor our enemies accuse us of failing to obey our Rule. We further command all subject brethren, of whatever condition, to accept this reform under obedience; any who refuse are to be stripped of active and passive voice, or punished still more severely if their superiors think fit.

Let consideration for God's honor impel you to this reformation, and in addition the certainty that unless you repel the attack by means of these weapons it will be the end of our Order, our religious observance, our monasteries, our way of life, and indeed our very selves. You, the provincial, must above all stand firm. Set yourself to the task, in season and out of season, knowing that you are working not for men only but for God, and that your efforts are spent not in a human cause but in one that is divine.

Letters as Augustinian General, 373-375

36. To an unidentified province

We, Brother Giles, assert all these things in the name of the Father, and of the Son, and of the Holy Spirit. Amen.

We issued orders last year that the habit, our customs, and community life were to be reformed. We heard, however, that there still remain certain places where the reform has not been completely carried through, and we therefore decided either to be present at the chapter or to send someone to implement a thorough reform. This proved impossible because Pope Leo X sent us to Germany to Emperor Maximilian, so throughout the month of April we were traveling with his camp and following the Emperor as he made for Italy with the Swiss.

We have now returned, and we recall to your minds that, as God is our witness, it behooves us to collaborate for the renewal of our congregation, and to pursue this end by every means at our disposal. We have promised to come in person, and to withhold no effort to secure this holy reformation.

A much more urgent situation has now developed, one which no longer merely encourages us to the task, but absolutely compels us. The Lateran Council, summoned by Julius II and conducted for the last three years by Leo X, is putting such pressure on us and has indeed declared war upon us so fiercely that, unless we amend ourselves by a most thorough and stringent reform and beg the favor and help of both God and men, it will be the end of our privileges, our freedom, and our entire Order.

We therefore lay vicar, priors, and all brethren under strict obligation to recognize the danger; to have regard for the interests of the Order, its freedom and your own selves; and to succor and defend these interests by the amendment of your lives, correction of your customs, dedicated service of God and continual prayer. In this great struggle, when a fierce storm has broken over the mendicants, you must not allow your own Order to be submerged and overwhelmed, nor consent to the disappearance and destruction of everything in our Order and its final dissolution.

Give instructions that this letter be read everywhere, and that prayers and supplications be offered for the defense of the poor against the powerful.

Letters as Augustinian General, 347-348   (1517)

37. To the monastery at Amelia — though they have not yet received it

We are aware that superiors, and any who accept a position of public authority, have been instructed to rule them with a rod of iron and break them like a potter's vessel; and indeed we have heard almost the same injunction from our sovereign lord the Pope and from our most reverend Protector. Nonetheless we have undertaken our administrative task not in order to break our brethren like pottery but rather to mend and strengthen whatever may have been broken; not in order to rule with iron rigor but to approach and solve all our problems in a humble spirit, using the therapeutic rod of the fear of the Lord. We are to be very gentle with everyone, while at the same time most zealous for the renewal of religious life.

We beg you, then, in the name of that charity urged upon us by our Lord in the gospel and by our holy Father at the beginning of our Rule, we beg you in the name of that salvation in view of which we were ordained to the priesthood, to establish the common life, a life regular, reformed, and holy. The three vows are to be observed faithfully, purely, and in their integrity. Religious life is founded on these vows; where they flourish, it flourishes too, but where they lapse, it decays. Our laws are to be read daily. Our Rule and constitutions are to be expounded and proclaimed either in chapter or at table; and you must organize community life in such a way that divergence from these laws may be as slight as possible.

We charge you as prior, more than all others, to give your mind to this, to bend all your efforts to it, to bring it to perfection by the exercise of all diligence, zeal, and care. Embrace as most valued brothers those whom you find docile and obedient. As for those whom you perceive to be rebellious and difficult, you must take care of them in love to the best of your ability, so as to win them for Christ and restore their souls from the pit of hell to the way of salvation. We long to convince you of that truth which the Lord, the Shepherd of shepherds, has made plain to ourselves, that an honest shepherd worthy of the name is one who will not only spend all his efforts for the saving of the sheep, but will even, if need be, sacrifice himself and lay down his life.

Devote your endeavors and your thoughts to these matters night and day. Write to us at once, and frequently, about brethren you find easy, or difficult, to deal with.

Farewell.

Letters as Augustinian General, 94-96   (Cimino)

38. *Postscript to an unidentified provincial*

We have, moreover, set our heart on studying any historical documents relating to our Order that may be extant. Accordingly we ask you to find out whether in any of the monasteries in your province there are ancient decrees, or books concerning our history, or any kind of records which seem to have an authentic look of antiquity. We beg you to search diligently for any such items and send us an accurate written account.

Letters as Augustinian General, 104-105

39. *To the monastery at Padua*

It is written in the sacred scriptures, *The ignorant will persist in ignorance*; and again, *Search the scriptures*. To priests who are to judge the earth (that is, the sins of earthly men) the command is given, *Receive instruction, you who judge the earth*. Moreover *the wage of sin is death*, and ignorance is the accomplice of sin; that is how, through the ignorance of our first parents, death entered the world. Just as ignorance is the death of the soul, so wisdom is undoubtedly its life. Accordingly Wisdom proclaims her own merit in the streets, *He who finds me will find life*; and this was said even before Wisdom put on our flesh. When, however, Wisdom had become incarnate, when the Word had been made flesh, he told us the same thing with his own lips; for in saying that he was the Truth he identified himself with Wisdom, and at once went on to call himself "the Way" and "Life."

Our monastery at Padua is educationally pre-eminent; it is the most suitable place for the pursuit of wisdom and the foremost in our whole Order. To the end that the wisdom of the serpent may not rear its head here, that serpentine cunning which is the enemy of both faith and life (for by faith the just man lives), we have, under divine inspiration, resolved that the wisdom which springs up and flourishes here should be the kind of wisdom which leads not to ruin through shameful conduct, but to happiness through virtuous life. It should be that very wisdom which proclaims to us, *Blessed are they who explain me*. And again, referring to the studious disposition of those who bend their efforts to the search for wisdom and keep vigil for her, she says, *Blessed is the man who daily watches at my door*. The Lord himself said to his apostles, *Blessed are the eyes which see what you see*, for they were men who had embraced a wisdom made lovely by holiness. The psalmist too sang, *Teach me goodness and discipline* — in that order — showing those who seek knowledge that goodness has priority.

The following instructions, then, are intended to insure that from this monastery, as from a sacred fountain, the whole Order may receive not merely knowledge, which when found in isolation serves only to puff people up, but also goodness. From this place may the eastern sun and the moon, that is, goodness and knowledge, arise and shed their light over the whole Order, and indeed the whole world. To this end we have in response to God's prompting laid down, and do now command, that religious life be lived in this place in all holiness and in accordance with the precepts of our laws, in such a way that our Rule and constitutions be observed with the greatest possible exactitude.

Anyone who disobeys either the prior or this command is to be dismissed. If the prior fails to expel a rebel, he shall not only be deposed from his office but shall also forfeit both active and passive voice for five years. Further, although we most earnestly desire that all our ordinances should be observed, the following are of special importance: divine worship, enclosure, silence, study, and the habit. Should anyone leave the monastery alone, if he be a brother of any rank who holds no degree he shall be dismissed; if he does hold any he shall be stripped of his degree. No one may leave the monastery for private purposes more than once a week, apart from attendance at ordinary lectures, and all shall ask a blessing on departure and return. Everyone, even the servants, shall have his own cell. No one may guide a novice, or speak with him. In the church and outside the monastery all shall bear themselves in seemly fashion as to their walk, hands, heads, and eyes. Anyone who acts otherwise shall not be sent out, even to lectures, until he has greatly improved his observance in this matter, both in going about and in classes.

Finally, let all other things be done in accordance with earlier legislation, and in virtue of holy obedience.

In issuing these commands we intend to encourage the good in every way, and to exercise all diligence and care in amending the evil.

(Padua, 24 February 1507)

The other precepts were of a kind common to all.

Letters as Augustinian General, 133-135

40. To. M. Paolo da Genazzano, *regent of studies at Naples*

Most dear son, we have been put into so difficult a position that no worse fate could possibly have befallen us; for to a studious person nothing is more precious than study, and certain it is that nothing has been traditionally regarded as more venerable. If any consolation remains to us in our grievous situation, it is only this: that along with the reform of divine worship and of a religious observance that has all but collapsed, we hope to promote the study of theology as effectively as possible.

We intend to employ all means and exert every effort to ensure that our young men be formed by a very thorough and exact education, and that these youngsters produce a good harvest. We shall reject the sluggish, the apathetic, and the drones; we shall fend off slothful and unprofitable animals from our mangers. We shall, to the best of our powers, prevent those who have made no progress in their studies from obtaining academic honors; heaven forbid that men who have not striven seriously and valiantly in the intellectual contest should win the wreath of success! It is impossible to overstate the stagnation that infects religious life, and the detriment it suffers, when people who have shown themselves unequal in effort, in studies, and in learning are put on the same level in the award of honors. Who would work all night and forego his sleep, if he believed that another, who sleeps not only all night but through a good part of the day as well, is to be adjudged his equal?

No indeed: industrious men undertake hard work with a view to winning what the indolent cannot win; and for this reason we have decided to seek out good, studious minds, and heap upon them kindness, favor, rewards, and honors. We shall deter from study others who are less suited to the noble arts, lest they attempt what is contrary to their natural bent.

You, for your part, already have distinguished studies to your credit, and your well-known mastery of the rudiments has inspired great hope in many people. You must bestir yourself, then. Lay aside all other cares and concerns; dedicate and give your whole mind henceforth to the sole business of making yourself the most outstanding, excellent, and admirable scholar in your academy. Gather together intelligent young men; read, dispute, and research; command them to engage in the struggle at all hours. You must be ever urging them, ever questioning, ever seeking. Never allow them to relax in these academic contests, never let them give up the struggle, never permit the signal for retreat to be sounded. Act in all matters as you would judge fitting for a strict commander as he trains, exercises, and disposes his troops, and habituates them to the use of arms.

If you will do all this, and thereby increase in them an honorable sense of purpose in their lives, showing yourself admirable no less for probity than for learning, there is nothing that we will refuse to do to further your efforts. You will find in the work a wonderful incentive for virtuous living. The more strongly we hear you to be committed to the task of which we have written, the more we for our part will praise, value, and honor you, and take thought for your advancement.

Write to us in full about all the students engaged in the struggle under your leadership, each at his own level. Tell us which among them have minds of high ability, which mediocre, of which you hope great things, and of which less. Report these things with the utmost accuracy.

Farewell. Cimino, 24 July 1507 (1506?)

We have sent this same letter to the community in Paris, and added a few points.

Letters as Augustinian General, 91-93

41. To the rector at Naples and others

As the deer thirsts for springs of water, so does my soul long for the Lord, the living fountain, yet my longing is not simply for my own sake. Most ardently do I desire that all our brothers should have the same yearning. Above all I long for a reformed and devoted Neapolitan community, in good spiritual health, beloved by God and men. Nothing could be more grievous to me than that things should turn out otherwise. You must believe that I never cease to think about Naples on all my journeys.

You, then — you who with fervent love rule this house — you must, if you have any love for me, take every possible care that nothing whatever be neglected in the observance we have enjoined. If, when you give orders accordingly, anyone opposes you, I command you in virtue of obedience not to tolerate him. If he is open to correction, then correct him; if he is defiant, cast him out. Should you act otherwise, be sure that you would be wronging both God and myself. I learned last year that certain fathers were resisting our holy reforming measures. If you detect anything of this attitude again in their words or actions, whether the person concerned be a master or not, we order you to obey the Rule and expel such a person from your fellowship, lest the arrogance of a rebellious mind infect the minds of your good sons. Read out the appointed penalties frequently; along with the Rule and constitutions you must be constantly drumming them into the brothers' memory.

Laws, however, are not merely to be known; they are to be kept. Hence you must be on the watch to make them effective; do your utmost to insure that all the brethren not only know the rules but also observe them. In virtue of obedience we lay upon them all the duty to obey the superior who enforces these rules, and never to infringe them by either word or deed. Should anyone dare to act otherwise he is to be regarded as a rebel against the Order: he shall not be admitted to the church, to table, or to disputations, until he has given public proof of repentance. Let everyone be convinced henceforth that we are more ready to expose ourselves to any deadly peril than to allow the most holy decrees of our Order to be scorned or neglected.

We speak so because the time for justice has come, the time when wounds in need of healing are to be revealed, not hidden. The Good Samaritan is our example in the treatment of an injured body: after long use of soothing oil we must resort to the astringency of wine. Hitherto there has been no man whose misdeeds have failed to find our forgiveness; henceforth there will be none whose wrongdoing we will condone. Until now we have never forsaken mercy; hereafter we shall never swerve from justice. There is a well-known proverb: Excessive kindness in doctors is a prescription for death.

Finally we would remind you that just as Peter was set over the apostles, you too are set over your brethren, and in each case the Lord has given two keys: the one (in our context) is the key of wisdom, the other that of holiness. To you both these powers have been entrusted: guard both keys day and night in such a way that those who profess religion reach the highest possible holiness, while those who dedicate themselves to literary pursuits attain the greatest possible wisdom, and all alike realize that those only will be acceptable who are both studious and upright, they alone will qualify for high honors.

Letters as Augustinian General, 139-141

42. Example of a letter appointing a regent of studies

Although we do not share the opinion which declares those who scrutinize heavenly intelligences to be happy in this life, we do nonetheless agree that love, and the charity which leads to happiness, are born of knowledge; we agree precisely insofar as such happiness is commonly given by God to people who have some degree of knowledge and understanding. If charity is the highest virtue, and the one which unites us to God, as the apostle tells us, then closest to the highest virtue must be that doctrine which instructs us and binds us to charity.

For this reason religious superiors have always considered it necessary to exercise the greatest care in selecting a man to take charge of the studies of young religious. Such a man needs erudition to teach them in a way that will sharpen their wits, seriousness and dignity to train them toward maturity. Temperately and by his own example he must inspire them to a good and happy life. Plato believes that the highest regard should be paid to the education of the young: the quality of the state in the future, he says, depends on the teaching given to young men; as the seed is sown in them in youth, so will the harvest be in their manhood.

With a view, then, to providing for the community and house of studies at Padua a man capable of bearing such a burden, we choose you, we appoint you regent, we create you instructor and teacher of the young, and we endow you with all the privileges which by law and custom regents have ordinarily enjoyed. In the name of the Father, and of the Son, and of the Holy Spirit.

We charge you to educate both parts of the human soul: the intellect from the writings of our brother Giles of Rome, and the will by the precepts of our father Augustine, inviting the intellect to acquire sacred learning and the will to build a holy life. It might seem that your office exists simply for academic purposes, yet, as the very name of regent suggests, we think it very appropriate to such an office that you rule conduct as well as giving lectures. Young people willingly imitate anyone to whom they listen and whose disciples they have become.

Accordingly, since we have committed so important a task to you personally, make every effort to satisfy us personally in the way you carry it out. If, as we hope, you justify our good opinion of you, we shall account you one of the blessed — blessed not, as our contemporaries would have it, by speculation and wealth, but, as the apostle teaches, in their hope and expectation of eternal life. Wisdom promised you this very happiness when she proclaimed, *Blessed are those who expound me . . .*

Letters as Augustinian General, 197-199

43. To the prior at Florence (M. Nicolaus)

Greetings. Day and night we are laboring at the business of reform. At the command of the Pope and our Protector we struggle, investigate, and think about nothing else but how to help our crumbling Order recover the splendor of its ancient dignity. It is incumbent on us so to labor lest we be at odds with God, with men, and with our own conscience; otherwise we who have made profession of religious life would be spurning the laws of religion.

We beg you, then, to call the brethren together at once and read out these laws, proclaim the sovereignty of the Rule, expound the common life from the constitutions, and see to it that the laws are complied with as soon as possible. The law of the Rule is under the authority of the holy apostles, being established to make it possible for us to imitate their life. Now the foundation of this apostolic life is the three vows, in which the essence of religious life consists. It follows that anyone who does not keep the Rule and his vows has lost the essential element of religious life and cannot enjoy its benefits.

Just as what is not human cannot have the faculty of laughter, so he who lacks the essence of religious life, which is to be found in observance of the vows, can certainly not keep the outward signs proper to it. If, then, we are to satisfy the demands of God, of our father Augustine, of our superiors, of our own salvation and our conscience; if we are to meet the demands of the laws, of honor, of the populace and our friends; if we are to act in their true interest; then we have no alternative: either we must dissociate the life of such persons from the religious state, or we must bring their life into harmony with religion and its laws.

To speak now more personally to you, for whom I have a special love: inasmuch as we deal with you in a more friendly and gentle way, you should be the more willing to play your part in this matter. In other places we have sought to further the reform by appointing men who were strangers to the district, for the less they are known locally the more vigorously they can act. Only Master Nicolaus, my superior at Florence, has been left undisturbed; he alone has been left without a visitator or a rector from outside. The truth, as anyone can see, is that at Rome we have appointed a non-Roman as superior, at Naples a non-Neapolitan, at Milan a non-Milanese, at Venice a non-Venetian, at Padua a non-Paduan, and at Perugia a non-Perugian. To this list may be added the prior of Rimini, whom we sent from Rome. As for Bologna and Siena, where the priors are my dear friends, since we did not introduce priors there we sent instead visitators from outside, which was extremely irksome to the priors. However, man is my friend and God is my friend, but God first, so to Bologna we have dispatched Master Mariano of Cave, a man scarcely acceptable to the prior, and to Siena Brother Seraphinus, vicar of the congregation.

There remains your own house, where, I hope, you who are dearest of all to me will do more of your own accord than others will under duress. We beg you, then, to respond in all generosity to our goodwill. As we have singled you out in friendship and love, so may we find you singularly zealous in the work of reform and the establishment of common life. That you will do this we beg you again and yet again; that it will come to pass we are exceedingly hopeful, for we have the greatest confidence in your goodwill.

Farewell, and that you may both undertake the task and bring it to perfection, may the Lord be with you.

Letters as Augustinian General, 203-204   (Cimino, 3 August, 1508)

44. Circular letter to the provinces of the Order on the common life

Our Lord Jesus Christ has warned us that it is wrong to break the commandments, whereas, he also teaches, anyone who keeps them enters into life. It follows that anyone who despises the commandments is hurrying toward death. Now a person who consents to the death of his brother is to be judged a murderer. We are resolved, then, to try every approach, and attempt whatever is within our power, to avert a death which would be both yours and ours.

What moves us to this resolution? The dishonor done to religious life and to our holy father Augustine moves us, for the misdeeds of an army are always attributed to its leader and commander, and a ruler who fails to correct the sins of evil men in his city is himself suspect of sin and evil-doing. We are moved too by public opinion, which thinks and speaks of us as the most degraded of men. The frequent quarrels between priests of our Order move us also, quarrels which spring from one source alone — our willingness to condone claims to private property in defiance of our law. We have not yet banished from our hearts that which, according to Plato and the Acts of the Apostles and the declaration of our Rule, is the cause of all evils: namely, the division between "mine" and "thine." Another sight which moves us is the wretched poverty of the monasteries, which has so greatly increased that in many places there has been no alternative but to abandon them, since crops have been pillaged and ruined. When each person looks after his own interests he neglects the common good; exclusive concentration on one's own affairs always tends to the detriment of the public weal. Finally it is the decline of sacred studies and the arts which moves us. When communities become poor they are hampered by lack of resources in the task of nourishing the minds of good young men and bringing them to fruitfulness; hence it has come about that religious life, which used to be lit up by the glory of very learned men wherever one looked, now lies skulking in the night of ignorance, listless and dumb. The harm which this base and wretched way of life has done to us can be seen most clearly from the fact that when our brethren, who wish to be called "observants," have safeguarded the common life, they have flourished in the very measure that we have deteriorated when we have despised it. By observing the law they gained monasteries, wealth, honors, and friendships in the same measure that we have lost all these by our neglect. If we shun our shared life, then our life will be shunned and hated by God and men.

Such, then, are our motives; and to them must be added the urging of our Holy Father and of our most reverend Protector, who daily declare that we shall never have done enough until there is but one way of life and one standard of observance throughout the Augustinian Order, indeed one sheepfold and one shepherd. With the Lord's help we shall expend all our labor, zeal, and loving care to bring this about.

Calling God to witness, therefore, together with the Blessed Virgin, our holy father Augustine, all the angels and saints and all humankind, we command you, the prior, in virtue of holy obedience, on pain of being adjudged a rebel and deprived of your office, that in this your monastery or province you establish the common life in such a way that, as ordained in the Rule, nothing whatever shall be called anyone's own, but everything held in common among you.

To the brethren, of whatever rank or status, we command, under the same penalties and also on pain of being stripped of their degrees if they hold any, or of suspension from the priesthood if they hold no degree, that as soon as they have heard our injunction in this present letter and the command of our father Augustine, they give up everything and within the space of three days free themselves for the unconditional observance of the three vows. Let them take care to live in future in a way conducive to their salvation, of which they seemed to be unmindful when they neglected their vows. We do not rely on our own judgment in issuing these commands, but act in the name of the Father, and of the Son, and of the Holy Spirit, Amen. If there be any who will not listen, we shall not tolerate them; but we shall embrace as sons and brothers those who obey.

Letters as Augustinian General, 267-269   (21 August 1508)

45. Example of formal confirmation of the election of a provincial and a statement of his duties

We, Brother Giles, most unworthy prior general, confirm and approve the provincial, the official appointments, and all the definitions and dispositions written above, subject only to this law and condition, that the provincial-elect shall, in the presence of the fathers of that community where he is when he receives this confirmation, swear to give to the reform all such attention as may be required to insure that everything laid down by our forbears in the Rule and constitutions be observed.

First: The brethren shall go to confession at least once a week; the Mass and the office shall be celebrated with the greatest reverence.

Second: Silence shall always be kept in the dormitory, the refectory, and the choir. After supper, and after the public prayer in church which follows it, together with the blessing with holy water, the psalms *To you, O Lord, have I lifted up* . . . and *Out of the depths*, for the living and the dead, there shall be no speaking until the hour of prime of the following day. This shall be the order of night prayer after supper, before the brethren retire to sleep: all shall assemble in choir, both the members of the community and any visitors staying in the house; all shall kneel and the prior shall begin, *I confess* . . . in which everyone shall join. Then the prior shall rise and say, *May almighty God have mercy* . . . Then he shall commend to their prayers the Church, Christendom, rulers, states, and the people of their own district, and shall continue, *Let us pray for our benefactors, both living and dead. O Lord, reward with eternal life all who have shown us kindness.* The response is, *Amen.* The brethren shall rise, and the hebdomadarian begin, *To you, O Lord, have I lifted up my soul;* then the prior shall say, *Our Father* . . . *and lead us not into temptation* . . . *Save your servants, men and women, who hope in you, God, etc. Lord, hear my prayer. And let my cry* . . . *The Lord be with you.* Response *And also* . . . *Let us pray: Stretch forth, O Lord, etc.* The opposite choir shall begin, *Out of the depths* . . . with *Give them eternal rest* . . . then *Our Father* . . . *and lead us not* . . . *May the souls of the faithful* . . . etc.

Third: The brethren's clothing shall be decent, not of silk or costly material, closed up and always black. No one at all shall ever wear a cap outside the monastery, but only a biretta made of four parts sewn together, with long flaps on each side. Their shoes shall not be exaggerated in style but close fitting, with some sign on the toes to distinguish them from those of secular persons.

Fourth: Goods already acquired shall be kept in a public place. Any goods which come in afterward, however they be obtained, shall not be held by the brethren but taken in charge by the procurator to be used for the needs of all.

Fifth: No one shall be named a graduate, whether master or bachelor, unless he has received letters of entitlement from the general chapter. At the time of chapter the fathers shall privately make recommendation for these, having due regard to the candidate's sufficient academic attainments and upright life; otherwise we might offend against canon law and fail to show proper respect for honors, which are to be awarded only to those who have good standing in religious life.

Sixth: Superiors, both of provinces and of houses, shall see that no familiar companionship be allowed to grow up between any brother and any person of whom evil suspicion may be entertained.

Seventh: No one is to be advanced to holy orders unless he has attained the legal age; nor shall anyone receive orders unless he has sufficient ability, is of upright life, and is publicly and solemnly professed. We wish the other injunctions contained in our laws to be observed also; and in order that this may be the more easily insured, the Rule shall be read every Friday, and on other days the constitutions, half way through dinner; for laws cannot be kept if people are ignorant of them.

Eighth: Every month the provincial shall write us a report on the progress of the reform, stating who obey and who resist, so that we may apply suitable remedies.

Provided that the provincial-elect shall have sworn in the presence of the fathers to observe all these things, we confirm all those acts of chapter mentioned above. In the name of the Father . . .

Letters as Augustinian General, 275-276

46. To Master Pascal of Venice

Your monastery, very rich and prosperous though it is, has sometimes suffered the fate which can nonetheless befall such houses, and been in want of necessary commodities before your very eyes. Often have you seen it short of money, and obliged to depend on the resources of others even to buy food. Very often too have you seen the novices go clad in rags; there have been unseemly delays in providing them with clothes, to their distress, the disgrace of the monastery and the amusement of onlookers. You have put your mind to resolving this problem, and urgently requested us to send letters of authorization empowering you to address it.

Your thoughts are holy and dutiful as in your good old age you ponder these matters; and we would concur with your wishes, in such a way as to save the monastery expense and to relieve the novices' shame. By these present letters, therefore, we give you permission to allot and set aside entirely, for the purpose of clothing the young men who shall be educated in the novitiate, any part of your income, from those goods which you now hold in the private store of things handed in, or from those you will hold subsequently whether from other items handed in or some estate you may perhaps buy later. We wish and command, however, that only the prior of the monastery, together with the prior of the community of

Saint Nicholas, shall have access to these monies; and he may use them for this purpose only.

Letters as Augustinian General, 296-297   (Rome, 19 November 1510)

Appendix IV

Giles of Viterbo on the Monastery of Lecceto

In 1962, under the title, De Ilicetana Familia (The Family of Lecceto), Francis X. Martin[1] published the text of a treatise by Master Giles of Viterbo addressed to the friars of Lecceto. Martin was careful to distinguish his treatise from another and earlier work by Giles, which was considered lost, the so-called Panegyricus Ilicetanus (Panegyric of Lecceto).[2] Then, in 1983, under the title, Trattato del Magistro Egidio Viterbese (Treatise of Master Giles of Viterbo), M. Benedict Hackett[3] published a copy of the missing work which he had discovered in 1982 in a manuscript of the Archivio di Stato in Siena.

Giles' reference to himself in The Family of Lecceto as a son of Viterbo suggested to Martin that the treatise was composed before June 1506 when Giles became vicar general of the Augustinian Order.[4] Similarly, the implication in the conclusion of the Panegyric of Lecceto that at the time of its composition Giles was a member of the congregation of Lecceto suggested to Hackett that the text should be dated 1503 to 1506, inasmuch as Giles probably became a member of the congregation in April 1503.[5]

The Family of Lecceto is a recension of the Panegyric of Lecceto, in that Giles retained the central portion of the Panegyric which deals with the nine most famous blesseds of the monastery and furnished it with a new introduction and conclusion. The introduction to the Panegyric deals with the origin of the monastery and congregation of Lecceto, while the introduction to The Family is an allegorical interpretation of the ilex trees which surround Lecceto and give it its name. The former shows Giles' keen interest in the legendary foundation of Tuscan eremitism by Augustine, while the latter demonstrates Giles' fusion of sacred and secular learning. The conclusions, while different from each other, are of much less consequence.

Probably the most interesting of all the items Giles treats is the volume of Augustinian Order history which belonged to the convent of Viterbo, but was taken by the prior general in spite of the protests of the friars, exposed to the perils of the sea, and lost in shipwreck. Deploring with Giles the loss of such a treasure, one can be glad if, as Hackett suggests, Giles' slender volume of excerpts from the manuscript has been conserved as part of a register in the Augustinian General Archives.[6]

The Treatise of Master Giles of Viterbo,
Professed Son of the Congregation of Lecceto,
on the Life and Sanctity of Its Blesseds

Introduction

Having implored the help of the Savior, we will draw up a list of the brethren who put off the old man and put on the new (Eph 4:24) in the Convent of the Holy Savior of the wood by the lake, which we call by the name of Lecceto. Fra Paraclito of Sant'Angelo, the best of men, often served as vicar of the congregation and very often as prior of this same

389

convent. With a similar intention, he investigated the antiquity of the place as accurately as possible and discovered here on the shores of Tuscany the beginnings of the monasticism which tradition says was inspired by Augustine. He also discovered that, because of the exceedingly long existence of the place, it was not possible to determine anything certain about the first fathers of Lecceto. They followed Augustine's way of life for so many centuries in this hermitage, that even their names had been wiped, nay, obliterated from the memory of man. Fra Paraclito therefore decided to write up from the most reliable records a list of the names of those who could be identified. And this proposal seemed even more worthy of his consideration, because long after the habitation of the first fathers according to the *Rule* of Augustine began, this holy and regular way of life continued to flourish among these ilex groves.

The enlightenment and sanctity of innumerable fathers of Lecceto was truly marvelous and almost incredible. Their most holy manner of life not only made them dear to God, but a source of amazement and wonder to the people because of the many great and marvelous signs which at diverse times took place among them.

But because they were more observant and zealous for righteousness than celebrity, for virtue above glory, for sanctity instead of reputation, and for God's approval rather than man's, they were more concerned about the conduct of a holy life than a favorable report of popular opinion. And they allowed little to be written about themselves, so that they could keep the works of the hermitage unblemished, not out of human respect, but solely for the love of God. For this reason, it came about that both the simplicity of the first hermits and lack of concern about events on the part of the later fathers deprived us and, as it were, begrudged us the precise knowledge of the glorious accomplishments of so many centuries.

A large volume on the antiquity of the Order was preserved for a long time at Viterbo. In spite of the protests of the fathers, this codex was taken by Master Mariano of Genazzano[7] and lost at sea in a storm which carried off all the general's effects, which Fra Serafino of Lecceto, then prior at Rome, was shipping to Naples. The ship foundered between Puteoli and Naples. Nothing survived of the book except some excerpts. It dealt with more than eight hundred years of history, from the foundation of the brotherhood by Augustine up to the pontificate of Innocent III.[8] It contained an account of the monasteries built along the whole coast of Africa, from the region of Hippo to the city of Jerusalem, gave detailed information about their founders, and cited dates. It gave the same kind of information about the maritime parts of Tuscany, so that, whenever seafaring brethren made for land because of a storm at sea, they could find refuge in one of their own houses.

I, Fra Egidio of Viterbo, culled many items from this volume at the order of the prior general, Mariano of Genazzano. These excerpts were redacted into a little book, so that anyone devoted to the study of our history could survey in depth the material copied from the codex. In this book we briefly considered the names of those who should be included (as we said above), because the memory is still fresh of how they abandoned human values, gave priority to the divine, and consecrated themselves to God. And although a reputation for great sanctity recommends many, the consensus of public opinion particularly favors the following men as blessed: Fra Bandino de' Balzetti Scotti, Fra Giovanni di Guccio Molli Incontri, Fra Pietro Salimbeni, Fra Niccolatio Bandinelli, Fra Iacomo Piccolomini, Fra Latino da Siena, Fra Niccolò Tini de' Mariscotti, Fra Antonio Alessandrini, all natives of Siena, and Fra Pietro da Val di Rosia, which is in the territory of Siena. Yes, these nine were generally held to be as illustrious above our other holy men as the sun surpasses the other stars in brilliance. And I have reported only those deeds of theirs that demonstrate this. Even if I should keep silence about these eminent men, the Lord himself has made them known by signs and wonders worked in their favor, because it is far more beneficial to imitate such men than to write about them. For their glory mortifies us very much. We are their successors, but so inferior to them. And yet our hearts are set ablaze by the example of our predecessors; it is as seemly to follow in their footsteps as it is unseemly to forget and neglect them.

The Family of Lecceto

Introduction

Fra Egidio of Viterbo, a hermit and most unworthy servant of the Lord Jesus, bids well-being in the Lord Jesus to his fathers at Lecceto.

Nothing is more meritorious for a religious than obedience. Notwithstanding, whenever I am ordered to depart from holy Lecceto, I seem, with a nearly flagging spirit, to leave my heart, my very self, affixed to the branches of its sacred ilexes. For this mount or, rather, this hillock, because of the very nature of its peculiar tree, has a certain character, an aura of sanctity, whereby it promises a most ample crop of the holiest men.

Both Theophrastus[9] and Pliny[10] have observed that some trees shed their leaves, while others do not. The evergreen or non- shedding trees have a stouter sap which is more stable for harvest and transport and has a higher caloric value because of its density,[11] whereas the deciduous or shedding trees have a sap which is more diluted because of its higher water content.

Are you not aware then that, in this wise, the nature of the laurel, the olive, and the ilex is symbolic of the love of charity? For what is love except a living flame, a fire of the heart. Indeed, no other form or symbol has been found more appropriate for love than flame and fire. Under this form, charity was imbibed by the apostles (see Acts 2:1-4). But the form of stability is most applicable to foundations and roots. Both forms are to be ascribed to the ilex tree, correctly it seems, because of both the caloric value and the stability of its nature.

There are, moreover, three trees which share this potency. It is held as certain among the learned that the oak, the laurel, and the olive represent three goods: the lowest, the median, and the highest, which are the goods of fortune, body, and soul.[12]

But riches are called the good of fortune. In the *Politics*[13] one learns of its twofold division into natural and artificial riches. Natural riches are certainly necessary for human functions, while artificial riches certainly are not. Through artificial riches, however, one acquires necessities. The former riches are food and clothing; the latter are the medium of exchange, by which victuals and all other necessities are procured. Various authors correctly observe that nature proffered acorns to man as his first food.[14] A certain author wrote that earth exchanged the Chaonian acorn for the rich wheat.[15] The oak tree therefore has the riches from which a sumptuous banquet was prepared for the still uncultivated and (as they say) golden world.[16] Not even the Republic of Socrates took issue with this meal.[17]

Next in order, the laurel is taken to represent the splendor, form, and ornament called the good of the body, which Ambrose treated extensively in his commentary on Genesis.[18]

Finally, the highest kind of good, which is attributed to the olive, is the good, neither of fortune nor of the body, but of the soul. In man, only the soul, not the body or a force in the body (as Aristotle writes[19]), has the capacity for heaven and heavenly things; rather the soul is present in the body as if holding a citadel (as Plato says[20]), conquering and subduing all things, just as olive oil permeates other fluids.

On the oak, therefore, are found the riches which afford no delight, but rather supply necessity; on the laurel, elegance and splendor; and on the olive, the source of that sublime liquid, the parent of light, which is the treasure of soul and mind. But you see all these things on the ilex, so very rich has nature made your tree. It supplies[21] acorns, the riches of the good oak; like the laurel, it never sheds the ornament of its branches; and it alone has the appearance of the olive, for it is so hoary that it confuses one's judgment, so that, for the moment, one might mistake its ramification and foliage for the olive's.

For the best of reasons, therefore, this tree has a religious significance:[22] it has embraced the three bases,[23] the foundations on the holy mountains on which the holy edifice of the Lord rises, the foundations of the apostles and prophets on which are built the walls of Jerusalem. And as in the feigning of the fables, you, like holy Amphions,[24] show the ilex tree to your sons and order them to learn poverty from its acorns, chastity and respect for the body from the abiding dignity of its leaves, and that loftiness of soul which is born of obedience and humility from its glossy brightness, which is not unlike the olive, for *he who humbles himself will be exalted* (Lk 14:11).

From the three Timaeus conflates the soul;[25] from the oneness of the three (one being an even and at the same time an uneven number) he deduces the soul's total harmony.[26] By the most precise reasoning you fill, equip, form, and so allure and motivate the souls of the most holy flock, triply joined together and coalesced by this threefold harmony, that, like stones squared to the line and the seven-foot rule, they spontaneously raise and align themselves into a spiritual edifice. These are large single pearls; these pearls from the Trapobani;[27] these beryls, emeralds, sapphires, and the others are the gems Moses (Ex 25:7), Ezekiel (Ez 27:16), and Isaiah (Is 3:20) spoke of aforetime, and John and the Lord (Mt 13:45-46) mentioned in the gospel. These are the stones Jacob anointed (Gn 28:18; 35:14), these, the flints with which Jesus Nave[28] circumcised at Gilgal (Jos 5:2-9), these, the twelve stones the priests took from the Jordan (Jos 4:1-9). These are the jewels set in the Lord's crown (Rv 14:14), sparkling with precious diamonds: the very walls of the City of God (Rv 21:11.18), constructed, not of Parian or Numidian marble, but of living stones.

Oh fortunate grove whose fortunes God foreshadowed in the eternal predestination, foretold by the prophetic tree in the story of the creation of the world (Gn 2:9; 3:3-7.11-12.22), and adorned in remote ages with the holiest of keepers. I pass over the legendary soothsayers of ancient Etruria, now our part of Tuscany, to whom Rome used to send its young men to acquire the lore of divination.[29] Rather, I proceed to more recent times to deal with our own concerns. For who does not perceive how very fortunate our land has been, insofar as we say that land is fortunate which is beloved of God, the object of his truly rare divine gifts.

It seems hardly possible that Aurelius Augustine, the most fruitful man the world has ever produced, would have been free to devote himself to sacred things, if he had not first been initiated and exercised in Tuscany in the rudiments of the divine. Extant on Monte Pisano,[30] at Centocelle,[31] and throughout Tuscany are the plainly discernible ruins of the habitations Augustine gave to his monks, where he himself sojourned. Your house began at that time; then the little mount with its canopy of ilexes offered its shade to those first fathers, where they were able to devote themselves to religious commentary in complete tranquility. The great Augustine died in the year 437,[32] about twenty years before the beginnings of the city of Venice.

Lastly, the entire history of Tuscany testifies that your hermitage and shrine was already flourishing and famous by the year 600, when the monstrous beast and feral faction of Muhammed was rising in the East. Through Lecceto, almost all of Tuscany was becoming amenable to the knowledge of God and to a change of heart and life. Tradition relates that the amazing austerity, frugality, temperance, and endurance of all things observed in those predecessors of yours was something wonderful. And when these things became commonly known, they attracted not only the people of Italy but the astonished barbarians too, who wondered if the hermits of Egypt and Syria had migrated to Tuscany to your Lecceto. Then people far and wide were stirred: they spread the word everywhere, sought out the place, approached the men, spoke to them face to face, looked to them for answers, and asked for peace and forgiveness, so that it became proverbial that "There are angels at Lecceto."

What should I say about these men who, eking out an existence among these trees, were brought to sanctity? I pass over in silence how many of them reached eminence. The Lord himself has made them known by signs and wonders worked in their favor. It is far more beneficial to imitate such men than to write about them. For their glory mortifies us very much. We are their successors, but so inferior to them. And yet our hearts are set ablaze by the example of our predecessors; it is as seemly to follow in their footsteps as it is unseemly to forget and neglect them.

[Common body of the two Treatises]

Who would dare to call into question the use of the epithet "saint" for Fra Pietro da Siena, who, they say, applied himself to divine contemplation so long and so intensely that his attention never wavered for even a moment. Who, I say, could remain unmoved, hearing about the continual illuminations Pietro received in prayer as he drank in the divine draughts. Unless he drove them away, certain people were wont to consult him like an oracle, inasmuch as he frequently foretold future events to them in secret. How many wars, how many insurrections and civil disturbances, how many plagues, how many troubles he predicted! So people would say of him: "I wish the saint would prophesy something good."

Furthermore, there is no one who does not marvel at the other Pietro identified as from Val di Rosia, from which he commonly receives the cognomen "Roscio." He wept over the Crucified with such a lamentation that no one ever saw him when he was not shedding tears. He was always fiercely opposed to laughter and jokes. If anyone accused him of sadness, as certain people did who cast up to him the words of the Apostle Paul: *God loves a cheerful giver* (2 Cor 9:7), he used to respond that he was a cheerful giver of tears; that gladness is an affair of the heart, not the eyes; that tears are caused, nonetheless, more by gladness than by sadness; and that it is not right to remain unmoved among so many great perils, and by no means right to say slaves have time for pleasure when their master has been nailed to the cross. And, in the same manner, in the midst of his weeping, he very frequently, in a tremulous voice, made use of the verse from the psalms: *They went away, went away weeping, carrying the seed; they come back, come back singing, carrying their sheaves* (Ps 126:6), and others like it. Not even hardened sinners could look at him weeping and not weep with him, so much did his weeping strike the human mind and heart.

I pass over in silence Fra Niccolatio Bandinelli who was never heard to say anything, except out of urgent necessity, because perpetual silence restrained his mouth.

What shall I say about Fra Iacomo Piccolomini, a member of the higher nobility, who slept on the ground, ate raw food, avoided wine, and wore garments not made of wool, but haircloth.

What about Fra Antonio Alessandrini, what about Fra Latino da Siena, both Sienese, both equal in sanctity, if not in age; the one serving by constant prayer, the other by charity for the brothers, even until death.

I will not dwell on the silence of Fra Bandino de' Balzetti Scotti who chose to surpass rather than imitate Fra Niccolatio. When he caught sight of the monastery's donkey being led away by a thief, he did nothing to prevent it himself nor did he tell anyone else about it, so that he would not cause a violation of the rule of silence. Instead, entering the church, he pressed his case with God by prayers and tears, and was given the victory. For the thief and the theft never got outside the ilex grove. They both stood immobile, until the thief realized what God was doing, and returned to give back the theft and ask pardon.

There is no one who does not know about Fra Niccolò Tini de' Mariscotti. He searched for beggars everywhere, to give them food and drink. After innumerable alms, as much grain was found in the granary as he had stored there during the summer. There was also much wine left in the cask, even though he gave so much wine away throughout the countryside that not even many casks would have sufficed. I will relate just one more incident from his life. A man who was an oblate of the monastery had hanged himself. Fra Niccolò, after he had labored in prayer the whole day, took him by the arm and restored him to life.

Thinking this would be enough, I was about to close with Niccolò. But I am reminded of the godly boy, Fra Giovanni di Guccio Molli Incontri, whose example makes it absolutely clear that no one of any age has not made wonderful progress here.

Come now, fastidious boy, small in years, but great, glorious, and remarkable in grace and divine friendship. Consider the case of this young man, you young men of good expectation, and realize no age is more suitable for inaugurating friendship with God than your tender age, which is far sweeter to God, because it is purer, freer, and timelier. Vice has not yet led callow insensibility astray; virtue may therefore sink its roots deeper. Accordingly, it is commonly said that John the Evangelist in his youth was the disciple Jesus loved. For love soars as ardently in green youth as fire flares in dry wood. Learn, O youths, from the example of a youth; take heed, you who oppose the new ranks of religious.

Draw near, most fortunate boy. Your delicate elegance occasioned a greater gift than subsistence on the "baked under the ashes" bread of the fathers. With what words of praise shall I speak of you? With what mark of honor shall I acknowledge you as the ornament and delight of Siena, of Tuscany, of Italy, of earth, and of heaven? You were the flower of your age, full of divine strength — a gentle youth of fruitful tenderness and wholesome gentleness! In countenance, you were graceful indeed, but, in your soul, much more full of grace. How that virtue pleased your crucified Savior, that strength which inured your flesh!

Although your genteel education did not foster discipline, you nevertheless entered the ilex grove with a great heart. But you were not able to bear the frugal peasant fare. Everything smelled; everything made you nauseous; everything offended your nose and eyes. You abstained at table because of your delicacy. No dish, no cup, no tablecloth seemed clean to you, so that, except for the occasional eggs, you would certainly have had either to leave or to starve. Your comrades had said to you: "What will you do when they send you to Siena where the only thing they are accustomed to serve at table are the loaves of moldy bread the little old women leave on the altar?"

You withdrew into your cell and purged yourself with simple boldness before the Crucified, asserting you had indeed come into a holy brotherhood, but no one could do more than his strength and nature allowed, and because your offense stemmed from the intolerable diet, you had to go home where the food was more acceptable, and no one is bound to the impossible, so God is not pleased with those who attempt it. Finally, you asked pardon. But you had showed it was better for you to consult your own interests when the law of the Church allowed it than to try to get away when it was no longer lawful. After all, no one could get a dispensation to return home when the year of novitiate was over. Thus, with the license of youth, you rationalized things. As if loosed from a vow, you burst from your cell, descend the steps, enter the garden, leave the enclosure, and come to the oaks of Mamre (Gn 13:18; 14:13). Though you are suspicious, there is nothing to hinder you.

But look, someone presents himself on the road, a man of noble mien and of a bearing too august to be merely human. With gladsome countenance, he accosts you and asks the reason for your departure. You tell it all. Still showing his gladness, he urges you to return. "For, in your case," he says, "it is not right to spurn the table of the poor, for I myself dwelt on earth for your sake and ate human food, the common, cheapest kind at that, even though I was God." Thereupon, the Savior showed himself as the boy had seen him depicted and had adored him. From his face and eyes he diffused the force of his divinity and, to the trembling and almost breathless boy, added: "But if you want condiments when you sit down to eat, I myself have prepared and brought this for you. You too will now accept this wound." He uncovered the wound hidden by his garment. "Cherish this," he said, "and here dip your food. This kind of condiment, O delicate boy, seasoned the meals of the apostles; this made fasting agreeable to my holy friends; this rendered steel, fire, and death itself sweet to the martyrs." And then so much light streamed from the wound that the boy fell down half-dead.

Rising at length, astonished at his tears and fright, he went back to those from whom he had fled. I entreat you, O radiant boy, how many tears you shed at the feet of the fathers, how you prostrated yourself before them. You lay on the ground, begging forgiveness and acknowledging you were otherwise unworthy of pardon. "Forgive me, O holiest of fathers," you cried, "forgive a most imprudent boy his unboyish fault. Chastise the sinner, but drive not the penitent away." Running up, they were all amazed at the extraordinary occurrence. When they tried to raise you up, you could not be budged off the ground. And hardly constrained to rise, you finally get up and relate the whole incident. And the good soul was so strengthened that our ilex grove, our Lecceto, never saw anything more humble, contemptible, and abject, or anything more holy, pure, and ardent.

The Treatise of Master Giles of Viterbo, Professed Son of the Congregation of Lecceto, on the Life and Sanctity of Its Blessed

Conclusion

You, therefore, most observant fathers, take note whose heirs we are, observe what predecessors we have had, perceive under what lofty auspices this family began. I have merely repeated what is in everyone's mouth. I have omitted noteworthy deeds done over so many centuries by innumerable men. But we have reviewed things attested and notarized in public records. We have not treated all these things equally, however. Rather we have emphasized things which have had a greater impact or have been available for examination and perusal in scholarly works.

I, Fra Egidio of Viterbo, complete my account up to the present by the addition of the dates of my subjects in the flux of time on earth and in heaven: Bandino de' Balzetti Scotti, to be sure, flourished in the year from the birth of Christ the Savior 1222; Giovanni di Guccio Molli Incontri, whom we discussed last, in 1290; and Niccolò Tini de' Mariscotti, whose prayer moved God to restore the dead man to life, in 1332. And the others whom we enumerated were all intermediates or priors of these men. And now I leave it to whom it may concern to write down in proper order what will ensue.

The Family of Lecceto

Conclusion

You, meanwhile, preserve the special character of your sacred tree. You know the verse of Scripture that a good soul will be like a tree which gives its fruit in due season (Ps 1:3). That this verse is applicable to your tree is proved by the following verse in the context, which adds: *and its leaf shall not fail.* In addition, the ilex has two very agreeable qualities, shade and fruitfulness. Shade is appropriate for meditation, for, as Virgil observes, "Under a dark ilex he ruminates the pale grass."[33] Fruitfulness is likewise indicated in the passage which reads that it is found under its ilexes. There it is possible to distinguish the breadth and the great number of your offspring. It was left written as a fact that this proliferation of such celebrated charisms drew even Saint Francis to the shade of the ilexes, where he sojourned a long time with the men of Lecceto, and it attracted many other famous people who wished to experience the spirit of the place directly.

Finally, you are aware how many men, like swarms of bees, have gone forth from you: the Order of Servites[34] and the Congregation which has its headquarters at Scopeto.[35] It remains for us to wake and to say with Jacob: This is truly a *holy place* (Ex 3:5), and *nothing other than the house of God and gate of heaven* (Gn 28:16-17). You have the keys to it. *Raise up your portals* (Ps 24:7.9), so that, when we come, we too may sing sacred hymns with you and your saintly sons in the midst of the angels: the princes, it is written, came first, together with the singers of psalms, *in the midst of the maidens playing tambourines* (Ps 68:24-25), that is, in the midst of the angels and holy souls who sing psalms to the Lord, who lives and reigns.

Introduction and translation by Joseph C. Schnaubelt, O.S.A.

Notes

1. F. X. Martin, "Giles of Viterbo and the Monastery of Lecceto: The Making of a Reformer," *Analecta Augustiniana* 25 (1962) 225-253.

2. *Ibid.*, 247-248.

3. M. Benedict Hackett, "A 'Lost' Work of Giles of Viterbo," in *Egidio da Viterbo, O.S.A., e il suo tempo*: Atti del V Convegno dell'Istituto Storico Agostiniano, Roma-Viterbo, 20-23 ottobre 1982, Studia Augustiniana Historica, No. 9 (Rome: Ed. *Analecta Augustiniana*, 1983), pages 117-136.

I wish to express my gratitude to Father Hackett for his assistance in solving various philological problems in Giles' Lecceto treatises.

4. Martin, *op. cit.*, 247.

5. Hackett, *op. cit.*, page 123.

6. AGA, Cc 37, fol 112r-116r. See Hackett, *op. cit.*, page 121.

7. *Catalogus Ordinis Fratrum Sancti Augustini* (Rome: Curia Generalis Augustiniana, 1976), pages 734-735: Mariano of Genazzano served as vicar general under the prior general, Anselm of Montefalco, from 1486 to 1496, and as prior general in his own right from 1497 to 1498.

8. A.D. 398/416 to A.D. 1198/1216. See Hackett, *op. cit.*, page 121.

9. Theophrastus, *Enquiry into Plants* 1, 9, 3.

10. Pliny, *Natural History* 16, 32-34. Hereafter cited as Pliny, N. H.

11. See, for example, Pliny, N.H. 16, 21-23.

12. See Plato, *Republic* 357, b-d.

13. Aristotle, *Politics* 1256, b, 40-25, a, 14. See 1253, b, 23; 1256, a, 1.

14. See, for example, Pliny, N.H. 16, 1, 6-13.

15. Vergil, *Georgics* 1, 8.

16. See Hesiod, *Works and Days* 109-127.

17. Plato, *Republic* 372, a-c.

18. Ambrose, *Exameron* 6, 8, 44 — 9, 76.

19. Aristotle, *On the Soul* 415, b, 9-10. See 405, a, 20; 405, b. 31-406, b, 14; 412, a, 20-30.

20. See Plato, *Republic* 436-441; *Phaedrus* 246-247.

21. The manuscript clearly has the plural form, *Dant*. However, the context certainly has as its subject the singular form, *arbor*. I have, therefore, taken the plural number of the verb, *Dant*, as an error, probably caused when the scribe misconstrued the forms, *bonae quercus*, which follow *dant*, as nominative plural, instead of genitive singular.

22. By the words: "this tree has a religious significance," *religiosa est arbor*, Giles was surely referring to the *Arbor Ilicetana*, a written work cited more than once by Thomas Herrera, *Alphabetum Augustinianum*, 2 vols. (Madrid, 1644), and Ambrogio Landucci, *Sacra Ilicetana sylva sive origo et chronicon breve coenobii et congregationis de Iliceto ord. erem. S.P. Augustini in Tuscia* (Siena, 1653). Giles was not referring to the painting of the tree and its fruits of holy friars which is found in the sacristy of the still extant hermitage of Lecceto, near Siena, Italy. The written work, set down in the form of a tree, assigned dates to the friars it recorded. But no dates are appended to the names of the friars in the painting. Moreover, the painting considerably postdates Giles. And it may be that the written work inspired the painted work.

23. Giles evidently had the Lecceto logo or seal in mind, which consists of three hillocks or bases. The central and highest hillock is surmounted by the cross of the Holy Savior, while each of the flanking hillocks is topped by an outward-leaning ilex. For an example, see Ambrogio Landucci, *Sacra Ilicetana Sylva*, page 7.

24. J. Thomas, *Universal Pronouncing Dictionary of Biography and Mythology* (Philadelphia, 1870; rpt. Detroit: Gale Research, 1976), I, 116: "A Theban prince, who received a golden lyre from Mercury, and cultivated music with such success that he built the walls of Thebes by the sounds he drew from that instrument, the stones arranging themselves obsequiously at his will. The meaning of this fable seems to be that by his eloquence and persuasive manners he prevailed upon his rude and hitherto intractable subjects to build the walls of their city. He married the famous Niobe." See C. Julius Hyginus, *Fabellae* 6 and 7; Horace, *Ars poetica* 394; Ovid, *Metamorphoses* 6, 221, 271, 402.

25. Plato, *Timaeus* 35.

26. *Ibid.* 37.

27. Modern day Sri Lanka, formerly Ceylon.

28. *Jesus Nave*, that is, the Greek form of the name Joshua, or Josue, son of Nun (Hebrew *Iehosua*).

29. Cicero, *On Divination* 1, 41, 92. See Valerius Maximus, *Memorable Deeds and Sayings* 1, 1.

30. Monte Pisano, the supposed site of Augustine's two year sojourn with the Tuscan hermits, must have been one of the hills to the north of Pisa toward Lucca (*Monti Pisani*). These hills were the location of a number of hermitages organized under the *Rule* of Saint Augustine. The mountain in question may once have been called *Eremiticus*, and it may be identical with the *Silva Livalia*, now commonly called Lupocavo (wolf cave). The monastery at Lupocavo is in ruins, but its church is maintained by the local populace as a center of pilgrimage. Lupocavo is certainly the earliest known unit of Tuscan hermits, and as the head of the congregation of hermits in the diocese of Lucca, Lupocavo may well have been the wellspring of the legend. See Arbesmann, "The Vita Aurelii Augustini Hipponensis Episcopi in Cod. Laurent. Plut. 90 Sup 48," *Traditio* 18 (1962) 343-344.

31. Located in the area northwest of the city of Rome in the old Roman Province of the Order of Saint Augustine, the celebrated hermitage of Centocelle is now in ruins, its church used as a shelter for animals. Father M. Benedict Hackett and two companions came on it, almost by chance, in a declivity about a mile east of Allumiere, which is approached by way of Civitavecchia. According to Benigno A. L. van Luijk, *Le Monde Augustinien du XIIIe au XIXe siècle* (Assen van Gorcum, 1972), page 41, the house was under the patronage of the Holy Trinity.

32. Giles is in error here, because Saint Augustine of Hippo died in the year 430.

33. Vergil, *Eclogues* 6, 54.

34. The Servite Order was founded in 1233, when Saint Bonfilius and his six holy companions left their native city of Florence to retire outside the gate of Balla in an area known as Cafaggio for a life of poverty and penance. Their connection with Lecceto, like the sojourn of Saint Francis of Assisi which Giles also mentions in his conclusion to *The Family of Lecceto*, seems to be completely unsubstantiated.

35. Ambrogio Landucci, *Sacra Leccetana selva, cioè origine, e progressi dell'antico, e venerabile eremo e congregatione di Lecceto in Toscana dell'ordine erem. del padre Sant'Agostino* (Rome, 1657), page 110, attributes the founding of the Congregation of the Canons Regular of Saint Augustine, called Scopetini, to Stephen Cioni, once a member of the Congregation of Lecceto. See Herrera, *Alphabetum Augustinianum*, II, 379-380.

Appendix V

Eclogues

The Eclogues constitute Giles' longest extant poems, totaling 431 lines. The first, in dialogue form, serves as a kind of autobiographical introduction to the other two, and is dactylic hexameter in form. The second, De ortu Christi Salvatoris, likewise in hexameters, begins as a dialogue but, once the narrative of the night of the Nativity is begun, turns into a narrative monologue. The third, De resurrectione Domini, employs the elegiac distich and is a miniature sermon on the resurrection. The Eclogues were composed by Giles sometime between midsummer of 1503 and early June of 1504, most likely at Martana, an island on Lake Bolsena. Martana was removed from the turbulence of the times and gave Giles at the same time a chance to renew his acquaintance with classical authors and to formulate his sentiments in the three eclogues he composed.

The political turmoil of the times, Giles' own hectic preaching schedule, his whole-hearted devotion to Ficinian Neoplatonism, his love of the classics, and his determination to seek the stability and solitude of the life of an Augustinian observant on Martana — all these combined to produce the Eclogues.

The Eclogues never made their way into print, either in Giles' lifetime or after, even though they continued to be mentioned in scholarly accounts of his writings. Moreover, the diffusion of the poems in manuscript form must have been very limited, since only two codices with copies of them have so far come to light, one in Naples and the other in Rome.

N (Neapolitanus) — Naples, Biblioteca Nazionale, MS V.F.20, sixteenth century 303 folios. The text of the Eclogues runs from fol. 22^r to fol. 34^r. Formerly part of the holdings of the monastery of S. Giovanni a Carbonara, the manuscript originally contained, in addition to the Eclogues, 329 letters written by, to, or about Giles and dating from the years 1498-1517. The last section of the codex, however, has been cut away, and this mutilation has resulted in the loss of 87 letters and thus reduced the total to 242. The text of the Eclogues is written in a very respectable Italian bookhand, with obvious cursive features, 22 lines to a full side. Unadorned capitals begin each line, and, since the script is relatively large, a verse may occupy one full line and part of a second. Eclogue II has the pentameter of the distich indented throughout. The regularity of the ductus, the general excellence of the text, and the almost total absence of corrections suggested the work of a practiced and careful scribe.

A (Angelicus) — Rome, Biblioteca Angelica, MS Lat. 1001, sixteenth century 314 folios. The text of the Eclogues extends from fol. 36^r to fol. 44^v. Like the preceding volume, this codex is a collection of Giles' correspondence, spanning the two decades of 1498 to 1517. It contains, together with the Eclogues, a total of 409 letters, arranged in eight books, and as such represents the largest single collection of correspondence. It reproduces the letters found in N, but does so in a different order. The text of the Eclogues is executed in an Italian cursive, with the number of lines on a full side varying from 21 to 31. A simple capital begins each line. In Eclogues I and II, the scribe has usually emphasized a change in speaker by beginning the first line of the new segment of dialogue in the left margin. For the first ten lines of Eclogue III, he has indented the pentameter of each distich, but

401

thereafter has abandoned this format. The number of errors which have crept into the text and the corrections made by the scribe while writing, along with variations in format, create an impression of somewhat hasty and not altogether careful work.

Eclogue I

Paramellus	Aegon

Paramellus

What great thoughts are yours as you take your ease in the quiet shade,
without anxiety over the state of our wretched times, O Aegon?
Everything is in disorder far and wide: the frenzy of war
throws everything into confusion, and nothing is safe from the soldier
in battle-gear.
But undaunted you can play on your hemlock pipes
and with stout heart make light of an unhappy destiny.

Aegon

You, too, if you wish, can scorn mad war's
armed array, grim looks, shafts and threats
and with stout heart make light of an unhappy destiny.
But your concern — too great, alas! — for flock and scanty herd
holds you back, as do your goats which graze on stony ground.

Paramellus

Tell me, please, O godlike Aegon, tell me,
if prayers which an old friend pours forth avail with you —
so may the Fates long preserve this state of peace for you,
so may your Muse ever enjoy sweet repose! —
tell me, I say, whatever way you wish,
how can this flock and how can these goats escape the turmoil.

Aegon

I saw, indeed, Paramellus, that all men long for peace
but few attain and hold it in possession.
I still remember, too, that while concern over my flock held me fast,
neither gladness touched my heart nor sleep my eyes.
Now I feared winter and the savage north wind, the ice and snow,
now summer's heat and the raging Dogstar, now rivers run dry,
now, too, disease from a neighbor's stall.
What? Need I mention the fury of constant warfare? The barbarians
hauling off booty
to the Cimbrians and carrying off our possessions to the distant shore?
No day passed without pitiable weeping and tears.
Hope proved deceitful, empty; and between fear and anguish
I was hard pressed, now from one direction, now from another,
and scarcely any life remained within me;
and so long as I remained too attached to my sheep and too attached
to my goats,

unending worry tore at my sad heart.
I had forgotten my own self, however, and so I did not see the very things
   of which I speak.
But see them I did when, in eager search of a goat that was wandering
   through unfrequented places,
   I beheld a nymph of surpassing loveliness.

Paramellus

Certainly this is what Mopsus, this is what Menalcas himself had long
   been recounting
   when they lamented your abandoning your father's fields, the herdsmen you knew,
   the groves and springs.
Your friend from Venice and Theones of Tuscany have lodged the same
   complaint,
   both dear friends of yours, both young, both skilled as well,
   the one in singing of the stars, the other in composing hymns of
   sacred love.
They told of going along with you to Euganean masters
   who taught the ancient lore of Arcadia.
They were surprised that old age had suddenly stolen upon one in his
   youth,
   and that one formerly so cheerful was dwelling now in gloomy
   caverns
   and had exchanged his lute for tears and his Muses for sighs.

Aegon

O tears so sweet to me and happy sighing!
Yes, sweet but not only to me,
   for often Chaonian doves join me as companions,
   often, too, the mourning turtle-dove. Philomela often forgets her old
   complaint
   and with melodious throat sings along with me.
And so have I been able to avoid the shepherd's brawls, insolent anger,
   bloodshed, and blood-stained swords.
What good does it do planting willows, what good training vines on the
   elm,
   what good grafting foster bough to bough,
      if at the same time the barbarian soldier seizes all these goods
      and a single hour seizes all a lifetime of labor has produced?
All, indeed, are familiar with and witness dreadful happenings such as
   these;
   but love of their flock makes them weak, wealth's deadly power
      gains control over them, and wickedly persuasive hope of
      possessing all

and the desire for pleasure, not satisfied by any means, deceives
  their spirit.
This is the cause of murder, this the cause of bloodshed, this the cause of
  every evil.

Paramellus

I recall that I once heard this in my tender years,
  years I wish would return for me with the returning sun!
Then on feast days there would come to our meadows
  farmers, doughty herdsmen and shepherds.
Here in the green shade of an aged plane tree, the godlike shepherds
  would vie in song and bind the victor's brow with the plane tree's
      boughs;
    and so they used to seek undying fame
    with pipes or practiced voice.
Some sang now of the happy crops, now of the gifts of Bacchus,
  the tending of the herd, the constellations of the turning earth,
  and the skill of bees in making honey.
Others sang of the portents of rain and of a coming storm —
  whether the fierce winds would make their assault from north or
      south.
Many sang of the paths of heavenly bodies — what the sun's position
  and changing phases of the moon bring on, what the five wandering
      planets bear,
  what the movements of the starry heavens pledge.
Yes, and others sang of hamadryads and dryads
  and of satyrs — part man, part goat — and of two-horned Pans,
  dream creatures of the woodlands and empty wantonness of an earlier
      age.
Present at these festivals, the mother and her little child
  would learn what custom would demand for all the year.
It was here that I saw Daphnis triumphant. The learned Muse
  awarded him the crown. He was endowed with such a charm of voice
      and face
    that all were firm in their belief that under human form,
    infused by favoring deity, there dwelt a spirit divine.
If, then, with Phoebus Daphnis in song had vied
  as the godlike swan in its last hour,
  all would have gazed like men confounded
  and clapped and touched the stars with cries
    so that the birds would fall lifeless at the excessive din.
Then Daphnis also sang what you yourself were singing.
"Shepherds," he said, "I give you warning: beware of seductive evil!
One should not fear Chimera's fiery power,
  nor Hydra, though wounded it rise more deadly against its foe,

nor Cerberus, though barking with three-mouthed voice,
nor Scylla of the deep nor dread Charybdis,
    as much as one should fear blind love of countryside and all
        unholy pleasure."
Thus Daphnis spoke, while woods and mountains rang aloud his name
    and the happy valleys praised him to the skies.
But come now, what advice have you yourself at last to offer
    so that I may follow in your steps and learn how not to sink beneath
        the waves?

Aegon

Indeed, I could have done this now, if you perhaps had been more brief.
But a sacred rite is calling me. The evening star is calling
    and nymphs already are returning from the hunt and fetching out
        their timbrels.
It is best to start the dance and sing praise to those on high.
The maidens beat and shake their sounding timbrels,
    and in their midst we sing the praises of the gods.
And if perchance our island once again shall see you,
    then will you learn still other things here by the shore
    or, should the air be cold, we shall enjoy the sun
    at the godlike maidens' shrine that is perched on high beneath the
        hollow rock.
The mossy benches are inviting and the very berry-clusters
    which hang from ivy that the stone with color paints.
Here it is I sing of olden shepherds and the holy herdsmen
    who pleasant pastures in the mountains of Jerusalem shared
        with nymphs and Muses
        whom they joined in common toil;
and, when I sing of Latins ravaging our ancient fields,
    tears check me as I sing with saddened voice.
But as the south wind with its wet blasts grows stronger
    and the lake heaves violent and seethes wild with waves,
    and as our skiff cannot be trusted in so vigorous a squall,
    you cannot leave from here today.
While the brisk south wind declines, stay here with us tonight.
We shall have venison, that game most pleasing to our nymphs.
Our ponds would also fish supply, if my embarrassment
    did not stand in the way. For so it does: and here I am,
    and an eager fisherman at that! But . . . we shall follow what is best.
Tomorrow, if perchance you please to listen, you will come to learn the
        rest—
    how wretched and how base one should consider it
    for me to be enslaved to cattle and to oxen wild.

Eclogue II
On the Birth of Our Lord

Meliboeus　　　　　　　　　Lycidas

Meliboeus

Let us sing, Lycidas, while we are here amid the shady hazel trees
　　and Phoebus' heat is blazing.
Phoebus doubles his heat so that shepherds will not cease their singing
　　and by breaking off their song forget the Muse.
He also takes delight in hearing himself frequently praised
　　　　　　　　on rustic pipes,
　　and so in his goodness inspires those who sing.

Lycidas

Let us sing, Meliboeus. We have come together here
　　　　　　　and both of us are skilled
alike in playing on our slender pipes and in composing verse,
　　something which few shepherds can do these days.
Yet, though I am still in my youth, that voice of mine all but fails me,
　　that voice so clear! Such long silence is harmful to one's voice.
You can recall how once in happier years
　　my shepherd's flute took second place to none.
You rivers and you laurels, you are my witnesses —
　　　　my witness, too, the plane tree —
and you beeches with bark inscribed recall
　　　　that often with my singing I linked the day with night.
But when I gazed on groves made radiant with a shining brightness in
　　　　　　　the night
　　and from a sacred chorus drank in its sacred sounds,
　　　　　my Muse took leave, as my voice fell still
　　　　　　and I set my pipes aside.

Meliboeus

What your father's flock was happy to have heard,
　　　　　　as you engaged in song,
　　no one may tell;
　　　　but these very groves, these mountains,
　　　　　　and these grottoes speak.
Arachynthus did not boast as much of Amphion's quill,
nor, though he calmed the shades of Erebus,
　　did Ismarus or Rhodope boast as much of Orpheus
　　　　as these fields have voiced their wondering awe of you,
　　　　　their poet.
Not Rhodope, not Ismarus lamented Orpheus's death

as these fields lament their poet's silence.
But, be this as it may, do tell me what I now so long to know —
    what chorus did you see, and in what groves?

Lycidas

Ask only what you may rightly ask, Meliboeus, and do not press that
            everything be spoken,
    for one may not tell everything to everyone.
Just as swine take no delight in leafy boughs, or kids in acorns,
    as wild game no food for cattle is, or pastures food for lions,
    as barley is not given to sheep, or grass to doves,
        so there is no single source of pleasure for us all,
and thus, what is sacred must not be entrusted to the unholy crowd.

Meliboeus

But I am not one to ask that things kept secret be disclosed —
nor was I urging that — but only that which can be heard without offense.
Do not rank me, indeed, with the senseless rabble and those dreadful folk
            who contemn the sacred.
For I faithfully perform our sacred rites, I often make my way to the
            temples of the gods,
and many a sacred victim falls in sacrifice within our shrine,
    just as my father taught me —
        what is there that parents have not taught!
I hate those whom you call the dreadful rabble and contemners
            of things sacred.
Let them suppose they know far more than others;
they then begin to make light of heaven, of the stars,
    of Tartarus, and of anyone who weaves sacred garlands
        for the shrines.
But, to the point — what did you come to know within those groves?

Lycidas

Hear the divine revelation of that happy night,
    a night than which no day will be more fair.
Listen reverently, O Meliboeus, and store what you hear deep within
            your heart.
I happened to be grazing lambs on the Palestinian hills,
and with me was Chrysillus, than whom no other would have been to
            me more dear,
    had he not in his folly burned with senseless love for Topila.
Thus did he destroy our old companionship.
Profligate love, alas, detests chaste love.
It was about the middle of the night,
    when the bright stars burned more clearly with unwonted brilliance.
There was no wind, nor was it cold, though fields were dusted white

> with frost,
and you, O Carmel, shivered beneath your snowy burden.
Then suddenly appeared a light. Day without the sun
seemed to have returned, save that the light
wrapped only our sheepfold with its brightness.
Then my companions arise, Thyrsis, and then good Menalcas,
and Chrysillus with Amyntas half-awake.
Nay more, in the midst of the brightness nymphs appeared.
Oh what lovely nymphs! What shining forms!
Then at that moment to me Chloe seemed unsightly,
and Phyllis even more,
though Chloe was truly beautiful and Phyllis surpassingly so.
Some hovered sporting and dancing in the air,
With stately, joyful step others danced in chorus.
Yet others thrummed with quill the strings of their melodious lutes
and rehearsed the Bacchic dance.
A gentle, sweetly flowing breeze stirred their snow-white robes
and soft tresses,
just as in spring in newly-growing fields
the Westwind stirs the crops
and with sweet murmur the happy plain sways
with rippling surface.
Meanwhile the nymphs also settled down upon the soft meadow
and gathered leafy greens and plucked flowers,
flowers which we scarcely ever see even at height of spring.
Some wove iris blooms for garlands,
others pale violets,
many white lilies or poppies mixed in with yellow marigolds.
Now narcissus blossoms and ruddy hyacinths are added,
myrtle, too, along with laurel greens.
Then, from every glen animals came forth,
stags and roe-bucks, and boar in company with lynx,
and — something you could scarcely credit even of one bound
by oath —
a wolf was seen in the midst of sheep, a lioness with goats.
Then the forests sounded forth: the cypress stirred their tresses,
and oaks and lofty-crested pines danced.
Now colorfully adorned with flowers of many hues and with flower
baskets filled,
the ethereal godlike maidens settled on the green
and spread soft couches of heaped flowers.
At the same time one, who shone forth from the whole band
as do lilies shining bright by grassy streams, spoke out:
"Strum with quill! Sound the timbrel!
Bring forth, my sisters, bring forth lyre and lute!

Let lyre and lute and timbrel sound!"
And they soothed the heavens with their inspired song.
This, O groves, this, O pasture lands, you heard with wonder
      and strange excitement.
The rivers heard, the waters of the blessed Jordan heard,
and it stopped motionless in full stream
    and drew back from the deep sea:
      then first it felt the honors that would come to it one day.
Why, the hills and unyielding mountains shook their heights
    and danced for joy, like lambs when their mothers come in sight.
And then the same godlike maiden who had begun before
    continued thus, while the bountiful earth
      and the heavens broke into applause.
Tell, O blessed Muses, of blessed ages tell!
Great and unheard of glory is born today to the stars on high
    and peace most serene to blameless lands.
For God has taken on a human face, among mortal men a mortal frame,
    and limbs that are subject to death,
        so that on earth he may gather the brave,
           those unconquered in war, and souls who guard
             standards of right,
           assemble them as heroes in an illustrious band,
           and lead them across to his native Olympus.
Tell, O blessed Muses, of blessed ages tell!
Little boy — if it is right to call a little boy
    one whom the heavens and those on high honor, reverence,
      and adore —
do you now really lie there helpless in the form of a child,
    offspring divine, God sprung from God?
You, little one, you are crying, naked on the barren ground, and seeking
      mortal breasts,
    a new-born babe, unrecognized by the ungrateful earth!
Tell, O blessed Muses, of blessed ages tell!
You, who shine like the golden sun in the vault of heaven,
      who renew the light of day for the eternal abodes
        of those on high,
      who grant a place at the heavenly banquet,
    you desire your mother now, you nurse on the milk of a mortal maiden
      and lie unknown in a gloomy grotto.
But we shall not call the maiden mortal — such great pledges these! —
    nor the grotto gloomy, with such a Lord there present.
Tell, O blessed Muses, of blessed ages tell!
One whom no power of nature holds enchained, whom the starry vault
    does not confine, the manger with its lowly hay holds close.
What have the cattle merited? What favor have you asses won?

Here is no Numa with Egeria, nor the darkness of the Corycian cave,
    here no Curetes' din, no resounding clash of bronze,
    here is no cave of Jupiter and no false tales of Crete.
Here is the true offspring of God, true Light from Light,
    eternal delight of the Father,
        in whom are the mighty elements of nature,
            sky and earth and air and sea,
    the model from which all nature broke as from its well-springs,
    the end toward which all nature finally runs,
        like rivers hastening to the open sea.
Tell, O blessed Muses, of blessed ages tell!
Behold the age of which the Sibyl's words
    and ancient prophecies of seers of old sang long ago.
The final age of Cumae's maiden has arrived.
She gave prophetic note that, war cast out, the world would find repose,
    that none would take up senseless arms
    or violate iron with flowing blood.
The days of which she sang have come: the Iron Age already wanes,
    ages of more precious metal start to flower,
    virtue grows bright and the Golden Age is come to life.
Tell, O blessed Muses, of blessed ages tell!
Sing, Maro, sing along with me! you, to whom as swan Mantua gave birth
    that in the final hour of a passing age
    you might, inspired by blessed Muse, sing sweetly of a happy age.
Only say not that the Great Months advance;
    let there be no Tiphys or another Argo, let not Achilles sail again to
            Troy.
For that is not the song of Cumae
    nor the words of holy Sibyl but forbodings of the man of Samos.
Tell, O blessed Muses, of blessed ages tell!
The impious traces of our age-old guilt will be ground away,
    and the serpent who devours and kills all things,
    breathing its viper's breath, will weaken and loose its poison.
Grow, O child! The throng of Elders will look on you, but a boy,
            giving judgment,
    teaching the path to heaven
    and hidden truths unknown to any ages of the past.
The flowing water will recognize the presence of divinity,
    water will change itself to wine,
    and in wonder your cups will bring Lyaean Bacchus from mid-stream.
Even on the surging sea you will walk dry-shod;
    at your passing across the deep, the sea will learn to be traversed
            without a boat
    and to bear and not to bathe your lightsome feet.
From here even to the bounds of Scythia, to the Britons in the west,

to the Ganges and to the remote Garamantian tribes
he will send his twelve companions, filled with a powerful Spirit,
chosen heroes, to bring his sacred rites straightway to all the world,
    to sing throughout the world of ages new
    and witness that on earth is born Olympus' king.
Tell, O blessed Muses, of happy ages tell!
To the dumb you will restore a ready speech, to the blind clear sight
    more promptly far than does Machaon's skill,
and by commanding nod restore the sick to health;
and thus will Chiron and the nymph Coronis' son hold their peace
    and Apollo look no more upon himself in admiration.
The ancients thought, Diana, that with your help
    the chaste Hippolytus in Pluto's hideous realm retraced his way,
    that Orpheus recalled Eurydice with his melodious lyre.
Beyond a doubt these are but tales which poetry contrives.
But true departed shades and naked souls of silent dead
    this child at graveside will call forth, as heaven stands in awe.
Why even the shades below, dread Tartarus, he will approach,
    and mastering the Furies, swing wide the dreaded gates.
Thence he will bear the spoils of Erebus, and breaking the chains,
    smash in the prison gates. Victor, he will free the shades
    and tear them from their bonds and fearsome dark.

Eclogue III
On the Resurrection of Our Lord

Now let us sing due praise to those on high and celebrate in song
　　the sacred mysteries: Christ now returns from the river Styx.
You, O lads, sing of the son, and you, O maidens, (sing) of his mother;
　　Virgin, draw near and favor bestow, you with your son.
Virgin, dry the tears from your eyes and drive out bitter sorrow;
　　a festive day calls only for feelings of joy.
That day orders man to leave tombs that lie empty,
　　that day orders Fates to give way to man,
the ashes to live again and souls to return to their bodies
　　one day when God will be judge.
What our ancestors could not believe would take place,
　　　　　　that already we see.
　　Look! What power has death? Christ is at hand!
And so, O death, you have no more rights: though dreadful you brandish
　　your scythe, the unholy throng hardly feels any fear.
Let timid cattle and sheep in terror tremble before you;
　　should you not know, a spirit divine holds sway in man's breast.
Heavenly minds are living within mortal bosoms:
　　there is nothing that heavenly mansions can fear.
Today, O death, you are yourself condemned to die. How fine at last
　　that now you learn at least to lay no hand on the divine.
Fallen is death. Now life returns. We live even now
　　in a Golden Age. Farewell now to trumpet and war and deceit!
Earth has thus far been ruled by its mere human settlers,
　　now it begins to be almighty home of spirits above.
Godlike Lady, rejoice at last — for you may — that your son
　　　　　　has been found;
　　yet 'twas he the whole world in omnipotence did found.
He had been from all eternity within the Father's bosom;
　　then he created his great work, mighty author of the world.
Here he stationed seas, the land and lofty sky, and heavenly bodies, too,
　　and gave them leave to move on their eternal ways.
To you, Phoebus, he appointed day, to you, O moon,
　　　　　　the darkness of the night,
　　and ordered you to go in turn, each on your path.
He ordered happy crops to spring forth from the earth,
　　　　　　forests to put out leafy branch,
　　fruit to grow ripe and so to bend the laden bough.
Rivers brought forth small fish, the seas from their depths the tunny,
　　while in the lofty heavens above there hovered the many-hued bird.
Then tales had not yet wailed Pandion's daughters,

not yet for Othrysian Itys had story made lament.
Not yet from her father's locks had Nisus' daughter the purple taken,
     not yet, O Nisus, did the sea-hawk live.
And still Aurora, in rosy chariot coming with team of four,
     filled every grove with voices of the birds.
The same Lord also made the sheep, the savage wolves and lions
     and all wild beasts with shaggy hides.
Then he made man and over all living creatures set him king,
     and man received the realm of nature subject to his sway.
In happy fields the man was placed with fair-haired spouse,
     where the meadows are green with their unending beauty of spring.
Here where climate serene under cloudless skies
     gladdens with perpetual flowers the fertile fields,
here where no illness, no toil or hardship abide,
     all happiness lives out the happy days.
Here happy folks live on in Golden Age,
     an Age of Gold whose seasons never end.
Earth does not fear those reckless sins of Jupiter —
     there nowhere can the power of gold grow base.
Though Jupiter into gems and into gold transform himself,
     still sinful Danaë's role no girl will play.
Though he may appear as snow-white swan and snow-white bullock,
     Leda and the Tyrian maid will recognize that trickery is concealed.
In these fields chaste pastimes only and pleasure chaste hold sway,
     here only chaste love excites the heart.
Those were the fields, O race of man, that God for you made ready,
     fields in which the power was given to live forever.
But this happy state our first parents came to grudge
     once they dared with hapless hand to pluck the fruit.
From that time on cast out from there we are thrust into barren fields
     where with death we are punished and with eternal exile.
Yet death and banishment could seem of small import;
     but, barking Cerberus, we are your prey.
Granted that fire and pain be to the wretched so very great,
     yet greater still that this admits no term.
All these ills unwholesome pleasure has brought on me and on my race.
     Alas! our world has nothing than this more harsh.
That pleasure our sires, their wretched race and line has damned
     and, unholy thing, has plunged them in the waters of the Styx.
To it is given what power the drugs of Aeaean Circe possess,
     what power the woman of Phasis with Haemonian art can wield.
Circe made bristled boars and bears and wolves
     and other beasts she was pleased to make;
age after age unwholesome pleasure the human race to Orcus drives
     and orders them to be without their native light.

But you, O God, who have always pitied suffering mankind,
  you, who abandon not the people that are yours,
toward wretched misfortune with help you hasten
  and, Greatest of Shepherds, you lift us, weak sheep.
First, in your effort to extinguish iniquity's fires,
  all things 'neath Deucalion's waters you swept.
Forthwith you called Abraham from the fold of Chaldaea
  and chose him for the gift of great friendship.
From the Pharian despot Moses and his people you snatched
  and, when the sea had been crossed, to him entrusted the Law.
Herders of sheep you summoned and made them magnificent kings
  and through many prophets you sang of things that would come.
All this in vain! That I may have life — Father! — oh you have to die!
  Lo! By birth you are mortal and as mortal must die!
But from Orcus and Erebus that day has returned you in power
  and the Furies has conquered and crushed.
No longer, then, Erebus and Orcus need we fear;
  to the entrance of Taenarus that day has set a block.

Translated by Edmund F. Miller, S.J.

Index

(for chapters 1 to 8)